Words of Love and Love of Words in the Middle Ages and the Renaissance

Medieval and Renaissance Texts and Studies

Volume 347

Words of Love and Love of Words in the Middle Ages and the Renaissance

Edited by
Albrecht Classen

ACMRS
(Arizona Center for Medieval and Renaissance Studies)
Tempe, Arizona
2008

© Copyright 2008
Arizona Board of Regents for Arizona State University

Library of Congress Cataloging-in-Publication Data

Words of love and love of words in the Middle Ages and the Renaissance / edited by Albrecht Classen.
    p. cm. -- (Medieval and Renaissance texts and studies ; v. 347)
    Includes index.
    ISBN 978-0-86698-395-2 (alk. paper)
    1. Love in literature. 2. Literature, Medieval--History and criticism. 3. Romances--History and criticism. 4. Literature, Modern--15th and 16th centuries--History and criticism. 5. European literature--Renaissance, 1450-1600--History and criticism. I. Classen, Albrecht.

PN682.L68W67 2008
809'.933543--dc22

                                            2008012099

∞
This book is made to last.
It is set in Adobe Kepler Std,
smyth-sewn and printed on acid-free paper
to library specifications.
Printed in the United States of America

Contents

INTRODUCTION
The Quest for Knowledge Within Medieval Literary Discourse: 1
The Metaphysical and Philosophical Meaning of Love
    ALBRECHT CLASSEN

CHAPTER 1
Concordia Virginitatis: Passionate Marriage in Paulinus of Nola, c. 25   53
    CYNTHIA WHITE

CHAPTER 2
Patronage and Erotic Rhetoric in the Sixth Century: The Case of   75
Venantius Fortunatus
    ROBERT LEVINE

CHAPTER 3
Fusion and Fission in the Love and Lexis of Early Ireland   95
    WILLIAM SAYERS

CHAPTER 4
Woman's Ways of Feeling: Lavinia's Innovative Discourse of/on/about   111
Love in the *Roman d'Eneas*
    RAYMOND CORMIER

CHAPTER 5
"Desire": The Language of Love in the Feminine in Heloise's Letters   129
    CARMEL POSA SGS

CHAPTER 6
The 'Sic et Non' of Andreas's *De Amore*   149
    BONNIE WHEELER

CHAPTER 7
Love of Language in the *troubadour* Poetry   169
    VALERIE MICHELLE WILHITE

Chapter 8
La dame et l'amour: les mots pour dire la beauté et la passion.   191
D'après un choix des *Chansons* de Guillaume d'Aquitaine et des
Lais de Marie de France
    Anna Kukułka-Wojtasik

Chapter 9
"De parler bon' eloquence": Words of Love in the *Lais* of Marie de France   217
    Karen K. Jambeck

Chapter 10
The Rhetoric of Love in the Romances of Gautier d'Arras   255
    Karen Pratt

Chapter 11
The Bitterness of Love on the Sea: Isolde's Amorous Discourse Viewed   275
through Gottfried's Crystalline Transparency
    Christopher R. Clason

Chapter 12
Songs of Love and Love of Songs: Music and Magic in Medieval   291
Romance
    Linda Marie Zaerr

Chapter 13
The Language and Culture of Joy   319
    Siegfried Christoph

Chapter 14
The Language of Love in Wolfram von Eschenbach's *Parzival*   335
    G. Ronald Murphy, S.J.

Chapter 15
When your Lover is the Virgin Mary: A New Approach to the   349
Cantigas de Santa Maria of Alfonso X of Castile
    Connie L. Scarborough

Chapter 16
Love of Discourse and Discourse of Love in Middle High German   359
Minnesang: The Case of the Post-Walther Generation from the
Thirteenth- through the Fifteenth Century
    Albrecht Classen

Contents vii

CHAPTER 17
   The Lover and His *Faus Semblant*: Technologies of Confession   379
   in the *Roman de la Rose*
      TRACY ADAMS

CHAPTER 18
   What Kind of Words are These? Courtly and Marital Words of Love   395
   in the *Franklin's Tale* and *Sir Gawain and the Green Knight*
      JEAN E. JOST

CHAPTER 19
   From Words of Love to Words of Hate in Two Medieval French Prose   421
   Romances
      STACEY L. HAHN

CHAPTER 20
   John Gower: Love of Words and Words of Love   439
      HARRY PETERS

CHAPTER 21
   How Love Took Reason to Court: Diego de San Pedro's *Prison of Love*   461
      SANDA MUNJIC

INDEX   477

INTRODUCTION:

THE QUEST FOR KNOWLEDGE WITHIN MEDIEVAL LITERARY DISCOURSE: THE METAPHYSICAL AND PHILOSOPHICAL MEANING OF LOVE[1]

ALBRECHT CLASSEN
University of Arizona, Tucson

Words of Love and Love of Words define premodern literature. This almost playful chiastic statement is not only ornamental, but goes to the heart of medieval and early modern culture, which can be characterized by the constant struggle for the appropriate words relevant for those ideals and values undergirding each society. The true heyday of the Middle Ages can be located in the twelfth century, when poets in the south of France discovered the theme of courtly love, which then quickly spread throughout Europe and became the dominant issue of all public discourse (including theology) far into the sixteenth century and beyond. However, medieval intellectuals as far back as the eighth century, if not even earlier, can be credited with surgical clearsightedness regarding the power of words they used in their writings to gain new understanding of themselves, their environment, and the transcendental. As the ninth-century Fulda abbot Hrabanus Maurus (ca. 780–856), one of Alcuin's most brilliant students, said: "What does it mean to place green rods of almond and plane before the eyes of the flock except to offer to the people the lives and lessons of the ancient Fathers as they appear throughout the Scriptures? . . . And when from these the bark (*cortex*) of the letter

---

[1] I would like to express my gratitude to Raymond Cormier, Karen K. Jambeck, and Karen Pratt for their critical reading of this introduction. I owe also thanks to Harry Peters and G. Ronald Murphy for their attention to details and providing me with last-minute corrections. Dr. Leslie MacCoull provided valuable corrections and suggestions in the final stage of copy-editing, which I greatly appreciated.

is taken away, the interior whiteness is shown allegorically."[2] His contemporary, the anonymous poet of the Old Saxon Gospel, *Heliand*, also written in Fulda, begins his account with the following words, interlacing the theological with the poetic, the philosophical with the historical:

> There were many whose hearts told them that they should begin to tell the secret runes, the word of God, the famous feats that the powerful Christ accomplished in words and in deeds among human beings. There were many of the wise who wanted to praise the teaching of Christ, the holy Word of God, and wanted to write a bright-shining book with their own hands, telling how the sons of men should carry out His commands. Among all these, however, there were only four who had the power of God, help from heaven, the Holy Spirit, the strength from Christ to do it. They were chosen. They alone were to write down the evangelium in a book, and to write down the commands of God, the holy heavenly word.[3]

The need to find words for ideas, emotions, observations, and thoughts is characteristic of human existence, and medieval poets were as keenly interested in conceptualizing their own identity through the poetic words as modern authors. The love of words thus proves to be the result of words of love artistically woven together, and this tapestry ultimately establishes the picture of human life. It is not enough to look backwards; instead we also need to remember and ponder on the past, as the anonymous poet of the *Nibelungenlied* (ca. 1210) formulated in the prologue to his epic: "We have been told in ancient tales many marvels of famous heroes, of mighty toil, joys, and high festivities, of weeping and wailing, and the fighting of bold warriors — of such things you can now hear wonders unending."[4] Several decades later, we come across other statements expressing similar observations. Dante Alighieri (1265–1321) strongly appealed to his audience to pay close attention to the deeper meaning of his words in *Inferno* 9.61–63: "O you who

---

[2] D. W. Robertson, *A Preface to Chaucer* (Princeton: Princeton University Press, 1963), 316–17; cf. William Sayers, "Breaking the Deer and Breaking the Rules in Gottfried von Strassburg's *Tristan*," *Oxford Germanic Studies* 32 (2003): 1–52; here 52. For a historical overview of early medieval missionary work, which also involved the reconquest of the written word for the Germanic world, see Roger Collins, *Early Medieval Europe: 300–1000*. 2nd ed. History of Europe (1991; Houndmills, Basingstoke, Hampshire, and New York: Palgrave, 1999), 249–61. For the tension between oral and literate, see Michael Richter, *The Formation of the Medieval West: Studies in the Oral Culture of the Barbarians* (New York: St. Martin's Press, 1994), 125–263; for a literary-historical perspective on early medieval Latin literature, see Linda Archibald, "Latin Prose: Latin Writing in the Frankish World, 700–1100," *German Literature of the Early Middle Ages*, ed. Brian Murdoch. The Camden House History of German Literature, 2 (Rochester, NY, and Woodbridge, Suffolk: Boydell & Brewer, 2004), 73–85. See also the other contributions in this volume.

[3] *The Heliand: The Saxon Gospel*. A Translation and Commentary by G. Ronald Murphy, S.J. (New York and Oxford: Oxford University Press, 1992), 3. See also *Héliand: Text and Commentary*, ed. James E. Cathey. Medieval European Studies, 2 (Morgantown: West Virginia University Press, 2002).

[4] *The Nibelungenlied*, trans. A. T. Hatto (Harmondsworth, Middlesex: Penguin, 1965), 17.

have sound understanding, / mark the doctrine that is hidden under / the veil of the strange verses!"[5] By the same token, Geoffrey Chaucer (ca. 1343–ca. 1400) signals to us in the *envoi* of the *Nun's Priest's Tale*: "Taketh the moralite, goode men. / For Seint Paul seith that al that writen is, / To oure doctrine it is ywrite, ywis; / Taketh the fruyt, and lat the chaf be stille."[6]

Of course, every writer and every poet throughout history has trusted in the power of his or her words and reached out to the audience, appealing to their sense of admiration for the magnificence of the creative word. The struggle between orality and literacy, however, which dominated the early Middle Ages,[7] was won by the book culture, and the triumph of the written word has reverberated throughout the Western world ever since.[8] Intriguingly, the public discourse of courtly love — at least in the vernacular as it began in Southern France in the early twelfth century — was as much focused on the power of the poetic word as on love itself, and a worthwhile hypothesis might be that the theme of courtly love was developed primarily as a venue for the exploration of new vehicles to accumulate intellectual influence and to determine the direction of society at large outside of the confines of the Latin Christian Church.[9] As Brian Stock has

---

[5] Here quoted from Chauncey Wood, "The Author's Address to the Reader: Chaucer, Juan Ruiz, and Dante," *Hermeneutics and Medieval Culture*, ed. Patrick J. Gallacher and Helen Damico (Albany: State University of New York Press, 1989), 51–60; here 52. Wood offers the following rumination: "While meaning is available on the veiled level, it is nevertheless veiled, so it is not available to everyone — rather it is accessible only to one kind of reader and not to another. . . . In a sense, then, to ask the reader to switch levels while reading a medieval poem is only a partial interruption, for apprehension continues changed but unbroken" (53–54).

[6] Geoffrey Chaucer, *The Canterbury Tales*, in *The Riverside Chaucer*, ed. Larry D. Benson, 3rd ed. (Boston: Houghton Mifflin, 1987), 4630–33.

[7] Brian Stock, *The Implications of Literacy: Written Language and Models of Interpretation in the Eleventh and Twelfth Centuries* (Princeton: Princeton University Press, 1983), emphasizes the emergence of a literate culture by the end of the eleventh century. C. Stephen Jaeger, *The Envy of Angels: Cathedral Schools and Social Ideals in Medieval Europe, 950–1250*. The Middle Ages Series (Philadelphia: University of Pennsylvania Press, 1994), attributes this shift from oral to written to the loss of the charismatic teacher type at the cathedral schools and the heretofore unknown degree of urgency to rely upon textbooks.

[8] For a collection of pertinent studies on this topic, see *The Book and the Magic of Reading in the Middle Ages*, ed. Albrecht Classen. Garland Medieval Bibliographies (New York and London: Garland, 1998).

[9] I have offered this and similar perspectives in Albrecht Classe *Verzweiflung und Hoffnung: Die Suche nach der kommunikativen Gemeinschaft in der deutschen Literatur des Mittelalters*. Beihefte zur Mediaevistik, 1 (Frankfurt a.M. et al.: Peter Lang, 2004). See also Kathryn Kerby-Fulton and Denise L. Despres, *Iconography and the Professional Reader: The Politics of Book Production in the Douce Piers Plowman*. Medieval Cultures, 15 (Minneapolis and London: University of Minnesota Press, 1999); as to dialectical thinking that determined the progression of the literary discourse, see Constance Brittain Bouchard, *"Every Valley Shall Be Exalted": The Discourse of Opposites in Twelfth-Century Thought* (Ithaca and London: Cornell University Press, 2003), esp. 57–75. In more than one way, the reflections in this introduction and the subsequent contributions represent the continuation of the investigations carried out at the first international symposium on Medieval and Early Modern Studies, held at the University of Arizona, April 2003, see the volume of proceedings: *Discourses on Love,*

observed, "Aspects of human relations that were once thought to deal with reality were now considered to deal only with words; hence a literature sprang up, not only glossing and supplementing textually interrelated forms of behavior, but also substituting, as literature, for patterns of life no longer thought to have validity."[10] This literature was part of a larger discourse community, and this community energetically worked toward establishing rational principles, logical strategies, and communicative operatives for the maintenance, improvement, and ultimately the perfection of their society. Our interest today in medieval words of love and hence in the poets' love of words is fundamentally grounded upon the inquiry of the extent to which humans can expand their potential, not through physical force, but through the power of the word. To quote Stock once again, "The Middle Ages are the period in which we can trace the forerunners of rationalization processes, as [Max] Weber suspected. More important, they were a time in which the debate about rationality began in a recognizably modern culture. To tell this story accurately, and without polemics, is to complete Weber's program. That is the challenge."[11]

It is my hope that this volume, based on an international symposium held at the University of Arizona, Tucson, in April 2005, will examine not only how premodern poets formulated ideas of love, but, more important, how the new idea of love had an impact on the fundamental system of communication, the development of new religious ideas (mysticism), modes of thinking (philosophy), concepts of language (linguistics), and perception of reality (epistemology). This symposium intertwined cultural aspects (words of love) with central issues of human hermeneutics (love of words). The chiastic approach to this investigation carried out by the contributors will be interdisciplinary and comparative by nature, and it promises to uncover many new dimensions of medieval and early modern perceptions of the self and key components of the intellectual and emotive analysis of the human environment.

In order to establish theoretical foundations for this collective enterprise, I will subsequently discuss some of the key components in the literary discourse of the high and the late Middle Ages focused on the dialectical tension between words and love. Traditionally, the first order would have been to examine the enormous contributions by St. Augustine (354–430), St. Anselm of Canterbury

---

Marriage, and Transgression in Medieval and Early Modern Literature, ed. Albrecht Classen. Medieval and Renaissance Texts and Studies, 278 (Tempe: Arizona Center for Medieval and Renaissance Studies, 2004).

[10] Brian Stock, *Listening for the Text: On the Uses of the Past*. 2nd ed. (1990; Philadelphia: University of Pennsylvania Press, 1996), 46.

[11] Stock, *Listening*, 139. For a discussion of medieval reflexivity, see Peter Czerwinski, *Der Glanz der Abstraktion: Frühe Formen von Reflexivität im Mittelalter* (Frankfurt a.M. and New York: Campus, 1989); for a critical discussion of his approach, see Albrecht Classen's review in *Amsterdamer Beiträge zur älteren Germanistik* 30 (1990): 172–77.

(1033–1109), Peter Abelard (1079–1142), and Thomas Aquinas (ca. 1227–1274), among many others.[12] Insofar as St. Anselm tried to prove the existence of God, however, he also laid the foundation of the rational exploration of love in its mystical and secular context.[13] Both philosophers and poets throughout the Middle Ages realized the epistemological relevance of the word in its myriad significations and strove for allegorical, tropological, and anagogical interpretations of the word in order to comprehend the meaning of life within a divine universe.[14] Nicholas of Lyra formulated this perhaps most clearly in a distich included in his *Postilla* on the Letter to the Galatians from ca. 1330:

> The letter teaches events, allegory what you should believe,
>
> Morality teaches what you should do, anagogy what mark you should be aiming for.[15]

Most writers outside of the medieval church, however, pursued an interest in the erotic, above all, which the contributions to this volume will illustrate from many different perspectives. Ultimately, the goal is to uncover the true nature of love

---

12 For a succinct overview, see David Herlihy, ed., *Medieval Culture and Society*. 2nd ed. (1968; Prospect Heights, IL: Waveland Press, 1993), 158–65; Clifford R. Backman, *The Worlds of Medieval Europe* (New York and Oxford: Oxford University Press, 2003), 231–52. See also the very useful summaries in G. R. Evans's *Fifty Key Medieval Thinkers*. Routledge Key Guides (London and New York: Routledge, 2002).

13 Marcia L. Colish, *The Mirror of Language: A Study in the Medieval Theory of Knowledge*. Rev. ed. (1968; Lincoln, NE, and London: University of Nebraska Press, 1983), 55–109.

14 Colish, *The Mirror of Language*, 222, emphasizes: "Augustine, Anselm, Aquinas, and Dante all adhere to the same doctrine of words as signs in the knowledge of God. In the theory of signification they all employ, being is prior to knowing. This presupposition is consistent both with the metaphysical bias of the classical philosophy from which they derived the theory and with their concentration on God as the object of knowledge and the intellectual light par excellence. They warrant their search for signs and analogues of God in nature, history, and human psychology with scriptural assertions proclaiming that the creation bears witness to God, and that it is a way of knowing him." We need to add, however, that the search for love (courtly and mystical) represented an essential complimentary aspect of this quest, perhaps best represented by Wolfram's Parzival in his eponymous romance and by Dante as the pilgrim in the *Divina Commedia*. See G. Ronald Murphy's contribution to this volume.

15 Quoted from Henri de Lubac, S.J., *Medieval Exegesis*. Vol. 1, trans. Marc Sebanc (1959; Grand Rapids, MI: Eerdmans, 1998–2000), 1. See also the insightful study by Friedrich Ohly, "On the Spiritual Sense of the Word in the Middle Ages," idem, *Sensus Spiritualis: Studies in Medieval Signifcs and the Philology of Culture*, ed. with an epilogue by Samuel P. Jaffe. Trans. Kenneth J. Northcott (Chicago and London: The University of Chicago Press, 2005; orig. 1958), 1–30. Ohly alerts us to the critical question also within the world of secular courtly literature pertaining to the fundamental epistemological issue at stake here, 27: "If the distinction between material and signification holds good for Chrétien de Troyes's Arthurian romances, then we are entitled to consider whether he did not see—more consciously than we have yet done—beyond the distinction of material and idea that was appropriate to his work to a possible signification of the meaning of individual motifs in his material."

poetry and love discourse as the critical vehicle for all human efforts in the interpretation of our physical and metaphysical environment, which surreptitiously establishes a profound connection with the religious again, whether we think of the vast body of mystical literature, or religious songs, such as King Alfonso X the Wise's *Cantigas de Santa Maria*.[16] This finds its perhaps most poignant expression in Gottfried von Strassburg's *Tristan*, where the narrator emphasizes, at the end of his prologue, "Today we still love to hear of their tender devotion, sweet and ever fresh, their joy, their sorrow, their anguish, and their ecstasy. And although they are long dead, their sweet name lives on and their death will endure for ever to the profit of well-bred people, giving loyalty to those who seek loyalty, honour to those who seek honour.... This is bread to all noble hearts. With this their death lives on. We read their life, we read their death, and to us it is sweet as bread."[17]

However, despite Gottfried's utopian conception of the power of language which serves, *mutatis mutandis*, to transmit utopian ideals of love, this desired perspicuity easily becomes opaque and ambivalent again, leaving behind those who do not belong to the inner circle of initiates, whereas the true lovers, it has been argued, fully understand the essential meaning of their own words, since love proves to be the strongest bond here in this world.[18] Friedrich Ohly argued that this identification with the Biblical allegoresis (e.g. on the Song of Songs 8:6–7) was the hallmark of the Middle Ages, and when modern science came in since the fifteenth or sixteenth century, the mysterium of human language was lost as well: "Wherever the communality of peoples in the Pentecostal language of allegory was broken up, that was where the death knell of the Middle Ages was sounded."[19] The chiastic correlation between words of love and love of words, however, might well indicate that Ohly's negative assessment would have to be reevaluated, if not rejected outright, although his observation that this allegorical and anagogical approach to the word, in its Biblical and poetic-secular context within the Middle Ages still could be upheld.[20]

---

[16] See the contribution to this volume by Connie Scarborough; cf. also Hildegard Elisabeth Keller, *My Secret is Mine: Studies on Religion and Eros in the German Middle Ages*. Studies in Spirituality, 4 (Leuven: Peeters, 2000).

[17] Gottfried von Strassburg, *Tristan*, trans. A. T. Hatto (1960; Harmondsworth, Middlesex: Penguin, 1984), 44; see C. Stephan Jaeger, *Ennobling Love: In Search of a Lost Sensibility*. The Middle Ages Series (Philadelphia: University of Pennsylvania Press, 1999), 105, 152, et passim. See also the contribution to this volume by Christopher R. Clason.

[18] Rüdiger Schnell, *Suche nach Wahrheit: Gottfrieds "Tristan und Isold" als erkenntniskritischer Roman*. Hermaea: Germanistische Forschungen, 67 (Tübingen: Niemeyer, 1992). Christopher R. Clason, in his contribution to this volume, examines the complex issue of ambivalence, ambiguity, and communication regarding the language of love in Gottfried's *Tristan*. In contrast to Schnell, he emphasizes how much the poet focuses on the communion of heart and mind as the basis for true love, carried by the unique words of love.

[19] Ohly, "On the Spiritual Sense of the Word," 30.

[20] See, for instance, the contribution to this volume by Sanda Munjic.

As we also know from the basic medieval teaching system, which consisted of the *trivium* and *quadrivium*, there are multiple levels of understanding, and only the true scholar knows how to penetrate the surface of words and things and to reach the deepest level of understanding, which approaches divine illumination within a human context.[21] The Spanish poet Juan Ruiz (1295/1296–1351/1352) makes abundantly clear that any communicative (verbal, gestures, images, music) exchange can lead to misunderstandings and confusions because the signs exchanged might have entirely different meanings for the respective receiver.[22] In the introduction to his *Libro de buen amor* (ca. 1340), he relates the tale of the learned Greek and the Roman ruffian who enter a theological debate but rely upon signs instead of words in order to avoid miscommunication. The debate actually takes place, but it proceeds in quite a different way from the one all involved would have expected. Whereas the Greek believes that his opponent has clearly demonstrated a profound understanding of the Christian religion, as indicated by his responses to his signs, the ruffian in reality trumped him and used a most naive gesture code of the street. For the Greek, the Romans have proved that they "truly deserve the Laws" (the Biblical text) because the opponent had indicated to him that God "held the world in His power, and that was right" (61). The ruffian, however, saw only gestures of violent threats and responded accordingly: "I answered that I would give him such a punch / that he would never be avenged in his lifetime" (63–64).[23]

Well before Ruiz, Andreas Capellanus had already forged the same path into the dialectics of human discourse when he promised to provide clear instructions about the *Art of Love* to his disciple Walter (ca. 1190). But even until the present day we are puzzled about the concrete meaning of his confessional sentence: "For I know, having learned from experience, that it does not do the man who owes obedience to Venus's service any good to give careful thought to anything except how he may always be doing something that will entangle him more firmly in his

---

[21] See the seminal study on this topic by de Lubac, *Medieval Exegesis*.

[22] For political gestures and rituals, see Gerd Althoff, *Inszenierte Herrschaft: Geschichtsschreibung und politisches Handeln im Mittelalter* (Darmstadt: Wissenschaftliche Buchgesellschaft, 2003), 274–97; idem, *Die Macht der Rituale: Symbolik und Herrschaft im Mittelalter* (Darmstadt: Primus Verlag, 2003); see also Corinna Dörrich, *Poetik des Rituals: Konstruktion und Funktion politischen Handelns in mittelalterlicher Literatur* (Darmstadt: Wissenschaftliche Buchgesellschaft, 2002); Christiane Witthöft, *Ritual und Text: Formen symbolischer Kommunikation in der Historiographie und Literatur des Spätmittelalters*. Symbolische Kommunikation in der Vormoderne (Darmstadt: Wissenschaftliche Buchgesellschaft, 2004). See also the contributions to *Medieval Concepts of the Past: Ritual, Memory, Historiography*, ed. Gerd Althoff, Johannes Fried, and Patrick J. Geary. Publications of the German Historical Institute (Cambridge and New York: Cambridge University Press, 2002).

[23] Juan Ruiz, *The Book of Good Love*, trans. Elizabeth Drayson Macdonald (London and Rutland, VT: Everyman, 1999).

chains."[24] Whereas Andreas seems to instruct Walter about the proper approach to love, he subsequently utters the most vile condemnation of courtly love, especially outside of marriage, although the major portion of his book emphasizes women's virtues, intellectual superiority, and strength. As recent scholarship has demonstrated, the *Art of Love* is not so much about love itself as about the discourse and the fascination with the dialectical nature of the word.[25] The more Andreas contradicts himself and establishes insurmountable obstacles in his discussion of the true nature of love versus marriage, of women's roles in men's lives and vice versa, the more he reveals his true interest in the paramount significance and yet also opaqueness of human language and, especially, poetic discourse.[26] In Constance Brittain Bouchard's words, "it would be more fruitful to consider his [Andreas's] approach as one analogous to that of the scholastics, in which both sides of the argument are presented. . . . As was the case both in works of literature and works of theology, Andreas found a narrative technique in a play of opposites."[27] As Bonnie Wheeler now argues, his critical source of inspiration might have been Abelard's *Sic et Non*.[28] The need to utilize words to come to terms

---

[24] Andreas Capellanus, *The Art of Courtly Love*, trans. John Jay Parry (New York: Columbia University Press, 1960), 27; see also Don A. Monson, *Andreas Capellanus, Scholasticism, and the Courtly Tradition* (Washington, DC: The Catholic University of America Press, 2005), who categorizes the entire work as a scholastic treatise, informed by Aristotelian ethics and twelfth-century dialectics; this analysis explains the entire work as the product of a logical mind that did not operate with irony (!) and argued most seriously with dialectic operatives, including the Third Book. See Albrecht Classen's review, forthcoming in *Mediaevistik*. Bonnie Wheeler, in her contribution to this volume, convincingly suggests Abelard's influence as a key element in the proper understanding of Andreas's *De amore*.

[25] Catherine Brown, *Contrary Things: Exegesis, Dialectic, and the Poetics of Didacticism*. Figurae (Stanford: Stanford University Press, 1998), 105: "His love (*dilectio*) for Walter thus makes the preceptor, like his literary lovers, both educator and seducer. Just as his lovers instruct each other in the fine points of *doctrina amoris*, so too Andreas teaches these principles to Walter in Books 1 and 2; and just as his male characters attempt to persuade their unwilling ladies to love them, so the preceptor in Book 3 attempts to persuade Walter to love not *domina* but *Dominus*, to leave the lady for the Bridegroom." See also Classen, *Verzweiflung und Hoffnung*, 53–107. Monson seems to misread particularly this section in Andreas's treatise, when he concludes, "Underlying the Chaplain's superficial about-face, a fundamental pessimism about the possibility of establishing a truly reciprocal love relationship remains constant throughout the treatise" (340).

[26] For a parallel situation in the correspondence between Abelard and Heloise, see Michael Calabrese, "Ovid and the Female Voice in the *De Amore* of Andreas Capellanus and the Letters of Abelard and Heloise," *Modern Philology* 95, 1 (1997): 1–26. For a more recent exploration of the female perspective reflected in Heloise's letters, see Carmel Posa's contribution to this volume.

[27] Bouchard, *"Every Valley Shall Be Exalted"*, 143. See also the excellent study by Kathleen Andersen-Wyman, *Andreas Capellanus on Love? Desire, Seduction and Subversion in a Twelfth-Century Latin Text*. Studies in Arthurian and Courtly Cultures (New York and Houndmills, Basingstoke: Palgrave Macmillan, 2007).

[28] See Bonnie Wheeler's contribution to this volume. For an English translation of Abelard's *Sic et Non*, see www.fordham.edu/halsall/source/1120abelard.html; for an alternative translation, see http://people.westminstercollege.edu/faculty/mmarkowski/Hall/Abelard.htm (both last accessed on March 1, 2006)

with the most powerful inner feeling humankind has ever experienced, erotic love, reverberates throughout almost all medieval narratives and lyrics dealing with the relationship between, on the one hand, man and woman, and, on the other, the human creature and the Godhead. Raymond Cormier, in his contribution to this volume, illustrates this phenomenon with his analysis of Lavinia's speech acts in the Old French *Roman d'Eneas*. These speech acts are induced by her profound love for Eneas, and she matures both intellectually and emotionally through her delicate and systematic analysis of her feelings. Without her own words of love, she would not have grasped the characteristic features of her own self and her power of giving her love to the leader of the Trojans.

We begin to understand that our previous observations cannot be limited to Andreas's and Juan Ruiz's texts. In fact, Dante plays with the same dilemma in his famous *Vita nuova* where he even goes so far as to choose another lady in order to hide his true love.[29] And in the explanation of one of his sonnets he realizes that love is much harder to describe than he himself had thought: "In the first [part] I speak of Love as he is in potentiality; in the second I speak of him as potentiality made actual."[30] Might it be that even Dante does not quite know what he is speaking about? Most unlikely; instead we ought to consider the ambivalence of his words as the very essence of the message of the poet who appeals to us to investigate the meaning of his text through multifold examinations, ruminations, and interpretations, offering an almost narcissistic interplay between reader and text without any possible conclusion because the process of reading/listening itself might be the fundamental purpose of all literary efforts.[31] Or should we trust the Wife of Bath in Geoffrey Chaucer's narrative in his *Canterbury Tales* as the experienced practitioner in matters of love (or sex)? She at least claims to be an authority in this regard, yet seems to contradict herself at every turn of her own account.[32] The many bookshelves filled with studies on how to understand the dexterous, feisty, evasive, yet energetic and decisive Wife of Bath speak to the very opposite, since the opaque attracts the intellectual mind, and the murky requires

---

[29] For a reading of this passage in terms of optics and allegory, see Suzanne Conklin Akbari, *Seeing through the Veil: Optical Theory and Medieval Allegory* (Toronto, Buffalo, and London: University of Toronto Press, 2004), 116–25. See also Karen Pratt's study on the works by Gautier d'Arras in this volume.

[30] Dante Alighieri, *La Vita Nuova*, trans. Barbara Reynolds (London: Penguin, 1969), 60.

[31] See Jean E. Jost, "Chaucer's Literate Characters Reading Their Texts: Interpreting Infinite Regression, or the Narcissus Syndrome," *The Book and the Magic of Reading*, ed. Albrecht Classen, 171–217; see also A. J. Minnis, *Magister amoris: The Roman de la Rose and Vernacular Hermeneutics* (Oxford and New York: Oxford University Press, 2001).

[32] Michael A. Calabrese, *Chaucer's Ovidian Arts of Love* (Gainesville: University Press of Florida, 1994).

further investigation, especially when the spiritual or intellectual gold seems to lure us into the dark.[33]

As I have observed in the introduction to *Love, Marriage, and Transgression*, "Love, marriage, and the various transgressive approaches to these topics were all based on and resulted from constant negotiations and reflected a most fertile exchange between and confrontation of many different discourses that vied for the dominant position at the courts . . . ."[34] Here, however, I suggest we take the next step and probe the issue much deeper, accepting the chiastic formula of 'words of love and love of words' as a spur to reach a new epistemological level in medieval hermeneutics.

Hugh of St. Victor advised us that two things prod us along in our quest of ultimate knowledge, "reading and meditation," and this meditation results from the fascination with the Word as an uncanny vessel of information and also as the key to the true essence of human life. This requires grammar, dialectic, and rhetoric, the triad of the *trivium*.[35] Hugh spoke as a teacher to his students, but his words were not hollow instructions for the disciplinarian. Instead, he reminds us that in order to "interpret the letter safely, it is necessary that you not presume upon your own opinion, but that first you be educated and informed, and that you lay, so to speak, a certain foundation of unshaken truth upon which the entire superstructure may rest . . . ."[36] But the surface of the text might confuse us, whereas the deeper meaning awaits us always at the end of profound research and meditation: "The divine deeper meaning can never be absurd, never false . . . ; the deeper meaning admits no contradiction, is always harmonious, always true."[37] As Ivan Illich describes Hugh's fundamental concept of epistemology: "The studious striving that Hugh teaches is a commitment to engage in an activity by which the reader's own 'self' will be kindled and brought to sparkle."[38] Moreover, in Illich's words, "Hugh asks the reader to expose himself to the light emanating from the page, *ut agnoscat seipsum*, so that he may recognize himself, acknowl-

---

[33] Gillian Rudd, *The Complete Critical Guide to Geoffrey Chaucer* (London and New York: Routledge, 2001), 165–69; *Geoffrey Chaucer: The Wife of Bath. Complete, Authoritative Text with Biographical and Historical Contexts, Critical History, and Essays from Five Contemporary Critical Perspectives*, ed. Peter G. Beidler. Case Studies in Contemporary Criticism (Boston and New York: Bedford Books of St. Martin's Press, 1996); *Chaucer's Wife of Bath's Prologue and Tale: an Annotated Bibliography, 1900 to 1995*, ed. Peter G. Beidler and Elizabeth M. Biebel (Toronto and Buffalo: University of Toronto Press, 1998).

[34] Albrecht Classen, "Love, Marriage, and Transgression in Medieval and Early Modern Literature: Discourse, Communication, and Social Interaction," *Discourses on Love, Marriage, and Transgression*, ed. idem, 1–42; here 30.

[35] *The Didascalicon of Hugh of St. Victor*, trans. Jerome Taylor (1961; New York: Columbia University Press, 1991), 82.

[36] *Didascalicon*, 144.

[37] *Didascalicon*, 149–50.

[38] Ivan Illich, *In the Vineyard of the Text: A Commentary to Hugh's Didascalicon* (Chicago and London: The University of Chicago Press, 1993; orig. in German, 1991 [here not mentioned]), 17.

edge his self. In the light of wisdom that brings the page to glow, the self of the reader will catch fire, and in its light the reader will recognize himself."[39]

In this volume we will explore the deeper meaning of the dialectical word pair 'words of love' and 'love of words,' reflecting upon the ultimate meaning of the literary discourse at large, as developed in the Middle Ages, focusing on the intriguing attraction which *logos* has exerted since time immemorial. Both the beginning of the Gospel of St. John and Dante's *Divina Commedia* speak to this phenomenon, the first relating the word to the divine itself, the latter to the erotic in its human dimension when he mentions Paolo's and Francesca's amorous transgression after having read the romance of *Lancelot* together, which led to their famous kiss. As Francesca tells the pilgrim Dante: "Sometimes our eyes, at the word's secret call, / Met, and our cheeks a changing colour wore / but it was one page only that did all."[40]

As much as Dante reflected his strong awareness of the erotic, hence also epistemological power of the word, so much was Roland Barthes, more than seven hundred years later, to point out the hermeneutic significance of the poetic expression reaching out for the spiritual meaning behind *logos*: "ce n'est pas l'écriture qui est littéraire; la Littérature est repoussée de la Forme: elle n'est plus qu'une catégorie; c'est la Littérature qui est ironie, le langage constituant ici l'expérience profonde."[41] Confirming this observation with respect to Jean de Meun's portion of the *Roman de la Rose*, David Holt comprehends this monumental poem as a literary enterprise to perceive, reflect, remodel, and critique reality: "The global fictional work, taken as an artistic expression, thus becomes a sort of reality statement at a secondary level. The entire critical activity, in fact, can be characterized as a struggle to transform fiction into history."[42] Hayden White's observations concerning this issue make the most sense here and deserve to be quoted at length:

> Narrative discourse, then, is as much "performative" as it is "constative," to use the terminology of early Austin, which Ricoeur favors at crucial junctures in his discussions of metaphoric language and symbolic discourse. And historical narrative, which takes the events created by human actions as its immediate subject, does much more than merely describe those events;

---

[39] Illich, *In the Vineyard*, 21.

[40] *The Portable Dante*, ed. Paolo Milano (1947; Harmondsworth, Middlesex: Penguin, 1985), V, 130–32.

[41] Roland Barthes, *Le degré zéro de l'écriture* (Paris: Editions du Seuil, 1953), 118. For studies pertaining to the similar phenomenon, now see the contributions to this volume by Christopher R. Clason, Linda Marie Zaerr, and G. Ronald Murphy, S.J., each focusing on a different corpus of texts. But I really would have to refer the reader to the entire volume, since all authors here address this issue in a myriad of fascinating ways.

[42] David Hult, *Self-Fulfilling Prophecies: Readership and Authority in the First "Roman de la Rose"* (Cambridge, London, et al.: Cambridge University Press, 1986), 99–100.

it also imitates them, that is, performs the same kind of creative act as those performed by historical agents.... This experience of historicality, finally, can be represented symbolically in narrative discourse, because such discourse is a product of the same kind of hypotactical figuration of events (as beginnings, middles, and ends) as that met with in the actions of historical agents who hypotactically figure their lives as meaningful stories.[43]

This struggle, however, as Marie de France had already confirmed in the prologue to her *Lais* (ca. 1170/1180), required particular challenges, and made the creation of hermeneutic veils necessary, otherwise the easy penetration of a text, or of any subject matter, would deceive and ultimately mislead the inquisitive mind. True poets transform history into fiction, and true historians make history out of fiction.[44] By the same token, medieval poets often competed with the theologians in their effort to gain access to the apophatic, whether we think of the *troubadours* and *Minnesänger*, or of the many mystical writers with their enormously poetic abilities.[45] As Eugene Vance observes with regard to Dante, "Dante's stance as a poet was to mark his autonomy with respect to the theologians but to emulate their goal of transcending what is temporal and material in human understanding (as well as what is discursive) in order to prepare the loving soul for its reunion

---

[43] Hayden White, *The Content of the Form: Narrative Discourse and Historical Representation* (Baltimore: Johns Hopkins University Press, 1987), 178–79.

[44] Hayden J. White, in his article "Historical Text as Literary Artifact," idem, *Tropics of Discourse: Essays in Cultural Criticism* (Baltimore and London: The Johns Hopkins University Press, 1978), 81–100; here 83, argues: "Histories gain part of their explanatory effect by their success in making stories out of *mere* chronicles; and stories in turn are made out of chronicles by an operation which I have elsewhere called 'emplotment.' And by emplotment I mean simply the encodation of the facts contained in the chronicle as components of specific kinds of plot structures, in precisely the way that Frye has suggested is the case with 'fictions' in general." See also his subsequent thoughts in the same article, 85–86. For the theoretical underpinnings of his concepts of history and fictionality, see the introduction to his *Metahistory: The Historical Imagination in Nineteenth-Century Europe* (Baltimore and London: The Johns Hopkins University Press, 1973), ix–xii, and 1–42. Some recent historians have seriously rebelled against these notion; see, for instance, Keith Windschuttle, *The Killing of History: How Literary Critics and Social Theorists Are Murdering Our Past* (New York, London, et al.: The Free Press, 1996), 227–51. But it seems to be a rather quixotic struggle because history as a subject matter is not under attack, whereas new methodologies and interpretive approaches are gaining in relevance, whether we think of the history of mentality or the interaction among the visual, the oral, and the written. See, for example, Peter Dinzelbacher, *Europa im Hochmittelalter 1050–1250: Eine Kultur- und Mentalitätsgeschichte*. Kultur und Mentalität (Darmstadt: Primus Verlag, 2003); Nancy Caciola, *Discerning Spirits: Divine and Demonic Possession in the Middle Ages* (Ithaca and London: Cornell University Press, 2003); Horst Wenzel, *Höfische Repräsentation: Symbolische Kommunikation und Literatur im Mittelalter* (Darmstadt: Wissenschaftliche Buchgesellschaft, 2005); *Visual Culture and the German Middle Ages*, ed. Kathryn Starkey and Horst Wenzel. The New Middle Ages (New York and Houndmills, Basingstoke, Hampshire, England: Palgrave Macmillan, 2005).

[45] See, for instance, the contributions to this volume by Valerie M. Wilhite and Anna Kukułka-Wojtasik.

with God."[46] Understanding, as Marie had earlier claimed, results from hard intellectual labor, from sharp analysis, at times even from illusions and distractions, hence from frustration, but ultimately from the unquenchable drive to learn the truth behind the allegory and the symbol, the gesture and the ritual: "It was customary for the ancients, in the books which they wrote ... to express themselves very obscurely so that those in later generations, who had to learn them, could provide a gloss for the text and put the finishing touches to their meaning. Men of learning were aware of this and their experience had taught them that the more time they spent studying texts the more subtle would be their understanding of them and they would be better able to avoid future mistakes."[47]

Those who do not study, or do not make any efforts in reaching a more complete understanding of the God-given signs in nature, or of words written on a page (*logos*), are subject to vice and sinfulness: "Anyone wishing to guard against vice should study intently and undertake a demanding task, whereby one can ward off and rid oneself of great suffering."[48]

Once we probe more deeply into Marie's concept of literature, we discover her ardent desire to express herself in the most eloquent terms and to formulate her thoughts in the most meaningful manner, as she says in the prologue to "Guigemar": "Whoever has good material for a story is grieved if the tale is not well told" (43), and then emphasizes that she relates her stories because she knows them "to be true" (43). As poet, she sees herself not only as an artist, but also, if not especially so, as the crucial link between past and future, as the conveyer of important accounts reflecting noble values and ideals: "The Bretons, who lived in Brittany, were fine and noble people. In days gone by these valiant, courtly, and noble men composed lays for posterity and thus preserved them from oblivion" (56). The poetic word serves as a bridge to fundamental truths, and its recreation and reformulation allow her to make known the truths contained in these words. Practically all of her *Lais* serve this purpose, especially because she perceives love to be the highest value in human life, and yet it is intimately connected with suf-

---

[46] Eugene Vance, *Marvelous Signals: Poetics and Sign Theory in the Middle Ages*. Regents Studies in Medieval Culture (Lincoln, NE: University of Nebraska Press, 1986), 256.

[47] Marie de France, *Lais*, trans. Glyn S. Burgess and Keith Busby (London: Penguin, 1986), 41. R. Howard Bloch, *The Anonymous Marie de France* (Chicago and London: The University of Chicago Press, 2003), 33, offers an interpretation that seems to read more into the text than what Marie is trying to say: "it is precisely the necessity of study and understanding that bears witness to a loss of original meaning that, God-given, required no interpretation." On the contrary, Marie argues that extensive study allows the scholar to reach ever-new levels of comprehension and meaning. For a very clear-sighted and cogent argument, also in remarkable contrast to Bloch's thesis, see Karen K. Jambeck's contribution to this volume.

[48] *The Book and the Magic of Reading in the Middle Ages*, ed. Albrecht Classen, 41; cf. Eric Jager, *The Book of the Heart* (Chicago and London: The University of Chicago Press, 2000); see also Karen K. Jambeck's contribution to this volume.

fering — both key catalytic components required for fundamental epistemological inquiry.

This suffering, the amalgam of all compounds transforming earthly material into spiritual matter, which deserves to be preserved for posterity, propels the poet to make those stories from the past known to her audience: "When the truth of this adventure was known, they composed the lay of *Le Fresne*" (67). There is a obvious urgency in Marie's telling of tales, since she knows the great importance of her compositions for the ethical and moral development of her society. The tragic history of Bisclavret's suffering as a werewolf and his betrayal by his own wife deserve to be remembered because they contain important lessons: "The adventure you have heard actually took place, do not doubt it" (72).

The pleasurable insight she achieves by relating these stories pertains to profound happiness and love, as she confirms in the epilogue to *Milun* (104). As she implies in the epilogue to *Eliduc*, ultimately, then, Marie confirms that love of words is tantamount to love of truth in its allegorical shape, and that the poet provides a most important service for her/his society in relating literary accounts which contain the secrets of life (126). This love of words — and it is the essence of all great literature — also occurs in Marie's *Fables* where she employs literary discourse for politico-didactic purposes, to teach the truth, or, to develop a textual mirror for the self-betterment of princes.[49] This concept of "betterment," however, needs to be contextualized and discussed in light of hermeneutics, intimately connected with the signification of the word itself. This, in turn, carries both theological and philosophical meanings which are open only to those who have acquired the necessary intellectual skills and the spiritual readiness to move into the metaphysical dimension, thereby turning into members of the highly elite community of those who love the word and use the word of love for their ideals.[50] To enter this community, however, the aspirant has to accept the dichotomies, ambivalences, opaqueness, and obscurity of the linguistic code, best expressed in the almost mundane term 'love.'

As Peter Allen observes with respect to Andreas Capellanus's *De amore*: "by giving Gualterius and his other readers the freedom to come to this understanding themselves [of their own existence], Andreas teaches them about their abilities and responsibilities, about their power and limitations."[51] Moreover, as Allen continues, reaching out for a global understanding of medieval secular literature at large: "These works of art were not seen as the equivalent of divine creation, but

---

[49] Karen K. Jambeck, "The *Fables* of Marie de France: A Mirror of Princes," *In Quest of Marie de France: A Twelfth-Century Poet*, ed. Chantal A. Maréchal (Lewiston, Queenston, and Lampeter: The Edwin Mellen Press, 1992), 59–106; here 94–95.

[50] Stock, *The Implications of Literacy*.

[51] Peter L. Allen, *The Art of Love: Amatory Fiction from Ovid to the Romance of the Rose* (Philadelphia: University of Pennsylvania Press, 1992), 77–78.

they could be a respite or a diversion from the constraints that religion imposed. Their very limitations were the elements that made them inviting for recreation and the free play of the imagination."[52] But we need to go one step further and realize the epistemological significance of the poetic word within medieval texts which, if properly espoused and employed, provides fundamental meaning and constitutes human existence.

The failure to read properly might have deadly consequences, beginning with the failure to grasp the essence of love. As Wolfram von Eschenbach illustrates in his fragmentary *Titurel* (ca. 1220), those who do not read properly are bound to die and cannot join the community of lovers because they fail in the demands on their social identity.[53] The same applies to political discourse in the Middle Ages which regarded language as the expression of a society's well-being whether in terms of a spiritual or secular orientation. For members of the church there was no doubt about the fundamental significance of the word in human life, because without it the knowledge of the divine could not be disseminated. Likewise Humbert of Rome (1200–1277), fifth master-general of the Dominican order, states, "Without preaching, which scatters the word of God like seed, the world would be sterile and produce no fruit."[54]

The apophatic (ineffable), however, is not a matter simply for theologians, but for love poets as well, especially because the erotic escapes easy definition and remains elusive of the intellectual and rational efforts to approach it with rational terms. Both the Godhead and the beloved, both the religious and the erotic experience, are caught in a linguistic dilemma, which Michael A. Sells calls "the *aporia*—the unresolvable dilemma—of transcendence."[55] To overcome this conflict, the speaker, or poet, has several options, such as to refrain from using language altogether, or to differentiate between human discourse and divine discourse, or to acknowledge the fact that there is something like an apophatic discourse. Refering to the Dominican teacher, preacher, and mystic—or was he a philosopher?—Meister Eckhart, Milem observes: "This aporia is not a problem for God but for human beings coming to grips with God's transcendence and ineffability."[56]

---

[52] Allen, *The Art of Love*, 78.

[53] Albrecht Classen, *Utopie und Logos: Vier Studien zu Wolframs von Eschenbach Titurel*. Beiträge zur älteren Literaturgeschichte (Heidelberg: Carl Winter Universitätsverlag, 1990), 115–22. See also the contribution to this volume by Ronald G. Murphy. He has elaborated his observations and thoughts in much greater detail in his book *Gemstone of Paradise: The Holy Grail in Wolfram's Parzival* (New York and Oxford: Oxford University Press, 2006).

[54] Vance, *Mervelous Signals*, 260.

[55] Michael A. Sells, *Mystical Languages of Unsaying* (Chicago and London: The University of Chicago Press, 1994), 2; Bruce Milem, *The Unspoken Word: Negative Theology in Meister Eckhart's German Sermons* (Washington, D.C.: The Catholic University of America Press, 2002), 6–7. See also the contribution to this volume by Valerie M. Wilhite.

[56] Milem, *The Unspoken Word*, 9.

Moreover, "Eckhart's speech uses apophatic discourse to emphasize its own status as language. In considering the problem of whether humans can speak about God, the sermon implicitly refers to itself as an attempt to do so."[57] The reference to mystical texts allows us to gain a profound understanding of the parallel problems with erotic discourse, since true love — whatever we might mean by this term — escapes linguistic definitions and challenges us both emotionally and intellectually to cope with our existence. Insofar as Eckhart, like most other mystics, reflects on his fundamental struggles with language, we begin to realize that talking about love also falls into the category of the apophatic. For love, there is no cataphasis, that is, no "knowledge of something by what is alike,"[58] since we cannot compare it with anything known to us in our material surroundings.

As Amy Hollywood observes, "Eckhart, then, creates a mystical symbolic system to describe the union of the soul and the divine and the way in which they may be mystically apprehended. Yet the source of mystical insight lies primarily in the subversion of this symbolic vocabulary and theological system through the use of logical self-contradiction, double paradigms, and referential shifts in which God and the soul become indistinguishable. Through this language, Eckhart attempts to create a nonreferential discourse, a form of speech that breaks through reified and delimited language and thought in order to demonstrate its limitations and to allow it to function in new ways."[59]

The Beguine Margaret Porete, or Porette, also reflects on this phenomenon in her mystical account, *The Mirror of Simple Souls*: "For love, I pray, says Love, that you listen with great attention of the subtle understanding within you, for otherwise all those who hear it will misunderstand it, if they are not so themselves."[60] The mystic, or the lover, experiences the self-liberation not through an act of its own volition, but through an act of grace: "We shall tell you how our Lord is in no way freed by Love, but Love is freed by him for our sakes, so that the little ones through you can hear of this, for Love can do all things, and not do wrong to anyone" (12). The realization of God's message does not happen through an assiduous learning process, but instead comes as a gift given by God; it requires a transgression of traditional, human approaches to hermeneutics which is possible only for the person who is graced with God's gifts: "The one whom God has given understanding of it knows that, and no one else, for no book contains it, nor can man's intelligence comprehend it, nor can any creature's laboring be rewarded by

---

[57] Milem, *The Unspoken Word*, 11; see also Amy Hollywood, *The Soul as Virgin Wife: Mechthild of Magdeburg, Marguerite Porete, and Meister Eckhart*. Studies in Spirituality and Theology, 1 (Notre Dame and London: University of Notre Dame Press, 1995),156–60.

[58] Conklin Akbari, *Seeing through the Veil*, 5.

[59] Hollywood, *The Soul as Virgin Wife*, 158.

[60] Margaret Porette, *The Mirror of Simple Souls*, trans. J. C. Marler and Judith Grant, and a foreword by Kent Emery, Jr. Notre Dame Texts in Medieval Culture, 6 (Notre Dame: University of Notre Dame Press, 1999), 10. See also the contribution to this volume by Valerie M. Wilhite.

understanding or comprehending it. Rather this is a gift given by the most High, into whom this creature is ravished through fullness of knowledge, and in her understanding she remains nothing" (17). Although it might be paradoxical, the more Margaret elaborates her mystical understanding of the Godhead and turns away from traditional learning, the more she also relies on words. These words, however, are no longer the result of a linear learning process, or their reflection; instead they are utterances of the mystically-inspired soul and rely as much on apophatic discourse as on cataphasis. When Reason inquires from Love what the rightful name of her Soul would be, Love offers the following litany: "The Very Wonderful: / The Unknown: / The Most Innocent of the Daughters of Jerusalem: / She upon whom all Holy Church is founded: / The Enlightened by Knowledge: / ... The Brought to Nothing in All Things through Humility / ... / Her last name is: Forgetting" (21–22).

More poignantly, Margaret goes so far as to discard all intellectual comprehension, which is insufficient in grasping the essence of her love for the Godhead: "If this Soul had all the knowledge and the love and the praise which ever were given and will be given of the divine Trinity, this would be nothing in comparison with what she loves and will love; nor will she ever attain to this love through knowledge" (25). She uses words, and yet knows only too well that her words cannot bridge the epistemological divide, because the mystical soul has no will of its own and cannot control its world, hence its own words: "The true meaning of what it says in so many places, that the Soul brought to Nothing has no will at all, and cannot want to have any at all" (27). Finally, when Reason queries Love about its own nature, we learn that the mystic relies on a dialectical approach to herself and words: "I am God, says Love, for Love is God, and God is Love, and this Soul is God through its condition of Love, and I am God through my divine nature, and this Soul is God by Love's just law" (41). Although Margaret discards logic as it normally appears in theological treatises, she offers the deepest possible insight into the mystical discourse between her own soul and the Godhead, and thereby she indicates the degree to which the words of love indicate the love of words as catalysts, or key holders, for a spiritual understanding of the Godhead.

This paradigm finds a significant confirmation in contemporary mystical texts, such as those by Mechthild of Hackeborn in *Liber Specialis Gratiae*:

> Igitur quanta Deus mirabilia in electis suis operatus sit, nullus sermo humanus poterit explicare, quantaque dona in anima ipsum fideliter amante diffuderit, lingua non valet promere; quam benigne quamque melliflue se illi exhibebat, sola feliciter experiri meretur.[61]

---

[61] Quoted from Margarete Hubrath, *Schreiben und Erinnern: Zur "memoria" im Liber Specialis Gratiae Mechthilds von Hakeborn* (Paderborn, Munich, et al.: Schöningh, 1996), 50.

[No human speech could explain what great miracles God has effected in those whom He had elected; and no tongue could express the great gift which he has poured into the loyally loving soul; she alone deserves to experience how mercifully and sweetly He has revealed Himself to her.]

Although the mystics regularly referred to the "Unsagbarkeitstopos,"[62] that is, their inability to express in human language what they had experienced in their encounter with the Godhead,[63] they actually reached new heights in exploring the epistemological power of words within their writings. The more they declared their inability to describe in human terms what they had witnessed, the more they revealed the enormous, unlimited potentiality of words. These are worldly, material utterances, but they purport to give voice to God's own messages: "ego sum in manu scribentium; in omnibus cooperator eorum et adjutor; sicque omne quod in me et per me veritatem dictant et scribunt, est verum" (I am in the hand of the scribes; I am in every respect their helper and assistant, and so everything that they write as truth in me and through me is really truth).[64]

Mechthild of Magdeburg described her relationship to the written word in different terms, realizing how hard it would be for her readers to understand her account. One simple reading of her book would not be enough; instead she urges her audience to read her book at least nine times, for it is only then that its meaning would be fully revealed.[65] Although *The Flowing Light* was certainly a product of Mechthild's own writing, she unmistakably emphasizes that her hand had been guided by the Godhead and that He wanted mankind to learn about Him through Mechthild's mystical account: "It shall be called a flowing light of my Godhead into all hearts that live free of hypocrisy" (39). In her prologue, she had emphasized the key component of all reading, a reading which requires respect, worship, intellect, and profound love: "This writing must be read in a pious spirit, however. It must be understood, as is the case with other holy writings, in a wholesome manner and in good faith. . . . Its author is the Father, Son, and Holy Spirit" (32). By way of communicating with the Godhead, the mystic overcomes the ancient tragedy of Babel and reconstitutes a linguistic, and then also spiritual, community of the human creature with God. Michel de Certeau has correctly characterized mystical discourse as "the anti-Babel, the quest for a common speech after

---

[62] Peter Fuchs, "Von der Beobachtung des Unbeobachtbaren: Ist Mystik ein Fall von Inkommunikabilität?," Niklas Luhmann and idem, *Reden und Schweigen*. Suhrkamp Taschenbuch Wissenschaft, 848 (Frankfurt a.M.: Suhrkamp, 1989), 70–100; Milem, *The Unspoken Word*; Steven Fanning, *Mystics of the Christian Tradition* (London and New York: Routledge, 2001), 76–77.

[63] This term was coined by Ernst Robert Curtius, *European Literature and the Latin Middle Ages* (1973; Princeton: Princeton University Press, 1990; orig. in German 1948), 159.

[64] Quoted from Hubrath, *Schreiben und Erinnern*, 54.

[65] Mechthild of Magdeburg, *The Flowing Light of the Godhead*, trans. Frank Tobin (New York and Mahwah: Paulist Press, 1998), 39.

its breakdown, the invention of a language of 'God' or 'of the angels' that would compensate for the dispersal of human languages."[66]

This intriguing operation is then realized, albeit only indirectly, through a highly complex process of involving the audience, inviting them in through the various types of genres utilized by Mechthild and the many different dialogues.[67] Not surprisingly, Mechthild defines her visionary experience in terms of writing and identifies the revelation as a letter, where she has her soul say, "'O Love, this letter I have written out of your mouth. / Now give me, Lady, your seal'" (43). But the mystic is told to remain quiet and to embrace the Godhead as her lover: "'Be silent, dear one, and speak no more. / Dearest of all maidens, let all creatures, myself included, / Bow down before you. / Tell my Lover that his bed is made ready, / And that I am weak with longing for him'" (43).

About one hundred and fifty years later, the English mystic Margery Kempe was to struggle with the same communicative problem in conveying her experiences in terms comprehensible to her audience, as she realized: "For ever the more slander and reproof that she suffered, the more she increased in grace and in devotion of holy meditation, of high contemplation, and of wonderful speeches and conversation which our Lord spoke and conveyed to her soul, teaching her how she would be despised for this love, and how she should have patience."[68] And a little later, she emphasizes, "Afterwards, when it pleased our Lord, he commanded and charged her that she should have written down her feelings and revelations, and her form of living, so that his goodness might be known to all the world."[69]

The details of the problems she encountered in attempting to record her visions and to receive the necessary help from learned scribes or clerics do not interest us here. What matters is her obvious attempt to find a medium and mechanism for her to reflect upon, to digest, and to relate her visions, translating the ineffable into the concrete of the written word. Her concern about coming to terms with her transcendental experience proved to be so overpowering that she finally managed to find the support from a priest who at long last could read the first, almost illegible, version and rewrite it: "compelled by his own conscience, he tried again to read it, and it was much easier than it was before."[70]

---

[66] Michel de Certeau, *The Mystic Fable*, trans. Michael B. Smith (Chicago and London: The University of Chicago Press, 1992), 157. Now see also Sara S. Poor, *Mechthild of Magdeburg and Her Book: Gender and the Making of Textual Authority*. The Middle Ages Series (Philadelphia: University of Pennsylvania Press, 2004), 22–56.

[67] Poor, *Mechthild of Magdeburg and Her Book*, 95.

[68] *The Book of Margery Kempe*, trans. B. A. Windeatt (London: Penguin, 1985), 34.

[69] *The Book of Margery Kempe*, 35.

[70] *The Book of Margery Kempe*, 38; see also Albrecht Classen, "The Literary Treatment of the Ineffable: Mechthild von Magdeburg, Margaret Ebner, Agnes Blannbekin," *Studies in Spirituality* 9 (1998): 162–87; here 167–68.

Both Mechthild and Margery manifest their irresistible desire to gain access to the written word because it guaranteed the perpetuation of their immediate access to the Godhead, or at least the memory of this unique experience. It would be erroneous, as feminists such as Sara S. Poor have suggested, to state that the mystic focuses on her own body as the site of the revelation.[71] Instead, these women fully realized the epistemological power of the word and made sure that their visions were recorded for posterity. Amy Hollywood observed this clearly with respect to Margaret Porete's testimony: "The book's authorship is pushed away from the human pen onto God because he gives the internal image to the Soul that is externalized in the form of the book."[72] It is possible to go as far back as to the visionary accounts of Hildegard of Bingen (1098–1179), who underscores that understanding of the apophatic is possible only through the word: "This is the infinite Word, which is in the Father before time, before the working of creation. In the glow of love, this Word was to become incarnate, in the course of time, miraculously and without stain or weight of sin, through the pure green vigour of the Holy Spirit in the dawn of blessed maidenhood. When you see the 'shining flame glow white,' it means that God's Word revealed its power as it were by catching fire: the whole of creation was roused by him and grew incandescent when the Word became incarnate in the dawn and brilliance of maidenhood, so that from the Word all the virtues and powers flowed in the knowledge of God when humanity came back to life in the salvation of souls."[73]

Although Hildegard obviously conceived "the Word" as a metaphorical expression, she derived it from her full understanding of the epistemological issues connected with the ineffable and with establishing a hermeneutic bridge to the transcendental. Intriguingly, she also asserted her own authority through letter-writing, hence through turning toward secular words exchanged between people. According to Beverlee Sian Rapp, "She was clearly aware of the effects of language and of the different responses that could be elicited by various forms of address and used these effects to her advantage."[74] As a corollary of her own realization of the ponderous weight of the word in mystical terms, Hildegard offers in her *Scivias* a whole discussion of the theological meaning of the word and relates it to the Holy Trinity: "A word has sound in order to be heard, force in order to be understood, and breath in order to be completed.... Therefore, just as there are the three components of the word, so also the heavenly Trinity is in one heavenly unity."[75]

---

[71] Poor, *Mechthild of Magdeburg*, 59.

[72] Hollywood, *The Soul as Virgin Wife*, 89.

[73] Hildegard of Bingen, *Selected Writings*, trans. Mark Atherton (London: Penguin, 2001), 12–13.

[74] Beverlee Sian Rapp, "A Woman Speaks: Language and Self-Representation in Hildegard's Letters," *Hildegard of Bingen: A Book of Essays*, ed. Maud Burnett McInerney. Garland Medieval Casebooks (New York and London: Garland, 1998), 3–24; here 11.

[75] Hildegard of Bingen, *Selected Writings*, 27.

To write down her visions, however, meant for her to create a container, or medium, for God's own words, since she conceived herself, as she says in a letter to Elisabeth of Schönau, as a "trumpet which only gives out a sound but does not work by itself, since it needs someone else to blow into it so that it will make a sound."[76] This sound itself represents a wonder, as Hildegard emphasizes in her *Scivias*, because it proves to be simply the audible representation of the Godhead and His Creation: "With the sounding of the words one wonder follows another, then human beings, struck by the grandeur of this miracle, tremble in body and soul, pondering, in their wonder at this miracle, their own weakness and frailty."[77] Nevertheless, Hildegard does not claim to be powerful enough to be God's mouthpiece and admits that no one here on earth can find enough words to represent God's wonders: "Who among all creatures can enumerate the works of God?"[78] Other mystics, such as Marguerite d'Oingt (d. 1310), offer significantly parallel images and demonstrate how much they were empowered through their visions to comprehend the fundamental epistemological and operational tools for human, but especially divine hermeneutics.[79]

Before I conclude these introductory observations, we need to return to our discussion of the significance of the word in its epistemological dimension within secular courtly literature because words of love and the love of words embrace both the religious and the erotic.[80] The Middle High German poet Walther von der Vogelweide (d. c. 1230) raised the seemingly simple, yet most fascinating question: "Saget mir ieman, waz ist minne?" (Could someone tell me, what is courtly love?).[81] Whereas most courtly love poets naïvely discuss their own feelings, their beloved, and other conventional motifs within this erotic discourse, according to the requirements of the specific poetic genre, Walther probes the deeper meaning and questions the relevance of the term itself. He inquires why love is so painful, and begs his audience to inform him about the true nature of this whole inexplicable phenomenon: "der berihte mich durch waz si tuot sô wê" (69.4; let him make known to me why it hurts so much).

---

[76] Hildegard of Bingen, *Selected Writings*, 81.
[77] Hildegard of Bingen, *Selected Writings*, 92.
[78] Hildegard of Bingen, *Selected Writings*, 146.
[79] Catherine Müller, "How to Do Things with Mystical Language: Marguerite d'Oingt's Performative Writing," *Performance and Transformation: New Approaches to Late Medieval Spirituality*, ed. Mary A. Suydam and Joanna E. Ziegler (New York: St. Martin's Press, 1999), 27–45.
[80] Walter Haug, "Gotteserfahrung und Du-Begegnung. Korrespondenzen in der Geschichte der Mystik und der Liebeslyrik," *Geistliches in weltlicher und Weltliches in geistlicher Literatur des Mittelalters*, ed. Christoph Huber, Burghart Wachinger, and Hans-Joachim Ziegeler (Tübingen: Niemeyer, 2000), 195–212.
[81] Walther von der Vogelweide, *Leich, Lieder, Sangsprüche*. 14., völlig neubearbeitete Auflage der Ausgabe Karl Lachmanns mit Beiträgen von Thomas Bein und Horst Brunner, ed. Christoph Cormeau (Berlin and New York: de Gruyter, 1996), 69, 1; the translations are my own.

For him, the term 'love' should be used only if it creates happiness: "minne ist minne, tuot si wol" (69.5; love is love, if she provides comfort), whereas the opposite would not deserve this name (69.6). Giving away his own rhetorical game, Walther then proceeds to explore the semantics of "minne" himself and suggests: "minne ist zweier herzen wünne: / teilent sie gelîche, sost diu minne dâ" (69.10–11; love is the joy of two hearts: when they share in this, then love is present). One heart alone, however, cannot sustain or develop love (69.12–13). This latter point provides the poet the necessary segue, or opportunity, to question his lady about whether she might have mercy on him and respond to his love. Walther confesses that his heart is too heavy with love and can no longer bear it alone (69.15). Not content with suffering love pangs without any hope from his lady, he appeals to her to make a clear decision, either to accept him as her lover or to state unmistakably that she would reject him. In this case he would let go of his wooing altogether: "unde bin von dir ein ledic man" (69.19; and will be a man separated from you). However, rejecting him would not be as easy as the lady might think, because without him she would not find any comparable poet: "daz dich lützel ieman baz geloben kan" (69, 21; hardly anyone can give better praise). His lady ought to know that the lover would not woo only to receive pain (69, 23) or to be dismissed by her as an unworthy candidate (69.25).[82]

The poet goes one step further when he defines his own role as courtly love singer as being the source of all cultural activities (72.31). Once his lady has turned her back on him, forcing him to end his singing, then the public entertainment, and also the essential discourse of love, come to an abrupt termination: "Hêrre, waz si flüeche lîden sol, / swenn ich nû lâze mînen sanc! / alle die nû lobent, daz weiz ich wol, / die scheltent denne âne mînen danc!" (73.5–8; O Lord, she will then suffer from much cursing when I stop my singing. All those who praise it now will complain bitterly without me being responsible for it). Of course, the lady is not any specific lady, but the court, or courtly society at large; hence Walther really talks about the relationship between himself and his audience, sharply admonishing them to pay him adequate respect and to honor him.[83] In other words, he is the creator of public honor and culture, and without his own words and melodies life will come to an end as they know it: "ir leben hât mînes lebennes êre: sterbet si mich, sô ist si tôt" (73.16; her life is determined by the honor of my life: if she kills me, she herself is dead). Of course, Walther does not examine the epistemological

---

[82] Heike Sievert, *Studien zur Liebeslyrik Walthers von der Vogelweide*. Göppinger Arbeiten zur Germanistik, 506 (Göppingen: Kümmerle, 1990), 43–58 (here referring to L. 49, 25 as an analogous poetic discourse); for a critical discussion of the current status in Walther research, see Horst Brunner, Gerhard Hahn, Ulrich Müller, and Viktor Spechtler, *Walther von der Vogelweide: Epoche – Werk – Wirkung*. Arbeitsbücher zur Literaturgeschichte (Munich: Beck, 1996), esp. 89–100.

[83] See Frederick Goldin's "Introduction" to Walther von der Vogelweide, *The Single-Stanza Lyrics*, ed. and trans. idem (New York and London: Routledge, 2003), 9–14.

dimension of his own singing, but he certainly demonstrates that courtly love poetry aimed much higher than only to the level of wooing a lady for the singer's, or the audience's, own, erotic sake. Walther challenges us to comprehend the meaning of love — of the words of love — and to understand our fundamental ability to formulate words of love as essential for the well-being of society in its communicative configuration.[84] Although as a highly professional poet he has been singing of love all his life, he admits in the end — albeit certainly as part of a rhetorical strategy — that he does not know what love is. But this formal admission also allows us to gain a new understanding of love discourse as apophasis:

> Diu minne ist weder man noch wîp,
> si hât noch sêle noch den lîp,
> sie gelîchet sich dekeinem bilde.
> ir nam ist kunt, si selbe ist aber wilde,
> und enkan doch nieman âne sie
> der gotes hulden niht gewinnen. (81, 31–36)

[Love is neither man nor woman, she has neither soul nor body, there is no image for her. We know her name, but she herself is foreign to us, yet no one can be without her who wants to gain God's grace.]

Walther signals that love is both erotic and spiritual, and that aspiring to love is tantamount to searching for the Grail, or for the Godhead within the mystical discourse. Words, language, and love intertwine here and represent a powerful epistemological and semiotic cluster that propels us forward in our quest for the ineffable. Life in its material dimension would be worthless without the spiritual; thus the discourse of love proves to be the ultimate, most powerful, and truly only significant enterprise for all human beings. As we should say once again, words of love and love of words join in a chiastic unity that represents the epistemological quest undergirding all human existence and elevates it above its material imprisonment, paving the way for the establishment of a human community, supported by the "joie de la curt," as Hartmann von Aue formulated, copying the words from his source, Chrétien de Troye's *Erec*.[85]

In light of this observation, we may conclude that many medieval poets like Walther, but also the mystics such as Mechthild of Magdeburg, Margaret Porette, and Hildegard of Bingen, regarded themselves as prophets who had to bring a new understanding of 'the word' to the world. Walther expresses this poignantly in his poem "Ir sult sprechen willekomen" (56.14): "der iu mære bringet, daz bin ich. / allez, daz ir habt vernomen, / dest gâr ein wint, nû vrâget mich" (56.15–17; the one

---

[84] Classen, *Verzweiflung und Hoffnung*, 167–220.
[85] See also the contribution to this volume by Siegfried R. Christoph.

who brings news, that is me. Whatever you have heard so far was nothing, now ask me).[86] Of course, Walther does not hide his irony, especially when he adds that he would tell his audience only bad news if they don't reward him properly for his singing: "wirt mîn lôn iht guot, / ich sage vil lîhte, daz iu sanfte tuot. / seht, waz man mir êren biete" (56.19–21).[87]

The true poet, whether worldly and erotically or mystically inclined, emerges as the harbinger of a utopian world, the world of love which finds its best expression in the word of love.[88] Both secular and mystical poets in the Middle Ages pursued this lofty goal and, as the preceding selection of texts has demonstrated, they seem to have realized their intentions to some extent, especially in connection with the insight that the human word gains value only when it reflects upon the apophatic and sings of the divine within the context of people's mundane existence, whether represented by the earthly beloved or by the mystical soul. As Alan of Lille (ca. 1128–ca. 1202) demonstrates in his famous *Anticlaudianus*, the ancient dream of man to achieve union with the divine is possible through the word, and the poet is called upon to give expression to that utopian idea: "The battle ceases, Victory falls to the New Man. Virtue rises, Vice sinks, Nature triumphs, Love rules, nowhere is there Disagreement but Agreement everywhere. For that blessed man guides the earthly kingdom with the reins of law, that man whom licentiousness does not impair, pride does not overcome, crime does not sully, the goad of wantonness does not urge on, guilt from fraud does not taint."[89]

But how would people ever find the way toward this utopia, this ideal world where all human potentials are realized, unless they resort to words and analyze their deeper meaning as firm guides toward the future? As Dante Alighieri says in his letter to Can Grande della Scala, "The sense of this work is not simple, but on the contrary it may be called polysemous, that is to say, 'of more senses than one'; for it is one sense which we get through the letter, and another which we get through the thing the letter signifies; and the first is called literal, but the

---

[86] For comparable statements by Middle High German poets, though mostly about their colleagues, see *Dichter über Dichter in mittelhochdeutscher Literatur*, ed. Günther Schweikle. Deutsche Texte, 12 (Tübingen: Niemeyer, 1970); see also Gerhard Hahn, "*dâ keiser spil*. Zur Aufführung höfischer Literatur am Beispiel des Minnesangs," idem and Hedda Ragotzky, ed., *Grundlagen des Verstehens mittelalterlicher Literatur: Literarische Texte und ihr historischer Erkenntniswert* (Stuttgart: Kröner, 1992), 86–107.

[87] Gerhard Hahn, "Walthers Minnesang," Horst Brunner, Gerhard Hahn, Ulrich Müller, Viktor Spechtler, *Walther von der Vogelweide*, 87–89, summarizes the standard interpretation of this song, which implies that the poet made a serious effort to regain his traditional position at the court of Vienna. Nevertheless, we cannot overlook the ethical implications of Walther's verses in the context of our investigation.

[88] For the medieval approach to utopia, see Tomas Tomasek, *Die Utopie im 'Tristan' Gotfrids von Straßburg*. Hermaea: Germanistische Forschungen, Neue Folge, 49 (Tübingen: Niemeyer, 1985), 32–39.

[89] Alan of Lille, *Anticlaudianus or the Good and Perfect Man*, trans. and comm. James J. Sheridan (Toronto: Pontifical Institute of Mediaeval Studies, 1973), 215–16.

second allegorical or mystic." Then, explicating a Biblical example, he explains further: "For if we inspect the letter alone, the departure of the children of Israel from Egypt in the time of Moses is presented us; if the allegory, our redemption wrought by Christ; if the moral sense, the conversion of the soul from the grief and misery of sin to the state of grace is presented to us; if the anagogical, the departure of the holy soul from the slavery of this corruption to the liberty of eternal glory is presented to us."[90] In defense of poetry, which, he asserts, is not the product of lying, Boccaccio went so far as to argue that fictional texts represent the truth hidden behind the veil of the literary word: "Clearly poets are not constrained by this bond to employ literal truth on the surface of their inventions." And: "So also a poet, however he may sacrifice the literal truth in invention, does not incur the ignominy of a liar, since he discharges his very proper function not to deceive, but only by way of invention."[91] In his treatise on Dante, Boccaccio offers an additional explanation, giving poetry the full weight that literary hermeneutics deserve: "And so to ensure that that which is acquired with labour should prove more pleasing, and should therefore be more carefully preserved, the poets concealed simple truth beneath many things which are apparently in opposition to it."[92] This idea had been expressed long before by Marie de France in the prologue to her *Lais*, discussed above; however, Boccaccio adds a new layer of critical discourse crediting the poet with a messianic and visionary power: "I say that theology and poetry can be spoken of almost as one and the same thing, when they share the same subject. Indeed, I will say even more: that theology is nothing other than a poetry of God."[93]

Medieval mystical discourse, courtly love poetry, courtly romances, and many other genres of narrative discourse reflecting upon the epistemological significance of the poetic word indicate that this awareness concerning the fundamental hermeneutics of the creative act of writing was generally shared, at least among the poets, though not necessarily among the theologians and other critics.[94] Whereas early medieval poetry seems little concerned with the individual creator of the text, from the twelfth century on we can clearly observe

---

[90] *A Translation of the Latin Works of Dante Alighieri* (1904; New York: Greenwood Press, 1969), 347–48 [translator is identified as Philip H. Wicksteed]. For a discussion of this important passage for the interpretation both of Dante's own *Divina Commedia* and other medieval texts, see *Medieval Literary Theory and Criticism c. 1100–c. 1375: The Commentary Tradition*, ed. A. J. Minnis and A. B. Scott with the assistance of David Wallace (Oxford: Clarendon Press, 1988), 383–87.

[91] *Medieval Literary Theory*, 432.

[92] *Medieval Literary Theory*, 497.

[93] *Medieval Literary Theory*, 498.

[94] See, for instance, Michael Bernsen, *Die Problematisierung lyrischen Sprechens im Mittelalter: Eine Untersuchung zum Diskurswandel der Liebesdichtung von den Provenzalen bis zu Petrarca*. Beihefte zur Zeitschrift für Romanische Philologie, 313 (Tübingen: Niemeyer, 2001), 35–57; see also Michel Zink, *The Invention of Literary Subjectivity*, trans. David Sices. Parallax: Revisions of Culture and Society (1985; Baltimore and London: The John Hopkins University Press, 1999), 45–60.

an intriguing awakening of the poetic 'I' and its efforts to reach out to the Godhead through its creativity. As Burt Kimmelman has perceptively observed, "A self-referentiality had inhered in the Augustinian epistemological system; this was later applied to a metapoetics in which poets increasingly tended to refer to and to carry on discussions about themselves as poets and about the possibility of making poetry that might reflect the true state of things in the world," or rather, as I might add, the other world.[95] When Hugh of Saint Victor discussed the essential nature of the Biblical text in his *Didascalicon*, he resorted to metaphoric language that allows us to comprehend how much the poetic text also contributes to the development of a cosmic universe where all pieces fit together to form an harmonious whole: "Therefore, the basis of this superstructure ought also to relate to allegory. The superstructure rises in many courses of stories, and each course has its basis. Even so, many mysteries are contained in the divine page and they each have their bases from which they spring."[96]

Indeed, whether we consider courtly love poetry, mystical revelations, theoretical discourse, or theological treatises, there is no doubt that medieval writers had a full understanding and appreciation of words of love as the medium of the love of words, hence of the fundamental hermeneutics connected with all creative work relying on human language.

We can conclude with another reference to Dante Alighieri, who offered a theoretical explanation of his poetry in the "Exposition" to his *Convivio*: "I say that in the stanza which begins HE DISCOVERS AN OPPONENT WHO DESTROYS HIM I intend to make plain that which my soul was speaking within me, namely, that which the long-established thought was saying against the new one."[97] Wisdom rests in the word, and the poet who loves words becomes a creator of wisdom because poetry is the ultimate vehicle of human epistemology in its central — even if apophatic — manifestation. There is no doubt that both medieval philosophers and theologians, and both jurists and artists, would have agreed. After all, love governs the world, as both Boethius in his *Consolatio Philosophiae* (2, m. 8) and Dante Alighieri in his *Divina Commedia* (*Inferno*, 1.38), among many other poets and philosophers have confirmed.

---

[95] Burt Kimmelman, *The Poetics of Authorship in the Later Middle Ages: The Emergence of the Modern Literary Persona*. Studies in the Humanities: Literature — Politics — Society, 21 (New York, Washington, D.C., et al.: Peter Lang, 1996), 35. See also N. S. Thompson, *Chaucer, Boccaccio, and the Debate of Love: A Comparative Study of the Decameron and The Canterbury Tales* (Oxford: Clarendon Press; New York: Oxford University Press, 1996), 49, referring to the first tale of the first day in Boccaccio's *Decameron*: "This tale is the one that introduces us to the world of ambiguous signs that constitutes the collection. The work shows a distinct lack of interest in the workings of the Divine Mind, and much prefers the comic workings of the human one." Holly Wallace Boucher, "Nominalism: the Difference for Chaucer and Boccaccio," *The Chaucer Review* 20, 3 (1985/1986): 213–20, offers parallel observations.

[96] *Medieval Literary Theory*, 78–79.

[97] *Medieval Literary Theory*, 405.

As early as the end of the third century of our era the Hermetic treatise *Asclepius* had already laid the foundation for the abstract notion that love and creation go hand in hand:

> It is through the Lord of all nature that the mystery of procreation has been invented for and bestowed on all things forever; in it the supreme charity, joy, mirth, desire and divine love inhere.... Love is therefore made in secret, so that the divinity manifesting itself in both partners in the act of love need not feel exposed to mockery.[98]

By the same token, we could argue that love as the fermenting agent of language extends into the creative sphere of all material things, and by accepting the conclusion that words of love translate into a love of words, we have come full circle, because love leads to the epistemological epiphany, and the poetic discourse proves to be the crucial medium to achieve this ultimate goal of human hermeneutics. This "theme of cosmic love," first fully developed by Boethius, reverberated throughout the entire Middle Ages and beyond, whether we think of Scotus Eriugena or William of Conches, Bernardus Silvestris or any of the major late medieval poets, such as Jean de Meun, Boccaccio, and Geoffrey Chaucer. Medieval love poetry and romance suddenly emerge as simply the other side of the same coin all the philosophers had discussed.[99]

The subsequent papers in this volume will pick up this discursive thread and trace it back to a wide range of literary documents from late antiquity to the Renaissance. Such a kaleidoscopic approach promises to yield far-reaching results, sensitizing us, above all, to the fundamental significance of the word of love, in both its written and oral performance. Central to this collection is the concept that the survival of all human societies through communication, the ultimate goal of language, is founded iin some way on words of love and love of words.

One of the hitherto unanswered questions regarding the enormously influential phenomenon of 'courtly love' in the Middle Ages pertains to its origin. When did public discourse accept the erotic as a valuable, noteworthy topic for the first time? Or, when did marriage emerge as more than a fairly simple matter of parental arrangement with the purpose of guaranteeing the continuity of the family and the creation of offspring within a legal framework? Cynthia White introduces an essential feature of medieval courtly love poetry in its incipient stage when she

---

[98] Quoted from Peter Dronke, *The Medieval Poet and His World*. Storia e Letteratura. Raccoltà di Studi e Testi, 164 (Rome: Edizioni di Storia e Letteratura, 1984), 448. See also the text excerpt online at www.gnosis.org/library/hermes2.html. For a brief introduction, see www.canadiancontent.net/en/jd/go?Url=http://www.sacred-texts.com/chr/herm/h-intro.htm (both last accessed on March 1, 2006).

[99] Dronke, *The Medieval Poet*, 456–75.

discusses the mingling of the genres of elegy and epithalamium in two poems that bridge the shift from classical pagan into early Christian Latin poetry.[100] Examining the *Epithalamium to Julian and Titia* of Paulinus of Nola (353–431 CE), she observes a unique and innovative blending of two genres, the classical elegy, which often ridicules and scoffs at marriage, and the epithalamium (song in praise of the bride or the wedding) in the vein of Statius (c. 45–96 CE). Paulinus resorted to this original combination of genres and topoi for specifically religious, i.e., Christian, purposes, but this did not tie his tongue into a knot, as the most sophisticated poetic arts employed by him clearly indicate. Whereas the elegiac verse traditionally served as a forum for the exploration of irrational passion and the rejection of marriage, the epithalamium glorified the very opposite; and Paulinus succeeded in interlacing both through the new focus on Christ as the spiritual bridegroom. Until Statius, the topos of the willing bridegroom and unwilling bride had been standard fare for the epithalamium, whereas the elegy thematized the willing groom and willing, though unattainable, bride. In his *Epithalamium to Stella and Violentilla*, Statius changed all that and offered the new perspective of the love-filled marriage — a literary foundation upon which Paulinus then could build and create his Christian poem informed by deep erotic passion.

Paulinus's epithalamium for Julian, son of Bishop Memor, and his bride Titia successfully drew from this new model and applied it to Christian teachings about the ideal marriage, here understood as Christ's union with the Church, predicated on asceticism and continence, hence aiming for *conjugal virginity*. Rejecting all the worldly pomp and luxuriousness of traditional elegies, Paulinus projects a value system determined by simplicity, modesty, and simple-mindedness as the essential conditions for the happily fulfilled marriage with Christ. This rejection, however, also proves to be a masterful manipulation of lyrical verses and rhetorical strategies, which reflects Paulinus's extraordinary love of words for his worship of Christ the Lord through words of love, purposefully inverting form and content.

Both Statius and Paulinus, though with rather oppositional intentions, signal a fundamental paradigm shift in the area of love and marriage, the former emphasizing the secular- erotic, the latter the erotic-religious, while both developing, each on his own, an intriguingly new platform for the discursive investigation of the relationship between love and marriage.

The deliberate misuse of words of love, however, can also be observed. The sixth-century poet Venantius Fortunatus, for example, whose panegyrics of love Robert Levine examines in great detail as an enormously ambivalent rhetoric of love, demonstrated early on that the language of love could be used for a wide range of purposes, using themes such as mutual respect, friendship, admiration, and ethical and moral ideals. As his love of words indicates, the poetic and rhetorical

---

[100] See also Jaeger, *Ennobling Love*, for insightful comments on pre-courtly eroticism.

arts emerge as the central tools for Fortunatus to create avenues and instruments for his own self-aggrandizement and self-indulgence. Autobiographical allusions within his panegyrics illustrate the extent to which this highly skilled poet knew how to manipulate language, casting himself as an intimate friend, as a trustworthy advisor, and as an absolute admirer of the persons to whom he dedicated his poems. Yes, Fortunatus reveals a deep love of words in his compositions, but he really utilizes his words of love for political, specifically highly self-centered, purposes. Should we then call him a sycophant, as Levine suggests? From a moral and ethical perspective that would certainly be the case. However, Fortunatus's panegyrics still prove to be masterpieces of euphony, dexterously developed and certainly pleasing to the ear, although his words of love reveal, particularly because they are the result of his love of words, an abject degree of delusion, deception, and illusion. A modern word for Fortunatus might be "spin-doctor."

Since this volume addresses its topic from a highly interdisciplinary perspective, we cannot leave out the world of Irish literature, in which the theme of love emerged very early, perhaps even long before it gained a foothold in continental medieval secular literature. Both words of love and love of words emerge as central aspects in many Old Irish narratives, which William Sayers here examines in great detail, offering highly valuable material for a comparative analysis. Intriguingly, however, some of the oldest texts primarily address hierogamy, that is, the union of the goddess of the land with her royal consort, whereas passionate, mundane love gained in relevance only later. But some of the early tales are specifically predicated on the love of words because a young woman and a young man test each other out regarding their ability to tell riddles and to create puns, before they agree on a union, which is made possible when he has met a series of heroic challenges.[101]

In numerous cases female representatives of the Otherworld demonstrate amatory interest in earthly male partners, which will find a surprising parallel in late medieval Spanish religious love poetry in the *Cantigas de Santa Maria* by King Alfonso X the Wise,[102] and in much of European bridal mysticism.[103] Another significant parallel proves to be the theme of the magical love-spot, which has the same effect as the transformative love potion as deployed in the pan-European *Tristan* tradition. Another aspect that sheds much light on the multiple connections between medieval Celtic and continental love literature proves to be scopophilia, mostly the woman's gaze from her window at the future lover who then feels a stirring of emotions in her. Sayers also calls attention to Old Irish debate poems

---

[101] For this pan-European motif with its profound epistemological significance, see Albrecht Classen, "Reading and Deciphering in Apollonius of Tyre and the *Historia von den sieben weisen Meistern*: Medieval Epistemology within a Literary Context," to appear in *Studi Medievali*.
[102] See the contribution by Connie Scarborough to this volume.
[103] See the contribution by Albrecht Classen to this volume.

involving a man and a woman poet discussing the meaning of love. Here the Provençal *tenso* offers an interesting parallel, despite differences. The differences mostly pertain to the emphasis on fissure in Irish love poetry, whereas courtly romances and courtly poems rather explore the dialectical meaning of love, embarking on a profound interiorization process, which was perhaps the greatest hallmark of the discourse on courtly love throughout the entire Middle Ages.

On another level, Sayers identifies numerous Irish texts that are predicated on the conflicts resulting from love at a distance, and on the potentially devastating effects of words of love on society at large, especially when the words are no longer intended as contractually binding, and as the basis for emotive commitments. Old Irish literature demonstrates that the public discourse of love, whether addressing hierogamy or regular love relationships between ordinary people, shares significant elements with romances and other works on the European continent.

Even the motif of the ugly hag who suddenly transforms herself into a lovely lady after having been kissed by the knightly champion, perhaps best represented in the "Wife of Bath's Tale" in Chaucer's *Canterbury Tales*, can already be discovered in Irish literature. How the European courtly poets learned of, and from, these Celtic antecedents or contemporary sources, remains, of course, a major question for future research. Here, at least, Sayers demonstrates the extent to which words of love and love of words are fundamental also for Old Irish literature, which, with its Welsh correspondences, must be reckoned a major font for much of medieval courtly literature.

Human language powerfully reflects the individual's mind-set, feelings, ideas, and thoughts. In contrast to early medieval heroes, who tended to be stoic, unreflective, and action-oriented, with the rise of twelfth-century courtly romances a new love of words injected a completely new dimension into medieval literature, offering surprising insights into the protagonists' interior world of emotions. As Raymond Cormier illustrates in his analysis of the speech acts by Lavine in the *Roman d'Eneas*, this young woman resorts to words of love in order to explore the feelings that the sight of Eneas has aroused in her. Arguing boldly for the relevance of this and other medieval narratives as literary mirrors for the modern analysis of selfhood, identity, and emotionality, Cormier reveals the potential of the love of words in the erotic context. Drawing from postmodern gender studies that focus on women's language and thought patterns, he observes that Lavine goes through a complex process of exploring her newly-discovered affection for Eneas, explicitly relying on a compound register of word-thought patterns that allow her to reach the full depths of her feelings and ultimately to formulate the ineffable phenomenon moving her, namely love. Particularly because Lavine has to fight against her mother's authority in choosing her own lover, the monologic yet simultaneously dialectic exploration of her sentiments finds powerful expression. Thus the intriguing love of words as expressions of her self empowers her to gain access to her own words of love, which in turn reflect her interior self. Consequently, Lavine acquires sufficient strength in this process to withstand her mother's urging to turn away from Eneas and to accept Turnus, the mother's preferred candidate.

Whereas Lavine emerges as a powerful projection of a female voice by a male composer, in Heloise's own letters to her lover, husband, and spiritual advisor Abelard we come across a much more radical position vis-à-vis female language, that is, a language of desire that accepts her own corporeality and embraces the erotic dimension as essential for the theological quest for the divine. In fact, as Carmel Posa argues in her contribution to this volume, desire for the transcendental can achieve its goal not only by way of renunciation of the body, or the physical self, which might be a male approach, as indicated by countless medieval statements in this regard. It might also be possible to realize one's spiritual and erotic desire by way of accepting the body, that is, through the body, as Heloise expressed it in her letters to Abelard.[104] Revolutionary as it might seem, the female epistolary author claimed that marriage and the monastic vow were not mutually exclusive, but rather complementary in their common goal, the love of God. Desire for the beloved, within marriage or outside, can, and ought to, guide the spirit in the right direction; hence Heloise's desire for Abelard was also a desire for God. As Heloise's intriguing words indicate, she firmly believed that true love relies on the integrity, or harmony, of body and soul, and her letter-writing supported her almost revolutionary perspective, as Lavine, in the *Roman d'Eneas*, would have certainly agreed, and as Isolde in Gottfried von Strassburg's *Tristan* would have also confirmed.[105] All three women embraced love as a physical experience within themselves, that is, within their bodies, and they turned to words as vehicles for coming to terms with this physical, and spiritual, love. Surprisingly, this holds true even though both Lavine and Isolde were undoubtedly male projections, whereas Heloise's authorship, though it continues to be questioned from various directions in modern scholarship, is generally held to be the voice of a real historical woman. The opposite perspective finds its expression in Abelard's letters,

---

[104] The discussion regarding the authenticity of Heloise's letters has continued, even despite, if not particularly because of, Constant J. Mews's *The Lost Love Letters of Heloise and Abelard: Perceptions of Dialogue in Twelfth-Century France*. With a translation by Neville Chiavaroli and idem. The New Middle Ages (New York: St. Martin's Press, 1999); see also *Listening to Heloise: The Voice of a Twelfth-Century Woman*, ed. Bonnie Wheeler. The New Middle Ages (New York: St. Martin's Press, 2000); see also Giles Constable, "Sur l'attribution des *Epistolae duorum amantium*," Académie des inscriptions et belles-lettres. Comptes-rendus des séances 4 (2001): 1679–93. For a highly critical perspective, see Peter von Moos, "Die *Epistolae duorum amantium* und die säkulare Religion der Liebe: Methodenkritische Vorüberlegungen zu einem einmaligen Werk mittellateinischer Briefliteratur," *Studi medievali* 3a serie, XLIV, 1 (2003): 1–115.

[105] Albrecht Classen, "Female Agency and Power in Gottfried von Strassburg's *Tristan*: The Irish Queen Isolde: New Perspectives," *Tristania* 23 (2005): 39–60.

so this unique correspondence emerges as a struggle of minds over the meaning of the body in the quest for spiritual happiness, or the fulfilment of human desires. The correspondence between these two outstanding intellectuals, both highly admired by their contemporaries and also by posterity, turns into a literary battlefield where fundamental theological issues and philosophical concerns regarding human desires and human corporeality are pitted against each other. It seems quite likely, as Posa demonstrates, that Heloise carried the victory through her skillful employment of these words of love, trumping even her own master who was so enamored by their mutual love of words that he could not fully comprehend the dialectic nature of Heloise's own words of love.

No investigation of the medieval discourse of love in its literary manifestation can be considered exhaustive if the attention is not turned toward Andreas Capellanus's treatise *De amore* at least once. Bonnie Wheeler does just that, but she offers one of the most far-reaching interpretations of this most complex and highly dialectical work from ca. 1190, if not later. Instead of either dismissing the third part as entirely separate from the first two, or focusing on the first two books only as a consistent teaching of courtly love, Wheeler argues convincingly that Andreas obviously followed the principles of Abelardian dialectics, as best expressed in his *Sic et Non*, arguing from both sides of the debate regarding love. Those, like Bishop Etienne Tempier of Paris, who vehemently condemned Andreas's treatise as the product of a vain mind, filled with loathsome follies relating it almost to such evil matters as necromancy, entirely missed the ironic, satirical, but above all dialectical nature of this text. Here love and words are so intimately intertwined that *De amore* might even be the explicit realization of the chiasm of "Words of Love and Love of Words." But each book stands on its own, containing almost violent forms of dialectics involving the two genders as disputants, demonstrating how much the obsession with the poetic word not only created words of love, but also, if not even more, a love of words. Instead of observing contradictory elements, especially with regard to the tension between the first two books and the third, Wheeler suggests that the treatise is completely predicated on contradiction itself, which is, however, an inherent element of both love and human language, constantly hovering between the 'yes' and 'no' in the Abelardian sense. However, this seeming instability of Andreas's discourse precisely establishes a basis for the exploration of human communication, and elevates rhetorics to the highest level of courtly existence,[106] granting the master of words profound respect for his intellectual abilities, and also love, the ultimate goal of all poetic language as pursued by male and female poets throughout the

---

[106] This is also the main thrust of Albrecht Classen's interpretation of Andreas's *De amore*, see Classen, *Verzweiflung und Hoffnung*, 53–107.

Middle Ages.[107] Nevertheless, Andreas also created difference in grammatical and social terms between the genders, but the contradictory nature of the entire treatise illustrates the extent to which all these categories and criteria are subject to debate and support the dialectical operations, even in the last, highly misogynist third book. After all, as Wheeler emphasizes, love as discussed by Andreas emerges as a function of the poetic and philosophical word, whereas the latter proves to be the translation of love's power into a manifest phenomenon.

Words of love prove to be, as Valerie Wilhite illustrates in her contribution, central vehicles both for secular, erotic poets and for mystical writers to come to terms with their ultimate quest. The experience of love commands a transformative power, or rather has an 'un-forming' impact on the individual in love, as Marguerite Porete, Jacopone da Todi, and Angela da Foligno demonstrate in their visionary accounts of encounters with the Godhead. The same can be claimed to be the underlying thrust of most courtly love poetry by the *troubadours* Gaucelm Faidit, Raimbaut d'Aurenga, and Bernart de Ventadorn, and, by the same token, by the *trouvères*, the German *Minnesänger*, and the Italian poets of the *dolce stil nuovo*. Love and language are two sides of the same coin, and the more mystical writers and courtly love poets strove to grasp the essence of the mysterium of their emotive experiences, the more they realized that their own self was dissolved and became part of the beloved, either the Godhead (Philippians 1:23) or the worshipped person. The love of words, in their poetic and religious dimension, replaces the traditional focus on the self and prepares the possibility of an erotic union with the 'Other.' The mystical revelation thereby proves to be a profoundly parallel experience to falling in love as understood by the *troubadour* poets, and others. But rapture, either religious or erotic — though the difference would be minimal — challenges the individual down to the core because human words, the essential catalyst of the self, are not readily available to express this ineffable experience. The apophatic, so to speak, determines both the mystical vision and the erotic passion, which forced both the mystical writers and the courtly love poets to search for a new language. Their words of love translated into a love of words,[108] both supported by a deeply-anchored desire for union with the beloved, which would ultimately overcome the fundamental binary oppositions of all human existence. This was perhaps best expressed by Dante in the third section of his *Divina Commedia*, the *Paradiso*, where the encounter with Beatrice leads him to the ultimate epiphany. However, as Wilhite suggests, the mystical account by Marguerite de Porete might well be identifiable as some of the very best erotic love literature ever composed in the Middle Ages because her words of love translated into an unsurpassable love of words in which the Godhead

---

[107] See especially the contributions to this volume by Valerie Michelle Wilhite, Christopher R. Clason, and Connie Scarborough.
[108] Classen, "The Literary Treatment of the Ineffable," 162–87.

manifests Himself. But Marguerite's vision ultimately displays surprising parallels to the feelings and ideas expressed by the *troubadours* because both erotic love and religious love aim for the union with the divine 'Other,' which human words can hardly, if ever, express adequately.

Courtly lovers — as the saying goes — love, but do not love themselves. Love, with a capital 'L,' as discussed by troubadours and their successors, is a god, Amors, who supports them as well as love poetry — or, troubadours' songs and tales and romances, and by the same token any other medium able to constitute love's proof and to make the poet or knight worthy of the lady's reward — and as love itself, as Anna Kukułka-Wojtasik explores in her contribution to this volume. Courtly poetry forms a closed circuit: the perfection of the poet who sings of love, and of the lady who gives value to love and herself: the more the form and music of the poem are perfected, the more the author and his love are glorified. Love corresponds to the poetry: the greatness of love becomes the splendor of the poetry: the lady's beauty is reflected in the formal beauty of the poem.

Poetry, in which love is lauded in public, is often accused of formalism, of the failure of the lyric, the repeated clichés, the same topoi, and the same motives. From a utilitarian perspective, this poetry is judged false or hollow because it is allegedly created only to provide, simultaneously, pleasure to the audience and secondarily to gain the lady's love. The troubadours, as well as verse narrators such as Marie de France in her *Lais*, inherit these formal limitations: they imitate the poetic and the courtly convention of their successors. But then they transcend these limitations and achieve a new understanding of the correlation between words of love and love of words because the linguistic and communicative investigation of the love discourse aspires to a novel goal, that of epistemology within the framework of medieval love poetry.

Kukułka's objective is to present, through the analysis of the portraits of the ladies and of the love which is vowed to them, the variety and the creativeness of this literature. The examination of the rhetoric of courtly poetics reveals the value and symbolism of this literature traditionally judged to be artificial. For this purpose she chooses a selection of Guillaume's songs and *lais* by Marie de France. In these works the ladies there are presented in different situations, excelling in their beauty, but often revealing psychologically and physically extraordinary features, and occasionally even supernatural powers. Often their beauty is described through the eyes of another person, as though the lover himself is unable to see it, or as though he does not deserve it. The recurrence of the rhetorical figures, the clichés of reveries, and the mechanical repetitions seem to be an expression of an obligatory ritual — the consequence of twists and turns of social and literal courtesy of the period. But all examples demonstrate how much these poets had truly grasped the ultimate function of human language, to illuminate, to communicate, and to glorify human existence.

The phenomenon of love is intimately connected with language, and the true command of language might be the implicit prerequisite for love, to paraphrase the title of this volume and to capture the sense of Karen K. Jambeck's contribution to this volume. One of the most interesting medieval poets, profoundly appealing to modern tastes, Marie de France explicitly discussed her fascination with language and the profound need to master it in order to comprehend the intricacies of love as explored in her magisterially composed *Lais*. As Jambeck's careful linguistic analysis reveals, Marie drew upon Latin literature, especially Ovid, and, of course, from the dominant courtly culture of her time, particularly in the world of the Angevin court of England with its triglossic condition. Jambeck offers, however, in clear contrast to previous scholarship, an innovative perspective on Marie's eloquence by applying principles of Pragmatics and Politeness Theory.

Examining the *lais Lanval, Yonec,* and *Equitan,* Jambeck argues that linguistic subtleties are essential to the successful expression of love. Love develops and grows into a stable, harmonious relationship, as Jambeck observes, only if the participants understand and observe linguistic practices that recognize and maintain "face," that is, both the "sense of self" and "public self-image." The opposite leads to catastrophes, as numerous negative examples in Marie's *Lais* indicate. In fact, aggressive language that leaves the opponent no room to maneuver might trigger the loss of love and can explode in the speaker's face.

In fact, as Jambeck indicates, a critical analysis of the *Lais* reveals Marie's command of language and her ability to portray its constructive and deconstructive effects, especially in exchanges between lovers. Attention to "positive face," for instance, invites the other into a love relationship, whereas the unmitigated linguistic "threat to face" derails emotions. In the *lais* of *Lanval* and *Yonec,* lovers achieve a high form of love related to truth and wisdom. In the case of Lanval and Arthur's queen, however, lack of attention to "face" translates into misadventure for both. Alternatively, as is the case in *Equitan,* the communication between the wooer, the king, and his lady, the seneschal's wife, transforms into linguistic bartering, a negotiation for self-gratification, which hence results in a deceptive form of love. Based on mercantile principles that commodify love, the relationship might well be successful for a while, but ultimately translates into tragedy for both.

Ultimately, then, as Jambeck's essay demonstrates, Marie was deeply concerned with the power of words as the critical instruments in establishing a good love relationship. The lovers' words need to be fed by a love of words — here the source being Marie's eloquence — which might well be the most important hallmark of human existence, and so of human love.

Whereas we traditionally associate love with intense poetic activity, especially because we assume that lovers talk intimately with each other, the actual situation for literary lovers, especially in their blissful union, might well be the very opposite, as Karen Pratt's discussion of Gautier d'Arras's *Eracle* and his *Ille et Galeron* indicates. In French romances of the twelfth century protagonists focus instead on their amatory suffering, which leads to an outburst of solitary reflections upon their extraordinary emotions. By contrast, when lovers achieve happiness, the need for words fades away because the experience of the ineffable is predicated on a different set of norms and ideals. Painful suffering from the pangs of love provides an important mechanism for introspection and an opportunity to examine the internal explosion of emotions, regularly leading to lengthy monologues about love. These monologues, however, serve also as important contributions to the public discourse on love, since they resemble propositions concerning the correct interpretation of this phenomenon, love. Gautier presents complex relationships, but the discussion of the emotions involved is not developed in amatory dialogue as much as we might expect, especially because actions, such as kissing, replace words of love. Those lovers who demonstrate considerable eloquence, such as Yvain in Chrétien de Troyes' eponymous romance, tend not to live up to their pledges of love and instead deceive their beloved. Honest lovers, on the other hand, no longer need words and can express their feelings in other ways, especially because love is apophatic.[109] The power of emotions appears to be overwhelming, hence they regularly turn toward a go-between, who provides a safe forum in which to explore the power of love.

Gautier's depiction differs from thirteenth-century German works, in which young lovers in particular examine carefully, and in close collaboration with each other, the meaning of love (Wolfram von Eschenbach's *Titurel*, Ulrich von Etzenbach's *Wilhelm von Wenden*, the anonymous *Mai und Beaflor*).[110] In Gautier's mid-twelfth-century romances, as Pratt demonstrates, only Ganor, Ille's second beloved in *Ille et Galeron*, represents a remarkable exception, as she deliberately and unabashedly expresses her feelings for Ille, almost in the vein of the protagonists in Andreas Capellanus's Latin treatise *De amore*. However, the norm proves to be considerable reticence in matters of love until the hero finds a quiet moment in which to analyze his feelings. In the case of Gautier two male protagonists seem to suffer from an inferiority complex. Yet Gautier also creates female characters who similarly prefer internal monologues to open dialogue with their desired partner, such as the Empress Athanaïs.

This hesitance on the part of the characters to approach the subject of love openly with the beloved, the solipsistic nature of their amatory monologues and internal dialogues, and especially the detailed commentary by narrators reveal

---

[109] Parallel cases might be the thirteenth-century Middle High German *Mauritius von Craûn* and the fourteenth-century Spanish *Libro de buen amor* by Juan Ruiz.

[110] Albrecht Classen, "Wolframs von Eschenbach *Titurel*-Fragmente und Johanns von Würzburg *Wilhelm von Österreich*: Höhepunkte der höfischen Minnereden," *Amsterdamer Beiträge zur älteren Germanistik* 37 (1993): 75–102.

how in the work of Gautier and his contemporaries a fascination with words is vital for the spiritual, emotional, and intellectual development of the self. This becomes particularly apparent in *Ille et Galeron*, because the male protagonist, who is loved by two women, has to cope with enormous emotional struggles that require extensive poetic elaboration by the author. Quite similar to Andreas's dialectical treatise on love and Thomas de Bretagne's *Tristan*, the profound conflicts in love — conjugal versus adulterous — presented by Gautier's romances provide an intriguing forum in which to examine the dialectical aspects of love varied perspectives, intricately weaving words of love with the love of words. This phenomenon involves at times deliberate gender reversals, offering additional ammunition in the poetic struggle to come to terms with both aspects, love and human language.[111] Whereas *Ille et Galeron* provides a literary platform on which marital love is idealized even within the world of the courts, *Eracle* offers a defense of adulterous love. But together these romances embrace a highly rhetorical discourse as the crucial vehicle to explore the meaning of love in its myriad manifestations, expressed in a kaleidoscope of poetic reflections.

Female experiences of love might well be more intense and all-consuming than those of the male, as Isolde in Gottfried von Strassburg's *Tristan and Isolde* (ca. 1210) and Heloise in her correspondence with Abelard seem to indicate. But as Christopher R. Clason emphasizes in his contribution to this volume, the critical point proves to be the linguistic competence of the female protagonist, the ability to embrace the ambivalent and the obscure, both key components of the experience of love. Tristan is used to employing his own linguistic code, often dubious and ambiguous for the purpose of self-protection, in his relationship with Isolde. Surprisingly, when love begins to connect these two figures, the linguistic challenge almost overpowers him, because the deceptive strategy no longer helps him to achieve his goal, which by now involves another person, his beloved. However, as we realize through Clason's complex analysis of Gottfried's *Tristan*, love is not gender-specific; but it does require the lover's intellectual ability to handle the epistemological challenge. Thus, words of love must also transform into a love of words, or into the realization of the hermeneutic relevance of the exchange, and human words of love, as the basis of fundamental truths, must stand up under such a critical examination.

As Clason argues in his essay, the intellectual and sensory battle between Tristan and Isolde focuses on the fundamental values of love and forces us, as listeners/readers, to investigate, in greater detail than even the medieval author might have been willing to grant, the essence of the words of love as the catalysts of love by themselves. As his discussion of Isolde's powerful words indicates, her

---

[111] Michelle Bolduc, "Transgressive Troubadours and Lawless Lovers? Matfre Ermengaud's *Breviari d'Amor* as a Courtly *apologia*," *Discourses on Love, Marriage, and Transgression*, ed. Albrecht Classen, 65–83; see also the Introduction and the other contributions to this volume.

initial resistance and subsequent acquiescence ultimately lead Tristan to a position where he fully comprehends the dialectical nature of love and perceives himself as an active player, despite the contradictory nature of the game upon which this love affair is predicated. Nevertheless, as Clason powerfully demonstrates, the female voice gains superiority and command over the love relationship, much like Heloise's voice in her relationship with Abelard, because of the subtle female control of the words of love. Whereas Tristan attempts to resort to his traditional role as teacher and male authority at large, Isolde insists on the predominance of her own female voice and resolutely takes charge of the discourse of love. Comprehension and mutual agreement are the ultimate goals of the discourse of love, as Gottfried's *Tristan* insinuates; hence the literary examination of love implies the philosophical quest for truth pertaining to society at large. Those who truly love each other, as Tristan and Isolde do, are the prime examples of how to establish the principal elements determining a functioning, that is, a communicative community, predicated on love. Love of words and words of love hence correlate with each other and produce an epistemological interrelationship, which medieval love poetry persistently addresses as its highest goal — hence the discursive character of almost all erotic literature. The chiastic relationship between love and words, or language and sentiment, directly pertains to the hermeneutic realization of the meaning of the poetic discourse.

Whereas most of the contributors to this volume focus on words and love — or love and words — Linda Marie Zaerr goes one step further and investigates the relationship between words of love and music of love, sometimes seen through the lens of magic, and very often through the lens of deception. Most medieval protagonists who excel as musicians, whether interacting as the highly educated and trained aristocratic entertainers they are, or disguised as professional jongleurs, utilize music for an aestheticization of their world and achieve a transformation of themselves and their social environment through playing music, mostly on the viol (*vielle*) and harp. As early as the eleventh-century Latin *Ruodlieb*, music proves to be not only a metaphor for love, but also, on a much higher level, a catalyst for love. This early courtly romance gave way to much more powerful literary examinations of the correlation between song and love, such as in the thirteenth-century *Le Bel Inconnu*. Obviously, as many other examples cited by Zaerr indicate, this miraculous phenomenon is predicated on the magic of the poetic word in interaction with musical performance. Protagonists who perform a song with a musical instrument reveal much about their social identity, and in this sense music emerges as an esoteric, yet revelatory language of highest significance within the courtly context because it relays truth and speaks of love. Jongleurs perform for money, whereas courtly knights perform for their lady. The same applies to female musicians, such as Fresne in *Galeran de Bretagne*, where Fresne gains access to her lover's heart and wins him as her husband through her superior and authentic playing and singing. When she sings, she sings from her heart, whereas the jongleurs play from their head. It is a language of love that leads to a love of music, and vice versa, the essence of the chiastic paradigm this volume explores in so many different ways. Yet ironically, the music of love can deceive others even as it most clearly discloses lovers to one another. In the *Roman de Horn* musical performance reveals the true identity of the player, which in turn transforms him into the one whom the female protagonist loves dearly, yet simultaneously that same music, transformed by disguise, deceives a lady into loving where love can never be returned.

Curiously, as Zaerr rightly observes, in one of the most haunting medieval erotic romances, Gottfried von Strassburg's *Tristan*, music serves as a disguise for the protagonist and it also contributes to various strategies of deception by both Tristan and an Irish competitor for Isolde, Gandin. Here music suddenly assumes an almost demonic function, bedeviling Tristan who utilizes it for soothing effects both on Isolde and on himself. But this threatens to destroy their love, whence Isolde, for one, destroys the mind-confusing music of the bell hanging from the neck of the magical dog Petitcreiu, refusing false happiness when she really ought to suffer from Tristan's absence. Even earlier, as we learn in Zaerr's analysis, the jealous courtiers had begun suspecting Tristan of sorcery, indirectly referring to his music as well. Somehow, the communication has broken down, and the chiastic paradox of words of love/music and music/love of words no longer seems to function. By contrast, Zaerr hastens to add, the role of music in the pan-European *Historia Apollonii*, here cited from its thirteenth-century Spanish version, was maintained as an ideal medium to speak to the listeners' hearts and to establish, or to maintain, the idyllic human community. A similar example can be found in *Aucassin et Nicolette*.

By the fifteenth century, however, music in romance could transform into a dangerous instrument in the hand of a sorceress, as in *Lybeaus Desconus*. And Tristram in Malory's *Morte Darthur* scarcely plays any music, and then only in a stage of lunacy. Music, in other words, proves to be an arcane language, difficult to grasp, malleable for many different functions, as is the case with the normal human language. Those who command music more than all others are regarded either as pure lovers or as evil magicians, but they surface, at any rate, as otherworldly figures because of their association with music.

As Siegfried Christoph reminds us in his contribution, the very essence of philology is predicated on the chiastic approach of 'words of love and love of words.' Nevertheless, as his careful analysis of the etymology of Middle High German 'vröude' indicates, the term 'joy' does not simply translate into its modern analogues, and instead we realize, once more, how complex medieval words can be because of their profound social meaning in a variety of contexts. 'Joy,' above all, signifies considerably more than simply 'individual happiness.' First of all, 'vröude' proves to be closely associated with love, but again not simply in a very personal context. Christoph's comparison with medieval and modern theological statements concerning 'joy' reveals its important connotation regarding the soul's experience, and perhaps also union, with the Godhead. Once again, we can observe that medieval mysticism and courtly love poetry share many elements, and the former might actually be identified as the crowning achievement of medieval literature at large. On the other hand, this does not entirely exclude the sensuous dimension of the term 'vröude,' or 'joy,' especially in its noteworthy variant 'Lust'or 'lust.' At any case, as Christoph concludes in the first part of his paper, 'joy' and 'lust' always carry with them a sense of anticipation, of expectation, and bring forth a considerable degree of energy in the person who experiences this sensation.

But the social dimension of 'joy' carries even more significance, as Christoph illustrates with the case of the "Joie de la curt" episode in Hartmann von Aue's *Erec*. Here, joy suddenly emerges as a central gauge of society's well-being, since without 'joy' there is no culture, no public entertainment, no happiness and harmony. And joy is associated with activity, particularly knightly prowess and chivalry, which Mabonagrin and his wife have occupied for themselves for much too long, not realizing that they created a virtual prison in which they are stuck, not able to depart from there until Mabonagrin will have been defeated by an opponent. Courtly ideals find their realization only through the dispensation of joy, that is, the public sharing of personal happiness through words and acts, or by inviting all other members of the court to participate in the communicative community.[112] Not by accident, we might say, Erec and Enite had similarly endangered the well-being of the entire courtly society because they had, as very young and inexperienced newlyweds, appropriated 'joy' all for themselves, which left all other members of the court disgruntled, disappointed, and even contemptuous, particularly because their 'joy' seemed to be exclusively sexual in nature and did not develop in any further sense. In other words, as similar scenes in contemporary romances, such as Gottfried von Strasbourg's *Tristan* indicate, even — if not especially — erotic love requires, if it wants to achieve its desired goal, a certain element of partaking and an openness toward society. The retreat into the isolated love cave (*Tristan*) or into the reclusive orchard (*Erec*) wreaks havoc because it puts two individuals in an extremely privileged position, whereas love ought to be the centerpiece of courtly culture, as perhaps best reflected in the problematic conflict in *Sir Gawain and the Green Knight*.[113] In this fourteenth-century Middle English alliterative romance the green belt, ultimately worn by all members of King Arthur's court, signals that the knights understand and sympathize with Gawain, and yet also enjoy the erotic experience/temptation that he had to

---

[112] See also the contribution to this volume by G. Ronald Murphy; see also Classen,*Verzweiflung und Hoffnung*, 2002.

[113] See the contribution to this volume by Jean E. Jost.

withstand while in his bedroom in castle Hautdesert, but not as voyeurs; instead they are participants in the public struggle for love and honor.

Hartmann von Aue specifically reflected on this critical need for society to know of, to share in, and to enjoy with the erotic lovers their 'vröude.' The words of love, so to speak, translate into a love of words, which represents the foundation of courtly culture at large. As Christoph poignantly underscores through his philological examination and his interpretive analysis, the complex nature of the term for 'joy' unmistakably relates the complex yet central function of the discourse of love for courtly society. It was neither a simple discourse for lovers nor a straightforward love for discourse, but instead always a combination of both, which sheds important light on the true meaning of courtly love — ultimately a platform for the establishment of harmonious, joyful, constructive, and stable relationships between all members of the court across the gender lines, beyond all age limits and even social levels.

The examination of medieval approaches to the *mysterium* of language mostly pertains to its use in literary discourse, though we would also be well advised to pay close attention to charms, legal texts, mystical texts, sermons, prayers, and other liturgical texts. But one of the key elements to establish a person's identity and relationship with the world through language consists of names. The love of words also extends to names, such as is the case in Wolfram von Eschenbach's masterpiece, *Parzival* (ca. 1205), in part based on Chrétien de Troyes' *Perceval*, in part, however, a truly genuine and original grail romance by this outstanding Middle High German poet. G. Ronald Murphy, S.J., proposes wonderful perspectives toward Wolfram's ingenious employment of names for his female characters. These have, as he argues most sensitively and convincingly, a direct impact on the protagonist's development from being still a child with all the typical psychological features of this stage in human life,[114] to a mature grown-up who understands how to operate within society, sharing and communicating with his fellow-beings. Moreover, as Murphy emphasizes, Parzival's interaction with these women — Herzeloyde, Sigûne, Condwîramurs, Cundrîe, and Repanse de Schoie — signals a specific learning curve from absolute self-centeredness toward ultimate sympathy and compassion, in close parallel to the parable of the Good Samaritan in the New Testament (Luke 10: 25–37).

Whereas traditional Wolfram scholarship has normally looked at Parzival's chivalrous accomplishments, interpreting this romance along the lines of most other courtly romance, Murphy suggests, and quite rightly so, that the true role in shaping Parzival's life, humanizing this young hero and transforming him into a new Good Samaritan, is given to these five women, as the deeper meaning of

---

[114] See *Childhood in the Middle Ages and the Renaissance: The Results of a Paradigm Shift in the History of Mentality*, ed. Albrecht Classen (Berlin and New York: de Gruyter, 2005), 12–13, 15, 41–42, 48, 57, 65.

their names indicates. Although many of the essential aspects and figures in Wolfram's romance can already be found in Chrétien's work, the German poet mostly assigned new and highly specific names to those women who have such a deep impact on Parzival's life. These names are profoundly symbolic and clearly indicate the process of how people ought to develop emotionally, intellectually, philosophically, and spiritually. What Parzival experiences intimately pertains to the impact of emotions on an individual from early childhood to adulthood, beginning — in Murphy's own terms — with maternal affection and pain, turning to fidelity to lover and family, then emotions regarding the guiding commitment of husband and wife (conjugal love), subsequently the acquisition of painful self-knowledge and shame, and finally the arrival, in fraternal style, at overflowing happiness. This development is clearly outlined through the names, which reflect Wolfram's strong interest in the power of words as catalysts for human life.

Murphy suggests that the deeper meaning of the names can be found by using a methodology that does not analyze these names in isolation, but rather by examining both their immediate environment as well as their role in the plotline. Those who love words also find words of love for their neighbors and practice this love as the Good Samaritan did and as the contexts of these ponderous names signal. In this sense, as we can see from Murphy's observations, Wolfram's *Parzival* does not really treat chivalry and knighthood in the Arthurian context, but instead focuses on love and compassion, sympathy and considerateness, but then also on communication and collaboration, as the careful analysis of the women's names in Wolfram's epic romance indicates.

The discourse of love, in both the Middle Ages and the Renaissance, was not univocal or one-dimensional, especially because it did not address only secular, physical topics. Our entire volume is dedicated to the exploration of this phenomenon, but most contributions focus primarily on non-religious narratives and poems. Connie Scarborough, on the other hand, invites us to consider the most intriguing interlacing of the erotic with the religious and to treat each as two sides of the same coin. This observation has been made many times with regard to medieval and early modern mystical narratives, perhaps best expressed in those mystical accounts based on the idea of bridal mysticism. Bernard of Clairvaux (1090–1153), one of the founders of this deeply eroticized language of mystical visions, provided the essential imagery which subsequent mystics throughout Europe far into the seventeenth and perhaps even eighteenth century, copied with great enthusiasm.[115] As James I. Wimsatt observes, "His emphasis on love for the body of Christ made Bernard a crucial figure in the medieval development

---

[115] For a recent overview, see Steven Fanning, *Mystics of the Christian Tradition* (London and New York: Routledge, 2001), 75–138; see Albrecht Classen's review in *Mystical Quarterly* 28, 4 (2002): 187–88; see also Peter Dinzelbacher, *Mittelalterliche Frauenmystik* (Paderborn, Munich, Vienna, and Zurich: Ferdinand Schöningh, 1992), 19–55.

of affective devotion to Christ the man, which centers particularly on his Passion.... He advocates this love not only for driving out inferior sensual affections, but also as the only way to the divinity of Christ."[116] But other poets also pursued this agenda, such as the Castilian King Alfonso X the Wise with his enormously fascinating *Cantigas de Santa Maria*, composed sometime during the king's reign from 1252 to 1284. Throughout the entire collection of Marian miracle stories and songs, we regularly discover an intriguing combination of the imagery and language characteristic of worldly, erotic love poetry, such as developed by the *troubadour* poets in the first half of the twelfth century, with profoundly spiritual, religious concepts. In fact, for Alfonso the veneration and adoration of the Virgin Mary became a cult of its own which was fundamentally predicated on secular love poetry, yet intended for a highly religious purpose. The kingly poet embraced the Holy Mother not only as a deity, but also as his mistress with whom he wanted to spend the rest of eternity.

Scarborough here convincingly illustrates the extent to which Alfonso relied very closely on all the basic concepts used by courtly love poets in their song compositions, whether we think of the lover's awe for his lady, her inaccessibility for her wooer, her physical and spiritual inspiration, the lover's willingness to sacrifice everything he owns and is on behalf of his lady, and the dream of the blissful union with the lady if she ever were to comply with the wooer's wishes — all this very similar to the functions assigned to Beatrice by Dante in his *Divina Commedia*. Curiously, however, yet intimately connected with the particular feature of mystically inspired Marian poetry, Alfonso's *cantigas* seem to reach a greater depth and foundation in their unmitigated and absolute dedication to the Holy Mother, which the poet certainly shared both with Bernard of Clairvaux's sermons and with the many religious-erotic accounts by late medieval mystics such as Mechthild of Magdeburg and Hadewijch of Brabant. In Alfonso's magisterial collection of Marian songs, the lover reaches unforeseen levels of emotional passion, concurrently drawing, as it seems, from both the physical-erotic and the religious-spiritual. A number of times the Virgin even emerges as a jealous mistress who steps in between the male voice and his worldly beloved, demanding priority over the earthly woman. Although Alfonso did not harbor negative feelings about marriage, he still projected the Holy Mother as far superior to all worldly women and appealed to his audience to follow his lead in his quasi-mystical pursuits. He even claimed that his particular devotion to the Virgin Mary provoked her to come to his assistance in the case of pernicious illnesses, performing particular miracles on his body.

---

[116] James I. Wimsatt, "St. Bernard, the Canticle of Canticles, and Mystical Poetry," *An Introduction to the Medieval Mystics of Europe*, ed. Paul E. Szarmach (Albany: State University of New York Press, 1984); 77–95; here 81. Of course, there are countless other studies on St. Bernard and his influence on late medieval mystics.

Words, then, whether religious or secular-erotic, provide the platform for the spiritual transcendence of our human existence. Insofar as King Alfonso heavily relied on the language of courtly love poetry, he masterfully achieved his goal of reaching out to the Holy Mother, transforming her, through the act of poetic imagination, and convincing her to accept him as her lover both in religious and even in worldly-erotic terms. Alfonso's words of love, then, truly prove to be the result of his love of words.

All poetry is predicated on the creative use of language with the purpose of indirectly revealing the apophatic dimension of this basic communication tool. In other words, we create poetry because there is no other medium available to reach out to the absolute Other, the Godhead. Medieval German love poetry, whether secular or religious, demonstrates, as Albrecht Classen argues in his contribution to this volume, that even basic rhetorical and linguistic features could be used to transcend the traditional limitations of language. But whereas those poets whose works have been collected in the famous *Des Minnesangs Frühling* and who flourished sometime between 1170 and 1200 have traditionally been hailed as the major spokespersons of Middle High German courtly love poetry, their late medieval successors have attracted considerably less attention, as if they were of lesser significance and artistic quality. One great exception, Oswald von Wolkenstein (1376/77–1445), has been mostly studied in light of his autobiographical (travel), musical, political, polyglot, and religious contributions, whereas his intriguing play with onomatopoesis, various (non-courtly) sound registers, and a highly unusual lexicon — all of it the true hallmark of his œuvre — has not received adequate attention. Significantly, however, his words of love, above all, prove to be most important vehicles for the investigation of late medieval and early modern amatory discourse. But he was not the only late medieval German poet who endeavored to experiment with a wide range of poetic elements and features. In fact the Wilde Alexander, Gottfried von Neifen, Reinmar von Brennenberg, Ulrich von Winterstetten, Ulrich von Singenberg, Hugo von Trimberg, and also some of the mystical writers such as Mechthild von Magdeburg and Hadewijch, incorporated intriguing and innovative strategies into their poetic discourse. Thus they demonstrated that they were not simply "epigonal" composers who had little to say to their audiences because they allegedly only copied from their great "classical" models. Through their creative exploration of words of love these late medieval German poets demonstrated their profound love of words and revealed the extent to which the dimension of the ineffable was, after all, accessible for themselves and their listeners/readers. They achieved this insight because they employed non-linear, non-analogic language for their erotic and mystical explorations that unexpectedly unearthed hitherto shrouded or unknown dimensions of human comprehension beyond the epistemological limits of the world of the courts.[117]

Those who love aim for a beloved other, and they instinctly realize that they need to resort to all their complete power of words to convince the other to return this feeling.

As Tracy Adams suggests, the lover in Guillaume de Lorris' part of the *Roman de la rose* involuntarily demonstrates that he has to suppress all his uncivilized, uncultured tendencies in order to impress his beloved; these changes are accompanied by the effacement of his self-consciousness. In Jean de Meun's continuation, the allegorical figures not only explicate the nature of love to the young man but also raise his level of self-consciousness again regarding the meaning of love. Faus Semblant, above all, makes the lover aware of the need to use the right words of love in order to achieve the desired goal, but in this process the lover also begins to question the validity of his own emotions because erotic language proves to be a manipulative game. Those who love must investigate whether they love for selfless reasons — pure, spiritual love — or whether they love because they are enamored of words of love. These words are regularly used to camouflage the hidden desires for sexual satisfaction, and Guillaume's portion of the text concludes before the deceptiveness of this strategy is revealed. However, Jean de Meun did not hesitate to rend this veil and to examine in detail the function of amatory language as a catalyst to achieve the ulterior goals of a more specifically sexual nature.

Guillaume's lover uses words of love, whereas Jean's lover, as Adams argues, employs his love of words to address his sexual and political ideals. In fact, in Jean's text, words of love increasingly turn out to be a pretext for the need to deal with the person's own sexual desires, whereas the erotic 'other' does not really matter. The Amant's love turns out to be lust, nothing else, although through his use of words of love he pretends to project authentic emotions. Nevertheless, as

---

[117] For a parallel approach to this phenomenon, though in English, Italian, and Latin literature, see Burt Kimmelman, *The Poetics of Authorship in the Later Middle Ages*; idem, "Ockham, Chaucer, and the Emergence of Modern Poetics," *The Rhetorical Poetics of the Middle Ages: Reconstructive Polyphony. Essays in Honor of Robert O. Payne*, ed. John M. Hill and Deborah M. Sinnreich-Levi (Madison, NJ: Fairleigh Dickinson University Press; London : Associated University Press, 2000), 177–205. As J. Stephen Russell poignantly observes, "From logicians to manuscript illuminators to controllers of the wool custom, medieval thinkers and writers and artists seem to see, in their fallen status as God's creatures, that all of their thoughts and words and expressions were uneasy negotiations between the world and their personal, wishful, anxious, muddled versions of it. Try as they might — through logic, allegory, iconography — to make their media behave themselves, honest medieval artists like Chaucer and Dante still struggled to express the world, knowing they could not help but express themselves as well in the effort" (*Chaucer and the Trivium: The Mindsong of the Canterbury Tales* [Gainesville, Tallahassee, et al.: University Press of Florida, 1998], 4). See Albrecht Classen's review in *Mediaevistik* 13 (2000): 527–29.

the *Roman de la rose* signals, the literary activity fulfills a specific purpose insofar as the erotic discourse makes possible the intellectualization of the feelings of lust and their transformation into something creative. In Jean's continuation, however, the Amant increasingly realizes, and also internalizes, that love is determined by the manipulative function of words serving the concrete goal of satisfying one's sexual lust. The literary discourse provides a forum to hide this physical intention and projects a deceptive screen for the self-conscious individual, who is now guided by Faus Semblant toward the confrontation with the countless contradictory emotional impulses in the field of love.

However, as Adams concludes, Faus Semblant also indicates the deceptive power of language within a religious context where the confessant is automatically implicated in being guilty of sinfulness when he talks about his love — perhaps because explicitly talking about love represents an inherent blasphemy since love, in its crystalline essence, at least as represented by Guillaume, is ineffable in nature. Nevertheless, in Jean's portion of the *Roman*, love discourse suddenly emerges as sinful, lustful, and purely sex-driven; hence love is destroyed through the use of false words of love because the love of words has triumphed after all — a metaphor of the rationalization that occurs through the growth of self-consciousness and the reflective treatment of love in its poetic, legal, and religious context.[118]

We have commonly assumed that the world of the courts was a world where courtly ideals and values were practiced through the employment of highly refined courtly language predicated on religious ethics, morals, and ideals. But a careful examination of some of the key texts in Middle English literature, such as Chaucer's "Franklin's Tale" and *Sir Gawain and the Green Knight* can unearth, as Jean Jost argues in her intriguing contribution to this volume, highly uncanny manipulative strategies, deception, ambiguities, duplicities, flatteries, devious discursive operations, and challenges of wit that easily transgress traditional gender roles and reverse social positions. In fact, courtly literature might be better described as an intellectual battleground where multiple voices, values, influential figures, and role models clash with one another, sometimes reconfirming one another, sometimes creating an explosive clash.[119] In the "Franklin's Tale," Dorigen's husband Arverargus at first assumes the air of a courtly lover in the vein of a *troubadour* poet, and pledges humility, service, and love to his wife. But then he abandons her for two years while traveling, and when he learns, upon his return, of her involuntary commitment to Aurelius, he suddenly assumes the attitude of a dominating, patriarchal husband who insists that she carry out his

---

[118] Karen K. Jambeck, "'Femmes et tere': Marie de France and the Discourses of 'Lanval'," *Discourses on Love, Marriage, and Transgression*, 109–45.

[119] See also Bonnie Wheeler's contribution to this volume; for further illuminations and discussions of this observation, see Brown, *Contrary Things*.

orders so that she can maintain her, but actually his own, honor. By the same token, Aurelius at first pretends to be a traditional courtly wooer, but when Dorigen rejects his pleading, he resorts to threats and blackmail. Ultimately, however, she proves to be nothing but the prize in the rhetorical battle between both men, and the victim, surprisingly, is not Dorigen, but courtly love and its chiastic code, the interlacing of words of love and the love of words.

Even more intriguing, following Jost's cogent train of thoughts, the courtly world, traditionally supported by its adherence to eroticized language, demonstrates an almost shocking underside, as illustrated by the intellectual struggle between the male protagonist and the lady Bercilak in *Sir Gawain and the Green Knight*. She powerfully manipulates Gawain into the position of a pawn of her eroticized rhetoric, forcing him to accept the position of the wooed courtly lady, whereas she herself assumes the role of the courtly knight because he is afraid of losing his life at the hand of the knight Bercilak. Moreover, the lady is happily married and utilizes courtly words of love only to seduce Gawain on behalf of her husband, which transgresses the norms of courtly love even further. Jost also points out the considerable influence of the Virgin Mary, whose knight Gawain has pledged to be. This allegiance stands in clear contrast to his submission to the lady Bercilak from whom he accepts her girdle as a means of preserving his life. Only when the protagonist finally learns the truth of the wager and realizes how much he has been deceived by the lady through her powerful and deceptive use of words of love, which directly appealed to his own love of words. Gawain, the traditionally glorified ideal courtly lover, releases a misogynistic diatribe because he has been shamed and ridiculed as a lover and as a man. But, as Jost concludes, both Chaucer and the *Pearl*-Poet indicate the extent to which they were attracted to and yet also disappointed by the traditional courtly love discourse, reversing, contradicting, and undermining its basic tenets and offering new perspectives toward communication as a mutually discursive, ethical, and spiritual operation of the highest order.

Words, depending on their meaning, are used in a pragmatic context, serving a strategic employment and a communicative function. They are important indicators of the social, ethical, moral, religious, and political developments of and within a society. Late medieval France underwent a profound crisis because of the Hundred Years War, a devastating power vacuum in the center because of weak royal leadership, almost an internecine civil war among the dukes of Orléans, Anjou, and Burgundy, a general malaise of the Catholic Church, and a subsequent flood of lawsuits, personal conflicts, public strife, and many other problems. How poets reflected on words of love can serve as a gauge of this deep sense of insecurity and anxiety among the public. Comparing the anonymous *Prose Lancelot* (1225) with Jean d'Arras's *Roman de Mélusine* (1393), Stacey L. Hahn reaches significant conclusions as to the meaning of words of love in both texts. Both prose novels are characterized by noteworthy thematic similarities, but major differences occur in these narratives, after a major catastrophe in the respective love relationship. Specifically related to the use of words of love, each author signals a major shift in the attitude and evaluation of oaths of love. In both romances the male protagonist ultimately rejects his female partner, and then seeks penance. However, in the *Prose Lancelot* the original relationship was based on adultery, whereas in the *Roman de Mélusine* the couple was married and had pledged oaths of loyalty to each other with the blessing of the Church. Both times the couple had found each other as a result of secret "criminal" activity and were bound together through some kind of magic. But tragically, the internalized conflicts ultimately erupt and force a wedge between both. Yet in the *Prose Lancelot*, where the principle of *fin'amors* still seems to be operative, at least in the first part of the tale, the young hero only has to return to the Church to confess his sin, in order to recover his peace of mind within a religious context. Lancelot confesses his sin in the Quest, but directly thereafter in the *Mort Artu* he falls into adultery again. It is only after Arthur has been killed at the end of the romance that he renounces love definitively.

Lancelot's disavowal of Guinevere in the *Quest* has no serious consequences for his society because their love affair had taken place outside of wedlock, so Lancelot does not really break an oath, and he only turns his back on his beloved upon the hermit's serious urging and after rational reflections. In Jean d'Arras's work, Raymondin, who is married to Mélusine, deliberately transgresses the taboo twice imposed on him by his wife, but each time in an irrational outburst that reflects his deep-seated anxieties concerning the fairy-woman and also his unmitigated sense of guilt over the accidental murder of his relative at the beginning of the novel. Publicly revealing his wife's true nature, Raymondin actually harms himself deeply and destroys his family, hence also his own happiness, not to mention that of Mélusine, who is expelled from human society and has to wait until the Day of Judgment for the absolution of her crime, parricide.

This repudiation has considerable consequences far beyond the narrative framework, since Jean d'Arras actually thematizes the dangers of destroying the fundamental commitment to words of love, and so to the love of words, that is, oaths, pledges, and other forms of ethical commitments. By abjuring Mélusine, Raymondin also abjures his own honor which is predicated on the ethical use of language in a communicative context. His lifelong suffering can thus be interpreted as an indication of the breakdown of the social fabric of late medieval French society.

Lancelot's repudiation of Guinevere, hence of adultery or *fin'amors*, was sanctified by the Church because it allowed the protagonist to return to the religious community and to preserve his own ethical principles. By contrast, Raymondin, perhaps representative of fourteenth- and fifteenth-century French society at large, turns his back on his own wife, his family, and his community, and then has to do penance for the rest of his life because his transgression destroyed all bonds with society. In a way, however, as Hahn emphasizes, only this catastrophic development could open an avenue for him to recover the love of words, though at the enormous price of the total victimization of his own wife and family. Paradoxically, however, this very catastrophe indicates the poet's deep love of words and his profound concern for the well-being of the communicative community. The considerable popularity of Jean's *Roman de Mélusine* indicates that this message was not lost to his audience.

At the end of the Middle Ages linguistic diversity increased, not only on a global scale, but also within individual territories. The English poet John Gower (ca. 1327–1408) impressively illustrates this phenomenon through his own trilingual poetry in which he relies on Middle English, Latin, and (Anglo-Norman) French, an unmistakable sign of his love of words and the epistemological power relayed through the linguistic diversity available to him and to his audience. Harry Peters examines, above all, Gower's *Confessio Amantis* — composed in English but using a Latin framework, with sprinklings of French loan-words — as an outstanding example of the deliberate use of three languages for individual purposes in the process of truth-finding, or *parrhesia*, that in turn involves various hermeneutic stages, each one operating with a different linguistic code. The same applies to Gower's ballads, composed in French and collected in a manuscript that includes other poems by Gower in Latin and English as well, where the soul-searching effort is also predicated on the incorporation of different languages. Overall, however, as Peters emphasizes, Gower proves to be a poet who had a strong sense of the three languages that served as the basis of his discourse concerning fundamental issues determining his society on every level and in every social class: love and marriage. The various types of discourses are of many different origins, but Gower magisterially orchestrated them all, combining and splitting them according to his own needs and purposes. Whereas the concepts of love and marriage traditionally seem to be straightforward and clean-cut, the careful examination of Gower's works reveals the extent to which medieval poets engaged in a highly complex discourse and opened up these concepts for public debate.[120] Gower knew exceedingly well how to utilize his three languages to conceptualize the dialectics of love and marriage, and to offer new, spiritualized ideals of both.

Even when we turn to the very late Middle Ages, the discursive element constitutive of many courtly romances and courtly love treatises, as originally developed by Andreas Capellanus (ca. 1190) and others, emerges once again, such as in the Spanish *Cárcel de amor*, first printed in 1492. Sanda Munjic illustrates,

---

[120] See also Bonnie Wheeler's contribution to this volume.

through a close reading of the highly contradictory approaches pursued by the various characters and the fictional *Auctor*, that this romance drew heavily from a wide range of legal, philosophical, theological, medical, sentimental, and rhetorical discourses and utilized them as an organon of freely available registers that were all predicated on love of words.[121] Even here, then, the chiastic paradigm of love of words drawing their energy from words of love comes to full fruition, demonstrating that the medieval tradition with its enormous fascination with and enjoyment of epistemological experimentation continued to hold sway even close to the end of the fifteenth century. Notwithstanding the clear focus on sentiments, passion, and love, the *Cárcel de amor* reveals the predominant undercurrent of ludic strategies operating with contradictory perspectives, discourses, and linguistic registers. Although the romance seems primarily to examine the development of emotions, Munjic's analysis reveals the dialectic nature of these emotions and their instrumentalization by the narrator for the exploration of hermeneutics within the amatory context. The fact that Leriano negotiates with Laureola about the nature of love and the possibility that she might grant her love to him under certain material conditions mercilessly uncovers the essence of the courtly discourse not as an exploration of the emotion of love, in the first place, but as the basis for the fundamental epistemological enterprise. The tragic development of the love affair in Chaucer's *Troilus and Criseyde*, for instance, would not have taken this course, at least not for Troilus, if the latter had been able to realize the degree to which words of love can be described, in essence, as the all-decisive and critical love of words — thereby embracing human language and its communicative function as the basis of human existence. But Munjic emphasizes that the reader of Chaucer's romance finds himself engrossed, hence engulfed by the text, whereas the reader of San Pedro's work is strongly encouraged to expose the operative strategies that determine the literal translation of words of love into love of words. The thirteenth-century Jean de Meun (*Roman de la rose*) and the fourteenth-century Juan Ruiz (*Libro de buen amor*) laid the foundation for such a literary approach to these epistemological investigations, and these are then fully developed in *Cárcel de amor*. Little wonder that it enjoyed such a long-term popularity far into the seventeenth century.

It is my pleasure to express my thanks to all contributors for their wonderful articles that truly help to expand our knowledge of one of the most important epistemological aspects characterizing medieval and early modern culture and literature: the public discourse of love. Any such scholarly enterprises as the symposium held at the University of Arizona, Tucson, April 29–30, 2005, upon which this volume is based to a large extent, would not be possible without financial

---

[121] For a historical-linguistic analysis of this phenomenon, but focusing on the work of Marie de France, see Karen K. Jambeck, "'Femmes et tere': Marie de France and the Discourses of 'Lanval'," 109–45.

assistance from various sources. I wish to acknowledge the generous support of the following sponsors: the University of Arizona Library and Department of Special Collections, the Office of the Vice President for Research at the University of Arizona, the University of Arizona Medieval Renaissance and Reformation Committee (UAMARRC), the Arizona Center for Medieval and Renaissance Studies (ACMRS, at Arizona State University, Tempe), and the University of Arizona Departments of German Studies, French and Italian, Linguistics, Classics, Spanish and Portuguese, and Russian and Slavic Languages.

I would like to dedicate this volume to my long-time friend and former doctoral advisor, Professor William C. McDonald, of the University of Virginia, who at an early point in my academic career helped me to rekindle the belief in the power and wisdom of the human language and demonstrated what the love of words can do when we return to the words of love as scholars, teachers, and friends.

CHAPTER 1

Concordia Virginitatis: Passionate Marriage in Paulinus of Nola

Cynthia White
The University of Arizona, Tucson

The *Epithalamium to Julian and Titia* of Paulinus of Nola (353–431 CE) may be considered a literary baptism of the great classical epithalamia.[1] It has been read as a proto marriage liturgy[2] and as an influential text in the burgeoning asceticism that characterized the fourth century.[3] Instead of Juno, Cupid, and Venus, Paulinus invites Pax, Pudor, and Pietas to the wedding. Instead of exhorting the newlyweds to amorous sport, the lascivious shouts that accompanied the *deductio sponsae* have been replaced with the cry "*Vivatis in Christo!*" The nuptial pair and the reader are called (ostensibly) to a new kind of pious marriage, dedicated to the love of Christ. Paulinus has not abandoned the traditional *topoi* of the genre, however; instead, he ironically plays upon the genre tensions between elegy and

---

[1] *Carmen* 25 in *Sancti Pontii Meropii Nolani Opera*, ed. Wilhelm August Hartel. Corpus Scriptorum Ecclesiasticorum Latinorum, 30.238–45 (Vienna: Tempsky, 1894). For an English translation, see P. G. Walsh, *The Poems of St. Paulinus of Nola*. Ancient Christian Writers, 40 (New York: Paulist Press, 1975), 245–53. Among the several Italian translations, see the very useful translation and commentary of Ombretta Pederzani, *Il talamo, L'albero e lo specchio: Saggio di commento a Stat. Silv. I 2, II 3, III 4* (Bari: Epiduglia, 1995), 13–145.

[2] Henri Crouzel, "Liturgie du mariage chrétien au Ve siècle selon l'Epithalame de Saint Paulin de Nole," *Mens concordet voci. Pour Aime-Georges Martimort a l'occasion de ses quarante annees d'enseignement et de vingt ans de la costitution Sacrosanctum Concilium* (Paris: Desclée, 1983), 619–26. For a more general discussion, see Lyndon Reynolds, *Marriage in the Western Church: The Christianization of Marriage during the Patristic and Early Medieval Periods* (Leiden: Brill, 1994).

[3] For this interpretation, see Salvatore Costanza, "Catechesi e poesia nei carmi XXII, XXV et XXXI di Paolino de Nola," *Crescita dell'uomo nelle catechesi dei Padri (età postnicena). Convegno di studio e aggiornamento, Facoltà di Lettere cristiane e classiche (Pontificium Institutum Altioris Latinitatis), Roma 20–21 marzo 1987*, ed. Sergio Felici. Biblioteca di scienze religiose, 80 (Rome: LAS, 1988), 237–56, and Andrea Ruggiero, *Paolino di Nola I Carmi*. Collana di testi patristici, 85 (Rome: Città nuova editrice, 1990), 25–27.

epithalamia in earlier classical poems, especially the epithalamium (*Silvae* 1.2) of Statius (*c.* 45–96 CE).[4]

In this paper I will treat first several *topoi* commonly found in the literary epithalamium[5] — the reluctance of the bride, the hymning of the bridal bower, the invocation of the wedding god Hymen, the encomia upon the beauty of the bride and the groom and their families, and the prayer for children that usually concludes these poems. Discussion of how he handled these conventions in his marriage song to Stella and Violentilla will reveal that Statius transformed the genre of epithalamium more significantly than any poet before him, especially in the way that he used mythology.[6] Most importantly however, he developed a new combination of the genres of elegy and epithalamia, heretofore separated: in his poem, he has infused the obligatory "love" of the marriage bond with the furor and passion of elegy. His poem in epic dactylic hexameter exhorts his friend Stella,[7] an elegiac poet, to marry his beloved Violentilla, an elegiac goddess, who according to the conventions of elegy should have remained a consuming but unconsummated passion.

Next, I will compare some of these characteristic *topoi* in the epithalamia of Statius and Paulinus. The encomium upon the bride with its detailed description of Venus' bower is a *topos* that enjoys expansive embellishment in the late antique epithalamia.[8] Stella's bride, Violentilla, possesses "egregium decus formae" (vv. 107–108; an outstandingly beautiful form); she is so lovely that even Venus marvels at her beauty, which, she says, "mihi dulcis imago prosiluit" (vv. 112–13; has bloomed into the sweet likeness of me). The dowry of Titia, on the other hand, in Paulinus's poem, is simply a dowry "puri luminis" (v. 42; of pure light). All the adornments of erotic love, that is, all the poetic conventions of elegy, which Statius had playfully interposed among his epithalamic hexameters, Paulinus no less playfully and no less skillfully rejects, but in elegiac couplets. His encomium upon Titia, a Christian bride, is devoted almost entirely to a long "elegiac" digression on Salome, "impia saltatrix" (v. 120; the wanton dancer), whose art, agile dance, and seductive and alluring dress avenge her mother's lust. The poetic description of

---

[4] For the text (based on Friedrich Vollmer, *Silvae* [1898]) and English translation, see *Statius Silvae*, ed. and trans. D. R. Shackleton Bailey. Loeb Classical Library (Cambridge, MA: Harvard University Press, 2003), 41–61.

[5] For an overview of the genre in Latin literature, see now Sabine Horstmann, *Das Epithalamium in der lateinischen Literatur der Spätantike* (Munich and Leipzig: K. G. Saur, 2004).

[6] Michael Roberts, "The Use of Myth in Latin Epithalamia from Statius to Venantius Fortunatus," *Transactions of the American Philological Association* 119 (1989): 321–48, attributes a new and novel role of the gods in human marriage to Statius's poem.

[7] On the relationship of Stella and Statius, fellow poets and friends, see G. Aricò, "Stazio e Arrunzio Stella," *Aevum* 39 (1965): 345–47.

[8] For Venus's excessively ornate bower as described in Claudian's *Epithalamium to Honorius and Maria*, see Gordon Braden, "Claudian and his Influence: The Realm of Venus," *Arethusa* 12, 2 (1979): 203–31.

her golden dancing shoes, her flowing and draped gown, the gems woven into her hair, even her leering spectators reveal that Paulinus is as skilled in the poetic art of metrical feet as Salome is "callida" (v. 130; skilled) "arte pedum" (v. 124; in the art of her feet), that is, her dance. Indeed, Paulinus's love of words has not at all been diminished (or stifled) by his love of God.

The earliest examples of the *topoi* of the classical epithalamia are found in Sappho's nuptial fragments;[9] but it is not until the third century that these *topoi* are codified by the rhetoricians Menander Rhetor and Pseudo Dionysius.[10] These early rhetoricians prescribe four components of an epithalamium: 1) an encomia upon the bride and groom that includes their family, upbringing, beauty, fortune, and disposition; 2) a hymn to the god of marriage and the wedding chamber; 3) a thesis upon the desirability of marriage; and 4) the final prayer for children. In addition, there are other persistent *topoi* in these marriage songs that are not included in the rhetorical handbooks, such as the separation of the bride from her mother and her community; the hymning of the Graces; and the bawdy taunts, called in the Roman tradition Fescennine verses.[11] These rhetorical and conventional elements of epithalamia generally correspond to the wedding ceremony,[12] which is a civic obligation *liberorum creandorum causa* (to have children) rather than a personal romance.[13]

At the rising of the evening star, the groom and the best man arrive at the bride's house. After a banquet she exits her home in a moment of splendor to join the procession to her new home. Riding in a wagon with the groom and best man, she is accompanied by a band of singing and dancing revelers, who escort her to the groom's home. This procession is called the *deductio in domum* and testifies

---

[9] For Sappho's poetry, see *Sappho et Alcaeus*, ed. Eva-Maria Voigt (Amsterdam: Athenaeum-Polak and Van Gennep, 1971); with an English translation, see *Greek Lyric*, trans. David A. Campbell, 4 vols. Loeb Classical Library (Cambridge, MA: Harvard University Press, 1982), vol. 1, Sappho and Alcaeus. Campbell includes poems 110a, 111, 104a, 105a, 105c, and 112–17 among the epithalamia.

[10] *Menander Rhetor*, ed. with trans. and commentary by Donald Andrew Russell and Nigel Guy Wilson (Oxford: Oxford University Press, 1981), 134–58, 365–68. *Cf.* Rudolf Keydell, "Epithalamium," *Reallexikon für Antike und Christentum* 5 (1962): 927–43.

[11] These are said to have developed from harvest songs. See Horace, *Epistles* 2.1.139–55 (in *Horace: Odes and Epodes*, ed. and trans. by Niall Rudd. Loeb Classical Library (Cambridge, MA: Harvard University Press, 2004).

[12] For an overview of the Greek ceremony, see John H. Oakley and Rebecca H. Sinos, *The Wedding in Ancient Athens* (Madison: University of Wisconsin Press, 1993), 3–47; for the Roman, see Gordon Williams, "Some Aspects of Roman Marriage Ceremonies and Ideals," *Journal of Roman Studies* 48 (1958): 16–29.

[13] On Roman marriage as a legal institution, see Susan Treggiari, *Roman Marriage: Iusti Coniuges from the Time of Cicero to the Time of Ulpian* (Oxford: Oxford University Press, 1991). On procreation as the primary purpose of the marriage, see David G. Hunter's focused study on Christian marriage and the *tabulae matrimoniales* in "Augustine and the Making of Marriage in Roman North Africa," *Journal of Early Christian Studies* 11, 1 (2003): 63–85; here 76–81.

to the legitimacy of the marriage.[14] Next, the Fescennine verses, taunts of a bawdy and lascivious nature (perhaps also apotropaic), are shouted at the couple.[15] At her new home the mother of the groom greets the bride and pours a mixture of nuts, figs, and dates over her to insure her fertility.[16] With her wedding torch the bride then lights the fire in the home of the groom. At this point the bride and groom enter the wedding chamber to consummate the marriage. Revelers sing loudly outside the chamber (Gr., thalamus from which we get the term *epithalamium* or "outside the wedding chamber"), which is beautifully decorated with flowers, cupids, and perfumes, and a doorman guards the door.[17] The next morning singing youths wake the couple[18] and a second day of festivities begins as the bride receives visitors, gifts, and her dowry. Songs and poems refer to each of the parts of the ceremony and were variously called *hymenaeoi, carmina nuptialia*, and *epithalamia*.[19]

As the classical and late antique poets deploy rhetorical and conventional elements of the songs associated with the ceremony, they consistently present marriage and passion as antithetical. Marriage is a social convention that benefits society by producing children for the state, and wedding songs in lyric or dactylic hexameter urge modest young brides to embrace their handsome grooms (at times, strangers) to this end. Passion, however, is an irrational emotion that is more often destructive than regenerative. Poems of passion and thwarted eroticism are written in elegiac verse and often mock and disdain marriage. In his

---

[14] This account from Diodorus Siculus 13.84 illustrates the sometimes extravagant nature of the procession: "Antisthenes.... when celebrating the wedding of his daughter gave a feast for all the citizens in the streets of the village — more than 800 teams followed in her succession. Most extraordinary was the lighting: All the altars in all the streets and sanctuaries were filled with wood and the shopkeepers were ordered to light them when the fire was lit on the Acropolis. So when the bride was led to her new home, the city was filled with light and the public roads did not have room for the crowd that followed." For the text and English translation, see *Diodorus Sicily*. Library of History, vol. 5 (Books 12.41–13), trans. Charles Henry Oldfather. Loeb Classical Library (Cambridge, MA: Harvard University Press, 1950).

[15] E.g., Catullus' epithalamium to Vibia Arunculeia and Manlius Torquatus 61.119–20, in *Catullus*, ed. Douglas F. S. Thomson (Toronto: University of Toronto Press, 1997), 134–43; here 139, "ne diu taceat procax / Fescennina iocatio" ("let not the merry Fescennine jesting be silent long"), calls for such ribaldry to begin.

[16] Cf. Plutarch, *Quaestiones Romanae* 279: "The bride should nibble a quince before going to the bridal chamber so that the first embrace may not be unpleasant." See *Plutarch. Moralia*, vol. 4, trans. Frank C. Babbit. Loeb Classical Library (Cambridge, MA: Harvard University Press, 1936).

[17] Sappho's epithalamic fragment 110a mocks the doorman's size, a warning to the revelers not to try to enter the wedding chamber: "The doorman's feet are seven fathoms long, and his sandals are made from five ox-hides; ten cobblers worked hard to make them."

[18] Theocritus's epithalamium (*Idyll* 18.56) to Helen and Paris refers to this custom: "Bolt the door for tomorrow morning the revelers will wake you at dawn." For the text, see *Theocritus*, ed., with trans. and commentary by Andrew Sydenham Farrar Gow, 2 vols. (Cambridge: Cambridge University Press, 1988).

[19] On possible distinctions, see Robert Muth, "Hymenaios und Epithalamion," *Wiener Studien* 67 (1954): 5–45.

epithalamium to Stella and Violentilla, Statius deftly combines these antithetical notions in an epithalamium for an elegist. Written in dactylic hexameter the poem defies genre conventions by introducing the themes of erotic love and irrational passion into the traditional *topoi* and the epic dactylic hexameter meter of the epithalamium. Paulinus, in his Christian epithalamium, likewise adapts epithalamic *topoi* for his own purposes. When he denounces pagan marriage, he seems to reject its rhetorical and literary tradition just as Statius had done before him. In fact, as we learn from close study of their poems, Paulinus is not only combining the antithetical notions of marriage and passion as Statius had already done, but, maintaining the ornate and labored trappings of the genre, he has transformed marriage. In Paulinus, marriage (and the marriage poem) is set in the elegiac meter, the meter of irrational passion and erotic love, but its message is asexual and dispassionate. The dialectics of rejection of marriage in favor of passion, on the one hand, which is the song of the elegist, and the rejection of passion in favor of marriage, which is the theme of the epithalamium, on the other, becomes in Paulinus a union with Christ. Through a dispassionate earthly union, the poet achieves a regenerative and passionate marriage to Christ, hence, a double immortality: that promised the Christian ascetic and that a poet hopes to achieve in writing verses that survive him.[20]

In his *Sermon on Marriage*, John Chrysostom, one of the four great fathers of the Eastern Church, speaks about weddings of his day and advises his audience to throw out the lewd songs, the corrupt melodies, the disorderly dances, the shameful songs, the diabolical display, the uproar, the unrestrained laughter, and the rest of the impropriety. Instead, he argues, they should consider how Isaac married Rebecca, how Jacob married Rachel. Scripture describes these kinds weddings, and how these brides entered the households of their bridegrooms: they gave banquets and dinners more lavish than usual, and invited their relatives to the weddings. Flutes, pipes, cymbals, drunken cavorting, and all the rest of the impropriety of his own time were avoided, including when people dance and sing hymns to Aphrodite, or songs full of adultery, the corruption of marriages, illicit loves, unlawful unions, and many other impious and shameful things.[21] These impious and shameful things are the stock features of the classical epithalamia of Sappho, Theocritus, and Catullus and contribute to its overriding theme, which is to encourage young couples, many of whom barely knew each other, to consider

---

[20] A common trope in classical literature, e.g., Horace, *Odes* 3.30, who upon completion of his three books of *Odes* claims to have carved out a monument more lasting than bronze, one that will withstand all the vagaries of time thus ensuring the immortality of the poet himself: "exegi monumentum aere perennius ... quod ... possit diruere aut innumerabilis annorum series et fuga temporum. non omnis moriar multaque pars mei vitabit Libitinam ...."

[21] St. John Chrysostom, *On Marriage and Family Life*, trans. Catharine Roth and David Anderson (Crestwood: St. Vladimir's Seminary, 1986), 81–88, here 81–82. Cf. Tomas Spidlik, "Il matrimonio, sacramento di unità, nel pensiero di Crisostomo," *Augustinianum* 17 (1977): 221–26.

marriage a civic obligation, to produce children for the state and as heirs of their own (usually aristocratic) family lines.[22]

For the ancients — as for so many medieval thinkers — marriage was a legal contract usually arranged by the couple's parents. The youth of the bride, and her strict seclusion and supervision made her a reluctant participant at the wedding; from its earliest appearance, the genre included a speech to persuade a young, frightened, and unwilling bride-to-be of the benefits of marriage. Sophocles' *Tereus* fragment 583 aptly expresses the dichotomy between this reluctance of the bride and the passion or romance we associate with marriage today:

> Young women have the sweetest existence
> known in the homes of their fathers . . . But
> when they reach puberty and are thrust
> away or sold away from ancestral gods
> and family it ends. Some go to strange
> men's homes, some to foreigners,
> some to joyless houses, some to hostile.
> All this once the first night has yoked us
> to our husband and we are forced to praise
> him and say that all is well.[23]

Apart from bridal reluctance, most wedding poems include an encomium on the bride's radiant beauty as this verse from one of Catullus's epithalmia illustrates: "ne qua femina pulchrior clarum ab Oceano diem viderit venientemprodeas nova nupta!" (*c.* 61.84–91; O new bride, come forth, for no maiden more lovely has ever risen to see the clear light of dawn coming from the ocean). Praise for the manly grace and strength of the groom is also a stock feature of these poems, as this verse from Sappho (fr. 112) illustrates: "O happy bridegroom, your form is graceful, your eyes gentle, and your handsome face is radiant with love." Venus, the Graces, and the wedding chamber also have a place in the epithalamia. These, sometimes together with the god of marriage, Hymen or Hymenaeus, are lavishly praised. Sappho's fragments 53 (hither, holy rosy-armed Graces, daughters of Zeus) and 128 (come here, now, tender Graces and lovely-haired Muses) invoke the Muses, Graces, Aphrodite, and the wedding alcoves to entrust to them the happy destiny of the bride.

---

[22] For Christians and non-Christians alike in this period, the essential purpose of marriage was to produce children, a doctrine that was born of Stoic opposition to vice, cf. William R. Schoedel, *Athenagoras: Legatio and De resurrectione*. Oxford Early Christian Texts (Oxford: Clarendon Press, 1972), here 81 and n. 1; for Augustine's many references in his sermons, see note 13 above.

[23] For the Greek text, see *Tragicorum graecorum fragmenta selecta*, ed. James Diggle. Scriptorum Classicorum Bibliotheca Oxoniensis (Oxford: Oxford University Press, 1998).

Some element of ribaldry that evolves into a prayer for children signals the poem's conclusion. Catullus addresses one of his epithalamia (c. 61) to real persons — Vibia Arunculeia and Manlius Torquatus. In closing, the poet wishes the couple a happy, harmonious marriage and offspring. They are enjoined to engage in amorous sport at will: *ludite ut lubet* (v. 204; play as you like!), with thousands of joys; but they are reminded that their amorous sport is to be a conscientious application to duty, that is, for the creation of legitimate children to perpetuate the name of the family: *non decet tam vetus sine liberis nomen esse sed indidem semper ingenerari* (vv. 205–08; it is not right for such an old family name to be without children, but rather should always be producing them). Thus passion is subordinate to the social structures of society and the good of the state. In Catullus c. 62, epithalamic themes — youth, sexuality, procreation, and mortality — play themselves out in a mock rhetorical contest between maidens and young men concerning the victory of marriage over virginity: the maidens wish the bride, a flower, to remain untouched and tenderly nurtured in seclusion that she may always be pleasing to boys and girls: "ut flos in saeptis secretus nascitur hortis ignotus pecori, nullo convulsus aratro quem mulcent aurae firmat sol educat imber multi illum pueri multae optavere puellae" (vv. 39–41; just as a secret flower is born in walled off gardens, unknown to sheep and overturned by no plow, which breezes caress, the sun strengthens, and rain causes to grow; many youths and many girls choose it); the youths argue that the maiden should be joined in wedlock in season: "cum par conubium maturo tempore adepta est cara viro magis et minus est invisa parenti" (vv. 57–58; but when in her bloom she is acquired in an **equal marriage** [*par connubium*], she is more dear to her husband and less hateful to her parents). This choral song — almost like the medieval *tenso* — foreshadows the conflict between virginity and marriage and the notions of equality between the husband and wife that are developing in the late antique epithalamia, especially in the epithalamium of Paulinus: "moxque suo factam sumsit ab osse parem" (v. 20; and soon he found an equal, made from his own rib).[24]

Apart from the epithalamia proper, there are several examples of epithalamic conventions in larger myths, poems, or stories. These texts are concerned with passion. Rather than upholding social conventions of marriage for the good of the state, the affairs of these texts are doomed to destruction. Such texts likewise employ the theme of separation and reluctance. In these, however, passion overwhelms the reluctant bride and the affair may be consummated, but outside the legitimate social code. In the epic *Argonautica* of Apollonius, for example, the

---

[24] Henri Crouzel, "L'epitalamio di San Paolino: il suo contenuto dottrinale," *Atti del Convegno XXXI cinquantenario della morte di S. Paolino di Nola (431–1981), Nola 20–21 marzo* (Rome: Herder, 1983): 143–48, and Remo Gelsomino, "L'Epitalamio di Paolino di Nola per Giuliano e Titia (Carme 25)," *Atti del Convegno XXXI cinquantenario della morte di S. Paolino di Nola (431–1981), Nola 20–21 marzo* (Rome: Herder, 1983), 213–30, emphasize the "new" equality in Paulinus's Christian marriage.

story of Jason and Medea contains an embedded hymeneal piece practicing many of the rhetorical conventions of the epithalamia proper.[25] In this marriage of passion, Medea is a near-eastern composite of sensuality and chthonic powers, a goddess-witch, who marries the mortal Jason to be discarded by him later. This is a destructive union because it is born of passion rather than civic duty. In Medea's case, the theme of bridal reluctance is played out against political betrayal. Medea is caught between her love for Jason (against all societal norms since he is both a foreigner *and* her father's enemy) and her loyalty to her family and country. In a touching soliloquy Medea plays the bride by participating in the preparatory nuptial sacrifices and rituals: she caresses her childhood bed and playthings and cuts a piece of her hair to leave for her mother, before sneaking off to sail away with Jason (*Argonautica* 3.284):

> She is torn but she is powerless to resist Erato,
> Muse of irrational love: When she first saw
> Jason, a speechless amazement seized her soul
> and deep in her heart a flame panted in anguish;
> remembrance left her and her soul melted with
> sweet pain.

In this and other epithalamic texts — not in the epithalamia proper although they employ many of the same literary conventions — it is easy to discern the elements of Roman elegy: love born of irrational passion, with its yearning, thwarted desires, and its hopelessness, is further identified by the elegiac meter, the metrical couplets made up of a line of dactylic hexameter with a complementary line of dactylic pentameter. Epithalamia proper, however, with their arguments for marriage and progeny in the interest of upholding the normative social structures, were usually written in dactylic hexameter, the meter of high, state poetry, like Vergil's *Aeneid*; but they were never written in elegiac couplets, the meter of passion and pain.[26]

That is, until Statius. Until the *Epithalamium to Stella and Violentilla*, the literary epithalamium was marked by the *topos* of bridal reluctance. Marriage was the union of a willing groom and an *unwilling but attainable* bride, taken against her will, with the blessing of society. The *topos* of the *willing but unattainable* bride was, instead, standard fare of elegy. Here the lover longed for his beloved and she for him, but their union was impossible. In the epithalamium of Statius we read, for the first time, of a marriage between an elegiac poet/lover and his beloved. Stella, himself an elegiac poet who has written elegies to Violentilla, longed for her, and

---

[25] For the Greek text and English translation, see *Apollonius Rhodius Argonautica*, trans. Robert Cooper Seaton. Loeb Classical Library (Cambridge, MA: Harvard University Press, 1990).

[26] Gabriel Laguna Mariscal, "Invitacion al matrimonio: en torno a un pasaje estaciano (*Silv.* 1.2)," *Emerita* 62 (1994): 263–87, argues that *Aeneid* 4.31–53 (Anna's suasoria to Dido urging her to marry Aeneas) was the inspiration for the *suasoria* of Venus urging Violentilla to marry Stella.

Concordia Virginitatis

suffered long nights desiring her is rewarded by marriage to her in a clever and humorous variation of genre conceits.[27] The poem breaks from its literary antecedents in important ways: Statius introduces panegyric song into the genre, and gives priority among hymeneal divinities to Venus, rather than to Juno.

Pavlovskis claims that Statius's epithalamium is the first example of a new hymeneal composition, "not intended for singing during the wedding."[28] I would add that Statius is the first to combine the passion usually reserved for elegy with the cooler sentiments of the "legitimate" marriage as it is represented in the genre of epithalamium. Texts of passion, until Statius's poem, were discretely limited to elegiac meter, or were embedded in larger narratives, such as Catullus, *c.* 64 — the epyllion to Peleus and Thetis — or the Jason and Medea episode of Apollonius's *Argonautica* mentioned above, but they were not epithalamia proper, the poems that called a couple to marry for the sake of procreation for the good of society. Statius melds the traditions when Stella wins Violentilla, the object of his passion, in marriage. Because Stella himself was an elegiac poet who wrote on erotic themes, we infer that he was committed to the poetry concerned with the furor of love, an unrequited, romantic, passionate union, but not the poetry of marriage. The witty employ of an epithalamium proper to extol his love for Violentilla, an affection that he had expressed in elegy, allows the disposition of rhetorical material and the narrative progressions typical of epic.[29] Appropriating the amatory conceits of elegy, the poem becomes a species of rhetorical panegyric whose theme is the glorification of married love.

Among the Muses that have come from Helicon with Apollo at the onset of the poem is *petulans Elegea* (line 7), whose limp identifies her as the same *Elegea* of the Ovidian tradition who lost a verse to Cupid:

> me miserum! certas habuit puer ille sagittas:
> uror, et in vacuo pectore regnat Amor.
> sex mihi surgat opus muneris, in quinque residat;
> ferrea cum vestris bella valete modis.[30]

> [Woe is me! That boy has sure arrows. I burn,
> and Love rules in my empty heart. Let my text
> stretch to six meters, then finish in five, and
> farewell harsh wars in your heavy meters.]

---

[27] Violentilla, for her part, yields as she warms to her elegiac admirer (vv. 139–40: *ipsam iam cedere sensi inque vicem tepuisse viro*).

[28] Pavlovskis, "Statius and the Late Latin Epithalamia," *Classical Philology* 60 (1965): 164–77.

[29] On Statius's use of the machinery and setting of epic for real and contemporary figures, see David F. Bright, *Elaborate Disarray: The Nature of Statius' Silvae*. Beiträge zur klassischen Philologie, 18 (Meisenheim am Glan: Hain, 1980), 7 ff.

[30] *Amores* 1.1.25–28. For the text, see *P. Ovidi Nasonis Amores Medicamina faciei femineae Ars amatoria Remedia amoris*, ed. Edward J. Kenney (Oxford: Oxford University Press, 1973).

So while Statius's Muses brandish the "solemnem thalamis coeuntibus ignem" (v. 5; solemn fire of conjugal) in their wedding torches, the "subitum ignem" (mounting passion[31]) typical of elegy is recalled. Just as Statius subtly mixes elegiac images with epithalamic, so does Elegy herself seek to mix amid the Muses unperceived, as the tenth:[32]

> quas inter vultu petulans Elegea propinquat
> celsior assueto divasque hortatur et ambit
> alternum furata pedem, decimamque videri
> se cupit et mediis fallit permixta sorores.
> [vv. 7–10; Elegy comes right up to them,
> with her brassy look, taller than usual.
> She hobnobs with the goddesses and
> hides her alternating foot. Hoping to be
> considered one of them she mixes
> right in with the sisters, an unperceived
> tenth Muse].

Although verses 19–23 seem distinctly epithalamic in their invocation to Love and Grace and in the imagery of the bridal chamber:

> nec blandus Amor nec Gratia cessat
> amplexum niveos optatae coniugis artus
> floribus innumeris et olenti spargere nimbo.
>
> [neither charming Love nor Grace cease
> to scatter you with countless flowers and
> a fragrant cloud as you embrace the
> delicate white limbs of your longed for wife]

this language is also the wedding imagery of Ovidian elegy: Phoebus arrives with festive garlands: *tibi Phoebus . . . serta ferunt* (vv. 17–19; Phoebus brings you garlands), but there is to be no forlorn sighing at the door of the beloved as is typical of elegy.[33] Instead, we read *pande fores!* (v. 17; open, doors!), for the love heretofore relegated to elegy has now come under new laws: *subiit leges . . . ille solutus amor* (vv. 28–29; that footloose love has come under laws). Here Venus is the handmaiden of Elegy. She leads the modest bride and prepares the nuptial chamber and tempers her own beauty so as not to outshine the bride: *dissimulata deam*

---

[31] *Amores* 1.2.9.
[32] There are only nine Muses.
[33] The elegiac *paraclausithyron* or "song outside the door of the beloved" is parodied here. For a study of the convention in Roman elegy, see Frank Olin Copley, *Exclusus Amator: A Study in Latin Love Poetry* (Madison: American Philological Association, 1956). See also Pederzani, *Il talamo*, 52–53.

Concordia Virginitatis

crinem vultusque genasque temperat atque nova gestit minor ire marita (vv. 14–15; hiding the fact that she is a goddess, she softens the radiance of her hair and face and eyes and is careful to appear smaller than the new couple). For her part, Violentilla is no longer a tender maiden, for she has been married and widowed already; so it is not marriage that she fears and shuns, but *thalami secundi* (v. 138; a second marriage). Therefore, her encomium, delivered by Venus, cannot take up her praise in the traditional terms of tenderness, modesty, and (appropriate) timidity. Acknowledging her fecund beauty, in this new encomium Venus makes everything, including Violentilla's beauty, second to her nobility of character (as striking a change as that our love poet Stella should marry!):

> hanc ego formae
> egregium mirata decus, cui gloria partum
>   et generis certabat honor, tellure cadentem
>   excepi fovique sinu. nec colla genasque
> comere nec pingui cerinem deducere anomo
> cessavit mea, nate, manus. mihi dulcis imago
> prosiluit. celsae procul aspice frontis honores
> suggestumque comae ...
> haec et caeruleis mecum consurgere digna
> fluctibus et nostra potuit considere concha ...
> huic quamvis census dederim largita beatos,
> vincit opes animo

> [vv. 107–22; How I have admired her, her peerless form in whom the ancestry and the honor of her noble line contended; I took her up as she fell from the earth, and I cradled her in my lap; nor has my hand ever ceased to beautify her neck and cheeks, or to give luster to her hair with rich balsam ... She has blossomed into my own sweet image. Look at the honor of her lofty brow and the glory of her hair ... She was worthy to rise with me from the blue waves and sit upon my shell ... and although I gave her abounding wealth, she will overcome her wealth by her soul.]

Elaborate praise of Venus forms a subsection of this encomium, an implicit comparison of the goddess and the bride.[34] When Statius zooms in, Venus is resting

---

[34] On the careful structure of the poem into thirteen sections and the crafted placement of the encomia of the bride and groom, see David W. T. C. Vessey, "Aspects of Statius' Epithalamion,"

in her heavenly bedchamber, faint, just released from the strong arms of her husband. She lies limp on the coverlets, with no particular plan in her heart as her attendant cupids flit about or settle on her bedposts. They await her bidding. Her son steps forward, and he delivers so persuasive a plea on behalf of love-struck Stella that Venus determines to intercede and make a love match between him and Violentilla. She lifts her *sidereos artus* (v.141; starry limbs), calls her doves, crosses her *superbum limen* (vv. 141–42; proud threshold"), harnesses her doves and rides off serenely happy through the clouds *gemmato temone* (v. 144; on a gemmed pole).

Venus approaches Violentilla's *domus*, the magnificence of which, by contrast, is elaborately described as *digna dea* (v. 147; worthy of a goddess):

> pandit nitidos domus alta penates
> claraque gaudentes plauserunt limina cycni. . . .
> hic Libycus Phrysgiusque silex, hic dura Laconum
> saxa virent, hic flexus onyx et concolor alto
> vena mari,l rupesque nitent quis purpura saepe
> Oebalis et Tyrii moderator livet aeni.
> pendent innumeris fastigia nixa columnis,
> robora Dalmatico lucent sociata metallo.
> excludunt radios silvis demissa vetustis
> frigora, perspicui vivunt in marmore fontes.
>
> [vv. 145–55; A tall house reveals shining interiors,
> and rejoicing swans flap on the bright entrance ways.
> Here there is Libyan or Phrygian marble, here the
> hard Laconian stone shines green; here is the
> changeable onyx and a vein the same color as the
> depth of the ocean; here stones shine that
> Oebalian purple and the moderator of the Tyrian
> bronze envy. Fastened pediments hang on
> innumerable columns; beams fastened with
> Dalmatian ore glitter. Cool currents from old
> trees block the sun, and crystal clear fountains
> are alive in the marble.]

Violentilla's *domus* is a self-contained *locus amoenus* of earthly riches that does not pale in comparison with that heavenly abode of Venus: *nitidis nec sordet ab astris* (v. 147; nor does it seem dingy even compared to the shining stars).[35] The

---

Mnemosyne, ser. 4, 25 (1972): 172–87. Cf. Stephen Thomas Newmyer, *The Silvae of Statius: Structure and Theme*. Mnemosyne, Bibliotheca Classica Batava : Supplementum, 53 (Leiden: Brill, 1979), 30 ff.

[35] *Cf.* Carole E. Newlands, *Statius' Silvae and the Poetics of Empire* (Cambridge: Cambridge University Press, 2002), 93–105. Newlands argues that the elaborate description of Violentilla's house

Concordia Virginitatis

visual symmetry between Venus' bower and Violentilla's house suggests an analogous syncretism between the heavenly and earthly bride. It is also an opportunity for the poet to reflect upon his craft. Just as the erotic sensibilities of Venus's bower are transferred to Violentilla's house, so is the erotic and adorned language of elegy transferred to the heroic and epic epithalamium.[36] As Venus leaves her tranquil mythological bower *plaga lactea serenati caeli* (v. 51; on the Milky Way of serene heaven) and enters the house of Violentilla to arbitrate in a real marriage, so are we meant to recall *Elegea permixta* leaving her accustomed metrical setting to arbitrate in an epic epithalamium. At their union, the god of marriage, Hymen, is present at the portal of the house now decorated for a wedding, ready to sing the *intactum carmen* (v. 238; new song), a mixture of elegy and epic epithalamium, as he leads a band of other poets celebrating the marriage in verse competition. Among these is Elegy. She is especially invited to sing the new marriage song:

> sed praecipue qui nobile gressu
> extremo fraudatis epos, date carmina festis
> digna toris.
>
> [vv. 250–52; but you especially who rob
> lofty Epic of its last foot, sing songs
> worthy of the marriage bed.]

Statius's poem is an epithalamium proper with all the standard conventions as they are laid out in the texts of the rhetoricians: a persuasive speech (delivered by Venus herself) to the reluctant Violentilla; encomia upon the bride and groom; a hymn to the god of marriage or to Venus; and the prayer for progeny. In these things Statius stands firmly in the epideictic tradition of the genre.[37] What is innovative is Statius's urging the elegiac poet Stella to marry and thus to reconcile his elegiac passion and erotic *furor* with the socially legitimate state of marriage. This is achieved by interweaving the epithalamia in dactylic hexameter with the conceits, conventions, and *topoi* of elegy. The *furor* that was associated exclusively with elegiac passion, elegiac meter, and a non-legitimate union, is now the impetus for the marriage. To sum up:

In vv. 3–10, the goddesses of marriage-songs (the Muses on Mt. Helicon), Venus *pronuba*, and the bride (more beautiful than the goddess herself) are summoned

---

(vv. 145 ff.) "serves the complex function of mapping the moral as well as the social and physical attributes of Violentilla upon architectural space" (94–95).

[36] For the patterned arrangement of words and the thematic repetitions in these kinds of descriptions, see the discussion in Betty Rose Nagle, *The Silvae of Statius* (Bloomington: Indiana University Press, 2004), 10–11.

[37] For the background and Statius's contributions to these epic praise poems, see Alex Hardie, *Statius and the Silvae* (Liverpool: F. Cairns, 1983), especially ch. 6, "The Epideictic Background," 74–102.

to the wedding. In addition, *Elegea* is introduced; she is *permixta* with the other Muses unperceived. At the onset Statius has changed the conventions of the epic epithalamium by this humorous addition of a tenth Muse and the conceits of the elegiac poetry she inspires.

Throughout the poem elegiac conventions are inverted, but in vv. 31–37, the closed door, the lover's sighs, the misery of thwarted love are overcome and the unattainable love is attained.[38] The doorkeeper who in elegy forbade the entrance of the lover has been banished, and no *lex*[39] or *pudor*, that is, neither the meter nor theme of epic, restrains him:

> pone o dulcis suspiria vates.
> pone: tua est. Licet expositum per limen aperto
> ire redire gradu. Iam nusquam ianitor aut lex
> aut pudor.
>
> [vv. 33–36; Put away your sighs, sweet poet, put
> them away: she is your own. You may now
> freely cross and re-cross the unguarded threshold.
> There is no doorkeeper, no restraint, and no shame.]

The proscriptive encomium of the groom, a feature of the rhetorical epithalamium, is likewise inverted in Statius's poem. Typically the groom is praised for his nobility and beauty, for his distinguished family, for his good fortune in his bride. Such an encomium is called the makarismos.[40] While such elements are in evidence here, Stella is primarily praised for his long-suffering, heart-sick yearning, as these comments of Cupid reveal: *quantos iuvenis premat anxius ignes . . .quantum me nocte dieque urguentem ferat* (vv. 81–83; What great fires the anxious youth repressed; what urging he bore from me day and night). Instead of his beauty and good fortune, Stella is praised for his attributes as an elegiac lover/poet. He is

---

[38] These are the telltale signs of elegy. On the paraclausithyron, or song outside the lover's door, see above n. 33.

[39] See Ruurd R. Nauta, *Poetry for Patrons. Literary Communication in the Age of Domitian*. Mnemosyne, Bibliotheca Classica Batava.; Supplementum, 206 (Leiden and Boston: Brill, 2002), 298–300; here 299 and n. 27. Nauta argues that the law is the dormant Julian Law against adultery, which Domitian had begun to re-enforce, and that Stella and Violentilla married because they were having an affair punishable by law. I understand in addition a metaphorical metric law, that is, that the genre constraints of form (*lex*) and content (*pudor*) have been inverted.

[40] See John J. Winkler, "Public and Private in Sappho's Lyrics," Helene P. Foley, *Reflections of Women in Antiquity* (New York: Gordon and Breach Science Publishers 1981), 73: *Makarismos* is the flattering comparisons/hymning of the bride, groom, and the families of the betrothed, the wedding chambers and alcoves, gods of marriage, marriage itself, and offspring, interspersed with stories of charm and love; Anne Pippin Burnett, *Three Archaic Poets* (Cambridge, MA: Harvard University Press, 1983), 237 and n. 15 "Marriage gave a particular man an experience like that of a divinity and in these moments he could be hailed with epithets that properly belonged to gods."; see Paolo Fedeli, *Catullus' Carmen 61* (Amsterdam: Gieben, 1983), 78–79 for a list of textual examples.

clarus de gente Latina est iuvenis, quem patriciis maioribus ortum nobilitas gavisa tulit (vv. 70-72; a distinguished young man of noble Latian lineage whom rejoicing nobility produced), named for the heavens in anticipation of his beauty: *praesagaque formae protinus e nostro posuit cognomina [Stella] caelo* (vv. 72-73; and named him with a name [Stella] from our heaven, the promise of his handsome form). He could have written epic songs extolling heroic deeds: *armiferos poterat memorare labores claraque facta virum et torrentes sanguine campos* (vv. 96-97; He could have commemorated warlike endeavors, the illustrious deeds of men and the battlefields running with blood), but instead he wrote love poetry: *sed tibi [Venus] plectra dedit mitisque incedere vates maluit* (vv. 98-99; but he gave his pen to you [Venus] and preferred to walk as a lighter muse). The praise typically accorded Hymen, the god of marriage, in an epithalamium, is bestowed upon Stella, and by analogy, elegy, or the marriage of passion, not social obligation.

The speech persuading marriage is significantly altered. In epithalamia the bride is reluctant but attainable; for marriage is a social obligation and a civic virtue. Here, the *suasoria* of Venus on the good of marriage, however, becomes an admonishment to Violentilla not to squander her youth but to make the most of fleeting beauty before time transforms it: *veniet iam tristior aetas. exerce formam et fugientibus utere donis* (vv. 165-66; A sadder time will come, so flaunt your beauty and use those fleeting gifts!) When Venus praises Stella for his poetic skill it is clear that marriage is no longer only a civic obligation for an unwilling bride. Rather, Venus, with persuasive rhetorical conceits, has inspired in Violentilla a passion born of the poetry Stella has addressed to her: *nam docta per urbem carmina qui iuvenes, quae non didicere puellae?* (vv. 172-73; What young men and what girls in all Rome do not know his polished verses by heart?). Civic obligation combined with the passion of elegy is neither an epithalamium nor an elegy. The poets who are invoked to sing songs of both Muses, that is, epic and elegy, worthy of this **new** marriage, however, are all elegists (vv. 252-54) — Philetas, Cos, Callimachus, Propertius, Ovid, and Tibullus. Although they are the poets of elegiac love and although they cheat noble epic of its final foot by writing in elegiac meter: *nobile gressu extremo fraudatis opus* (vv. 250-51; you steal the last foot from noble epic), they are nonetheless the ones encouraged to write songs worthy of the wedding feast: *date carmina festis digna toris* (vv. 251-52; Sing songs worthy of the decorated marriage beds!).

The final passage prays for fruitful union, the typical conclusion of an epithalamium, but here, the bride is to remain ever young, ever beautiful, unmarred by childbirth. So while the poet has attained the beloved for whom he yearned (in elegiac poetry) in a legitimate union (in an epithalamium), he also has retained his mistress in her eternal youth and beauty, qualities unique to the elegiac mistress, who forever remains untouched, inviolably lovely, and pined after: *sic damna decoris nulla tibi, longae virides sic flore iuventae perdurent vultus tardeque haec forma senescat* (vv. 275-77; So may your beauty suffer no loss, and the fresh glow of youth abide upon your countenance, and your beauty age slowly.) And so does Violentilla remain in Statius's poem, as immortal in the poetry of marriage as the poet's elegiac mistress is in the poetry of passion.

Paulinus of Nola's fifth century[41] epithalamium for Julian, Son of Bishop Memor, and his bride Titia, is an overtly Christian epithalamium, an attempt to expunge "pagan" imagery from the genre in favor of a pious union dedicated to the love of Christ. Sexual lasciviousness, mythological gods and goddesses of marriage — Juno, Cupid, and Venus — are rejected, and Pax, Pudor, and Pietas are invoked in their places. The rhetorical conventions so carefully defined by Pseudo Dionysius and Menander Rhetor and still evident in the poem of Statius are transformed by Paulinus: the encomia upon the bride and groom, and the praise of marriage draw upon biblical analogies — the story of Adam and Eve, the examples of Sara, Rebecca, and Mary, the Pauline passages on marriage;[42] and Christ and Concordia replace Juno as bridesmaid to perform the *dextrarum unctio*. This new kind of sacred marriage, however, is not cast in the heroic meter of virtue, pudor, and epithalamia, but in the meter of passionate, irrational, and painful love, the elegiac couplet. If Statius's epithalamium is epic in form and private in its design, Paulinus's is elegiac in form but epic and even sacred in design. In a movement from contractual to sacramental a new spirituality of marriage based upon ideals of asceticism and continence is born and gives rise to the notion of the marriage of Christ with the Church in a mystic fusion of spirit.[43] The rhetorical features of the late Latin poems as well as the *topoi* of the Greek and Roman examples are identifiable, some transformed into the service of the propagation of a Christian marriage and ceremony, others, a clear rejection of "pre" or "non" Christian *topoi* and rhetorical elements.[44] Paulinus's poem is overtly Christian and his stern admonishments against worldly pleasures, including the joys of earthly marriage, call for a new nuptial ideal — *concordia virginitatis*, conjugal virginity.[45]

Upon closer reading, however, those admonishments might strike the modern reader as almost fanatical, for Paulinus enjoins the reader to avoid sin

---

[41] According to Pierre Fabre, *Essai sur la chronologie de l'oeuvre de Saint Paulin de Nole* (Paris: Belles Lettres, 1948), 122–23, the likely date is between 400 and 404, when the Julian Eclanum mentioned in the poem was a lector.

[42] See Richard A. Batey, *New Testament Nuptial Imagery* (Leiden: Brill, 1971), ch. 2, "Paul's Bride Image," 12–19, and ch. 3, "Deutero-Pauline Nuptial Imagery," 20–37.

[43] This collection of patristic texts on the evolving notions of marriage contains several such interpretations: *Marriage in the Early Church*, ed. and trans. David G. Hunter (Minneapolis: Fortress Press, 1994).

[44] Camillo Morelli, "L'epitalamio nella tarda poesia Latina," *Studi italiani di Filologia classica* 18 (1910): 319–432.

[45] This is a reflection of the love between Christ and his church where carnality is sublimated to a mystical fusion of souls. Cf. Gelsomino, "L'Epitalamio di Paolino," 227–30 and Carlo Tibiletti, "Nota teologica a S. Paolino di Nola (carmen 25, 189)," *Augustinianum* 18 (1978): 389–95.

Concordia Virginitatis 69

with all the rhetorical artifices and lascivious sensual detail of the classical and late antique epithalamia.[46] In the same way that Robert Levine's explores the sincerity of Venantius Fortunatus's panegyrics in his contribution to this volume, on patronage and erotic rhetoric in the poems of Venantius Fortunatus, we should question the sincerity of Paulinus's *concordia virginitatis* in elegiac distichs.

Statius begins his poem by inviting, in dactylic hexameter, the Muse Elegy into the genre. Together with the Graces and Loves, typically invited to decorate the wedding bower with blossoms and perfumes (vv. 19–21), Statius also invites Phoebus, Bacchus and Mercury to bring garlands and join in the decorating (vv. 17–19). These are not the gods who usually attend a wedding, but the gods of lost love, unrequited love — the gods of elegy. Paulinus begins his poem by dismissing, in elegiac meter, not only the Muse Elegy, whom Statius, in dactylic hexameter, had invited into the genre, but also the hymeneal parade and decorations, which, as they are expressed here, are more the literary motifs of elegy and the elegiac serenade than the nuptial celebration: "nulla per ornatas insultet turbas plateas nemo solum foliis, limina fronde tegat. nulla peregrines fragret nidoribus aura... nolo supervacuis ornentur fercula donis" (vv. 31–39; No crowd should gather to dance in festooned piazzas, nor to cover the ground or thresholds with garlands; there should be no hint of foreign perfumes, no trays of gifts). Such *topoi*, while they echo the patristic tracts that eulogize virginity,[47] also invoke the more general literary program of elegiac love, love without emotional entanglements and concerned with beauty and sexual pursuit rather than marriage. This is the vivid imagery of the elegiac *komos*, the procession of drunken young men who make their way singing to the home of a young woman, sometimes to serenade her and sometimes to wait outside her door: wine, song, garlands, pipes and torches of drunken revelry and thwarted love.[48] It is this tradition — elegiac, Bacchic, Apollonine, and Mercurial that Paulinus dismisses, with their elaborate rhetorical trappings, the very trappings that allow him to describe the elegiac serenade in

---

[46] André Basson, "A transformation of genres in late Latin literature: classical literary tradition and ascetic ideals in Paulinus of Nola," *Shifting Frontiers in Late Antiquity*, ed. Ralph W. Mathisen and Hagith S. Sivan (Brookfield, VT: Variorum, 1996), 267–76, has argued that despite Paulinus's new religion he could not turn his back on the conventions of classical literature. The conclusions of Anna Sbrancia, "L'Epitalamio di S. Paolino di Nola," *Annali della Facoltà di Lettere e Filosofia dell'Università di Macerata* 11 (1978): 83–129; here 124, and Gelsomino, "L'Epitalamio," 214, concur: Paulinus has written a new kind of marriage song advocating a new kind of marriage within the rhetorical structure of the classical epithalamia.

[47] On virginity in the early church, see Peter Brown, *The Body and Society: Men, Women, and Sexual Renunciation in Early Christianity* (New York: Columbia University Press, 1988).

[48] On the origin of the *komos*, the evening (or early morning) procession of a group of drunken young men to the home of a young woman, to serenade her, or to wait as a lovesick attendant outside her door, see ch. 2, "Erotic Epigrams: The kw>mo" and the Paraklausivquron," in Sonya Lida Tarán, *The Art of Variation in the Hellenistic Epigram*. Columbia Studies in the Classical Tradition, 9 (Leiden: Brill, 1979), 52–110.

full detail, the same trappings that Statius, in his novel treatment of the epithalamium, had developed in his epithalamium.

The notions of the separation of the bride from her family, or the bride as abducted, so important in the early texts, in Paulinus are dismissed in three distichs with Biblical overtones:

> auxilioque viri divino munere factam
> lector coelesti discat ab historia;
> inque vicem mulier, sancto sit ut aequa marito
> mente humili Christum in conjuge suscipiat
> crescat ut in sanctum texta compagine corpus,
> ut sit ei vertex vir, cui Christus apex.

> [vv. 143–48; Let the lector learn from celestial history that his wife has been made as a helpmate of her husband by divine gift. And let the woman in turn take up Christ in her marriage with humble heart, that she may be an equal to her holy husband; that she may grow into his holy body woven by his rib, that her husband may be a vertex to her, to whom Christ is the apex.][49]

The invocation to, or hymning of, Venus and the gods of marriage is included only to be rejected: *absit ab his thalamis vani lascivia vulgi, Juno, Cupido, Venus, nomina luxuriae* (vv. 9–10; Let the lasciviousness of the vain crowd be absent from these marriage chambers — Juno, Cupid, Venus, the names of Luxury). Shortly thereafter an invocation to Christ replaces the usual call to Hymen, the god of marriage: *seria tranquillis agitentur gaudia votes Christus ubique pii voce sonet populi* (vv. 29–30; Let our serious joys be impelled by tranquil prayers; let Christ everywhere be sung with the voice of a pious people).[50] Festooned streets and the garlanded bedchamber, dancing graces, attendant nymphs, and feasting have no place in the new wedding song of Paulinus, a song that God has made sacred *proprio ore* (v. 15; with his own voice) and which the poet sings *novo ore* (v. 23; with a new voice):[51]

> nemo solum foliis, limina fronde tegat.
> ne sit Christicolam fanatica turba per urbem.

---

[49] *Cf.* Gn 2.18; Eph 5.29–32.

[50] For these and other invocations in the poem, see Joseph A. Guttilla, "Preghiere e invocazioni nei *Carmi* di S. Paolino di Nola," *Annali del liceo classico* 28–30 (1991–1993): 93–188; here 170–74.

[51] The novelty of Paulinus's treatment vis à vis the "pagan" epithalamium is taken up in Jan Adriaan Bouma, *Het Epithalamium van Paulinus van Nola. Carmen XXV met inleiding, vertaling en commentaar* (Assen: Van Gorcum, 1968).

Concordia Virginitatis

nolo profana pios polluat ambitio.
nulla peregrinis fragret nidoribus aura:
cuncta pudicitiae munditias oleant....
nolo supervacuis ornentur fercula donis:
moribus ornatur, non opibus probitas.

[vv. 31–40; Let no one cover the ground with
flowers and the thresholds with greens. No
fanatic crowd should be present in the city in
which Christ [not Hymen] dwells. I do not
want profane greed to pollute the pious.
Let no breeze scent the air with foreign
sacrifices but let every elegance of modesty
[*pudicitiae*] be redolent..... I do not want trays
piled with meaningless gifts; let goodness be
decorated with character not wealth.]

The encomium upon the groom (vv. 91–98) takes the form of paternal advice: Julian should spurn the cares of decorous form and devote himself to books that contain examples from the Old Testament and from the lives of the saints: "compensavit enim Christus tibi largiter ornans perpetuis pulchram divitiis animam ... spe, pietate, fide, pace, pudicitia. sermo Dei argentum est, et sanctus Spiritus aurum mentibus et gemmae clara bonorum operum" (vv. 93–98; Christ has bountifully compensated your fine soul with the perpetual riches ... of hope, piety, faith, peace, and modesty. The word of God is silver and the Holy Spirit gold; to your minds gems are the brightness of good works).

The encomium upon the bride catalogs then dismisses the vain display of nuptial pomp, among which are named make-up, jewels, blond hair tint, purple silk tied coyly about her waist, fancy hair, styled high, perfumed and golden sandals (vv. 41–90). Instead of this worldly party attire, Paulinus tells us that the bride will be pleasing if she is simply adorned with an elegant interior, that is, a character (*ingenium*) decorated with a salvific dowry: "Interiore magis mundo placitura colatur comta salutiferis dotibus ingenium" (vv. 49–50; Let her be cherished more for her pleasing interior grace, a character that has been adorned by a dowry of salvation).[52]

In Statius's encomium upon the bride Violentilla, her singular beauty is praised; Venus herself has graced her face and neck and combed her hair with rich balsam; Venus herself marvels at the dignity of her high brow and her high-piled

---

[52] There are several patristic texts on the topic, e.g., Tertullian, *De cultu feminarum*. Corpus Christianorum Series Latina, 1; Cyprian, *De habitu virginum* (Corpus Scriptorum Ecclesiasticorum Latinorum 3), et al. For other corollary texts, see Walsh, *The Poems of St. Paulinus*, 400–01 and nn. 19–20.

hair: "nec colla genasque comere nec pingui crinem deducere amomo cessavit mea ... manus ... celsae procul aspice frontis honores suggestumque comae" (vv. 110–14; Nor had my hand ceased to adorn her neck and face, nor to braid her hair with rich balsam ... Look, even from here you can see the honor of her high brow and her high-piled hair). She is, claims Venus, "dulcis imago mihi" (v. 112; her own sweet image). There are not enough ways to praise her — the encomium extends from vv. 102–37 — nor enough beautifully dyed garments of purple or gemmed necklaces for her. If Bacchus had seen her, he would have abandoned Ariadne: "Cnosida desertam profugus liquisset et Euhan" (v. 133; Euhan too would have fled and left the Cnosian girl [Ariadne] abandoned); and, for Violentilla, Jupiter would disguise himself to deceive Juno: "pennas et cornua sumeret aethrae rector, in hanc ver<s>o cecidisset Juppiter auro" (vv. 135–56; Jupiter himself would take on wings or horns, or would have fallen into her [Violentilla's] lap transformed into gold). Yet, for all her beauty and wealth, we learn that Venus considers her soul her greatest asset: "vincit opes animo" (v. 122; She surpasses her wealth with her soul).

The dowry of Titia, on the other hand, in Paulinus's encomium to the bride (vv. 41–90) should be simple and unostentatious. The bride should shudder at costly and ostentatious garments: "horreat inclusas auro, vel murices vestes" (v. 43: let her shudder at dresses woven with gold or purple); the gold of her garment should be, instead, the purity of God: "aurea vestis huic gratia pura Dei est" (v. 44; her golden dress is the pure grace of God). She should spurn splendid jewelry: "respuat et variis distincta monilia gemmis" (v. 45; she should spurn necklaces studded with varied gems); and she should cultivate a character that can claim salvation as her dowry rather than desiring precious gems or silk gowns: "non cupiat lapidum pretium non vellera serum" (v. 51; let her not desire precious stone or a cloak of silk). These kinds of displays and excess only cheapen the Christian bride of Paulinus's poem: "sordescit *nitidis corporis exuviis*" (v. 58; with such gleaming excess of her person she becomes sordid). By these few examples in the encomia to the brides of their respective poems, we see again that all the adornments of erotic love elegy that Statius ironically interposed among his epithalamic hexameters Paulinus ironically rejects in elegiac meter.

In a digression similar to that of Statius's elaborate description of Violentilla's house, Paulinus takes forty verses to compare the extravagantly adorned (non-Christian) bride to the alluring Herodias as she danced before her father and his guests.[53] In golden slippers and an enticing, flowing robe, with her hair unbound and wrapped in gems, inspired by an avenging lust, Herodias dances, clever in her *arte pedibus* (v. 124; nimble feet), a play upon the poet's metrical (and Herodias's

---

[53] Rosanna Bertini Conidi, "La figura di Salome in Paolino di Nola (carm. 25). Sul comportamento etico femminile," *Studia Ephemeridis Augustinianum* 53 (1996): 533–42, argues that dancing itself was as offensive to the Church fathers in the tradition of earlier Stoic writers.

dancing) foot. His poem is ostensibly a rejection of the art of [metrical] dancing, that is, a rejection of Statius's clever fusion of elegiac erotic themes in epithalamic poetry. But when he writes of the *seria gaudia* (v. 29; serious joys) of the *sanctum foedus* (vv. 27–28; sacred marriage pact) in elegiac couplets rather than in epic hexameters, he invites the reader to appreciate the irony. On the model of Statius, form and content have been purposefully inverted.

Finally let us consider the conclusion of an epithalamium, the prayer for progeny. Statius offers a twist upon the epithalamic tradition when he prays that Violentilla's beauty suffer no harm in childbirth and that her lovely form be slow to age, in short, that she have children but remain an eternally young and seductive elegiac mistress. The final words, "tardeque haec forma senescat" (v. 277; may her beauty [*forma*] age slowly), hope not only for Violentilla's lovely form to age slowly, but also that the poet's unique poetic combination — epithalamic form with elegiac content — should age slowly and thus grant its author immortality. Paulinus cleverly transforms the conceit. He asks that the same love by which the Church holds Christ and with which Christ nurtures the Church bind the newlyweds. He asks that the couple live in "concordia virginitatis" (v. 233; harmonious virginity), not the regenerative virginity of Statius's elegiac bride, but a sanctified virginity. Or, if this is not possible, he asks that the children born in this marriage be sacred offspring of a priestly race: "Casta sacerdotale genus[54] ventura propago" (v. 236; chaste offspring who will be born into a priestly family).

The poem ends with four pentameter lines that break the metrical pattern and polyptotonically play on the words *Memor* and *memor*. The repetition of the word *domus* four times in two verses (vv. 237–38) invites readers familiar with the elaborately described house of Violentilla to compare it to the simple, elegant, pure, yet seductive house of Memor, the bishop of Capua and father of the groom:

Et domus Aron sit tota domus Memoris
Christorumque domus sit domus haec Memoris.
Esto et Paulini Therasiaeque memor[55]
et memor aeternum Christus erit Memoris.

[vv. 237–40; Let the whole house of Memor
be the house of Aron, and may this house of
Memor be a house of Christians. Let him be

---

[54] Titia is marrying into a priestly family: Memor is Julian's father but also Bishop of Capua. Julian became Bishop of Eclanum. See Carlo Tibiletti, "Paolino di Nola e famiglie di 'clerici,'" *Vichiani* 11 (1982): 305–10.

[55] Paulinus and his wife Theresa lived in ascetic harmony from 394 when he became a cleric (and ultimately bishop of Nola) at least until 408. On his internal struggle as he came to this decision and the evidence for it in his correspondence with Ausonius, see ch. 4, "Renunciation and Ordination," in Dennis E. Trout, *Paulinus of Nola. Life, Letters, and Poems* (Berkeley: University of California Press, 1999), 78–103.

mindful of Paulinus and Theresa and
Christ will be eternally mindful of Memor.]

The promise to Memor of *memor aeternum* (v. 240; eternal life in Christ) is predicated upon the *memor Paulini*, that is the life of the poem (v. 239; mindful of Paulinus): as long as Paulinus's poem lasts, so long will Christ be *memor* of the house of *Memor*, here established by his son's marriage to Titia.

In words of love, Statius immortalized Violentilla as an elegiac mistress in an epithalamium, while incidentally claiming for himself the immortality a poet achieves when his verses live beyond him. Also in words of love, Paulinus immortalized his wife, Theresa, in an elegiac poem, claiming for them both the immortality hoped for by ascetic Christians, in addition to the immortality a poet achieves when his verses live beyond him. Both poets' love of words, however, has immortalized the poetic tension between love and marriage. This tension was first playfully exploited in Statius' epithalamium to Stella and Violentilla, and then infused with the love of Christ in Paulinus's epithalamium to Julian and Titia, the *locus classicus* for the same tension between love and marriage in medieval courtly love poetry.[56]

---

[56] Cf. C. Stephen Jaeger, *Ennobling Love*. Middle Ages Series (Philadelphia: University of Pennsylvania Press, 1999).

Chapter 2

Patronage and Erotic Rhetoric in the Sixth Century: The Case of Venantius Fortunatus

Robert Levine
Boston University

Many of the papers in this volume are concerned with religious, philosophical, linguistic, and epistemological aspects of medieval erotic rhetoric; this paper is concerned with a more practical aspect — the use of "sweet talk" for material gain. Panegyric, often considered the lowest of literary activities,[1] is the obvious place to look for instances of such activities, and Venantius Fortunatus's (c. 531-c.609) efforts in the genre have been surprisingly successful, since his *Carmina* have moved several of his most attentive modern readers to admire the sincere, authentic, passionate nature of the self-proclaimed *novus Orpheus's*[2] expressions of *amicitia*. An Italian, born in Treviso, trained at Ravenna, who came to France, ostensibly to pay homage to Saint Martin, but not incidentally to escape the political strife in his native land, Fortunatus is best known for composing two major hymns, "Vexilla Regis Prodeunt" and the "Pange Lingua,"[3] but he also composed panegyrics for Bishop Gregory of Tours, as well as for other ecclesiastical figures and powerful aristocrats, both men and women. These poems have received less

---

[1] "Panegyricum est licentiosum, et laciniosum genus dicendi in laudibus regum, in cujus compositione homines multis mendaciis adulantur. Quod malum a Graecis exortum est, quorum levitas instructa dicendi facultate et copia incredibili multas mendaciorum nebulas suscitavit" (Isidore of Seville, 6.VIII.7: Panegyric is a contemptible way of speaking in praise of kings, in the course of whose composition men are glorified mendaciously. The Greeks developed the wretched thing, raising many clouds of lies with remarkable, well-trained skill).

[2] *Venance Fortunat, Poèmes,* texte établi et traduit par Marc Reydellet (Paris: Les Belles Lettres, 1994), 4.

[3] *Venance Fortunat*, 5–52, 57–58.

attention, and the judgments made about them in the last hundred and fifty years have been both positive and negative.

For example, Judith George admires the sincerity[4] of *Carmina* 8.19, in which Fortunatus thanks Gregory for lending him a villa:

> ... poem 8.19 is more than a mere tribute from a poet to his patron. In its literary echoes of the ascetics' use of erotic terminology to express loving friendship, it is a tribute of great feeling to Gregory. There is respect for him as pastor and patron, but there is also personal love.[5]

George's assertions imply that Fortunatus's poems show signs of sincerity, authenticity, and accuracy (three words often invoked in the search for truth), qualities that can be dangerous, unless well disguised, for writers dependent upon patronage.

> In addition, *Carmina* 8.19, in which Fortunatus uses *amor* once, and addresses Gregory merely as *care,* "my dear one," it certainly seems to be the work of a cold fish when compared to the extravagant expression of passion provided in mere prose by Paulinus in the opening of his *Epistle* xxiii, 8.19:
> Si potest mare superfluere obices suos , et quaecumque naturalem plenitudinem servant, incrementum temporale sentire, potest et caritas in te nostra cumulari ... sollicitas potius gulam caritatis tantoque minus exples gratia litterarum, quanto majorem sedulitate ipsa et humanitate sermonis tui causam suggeris, te ipsum .... Nam quantus quantus es, qua mente, qua lingua es, totus desiderium es: et mihi dulcedinem Christi sapis ut hortus mihi, *ut odor agri pleni* , quem in odorem unguentorum illius currendo legisti. (*PL* CXI, 256–257)

> [If the sea can overflow its barriers, if all that is naturally full can experience a short-lived increase, then my love for you can be enhanced ... you awake the gluttony of my love. Your failure to satisfy me with the pleasure of your letters is all the greater because by the very diligence and kindness of your words you awake in me a greater desire for seeing you in the flesh .... All

---

[4] The classic work on sincerity is Henri Peyre, *Literature and Sincerity.* Yale Romanic Studies, 2nd Series, 9 (New Haven: Yale University Press, 1963); Lionel Trilling, *Sincerity and Authenticity* (Cambridge, MA: Harvard University Press, 1972), is also intermittently useful. Harry Frankfurt's recent brief treatment of the topic is playfully provocative: Facts about ourselves are not peculiarly solid and resistant to skeptical dissolution. Our natures are, indeed, elusively insubstantial — notoriously less stable and less inherent than the natures of other things. And insofar as this is the case, sincerity itself is bullshit. (Harry Frankfurt, *On Bullshit* [Princeton: Princeton University Press, 2005], 66–67). See also Judith George, "Venantius Fortunatus: Panegyric in Merovingian Gaul,"*The Propaganda of Power: The Role of Panegyric in Late Antiquity,* ed. Mary Whitby (Leiden: Brill, 1998), 225–46.

[5] Judith W. George, *Venantius Fortunatus: A Latin Poet in Merovingian Gaul* (Oxford: Clarendon Press, 1992), 130.

of you, mind and tongue, I long for. Your savour is for me the sweetness of Christ, like a garden or the smell of a plentiful field.... [6]]

Though he chooses not to match Paulinus's hyperbole in 8.19, Fortunatus provides a more heated rhetoric elsewhere; for example, two poems to Dynamius reflect what George calls "the tradition of the passionate expression of an ascetic friendship."[7] Poem 6.9, to Dynamius, written in 567, while Fortunatus was still at Metz, but after Dynamius had returned to Marseilles, contains the startling assertion, *Vulsus ab aspectu, pectore junctus ades*: "torn from my sight, you are joined to my breast," the image of Siamese twins certainly outdoes its classical source or analogue, Horace's less graphic tribute to Vergil: *Et serves animae dimidium meae*, "you keep one half of my soul."

However, Fortunatus uses Horace's line in 7.20, a poem to Sigmund, an officer perhaps in the service of Sigebert, for whom he declares himself steady in love, and panting for news about his *care*; the poem ends with Fortunatus declaring that Sigmund is *pars animae dimidiata meae*:[8]

> Quid geris, oro, refer; tamen, ut queo longius opto,
> Uiuas *pars animae dimidiata meae*
> [But please tell me what you are doing; I wish that you, one half of my soul, may live as long as possible.]

In 6.10.48, he addresses Dynamius with a variation of the formula, *animae pars mediata meae*, either unaware or heedless of the dogmatic, categorical rejection of the possibility of *amicitia* between men of unequal social rank that Jerome makes, using Horace's very words as an example of deceit:

> Amicitia pares aut accipit, aut facit: ubi inaequalitas est, et alterius eminentia, alterius subjectio, ibi non tam amicitia, quam adulatio est. Unde et alibi legimus: Sit amicus eadem anima. Et Lyricus pro amico precans: *Serves*, inquit, *animae dimidium meae (Horat.)*. Nolite ergo credere in amicis, id est, his hominibus, qui de amicitiis sectantur lucra.[9]

[Friendship assumes or makes men equal; where there is inequality, and one man is above and the other below, there is no friendship, but adulation. That is why we read elsewhere, "a friend may be the same soul." And the poet asks

---

[6] Trans. by P. G. Walsh, *Letters of St. Paulinus of Nola*, vol. II (Westminster, MD: Newman Press, 1968), 1, 2.
[7] George, *Venantius Fortunatus*, 1992, 143.
[8] Horace, *The Odes and Epodes*, ed. and trans. C. E. Bennett (Cambridge, MA: Harvard University Press, 1968), 1.3.8 and 2.17.5.
[9] Jerome on *Micah* II, *PL* 25, c.1219C

his friend, "keep one half of my soul." Therefore do not have faith in friends, that is, men who try to make money from friends.]

In another epistle to Dynamius (VI.10), paraphrased by Judith George as, "The two men are set in the literary world of lovers cruelly separated by malign and cosmic forces ... ",[10] Fortunatus credits his addressee's verse with the powers of intestinal penetration:

Interiora mei penetrans possessor agelli,
Felix perpetue, dulcis amice, uale.

[penetrating the depths of my little field, remain forever happy, sweet friend.]

Fortunatus relentlessly relies on corporeal imagery to give the impression or illusion of intense love, a strategy that is more vivid in his poems addressed to male patrons than to his passionate expressions of *amicitia* to Agnes and Radegund. The use of erotic terminology often disturbs and confuses readers; in addition, Fortunatus's use of an ascetic strategy does not guarantee the genuineness of his feeling for Gregory, since no evidence of his asceticism has survived, while considerable evidence of his sensuality recurs throughout his verse and prose. One of the better known examples occurs in VI.vii, when the poet rhapsodizes about eating apples:

Quod petit instigans auido gula nostra baratro,
excipiunt oculos aurea poma meos.
Undique concurrunt uariato mala colore,
Credas ut pictas me meruisse dapes.
Uix digitis tetigi, fauce hausi, dente rotaui,
Migrauitque alio praeda citata loco.
Nam sapor ante placet, quam traxit naris odorem
Sic uincente gula, naris honore caret.

[Since our appetites, stirring us on, hunt in the great depths, the golden apples capture my eyes. Apples of all colours come piling in from all sides, so you would think I had earned a painted feast. Scarcely had I touched them with my fingers, put them in my mouth, rolled them between my teeth, and the booty, set in motion from that spot, sped down into my belly. For the flavour delighted before it attracted the nose's scent ; so the gullet won, whilst the nose lost its glory.][11]

---

[10] George, *Venantius Fortunatus*, 1992, 144.
[11] George, *Venantius Fortunatus*, 1992, 52.

Patronage and Erotic Rhetoric in the Sixth Century

In a poem to the nun Agnes, whom he apostrophizes as "O uenerandus amor," he expresses the pleasure he feels upon discovering the imprint of her fingers on the cheese she has sent to him:

> Aspexi digitos per lactea munera pressos,
> Et stat picta manus hic ubi crema rapis.
> Dic, rogo, quis teneros sic sculpere compulit utres,
> Daedalus an vobis doctor in arte fuit?
> O venerandus amor, cujus , faciente rapina,
> Subtracta specie, venit imago mihi.
> Spes fuit haec quoniam tenui se tegmine rupit,
> Nam neque sic habuit pars mihi parva dari.
> Haec facias, longos Domino tribuente per annos,
> In hac luce simul matre manente diu. (XI.xiv)

[I observed the fingerprints over the milky gifts, and your hand remained imprinted here where you pick up the butter pat. Tell me, please, who encouraged your gentle fingers to fashion in that way? Was Daedalus your teacher in this art? O revered love, whose image comes to me, though the mould has been stolen away. But my hope was in vain, for this image broke up in its flimsy covering. Thus not even a small part could be given to me. May you make these over the long years the Lord gives you, with our mother abiding long with you in this life.][12]

Lines like these moved Richard Koebner to admire Fortunatus's delicate understanding of the sensuality of feminine celibacy:

> Fortunatus stand sinnlichem Fühlen nicht fern, das beweisen seine Gedichte in ihrer Zährtlichkeit, in ihrem Verständnis für das erotische Moment der Nonnenandacht und überhaupt für das Fühlen der Frau.[13]

More than a century ago Paul Nisard ended his book on Fortunatus with an impassioned fifteen-page defense of the sincerity and purity of Fortunatus's *amicitia* not with Gregory, or with Dynamius, but with the nuns Agnes and Radegund; about poems XI.9,10, Nisard categorically asserts:

---

[12] *Venantius Fortunatus: Personal and Political Poems*, trans. Judith George. Translated Texts for Historians, 23 (Liverpool: Liverpool University Press, 1995), 106.

[13] "Fortunatus was no stranger to sensual feelings, as his poems demonstrate, in their tenderness, in their understanding of the erotic component of a nun's devotion, and in their general understanding of a woman's feelings." Richard Koebner, *Venantius Fortunatus: seine Persönlichkeit und seine Stellung in der geistigen Kultur des Merowingerreiches* (Leipzig: B. G. Teubner, 1915), 46.

> C'est une protestation pleine de dignité et de mesure; c'est l'accent de la vérité dans sa candeur intrépide et modeste, c'est l'expression de la tendresse même qui trouve l'éloquence pour se relever...[14]

On the other hand, by calling for "douce tolérance" toward Fortunatus's "galanterie,"[15] he concedes the possibility that the poet was less than entirely sincere, and Nisard goes even further when he complains about the poet's compulsive desire to please, "il voulait plaire et toujours plaire, mettant presque cette qualité au-dessus de celle de poète et s'y laissant aller jusqu'à la bassesse."[16] Nisard, however, like George, neglects to consider the complexity as well as the ambiguity generated by a priest establishing *amicitia* with patronesses who were nuns, one of whom was also, not incidentally, a former queen.[17] Fortunatus himself acknowledges part of the problem, and perhaps protests too much, when he insists that the intense nature of his feelings for Agnes, although it involves *amor*,[18] is like that which one feels conventionally for a mother and a sister, i.e., spiritual, not physical. Again, to represent the intensity of his feeling, he invokes breasts and the womb:

> Mater honore mihi, soror autem dulcis amore,
> quam pietate fide pectore corde colo,
> caelesti affectu, non crimine corporis ullo:
> non caro, sed hoc quod spiritus corporis amo. (XI.vi 1–4)
> testis adest Christus, Petro Pauloque ministris,
> cumque piis sociis sancta Maria uidet,
> te mihi non aliis oculis animoque fuisse,
> quam soror ex utero tu Titania fores,
> si uno partu mater Radegundis utrosque,
> uisceribus castis progenuisset, eram,
> et tamquam pariter nos ubera cara beatae
> pauissent uno lacte fluente duos.
> heu mihi damna gemo, tenui ne forte susurro
> impediant sensum noxia uerba meum;

---

[14] "Iit is a protestation full of dignity and measure, it has the accent of truth in its bold and modest directness, it is an expression of tenderness which even finds the eloquence to enoble itself." Charles Nisard, *Le poète Fortunat* (Paris: H. Champion, 1890), 189.

[15] Reydellet, *Venance Fortunat, Poèmes,* lvi–lvii, also admires Fortunatus's expressions of friendship, asserting that they are warmer than what is found in Sidonius or Ennodius.

[16] Nisard, *Le poète Fortunat*, 139–40.

[17] See Jacques Fontaine, "Hagiographie et politique," *Revue d'histoire de l'Eglise de France* 62 (1976): 113–40; here 115: "Radegonde ait été à la fois hors du monde et dans le monde."

[18] Chaucerians will recall the profound ambiguity of *amor* inscribed on the Prioress' brooch, ll. 160–62 of the General Prologue to the *Canterbury Tales*.

sed tamen est animus simili me uiuere uoto,
si uos me dulci uultis amore coli.[19]

[Mother to me in honour, sister sweetly loved, whom I esteem with devotion, faith, heart and soul, with heavenly affection, and not with any bodily sin; I love, not in the flesh, but what the spirit yearns for ... Christ is my witness, with Peter and Paul by His side, and holy Mary looking on with her godly host, that you were nothing other to me in sight and spirit than if you had been my sister by birth, Titania, and as if our mother Radegund had given birth to both of us in a single delivery from her chaste womb, as though the dear breasts of the blessed mother had nurtured the two of us with a single stream of milk. Alas, I bewail my danger, the fear lest by a slight whisper malicious words thwart my feelings ; but yet it is my intent to live with the same hopes, if you wish me to be cherished with sweet love.][20]

To infer, then, that Fortunatus exploited erotic terminology to produce the effect it clearly had more than 1300 years later on nineteenth- and twentieth-century scholars such as Nisard, Koebner and George, and may or may not have had on its original recipient, does not require strenuous effort. In any event, a friendship between a man as powerful as Bishop Gregory and a man far more economically and socially vulnerable than his significant predecessors in panegyric (Paulinus [353–431 A.D.], Ausonius [310–394?], Sidonius [430–479?], were from wealthy, aristocratic families) was as complex in the sixth century A.D. as it was between Maecenas and Horace in the first century B.C..[21]

Recent work on patronage and poetry later in the Middle Ages tries to establish a less sentimental perspective on the problem. In the process of examining eleventh- and twelfth-century courtly behavior, C. Stephen Jaeger argues that "The language of favor relationships at court was the language of love."[22] As described by Lynn Staley, Ricardian speech-acts in fourteenth-century England also resemble Merovingian behavior eight centuries earlier:

... the *language* of love is social and should be understood as practiced within a set of conditions that, in the case of the medieval court, cannot be

---

[19] *Venanti Honori Clementiani Fortunati Opera Poetica*, ed. F. Leo. Monumenta Germaniae Historica, 4, 1 (Munich: Monumenta Germanicae Historica, 1881), 260–61.
[20] *Venantius Fortunatus: Personal Poems*, trans. George, 1995, 52.
[21] For a discussion of the necessity of understanding the complex nature of *amicitia* in Horace, see I. M. Le M. Du Quesnay, "Horace, *Odes* 4. 5," *Homage to Horace: a Bimillenary Celebration*, ed. S. J. Harrison (Oxford: Clarendon Press, 1995), 128–87.
[22] C. Stephen Jaeger, *Envy of Angels: Cathedral Schools and Social Ideals in Medieval Europe, 950–1200*. The Middle Ages Series (Philadelphia: University of Pennsylvania Press, 1994), 104.

understood without reference to power and to the terms of social harmony that power produces.[23]

Expressions of affection, then, between two unequals, as Jerome insisted, stand virtually no chance of being reliable testimony to authentic feeling.

Some recent work on Horace's relationship to Maecenas has attempted to free him from the demands of sincerity. According to D. P. Fowler,"any concern for 'sincerity' or even 'authenticity' is a blind alley."[24] According to Gregson Davis, the only authenticity that can be claimed for Horace is as "an authentic composer of lyric song."[25] In his vigorous search for patronage, Fortunatus, whom George calls " a poet of Horatian pedigree,"[26] demonstrates a blatant, compulsive desire to please ("il voulait plaire et toujours plaire, mettant presque cette qualité au-dessus de celle de poète et s'y laissant aller jusqu'à la bassesse"),[27] making himself a far more vivid example than Horace of what Vasily Rudich, in his study of Lucan, calls, "the rhetoricized mentality":[28]

> ... by definition, the rhetoricized mentality is indifferent to truth and falsity and resists any attempt at consistency.... The forms it takes differ in different contexts, but it always helps to privilege manner over matter, ideas over facts, and fiction over truth.[29]

The most dramatic, if not notorious example of Fortunatus's indifference to truth occurs in *Carmina* 6.5, a lament for the death of Galswinth, who, according to Gregory of Tours, had been murdered by her husband Chilperic, enraged at her refusal to accept Fredegund's rival presence (576 A.D.). As Kurt Steinman has pointed out:

---

[23] Lynn Staley, *Languages of Power in the Age of Richard II* (University Park: Pennsylvania State University Press, 2005), 57.

[24] D. P. Fowler, "Horace and the Aesthetics of Politics," *Homage to Horace*, 248–66; here 249. But the most complex discussion of patronage and poetry in Horace occurs in Phebe Bowditch, *Horace and the Gift Economy of Patronage* (Berkeley: University of California Press, 2001), particularly in the chapter "From Patron to Friend," 161–210.

[25] Gregson Davis, *Polyhymnia: The Rhetoric of Horatian Lyric Discourse* (Berkeley: University of California Press, 1991), 247.

[26] George, *Venantius Fortunatus*, 1992, 181.

[27] Nisard, *Le poète Fortunat*, 139–40.

[28] Vasily Rudich, *Dissidence and Literature under Nero: The Price of Rhetoricization* (London: Routledge, 1997), 156–69, et alibi. Stephen Hinds's description (*Allusion and Intertext: Dynamics of Appropriation in Roman Lyrics* [New York: Cambridge University Press, 1998], 86) of Lucan, "... a poet whose voice is so immoderate that his modern critics can variously accuse him of excessive obsequiousness to Nero, excessive hostility to Caesarism, and both in the same poem ...," suggests that the first-century poet and Fortunatus may have found themselves in similar predicaments.

[29] Rudich, *Dissidence and Literature*, 156.

dass ein anonymes Schicksal, nicht der Wille Chilperichs für die Tat verantwortlich gemacht wird, entbehrt das Gedicht im entscheidenden Punkt durch das Verschweigen des Täters der historischen Wahrheit.[30]

Steinman goes on to point out that Fortunatus blames only *improba sors* for her death, borrowing the phrase from Lucan IV.503, perhaps because those who live under tyrants find it safer to blame impersonal forces than individual human beings.

In his paper on the strategies of lament and consolation in 6.5, Gregson Davis adds the complexities of genre to the problem of determining Fortunatus's concern with the truth, focusing upon the elaborate obfuscation of the style of the poem:[31]

> The very elaborateness and profusion of the lament in contrast to the curtailed consolation are a clear index that something gross and unnatural has occurred" (Davis 120). "The framework of lament which Fortunatus adopts with minor modifications is that of Classical amatory style as exemplified by the erotic *epyllion* of Latin epic and elegiac poets (Davis 125).[32]

The result is a strange mingling of epithalamium and funeral oration, compounded out of erotic topoi, ornamented with alliteration and *annominatio*, and concluding with an intensely carnal embrace of mother and daughter that falls just short of the child crawling back into her mother's womb:

> Cum primum algentes iungi peteretur ad arctos,
> regia regali Gelesuinta toro,
> Fixa Cupidineis caperet ut frigora flammis,
> Uiueret et gelida sub regione calens,
> Hoc ubi uirgo metu, auditu que exterrita sensit,
> Currit ad amplexus, Goisuinta, tuos;
> Tunc matris collecta sinu, male sana reclinans,
> Ne diuellatur, se tenet, ungue, manu.

---

[30] "... that an anonymous fate, not the will of Chilperic, is blamed for the deed deprives the poem, at a decisive point, by remaining silent about the perpetrator, of historical truth." Kurt Steinmann, *Die Gelesuintha-Elegie des Venantius Fortunatus (Carmen VI 5): Text, Übersetzung, Interpretation* (Zürich: Juris Druck + Verlag, 1975), 182–83. Heinz Hoffman has pointed out that panegyric tends to suppress historical reality in the panegyric epic of Fortunatus's contemporary, Corippus, as well as what Hoffman calls Fortunatus's "hagiographisches Martinepos," "Überlegungen zu einer Theorie der nichtchristlichen Epik der lateinischen Spätantike," *Philologus* 132 (1988): 101–59; here 105.

[31] Gregson Davis, "*Ad sidera notus*: Strategies of Lament and Consolation in Fortunatus's *De Gelesuintha*," *Agon* I (1967): 118–34.

[32] Davis, *Polyhymnia*, 120, 125; see also Sven Blomgren, "Der P. Papinii Statii apud Venantium Fortunatum vestigiis," *Eranos* 48 (1950): 57–65.

Brachia constringens nectit sine fune catenam,
Et matrem amplexu per sua membra ligat.
Illis uisceribus retineri filia poscens,
Ex quibus ante sibi lucis origo fuit.
Committens secura ejus se fasce leuari,
Cujus clausa uteri pignore tuta fuit. (ll. 23-36)

[When first royal Galswinth was sought in marriage for a regal bed in the chill north (when, transfixed by the fires of Cupid, she here desired the cold and lived well warmed in an icy realm), when the maiden, beside herself with fear and with what she heard, realised this, she fled to your embrace, Goiswinth; then, with mind disturbed, lying enfolded in her mother's embrace, she clung with nail, with hand, so that she would not be dragged away. Bringing her arms together she wove a chain without a rope and bound her mother in her embrace with her own limbs, demanding as a daughter to be kept still by that flesh from which earlier the beginnings of her life had been; entrusting herself in confidence to be cared for by her royal power, in whose womb she had been safe and secure.][33]

This grotesque sequence is a vivid illustration of Fortunatus's frequent reliance on "body language" to intensify whatever emotional impact he wants to generate. Even (or unavoidably) when he composes a poem on virginity, "the flavour is decidedly erotic."[34]

In addition to his steady reliance on images of "the lower bodily stratum,"[35] Fortunatus relies on euphony, and specifically alliteration, to create the illusion of intensity. The first four lines of XI.6 show some of the things that he can do with the letter "c",

Mater honore mihi, soror autem dulcis amore,
quam pietate fide pectore corde colo,
caelesti affectu, non crimine corporis ullo:
non caro, sed hoc quod spiritus corporis amo. (XI.vi 1-4),

---

[33] *Venantius Fortunatus: Personal and Political Poems*, trans. George, 41. See now M. Rouche, "Autocensure et diplomatie chez Fortunat, à propos de l'élégie sur Galeswinthe," *Venanzio Fortunato tra Italia e Francia: atti del convegno internazionale di studi: Valdobbiadene 17 maggio 1990 - Treviso 18–19 maggio 1990*, ed. Tiziana Ragusa and Bruno Termite (Treviso: Provincia di Treviso, 1993), 149–59; also Sven Blomgren, "Bemerkungen zur Gelesuintha-Elegie des Venantius Fortunatus," *Eranos* 81 (1983): 131–38. More than a thousand years later Spenser and Milton will emphasize the grotesque implications of the image in their representations of Error and Sin (*Fairy Queen* I.i.xv; *Paradise Lost* II, 649 ff.).

[34] J. M. Wallace-Hadrill, *The Frankish Church*. Oxford History of the Christian Church (Oxford: Clarendon Press; New York: Oxford University Press, 1983), 84. Venantius Honorius Clementianus Fortunatus, *Poésies mêlées* ed. and trans. Charles Nisard and Eugène Rittier (Paris: Firmin-Didot, 1887), Dissertation Préliminaire, 28.

[35] A phrase popularized by Mikhail Bakhtin, in *Rabelais and his World* (Cambridge: M. I. T. Press, 1968), passim.

although they of course fall far short of the encomium of Charles the Bald composed more than 300 years later by the musical Hucbald; the entire poem, every word of which begins with " c," exceeds 130 lines.[36]

Even in prose Fortunatus cannot restrain his penchant for alliteration: "dum captivi solvere lora cupio, me catena constringo."[37] But his works in verse far outnumber those in prose; in the very first poem in the latest edition, Fortunatus limits himself to the pleasures of assonance in the first line, provides alliterating g's in the second line, and then bursts out with four v's in the third line:

> Antistes domini, meritis in saecula uiuens,
> Gaudia qui Christi de grege pastor habes,
> Cum te Uitalem uoluit uocitare uetustas ... (I.i)

> [Bishop of the Lord, living through the ages because of your worthy deeds, who possesses joys as a shepherd of the flock of Christ, since your parents wanted to name you Vital . . . .]

In *Carmina* IV.xxii, an epitaph for two brothers buried alongside their mother, he does not match the bathos of Ennius' *O Tite, tute, Tati, tibi tanta, tyranne, tulisti*, but

> Non flenda infantia fratrum
> Simili sunt sorte sepulti
> [baby brothers not to be wept for, buried by the same fate]

shows great aptitude in the art of sinking.[38]

But his greatest self-indulgence occurs in *Carmina* X.ix, a poem on Childebert, in which Fortunatus compounds alliteration with polyptoton and assonance through the first ten lines of a fourteen-line poem, using his prosodic ornaments the way desperate amateur fiddlers use vibrators:

> Rex, regionis apex, et supra regna regimen,
> Qui caput es capitum, vir capitale bonum.
> Ornamentorum ornatus, ornatius ornans,
> Qui decus, atque decens, cuncta decenter agis.
> Primus, et a primis, prior et primoribus ipsis,
> Qui potes ipse potens, quem iuvat Omnipotens.

---

[36] *PL* CXXXII, c. 1041–45.

[37] In a letter to Syagrius, *PL* 88, c.194a; Cf. Max Manitius's judgment, " ... aber zu einer stehenden Form ist bei ihm die Alliteration geworden, die er manchmal in störender Weise verwendet . . . . " *Geschichte der lateinischen Literatur des Mittelalters* (Munich: Beck, 1911), vol. I, 177.

[38] See L. P. Wilkinson, *Golden Latin Artistry* (Cambridge: Cambridge University Press, 1963), 25–28, for a sketch of the kinds of difficulties that arise when one tries to assess aesthetically the use of alliteration.

Dulcia delectans, dulcis, dilecta potestas,
Spes bona, vel bonitas, de bonitate bonus.

Digne, nec indignans, dignus, dignatio dignans,
Florum flos florens, florea flore fluens.
Childeberte cluens haec Fortunatus amore,
Paupere de censu pauper et ipse fero.
Audulfum comitem commendo supplice uoto,
Me quoque; sic nobis hic domineris apex.

[King, leader of the area, and reign above kingdoms, you are the head of heads, a man who is true chief good, the ornament of ornaments, which ornaments more ornately, you who are the glory, and glorious, lead all things gloriously, first, (etc., *ad nauseam*)].

The link early in this passage between power and ornament clearly is second nature for a poet dependent on patronage.

The indulgence in sonic ornament that characterizes the *Carmina* also runs rampant in the *Life of Saint Martin*, where the poet indulges his fondness for alliteration to the greatest extent, producing lines in which every word alliterates, and polyptoton and assonance abound:

Foedere fida fides formosat foeda fidelis (I.506)[39]

[faithful faith, strengthened by divine pact, made ugliness lovely]

Having restrained himself for the first seventeen lines of the poem, Fortunatus unleashes:

prudens prudenter Prudentius immolat actus.[40] (Leo 296)

[wise Prudentius wisely heaped up an offering of their deeds]

Athough the *Carmina* contain, as his most recent editor and translator asserts,[41] the most personal work of Fortunatus, the *Life of Saint Martin*, becomes urgently personal when Fortunatus introduces himself into the poem, experiencing the

---

[39] As quoted by Guido Maria Dreves, *Hymnologische Studien zu Venantius Fortunatus und Rabanus Maurus*. Veröffentlichungen aus dem Kirchenhistorischen Seminar München, Reihe III, 3 (Munich: J. J. Lentner, 1908), 23. Earlier Christian poets had shown greater restraint: for what was common practice for Paulinus of Nola, Ausonius, and Juvencus; see R. P. H. Green, *The Poetry of Paulinus of Nola: A Study of His Latinity*. Collection Latomus, 120 (Brussels: Latomus, 1971), 104–05.

[40] Solange Quesnel, ed. and trans., *Vie de Saint Martin* (Paris: Les Belles lettres, 1996).

[41] Reydellet, *Venance Fortunat, Poèmes,* xviii, calls it " l'œuvre la plus longue et la plus personnelle de Fortunat, celle où révelent le mieux les qualities de l'homme et de l'écrivain."

Patronage and Erotic Rhetoric in the Sixth Century   87

miraculous ophtalmological powers of the saint. First he describes the miraculous cure that occurred when Paulinus stood before the picture of Martin:

> Paulinique oculum tetia caligine mersum
> inpositis manibus radius penetrauit acutus
> atque **serena** dies detersa nube refulsit,
> lumen et emicuit facies non lusca gemellum
> Martini digitis oleo manante lucernae,
> cuncta salutifero superans collyria tactu. (II.38–43)

[The sharp ray penetrated Paulinus' eye, buried in a dark cloud (leucoma), when Martin placed his hands on it, and the serene day gleamed when the cloud had been removed, and the light shone on his face, no longer blind. From Martin's fingers flowed oil whose touch surpassed all unguents.]

Fortunatus's hexameters certainly outdo the rhetoric of his model, Sulpicius Severus's account in plain prose of how Martin healed Paulinus's eyes:

> Paulinus vero, vir magni postmodum futurus exempli, cum oculum graviter dolere coepisset, et jam pupillam ejus crassior nubes superducta texisset, oculum ei Martinus peniculo contigit, pristinamque ei sanitatem sublato omni dolore restituit.[42]

[Paulinus, a famous man, who in the future was destined to be an example, suffered grievously in one of his eyes, of which the pupil was already obscured by a thick film. Martin touched the eye with a sponge, delivered his friend entirely from all suffering, and restored to him his previous good health.]

After describing the church and the picture of Martin on the wall, Fortunatus goes on to insert a description of his own healing by St. Martin: [43]

> huc ego dum propero, ualido torquente dolore,
> diffugiente gemens oculorum luce fenestris,
> quo procul ut tetigi benedicto lumen oliuo,
> igneus ille uapor marcenti fronte recessit
> et praesens medicus blando fugat unguine morbos. (IV.694–98)

---

[42] *Vita Martini* 19.3/4: www.thelatinlibrary.com/sulpiciusseverusmartin.html (last accessed on March 1, 2006); Sulpicius Severus is himself by no means a restrained hagiographer; see Clare Stancliffe, *St. Martin and his Hagiographer: History and Miracle in Sulpicius Severus* (Oxford: Clarendon Press, 1983), 183–202 *et alibi*.

[43] *Vita Martini* 4.689–701.

[I quickly came closer, in great pain, groaning because light was fleeing from the windows of my eyes. As soon as I touched my eyelids with the consecrated oil, the fiery cloud disappeared from my face, and the physician drove off the malady with his mild unguent.]

The relatively chaste rhetorical restraint of this passage, particularly the fastidiously reduced alliteration, suggests that one of Fortunatus's strategies for generating the illusion of truth was to strip away some of the most obvious ornaments, although he does add the presence of a mysterious light, which he might have borrowed from any number of Biblical passages representing divine intervention, to the description of his own cure.[44]

Wallace-Hadrill[45] accepts the autobiographical insertion as factual, but Marc Reydellet categorically asserts that "... le visite au tombeau de saint Martin ne fut qu'un prétexte.... chargé de ce qu'un pourrait nommer une offensive de charme."[46] In her edition of Fortunatus's *Life of Saint Martin*, Solange Quesnel also is struck by Fortunatus's attempt to "charm,"[47] but Brian Brennan provides the strongest contextual support for skeptical resistance:

In an age ever ready for miracle stories, what better way would a poet have of gaining the attention of bishops and clergy, as well as the interest of the Bishop of Tours, one of Gaul's most important metropolitans, than association with Martin, the most popular of Gallic saints and the patron of Tours.[48]

In addition, as Giselle de Nie has pointed out, "Fortunatus's story is the first in the West, and as far as I know the only one in this period, explicitly to mention an expression of the healing 'presence' of a saint through his picture, rather than a relic or a tomb."[49]

Writing himself into Martin's life, Fortunatus's self-impersonation[50] also provides material for answering yes to the rhetorical question Paul De Man asked twenty-six years ago:

---

[44] Cf. *Acts* 9.3–4, 22.6–16, 26.12–18; *John* 1.1–41; *Isaiah* 42.6–7.
[45] Wallace-Hadrill, *The Frankish Church*, 82.
[46] Reydellet, *Venance Fortunat, Poèmes*, xv.
[47] Quesnel, *Vie de Saint Martin*, xi.
[48] Brian Brennan, "The Career of Venantius Fortunatus," *Traditio* 41 (1985): 49–78; here 55.
[49] Giselle de Nie, *Word, Image and Experience: Dynamics of Miracle and Self-Perception in Sixth-Century Gaul*. Variorum Collected Studies Series, 771 (Burlington: Ashgate/Variorum, 2003), chapter XII, 110.
[50] As Gerald A. Bond uses the term in *The Loving Subject: Desire, Eloquence, and Power in Romanesque France*. Middle Ages Series (Philadelphia: University of Pennsylvania Press,1995), passim.

Patronage and Erotic Rhetoric in the Sixth Century

> We assume that life produces the autobiography as an act produces its consequences; can we not suggest, with equal justice, that the autobiographical project may itself produce and determine the life and that whatever the writer does is in fact governed by the technical demands of self-portraiture and thus determined, in all its aspects, by the resources of the medium?[51]

The Life of Saint Martin is, of course, like all hagiography, a panegyric, a genre in which accuracy, sincerity, and truth are not primary requisites.

An example of Fortunatus's ruthless disregard of accuracy, perhaps more blatant than his elegy for Galswinth, occurs in 9.1, a panegyric of Chilperic composed in 580, in what some have seen as a betrayal of Gregory of Tours, who had called King Chilperic the "Nero nostri temporis et Herodes."[52] Others, however, have argued that it was a clever way of smoothing things out between Gregory and Chilperic. Whatever his purposes, offering an accurate representation of historical reality was not one of them; Steinmann asserts categorically that one of them certainly was self-serving:

> Im Panegyricus auf Chilperic Chilperich I.X.1, der im Zusammenhang mit der Biographie des Dichters schon kurz besprochen wurde, nimmt F. Zuflucht zu Lügen und Vertuschung der Wahrheit, um im Auftrag des Episkopats den brüskierten König versöhnlich zu stimmen.[53]

Since he is not reliable about the details of his own life, nor sincere about the emotions he expresses, what remains is the proposal that he is meticulous about his craft. Significantly, Nisard says that Fortunatus *nearly* placed pleasing people above poetry; one apparent example of this virtue occurs during a panegyric of bishop Bertram of Bordeaux. After heaping twelve lines of hyperbolic praise on the bishop himself, Fortunatus is unable to restrain himself from injecting some literary criticism:

> Sed tamen in uestro quaedam sermone notaui
> Carmine de ueteri furta nouella loqui;
> Ex quibus in paucis superaddita syllaba fregit,
> Et pede laesa suo musica cloda gemit. (III.xviii 13–15)

---

[51] Paul de Man, "Autobiography as De-facement," *Modern Language Notes* 94 (1979): 919–30. Another useful contrast, between organic and morphological elements in medieval autobiography, is offered by Georg Misch, *Geschichte der Autobiographie* (Bern: A. Francke, 1949), vol. II: *Das Mittelalter*. Part I: *Die Frühzeit*, 21–22.

[52] *Historia Francorum* VI.46 www.thelatinlibrary.com/gregorytours6.html (last accessed on March 1, 2006).

[53] "In the panegyric for Chilperic 1 X 1, about which we just spoke, F.(ortunatus) takes refuge in lies, covering up the truth, at the express order of the bishop, to conciliate the snubbed king," Steinmann, *Die Gelesuintha-Elegie des Venantius Fortunatus*, 200.

[But I see that some of the lines have been stolen from an old poem, and the music of the verse is hobbled by a miscounted foot.]

First to accuse him of plagiarism (*furta* in this context seems stronger than "borrowed"), then of composing verse whose music simultaneously limps and groans because of an inability to count syllables — surprisingly blunt charges for panegyric — suggest that Nisard's *presque* was the right word; for the *novus Orpheus*, poetry might sometimes have been even more important than pleasing patrons. In his panegyric of King Charibert, Fortunatus praises the king's eloquence, but not his verse (VI.2.97–100). But Chilperic receives extensive praise not only for his religious faith and administrative fairness, but also for his literary accomplishments, an area in which Gregory had disdainfully dismissed the king.[54]

More complex, however, is the poem in which Fortunatus compliments Radigund for her verse, connecting *sinceros* with gustatory delight, declaring their breasts or hearts (George here translates *pectora* as singular, consciously or unconsciously intensifying the intimacy) linked:

In breuibus tabulis mihi carmina magna dedisti,
Quae uacuuis ceris reddere mella potes;
Multiplices epulas per gaudia festa ministras,
Sed mihi plus auido sunt tua uerba cibus:
Uersiculos mittis placido sermone refectos,
In quorum dictis pectora nostra ligas.
Omnia sufficient aliis quae dulcia tractas,
At mihi **sinceros** det tua lingua fauos.
Supplico me recolas inter pia uerba sororum,
Uerius ut matrem te mea uota probent:
Omnibus et reliquis, te commendante, reformer,
Ut per uos merear quod mea causa rogat.[55]

[You have given me great verse on small tablets, you can create honey in the empty wax; you bestow a feast of many courses in the joyful festivities, but your words are sustenance to me for which I am even more eager, you send little verses composed of charming speech, by whose words you bind our heart. All the delicacies you produce are sufficient for the others, but to me may your tongue grant pure honey. I pray that you remember me among the holy words of the sisters, that prayers for me make you my mother all the more truly; through your commendation, may I be restored to all the others, that I am worthy to attain through you what my plea requests. [56]]

---

[54] *Historia Francorum*, 4.51, 5.39, quoted from www.thelatinlibrary.com/gregorytours6.html (last accessed on March 1, 2006).
[55] Appendix xxxi, Nisard, *Poésies mêlées*, 1887, 281.
[56] *Venantius Fortunatus: Personal and Political Poems*, trans. George, 120–21.

Translating *sinceros* as "empty"—it is a pun: sin - cere: "without wax [cerum]"—loses the physical quality of honey, that is, it is clear, or pure, and sensually pleasing, qualities Fortunatus often associates with women in general (and typically medieval, in accord with the theories propounded on the third function by Dumézil and Duby),[57] and with Agnes and Radegund specifically; he also arranges for *uerius* to appear two lines later, reinforcing the connection between sincerity and truth; finally, he balances the potentially hyperbolic *carmina magna* of the first line of the poem with the reductive *versiculos*, a word that might imply that her lines are not *aere perennius*, and that he has not categorically sacrificed his artistic standards to please the queen who became a nun.

Fortunatus's use of *sinceros* in this poem and elsewhere in his verse, where he often links "sincerity" with "serenity," may signify more than his relentless appetite for alliteration, since "sincerity" and "serenity" provide two of the three elements juxtaposed with the third element, "truth," by Augustine in an explication of the book of *Genesis*, where he speaks of the clarity and serenity of the sky as analogues for the truth, and specifically as qualities to be found in virtuous creatures:

> Quapropter non absurde existimari potest firmamentum coeli in divinis Scripturis usque ad haec spatia vocari, ut et ille aer tranquilli simus et sincerissimus ad firmamentum pertinere credatur. Hoc enim nomine firmamenti, ipsa tranquillitas et magna pars rerum significari potest. Unde etiam illud dici pluribus in Psalmis existimo: *Et **veritas** tua usque ad nubes* (Psal. XXXV, 6; et LVI, 11). Nihil est enim firmius et *serenius veritate*. Nubes autem sub ista *sincerissimi* aeris regione concrescunt. Quod quanquam figurate dictum accipiatur, ex his tamen rebus scriptum est, quae habent ad haec quamdam similitudinem; ut corporea creatura constantior et purior, quae a summitate coeli usque ad nubes est, *veritatis* figuram recte habere videatur, id est usque ad aerem caliginosum et procellosum et humidum.[58]

[For this reason it is plausible to consider the firmament of the sky in holy scripture as the space up to this region, so that this most peaceful and clearest air may be believed to belong to the firmament. Therefore, by the name

---

[57] For a discussion of these terms, see Georges Duby, *The Three Orders: Feudal Society Imagined* (1978; Chicago: The University of Chicago Press, 1980). Duby develops the scheme, originally devised by Georges Dumézil. The latter points out that one function is more difficult to define, the one associated with the categories of labor and fecundity (*L'idéologie tripartie des Indo-Européens*. Collection Latomus, 31 [Brussels: Latomus, 1958], 19. See also Jean Flori, *L'Essor de la chevalerie: Xie–XIIe siècles*. Travaux d'histoire éthico-politique, 46 (Geneva: Droz,1986), for an attempt to apply tri-functionality to a study of feudal ritual; Joel H. Grisward's *Archéologie de l'épopée médiévale: structures trifonctionnelles et mythes indo-européens dans le cycle des Narbonnais*. Bibliothèque historique (Paris: Payot, 1981), offers an application of trifunctionality to a specific medieval genre. See also Robert Levine, "Baptizing Pirates: *Argumenta* and *Fabula* in Norman *historia*," *Mediaevistik* 4 (1991): 157–78.

[58] *PL* 34, c. 239.

"firmament" this peacefulness and the great part of things may be signified. It is for this reason I believe that it is said in several psalms: "your truth reaches to the clouds" (Ps. 35:6; 56:11). Nothing is stronger and clearer than the truth. Although it is meant figuratively, it is written about things which bear some resemblance to these words; then bodily creation, more constant and purer, which stretches from the top of the sky down to the clouds, seems to be an appropriate figure for the truth, that is, up to the dark, stormy, wet air.]

In another work, arguing that Julian has not understood the difference between love and lust; Augustine also chains "serenity", "sincerity", and "truth":

> Audi ergo apertam sententiam meam, et intellige vel sine intelligere alios, non offundendo caligines nebulosae disputationis *serenitati sincerissimae veritatis*.

> [Hear my open declaration, and understand it, or permit others to understand, raising no more mists of obscurity about the serenity of the most sincere truth].[59]

In Augustine's Epistle 242, the three words occur in two consecutive sentences, with "truth" occurring twice in the second sentence:

> Ita excedentes animalis hominis caliginosas imagines, ad *serenitatem* illam *sinceritatem*que veniemus, qua videre possimus quod dici non posse videmus.

> 5. Nam libello quem dignatus es mittere, si mihi sit otium, facultasque tribuatur ad singula respondere, arbitror te cogniturum tanto minus quemque vestiri lumine **veritatis**, quanto magis sibi videtur nudam depromere *veritatem*.[60]

> [Thus going beyond the nebulous images of the human animal, we may come to that serenity and sincerity by means of which we may see what cannot be said. For by this little book which you have deigned to send, if I have the time and ability to reply in detail, I think that you will understand that the less one is wrapped in the light of truth the more he seems to himself to partake of truth directly.]

Augustine, in turn, may have been following the third-century commentary on I *Corinthians* v.vii in which Cyprian links truth and sincerity:

---

[59] *Contra Julianum*, liber quintus. caput ix. 37; trans. from *Against Julian*. trans. Matthew A. Schumacher. Fathers of the Church, 16 (New York: Fathers of the Church, 1957), vol. 16, 281.
[60] *PL* 33, c. 1053.

XVI. . . . Itaque festa celebremus, *non in fermento vetere, neque in fermento malitiae et nequitiae, sed in azymis sinceritatis et* veritatis (I Cor. V, 7). Num inceritas perseverat et *veritas* quando quae *sincera* sunt polluuntur colorum adulteriis et adulterinis medicaminum fucis in mendacium *vera* mutantur?[61]

[Therefore let us keep the feast, not with old leaven, neither with the leaven of malice and wickedness, but with the unleavened bread of sincerity and truth." But are sincerity and truth preserved, when what is sincere is polluted by adulterous colours, and what is true is changed into a lie by the deceitful dyes of medicaments?][62]

If we accept the nexus of serenity, sincerity, and truth as a patristic commonplace, developed and expanded from its appearance in the New Testament, then Fortunatus's use of the word *sinceritas* is clearly taken from the letter, not from the spirit.

An Italian understandably anxious in Merovingian Gaul, Fortunatus was a perpetually oscillating self-impersonator who made use of the rhetoric of passionate friendship, a subdivision of the rhetoric of sincerity, developed in antiquity and transmitted by Augustine and others, to win friends, and, eventually, a bishopric.[63] Sentimental in several senses of the word, a textbook illustration of the rhetoricized mentality, he manipulated a sensual vocabulary through several genres of poetry; the only passionate attachment that can be demonstrated from his secular poetry is to poetry itself; prosodic competence was (though discontinuously) more important than pleasing patrons; otherwise, the *novus Orpheus* was, to borrow Wallace Stevens' phrase, a "bawd of euphony."

---

[61] *PL* IV, c. 455b.

[62] Translation from www.intratext.com/IXT/ENG0280/_PH.HTM (last accessed on March 1, 2006).

[63] Michael Roberts shows how well Fortunatus serves his masters, even when writing a poem about a river, in "The Description of Landscape in the Poetry of Fortunatus: The Moselle Poems," *Traditio* 49 (1994): 1–22; here 22: "the scenery of the Moselle valley serves to idealize and hypothesize the cultural systems that have Fortunatus's addressees at their head...The elements of this system are present in the *Mosella*, but diffused with ambiguous evaluation. In Fortunatus they are employed, for the most part unproblematically, to legitimate the new powers in Merovingian Gaul."

CHAPTER 3

Fusion and Fission in the Love and Lexis of Early Ireland

William Sayers
Cornell University

Although conceptions of courtly love are judged to have originated in the south of France, conceivably under Hispanic-Arabic influence,[1] much of the narrative matter of medieval French and other romance, motif as well as plot, has associations with Celtic Britain and Ireland. On the level of story-line and onomastics this is well-charted ground. Let the Irish story of Diarmaid and Gráinne or Welsh mentions of Drystan and their relation to the romance of Tristan and Yseut stand as example.[2]

But there has been little effort to explicate the nature of the human love that informs these Celtic stories and may have influenced the subsequent French and Anglo-Norman retellings. Is it to be equated with unreflected physical passion? lust for corporal and other power? or fate, realized through the infraction of tabu? Product of an honor society or threat to it? The Irish language provides a vantage point from which to address these questions, since it is informed by a passionate native lexicophilia that offers a perspective nearly unique in medieval European vernaculars. The early medieval Irish love of words includes specialized alphabets, arcane lexical registers, sets of classifiers, lists of synonyms, monolingual glossing, and so on, but also a science of etymology — "etarscarad," 'separating,

---

[1] See, for instance, the contribution of Anna Kukułka-Wojtasik to this volume.
[2] An early study and conventional reference point is James Carney, "The Irish Affinities of Tristan," Idem, *Studies in Irish Literature and History* (Dublin: Dublin Institute for Advanced Studies, 1955), 189–242. The anonymous medieval Irish texts discussed in this essay are in the main preserved in codices from the twelfth century and later, although linguistic features point to written antecedents from as early as the eighth century. It is then not possible to date the tales in quite the same way as is conventionally attempted for their continental European analogues. See also Peter K. Stein, *Tristan-Studien*, ed. Ingrid Bennewitz (Stuttgart: S. Hirzel, 2001), 14–17.

cutting between' — based on the division and the often fanciful re-identification, semantic rather than phonological, of constituent word-parts by the members of the literate learned class. Thus many key terms in the early Irish language of love might be imagined as having one or more critical glosses.

This essay approaches scenes of love and loss in Celtic story — the fusion and fission of its title — with attention to the amorous and erotic vocabulary (fusible, fissionable), not least as deployed by empowered female actors. In this review of texts from the mythological cycle, from the Ulster and kings' cycles, and finally from the Fenian cycle, the precocity of the vernacular Irish literary tradition, compared to the Occitan and Old French tradition must be emphasized. This might be imagined as a movement from archaic mythic paradigms of the interrelation of male and female to secularized but still legendary accounts of falling in love and looking back on love among human women and men. Observations and conclusions will assist in re-addressing the medieval European literature of love through a technique of triangulation that incorporates northwestern as well as southern European perspectives.

A first example is from *The Second Battle of Mag Tuired* (*Cath Maige Tuired*) and concerns the conception of one of the principals. The maiden Ériu sees a handsome man approach in a silver ship.

> The man said to her, "Shall I have an hour of lovemaking with you?" "I certainly have not made a tryst with you," she said. "Come without the trysting!" said he. Then they stretched themselves out together. The woman wept when the man got up again.
>
> "Why are you crying?" he asked. "I have two things that I should lament," said the woman, "separating from you, however we have met. The young men of the Túatha Dé Danann have been entreating me in vain and you possess me as you do." "Your anxiety about those two things will be removed," he said. He drew his gold ring from his middle finger and put it into her hand, and told her that she should not part with it, either by sale or by gift, except to someone whose finger it would fit. "Another matter troubles me," said the woman, "that I do not know who has come to me." "You will not remain ignorant of that," he said. "Élatha mac Delbaith, king of the Fómoire, has come to you. You will bear a son as a result of our meeting."[3]

Now, Ériu is to be seen as a goddess of territorial sovereignty, the origin of the name for Ireland, in fact, and Élatha is king of one of the supernatural races that once peopled Ireland. This is then not properly a scene of courting but of hierogamy, between the land and its royal consort and ruler, literally geopolitics, and

---

[3] *The Second Battle of Mag Tuired: Cath Maige Tuired*, ed. and trans. Elizabeth Gray. Irish Texts Society, 52 (Dublin: Irish Texts Society, 1983), 26–29.

thus it involves testing and contractual agreement, not love as might be conventionally conceived.[4] Identities are established only after the act, and this seems to be choice on the man's part. But is it infatuation, compulsion, or recognition on the woman's part? Her reticence makes this difficult to answer. This scene is given a coarse replay later in the tale, when the Dagda, the Good God, after a huge meal of porridge, couples with a girl with preternatural powers who also seems an incarnation of the land. The dialogue is now mocking, coercive, as she seeks to mount a defense against the invaders, but the outcome is the same.

In another tale from the Mythological Cycle, the *Wooing of Étaín* (*Tochmarc Étaíne*), Eochaid, king of Ireland, seeks out a maiden who is reputed to be worthy as his wife, what the later folklore would make into a "fairy wife." He finds Étaín washing at a fountain, the narrative pretext for a lengthy detailed description of her body, representative of a descriptive sub-genre preserved into medieval European romance, as in the works by Chrétien de Troyes. The portrait can be explored as a catalogue of what is lovable and also of how language can be deployed to capture such loveliness. Desire seizes the king at once. He addresses the girl and learns her identity. Then immediately: "Shall I have an hour of dalliance with you?" "It is for that I have come here under your protection" (i.e., she assumes the king guarantees her security while traveling).[5] She says that although courted by nobles of the Otherworld she had loved him since a child for his splendor. The king promises lifelong monogamy, a bride-price is negotiated with the maiden, and she returns with him to Tara as bride and consort.[6] In the subsequent story her brother-in-law Ailill falls in love with her and begins to pine away in love-sickness. Étaín is prepared to provide relief, but a man who identifies himself as Mídir intervenes and prevents Aillil from going to the tryst. Clearly a supernatural being, he says that in an earlier life Étaín had been his wife and now asks whether she will rejoin

---

[4] Central studies of the tale are Elizabeth A. Gray, "*Cath Maige Tuired*: Myth and Structure," *Éigse* 18 (1981): 183–209, 19 (1982): 1–35, 20 (1983): 230–62; Tomás Ó Cathasaigh, "*Cath Maige Tuired* as Exemplary Myth," *Folia Gadelica*, eds. Pádraig de Brún, Seán Ó Coileáin, and Pádraig Ó Riain (Cork: Cork University Press, 1983), 1–19; and John Carey, "Myth and Mythography in *Cath Maige Tuired*," *Studia Celtica* 24–25 (1989–1990): 53–69. For the goddess of territorial sovereignty see R[isteard]. A. Breatnach, "The Lady and the King: A Theme of Irish Literature," *Studies* [Ireland] 42 (1953): 321–36; Proinsias Mac Cana, "Aspects of the Theme of the King and Goddess in Irish Literature," *Études Celtiques* 7 (1955–1956): 76–114, 356–413, 8 (1958–1959): 59–65; Máire Bhreatnach, "The Sovereignty Goddess as Goddess of Death?," *Zeitschrift für Celtische Philologie* 39 (1982): 243–60; and Máire Herbert, "Goddess and King: The Sacred Marriage in Early Ireland," *Women and Sovereignty*, ed. Louise Olga Fradenburg (Edinburgh: Edinburgh University Press, 1992), 264–75.

[5] Translated as *The Wooing of Etain*, in *Ancient Irish Tales*, ed. Tom Peete Cross and Clark Harris Slover (New York: Henry Holt, 1936), 82–92; Irish text published as *Tochmarc Étaíne*, in *Lebor na hUidre: Book of the Dun Cow*, eds R. I. Best and Osborn Bergin (Dublin: Hodges, Figgis, 1929), 323–32. Discussion of the tale in Myles Dillon, "Tochmarc Étaíne," *Irish Sagas*, ed. idem (Cork: Mercier, 1968), 11–23.

[6] On the legal dimension of marriage, see Fergus Kelly, *A Guide to Early Irish Law* (Dublin: Dublin Institute for Advanced Studies, 1988), 70–73.

him.[7] She replies that she will not exchange the King of Ireland for someone whose kin and lineage are unknown to her. Mídir explains that he had caused Ailill to be infatuated with her but at the same time had impeded him from coming to the assignation in order to preserve Étaín's honor. In the fragmentarily preserved tale Mídir does eventually successfully reclaim his former wife, albeit without further significant dialogue with her, and they retreat to the Otherworld.[8]

In the tale from the Ulster Cycle of Cú Chulainn and Emer (*The Wooing of Emer, Tochmarc Emire*), two young people learn of each other's merit and thus their love is based on reputation but also communications.[9] Appearance and status both count, and the hero's approach in a war chariot is given prominence through what is called the watchman device (teichoscopy), where a maid reports on what she sees and the more astute Emer can provide an identity.[10] Cú Chulainn's suit and suitability are thus established narratively, through the third-party description and Emer's identification. This might be called the pre-vocalization of desire, a woman literally talking herself into love.[11]

Speech skills are given prominence in the first conversation between the two young people. In discussing Cú Chulainn's itinerary and reason for coming, he and the girl speak in puns and codes, and make extensive reference to legendary place-name lore in order to test one another and disguise the content of their exchange from Emer's maidens.[12] When each has successfully impressed the other with an account of upbringing and training, Emer sets a number of heroic conditions that Cú Chulainn must meet before he can claim her as a bride. When the suitor remarks on the attractiveness of Emer's breasts, glimpsed over the yoke

---

[7] On extramarital relationships, see Thomas Owen Clancy, "Fools and Adultery in Some Early Irish Texts," *Ériu* 44 (1993): 105–24.

[8] For a fundamental orientation to the Irish conception of the Otherworld, see Proinsias Mac Cana, "The Sinless Otherworld of *Imramm Brain*," *Ériu* 27 (1976): 95–118, and Tomás Ó Cathasaigh, "The Semantics of 'síd'," *Éigse* 17 (1977–1978): 137–55.

[9] *The Wooing of Emer*, in *Ancient Irish* Tales, 153–71; *Tochmarc Emire*, in *Compert Con Culainn and Other Stories*, ed. A. G. van Hamel, Mediaeval and Modern Irish Series, 3 (Dublin: Dublin Institute for Advanced Studies, 1933), 16–68. The mutual assessment of suitor and maiden is typical of heroic epics and in particular of bridal-quest stories.

[10] The watchman device was first so identified and explored by James Carney, "The Watchman Device," as part of "The External Elements in Irish Saga," chap. 7 in idem, *Studies in Irish Literature and History*, 305–21, and further documented in Welsh and Irish in Patrick Sims-Williams, "Riddling Treatment of the 'Watchman Device' in *Branwen* and *Togail Bruidne Da Derga*," *Studia Celtica* 12/13 (1977–1978): 83–117. For its apparent transferral to the Norse world, see William Sayers, "An Irish Descriptive Topos in *Laxdœla Saga*," *Scripta Islandica* 41 (1990): 18–34.

[11] See, for a medieval French equivalent, the contribution of Raymond Cormier in this volume.

[12] See Doris Edel, *Helden auf Freierfüssen: 'Tochmarc Emire' und 'Mal y kavas Kulhwch Olwen.' Studien zur frühen inselkeltischen Erzähltradition* (Amsterdam, New York, NY: North Holland, 1980); William Sayers, "Concepts of Eloquence in *Tochmarc Emire*," *Studia Celtica* 26–27 (1991–1992): 125–54; and Joanne Findon, *A Woman's Words: Emer and Female Speech in the Ulster Cycle* (Buffalo and Toronto: University of Toronto Press, 1997).

of her gown, with the image "Fair is the plain, the plain of the noble yoke," a reference to the turret-topped double yoke used with the team and early Irish war cart, she replies:

> "None comes to this plain who does not go without sleep from summer's end to the beginning of spring, from the beginning of spring to May-day, and again from May-day to the beginning of winter."[13]

Thus we have a very formal exterior with the subjacent potential, in reality not far from the surface, of physical passion — a little like the geisha's unpowdered patch of skin on the back of her neck. The hero meets these and other conditions. After a year on watch outside the stronghold of Emer's father, he leaps into the enclosure, kills the defenders, and abducts Emer, all according to the conditions set earlier.

The story of Froech and Finnabair (*The Cattleraid of Froech, Táin bó Fraích*), in which the girl's father tries to rid himself of an unwelcome suitor by sending him on an errand into a lake with a monster, is also founded on the notion of love as prompted by repute. Again, the elaborate description of the approaching suitor seems to vouchsafe his claim on the girl's love as much as on the public's sympathy.[14]

In another tale from the Ulster Cycle, *The Wasting Sickness of Cú Chulainn (Serglige Con Culaind)*, Cú Chulainn is now married to Emer.[15] At Samhain, the Christian All Hallows Eve and the interstice between the light and dark halves of the Celtic year, when interaction with the Otherworld is more common and more fraught with danger, a flock of aquatic fowl settles on a lake. Cú Chulainn brings down a number of them with his sling and distributes them to the women at the assembly, but gives none to his wife. Next time, he promises her. Two birds joined by a gold chain fly overhead and their song causes the host to fall asleep,

---

[13] Compared to the archaeological evidence, for which see Barry Raftery, "Iron-age Ireland," *Prehistoric and Early Ireland*, ed. Dáibhí Ó Cróinín, Vol. 1 of *A New History of Ireland* (Oxford: Oxford University Press, 2005), 134–81; here 147f., very idealized concepts of the early Irish war-cart or "chariot" have been preserved in the literature; see David Greene, "The Chariot as Described in Irish Literature," *The Iron Age and the Irish Sea Province*, ed. Charles Thomas, Council for British Archaeology, Research Report 9 (London: Council for British Archaeology, 1972), 59–73; William Sayers, "Old Irish *Fert*, 'Tie-pole', *Fertas* 'Swingletree', and the Seeress Fedelm," *Études Celtiques* 21 (1984): 171-83, and idem, "Textual Notes on Descriptions of the Old Irish Chariot and Team," *Studia Celtica Japonica* 4 (1991): 15–35. For an element of the historical background, see Raymond Cormier, "Early Irish Tradition and Memory of the Norsemen in the Wooing of Emer," *Studia Hibernica* 9 (1969): 65–75.

[14] *Die Romanze von Froech und Findabair: Táin bó Froích*, ed. and trans. Wolfgang Meid (Innsbruck: Institut für Vergleichende Sprachwissenschaft der Universität Innsbruck, 1970). For an early appreciation, see James Carney, "Composition and Structure of TBF," in idem, *Studies in Irish Literature and History*, 1–65. On the matter of first impressions, see Michael Herren, "The Sighting of the Host in *Táin Bó Fraích* and the *Hisperica Famina*," *Peritia* 5 (1986): 397–99.

[15] *The Wasting Sickness of Cu Chulaind*, in *Early Irish Myths and Sagas*, trans. Jeffrey Gantz (Harmondsworth: Penguin, 1981), 153–78; *Serglige Con Culainn*, ed. Myles Dillon, Mediaeval and Modern Irish Series, 14 (Dublin: Dublin Institute for Advanced Study, 1953).

but Cú Chulainn is intent on hunting them despite his wife's warning. His three casts fail and he walks off dejected, then falls asleep too. Now follows a compelling and extraordinary scene. "While sleeping he saw two women approach: one wore a green cloak and the other a crimson cloak folded five times, and the one in green smiled at him and began to beat him with a horsewhip. The other woman then came and smiled also and struck him in the same fashion, and they beat him for such a long time that there was scarcely any life left in him." Cú Chulainn must take to his bed for a year. Then the woman in the green cloak explains that, despite the beating for hunting the supernatural birds, it is his friendship and military aid that they wish.

An Otherworld woman, Fand, has been abandoned by her husband, Manannán mac Lír, elsewhere more explicitly the god of the sea, and she has now given her love to Cú Chulainn. Here too we observe the curious amorous interest of supernatural beings in human partners. She will be sent to Cú Chulainn by the Otherworld king in exchange for a day's fighting against his enemies. Cú Chulainn's wife now accuses him of being sick with love, rather than being the object of supernatural attention. Clearly the hero is meant to experience some discomfort at being so manipulated by a woman. Cú Chulainn agrees to fight and is later described and praised by Fand in conventional epic terms. He is individualized by his physical properties, e.g., seven pupils in his eye. Yet personality and psychology as understood today do not enter the picture, and the nature of female desire is not explored. Cú Chulainn then sleeps with Fand and stays with her for a month. But his wife's jealousy and her recriminations over how easily a marriage goes stale oblige Cú Chulainn, very reluctantly, to surrender his Otherworld beloved, who is eventually taken back by her husband Manannán. Social concerns are never very distant in this tale of love and loss. "Fand began to cry and grieve, for being abandoned was shameful to her; and she went to her house, and the great love she bore Cú Chulainn troubled her."[16] Cú Chulainn experiences a bout of madness in the wilderness, but Manannán eventually shakes a cloak of forgetfulness between the two former lovers.

Two tales, one from the Ulster Cycle, the other from the Cycle of Finn mac Cumail, are built on the plot motif of a girl destined for an older man who makes her own choice and articulates it, even precipitating the action that will be seen as abduction or elopement. Here the reputation of the older man is outweighed by the sheer physical attractiveness of the younger one. Unable to compete on a level playing field, the rejected older man, king or leader of a warrior band, must resort to treachery. The young man is killed and the girl dies of grief.

---

[16] For an early contribution to one of the questions underlying this essay, see Raymond Cormier, "La lamentation de Fann et l'hypothèse des sources celtiques de l'amour courtois," *Le Moyen Âge* 75 (1969): 87–94.

In the first of these tales, *The Exile of the Sons of Uisnech* (*Longes mac n-Uislenn*), the young Deirdre sees a calf being slaughtered in the late fall, the spilled blood attracting a raven.[17] In the stark chromatism of the scene she is reminded of the warrior Naoíse, his hair as black as the raven's plumage, his skin as white as the snow, his cheek as red as the blood on it. Here it is worth recalling that in the material societies surrounding these stories, the details of human and animal sexuality were well known to all, and thus there was an immediate, uncomplicated explanation for lust in humans as there was for heat in animals. But just as society, in its own best interests, must surround sexuality with the constraints of culture, so story-telling must complicate the issue. One way was to employ metonymy to explain the inexplicable, that a young man like Diarmaid (see below) had a supernaturally ascribed "love spot" that made it impossible for women not to love him. The familiar love potion, inadvertently ingested, is also an exteriorizaton and depersonalization of this feature of inherent lovability, as reflected in the entire European Tristan tradition. Deirdre's observation, however, which finds verbal expression in a comment to her nurse, puts epistemological experience refined by speech and art in the service of love. After increasing her stake in the affair by elaborating the striking triple simile, how could she not love Naoíse? In a sense, she has talked herself into it. The words of love that are exchanged before marriage or the illicit consummation of passion are generally few, a simple catalyst. Courting is abrupt, even if the dimension of pre-nuptial agreement is never absent. Deirdre, for example, seizes the reluctant Naoíse by the ears and threatens him with a life of shame unless he elopes with her. The social and gender-based disparity of the couple makes it impossible for the male not to act, since he has no suitable way to silence or otherwise overcome his critic. This is a kind of negative female verbal empowerment, to which we shall return. In parallel to seemingly uncomplicated human sexuality in contrast to reflected, culturally constructed love, the eloping young lovers, like the later Tristan and Yseut, find a welcome refuge in nature but in the end, like a constant diet of game without salt, it is not sufficient, is too simple, and the richer complications of culture and company, which include adultery, jealousy, covert action, and so on, recall them to society where they will be betrayed. Thus, the old saw "You cannot live on love alone" takes on a deeper meaning, when love alone proves too thin a cultural diet.

---

[17] *The Exile of the Sons of Uisnech*, in *Ancient Irish Tales*, 238–47; *Longes mac n-Uislenn*, ed. and trans. Vernam Hull (New York: Modern Language Association, 1949). Important studies are S. Bryson, "The Tale of Deirdre," *Emania* 5 (1988): 42–47; 6 (1989): 43–47; 7 (1990), 54–58; Máire Herbert, "The Universe of Male and Female: A Reading of the Deirdre Story," *Proceedings of the Second North American Congress of Celtic Studies*, ed. C. J. Byrne, M. Harry, and P. Ó Siadhail (Halifax: St. Mary's University, 1992), 53–64; and Cornelius J. Buttimer, "*Longes mac nUislenn* Reconsidered," *Éigse* 28 (1994–1995): 128–32. On the slaughtering scene, see Maria Tymoczko, "Animal Imagery in *Loinges mac nUislenn*," *Studia Celtica* 20–21 (1985–1986): 145–66.

A second tale on a similar theme, *The Pursuit of Diarmaid and Gráinne*, with its many parallels to the story of Tristan and Yseut, appears to have been widely known already in the early medieval period.[18] Our first complete text, as distinct from some archaic fragments, is from the early modern period and does not authorize a sharp focus on the terminology of love, although some general observations can be ventured. Gráinne, the daughter of King Cormac, asserts she is willing to take as husband the man who is suitable as her father's son-in-law. But she takes an aversion to the older Finn on first sight and says she might be more suitably offered to his son Oisín. After drugging all but two of the men at the feast she asks whether Oisín will accept her courting. But he will not act against Finn's interests. Gráinne then asks Diarmaid, a young warrior in Finn's service. But Diarmaid will not accept Gráinne's courting either. Oisín may have been a straw man in this context, who had to be asked first to set up the paradigm, both narrative and psychological-ethical, for Diarmaid. Gráinne then puts a kind of curse or "bond" on Diarmaid, although the Irish word "geis" is most often rendered "tabu." He will suffer the pains of women in childbirth and the "vision of a dead man over the water," whatever this may be, plus reproaches, if he fails to elope with Gráinne. "Why me?" asks the distraught Diarmaid. Gráinne then tells of having seen Diarmaid from the window of her bower the previous day when the young man was engaged in hurling. "Who is that blooming, sweet-spoken man with the curling jet-black hair and the two crimson red cheeks, on the left hand of Oisín son of Finn?" (9) she had asked and so learned his identity. The first set of descriptors in Irish ("buileach binn-bhriathrach") are alliterating terms, a bisyllabic word followed by a compound, which is in turn composed of one monosyllabic and one bisyllabic element. Thus the moment of infatuation is closely allied with verbal expression of the features that precipitate this love. Here we have the same colors and male ideal as with Naoíse, but seen for the first time, not in simile-driven recall. She says that she loved him on sight. Thus, the lovers, if this term applies, are caught in rather different sets of constraints: Gráinne's aversion to Finn, her physical attraction to Diarmaid, and the necessary surrender of a life as the wife of the leader of the warband; Diarmaid's ethical-magical bind, in which he is forced to weigh unfaithfulness to Finn against the tabu and the shaming situation we had seen with Deirdre and Naoíse.

As seen above, some of the interaction between lovers-to-be may be put under the heading of interpellation, a challenge raised in the transient parity of intimate dialogue. Who, then, might be better equipped to speak words of love from a love

---

[18] *The Pursuit of Diarmuid and Gráinne*, in *Ancient Irish Tales*, 370–421; *Tóraigeacht Dhiarmada agus Ghráinne*, ed. Nessa Ní Shéaghdha. Irish Texts Society, 48 (Dublin: Dublin Institute for Advanced Studies, 1967). A fundamental study is R. A. Breatnach, "The Pursuit of Diarmait and Gráinne," *Studies* [Ireland] 47 (1958): 90–97; synopsis and comment in idem, "Tóraigeacht Dhiarmada agus Ghráinne," *Irish Sagas*, 138–51.

of words than two poets, a woman and a man? The tale of Líadan and Cuirithir now consists of a series of quatrains mostly in the voices of these two principals, quatrains conceivably composed by more than a single author.[19] As well as the composite, potentially inconsistent, portraits this naturally produces, the narrative framework is the most rudimentary, so that the story line is not assured. In these circumstances, only relatively little of relevance to our topic can be gleaned from the attractive verses. What seems to happen is this: The two poets meet, and the man, Cuirithir, suggests their union because of the wonderful offspring they are sure to have. We have seen other Irish tales that begin where a modern pulp romance would end. The female poet, Líadan, declines in order to pursue her career. What she says is that beginning a relationship would disrupt her circuit of aristocratic residences; Líadan is on the road, moving from one noble patron to another. She asks that he meet her at her home, later, instead. Then, inexplicably, she seems to have taken the veil, and perhaps Cuirithir also gives up his profession. First, another poet and fool, Mac Da Cherda, whose name means "lad of two arts," is asked to plead on Cuirithir's behalf. Mac Da Cherda and his counterparts in Irish story are holy fools, of great insight and prescience, almost proxies for kings in their relations with the kingdom. His covert message to Líadan, punning on names, appears to have no result. Then the couple put themselves under the spiritual direction of a Christian cleric, Cummine.

This replacement of the fool, with his pagan origins, by the ecclesiastic, with a differing ideological agenda, is frequent in the kings' tales.[20] Cummine tries to mediate the relationship between the two, even giving them a night alone to talk things through, albeit with a young student sleeping between them. Finally, Cuirithir goes into self-imposed exile, while the nun Líadan grieves her loss, passing her days on the flagstone where her lover had spent his time. On her death it is placed over her own tomb. The unfulfilled love, which after the initial offer of a union never takes the form of dialogue, is expressed in verses such as "Curithir, once the poet, / I loved; the profit has not reached me" or "Of late / since I parted from Liadain, / Long as a month every day, / Long as a year every month." "A roar of fire has split my heart." Líadan denies physical intimacy: "That Friday / there was no stretching out on fields of honey, / on the fleece of my little rug, / Between the arms of Cuirithir" (adapted from Meyer). Líadan's regret is best captured in

---

[19] *Liadain and Curithir* [*Comracc Liadaine 7 Cuirithir*], ed. and trans. Kuno Meyer (London: Nutt, 1902); excerpts in Gerald Murphy, *Early Irish Lyrics: Eighth to Twelfth Centuries* (Oxford: Clarendon, 1956), 83–85. I am grateful to fellow conference participant Raymond Cormier for recalling this understudied text to my attention.

[20] See William Sayers, "Deficient Royal Rule: The King's Proxies, Judges, and the Instruments of his Fate," *Scéla inna Ríg: The Irish Kings' Cycles*, ed. Daniel Wiley (Dublin: Four Courts Press, forthcoming in 2006).

the story's most famous line: "Nech ro-charus ro-cráidius" — "The one whom I have loved I have vexed."[21]

Here we may briefly summarize the foregoing and note that while some of the processes of love are inarticulate, others are very articulate, albeit often in the language of contract. The nature of sentiment, love in particular, is never questioned, only its effects, what one does about it. The dialectical dissection of amorous feelings that we find in Chrétien, *Cligès* being a good example, is quite foreign to Celtic story. It would appear that traditional oral story does not promote interiorization and the creation of distinctive personality, even though we find the rare monologue. Self-reflection, so evident in French romance, seems to be the product of the literate tradition and in particular the product of the schools and their practice of dialectic.

But if the words that generate amorous and erotic fusion are few, those of fission are many and long, since loss and grief are open-ended. Before considering an example, we might ask who is the public of a "keen," recalling that the word entered English from Celtic.[22] Keening follows an established pattern, with fixed stylistic devices, such as the apostrophe of the lost one, encomium, and so on. What traces of the nature of love as understood by protagonists can be recovered in what is usually a female retrospective? Deirdre's lament recalls life in the forest and the beauty of men's voices. But this "back to the land" motif is really the theme of the poem, which certainly post-dates the central story, and love is only an incidental.

In the Fenian corpus, Cáel qualifies to win the fairy Créde because he can compose a poem describing and praising her material wealth, although he has had it ghost-written by his foster-mother.[23] When he is announced, Créde is businesslike: "We have heard tales of him but have not seen him. Does he have my poem ready?" The poem describes things Cáel had never seen, so that its truth is anticipatory. Intended for a public of Cáel alone, the poem opens the way to the boudoir. But Cáel is then drowned at the Battle of Ventry and his body washes ashore. Créde's consequent lament shares many formal features of the earlier wooing poem. The keen is retrospective and is a monologue. The poem is a fine example of the pathetic fallacy, as the creatures of wild lament the loss of Cáel. "Sad is the crash of the wave against the southern coast, / And I, whose time has come, am

---

[21] See P[atrick]. L. Henry, "Líadan and Guðrún: An Irish-Icelandic Correspondence," *Zeitschrift für Celtische Philologie* 27 (1958–1959): 221–22.

[22] For a comparative overview, see Richard P. Martin, "Keens from the Absent Chorus: Troy to Ulster," *Western Folklore* 62 (2003): 119–42.

[23] *Tales of the Elders of Ireland* (*Acallam na Senórach*), trans. Ann Dooley and Harry Roe (Oxford: Oxford University Press, 1999), 25–28; *Agallamh na Senórach*, in *Silva Gadelica*, ed. and trans. Standish H. O'Grady, 2 vols. (London: Williams and Norgate, 1892), completed by Whitley Stokes, *Acallamh na Senórach*, in idem, *Irische Texte, mit Übersetzungen und Wörterbuch*. Series 1, Vol. 4, Fasc. 1 (Leipzig: S. Hirzel, 1900), no page numbers.

now destroyed by grief." Cáel's beauty and prowess are eulogized, that is, moved toward a kind of Platonic ideal. They are personal only in their uniqueness. Créde does not analyze her love and barely her grief. "I grieve for the warrior's death, for the one who lay with me." The keen is not interrogative; it recalls past events but does not explore feeling. This absence of heightened emotion recalls the doubtless apocryphal story of a folklore collector inquiring why the traditional Appalachian songs of love and loss were sung so unfeelingly and learned that it was the audience's part to supply the emotion.

From these dialogue scenes in the Irish narrative corpus can be gleaned a small erotic and amorous lexicon concerned with love and its loss, a lexicon that sounds quite contemporary in English translation. The exact semantic and affective charge of the Irish originals is, however, our present concern. The work known as *Cormac's Glossary* is ascribed to Cormac Uí Cuilennán, king-bishop of Cashel in the tenth century. Entries typically consist of a head word in Irish followed by a synonym, and then an etymology in Latin or Irish of either the head-word or its gloss. For example, "cride" 'heart' from its trembling ("crith").[24] But however promising this example, we look in vain for the vocabulary of the heart. The clerical bias of the work, with its preferential treatment of legal and ecclesiastical terms, against a background of many everyday concepts, means that love is present only in its absence, with several entries for virgins and prostitutes.[25] This is all the more vexing when the glossary provides so much information on the pagan Irish past, gods, goddesses, feast days, prominent places, and the like. This was clearly thought less a threat to devotional purity than talk of love would be to the social order. Typical of this approach is the entry "lánomain" 'married couple,' i.e., "lanshomain" 'full property of each other.'[26] But this at least confirms the concern for the contractual dimension of formal and less formal sexual unions that we had seen in the tales. The misogynistic strain of Irish gnomic literature is even more evident in the work named for the legendary king Cormac, *The Instructions of Cormac* (*Tecosca Cormaic*).[27] Here there is much that describes the ideal leader but nothing that relates to lovers; rather, female nature is vehemently condemned.

---

[24] *Sanas Chormaic: Cormac's Glossary*, trans. J[ohn] O'Donovan, ed. Whitley Stokes (Calcutta: Irish Archaeological and Celtic Society, 1868), 34; *Sanas Cormaic: An Old-Irish Glossary*, ed. Kuno Meyer, in *Anecdota from Irish Manuscripts* 5 (Dublin: Hodges and Figgis, 1913, repr. Felinfach: Llanerch, 1994), 23. The etymologizing practice was adapted from Isidore of Seville's *Etymologiae*, now most readily consulted in San Isidoro de Sevilla, *Etimologías*, ed. and trans. José Oroz Reta and Manuel-A. Marcos Casquero, 2 vols. (Madrid: Editorial Católica, 1982–1983).

[25] See Paul Russell, "The Sounds of Silence: The Growth of Cormac's Glossary," *Cambridge Medieval Celtic Studies* 15 (1988): 1–30.

[26] *Sanas Chormaic*, ed. Stokes, 102; *Sanas Cormaic*, ed. Meyer, 69.

[27] *Tecosca Cormaic*, published as *The Instructions of King Cormac mac Airt*, ed. and trans. Kuno Meyer (Dublin: Hodges, Figgis, 1909). See the fresh translation, *The Counsels of Cormac: An Ancient Irish Guide to Leadership*, trans. Thomas Cleary (New York: Doubleday, 2004).

We find a less intentional but still revelatory statement on the cause of love in an instance of lexical evolution. The phrase "grád écmaise" 'immoderate love' (of the kind caused by a love potion or love spot), based on the negated form of "coimse" 'moderate,' was, as a consequence of contact with other literary motifs, believed derived from "écmais" 'absence,' so that the phrase took on the meaning of love at a distance, usually based on reputation.[28]

Yet love and lust's potential as societal destabilizer were clearly observed. Here is the apocalyptic vision of the Morrígan, the Great Queen, at the conclusion of the *Second Battle of Mag Tuired* of an ill-ruled world, one in which breach of contract, adultery, and extra-matrimonial love are well-recognized threats. It is strikingly consonant with the words of the seeress in the Old Norse *Völuspá*, with the words of the loathly maiden in Chrétien's *Perceval* or Wolfram's *Parzival*, and, broadly speaking, with the end of Arthur's reign.

> I shall not see a world which will be dear to me: summer without blossoms, cattle will be without milk, women without modesty, men without valor, conquests without a king . . . woods without mast, sea without produce . . . false judgments of old men, false precedents of lawyers, every man a betrayer, every son a reaver, the son will go to the bed of his father . . . an evil time (73).

In conclusion, what was the bequest of Celtic story-telling to medieval European romance? Before addressing this question, it will be noted that this essay has not broached the subject of how such putative transmission might have occurred. After more than a century of intensive study, our texts and their historical background have left us no better informed on supposed bilingual Breton storytellers or Welsh bards.[29] Yet a thorough inventory of the matter transferred, particularly on the ideological level, may assist in recreating the circumstances of reception and adaptation among poets, patrons, and patronesses. Back then to our question: what does medieval European literature owe to Celtic story-telling? Plot, theme, and motif, as represented by courting dialogue and other tests, love-triangle, love-potion or equivalent, and irresistible passion are certainly there. The Celtic words of love are probative, challenging, contractual before love's physical consummation, then drop off the screen in the course of love's true or untrue

---

[28] M. A. O'Brien, "Ir. *grád écmaise*," No. 17 in "Etymologies and Notes," *Celtica* 3 (1956): 168–84; here 179.

[29] See the thorough and disinterested review of evidence in Patrick Sims-Williams, "Did Itinerant Breton *Conteurs* Transmit the *Matière de Bretagne*?" *Romania* 116 (1998): 72–111. National unity and an effective high-kingship over all Ireland remained an elusive goal during the Middle Ages, and the concept of sovereignty retained strong local associations. Yet, at the same time, the standardized literary language of early Ireland, not least in its love stories, reveals an impressive degree of cultural homogeneity, which would have been an important factor in the putative spread of these stories to the medieval romances of Britain, France, and Germany.

course, and return only in the non-analytical unidimensionality of grief. At the opposite pole from phenomenology, love is exteriorized—something that is out there—rather than being the object of analysis by either lover or author. We have portraits of loveliness but none of love. The love of words is certainly evident in the lexically enriched descriptions of approaching suitors or recalls of the lovers' life in the wilderness, but the learned fascination with native vocabulary proves disappointing when we look to the lexicon of love, because the analysis of sentiment is generally not a concern. But part of the language of love is certainly the language of contracts, in which negotiation creates a momentary parity between female and male. Coincident with love, there is always the question of who is worthy of whom. It will be in the much more extensive analysis of love—words of love and words on love rather than love of words—that European romance will most distinguish itself from Celtic story.

This said, another important feature that is carried over into later European romance is the reflexes of the Celtic goddess of territorial sovereignty, in several important dimensions. Although there is no hint in Irish story that anything like love service had transcendent capacity, the royal consort's faithful husbandry of the land and his divine spouse did find expression in justice, bravery, and generosity, thus putting human action in harmony with divine power. Originally the selector of the best-suited royal candidate and a future partner in a hierogamy of land and lord, the goddess lives on in romance in the lady as arbiter of the knight's conduct. Here the love that had been subjacent in Celtic story—taken for granted as something as ordinary as sexual drive—is moved 180 degrees on the board and the knight, who in his Celtic guise served his land and people, now serves a nearly abstracted mistress and love itself.

The many female portraits that we first see in the romances of antiquity, in the works by Chrétien de Troyes, and in the *Lais* by Marie de France undeniably have classical antecedents but display a parallel line of descent from Celtic story and from the figure of the goddess. They are among the most attractive conjunctions of words of love and love of words in both Celtic and continental literature. Words of love—who may utter them? Although European romance has scenes of confrontational dialogue led by a woman, such as the judgmental damsel in *Perceval* or Lunette in *Yvain*—which in their provocation to action remind us of Deirdre taking Naoíse by the ears and coercing an elopement—women are more often situated in silence, yet are always latent speakers. Like Érec's Énide, they may be condemned to muteness but still venture comment, and then with considerable emotional force.[30] Although the structures and strictures of courtly

---

[30] For an analysis of the communicative aspect in the Middle High German text, *Erec*, by Hartmann von Aue, see Albrecht Classen, *Verzweiflung und Hoffnung: Die Suche nach der kommunikativen Gemeinschaft in der deutschen Literatur des Mittelalters*. Beihefte zur Mediaevistik, 1 (Frankfurt a.M., Berlin, et al.: Peter Lang, 2002), 109–66.

love authorized a degree of female verbal power, it is nonetheless in the intimate sphere of women's chambers rather than in the larger geopolitical sphere of the Celtic goddess.[31]

By way of an epilogue, here is a classic two-part portrait of the Irish goddess. The story of Níall (the future King Níall of the Nine Hostages) and his half-brothers recounts trials set by the smith and sorcerer Findchenn in order to determine the lads' relative suitability for the kingship. In the second trial they are sent hunting with new weapons. Thirsty after the meal of grilled fresh meat, they go one at a time to seek for water. Each finds a well guarded by an ugly hag who demands a kiss in exchange for water. In a conventionally organized portrait she is described as follows:

> This is how the hag looked: as black as charcoal was her every part and her every joint from the top of her head down to the ground. Like the tail of a wild horse was the bristling gray shock of hair that sprouted from the crown of her head. The acorn-laden live branch of an oak would have been severed by the sickle of green teeth that stretched around her head to her ears. She had smoke-dark eyes and her nose was crooked, with cave-like nostrils. Her body was all sinewy and spotted with festering sores, and her shins were bowed and crooked. Her knees were swollen, her ankles knobby, her green-nailed feet as wide as shovels. The appearance of the hag was truly loathsome.[32]

Only Níall is brave enough to exchange a kiss and even offers sexual congress.

> So then Níall went to look for water and he too came on the same spring. "Water, woman!" said Níall. "I'll give you some," she said, "but give me a kiss." "I'll both give you a kiss and lie with you." Then he throws himself down on her and gives her a kiss. But then, when he looked at her, there was not in the wide world a maiden whose bearing or appearance was more attractive than hers. Like fresh-fallen snow in the rays of the sun was every part of her from crown to sole. Full and regal were her forearms, her fingers long and tapering, her legs straight and fair-skinned. Two square-toed shoes of white metal were between her soft white little feet and the ground. She wore a rich, deep-purple mantle, with a brooch of polished silver holding the fold. She had bright, lustrous teeth, large and queenly eyes, and lips as red as Parthian

---

[31] Albrecht Classen address the issue of female agency in "Female Agency and Power in Gottfried von Strassburg's *Tristan*: The Irish Queen Isolde: New Perspectives," *Tristania* 23 (2004): 39–60.

[32] My translation, building on "Echtra mac Echdach Muigmedoin: The Adventures of the Sons of Eochaid Mugmedon," ed. and trans. Whitley Stokes, *Revue Celtique* 24 (1909): 190–203. Less on the topic of sovereignty and more concerned with esthetics is Grace Neuville, "Beauté et laideur féminines dans la poésie courtoise d'Irlande," *Le Beau et le laid au Moyen Âge*. Senefiance 43 (Aix-en-Provence: Université de Provence, 2000), 401–11.

leather. "Many a guise, woman," said the lad. "True enough," she said. "Just who are you?" he said. "I am Sovereignty," she said.

The diptych, with its words of loathing and of love, illustrates the basic Celtic conception that love of the land, at its foulest and fairest, must precede its effective and just rule.[33] Such love and rule of the land includes the language spoken in it. The amorous and erotic vocabulary of early Ireland is then inextricably tied to notions of legitimate sovereignty and conjugal regal relations with divine power.

---

[33] For this motif in Middle English literature, see Jean Jost, "Margins in Middle English Romance: Culture and Characterization in *The Awntyrs off Arthure at the Terne Wathelyne* and *The Wedding of Sir Gawain and Dame Ragnell*," *Meeting the Foreign in the Middle Ages*, ed. Albrecht Classen (New York and London: Routledge, 2002), 133–52.

CHAPTER 4

WOMAN'S WAYS OF FEELING: LAVINIA'S INNOVATIVE DISCOURSE OF/ON/ ABOUT LOVE IN THE *ROMAN D'ENEAS*

RAYMOND CORMIER
Longwood University, VA

Tu autem cum oraveris, intra in cubiculum tuum, et clauso ostio, ora Patrem tuum in abscondito: et Pater tuus, qui videt in abscondito, reddet tibi.

[But thou, when thou prayest, enter into thy closet, and when thou hast shut thy door, pray to thy Father which is in secret; and thy Father which seeth in secret shall reward thee openly. — Matthew 6:6]

Odd as it may seem, some of us these days perceive similarities or parallels among the ancient, medieval, and modern worlds. I am forever struck by analogies, especially in contemporary popular culture. But if, as C. Stephen Jaeger wisely puts it, "ennobling love" has disappeared forever from our lives, only to be pursued as a lost sensibility,[1] nevertheless I think certain features of present-day thought harbor relevance and connections to the literary study of pre-modern texts.[2] My

---

[1] C. Stephen Jaeger, *Ennobling Love: In Search of a Lost Sensibility*. The Middle Ages Series (Philadelphia: University of Pennsylvania Press, 1999). This paper was prepared for and first presented at a symposium, "Words of Love and Love of Words," organized by Albrecht Classen, University of Arizona, 28 April–1 May 2005. I am grateful to Albrecht Classen for his reception and comments, and to the participants for their insights and sound advice, most especially to Professors Tracy Adams, Bonnie Wheeler, Jeremy Du Q. Adams, Maria-Claudia Tomany, Ronald Murphy, S.J., Karen Jambek, Julia Shinnick, and Christopher Clason.

[2] For a number of examples, studied from both a medieval and a modern perspective, see *Medieval German Voices in the 21st Century: The Paradigmatic Function of Medieval German Studies for German Studies*, ed. Albrecht Classen. Internationale Forschungen zur Allgemeinen und Vergleichenden Literaturwissenschaft, 46 (Amsterdam and Atlanta: Editions Rodopi, 2000).

two- or three-pronged approach here takes on first a feminist recuperative reading strategy, like that "re-vision" proposed by Adrienne Rich. It is an "act of looking back, of seeing with fresh eyes, of entering an old text from a new critical direction," writes Rich. "[F]or women [such an endeavor is] far more than a chapter in cultural history: it is an act of survival." Epitomizing this act of survival is the enormously difficult and risky task of excavating women's voices from ancient texts.[3] Next, and perhaps more important, I refer to the vivid and compelling descriptions of research results from recent cognitive psychology on girls and women. Then, my *tertium quid* is a literary sample text that comes from a well-known and vibrant *amplificatio* devoted to an emblematic heroine of romance, redolent with Ovidian love terminology. (One might say she, i.e., Lavine stands — like a "back-running brook" — between Ovid's fictional Medea and the historical Eleanor of Aquitaine.) My re-visioning experiment in the following pages will apply a template from *Women's Ways of Knowing* (from both the original 1986 publication [ed. Belenky, et al.] and the 1996 follow-up [ed. Goldberger, et al.]) to the second half of the twelfth-century *Roman d'Eneas*, particularly to the celebrated Lavinia scenes illustrating ideally, I think, the extraordinarily innovative high medieval French female voice, heard loud and clear. Perhaps our investigation will unveil some hidden fruit.[4]

In the field of epistemological and developmental psychology, the multi-authored landmark study, entitled *Women's Ways of Knowing* underscored some of the important gender differences regarding psychological maturation involving separation and individuation, as well as highlighting how women perceive truth in a subjective, empathetic, and connective mode, whereas ideas are viewed

---

[3] Adrienne Rich, "When We Dead Awaken: Writing as Re-vision," *Adrienne Rich's Poetry and Prose: Poems Prose Reviews and Criticism*, ed. Adrienne Rich, Barbara Charlesworth Gelpi, and Albert Gelpi (New York: Norton, 1993), cited by Judith Fletcher, review of L. O'Higgins, *Women and Humor in Classical Greece*, Bryn Mawr Classical Reviews, 2004.12.22. Available online at: http://ccat.sas.upenn.edu/bmcr/2004/2004-12-22.html. Last accessed on March 1, 2006. See now also Stephen G. Nichols, "Writing the New Middle Ages," *PMLA* 120, 2 (2005): 422–41; here 423–24, for a slightly different idea of re-visioning or refraction. See also Albrecht Classen, *Late-Medieval German Women's Poetry: Secular and Religious Songs* (Rochester, NY: D.S. Brewer, 2004), for a discussion of these points from a Germanist perspective. See also Joan Ferrante, *Epistolae: Medieval Women's Latin Letters*: http://chnm.gmu.edu/wwh/w/17/wwh.html (last accessed on April 7, 2006).

[4] Albrecht Classen "Introduction: The Quest for Knowledge," in this volume, MS p. 2]. See also, for courtly discourse, idem, "Wolframs von Eschenbach *Titurel*-Fragmente und Johanns von Würzburg *Wilhelm von Österreich*: Höhepunkte der höfischen Minnereden," *Amsterdamer Beiträge zur älteren Germanistik* 37 (1993): 75–102. Though, according to Classen (per litt., 26 June 2005), it remains a real desideratum, detailed comparison of Lavine's discourse with romance characters like Chrétien's Enide, Soredamors, Fenice, Wolfram's Sigune and Schionatulander, then Mai and Beaflor, or with Heinrich von Veldeke's Lavinia cannot be carried out in these few pages. For Heinrich, see, however, pp. 8–9. I plan to expand my comments on Chrétien's romances and on Marie de France's *Lais* in a subsequent version of this paper, to be incorporated in a forthcoming monograph *La Genèse du roman français médiéval* (Ch. 7, La Tour de Lavine). My thanks to Karen Jambek for the suggestion in regard to Marie de France.

as externals.[5] In this context, we will give our attention to the heroine's extensive emotive and emotional discourse on nascent love in an anonymous French romance that freely adapts Virgil's *Aeneid*. The character Lavine (Virgil's Lavinia) provides abundant textual experimental and elaborate experiential self-analyses (about 1700 octosyllabic lines, including segments devoted to Eneas's developing love — which we will very briefly consider; see below).[6] These may be viewed, in the context of rich and burgeoning contemporary spirituality, as mystico-religious examinations of conscience: they bridge the epistemological and hermeneutical divide (see Classen, "Introduction," 15–21). Indeed, and perhaps more significantly, the period we are examining has been targeted by Susan Smith as a

---

[5] *Women's Ways of Knowing: The Development of Self, Voice, and Mind*, ed. Mary F. Belenky, Blythe McVicker Clinchy, Nancy Rule Goldberger, and Jill Mattuck Tarule (New York: Basic Books, 1986; hereafter *WWK*), 69; see also, Carol Gilligan, *In a Different Voice: Psychological Theory and Women's Development* (Cambridge: Harvard University Press, 1981); *Knowledge, Difference, and Power: Essays Inspired by Women's Ways of Knowing*, ed. Nancy Rule Goldberger, Jill Mattuck Tarule, Blythe McVicker Clinchy, and Mary Field Belenky (New York: Basic Books, 1996; hereafter *KDP*). The latter was reviewed in depth by Marion Nesbit, "Connected Knowing and Developmental Theory," *ReVision*, 22, 4 (Spring 2000): 6–14. The work of the *WWK* collaborative derives in part from the earlier, now classic work by William G. Perry, Jr., *Forms of Intellectual and Ethical Development In the College Years: A Scheme* (1968; New York and Chicago: Holt, Rinehart and Winston, 1970). See also, more recently, Joanne Ardovini-Brooker, "Feminist Epistemology: A Reconstruction and Integration of Women's Knowledge and Experiences," *Advancing Women in Leadership Journal* No. 7, Summer 2000. Consulted online at www.advancingwomen.com/awl/summer2000/index.html (last accessed on March 1, 2006); cf. *Scrutinizing Feminist Epistemology: An Examination of Gender in Science*, ed. Cassandra Pinnick, Noretta Koertge, and Robert Almeder (New Brunswick, NJ: Rutgers University Press, 2003), reviewed by Elizabeth Anderson www-personal.umich.edu/%7Eeandersn/hownotreview.html (last accessed on March 1, 2006); and, from a very different angle as well, Isabelle Fortier, "Pouvoir, compétence et féminité: Expérience d'ingénieures en gestion," *Recherches féministes: Science, ingénierie et technologie* 15, 1 (2002) at: www.fss.ulaval.ca/lef/revue/ (last accessed on March 1, 2006). Not irrelevant here to Lavine's ultimate success is Daniel Goleman's *Emotional Intelligence: Why It Can Matter More Than IQ* (New York: Bantam, 1995): emotional intelligence comprises certain core competencies, like self-control and self-awareness, altruism and empathy, personal motivation and self-mastery, social expertise, and the ability to love and be loved by friends, partners, and family members. Goleman observes (281–82): "People who possess high emotional intelligence are the people who truly succeed in work as well as play, building flourishing careers and lasting, meaningful relationships." Scientific research continues to probe these matters: see Patricia J. Bauer, et al., "Representation of the Inner Self in Autobiography: Women's and Men's Use of Internal States Language in Personal Narratives," *Memory* 11 (2003): 27–42 (women use more emotional terms for recall); cf. also Larry Cahill, "His Brain, Her Brain," *Scientific American.com*, April 25, 2005 (May 2005 issue), suggesting differences in architecture and activity of male and female brains www.sciam.com/article.cfm?articleID=000363E3-1806-1264-980683414B7F0000&ref=sciammind (last accessed on March 1, 2006).

[6] *Eneas: Roman du XIIe siècle*, ed. J. J. Salverda de Grave (Paris: Champion, 1925–1927), vv. 7857–9274; 9313–42; 9839–10090. *Eneas: A Twelfth-Century Romance*, trans. John A. Yunck (New York and London: Columbia University Press, 1974). See David Scott Wilson-Okamura, "Lavinia and Beatrice: The Second Half of the *Aeneid* in the Middle Ages," *Dante Studies* 119 (2001): 103–24; here 113–17, for muscular arguments in regard to our text's *Nachleben* and especially for Dante's knowledge and exploitation of the *Eneas*.

time of attack on "father speech," with powerful female-identified voices raised, like that of Heloise.[7]

For Lavine's crisis-like words of love, I have observed (within the amplification in question — more than a tenth of the text) some nine stages or stations, from naïveté and rejection of that "sweet malady," to a happy resolution and realization of transcendence in love. Along the way, the bold ingénue emerges, through a seeming *psychomachia* and through a time-stopping martyrdom of love and lost in multiform dialectic confusion over right and wrong, fate, chance and willfulness, reason and folly, love and hate, shame or arrogance, suicide or survival. Taking place in the enclosed tower-room above the armed conflict raging below, each phase of quiet, cloister-like intimacy is interlaced with punctuating exterior battle scenes occurring in Italy.[8] But also, and more important for us, Lavine makes oscillating inner probes of conscience, as if a visualization of Ovidian love lyric, accompanied by thoughts and the experience of love's suffering and pain, the need for love's mutuality, as well as her own self-doubt and desire for fidelity, devotion, and belonging. Besides which, the dialectic in soliloquy (or interior dialogue) is dynamic here and possesses the contingencies of a living conversation, and is thus non-linear, with typical interruptions and revisions. As Harry Peters's essay on Gower in this volume reminds us, both Lavine's (and Eneas's) confession-like interior monologues, like "dialogues of trust," reveal inner truths and self-knowledge — Foucaldian parrhesia, *avant la lettre* perhaps. That is, "franc-parler" in French, and in German, "Freimütigkeit." Lavine, alone, seeks to persuade herself eloquently yet in a non-lyrical mode, as Karen Pratt might put it.[9]

While the following pages concentrate on the French Lavine, I think it would be appropriate to include some observations on her counterpart as described in Heinrich von Veldeke's *Eneasroman* (= *Eneide* or *Eneit*). For the French Lavine, the accompanying chart (see Appendix) lays out a brief overview of her nine stages of inner development, discussed below. Each passage in question also includes key words that anchor the individual episode described.

* * *

---

[7] Susan L. Smith, *The Power of Women: A Topos in Medieval Art and Literature* (Philadelphia: University of Pennsylvania Press, 1995), 34–44.

[8] See R. J. Cormier, "Le *Roman d'Enéas* et la formation des critères du roman médiéval," *Atti: dal XIV Congresso internazionale di linguistica e filologia romanza*, Naples, Italy, April 1974 (Naples and Amsterdam: J. Benjamins, 1981), 353–60, for a discussion of the alternating or interlace structure of these both warlike and courtly scenes. Cf. Joan G. Haahr, "Justifying Love: The Classical *Recusatio* in Medieval Love Literature," *Desiring Discourse: The Literature of Love, Ovid Through Chaucer*, ed. James J. Paxson and Cynthia A. Gravlee (Selinsgrove, PA: Susquehanna University Press, 1998), 39–62; here 50–51 (a different approach how to love "*legitimizes* the dynastic impulse," 51).

[9] See Karen Pratt's contributions to this volume, 260

"Feminism is a stool with many legs," observed Stephen Metcalf.[10] Like an enigmatic, "cognitive illusion," gender differences seem still to draw on sources from both nature *and* nurture. Now this is not the place to enter the fray between the "essentialists" and the "constructivists" in Women's Studies. (Over ten years ago, the French medievalist Sarah Kay cautiously warned us against confusing sexual identity and gender identity.) I will reiterate merely the salient themes I have discovered on the broad subject of women, cognition, and emotion. *Women's Ways of Knowing* argues for five arbitrary and sometimes untidy tendencies in the development of genderized perspectives on personal experience: *silence* (a passive position of mindlessness and voicelessness vis-à-vis authoritative others); *received knowledge* (not created knowledge but parroting what is known from external authority); *subjective knowledge* (truth as "personal, private, and subjectively ... intuited," 15); in *procedural knowledge* the learner acts from an internalized truth, without objectivity, voicing challenges to external authorities that differ from what is known subjectively, and herein lie the procedures of *separate knowing* vs. *connected knowing*; finally, *constructed knowledge*, where connected knowing allows the subject to understand contextual clues and create knowledge, however tentative, thus finding authority and autonomy within the self.

Belenky et al. suggest that these rather unsystematic and dynamic gender-coded stages offer an alternative epistemology that yet contrasts with typically male "separate knowers" who appear more inclined toward combative, impersonal, and objective approaches, using agonistic verbal sparring and delighting in adversarial debate. In this regard, one may possibly think of the assertive speech by Eneas (vv. 9343–94) before King Latinus, in which the newly confident hero, deeply aware of Lavine's love, transformed and now emboldened by its "sweet and noble bread" (Classen, "Introduction," 6), is about to clash in single combat with Turnus. He recounts his career path (so to speak) and *raison d'être* and lays down his conditions, whether victorious or defeated. From a male-oriented perspective, Eneas underwent an earlier transformation as well, and his journey to the Underworld helped him resolve any remaining doubts about the relevance of his mission: his maturation, as Bernardus Silvestris, following Fulgentius, interprets Virgil, involves abandoning passion and acquiring wisdom.[11]

---

[10] Stephen Metcalf, "'Florence of Arabia': Hello Matar, Hello Fatwa," *The New York Times Book Review*, Sunday October 10, 2004, 1–3; here 2 [review of Christopher Buckley, *Florence of Arabia*].

[11] Cf. Sarah Kay, *The Chansons de geste in the Age of Romance: Political Fictions* (Oxford: Clarendon Press, 1995), 35. See also Walter Ong's important synthesis, *Orality and Literacy: The Technologizing of the Word* (London and New York: Methuen, 1982), a watershed study preceded by his influential *Rhetoric, Romance, and Technology: Studies in the Interaction of Expression and Culture* (Ithaca, NY: Cornell University Press 1971), and its sequel, *Interfaces of the Word: Studies in the Evolution of Consciousness and Culture* (Ithaca, NY: Cornell University Press, 1977). For an analysis of the words of love uttered by Eneas, see Raymond Cormier's *One Heart One Mind: The Rebirth of Virgil's Hero in Medieval French Romance*. Romance Monographs 3 (University, MS: Romance Monographs,

Regarding Lavine's character, the contemporary linguistic-pragmatics work of Deborah Tannen seems to confirm these oppositional hypotheses; she writes as follows in a lengthy but fascinating report:

> I believe [. . .] systematic differences in childhood socialization make talk between women and men like cross-cultural communication, heir to all the attraction and pitfalls of that enticing but difficult enterprise. My research on men's and women's conversations uncovered patterns similar to those described for children's groups. For women, as for girls, intimacy is the fabric of relationships, and talk is the thread from which it is woven. Little girls create and maintain friendships by exchanging secrets; similarly, women regard conversation as the cornerstone of friendship. So a woman expects her husband to be a new and improved version of a best friend. What is important is not the individual subjects that are discussed but the sense of closeness, of a life shared, that emerges when people tell their thoughts, feelings, and impressions. Bonds between boys can be as intense as girls', but they are based less on talking, more on doing things together. Since they don't assume talk is the cement that binds a relationship, men don't know what kind of talk women want, and they don't miss it when it isn't there. Boys' groups are larger, more inclusive, and more hierarchical, so boys must struggle to avoid the subordinate position in the group. This may play a role in women's complaints that men don't listen to them. Some men really don't like to listen, because being the listener makes them feel one-down, like a child listening to adults or an employee to a boss.[12]

1973), 166–78 (Eneas as hero), 212–13 (the love hero), 241–48 (his epiphany through love), 260–64 (his inner self). As Classen ventures, the medieval love hero's words embody a rebirth in and through love, thus expanding his human potential (see Classen, "Introduction," 4). But, the hero's courtship, it can be argued, is completely unnecessary and gratuitous! He is *fated* to own the land and wed "the maiden"! But how much sweeter it is if the principals love one another; cf. Tracy Adams, *Violent Passions: Managing Love in the Old French Verse Romances*. Studies in Arthurian and Courtly Cultures (New York: Palgrave Macmillan, 2005), 138–39 (galley pages; I am grateful to Prof. Adams for sharing these proofs in advance of publication). Moreover, Eneas seems also to follow, willy-nilly, the developmental stages outlined in the "Perry Scheme" (see n. 4, above). For precisely contemporary parallels, see Bernardus's mid-twelfth century *Commentary on the First Six Books of the Aeneid of Vergil commonly attributed to Bernardus Silvestris*, ed. Julian Ward Jones and Elizabeth Frances Jones (Lincoln: University of Nebraska Press, 1977). Moreover, Adams, in this volume, writes of Amour's lessons in *cointise* ("charm, gentility" — "The Lover and Faus Semblant," 381–82), and this reminds me that I have argued elsewhere that the homophile warrior Eneas is "tamed" not only by love but also by the accusations of sodomy (Raymond Cormier, "Taming the Warrior: Responding to the Charge of Sexual Deviance in Twelfth-Century Vernacular Romance," *Literary Aspects of Courtly Culture*, ed. Donald Maddox and Sara Sturm-Maddox (Cambridge: D. S. Brewer, 1994), 153–60; see also Suzanne Kocher, "Accusations of Gay and Straight Sexual Transgression in the *Roman de la Violette*," *Discourses on Love, Marriage, and Transgression in Medieval and Early Modern Literature*, ed. Albrecht Classen. Medieval and Renaissance Texts and Studies, 278 (Tempe, AZ: Arizona Center for Medieval and Renaissance Studies, 2004), 189–210.

[12] Quotation from Deborah Tannen's web page at: www.georgetown.edu/faculty/tannend/sexlies.htm (last accessed March 1, 2006). This article also appeared in *The Washington Post*, June 24,

To these male-female communication styles and tendencies I would add — anecdotally and in no absolute or scientific way — that what is reticent, indirect, personal, human, caring, and related to the intuitive, to intimacy, and to interiorization belong to the realm of constructed knowledge.[13]

* * *

In the Appendix, as noted, Lavine's appearance begins with an interview initiated by her queen mother. I: The dialogue revolves around the nature of love, especially nascent love, and here the queen introduces Turnus's viability as a potentially devoted spouse, and Eneas as a dangerously inappropriate one. II: Lavine's first extended love soliloquy in solitude is ignited by the appearance of the hero on the battlefield.[14] III: Lavine's "martydom of love" continues through the night as she apostrophizes Eneas and, in his absence, asks herself repeatedly if she should declare her love. IV: Here Lavine confesses her love for Eneas in a scene throbbing with emotionality, followed by her mother's violent, crude and scolding accusations leveled at the Trojan.[15] V: Having learned that night of her love for him, Eneas,

---

1990. See also *eadem*, "Agonism in Academic Discourse," *Journal of Pragmatics* 34, 10–11 (Oct.–Nov. 2002): 1651–69.

[13] My hints here in regard to the presence, concerns, and contributions of women, especially in the public and political sphere (particularly health care, aging and education), rely upon a stimulating lecture by Anita Perez Ferguson, "Women Seen and Heard," Woodrow Wilson Foundation Visiting Fellow, Longwood University, 31 March 2005. Gilligan, *In a Different Voice,* establishes the non-hierarchical and relationship-linked female perspective that stresses caring, self-sacrifice and compassion (125–26, 131–32). Worthy of study, like "shining flames" that "glow white" (v. Classen, Introduction, 20), Lavine's distinctive voice recalls that of her contemporary, Hildegard of Bingen and her revolutionary conservatism, for which see John Van Engen, "The Voices of Women in Twelfth-Century Europe," *Voices in Dialogue: Reading Women in the Middle Ages,* ed. Linda Olson and Kathryn Kerby-Fulton (Notre Dame, IN: University of Notre Dame Press, 2005), 199–212; here 206.

[14] It is not music here but Eneas's overwhelming beauty that sparks Lavine's scopophilia; see, in this volume, L. Zaerr's "Songs of Love," 306–7.

[15] The queen's anger over the confession might be taken as another type of "emotion talk;" cf. Stephen D. White, "The Politics of Anger," *Angers Past: The Social Uses of an Emotion in the Middle Ages,* ed. Barbara H. Rosenwein (Ithaca, NY: Cornell University Press, 1998), 127–52; here 132–39. See also Rosenwein's challenging and controversial "Worrying about Emotions in History," *The American Historical Review* 107, 3 (821): 821–45. Carol Magner, in a presentation at The Open University, "The Destructive Potential of Anger: An Ancient Theme Given New Life in Heinrich von Veldeke's *Eneasroman*," 7–9, demonstrates convincingly how Heinrich's Amata (and especially Turnus) exhibit much more irrational rage, madness, and fury than in the antecedent Old French version; they are linked by *unminne*, just as Eneas and Lavine/Lavinia are joined by *minne* (The Reception of Classical Texts and Images, Conference, Milton Keynes, U.K., Jan. 1996 — The Reception of the Texts and Images of Ancient Greece in Late Twentieth-Century Drama and Poetry in English, Department of Classical Studies, The Open University) www2.open.ac.uk/ClassicalStudies/GreekPlays/conf96/magnerabs.htm (last accessed on March 1, 2006) 8. See also William C. McDonald, "Turnus in Veldeke's *Eneide*: The Effects of Violence," *Violence in Medieval Courtly Literature: A Casebook,* ed. Albrecht Classen (New York and London: Routledge, 2004), 83–95, for much more focused detail on the dark political, tactical, and legal behavior of Turnus, a rash, vengeful, and suicidal character, given to self-deceptive rage. At our symposium in Tucson, Tracy Adams reminded me that the queen (Amata in Virgil) can

lovesick and suffering, experiences his own *amour-religion* — with its pangs and symptoms, an echo of Lavine's. VI: The pining and weakened hero stands beneath the tower, gazing at Lavine as each smiles, sighs, and trembles. VII: Drawing on *Aeneid* 12, the narrative tells of Eneas's physical wounding (metonymy for the love wounds in his heart), then of the struggle between him and his Rutulian nemesis, Turnus. VIII: Lavine expects to see the victorious hero return, but his absence leads her to self-reproach for her impulsive declaration of love. IX: Eneas, understanding now the full and exemplary significance of his own life, realizes he should have gone to see Lavine after the battle; he regrets his error, thinking that he will seek her forgiveness as the marriage date is set for a week hence.

In Heinrich von Veldeke's somewhat later German version, I have noted, thanks to Fisher's detailed commentary, about eight major (and therefore interesting) divergences from the Old French version: i) with regard to Lavine, only the *Eneas* uses the "eyes of the heart" metaphor explicitly (Fisher, *Eneas*, 68); ii) only the French heroine deploys a great deal of "genuine" interior monologue (69, 70); iii) Heinrich stresses physical torments and lack of appetite before bedtime, but in the *Eneas* Lavine is tormented during the night as well; iv) Heinrich's queen is more restrained and circumspect in her insults of Eneas with regard to his homosexuality, described in explicit and coarse terms in the French version; v) Heinrich's Lavinia seems more concerned with her honor, so that, for example, the erotic idea of her entering Eneas's tent barefoot is unqualified; vi) cf. the passage below, where Lavine feels humiliated and disappointed that the hero has neglected her: Heinrich has omitted this concern; vii) The French version details the psychology and physiology of the "martyrdom of love" suffered by the hero near the end of the poem (vv. 9929–10078), whereas Heinrich has skipped over this; viii) King Latinus issues the wedding invitations in the Old French version, but for Heinrich, it is Eneas himself who carries out this task.[16]

Now, let us take a brief look at three short selections in which the French Lavine speaks of her feelings and intentions, the first from our second movement, the second and third segments from the eighth. The first passage is chosen particularly to emphasize the dialectic nature of Lavine's inner debates (vv. 8073–81):

---

hardly represent "patriarchal authority" in the Foucaldian sense: she is a woman herself and disagrees with the prophecy embraced by King Latinus. Yet, to my mind, she seems to stand for a more political, non-oracular authority.

[16] For Heinrich von Veldeke's *Eneit*, see Rodney W. Fisher, *Heinrich von Veldeke, Eneas: A Comparison with the Roman d'Eneas, and a Translation into English*. Australian and New Zealand Studies in German Language and Literature, 17 (Bern and Frankfurt: Peter Lang, 1992), 79. For the text, see *Heinrich von Veldeke: Eneasroman*, ed. and trans. Dieter Kartschoke (Stuttgart: Reclam, 1986). On the whole subject, and from a psychological viewpoint, see Jeff Joireman, "Empathy and the Self-Absorption Paradox II: Self-Rumination and Self-Reflection as Mediators Between Shame, Guilt, and Empathy," *Self and Identity* 3, 3 (2004): 225–38, which demonstrates how self-selection mediates the correlation between guilt and perspective taking.

> She began to perspire, then to shiver and to tremble. Often she swooned and quaked. She sobbed and quivered; her heart failed; she heaved and gasped and gaped: Love had indeed placed her in his service! She cried and wept and sighed and moaned. She did not know who was doing this to her, who was so agitating her heart.[17]

Clearly, her martyrdom of love involves genuine physical suffering and is expressed in verbs that pulsate throughout the description. In this volume, Tracy Adams cites a very similar symptomology from the mystical realm of Richard of St. Victor ("The Lover and His *Faus Semblant*," MS, p. 4).

> Now that Lavine realizes she cannot keep herself from loving Eneas, she exclaims in stichomythia (vv. 8134–40): 'Foolish Lavine, what have you said?' / 'Love for him torments me very much.' / 'But you will escape it if you flee.' / 'I cannot find it in my heart to flee.' / 'You were not so wild (*farouche*) yesterday.' / 'But now Love has completely overcome me.' / 'You have protected yourself very poorly.'[18]

The transformation through love that Lavine undergoes arises from a "force from outside," as L. Zaerr remarks in this volume ("Songs of Love," 317).

Secondly, as Eneas leaves and Lavine has just fallen for him, she states — speaking alone in her tower overlooking the battlefield — that the apparently heartless Trojan is taking away her heart:

> "'My heart is going away with him. He has taken it out from within my breast. Beloved, will you never return? Your friend means very little to you. Can I not have a gentle look or a sweet glance from your direction? My life is all in your hands. But how can it matter to you, since you are not certain that I love you with a true heart? I will not trust a messenger, by whom I might make you know that you can have my love. Nevertheless, I would find a way to tell you, but I fear that you would hold me to blame for it if I sent you my love first, and since you would have me without resistance (for that would be less than a little), you would say that I might later make elsewhere such an advance as I had made toward you, and that I was fickle (*noveliere*) in

---

[17] Vv. 8073–81: "Ele comance a tressüer, / a refroidir et a tranbler, / sovant se pasme et tressalt, / sanglot, fremist, li cuers li falt, / degiete soi, sofle, baaille: / bien l'a Amors mise an sa taille! / Crie et plore et gient et brait; / ne set ancor qui ce li fet, / qui son corage li comuet." See in this volume Christopher Clason's "The Bitterness of Love on the Sea," 280, for an analogous description of the power of love in Gottfried's *Tristan*. Lavine's is clearly a "glorious passion;" see Nichols, "Writing;" for the suffering female body as a "psychohistorical concept," 429.

[18] Vv. 8134–40: "'— Fole Lavine, qu'as tu dit? / Amors me destrointe molt por lui. / Et tu l'eschive, se lo fui ! / Nel puis trover an mon corage. / Ja n'eres tu ier si salvage. / Or m'a Amors tote dontee. / Molt malement t'en es gardee [...].'" For similar interior debates, both eloquent and powerful, in the work of Gautier d'Arras, see Karen Pratt's contribution to this volume, 272.

love. Do not think this at all, my love: I shall be your love forever. I will never change my love for you. Be secure; if I have you, I will never love any man but you. Never be jealous of me.'"[19]

Finally, after the duel and the death of Turnus, the victor leaves the battlefield but does not return first to the tower to acknowledge or come to talk to her. Lavine laments her situation, fearing Eneas the victor will be cruel to her:

"'I will have no one to aid me, and he will show great haughtiness. Whether he loves me little or much, he will always show me the appearance of great pride and cruelty. He will reproach me often because I was impulsive in my love of him, and he will hold me for *a lover of change (noveliere)*. I will have haughtiness from love: he will win in the end.' . . . 'Foolish Lavine, do not be angry if he wins in the day and you at night.'"[20]

The second speech will be repeated in interior monologue virtually verbatim by Chrétien's Soredamors in his *Cligés* romance, dating from the 1170s (cf. vv. 956–1038).[21] In Heinrich's version, Lavinia feels "surprise and disappointment" at this point over the Trojan's neglect, an important omission, which emphasizes more her honor. Indeed, the French Lavine's expression of emotion in this scene displays a much broader range than is found in Heinrich — such as fear for the possible political dangers if Eneas does not reciprocate her love, and her resulting thoughts of suicide.[22] So that on the one hand, Lavine's love pangs and, on the other, Eneas's arc of suffering, equalize these lovers. Following Robert Levine, "Erotic Rhetoric" (in this volume, 77-78),both Lavinia and Eneas — French or German — become

---

[19] Vv. 8353–80: "'Mes cuers avoc lo sien s'en vait, / desoz l'eisselle lo m'a trait. / Amis, vos ne retorneroiz mie? / Molt vos est po de vostre amie. / Ne puis avoir de vostre part / un dolz sanblant n'un bel regart? / Ma vie est tote antre voz mains. / Cui chalt, quant vos n'iestes certains / que ge vos ain de bon corage? / Ne m'en acrerai an mesage / par cui vos feïsse savoir / que m'amistiez poëz avoir; / et nequedan ge troveroie / par cui mander; mais ge crienbroie / que vos m'an tenissiez par propere, / se vos mandoie amor premere, / et quant m'avroiz sanz contredit / car ce sera jusqu'a petit), / vos diriez qu'itel atrait / come j'avroie vers vos fait, / redeüsse ge faire aillors, / novellerie fust d'amors. / Amis, ce ne quidiez vos mie; a toz jors serai vostre amie, / ja vostre amor ne changerai; / soiez segur: se ge vos ai, / ja n'amerai home fors vos, / ne soiez ja de mei jalos.'" The innovation here (besides the extraordinary use of the *verbal conditionals*) is that the female is taking the first step, declaring her love, come what may. The act will put her "on top" (for which theme, see Cormier, *One Heart One Mind*, 213–16).

[20] Vv. 9857–68: "'Ge ne m'avrai de coi aidier, / si me demenra grant dongier; / ou s'il m'aime ou po ou grant, / toz tens me fera il sanblant, / de grant orgoil, de grant fierté: / sovant me sera reprové / que de s'amor fui prinsaltiere / et me tanra por noveliere; / le dongier avrai de l'amor, / il an ventra au chief del tor. / Fole Lavine, ne t'enuit, / s'il vaint lo jor et tu la nuit.'"

[21] *Cligés*, ed. and trans. Philippe Walter in Chrétien de Troyes, *Oeuvres complètes*, ed. Daniel Poirion, et al. Pléiade (Paris: Gallimard, 1994), 170–336 (notes 1114–70); here 196–98.

[22] Likewise, in Chrétien's *Erec et Enide*, Arthurian romance dating from ca. 1170, Enide laments, debates, and deliberates fearfully within herself, regrets her pride, and even contemplates suicide — most of which interior monologues revolve around her dilemma vis-à-vis Erec.

equals by means of the love episodes, and the sincere expression of affection, such as it is, authenticates their love. As Gottfried von Strassburg puts it so poetically, "They who were two and divided now became one and united."[23]

We turn back now to a medieval literary creation — one woman's feelings and our cognitive template. The gamut of agitated emotions that our heroine experiences — dread, distress, resentment, remorse, even joy finally — impinges upon her physically, psychologically, and physiologically. They are "strange alterations," as Timothy Hampton puts it.[24] We are told and she tells us that sensory qualities and bodily sensations, e.g., tears, sighs, moans, paleness, yawning, weakness, feverish burning and shivering, and mortal pangs (vv. 8073–8100), all lead to a kind of mind-body awareness (*KDP*, 105), wherein her feelings, recapitulated for the reader-listener through interior monologue and dialogue, lead to a preliminary stage of self-consciousness. As feminist Sarah Ruddick asserts, "Knowing is not separated from feeling; emotion is not only a spur but often a test of knowledge" (*KDP*, 261). Lavine's initial introspection takes her beyond the stage of *silence*, so that she would no longer maintain that " the source of self-knowledge is lodged in others — not in the self" (*WWK*, 31). Indeed, the negotiating interview with her authoritative and threatening mother stimulates the maiden's further self-analysis: as Vygotsky has argued, exterior dialogue is an essential antecedent to interiorization and inner dialogue; like a megaphone, outer speech is a requisite for inner (*WWK*, 33). In this case, it is the queen herself who plays the role of the legitimizing, culturally (and politically) sanctioned policy-maker (her views are "authorized" in the sense meant by Michel Foucault) (*KDP*, 87).

To recapitulate: a passive position of received knowledge vis-à-vis authority (here, the queen) is followed by Lavine's insight into inner truth as privately and intimately "intuited" (*WWK*, 15). Acting from this internalized truth (that she loves and will love Eneas notwithstanding any pain or suffering or shame), Lavine's acquisition of *procedural knowledge* allows her to see that she can act upon the subjective, internalized truth, not only by voicing challenges to external authorities that differ from what is known subjectively, but also by taking measures and choosing terms, i.e., by declaring her love of Eneas in spite of the dangers associated with such behavior. Herein lie the procedures of *separate knowing* vs. *connected knowing*. Finally, by means of *constructed knowledge*, Lavine understands all the contextual clues and *creates* knowledge, however tentative, thus finding authority and autonomy within herself, i.e., deeper and enlightened meaning).[25]

---

[23] Cited by Christopher Clason in this volume, "The Bitterness of Love on the Sea," 288.

[24] Timothy Hampton, "Strange Alteration: Physiology and Psychology from Galen to Rabelais," *Reading the Early Modern Passions: Essays in the Cultural History of Emotion*, ed. Gail Kern Paster, Katherine Rowe, and Mary Floyd-Wilson (Philadelphia: University of Pennsylvania Press, 2004), 272–93, 354–58; here 280–81.

[25] (see Classen, "Introduction," 10–12.

Perhaps not so incidentally, with regard to interiority and the female perspective, links between twelfth-century women religious and Augustine's *Confessiones*, as Linda Olson has recently speculated, may be observed in the spiritual directions by Goscelin, Anselm, and Aelred, so that the nuns were not excluded from the "male paradigm" of "personal devotional literacy in which reading is a predominantly internal process laden with affection and undertaken to enhance the spiritual progress of the individual" ("Women," 92). Olson further connects as well the type of interiority encouraged by Augustine's classic to the subjective religiousness principally aligned with medieval women; one might say the *Confessions* were the textual flame that "ignited affective piety" (96).[26]

Lavine defiantly declares her love of Eneas (and declares it *to* him as well) in spite of her mother's imprecations. Here we may note her energy and "openness to novelty" (*KDP*, 77), because she is breaking with her innocent past (*KDP*, 81). Lavine has learned about herself through "*inward* listening and watching" (*KDP*, 85), and has thus embraced a *constructivist* approach: consultation and self-awareness, empathy with "the other" — to be known and understood (*KDP*, 141). In Lavine's own voice, reasonable moderation and then foolish abandon interrupt each other, the dialectic and debates alternating ostensibly between two states or modes of thought, Reason and Folly (vv. 8134–50) — not unlike an Abelardian *Sic et Non*. It is as if she is caught speaking deep within her imagination to the two sides of her inner self, each one putting forth an observation to be examined by the other.[27] Such formal logic leads to an emergence of common agreement — and Lavine's inward truth is thus revealed, and I think fruitfully.

Bonnie Wheeler's contribution in this volume on Andreas Capellanus's *De Amore* focuses on what has been called the "palinode" (Book III) of that treatise, and it provides us with a fuller context to understand Lavine's psychic and tilting oscillations — to be seen also, I believe, in light of Medea's wrenching soul-searching (see Ovid, *Metamorphoses* 7.7–455, esp. 62–71, 144–48). Without harking back to Prudentius's allegorical *Psychomachia* (ca. 400 A.D.) which sketches faith's struggles, especially against idolatry and pagan vices, bolstered by the cardinal virtues, we should listen to the letters — closer in time — of St. Anselm (1033–109). As Krüger has recently argued, he is the influential innovator of a kind of exis-

---

[26] Linda Olson, "Did Medieval English Women Read Augustine's *Confessions*? Constructing Feminine Interiority and Literacy in the Eleventh and Twelfth Centuries," *Learning and Literacy in Medieval England and Abroad*, ed. Sarah Rees Jones. Utrecht Studies in Medieval Literacy, 3 (Turnhout: Brepols, 2003), 69–96. See Brian Stock, *After Augustine: The Meditative Reader and The Text* (Philadelphia: University of Pennsylvania Press, 2001), 56–70, for a more thorough examination of these tensions and of the matter of "self-representation" and the "independent self," from St. Paul down through Abelard and Heloise, Christine of Markyate, St. Francis, and Petrarch.

[27] This is an emotional "tug-of-war" within Lavine's soul; for parallel cases, see Karen Pratt's contribution to this volume, 272–73.

tential understanding of human personality and conscience, a socio-political self and a subjective, moral self.[28]

On this same subject, the pioneering study of dialectical reasoning and casuistry in this period by Tony Hunt, proclaims that "[d]ialectic is both part of the subject of much courtly literature and a heuristic tool for its interpretation" (128). Sarah Kay in her *Courtly Contradictions*, writing in a highly theoretical mode, adroitly applies dialectic concepts of contrariety and contradiction (41) to a wide variety of texts, including the infamous Troubadour, Guillaume IX "bifrons" (43–44); and she underscores as well an Aristotelian opposition between *wisdom* (or reason) and *folly* in the *Eneas*.[29]

To return at last to the template of Ruddick (*KDP*, 248–73; see note 4), the notion of "connected knowing" means acquiring knowledge by entering the belief world of another person (though this view is now criticized by some as contributing to a gender-determined system of learning). In her search for perspicuity (Classen, "Introduction," 6), Lavine repeatedly imagines herself inside the heart

---

[28] One of Wheeler's arguments maintains the lack of hermeneutic synthesis within the Latinate dialectic hierarchy, a synthesis achieved perhaps in the vernacular, especially by a Chrétien de Troyes. See further Andrew Taylor, "A Second Ajax: Peter Abelard and the Violence of Dialectic," *The Tongue of the Fathers: Gender and Ideology in Twelfth-Century Latin*, ed. David Townsend and idem. The Middle Ages Series (Philadelphia: University of Pennsylvania Press, 1998), 14–34; here 20, 23, 26–29, on the combative, bellicose, and aggressive "ritualized violence" of *disputatio* in dialectic argumentation; Taylor hypothesizes that this may be compensatory for "celibate noncombatants" (30). In this light, Lavine becomes perhaps more male with her dialectic-style discourse, a perfect match for the once-warrior hero, the lovesick Eneas. See also Tony Hunt, "Aristotle, Dialectic, and Courtly Literature," *Viator* 10 (1979): 95–130; here 128. For Anselm, see Thomas Michael Krüger, *Persönlichkeitsausdruck und Persönlichkeitswahrnehmung im Zeitalter des Investiturkonflikte: Studien zu den Briefsammlungen des Anselm von Canterbury;*. Spolia Berolinensia, 22 (Hildesheim: Weidmann, 2002), 215–29.

[29] Sarah Kay, *Courtly Contradictions: The Emergence of the Literary Object in the Twelfth Century* (Stanford, CA: Stanford University Press, 2001), 48–49. See also Gerhild Scholz Williams, "Against Court and School: Heinrich of Melk and Hélinant de Froidmont as Critics of Twelfth-Century Society," *Neophilologus* 62 (1978): 513–26; here 523: extrovertive and sceptical learning and dialectic (taken as an enemy of the contemplative life) may be said to provide a broad socio-religious context for the rise of interior debate. All these points — relative to Lavine's love discourse and its dualistic taxonomy — deserve further study, especially in light of the study by Constance Brittain Bouchard, *"Every Valley Shall Be Exalted": The Discourse of Opposites in Twelfth-Century Thought* (Ithaca, NY: Cornell University Press, 2002), which stresses omnipresent conflict and dissonance. It is my intention to develop the parallels among Lavine's discursive disquisitions, the intentionality notions in Abelard's *Ethica*, and its attempt at "harmonizing the [theological] contradictions," for which see J. G. Sikes, *Peter Abailard* (Cambridge: Cambridge University Press, 1932), 76ss., on the *Sic et Non*. See the editions of these works: *Peter Abelard's Ethics: An Edition with Introduction, English Translation and Notes*, ed. D. E. Luscombe (Oxford: Clarendon Press, 1971); *Peter Abailard: Sic et Non, A Critical Edition*, ed. Blanche Boyer and Richard McKeon (Chicago: University of Chicago Press, 1977).-Cf. Barbara M. Stafford, "Leveling the New Old Transcendence: Cognitive Coherence in the Era of Beyondness," *New Literary History* 35, 2 (Spring 2004): 321–38, which aims toward temporal and spatial convergence in cognitive science and neurobiology, while arguing that our "contemporary technonoetic culture [...] is [still] rooted in the binary hyper-logic of transcendence." See also Classen, "Introduction," 15–19, on the "ineffable."

and soul (and tent!) of Eneas, trying to outguess his cool behavior, to anticipate his moves (or lack thereof), and to understand the few leads and hints he has given her about his feelings. In the socio-political sphere, as Duby suggests, this whole amorous game augured for acceptance of a new courtesy and civility in male-female relations.[30] Like a see-through mirror, the romance genre provided serious recreation for its audience — just as its descendant does today. Psychologically, Lavine's "emotion talk" powerfully articulates as well her needs — her need for security, for belonging, and for esteem, as Dominique Chapot has recently expressed it.[31]

Thus it may be said, by way of conclusion, that one woman's ways of feeling confirm that Lavine matures, learns about herself and about love, not from any exterior motive or incentive, but through feeling — all declared through words of love — and all, by the way, carried out in a prayer-like and secretive place, the "closet" of Scripture, Lavine's tower room and window, where she is "rewarded," as Matthew puts it. Like old wine in new skins, the seminal medieval romance comes alive in its new framework. We could in the end define Lavine's own personal and subjective version of the truth according to the paradoxical poem of Robert Frost, whereby "speaking of contraries," like a "tribute of the current to the source," allows her finally to comprehend and embrace life and love completely — all the while tacking toward a harmonious utopia with her beloved.[32]

By studying Lavine's words of love, we have re-visioned our heroine and the *Roman d'Eneas* from a new viewpoint. Like the eternal human search for Jaeger's "lost sensibility," Lavine's quest for self-knowledge and identity anticipates, *de loin* to be sure, the potent European notion of individualism, that powerful and novel idea that led to progress for humankind. Apparently, only those who learn the secrets of human language in all its epistemological dimensions can also reach out and embrace the secret of love. Indeed, this is where the words of love metamorphose into the love of words.

---

[30] Georges Duby, *Women of the Twelfth Century*. I: *Eleanor of Aquitaine and Six Others*, trans. J. Birrell (Chicago and London: The University of Chicago Press, 1997), 96–99. Cf. Classen, "Introduction," 8–10.

[31] Dominique Chapot, *Emois en moi: Se réconcilier avec ses émotions*. (Paris: Seuil. 2005). Cf. Nichols, "Writing the New Middle Ages," 423–24. Relevant also is the major study by Gerd Althoff, "Empörung, Tränen, Zerknirschung: 'Emotionen' in der öffentlichen Kommunikationen des Mittelalters," *Frühmittelalterliche Studien* 30 (1996): 60–79 (Latin context, post-Carolingian).

[32] Robert Frost, "West-running Brook," idem, *North of Boston: Poems (1915)*, ed. Edward Connery Lathem (New York: Dodd, Mead, 1977).

APPENDIX

Lavine's Nine Love Episodes, vv. 7857–10090
[Interlaced between the death and burial of Camilla
and Eneas' wounding and final, mortal duel with Turnus]

I (vv. 7857–8024). On the morning of the first day, the queen mother and her daughter meet in an interview. In this first encounter, fraught with *quiproquo*, the queen, as a voice of authority, while expounding on the nature of love, clearly wishes to impose her will upon Lavine in a win/lose model. She threatens to kill her, saying that Eneas wants to take the maiden by force, all the while explaining Love's nature, pleasures and pains — that "sweet malady." The dutiful daughter expresses her fear of suffering, i.e., a fear of knowing her true self. (We assume that in the axiomatic equation love = life, then self-knowledge is at issue here). Key Word of Love: *salvage* (*Molt ert salvage la meschine*), "The maiden was very stubborn" [trans. Yunck], v. 8021; better: untamed or haughty toward love; the opposite of timid — because of her fear of suffering. Elsewhere: *estrange* toward love; vv. 8116, 8138, 8308 [and cf. vv. 8025–46: Eneas on parade.]

II (vv. 8047–82). During a truce between the armies, that afternoon (vv. 8047–56), from the tower, Lavine alone and in a state of confused admiration, falls in love with the hero as he marches past and, until nightfall, continually (though briefly here) examines her Ovidian motivations through self-interrogation and mental oscillations — between safe exterior (read: public) reason and wild, uncontrollable (read: private) inner passion, yearning nevertheless for clarity and understanding of her emotions. Key Word of Love: *saiete* (*la saiete li est colee / desi qu'el cuer soz la memelle*), "The arrow had struck her as deep as the heart beneath her breast" [Yunck], vv. 8066–67. This is a foreshadowing of the arrow-messenger scene.

III (8083–444). Late that afternoon and night, alone in her room, Lavine suffers what has been called a "martyrdom of love," embellished with a 300-line interior monologue (vv. 8083–380). She continues, then, in bed. The expression "martyrdom of love" is a kind of descriptive, literary calque on mystical torment. Key Word of Love: *partir* (*Puet lan donc si partir amor*), "Can one thus share one's love?, v. 8281; cf. also v. 8270. Cf. Chrétien de Troyes, *Cligés*, 4366–526).[33]

IV (vv. 8445–864). The next morning the queen returns for a second interview, filled with questions. The maiden, noticeably suffering the pangs of her passion, now makes her throbbing confession of love, to which the mother retorts

---

[33] Chétien de Troyes, *Cligés*, ed., trans. Philippe Walter in *Chrétien de Troyes: Oeuvres complètes*, ed. Daniel Poirion, et al. Pléiade (Paris: Gallimard, 1994), 170–336 (notes 1114–70); (Fenice). See Aimé Petit, "Nuits blanches dans les romans antiques," *Revue des Langues Romanes (L'Imaginaire de la nuit au Moyen Age)* 106, 2 (2002): 295–314; here 305–10.

angrily with her famously crude and vulgar insult of the "faithless Trojan sodomite," Eneas. In spite of this warning, later in the day, a determined Lavine sends a letter declaring her love to the hero (vv. 8767–8864). Key Word of Love: *vive* (*ja vive ne m'avra Turnus*), "Turnus will never possess me alive," v. 8748. The suicide theme is introduced here.

V (vv. 8865–9118). At dusk, Eneas, having read and considered the love letter and ostensibly smitten, returns to his tent where, realizing the significance of Lavine's actions and gestures (she blows him a kiss), he spends the night suffering a similar symptomology, again a martyrdom of love (vv. 8908–9118). Key Word of Love: *savor* (*mes nel senti, ne il ne sot, / de quel savor ert li baisiers*), "nor did he know of what savor the kiss was" [Yunck], vv. 8880–81. Cf. *WWK*, 100–02 on *connaître* vs. *savoir*. See Classen, "Love of Discourse" in this volume (MS p. 12), on word play like this in late medieval German (realistic) lyric. See as well Etienne Wolf, *La Lettre d'amour au Moyen Age* (Paris: NIL, 1996), on the usually "equivocal" medieval love-letter.

VI (vv. 9119–274). On the morning of the third day, Eneas is still lovesick (vv. 9119–204). Lavine returns to the tower window and very anxiously awaits the hero, who arrives finally at mid-afternoon (vv. 9205 ff.). Key Word of Love: *hardemant* ('*hardemant me done m'amie*'), "My beloved gives me boldness" [Yunck], v. 9056. This word introduces the chivalry topos. For the tower-window image, see Theodore Ziolkowski, *The View from the Tower: Origins of an Antimodernist Image* (Princeton: Princeton University Press, 1998), 5–40; A. Petit, "Estre a la fenestre dans le *Roman d'Eneas*," *Par la fenestre: Études de littérature et de civilisation médiévales*, ed. Chantal Connochie-Bourgne, *Senefiance-CUER MA* (Aix-en-Provence: Publications de l'Université de Provence, 2003), 345–56.

VII (vv. 9275–838). Later (the same day? the next morning?), the peace truce fails. Eneas is wounded by a stray arrow, and preparations follow for the final single combat between Eneas and Turnus, which then ensues. After the victory, the wedding-date is set eight days hence. Key Word of Love: *dolut* (*La plaie li dolut formant*), "The wound pained him greatly" [Yunck], v. 9475. The real wound stands as metonymy for the wound of Love.

VIII (vv. 9839–922). Later (that afternoon?), Lavine, in the tower, who saw and heard the events on the battlefield below, is disturbed that Eneas the victor did not come to see her after the victory. Key Word of Love: *noveliere* (. . . *sovant me sera reprové / que de s'amor fui prinsaltiere / me tanra por noveliere*), "He will reproach me often because I was impulsive in my love of him, and he will hold me for a lover of change" [Yunck], i.e., impatient, fickle, forward, "forthputting"?-vv. 9862–64. Innovation (i.e., potentially heretical) comes to have a pejorative connotation during the Reformation. Martial's epigram (8.12.3–4) reinforces the Pauline dictum about wives: *Inferior matrona suo sit* . . . ([. . .] a woman should always be beneath her husband / Otherwise they won't be equal in their relationship) — ed. and trans. Erich Segal in *Plautus: Four Comedies* (Oxford: Oxford University Press, 1996).

IX (vv. 9923–10090). Eneas spends that night in self-interrogation over his love. The wedding will occur seven days later. Key Word of Love: *escamonie* ('*Corroz qui trop ne dure mie / est a amor escamonie...*'), "Anger which does not last too long is a great medicine for love ...." [Yunck], vv. 9981–82. This lexicographical hapax in the *Eneas* typifies the author's wide-ranging borrowings, this no doubt from Pliny's *Natural History*.

CHAPTER 5

"Desire": The Language of Love in the Feminine in Heloise's Letters

Carmel Posa
sgs. Melbourne College of Divinity (Australia)

The concept of "desire" elicits a variety of reactions when spoken of particularly in relationship to theological principles of Christian living and spirituality. Desire can have both positive and negative connotations. In traditional Christian thinking one can legitimately focus one's desire on God, yet worldly desires, particularly related to the body, are considered base and removed from the ultimate goal of human longing. Bernard of Clairvaux (1090/91–1153), a master of spiritual writing in the medieval era, writes about how one comes to love God through this language of desire. Desire isn't evil in and of itself, but if its object is "evil, illicit, carnal or worldly"[1] it is an obstacle to spiritual growth, for only the soul is the privileged site for loving God. Bernard, in a language reminiscent of Platonic or Neoplatonic thought, claims that:

> For the love by which one loves spiritually, whether its object is God, or an angel, or another soul, is truly and properly an attribute of the soul alone. Of this kind also is the love of justice, truth, goodness, wisdom, and the other virtues. But when a soul loves — or rather yearns for — anything of a material nature, be it food, clothing, property, or anything else or a physical

---

[1] Cf. Michael Casey, *A Thirst for God: Spiritual Desire in Bernard of Clairvaux's Sermon on the Song of Songs*, Cistercian Studies Series, 77 (Kalamazoo: Cistercian Publications, 1988), 65. The Latin text of any Bernardine sources are taken from Jean Leclercq, Henri Rochais, and C. H. Talbot, ed., *Sancti Bernardi Opera*, 8 vols. (Rome: Editiones Cistercienses, 1957–1977). (SBO). The sermons will be indicated by the standard abbreviation of the individual work and its reference within *SBO*. For the English translations I have used the four volumes from the Cistercian Fathers Series. *Bernard of Clairvaux: On the Song of Songs*, trans. Killian Walsh and Irene M. Edmonds, Cistercian Fathers Series 40, 4 (Kalamazoo: Cistercian Publications, 1980).

or earthly nature, that love is said to pertain to the flesh rather than to the soul.[2]

Though the body plays a functional part in this quest, the recognition of the body's intimate or essential involvement in the love of God is missing from Bernard's thought. Disconnecting the role of the body from that of the soul, he states that, "It is not with the steps of the feet that God is sought but with the heart's desires . . . ."[3]

Heloise of the Paraclete (d. 1164) lived the better part of her life as a monastic. Her early education took place in the Benedictine convent of Argenteuil. After her famous and passionate yet brief love affair with Peter Abelard (1079–1142), she returned to Argenteuil (ca. 1117/18) and later became the abbess of the Paraclete Benedictine community, founded by Abelard himself (ca.1129). When we investigate the concept of "desire" in relation to Heloise and her writings to Abelard,[4] we are faced with many puzzling and problematic questions and conclusions. Here is a woman who seems to have let loose her desires with unbridled passion. Here is a Christian whose desire seems to be clearly other than for God. Here is a renowned monastic leader whose desire seems no less than publicly scandalous and far from edifying. Given such obvious ambiguity and seeming contradiction, is it worthwhile analyzing Heloise's writing a little more closely? As Mews asserts in relation to her first letter, "As with Abelard's account, reading her [Heloise's] letter simply as an outpouring of the 'the heart' ignores the rhetorical skill with which she formulates her ethical argument."[5] Perhaps we can go even further and read her letters from a different perspective altogether in order to see if the voice of this famed abbess contains a deeper clarity that uncovers to us the justification for her acclaim as an extraordinary woman, Christian, and religious leader of history.[6]

---

[2] ". . . quod vere et proprie ad solam pertineat animam illa dilectio qua aliquid spiritualiter diligit, verbi gratia Deum, angelum, animam. Sed et diligere iustitiam, veritatem, pietatem, sapientiam virtutesque alias, eiusmodi est. Nam cum secundum carnem quippiam diliget, vel potius appetit, anima, verbi gratia cibum, vestimentum, dominium, et quae istiusmodi sunt corporalia sive terrena, carnis potius quam animae amor dicendus est," *Sermo super Cantica canticorum* (hereafter *SC*) 75.9; (*SBO* 2:252, 11–13)

[3] "Non pedum passibus, sed desideriis quaeitur Deus," *SC* 84.1 (*SBO* 2:3003, 12–16).

[4] See Suzanne Wayne, "Desire in Language and Form: Heloise's Challenge to Abelard," *Translating Desire in Medieval and Early Modern Literature*, ed. Craig A. Berry and Heather R. Hayton. Medieval and Renaissance Texts and Studies, 294 (Tempe, AZ: Arizona Center for Medieval and Renaissance Studies, 2005), 89–107.

[5] Constant Mews, *Abelard and Heloise*. Great Medieval Thinkers (Oxford and New York: Oxford University Press, 2005), 152.

[6] See Christopher Baswell, "Heloise," *The Cambridge Companion to Medieval Women's Writing*, ed. Carolyn Dinshaw and David Wallace. Cambridge Companions to Literature (Cambridge and New York: Cambridge University Press, 2003), 161–71.

Albrecht Classen, in his introduction to this volume, refers to the teaching methods of Hugh of St. Victor for reading a text. He notes that "... the surface of the text might confuse us, whereas the deeper meaning awaits us always at the end of profound research and meditation." Quoting Hugh, Classen observes: "The divine deeper meaning can never be absurd, never false ... the deeper meaning admits no contradiction, is always harmonious, always true."[7] I want to suggest that, in our own time, it is possible to read the correspondence of Heloise and Abelard from a deeper level of meaning, that is, from a theological and philosophical perspective of the body, particularly the "reasoning female body," and bodies as articulated by the psychoanalytic perspective of sexual difference and alterity in the writings of the French feminist philosopher Luce Irigaray. What becomes evident and highly significant in this reading is Heloise's distinctive use of language, in particular her language of love. Heloise's refusal to erase the concepts of essential embodiment and sexual difference[8] throughout her dialogue with Abelard is maintained through the creation of a space for the language of desire, in contrast to Abelard's emphasis on the more traditional language of renunciation. As such, Heloise's twelfth-century use of, and struggle with, language could be said to be analogous, in many ways, to the task involved in Irigaray's modern philosophical critique.[9]

Irigaray asserts that, in Western culture at least, woman and femininity have been defined within the framework of masculine discourse. This "master" discourse is structured on a metaphoric symbolization that implies a sacrifice and repression of meaning and sets up the danger of a system of inherent dualities. Irigaray claims:

> In the system of production that we know, including sexual production, men have distanced themselves from their bodies. They have used their sex, their language, their technique, in order to go further and further in the construction of a world which is more and more distant from their relation to the corporeal.[10]

---

[7] Classen, "Introduction," 10.

[8] By using the term "essential" embodiment and sexual difference, I am drawing on Irigaray's position vis-à-vis the nature of the feminine body. Serene Jones has classified Irigaray's position as "strategic essentialism", a position that takes account of both the constructivist and purely essentialist positions. Cf. Serene Jones, "Divining Women: Irigaray and Feminist Theologies," *Yale French Studies* 87 (1995): 42–48.

[9] For my arguments here, I will be drawing primarily from the following works by Irigaray: *This Sex Which Is Not One*, trans. Catherine Porter and Carolyn Burke (Ithaca: Cornell University Press, 1985); *An Ethics of Sexual Difference* (London: Athlone Press, 1993). I will also draw on her work as summarized in Elizabeth Grosz, *Sexual Subversions: Three French Feminists* (North Sydney: Allen and Unwin, 1989).

[10] Luce Irigaray, *Le Corps-à-Corps Avec La Mère* (Montréal: Les Editions de la pleine lune, 1981), 83–84. Cited in Grosz, *Sexual Subversions*, 118.

The language of denial and renunciation in the history of Christian spirituality is central to this thinking. Irigaray suggests that feminine desire is to be found in a yet-to-be-claimed language that retrieves the body, a different body, the body of the female, autonomous in its own right, and not considered simply from the perspective of masculine discourse or even primarily from a biological perspective.[11] In Irigaray's own poetic mode of expression she warns us:

> If we don't invent a language, if we don't find our body's language, it will have too few gestures to accompany our story.... Asleep again, unsatisfied, we shall fall back upon the words of men — who, for their part, have 'known' for a long time. But not our body. Seduced, attracted, fascinated, ecstatic without becoming, we shall remain paralyzed.[12]

From a feminist perspective, the language of desire, which has been assessed so often in the negative by patriarchal definitions and symbolization in both philosophy and theology, can be freed from these masculine constraints. Once this is achieved through the appreciation of the symbolic nature of feminine discourse, the concept of desire can be legitimately in-corporated into the story of women's subjectivity in general and women's spirituality in the Christian tradition in particular. It is this in-corporation of desire that we discover in the re-reading of Heloise's letters.

As a medieval woman, steeped in Christian principles, Heloise creates a space for the language of "desire" that is fundamentally a theological reading of the human person, and specifically the female human person. Graham Ward describes this concept of difference and its relationship to desire in terms of its theological foundation:

> Only where there is space, where there is distance, where there is *difference* can there be love, which *desires*, which draws, which incorporates ... the doctrine of creation is founded upon a fundamental difference in which desire and love can operate ... In the beginning God created a process of separation ... Desire is built, then, into the substructure of creation; and, in that, creation is an image of *desire and difference* within the Trinity itself.[13]

In the light of this fundamental theological principle, a principle that posits a God who, as threefold, is relational by very nature, it is possible to construct a theological understanding of women's desire, and thus the language of love, in

---

[11] The body here refers to its articulation at every level: psychic, social, religious as well as biological.

[12] Irigaray, *This Sex Which Is Not One*, 214.

[13] Graham Ward, "Divinity and Sexuality: Luce Irigaray and Christology," *Modern Theology* 12, 2 (1996): 221–37; here 228–29. Emphasis added.

terms of an essential "difference" in the perception of the body, a perception that focuses on embracing the body in the spiritual journey, rather than its denial or renunciation. It is precisely in longing, in desire, that the feminine finds her voice in order to speak "Words of Love" which enables true and authentic subjectivity for women and, as a consequence, the possibility of fully entering into relationship with a God who is love.

THE VOCABULARY OF DESIRE AND RENUNCIATION IN CHRISTIAN SPIRITUALITY

From Gregory the Great, dubbed the Doctor of Desire, and Benedict of Nursia, father of the monastic tradition that Heloise and all in her day inherited, to Heloise's contemporary, the Doctor of Love himself, Bernard of Clairvaux, the theme of desire has had a somewhat ambiguous position in the working out of Christian spirituality. As noted above, desire is to be unbridled in relationship to God, yet eradicated with respect to all else. As a consequence, desire's focus has often led to a separation of God's position vis-à-vis humanity. Earthly desires are considered base and distracting from our primary desire, which should be the love of God.

That the desire of, and for, the body or things of the world should be seen as an obstacle to desire for God is a product of an undeniable Western disdain and mistrust of created reality and particularly of the body's ability to enter into divine activity in and of itself. This is hardly a celebration of the intrinsic value of our created being. In spite of the fact that the "Word" himself took on the body out of love for humanity, the priority of the soul over the body is always paramount. Body and soul are not the integrative unit that we discover when we listen carefully to the voice of Heloise.

It is the language of "renunciation" and its inherent psychological dynamics that is at issue here, not so much the fundamental basis underlying the concept itself. Renunciation fundamentally involves the denial of self in preference for the other. It aims at the expansion of the heart and the capacity to love the other. It is a renunciation that leaves the subject with only one object of desire, the desire for God, but it is a renunciation that symbolizes "sacrifice and repression," rather than a language which might "integrate and harmonize."

The questions remain: "Can this 'single-hearted' focus on the desire for God, be expressed in language other than renunciation?" Is it possible to escape that "linguistic dilemma" described by Classen in his introduction that exists between "both Godhead and the beloved, both the religious and the erotic experience?" (15) "Can our attitude to theological desire be remodeled by Heloise's insights and attempts at feminine discourse?" It is my contention that the dichotomy between our innate desire for the divine and the so-called "worldly desires" dangerously lurking in the language of renunciation is exposed by the language that incorporates and harmonizes desire and the body, the immanent and the transcendent, in the letters of Heloise of the Paraclete.

THE VOCABULARY OF DESIRE IN HELOISE'S LATER CORRESPONDENCE

Though the language of renunciation is not totally absent from Heloise's rhetoric, it is certainly overshadowed by her vocabulary of desire. In Heloise's first letter to Abelard,[14] her response to his *Historia calamitatum,* she seeks to establish a sense of wholeness for her identity. She understands this desire for wholeness from the standpoint of having something missing to her being, and the missing element for her is her husband and the founder of her community, Abelard. This desire does not demand that she or her community should renounce Abelard, but that they should share in his struggles and he in theirs. Her vocabulary is expressed in terms of hope, a hope that Abelard might in some way connect with her and the community: "Per ipsum itaque qui te sibi adhuc quoquo modo protegit Christum obsecramus, quatinus ancillulas ipsius et tuas crebris litteris de his in quibus adhuc fluctuas naufragiis certificare digneris" (And so in the name of Christ, who is still giving you some protection for his service, we beseech you to write as often as you think fit to us who are his handmaids and yours about the vicissitudes you are still experiencing).[15]

Abelard has been remiss in his duty to Heloise and the community, or, more accurately, he has been remiss in his love for them. His neglect has caused a rupture in the community's and Heloise's identity, and she insists that he now has a duty to heal these wounds. His desire, were he true to his own identity as husband to Heloise and father to the community, should be for her and the community's well-being: "Hujus quippe loci tu post Deum solus es fundator, solus hujus oratorii constructor, solus hujus congregationis edifficator" (For you after God are the sole founder of this place, the sole builder of this oratory, the sole

---

[14] All references to the Letters of Heloise and Abelard are taken from the Latin edition of the letters by Eric Hicks, ed., *La vie et les epistres, Pierres Abaelart et Heloys sa fame, Traduction du XIIIe siècle attribuée à Jean De Meun, avec une nouvelle édition des textes latins d'aprés le ms. Troyes Bibl. Mun. 802. Introduction, Texts*, vol. 16 (Paris: Champion, 1991), and the revised English translation by Betty Radice, *The Letters of Abelard and Heloise*, ed. Michael Clanchy (London: Penguin, 2003); see also Glenda McLeod, "'Wholly Guilty, Wholly Innocent': Self-Definition in Heloise's Letters to Abelard," *Dear Sister: Medieval Women and the Epistolary Genre*, ed. Karen Cherawatuk and Ulrike Wiethaus. The Middle Ages Series (Philadelphia: University of Pennsylvania Press, 1993), 64–86.

[15] *Ep.* 2, ed. Hicks, 46 (trans. Radice, 48).

creator of this community).[16] This triple formula will be repeated to even greater effect in her last letter of this correspondence.

Oscillating as she does between her own personal voice and that of the representative communal voice, her desire for Abelard simply symbolizes and encapsulates the desires and needs of the whole feminine community, and, as such, justice is embedded into her desire and that of the community: "... ut ceteras omittam, quanto erga me te obligaveris debito pensa, ut quod devotis communiter debes feminis, unice tue devotius solvas" (Apart from anything else, consider the close tie by which you have bound yourself to me, and repay the debt you owe a whole community of devoted women by discharging it the more dutifully to her who is yours alone).[17]

Heloise puts her argument surrounding her desire for Abelard's presence in at least his provision of letters, in the context of the desire for God of holy women of old and the care given them from the Church Fathers. Why, then, should her desire and that of her community be left unacknowledged, given the tradition of this wholesome love between holy women of old and the great Fathers of the Church?

Furthermore, Heloise has recourse not just to this one holy precedent from church history. She considers herself lawfully married to Abelard. For Heloise each state, her marriage bond and her monastic vows, is incorporated into the other, and she draws his attention to this when she remarks: "... cui quidem tanto te majore debito noveris obligatum quanto te amplius nuptialis federe sacramenti constat esse astrictum et eo te magis michi obnoxium quo te semper, ut omnibus patet, immoderato amore complexa sum" (Yet you must know that you are bound to me by an obligation which is all the greater for the further close tie of the marriage sacrament uniting us, and are deeper in my debt because of the love I have always borne you, as everyone knows, a love which is beyond all bounds).[18] Clearly, Heloise does not identify with any renunciation of her marriage vows, and neither do they appear as in any way in conflict with her monastic vows to God and the community.

Numerous scholars have researched various aspects of marriage and concubinage in the medieval world.[19] What is important to note is that even

---

[16] *Ep* 2, ed. Hicks, 47 (trans. Radice, 49).
[17] *Ep.* 2, ed. Hicks, 48 (trans. Radice, 50).
[18] *Ep.* 2, ed. Hicks, 48 (trans. Radice, 50).
[19] Cf. C. N. L. Brooke, *The Medieval Idea of Marriage* (Oxford: Oxford University Press, 1989); David. L. d'Avray, *Medieval Marriage; Symbolism and Society* (Oxford: Oxford University Press, 2005), and *The Discourse on Love, Marriage, and Transgression in Medieval and Early Modern Literature*, ed. Albrecht Classen. Medieval and Renaissance Texts and Studies, 278 (Tempe: Arizona Center for Medieval and Renaissance Studies, 2004); see also Albrecht Classen, *Der Liebes- und Ehediskurs vom hohen Mittelalter bis zum frühen 17. Jahrhundert*. Volksliedstudien, 5 (Münster, New York, et al.: Waxmann, 2005).

though it was understood that marriage vows were lesser superior than the vows made by religious and that religious vows superseded previous vows, Heloise's position is explicitly supported by Peter the Venerable of Cluny (ca.1094–1156), one of the foremost respected black Benedictines of the age and head of the Abbey of Cluny. After Abelard's death he writes to console her:

> Hunc ergo uenerabilis et carissima in domino soror, cui post carnalem copulam tanto ualidiore, quanto meliore diuinae caritatis uinculo adhesisti, cum quo et sub quo diu domino deseruisti, hunc inquam loco tui, vel ut te alteram in gremio suo confouet, et in aduentu domini, in uoce archangeli, et in tuba dei descendentis de caelo, tibi per ipsius gratiam restituendum reseruat.
>
> [Him, therefore, venerable and dearest sister in the Lord, him to whom after your union in the flesh you are joined by the better, and therefore stronger, bond of divine love, with whom and under whom you have long served God: him, I say, in your place, or as another you, God cherishes in his bosom, and keeps him there to be restored to you through his grace at the coming of the Lord, at the voice of the archangel, and the trumpet-note of God descending from heaven.][20]

Peter the Venerable here eloquently confirms the final validity of Heloise's integrated view of her marriage and monastic vows, with God sealing their love at the end of the ages.

God is not simply ignored or denied by Heloise in her desire for Abelard. She clearly understands herself and her community as handmaidens of God.[21] She is arguing that the severing of ties does not leave one free to pursue a more purely motivated desire. It ruptures the identity and falsifies the endeavor. She entreats Abelard: "Per ipsum itaque cui te obtulisti Deum te obsecro ut quo modo potes tuam michi presentiam reddas, consolationem videlicet michi aliquam rescribendo, hoc saltem pacto ut sic recreata divino alacrior vacem obsequio.... Quanto autem rectius me nunc in Deum" (And so, in the name of God to whom you have dedicated yourself, I beg you to restore your presence to me in the way you can by writing me some word of comfort, so that in this at least I may find increased strength and readiness to serve God. . . . Is it not far better now to summon me to God).[22] What we must be aware of is that Heloise recognizes her

---

[20] *Ep.* 115 in *The Letters of Peter the Venerable,* ed. Giles Constable, 2 vols. (Cambridge, MA: Harvard University Press, 1967), 307–08, trans. Radice, 223.

[21] "Per ipsum itaque qui te sibi adhuc quoquo modo protegit Christum obsecramus, quatinus ancillulas ipsius et tuas crebris litteris de his in quibus adhuc fluctuas naufragiis certificare digneris" (And so in the name of Christ, who is still giving you some protection for his service, we beseech you to write as often as you think fit to us who are his handmaids and yours), *Ep* 2. Hicks, 46 (Radice, 48).

[22] *Ep.* 2, ed. Hicks, 53 (trans. Radice, 54–55).

The Language of Love

love and desire for Abelard as not incompatible with, but integral to, this desire for God and not a step to be overcome in the ascent to God.

Heloise sets her barb against Abelard with a contrast between their positions vis-à-vis desire, using the negative term "lust" (*concupiscentia*): For herself she states: "Nichil umquam — Deus scit! — in te requisivi; te pure, non tua concupiscens" (God knows I never sought anything in you except yourself; I wanted simply you, [*concupiscens* — lusting for] nothing of yours).[23] For Abelard she says: "Dicam: concupiscentia te michi potius quam amicitia sociavit; libidinis ardor potius quam amor" (It was [lust] desire, not affection, which bound you to me, the flame of lust rather than love).[24] This is desire based on lust, not love. It is worldly (fleshly) desire for the self, not embodied desire for the other. Heloise desires to know that this accusation she is hurling at Abelard is a fiction and that his desire is as pure and as embodied as hers.

In contrast, Abelard's somewhat self-absorbed language of his Letter III ignores Heloise's particular condition, and focuses primarily on his own precarious existence. Anxious for divine aid in his insecure predicament, Abelard uses the traditional language of renunciation of desires: "Quarum tam abstinentia quam continentia deo sacrata, quanto ipsi gratior habetur, tanto ipsum propitiorem inveniet" (The more God is pleased by the abstinence and continence which women have dedicated to him, the more willing he will be to grant their prayers).[25]

Having made little impression on Abelard through the expression of her desires, Heloise intensifies her rhetoric of desire in her next letter to him. Her language now involves the rich and emotive vocabulary of grief, anguish, suffering, contrition and memory through the experience of both the absence and the loss of Abelard to herself and to her community, moving again freely between her own particular voice, her "I," and the general voice of her community, i.e., "we."

Heloise's desire is expressed in the vocabulary of "suffering" and penitence: " . . . et quod tu ad horam in corpore pertulisti, ego in omni vita — ut justum est — in contritione mentis suscipiam, et hoc tibi saltem modo, si non Deo, satisfaciam" (. . . and what you suffered in the body for a time, I may suffer, as is right, throughout my life in contrition of mind, and thus make reparation to you at least, if not to God).[26] What Abelard suffers in his castration is temporary and in fact ultimately healing for his sins. For Heloise, who has not undergone the loss of the site of bodily desire, the suffering continues and she argues that what she suffers through this unrelenting desire for Abelard is a path by which she can atone for his suffering and her own sins. Because of the absence of Abelard's comfort, however, Heloise's desire to make reparation to God is unfulfilled:

---

[23] *Ep.* 2, ed. Hicks, 49 (trans. Radice, 51).
[24] *Ep* 2, ed. Hicks, 51 (trans. Radice, 53).
[25] *Ep.* 3, ed. Hicks, 57 (trans. Radice, 59).
[26] *Ep.* 4, ed. Hicks, 65 (trans. Radice, 67).

"... qua penitentia Deum placcare valeam non invenio, quem super hac semper injuria summe crudelitatis arguo et ejus dispensationi contraria" (... I can find no penitence whereby to appease God, whom I always accuse of the greatest cruelty in regard to this outrage).[27] It is because of the unfulfilled nature of desire that Heloise can so freely rage against God, against herself, and against Abelard.

Heloise's position here rests once more on the understanding of her integrity. There is no point in repentance when there is no integrity between body and the mind: "Quomodo etiam penitentia peccatorum dicitur, quantacumque sit corporis afflictio, si mens adhuc ipsam peccandi retinet voluntatem et pristinis estuat desideriis?" (How can it be called repentance for sins, however great the mortification of the flesh, if the mind still retains the will to sin and is on fire with the old desires?).[28] At this juncture, Heloise uses *desiderium*, not *concupiscentia*. Can this be because this desire she has for Abelard is not something that she considers sinful?

In fact, Abelard's language of renunciation is not the language with which Heloise or her community can imagine their monastic endeavor, particularly if it requires that they deny their intimate and embodied connection to Abelard. They cannot bring themselves to repent of the desire for this relationship, as to deny this connection, and the desire for it, would be to deny their own identity. And so begins Heloise's shocking confession of her overtly embodied desire for Abelard, a desire that she cannot bring herself either to deny or condemn: "In tantum vero ille quas pariter exercuimus amantium voluptates dulces michi fuerunt ut nec displicere michi nec vix a memoria labi possint. Quocumque loco me vertam, semper se oculis meis cum suis ingerunt desideriis, nec etiam dormienti suis illusionibus parcunt" (In my case, the pleasures of lovers which we shared have been too sweet — they cannot displease me, and can scarcely shift from my memory. Wherever I turn they are always there before my eyes, bringing with them awakened longings [desires] and fantasies which will not even let me sleep).[29] Heloise can find no way to repent of this desire, and she struggles to find a way to incorporate it into her present identity because of her conviction that incorporation is required for wholeness. It is this incorporation that drives Heloise's desire, and it can only be achieved through Abelard's acknowledgment and appreciation of this desire. As Morgan Powell also maintains, in the hermeneutic of these letters there is "... the voice of a nascent spirituality that seeks the assimilation of human sexual desire to the love of God."[30]

---

[27] *Ep.* 4, ed. Hicks, 65–66 (trans. Radice, 68).
[28] *Ep.* 4, ed. Hicks, 66 (trans. Radice 68).
[29] *Ep.* 4, ed. Hicks, 66 (trans. Radice, 68).
[30] Morgan Powell, "Listening to Heloise at the Paraclete: Of Scholarly Diversion and a Woman's 'Conversion'," *Listening to Heloise: The Voice of a Twelfth-Century Woman*, ed. Bonnie Wheeler. The New Middle Ages (New York: St. Martin's Press, 2000), 255–86; here 278.

The Language of Love 139

This "unfulfilled" desire is also what makes her life a sham: "Castam me predicant, qui non deprehendunt ypocritam; munditiam carnis conferunt in virtutem: cum non sit corporis sed animi virtus" (Men call me chaste; they do not know the hypocrite I am. They consider purity of the flesh a virtue, though virtue belongs not to the body but to the soul).[31] Yet she upends this own condemnation of herself when she questions the nature of this very hypocrisy: "... aliquid laudis apud homines habens, nichil apud Deum mereor, qui cordis et renum probator est et in abscondito videt. Religiosa hoc tempore judicor in quo jam parva pars religionis non est ypochrisis, ubi ille maximis extollitur laudibus qui humanum non offendit judicium" (I am judged religious at a time when there is little in religion which is not hypocrisy, when whoever does not offend the opinions of men receives the highest praise).[32] Here she obliquely criticizes the society in which she lives, as her contemporary Hildegard of Bingen does more openly and directly in her many letters.[33] Heloise proceeds to put forth a summary of her position vis-à-vis acceptable behavior in the eyes of God, i.e., to do none harm.[34] Yet even so, all behavior must have at its fundamental foundation the "love of God": "... sicut scriptum est: 'Declina a malo, et fac bona.' Et frustra utrumque geritur quod amore Dei non agitur" (... as it is written: 'Turn from evil and do good' [Ps. 33:15]. Both are vain if not done for love of God).[35] This must be the basic orientation for Heloise; the interior intention based on love, if her behavior is to have any integrity.

Heloise insists that Abelard must recognize her desires as real and substantial, and that her holiness lies not in some vainly sought perfection and unlooked-for praise, but in her humility, her honest desire to be known for what she really is: "Tanto autem michi tua laus in me periculosior est quanto gratior, et tanto amplius ea capior et delector quanto amplius tibi per omnia placere studeo. Time, obsecro, semper de me potius quam confidas, ut tua semper sollicitudine adjuver" (To me your praise is the more dangerous because I welcome it. The more anxious I am to please you in everything, the more I am won over and delighted by it. I beg you, be fearful for me always, instead of feeling confidence in me, so that I may always find help in your solicitude).[36]

---

[31] *Ep.* 4, ed. Hicks, 67 (trans. Radice, 69).
[32] *Ep.* 4, ed. Hicks 67 (trans. Radice, 69). Cf. Wayne, "Heloise's Challenge," 95–96.
[33] Compare Hildegard's stronger position in this respect, e.g., in *Letter* 19, in Hildegard of Bingen, *The Letters of Hildegard of Bingen*, trans. Joseph L. Baird and Radd K. Ehrman. Vol. 1 (New York and Oxford: Oxford University Press, 1994), 71. Baird and Ehrman's translation is based on the first volume of the critical edition of Lieven Van Acker ed, *Hildegardis Bingensis Epistolarium*: Prima Pars. *Corpus Christiamorum: continuatio medievalis,* vol. 91 (Turnhout: Brepols, 1991). Hildegard reveals to us a woman profoundly disillusioned with the institutional church to the extent that in her major work, *Scivias*, she even envisages the Antichrist coming forth from the womb of the Church, *Ecclesia*, herself. Cf. Carmel Posa, "Keeping Vigil on the Edge," *Tjurunga* 62 (2002): 69–91.
[34] Cf. *Ep.* 4, ed. Hicks, 67 (trans. Radice, 69).
[35] *Ep.* 4, ed. Hicks, 67 (trans. Radice, 69).
[36] *Ep.* 4, ed. Hicks, 68–69 (trans. Radice, 70).

As in the previous letter, Heloise's underlying desire is a resolution of her conflict, and a resolution that desires a God who will not ask of her the denial of her love for Abelard, but one who will accept mercifully the longings of a very ordinary human heart: "Nolo me ad virtutem exhortans et ad pugnam . . . Non quero coronam victorie; satis est michi periculum vitare. Tutius evitatur periculum quam committitur bellum. Quocumque me angulo celi Deus collocet satis michi faciet" (I do not wish you to exhort me to virtue or summon me to battle. . . . I do not seek a crown of victory; it is sufficient for me to avoid danger, and this is safer than engaging in war. In whatever corner of heaven God shall place me, it will be enough for me).[37] This very moving posture of humility assumed by Heloise highlights Abelard's own position of spiritual pride. His inability to console Heloise stems from his failure to recognize his own love for her because it seems to him incompatible with his quest for spiritual perfection, a quest that contrasts with Heloise's humble recognition of the inner truth of her identity.

Abelard's response to these impassioned pleas from Heloise begins with an obvious generalizing of their relationship: "Sponse Christi, servus ejusdem" (To the bride of Christ, from His servant).[38] In this letter he intends to provide Heloise with the encouragement she seeks and to set her straight on a number of issues concerning her rebuke of him. Though he states that he does not intend the letter to be a justification of himself, this is precisely the tone of much of it.

Abelard proceeds to allegorize away the particular body of Heloise with its carnal desires, using the metaphor of the Ethiopian bride in his exegesis of the Song of Songs. As Peggy McCracken maintains: "Abelard describes an abstract body-as-metaphor" for the spiritual life, and thus, " . . . effaces gender in the description of the Christian subject . . . ."[39] In this letter he urges her to transcend the space that has been left in her and, through prayer, to spiritualize that space through a hunger for God alone, her true bridegroom. All desire is to be transformed into a disembodied desire for God alone. Heloise is now a widow, counted among the holy widows of the Church, clothed in the black habit of her sinful and abject body, yet a white lily of virtue and humility within.

For Abelard there is no room for any consideration of justice for the body and its desires, and he later continues this metaphorical erasing of Heloise's feminine body through the spiritualizing of female motherhood and thus the maternal body, a moment that must have proved particularly painful for Heloise.

The fiction that Heloise desires to be relieved of is proved to be a reality by Abelard in his cruel attempt to drag Heloise into this spiritualized focus on God's love through his own denial of love: "Amabat te ille veraciter, non ego. Amor meus

---

[37] *Ep.* 4, ed. Hicks, 69 (trans. Radice, 71). Cf. Wayne, "Heloise's Challenge," 105.
[38] *Ep.* 5, ed. Hicks, 70 (trans. Radice, 72).
[39] Peggy McCracken, "The Curse of Eve: Female Bodies and Christian Bodies in Heloise's Third Letter," *Listening to Heloise*, 217–31; here 218.

qui utrumque nostrum peccatis involvebat, concupiscentia, non amor dicendus est. Miseras in te meas voluptates implebam, et hoc erat totum quod amabam" (It was He who truly loved you, not I. My love, which brought us both to sin, should be called lust, not love. I took my fill of my wretched pleasure in you, and this was the sum total of my love).[40] Abelard's letter embraces the traditional language of renunciation and spiritual perfection with its images of sacrifice and repression. His desires are now focused on a disembodied desire for God, and any recognition of Heloise's or his own more overtly sensual desires is not possible and even unthinkable for Abelard, and, in a reversal of Benedict's Biblically-inspired summit of humility, he reveals his own "fear which casts out love."[41] As Timmerman summarizes in her study on desire in the spiritual life: " . . . those who deny their bodies and their feelings, thinking that the real self is the mental subject, are never wholly available. Some part, the vital, spontaneous part, is always under constraint. Touch is always feared."[42]

The third letter from Heloise has been interpreted as the moment when she "abandons the passionate speech of desire that characterizes her first two letters . . . ."[43] Yet, on the contrary, the desires of Heloise simply shift from a mostly personal tone to that of her communal mood. Heloise's voice is not sacrificed for the voice of the Abbess.[44] In her transfiguration into the body of the community, Heloise expresses exactly the same desires using the same arguments as she had in her previous letters, concerning the ethics of intention, the struggle with the body, its feminine specificity, and the need to recognize this body's relationship to Abelard; but now she *is* the communal body.

Heloise had desired that Abelard give her some comfort through his concrete recognition of their relationship and particularly of the history of their relationship held within their memory, their personal history. Now, as the communal body, she again desires this same concern from him through his provision of a history of monastic women: "Omnes itaque nos Christi ancille et in Christi filie tue duo nunc a tua Paternitate supplices postulamus, que nobis admodum necessaria providemus. Quorum quidem alterum est ut nos instruere velis unde sanctimonialium ordo ceperit, et que nostre sit professionis auctoritas" (And so all we handmaids of Christ, who are your daughters in Christ, come as suppliants to demand of your paternal interest two things which we see to be very

---

[40] *Ep.* 5, ed. Hicks, 84 (trans. Radice, 86).
[41] Cf. RB 7:67: *ad caritatem Dei . . . quae perfecta foris mittit timorem . . .* (. . . the perfect love of God which casts out all fear).
[42] Joan H. Timmerman, *Sexuality and Spiritual Growth* (New York: Crossroad, 1992), 37.
[43] McCracken, "The Curse of Eve: Female Bodies and Christian Bodies in Heloise's Third Letter," 217.
[44] Cf. J. T. Muckle (ed.), "The Personal Letters between Abelard and Heloise," *C.S.B. Mediaeval Studies* 15 (1953): 47–95; here 59, D. W. Robertson, Jr., *Abelard and Heloise* (1972; London: Millington, 1974), 54.

necessary for ourselves. One is that you will teach us how the order of nuns began and what authority there is for our profession).[45]

Similarly, Heloise desires that the female body be taken into account with her request for a Rule specifically gendered, that is, for women's bodies, the details of which she then proceeds to describe herself. This request is no more than the communal form of the request that Heloise made previously for the inclusion of her particular feminine body and its desires within their own personal dialogue. As the communal body, Heloise, rather than denying herself and her desires, expands both, and in so doing concretely highlights the nature and difference of the feminine body.[46]

Her community desires to live authentic lives, and they cannot do this without positing their subjectivity, a subjectivity in difference. In contrast to Abelard, Heloise achieves this authentification by avoiding any meditation on metaphorical interpretations of the individual soul in the religious endeavor. Metaphorical readings invariably abstract the body and eliminate its subjectivity. By contrast, Heloise is determined to harmonize the body's many desires and needs with the spiritual quest for God.

The whole of this letter, as in the previous letters, concentrates on the difference between men and women. Women are different in bodily, mental, and spiritual strength.[47] Their bodily functions are different and thus have different needs with regard to clothing.[48] They are "protected by greater sobriety"[49] with regard to food and drink.[50] They are more vulnerable to their own bodily desires.[51] They are less capable of the physical labor demanded by the Rule.[52] Of course, one may wish to dispute all these claims from our own modern and scientific perspective; however, in the light of Heloise's purpose we shouldn't be led away from her primary aim here. She is setting up a case for women and their difference, not arguing their inferiority. Indeed, she claims, obliquely at least, a superiority of women living the Benedictine life:

---

[45] *Ep.* 6, ed. Hicks, 89 (trans. Radice, 94).

[46] Further to this argument, see Carmel Posa, "Specialiter: The Language of the Body and Bodies in the Letters of Heloise," *Magistra: A Journal of Women's Spirituality in History,* 11, 1 (Summer 2005): 3–25.

[47] Cf. *Ep.* 6, ed. Hicks, 89 (trans. Radice, 94), and elsewhere.

[48] Cf. *Ep.* 6, ed. Hicks, 94 (trans. Radice, 99). McCracken unpacks Heloise's concentration on the menstruating body and claims that Heloise highlights this aspect in order to articulate clearly sexual difference. Cf. McCracken, "The Curse of Eve: Female Bodies and Christian Bodies in Heloise's Third Letter," 222.

[49] Cf. *Ep.* 6, ed. Hicks, 94 (trans. Radice, 99).

[50] Cf. *Ep.* 6, ed. Hicks, 94 (trans. Radice, 99).

[51] Cf. *Ep.* 6, ed. Hicks, 89–90 (trans. Radice, 94–95).

[52] Cf. *Ep.* 6, ed. Hicks, 104–05 (trans. Radice, 109–10).

The Language of Love

> Satis nostre esse infirmitati et maximum imputari debet, si continenter ac sine proprietate viventes, et, officiis occupate divinis, ipsos Ecclesie duces vel religiosos laicos in victu adequemus, vel eos denique qui Regulares Canonici dicuntur et se precipue vitam apostolicam sequi profitentur.
>
> [It should be sufficient for our infirmity, and indeed, a high tribute to it, if we live continently and without possessions, wholly occupied by service of God, and in doing so equal the leaders of the church themselves in our way of life or religious laymen or even those who are called Canons Regular and profess especially to follow the apostolic life].[53]

And she rightly accuses men as deserving of less admiration when she states that: "Providendum itaque nobis est ne id oneris femine presumamus, in quo viros fere jam universos succumbere videmus — immo et deficere!" (We must therefore be careful not to impose on a woman a burden under which we see nearly all men stagger and even fall).[54] In fact, what she seems to achieve here is the overturning the twelfth-century understanding of "women's weakness."[55]

Not to consider "difference", and sexual difference in particular, is totally unreasonable and unjust for Heloise and her times, as it was for Benedict in his times: "Perpende itaque quam longe absistat ab omni rationis discretione ejusdem Regule professione tam feminas quam viros obligari, eademque sacrina tam debiles quam fortes onerari" (Consider then how far removed it is from all reason and good sense if both women and men are bound by profession of a common Rule, and the same burden is laid on the weak as on the strong).[56] Heloise's own tragic experience and her own good sense make it all too obvious to her what the differences are between men and women. Equality, particularly equality of virtue, should not be judged simply by rigid adherence to the same set of Rules. This is not justice! It is not love! It was not even what Benedict himself intended. Rather context bears heavily on this judgment as she points out that even the men of the past, with their wives in tow, reached esteemed and model degrees of virtue.[57] This is surely a barb aimed at Abelard's disposal of his own wife.

It appears that Heloise knows the flexibility of the Rule better than anyone in her own time. She remains totally within the dictates of the rule itself in her critique, particularly when she points out to Abelard that even Benedict's own desire is for a Rule that adapts to the context in which it finds itself. "Hujus autem discretionis beatus non immemor Benedictus, tanquam omnium justorum

---

[53] *Ep.* 6, ed. Hicks, 95 (trans. Radice, 100).
[54] *Ep.* 6, ed. Hicks, 96 (trans. Radice, 100).
[55] Heloise uses the word *infirmitas*, weakness, rhetorically in many of her references to women's position vis-à-vis the Rule of Benedict throughout Letter 6 of her correspondence
[56] *Ep.* 6, ed. Hicks, 92 (trans. Radice, 97).
[57] Cf. *Ep.* 6. Hicks, 93. (Radice, 98).

spiritu plenus, pro qualitate hominum aut temporum cuncta sic moderatur in Regula ut omnia, sicut ipsemet uno concludit loco, mensurate fiant" (Benedict, who is imbued with the spirit of justice in everything, has this discretion in mind when he moderates everything in the rule according to the quality of men or the times so that, as he says himself at one point, all may be done in moderation).[58] She also scrupulously examines the Rule for its inherent adaptability in all its manifestations and then, as a faithful Benedictine abbess, as she was a faithful lover, applies it to her own context: "Quid, obsecro — ubi iste qui sic ad hominum et temporum qualitatem omnia moderatur, ut ab omnibus sine murmuratione perferri queant que instituuntur — quid, inquam, de feminis provideret, si eis quoque pariter ut viris regulam institueret?" (What, I wonder, when he adapts everything to the quality of men and seasons, so that all his regulations can be carried out by everyone without complaint — what provision would he make for women if he laid down a Rule for them like that for men?).[59] She is not proposing the indiscriminate disposal of the Rule itself, but its transfiguration into the context of women. Heloise desires this "justice" of Benedict and his Rule for her own female community as reflective of the injustice perpetrated against love in their personal lives. As abbess, just as lover, her desire for justice is expressed in the recognition of their sexual difference.

Heloise's spirituality and her critique of the Benedictine Rule must also be viewed in the light of various reform movements in monasticism that were in full swing around her at the time.[60] She stands within the midst of the endless controversies between the spiritual interpretation of the Rule by the black Benedictines of Cluny and the uncritically strict adherence to the demands of this primitive Rule by the white Cistercians, headed by Bernard of Clairvaux.[61] Mews describes Heloise's position as " . . . a subtle critique of those Cistercian reformers who considered that failing to observe the Benedictine rule to the letter was to permit corruption of monastic ideals . . . ."[62] Within this milieu, Heloise attempts to make a case for adapting, and even rewriting, the Holy Rule for women. As Peter

---

[58] *Ep.* 6, ed. Hicks, 91 (trans. Radice, 96).

[59] *Ep.* 6, ed. Hicks, 92 (trans. Radice, 97).

[60] Reforms in monasticism had been the mark of the eleventh century and included figures such as Romuald and the Camaldolese movement, Peter Damian with his tireless emphasis on the eremitical lifestyle, Bruno and the Chartreuse charterhouse, Robert of Molesme and Stephen Harding with the beginnings of the Cistercian reform, and the developments undertaken by the great abbots of Cluny. These movements continued into the twelfth century and witnessed the breakneck expansion of the Cistercian Order under Bernard of Clairvaux, as well as the attempts of Robert of Arbrissel and Gilbert of Sempringham to establish viable orders for men and women. For a summary of these movements see Peter King, *Western Monasticism: A History of the Monastic Movement in the Latin Church*. Cistercian Studies Series, 185 (Kalamazoo: Cistercian Publications, 1999), 131–228.

[61] For a recent, refreshingly critical biography, see Peter Dinzelbacher, *Bernhard von Clairvaux: Leben und Werk des berühmten Zisterziensers* (Darmstadt: Primus, 1998).

[62] Mews, *Abelard and Heloise*, 59.

Dronke asserts, "even though she had been forced into taking the veil, [she] had also developed a willing concern with every aspect of womanly monastic life."[63] But in doing this, Heloise is presenting us with a woman's voice, with a woman's desires, in the sea of voices from the male monastic world.[64] Her complaint is that the Rule is not inherently a literalist universal Rule and should not be understood as such. Her desires, consistent with what had previously been the basis of her arguments in her previous letters, are expressed, not in terms of Rules or even in terms of interpretation of Rules, but rather in terms of one's interior motivations or intentions, intentions that are primarily concerned with the adherence to love, not rules.

"Love" itself should be the focus of one's desire, and this is precisely what Heloise identifies as missing in the world. In a pointed remark Heloise claims universally what she had previously accused Abelard of personally[65] when she states, "... et juxta illud Veritatis, ipsam karitatem non tam multorum quam fere omnium refriguisse" (... in the words of Truth, amongst many or indeed almost all men love itself has grown cold [Matt. 24:12]).[66] For Heloise in her letters as for Marie de France in all her *Lais*, and many of the other writers discussed in this volume, love alone is what justifies one's being. Renunciation or sacrifice may well be inherited into the bargain, but they are not the primary aim.

The Rule, as Benedict himself asserts, is not an end in itself, but only a beginning.[67] If these Rules do not serve the end, which is love, and they don't do so in every detail for women, then they should be altered or simply ignored, as they hinder rather than help the desire for God which is the Christian's true endeavour, nothing more and nothing less: "Atque utinam ad hoc nostra religio conscendere posset ut Evangelium impleret, non transcenderet, nec plusquam christiane appeteremus esse" (Would that our religion could rise to this height — to carry out the Gospel, not to go beyond it, lest we attempt to be more than Christians).[68] Contrary to Mews's assertion that Heloise's critique goes "... beyond the Rule of Benedict to Scripture itself to find authority for the religious life,"[69] Heloise adheres firmly to the Rule's own position vis-à-vis the superiority of Scripture. In sharp contrast to Abelard's position in Letter V, Heloise reinstates the primacy and inexorable presence of the body and its needs, which he had totally erased,

---

[63] Peter Dronke, *Women Writers of the Middle Ages* (Cambridge: Cambridge University Press, 1994), 130.

[64] Marie de France, here cited from the English translation, *The Lais of Marie de France*, trans. with an intro. by Glyn S. Burgess and Keith Busby (London: Penguin, 1986).

[65] Cf. *Ep.* 2, ed. Hicks 51 (trans. Radice, 53).

[66] *Ep.* 6, ed. Hicks, 96 (trans. Radice, 101).

[67] Cf. *RB* 73:8

[68] *Ep.* 6, ed. Hicks, 93 (trans. Radice, 98).

[69] Mews, *Abelard and Heloise*, 159.

and she justifies her argument for change by drawing on the Gospel's primary focus on love.

Heloise ends this final letter with a last appeal to Abelard, an appeal that very astutely draws on Abelard's own theological concern and aptly draws together her desire for love in its ultimate and most Christian expression. Extending the triple formula she used in her first letter,[70] she unashamedly inserts her desires into a clearly Trinitarian formula in order to exhort Abelard to embrace these same desires and the desires of the community: "Tibi nunc, domine, dum vivis, incumbit instituere de nobis quid in perpetuum tenendum sit nobis. Tu quippe post Deum hujus loci fundator, tu per Deum nostre congregationis es plantator, tu cum Deo nostre sis religionis institutor" (It is for you then, master, while you live, to lay down for us what Rule we are to follow for all time, for after God you are the founder of this place, through God you are the creator of our community, with God you should be the director of our religious life).[71] Heloise's love is the love that the Trinity, God herself, has built into the fabric of creation.

CONCLUSION

If what Ward posits is true, that "desire is built into creation"[72] through the love of God, who is a trinity of love, then to deny desire is part of the essence of human sinfulness. In Heloise's letters to Abelard, we are confronted by a startling re-orientation for the place of both love and desire in monastic and Christian spirituality, a re-orientation that dares to take stock of the human condition from the feminine perspective and develops a language that enables women to insert themselves into a love for God through their own unique subjectivity, a subjectivity which does not need to bypass or transcend the body and its desires.

In these letters, Heloise obliquely justifies her own personal position vis-à-vis her love for Abelard. Shifting the traditional language of renunciation from its "position of mastery,"[73] Heloise presents an alternative and equally valid vocabulary by which one can achieve true "love of God." In this alternative position, Heloise moves from a spirituality that focuses on "liberation from desire" to that which values the "liberation of desire."[74] As Black's analysis of desire suggests: "The former is insatiable self [promoting ego], compulsive, addictive, and gives desire a bad name. The latter gives one's story a chance to move on. Risk, in

---

[70] Cf. *Ep.* 2, ed. Hicks 47 (trans. Radice, 49).
[71] *Ep.* 6, ed. Hicks, 106 (trans. Radice, 111).
[72] Graham Ward, "Divinity and Sexuality: Luce Irigaray and Christology," 228–29.
[73] A term used throughout by Irigaray, *This Sex Which Is Not One*.
[74] I have borrowed the naming of these two positions from Sebastian Moore, *Jesus the Liberator of Desire* (New York: Crossroad, 1989), 92.

fact, is the refusal to forget desire."[75] Heloise risks this freedom of desire and in so doing expands her desires through her personal issues to those of the larger female body, the community. Heloise's recognition of desire brought life to both her and her community, whereas in running away in denial of the love born of desire, Abelard bred only strife for himself in his failed attempts to be a monastic leader of his age.[76]

This love which Heloise positions as primary, is achieved not through the repression of other loves but through their incorporation into "Love" itself, a love that Heloise has shown to be humble in its honest expression, embodied in its context, and selfless and disinterested in its orientation, and stubbornly refuses to be denied. Here is a spirituality that finds integrity for the human person's desire to love, in and through our essential embodiment. It is a spirituality that Timmerman appeals to when she states:

> It is not the renunciatory lifestyle that produces grace, but the response to grace that takes forms sometimes of detachment and sometimes of attachment. In the history of spirituality, perhaps because it was largely written or censored by men, perhaps because of the exegetical tradition, letting go, detachment, has been interpreted to have greater intrinsic value. But the movements of the Spirit toward embodiment, engagement, or taking hold are fruit equally of grace.[77]

This voice of a monastic woman from the twelfth century is not one that should shame us or confuse our understanding of the spiritual quest. Heloise's position frees us from that "master discourse" that is so pervasive of our expression and all too obvious in the unhealthy and dangerous results of sexual repression that plague the religious world in particular and the wider world in general to this day. Heloise enables the re-imagining of human desires in a feminine key, a key that does not repress, but rather harmonizes the spiritual and the material dimensions of human love in the pursuit of Christian integrity.

Irigaray makes the claim that "Feminine pleasure has to remain inarticulate in language, in its own language, if it is not to threaten the underpinnings of logical operations [i.e., male speech]. And so what is most strictly forbidden to women today is that they should attempt to express their own pleasure."[78] That Heloise should dare to attempt to express her own pleasure, her desires and those

---

[75] Peter Black, "The Broken Wings of Eros: Christian Ethics and the Denial of Desire," *Theological Studies* 64,1 (2003): 106–26; here 118.

[76] Cf. ibid., 126. For a modern perspective on this relationship, see the fictional text by Luise Rinser, *Abelard's Love* (1991). For a critical study of this novel, see Albrecht Classen, "Abelard and Heloise's Love Story from the Perspective of their Son Astrolabe: Luise Rinser's Novel *Abelard's Love,*" *Journal of the Rocky Mountain Modern Language Association* 57, 1 (2003): 9–31.

[77] Timmerman, *Sexuality and Spiritual Growth*, 33.

[78] Irigaray, *This Sex Which Is Not One*, 77.

of her female community, or that we should dare to interpret those pleasures and
desires as constitutive of her Christian identity, is to dare to have a different "Love
of Words" so as to speak in different "Words of Love," words that are the "love of
God," in, through, and with our bodies.

CHAPTER 6

THE 'SIC ET NON' OF ANDREAS CAPELLANUS'S *DE AMORE*

BONNIE WHEELER
Southern Methodist University, Dallas

Is there any work that explores that high medieval play on 'words of love' and 'love of words' more explicitly than does Andreas Capellanus's love treatise *De Amore*?[1] Andreas's passionate love-casuistry is verbally dazzling, but readers are reasonably mystified by the combination of vehement attachment and violent contempt with which the cleric figures heterosexual human love. In the first two of his tract's three books, Andreas is conventionally thought to embrace the value of human love when he explores what love is, and how it is to be sought, achieved, and sustained. In his third book, however, he reviles heterosexual passion in favor of male homosociality and (better yet) the love of God. Many scholars find an absolute cleavage between the first two books and the final one, variously describing Andreas's only known work as a codex of so-called "courtly love," inconsistent, ironic, scholastic, or satirical.[2]

---

[1] I use *De Amore* as the treatise's easiest standard title. This first segment of this essay was presented as "Andreas's *Sic et Non*" at a 1990 Kalamazoo session with Don Monson. York University and the Pontifical Institute of Medieval Studies at the University of Toronto kindly invited me to lecture on Andreas's use of nuptial imagery. I am indebted to Albrecht Classen, not only for his incisive recent work on Andreas (very much in the vein of this essay) in *Verzweiflung und Hoffnung: Die Suche nach der kommunikativen Gemeinschaft in der deutschen Literatur des Mittelalters*. Beihefte zur Mediaevistik, 1 (Frankfurt a. M. et al.: Peter Lang, 2002), esp. sec. 2.14 and sec. 2.20, but also for his organization of this volume and his patience with this contributor. I am pleased that a book-length study, Kathleen Andersen-Wyman's *Andreas Capellanus on Love? Desire, Seduction and Subversion in a Twelfth Century Latin Text*, will soon appear in my book series, Studies in Arthurian and Courtly Cultures (New York: Palgrave Macmillan, forthcoming).

[2] This includes Don A. Monson, *Andreas Capellanus, Scholasticism, and the Courtly Tradition* (Washington, DC: The Catholic University Press, 2005). Only by the *De Amore* is Andreas known to us; his dates are elusive. He may have been, as the scholarly tradition used to assume, one André listed in records of the court of Countess Marie of Champagne (1145–98), daughter of Eleanor of Aquitaine

It is not just modern readers who find Andreas troubling. To his famous Condemnation of 1277, Étienne Tempier, bishop of Paris, appended an inexplicit denunciation of the *De Amore*. We still speculate about *why* a tract that advocates the love of God above the love of women was judged so dangerous. Hints may be found in Tempier's own words:

> We have received frequent reports, inspired by zeal for the faith, on the part of important and serious persons to the effect that some students of the arts treat and discuss, as if they were debatable in the schools, certain obvious and loathsome errors, or rather vanities and lying follies [Ps. 39:5], which are contained in the roll joined to this letter.... For they say that these things are true according to philosophy but not according to the Catholic faith, as if there were two contrary truths and as if the truth of Sacred Scripture were contradicted by the truth in the sayings of the accursed pagans.... By this same sentence of ours we also condemn the book *De Amore*, or *De Deo Amoris*, which begins with the words *Cogit me multum*, and so on, and ends with the words, *Cave, igitur, Galtere, amoris exercere mandata*, and so on.[3]

Recent scholars seize upon Tempier's perception of "contrary truths" to rationalize the bishop's attempted extirpation of Andreas, just as past scholars found sufficient rationale in Andreas's problematic "morals."[4] Helen Solterer surmises that Tempier thought "the danger lay in representing (falsely) the subject of mastering women as a reputable clerical concern."[5] The appeal to pagan authority deepened

---

and Louis VII of France, and the second wife of Count Henry the Liberal, who ruled that cosmopolitan principality between 1152 and 1181; he may thus have been the earliest theorist of *fin'amors*: see J.F. Benton, "The Court of Champagne as a Literary Center," *Speculum* 36, 4 (1961): 551–91. He may, however, have written a generation or two later, in the Paris of Philip Augustus (1180–1223), for an audience shaped by the bumptiously assertive clerical culture of the young University of Paris, and he may have been satirizing romantic love and aristocratic lay culture rather than proposing anything in the way of a theory: see John Baldwin, *The Language of Sex: Five Voices from Northern France around 1200*. The Chicago Series on Sexuality, History, and Society (Chicago and London: The University of Chicago Press, 1994). Alternately, he may have written even later, perhaps around 1230, and chosen the *nom de plume* Andreas because of a poem, now lost, recounting the love of one Andreas of Paris for the hopelessly exalted Queen of France: see Peter Dronke, "Andreas Capellanus," *The Journal of Medieval Latin* 4 (1994): 51–63. Consult Monson, *Andreas Capellanus*, for fuller bibliographical details than found in this essay.

[3] For Tempier, see *La condemnation parisienne de 1277*, nouvelle édition du texte latin, traduction, introduction et commentaire par David Piché; par la collaboration de Claude Lafleu (Paris: Vrin, 1999).

[4] Yet in 1290 Drouart la Vache found Andreas's Latin treatise so amusing that he undertook to translate it into French. See Robert Bossuat, *Li libres d'amours de Drouart la Vache* (Paris: Champion, 1926) and D. W. Robertson, *A Preface to Chaucer: Studies in Medieval Perspectives* (Princeton: Princeton University Press, 1962), 400. For analysis of scholarship on double or contrary truths, see Catherine Brown's indispensable *Contrary Things: Exegesis, Dialectic, and the Poetics of Didacticism*, Figurae: Reading Medieval Culture (Stanford: Stanford University Press, 1998).

[5] Helen Solterer, *The Master and Minerva: Disputing Women in French Medieval Culture* (Berkeley: University of California Press, 1995), 42.

The 'Sic et Non' of De Amore

the problem, since the "banter between male/female speakers" in a "playful ... Ovidian ... dialogue between men and women"[6] was far from exemplary as a matter of method in schools dedicated to the training of clergymen. Catherine Brown remarks that Tempier "was certainly correct, for the *De Amore*'s fictionalization of truth makes it not ultimate referent but textual effect."[7] Brown's insight acknowledges one pole of this baffling exercise of truth's complicity with rhetoric — in Andreas's case, the fictive rhetorical assertion of clerical masculinity. Like Abelard, another northern French cleric, the author we know as Andreas Capellanus chose dialectic as the central strategy for his assertion of masculine power.[8] Tempier, I suggest, played the role of Abelard's Bernard of Clairvaux to Andreas: both judges found orthodoxy itself threatened by dialectical multiplicity. Further, in such judges' view, virtuous orthodoxy and the pursuit of sexual passion were antithetical — unless passion cross-dressed in the nuptial metaphorics of spiritual rapture.

The twelfth century celebrated, as have few other moments in recorded Western history, sacred and sexual desire as inspiration and goal. The paradigm of human heterosexual love ordered internal and external quests for meaning.[9] Secular currents of thought bound together the ancient view — of sexually passionate love as a form of pathological suffering — with a new view of such passion as therapeutic and ennobling. In the context of the Christian ethical tradition, desire was to be regulated and swiftly channeled to spiritual goals. The mystical traditions wrapped fleshly passions into allegorized spiritual yearnings. Andreas implodes these ideas of passion, and perhaps this helps explain why Tempier disapproved. The bishop may have noticed how Andreas subverts established paradigms of theological as well as socio-sexual discourse by exposing their premises. From the first to the final clauses of the *De Amore*, Andreas both solicits and undermines desire.

Andreas no more defends *fin'amors* in the first books than he defames it in the third. Those who lump Books One and Two together as celebrations of love ineluctably mark out the final book as an anomaly, but I seek here to demonstrate that all three books together constitute a warning to Walter and other readers to recognize love's attractions and fear love's costs. Book Three maintains the work's intellectual thrust: Andreas plunders available traditions simultaneously to posit and undermine each of his assertions. With Andreas, it is always yes *and* no. In this essay, after reflections on the tract's dialectical structure, I consider each of

---

[6] Solterer, *The Master and Minerva*, 36.

[7] Brown, *Contrary Things*, 109.

[8] On Abelard and clerical masculinity, see Bonnie Wheeler, "Origenary Fantasies: Abelard's Castration and Confession," *Becoming Male in the Middle Ages*, ed. Jeffrey Jerome Cohen and eadem. The New Middle Ages, 4 (New York: Garland, 1997), 109–28.

[9] See the contribution by Carmel Posa to this volume.

Andreas's three books in turn as I push toward my final point about Andreas's probe into the traditional parable of the Wise and Foolish Virgins.

The *De Amore* is a specialist's unfolding display of various disciplines that compose the clerical trades. And not mere display: this deconstructionist fantasy is a "sic et non" that reveals simultaneously the limits of the tools of the trade. The witty master uses the subject of passion as the provocation for a set-text on the *trivium*. The *trivium* training of Book One gives way to the logical, legal, and fictive mechanics of Book Two, and then to the homiletic and theological modes of Book Three.

The tract's three books approach love and desire from different disciplinary modes that embody dialectic in practice. From the grammar of love to its varieties of oratory, the whole is suffused by dialectic in the Abelardian mode.[10] Scholastic synthesis, required from Gratian (1140) onward — indeed, since the *Panormia* of Ivo of Chartres — is absent in Andreas just as it is in Abelard's *Sic et Non*. Each book of the *De Amore* generates its own "sic et non" as each book contains and unmasks its own position. Why? Abelard argues that "by doubting we come to inquiry, and by inquiry we perceive truth."[11] As Haskins succinctly states, "the stimulating of discussion among his pupils seems to have been Abaelard's primary object, but the emphasis upon contradiction rather than upon agreement and the failure to furnish any solutions, real or superficial, tended powerfully to expose the weaknesses in the orthodox position and to undermine authority generally."[12]

Andreas's three books together stand as a collation of discordant responses and advice, played out in shifting rhetoric between dueling sexes and classes. One interpretive problem lies in reading the work as "aut sic aut non"[13] rather than by Abelard's formulation, "sic et non," both the one and the other. Understanding does not require synthesis; the meaning that issues from Abelardian

---

[10] *Petri Abælardi Opera*, ed. Victor Cousin, 2 vols. (Paris: A. Durand, 1849–1851); Peter Abailard, *Sic et Non: A Critical Edition*, ed. Blanche Boyer and Richard McKeon, 7 fascicles (Chicago: University of Chicago Press, 1976–1977); an abbreviated English translation an be found at http://www.fordham.edu/halsall/source/1120abelard.html (last accessed February 28, 2006). On Andreas's Abelardian dialectic, see Tony Hunt, "Aristotle, Dialectic, and Courtly Literature," *Viator* 10 (1979): 95–129; N. De Paepe, "'Amor' und 'verus amor' bei Andreas Capellanus," *Mélanges offerts à René Crozet . . . à l' occasion de son 70 anniversaire, par ses amis, ses collèques, ses élèves*, ed. Pierre Gallais and Yves-Jean Rion. Cahiers de civilisation médiévale, 2 vols. (Poitiers: Société d' études médiévales, 1966), 2:911–17.

[11] Abailard, *Sic et Non*, ed. Boyer and McKeon, 1:89.

[12] Charles Homer Haskins, *The Renaissance of the 12th Century* (Cambridge, MA: Harvard University Press, 1927; repr. Meridian Book [Cleveland: World Publishing Company, 1957]), 355.

[13] Brown, *Contrary Things*, 93–94, views the *De Amore* as a "kind of summa" that results from Andreas's compilation of "all the pertinent opinions on any given question." She concludes that the *De Amore*'s "endlessly provocative structure . . . forces one to respond to its doctrine 'aut sic et non.'" But I disagree that "Abelardian hermeneutic rules offer little help in a text like this, in which opposing propositions are at once mutually exclusive and mutually coimplicated" since I think this is Abelard's and Andreas's shared technique.

dialectic — including Andreas's version in the *De Amore* — relies on the sustained preservation of multiple possibilities. Access to greater truth or meaning paradoxically requires destabilization so as to admit the simultaneous presence of contradictory positions: pure dialectic not based on the need for synthesis allows readers to celebrate truth in difference.[14]

This didactic, purportedly systematic, exploration of the nature, practices, and rules of love is a mosaic composed of stones quarried from texts of various sorts — etymological, oratorical, amatory, philosophical, juridical, folkloric, religious, and mystical — from Ovid forward, but particularly indebted to the clerical production of its own cultural mores.[15] Not surprisingly, the treatise emerges from a cultural nexus that forged public institutional life: the elevation of the clerical class and the exclusion of women were powerfully yoked. This tract on love is also a sustained meditation on the strategies by which the male 'chattering classes' gain masculine empowerment in the increasingly stratified culture of high medieval France.[16] The *De Amore* is a useful social document: in its ineluctably gendered disputation between men and women, the tract also provides a snapshot of the clerical struggle for status.

Andreas's application of dialectic alternates "yes" and "no," unfastening unitary truths while dissecting desire in parsing the human games of love. Love is consequently always represented as unachieved: desire is motion that ends when the object of love is achieved. Hence desire, like Abelardian dialectic, must not come to rest or it will lose its meaning and force. Andreas's passionate words of seduction — simultaneous panegyric and threat — reflexively praise the speaker as much as the recipient. In Book One, Andreas's lovers neither succeed nor admit total defeat — and they are rarely categorically repulsed. Desire thrives between the "yes" and the "no," and dies only when presented absolute affirmation or rejection: passion is an ideal subject to demonstrate intellectual motility.

---

[14] Hunt, "Aristotle, Dialectic, and Courtly Literature," 104, urges an evaluation of Andreas's treatise in accord with Abelard's methods to determine "whether its principal significance lies in the rhetorical expression of truth or the intellectual stimulus to he pursuit of truth, hence whether it leads to affirmation or interrogation."

[15] To place Andreas in fuller European Ovidian context, consult Anna Marie Finoli, *Artes Amandi da Maître Elie ad Andrea Capellano* (Milano-Varese: Istituto editoriale cisalpine, 1969); Ingeborg Glier, *Artes amandi: Untersuchung zu Geschichte, Überlieferung und Typologie der deutschen Minnereden*. Münchener Texte und Untersuchungen zur deutschen Literatur des Mittelalters, 34 (Munich: Beck, 1971), and Dronke, "Andreas Capellanus."

[16] Constance Brittain Bouchard argues that the "chief difficulty with seeing [this] work as a description of love among the aristocracy is that it was written at least in part as a sophisticated satire on both his society and recent intellectual trends . . . [and] as a commentary on the then-current vogue for scholastic argumentation and categorization, as well as on the romances that were becoming popular in his time. . . . [The work] makes much more sense as a parody of the scholastic method of argumentation, in which the philosopher or legal scholar was required to provide arguments both for and against a proposition," *"Strong of Body, Brave and Noble": Chivalry and Society in Medieval France* (Ithaca and London: Cornell University Press, 1998), 141.

Are words of love Andreas's subject? Yes. Is love of words his subject? Yes. In his Preface, Andreas quickly expresses anxiety about amatory love. Consistently casting love in terms of warfare, slavery, and suffering that threatens men by causing them anxiety and forfeit of free will, Andreas only reluctantly — and for the sake of his affection and concern for his friend Walter — agrees to compose the treatise:

> I cannot express to you in words the seriousness of this situation, and the mental anxiety it causes me.... So though dwelling on such topics seems hardly advisable, and though the man of sense shows impropriety in making time for such hunting as this, the affection that binds us makes me utterly unable to oppose your request.[17]

Andreas opens Book One by defining his system for analyzing love: "First we must see what love is, why it is so called, and its effect; between what persons it can exist; how it can be obtained, kept, increased, diminished, and ended; how reciprocated love is recognized; and what one lover should do if the other is untrue" (33). The definition of love as suffering is reinforced and undermined by cunningly defective etymology.[18] Rubrication tightly follows standard scholastic mode.[19] Yet despite its ubiquitous categorization, the *De Amore* challenges the very order it asserts. Andreas's courtship principle is clear: words do it. "Eloquence of speech frequently impels the hearts of indifferent persons to love. The adorned language of a lover usually unleashes love's darts; it creates a good impression about the speaker's moral worth. I shall take the trouble to explain to you as briefly as I can how this takes place" (45). His instructions center on how men choose rhetorical strategies; to be competently masculine is to manipulate rhetoric. This notion of rhetorical substantiality is consistent throughout the *De Amore*: true masculine power is the ability to arrange words into a reality that obscures what is undesirable or detrimental, and propels its audience into compliance. Whether overtly dominant or apparently collaborative, this clerical style of control necessitates complicity between clerics and women, which thus instantiates the clerics' defective masculinity *vis-à-vis* their knightly counterparts.

Andreas faces a critical problem: in a culture in which power belongs to the warrior male, how can non-warriors — particularly unmarried clerics — be manly

---

[17] *Andreas Capellanus On Love*, ed. and trans. P. G. Walsh. Duckworth Classical, Medieval, and Renaissance Editions (London: Duckworth, 1982), 31. All in-text references refer to this parallel-text edition by page number; with few exceptions, space limits require use of English translations.

[18] Paolo Cherchi, *Andreas and the Ambiguity of Courtly Love*. Toronto Italian Studies (Toronto and Buffalo: University of Toronto Press, 1994), 28–29, cites Andreas's use of contemporary medical authorities rather than Ovid or patristic sources on love as *passio*, suffering, a breach or a wound. Intense meditation precipitates the speaker-sufferer into a narrative of pathological desire; for reasons perhaps as prophylactic as rhetorical, story replaces sex.

[19] "Quid," "quis," and "qualiter," as Baldwin notes: *The Language of Sex*, 17.

and hence claim manly empowerment? Andreas's answer is identical to Abelard's: wield rhetoric as a singing sword. For Andreas, rhetorical control is a condition for manhood. The *De Amore* exposes, sometimes quite explicitly, the overriding anxiety of Andreas's professional class *vis-à-vis* the most highly privileged sector of the twelfth-century elite, and it also presents a strategy for achieving control of its insecure situation. The technology of this strategy is the manipulation of rhetorical finesse, with the objective of establishing complicity with women who, once subdued, will be erased — an exploitative alliance seething with misogyny. Andrew Taylor points out that for Abelard's contemporaries "the ritualized violence of disputation provided an alternative to actual physical violence."[20] For medieval European clerics, initiation to rhetorical disputation functioned as a male rite of passage.[21]

Disproportionately meager lines are given to illustrations of love in Book One, though it reads as a handbook for gender-appropriate speech, defining acceptable male and females roles through witty thrust and parry. Games of love are proving grounds for an assertive masculinity and defensive femininity. Yet if men achieve full manliness not by war or physical ardor but when they learn to control women by rhetorical splendor, then there is no man in this text. In Book One, women remain uncontrolled, defensive, but quite capable of parrying the verbal thrustsof their interlocutors.

The dialogues of Book One stand as the centerpiece of the treatise and constitute more than half of the whole tract. A strict division of social class orders the eight dialogues, and Andreas presents an unequivocal basis for structuring the dialogues in this manner: "Women belong either to the common stock or to the nobility or higher nobility. So too with men — they are either common, or noble, or of the higher nobility, or of the highest nobility" (17).[22] Such rules of social ranking, like rules of love, are Andreas's inventions. He generalizes in order to define, ironically setting absolutes that are themselves plagued with contradictions and inconsistencies: "[A] man attached to a wife who is more or less noble than himself does not change his rank, whereas a woman bound to a husband changes her

---

[20] Andrew Taylor, "A Second Ajax: Peter Abelard and the Violence of Dialectic," *The Tongue of the Fathers: Gender and Ideology in Twelfth-Century Latin*, ed. David Townsend and idem. The Middle Ages Series (Philadelphia: University of Pennsylvania Press, 1998), 14–34; here 29–30. See also Jo Ann McNamara, "The *Herrenfrage*: The Restructuring of the Gender System, 1050–1150," *Medieval Masculinities: Regarding Men in the Middle Ages*, ed. Clare A. Lees, with assistance of Thelma Fenster and Jo Ann McNamara. Medieval Cultures 7 (Minneapolis: University of Minnesota Press, 1994), 3–31.

[21] Abelard's adult description of his adolescent choice of an intellectual career is the classic instance: "I gave up completely the court of Mars so as to be brought up in the lap of Minerva.... I put the conflicts of the disputation over and above the trophies of combat," *History of My Calamities: The Letters of Abelard and Heloise*, trans. Betty Radice (London and New York: Penguin, 1974), 58.

[22] Cherchi, *Andreas and the Ambiguity of Courtly Love*, 33, recognizes Andreas's limited system of social mobility: "[W]hile for men there is no social mobility, for women it is possible to move on the social ladder just by marrying someone of different rank."

nobility according to his rank. A male's nobility can never be changed by marriage with a woman" (47). Andreas adds the partition of gender to his taxonomy of rank, both revealing and creating social imperatives generated by the gap between male and female.

Gender opposition is not simply for Andreas a grammatical given: he takes care to label his male interlocutors *homines,* the generic term for the human being, not *viri,* the specific term for the masculine gender. Their female respondents are *mulieres,* possessing simply their sub-general specificity of their grammatical gender. In such a system, which assumes not difference but identity as normative, the female falls under the category of the non-normative, even the abnormal.[23] This grammatical premise expresses itself in Andreas's treatment of women as if they are devoid of desire, but perfect receptacles for it: such an object — at once grammatical and rhetorical — is the Lady as Andreas invents her. Men love; women are loved.

Andreas's "sic et non" persists: though he highlights a social system with an inflexible, one-way mobility, his statements about rank also contradict his assertions of gender interaction. A woman, according to Andreas, has no power to effect a change in rank either for herself or for a man. Furthermore, a woman's own status is strictly defined by the men to whom, whether through blood or matrimony, she is connected. Andreas describes social determinants of female rank: "The common woman requires no explanation. The noble woman is descended from the blood of a vavasour or lord, or is the wife of one of these. The woman of higher nobility is so called if she is the daughter of a line of lords" (47). A man may be stranded in the social station to which he is born, but at least he possesses the power to alter the standing of the woman he marries.

Regardless of social class, a man has the prerogative of speech: in the dialogues, even a common man has the right to address a noble lady and attempt to persuade her with his words. A man should develop his command of rhetoric in order to attain his desires, but, as he recommends this strategy, Andreas exposes its falsity as a linguistic game. The text, like Penelope's weavings and lover's pleadings, is full of making and unmaking.

The treatise's ostensible recipient is a man who has asked for instruction on how to approach a woman; correspondingly, the dialogues are invariably initiated by the male: "*homo ait*" always precedes "*mulier ait.*" In the tradition of debate poems, Andreas's male speaker has the right to address a woman who speaks only in reply. Andreas imitates conventions in which language serves as a

---

[23] For a rich study of grammar and gender, see Jan Ziolkowski, *Alan of Lille's Grammar of Sex: The Meaning of Grammar to a Twelfth-Century Intellectual.* Speculum Anniversary Monographs, 10 (Cambridge, MA: The Medieval Academy of America, 1985).

masculine tool of aggression and a feminine mode of defense.[24] The odd relationship between gender and social class is revealed in the male privilege that allows even the common man to address the lady of highest nobility. She, conversely, responds to him only after his commencing words have activated her voice, but no woman refuses to respond. Helen Solterer discusses the literary *topos* of the woman respondent in the Provençal *tenso* which also depicts "the woman . . . in a position of resisting the man's onslaught."[25] Women in the *De Amore* are no more "disembodied voices"[26] than are men. Dialectic dialogues keep the air crackling with tension: word may substitute for action, but no man succeeds, no woman submits. Andreas's women successfully defend themselves against the male offensive: none of the women assent to the requests put to them by male speakers.

Andreas invents the notion of class as we moderns understand it just as he styles ideas about gender.[27] His discourse is gendered by such questions as: What must men do (or say) to appear manly? And how must women behave to appear womanly? But he also refines questions about social class: What postures are appropriate for men and women of different social classes? He notably places clerics at the top of the social structure: "[W]e find one rank more in men than in women, because there is one type of man of the highest nobility, for example the cleric" (47).

The effeminate cleric stands in stark opposition to the manly warrior. The man of higher nobility, now in the role of a cleric, seeks to counter the woman's charges of effeminacy and redeem — even exalt — his profession. First he defends the clerics against those who disqualify them from the games of love. Even clerics, he asserts, are "subject to the temptations of the flesh like other men." This susceptibility supposedly validates his love suit. "This is why, if I seek the love of some woman, she cannot reject me on the excuse that I am a cleric. No, I shall prove to you with irrefutable logic that the cleric should be chosen for love in preference to a layman" (185). In one sentence the speaker demotes himself to the common mortal weaknesses of the laity, and in the following (a dialectical pronouncement

---

[24] Toril Moi, "Desire in Language: Andreas Capellanus and the Controversy of Courtly Love," *Medieval Literature: Criticism, Ideology, and History*, ed. David Aers (New York: St. Martin's Press, 1986), 11–33; here 23–24, observes that "it is the lover who does most of the talking: the lady, although obviously capable of a quick repartee, limits her remarks to shrewd criticism of the lover's points, and hardly ever instigates new topics of her own,"

[25] Solterer, *The Master and Minerva*, 7.

[26] Michael Calabrese, "Ovid and the Female Voice in the *De Amore* and the Letters of Abelard and Heloise," *Modern Philology* 95, 1 (August 1997): 1–26; here 15, proposes what I take to be one pole of interpretation of Andreas's women. He understands the women's voices as both radically empowered and indicative of "medieval clerical imaginings of women's language, moral capabilities, and relations to men."

[27] For an amusing American view of class, see Paul Fussell, *Class: A Guide through the American Status System* (New York: Simon & Schuster, 1992), which shows how uneasy modern academics and intellectuals are about social placement.

made possible by the flaws assumed in the first sentence), he exalts his group as not only eligible but superior lovers. The cleric's tongue translates the knight, usually the embodiment of courtly virtues and manly prowess, into a tainted, second-class man. Fighting no longer stands as an essential indicator of masculinity, although the noble woman contends that a man must be prepared "to show fierceness against those who war on him, delight at the varying strains of battle, and application to the grinding toil of wars" (185). Instead, the activity of warfare blights potential masculine clerical perfection:

> As for fighting battles, God has forbidden us to do this, so as to keep our hands ever innocent of bloodshed, and so that we may not be rejected from His service as unworthy because we have shed blood. The man polluted by bloodshed is rejected from God's service. (189)

Through this verbal oscillation, the man of highest nobility upturns the noble woman's charge. He has equalized the cleric and the warrior as subjects that are desiring and thus sufficiently masculine to be considered eligible lovers. What stands between the cleric and the warrior is no longer the warrior's superior prowess, but the cleric's superior spiritual dedication. The warrior is somehow fatally flawed in this respect. According to this disputant's reasoning, the warrior is less worthy of a woman's love, just as one seeking to serve God would be rejected because tainted by the blood of battle. The cleric slyly qualifies his excuse for refusing martial activity: "If this reason did not prevent me, nothing in the world would be more pleasant for me than to practise deeds of war and show my boldness of heart" (189). So the cleric shares the warrior's masculine yearnings for battle. By his greater strength and dedication to God's service, however, he restrains these desires. The shared desire for women, however, does not need to be subdued.

The cleric is further exalted by his superior study. Having learned the lessons of scripture, the "cleric is seen to be more careful and wise in all things than the layman. He orders himself and his affairs with greater control, and is accustomed to governing everything with more fitting measure; because he is a cleric he has knowledge of all things, since scripture gives him this expertise. So his love is accounted better than the layman's, because nothing on earth is established to be so vital as that the lover should have experience in diligent application to all things" (185). This statement completes the transvaluation of martial prowess into learned pursuits, while the assertion of clerical omniscience, "knowledge of all things," also bolsters Andreas's own credibility as an authority on love. Simultaneously, Andreas's credibility is undermined since he speaks as a self-aggrandizing codifier whose ventures in sexual love are incongruous in relation to his supposed vocation.[28]

For Lacan, courtly love is a masculine game played in the absence of real sexual relationships with women, a sort of fantasy-world for men, complete with a built-in guarantee that desire will continue: the result is the non-definitive "no." As in classic patriarchal systems, Andreas's men have the power to choose, act, and speak, and women the power to postpone submission. Even the commoner in the second dialogue of Book One refuses to take a woman's rejection as a definitive answer. "In spite of your dismissive words," he says, "I shall not abandon my designs on your love as long as I live" (114). Attempted rejection is not definitive but serves to heighten desire.

Duration of speech is a reflex of class: social scale is replicated in verbal scale as both men and women in upper social registers demonstrate virtuoso capacities to sustain prolonged conversations about positions they will not assume. None of the dialogues result in acceptance of the suitor. If, therefore, Book One is (as advertised) an exercise in how love is obtained, it is notably unsuccessful. What is obtained is conversation, discourse about desire, about the need for male empowerment and female submission.[29] The dialectic strategies of Book One maintain a double thrust on the nature of proper argument and on the ostensible subject of love. The 'order of right reason' and procedures for proper argument pre-empt sentimental sighs in Book One's love talk. The discourse of love and all its rules obscure the physical gap between the desiring subject and his desired object, resulting in what Lacan calls "an altogether refined way of making up for the absence of sexual relations by pretending that it is we who put an obstacle to it."[30] It is thus a tactic not dissimilar to Freud's *fort/da* game — and, of course, Abelardian disputation — in which a difficulty is generated in order for the vulnerable ego to gain control. Moi interprets Andreas's figuration of love as an even more exclusive power struggle. The male speaker wages an artificial war that he has created *himself*, and he uses language as his weapon.[31] In this view, the woman is completely eclipsed from the equation, leaving the man narcissistically struggling to command his words in order to attain mastery altogether separate from the power that a woman can grant him.

---

[28] For other instances of Andreas's self-reference, see *De Amore*, 117, 153.

[29] Michael Cherniss, "The Literary Comedy of Andreas Capellanus," *Modern Philology* 72 (1975): 223–37; here 233, remarks that "in courtly literature it is at least assumed that the suitor will prove his *probitas* by his deeds, while here verbal facility is supposedly all success required."

[30] Jacques Lacan, *Female Sexuality: Jacques Lacan and the école freudienne*, ed. Juliet Mitchell and Jacqueline Rose (New York: W. W. Norton, Pantheon Books, 1982), 141.

[31] "By dominating the word, [the lover] gains a phallic power that contradicts his seemingly humble stance toward the lady. This mastery is only achieved, however, by the most humble submission to the inflexible rules of scholastic rhetoric," Moi, "Desire in Language," 24.

Yet it is compelling to conjure the other end of the dialectical imaginary: perhaps Lacan is only partially right. Courtly love may not merely be the displacement of sexuality into discourse but also the placement of discourse into sexuality. Talking is pleasurable: the discourse of desire sets (at least) its male speaker on the cusp of gratification. If women are ferociously mocked, they are also adored. If women are complicit, they are also unsubmissive. The superiority of the male masters is never really in doubt (despite the servant masks they wear), and the narcissism of the male covers a blatantly rhetorical game. But, like all games, it does more than merely pass the time. Andreas plays misogynistic tricks. Equal in the dialectic, however, is his celebration of passion as a life-sustaining goal.

The method conflates convention and nature, but, by the codification of purportedly natural distinctions as speech lessons, Andreas exposes the dialectical method by which the unnatural is naturalized. His male lovers grant an elevated position to the women with whom they carry on conversation so long as they participate in the discourse of desire. Even the man of higher nobility tells the common girl that he is at her mercy:

> I pray with full confidence that your decision may do me no injustice. For whilst it is true that no man can fully manifest to a lady (*alicui*) his honourable intentions, it is equally the case that any woman (*quaelibet mulier*) may reject a suitor, whoever he may be (125).

If a woman, however, attempts to reject a suitor, the man verbally threatens and manipulates her. The noblewoman laboring to reject the nobleman in the fifth dialogue of Book One anticipates Andreas's final position in Book Three:

> It is very easy to discover the entrance to the court of Love, yet difficult to abide there, because of the pains poised above lovers; but people find it impossible and insuperably hard to leave because of the acts of love which they crave. Once he has truly entered Love's court, a lover can say yea or nay to nothing except the fare placed before him on Love's table, and that which can please his partner in love. So a court of that kind we should not approach; we should totally avoid entering such a place from which it is not possible to leave freely.... Hence the court of Love is rightly hateful to my eyes, so you, my brother, must seek love elsewhere (101).

In reply, the male suitor presents an image of the Palace of Love with its zones of Pleasance, Wetness, and Dryness, describing in pointed physical detail the fate of "unnatural" women who refuse to cooperate with masculine desire. Faced with these hellish tortures, the noblewoman seemingly changes her mind:

> If your assertion is true, it is a splendid thing to devote oneself to the services of Love and highly dangerous to set oneself against his commands. So

The 'Sic et Non' of De Amore

> whether your account is true or false, your narrative of fearful punishment terrifies me. Accordingly, I do not wish to remain outside the army of Love, but to be joined in his devoted company, and to find myself a home at the southern gate .... Therefore I shall take pains to discover the man who is worthy to enter, and once I have pondered and discovered the truth, I shall let him in (119).

Through fear, the feminine is contained, naturalized into acquiescence: the 'Lady' who submits to desire is divorced from the Woman who experiences physical yearnings and sexual desire. Andreas did not invent this discursive posture, though he engraves 'ladylike' behaviors more deeply than did the literary traditions on which he drew. As the man of higher nobility affirmed early in his debate with a common woman, "frigidity is dominant in a woman whereas in men there is a natural innate heat" (175). By an interesting projection, Andreas's game now imposes on these frigid ladies the exercise of the rhetorical rationality he seems at first to claim for the superior, normative male sex. As men incarnate the heat of nature, women must now embody several modes of cultural coolness. Women must first counter male lustfulness with modesty, then impose the requirements of economic rationality (is there enough money?) and of social hierarchy. If she is made to seem enigmatic or capricious, those variants of frigidity are simply misperceptions (*méconnaissances,* Foucault might say) of her cultural duty to lift up and civilize, even ennoble, male animality in this potential exchange.[32]

Whatever the social status of his interlocutors, Andreas's figuration of love does not fulfill his claim that love ennobles. Herein lies a fundamental inconsistency: Andreas's lovers declare that love is the origin and cause of all good, but Andreas himself has defined love as a *passio,* a disruptive and deforming suffering. How then can it be a cause of good? For modern readers, such love cannot be a final cause of anything good; indeed it must be nearly the contrary.[33] So what does Andreas mean when he and his characters speak of *amor*? Dronke has remarked how startlingly absent from Andreas's treatise is any idealization of the beloved, indeed, any statement of idealized love, so typical of the romance tradition as a whole:

> Insofar as his dialogues allude to such idealism at all, it is blatantly part of a seducer's strategy to get a woman into bed — there is not a trace of tenderness, or of reverence.... There is a coarsely cynical element in Andreas's text that determines the attitude to women, to love, and to ecclesiastical notions of morality.[34]

---

[32] Calabrese, "Ovid and the Female Voice," 15; Moi, "Desire in Language," 22.
[33] Cherchi, *Andreas and the Ambiguity of Courtly Love,* 37–38.
[34] Dronke, "Andreas Capellanus," 59–60.

These games of love-casuistry are irreverent, power-driven and frustrating, but I would argue that this is only part of the dialectical story. To perform well, men must seek and speak their desire to the all-judging Lady. Using flattery, evoking jealousy, but remaining generally well mannered, the lover spurs himself to deliver carefully practiced speeches — only to have the woman say, "Not yet." Female resistance in the dialogues conjures and deepens desire. The wound of Love in *De Amore* is in part emptiness, an opening that is filled by language. Literary seduction-games are sheer fraudulence, strict literary conventions, that are simultaneously evocative, self-revelatory, and akin to the fictive dimension of poetry. These games conjured into being a culture that subdued women while wooing them. That brand of culture taught all men, not just clerics, that their tongues and pens were sex organs. Such is the relentless power of imagination, even when Aphrodite goes missing.

Why do all of Andreas's lovers fail to secure the grace of their beloved women? In Book One, Andreas's lovers woo but do not win. There is no closure, no happy or unhappy ending. Is Andreas thus playing a cynical or comic game when he reveals the ruses by which men and women speak of sex in veiled terms? Many think so.[35] But I find a hard kernel here in the "sic": Desire remains inchoate (though sharply physical) until shaped by language: love casuistry then intensifies desire, and the dialectic of love and words continues its passionate cycle. Andreas displaces sex into language. None of his pairs agree to love, but merely to talk about it. Language rises from the crucible of gender and class to mediate human desire.[36]

Book Two crafts the same distinctions between the genders and social classes, but casts the amorous fiction juridically into precepts, precedents, court decisions, and secular exempla. Andreas projects a pretense of juridical resolution, evoking legal pronouncements as if law could resolve the complications of desire but simultaneously revealing the inability of legal pronouncements to harness a thing so slippery and mutable as desire.[37]

Andreas's plan in Book Two is set in a framework of failure. Love is found in the fissures. The blissful time of love falls in the gap between Books One and Two: no happy lovers frolic on the pages of the *De Amore*. Andreas occludes amatory success between the open-ended dialogues of Book One and the downward spin described in Book Two. Even the Arthurian quest, a tale in which readers expect

---

[35] Cherniss, "The Literary Comedy of Andreas Capellanus," 231, calls the dialogues "elaborate comic exercises in the rhetoric of flattery and persuasion."

[36] Classen, *Verzweiflung und Hoffnung*, 81–105, identifies this as the basis for the establishment of human communication, which in turn proves to be the fundamental condition for a constructive community.

[37] While Book Two is not a true legal treatise, it reflects a society increasingly ordered by legal procedures that depended on rhetoric and reason — empowering venues to which educated clerics like Andreas were naturally well suited, and in which they were becoming increasingly experienced. Juridical terms and concepts appear often, e.g., "obligata" (266), or breaking faith (233).

The 'Sic et Non' of De Amore 163

to find scenes of happy lovers, reinforces the deletion of amatory love: the hero successfully achieves his quest, but his beloved only cursorily grants him her love (Andreas gives no details) while the sensuous and unconquered — but beckoning — fairy-woman awaits him in the forest. Desire flees just as it comes within his grasp.

In Book One, Andreas demonstrated persuasive and coercive techniques by which men ingratiate themselves with women, aiming to achieve their compliance; now he turns to the matter of maintaining desire. Book Two is often mistaken as a "how-to-keep-her" handbook, as P. G. Walsh calls it. But, as it is titled in the manuscript, this is a study in how love can be sustained. Once women relent, how can men craft continued amatory interest? Once you have her, how do you manage to want her? In the first six sections of Book Two, Andreas details techniques for maintaining male desire from seemingly inevitable erosion. He toys with the ancient, paradoxical insight that the fulfillment of desire is its death. What he adds to this mix is another paradoxical insight about how to keep untrammeled desire alive through strict discipline. Just as the lovers fail in Book One, Andreas seems also to predict failure in Book Two.

The careful ordering of the stages of love's diminishment suggests that Andreas aimed to inscribe a prediction into his narrative: desire wanes despite the games — including his own precepts — contrived to perpetuate it. Yet Andreas's scenarios and recommendations are also laden with contradiction. There is never an unambiguous codification of a proper way to preserve a love affair. Instead Andreas strikingly presents the fine line between behaviors that advance love and those that destroy it. Even the juridical summary of love's thirty-one Rules of Love opposes much of Andreas's previous advice. This weirdly oscillating codification (oddly, the most frequently reproduced summary of what is taken to be "courtly love") summarizes Andreas's pretense of juridical resolution. On the one hand, "Love does not usually survive being noised abroad" (283), but on the other, Andreas states the contrary: "Each lover should also harp publicly on the praises of his partner" (225). How can such contradictions be resolved? Andreas entraps his lovers in rhetorical anxiety, placing them in between two courses of speech and speechlessness such that each hazards the possibility of failure. The impasse between singing praises and clandestine worship, like other oppositions in Book Two, is mediated by an injunction for moderation. But "it is not appropriate to make her name echo with windy, often repeated recollections of her." What is enough? What is too much? The intimation of precision amplifies rather than soothes a lover's apprehensions. A lover must have impeccable verbal finesse and social intuition, seeking exact amplitude while fearing he will miss the mark and be spurned for his artlessness.

Andreas's ladies are supposed to be powerful dispensers of gracious acceptance as well as objects of yearning adoration, but they do little such dispensing in Andreas's treatise. Book Two contains twenty-one cases of amatory disputes in the "time-honored clerical tradition of *jeux d'esprit*,"[38] purportedly arbitrated by royal ladies. This series of judgments presents Andreas's legalistic re-enactment of the Pleasance story in Book One: women who defy male desire are tortured. In Book Two, women are again punished, but this time their degradation is all the more bitter since it is other women who damn them. These judgments serve to bind men and women to desire through discourse, but also implicate women as co-conspirators against their own sex in Andreas's plan for clerical empowerment. In case after case, women make the wrong decisions: choosing the less worthy of two lovers, extending hope with no intention of granting love, rejecting a faithful lover for a new one, and greedily accepting gifts in the manner of harlots. Collectively the judgments construct a catalogue of bad women, presenting to Walter and other aspiring lovers the many sufferings inflicted by unjust women. The judgments also constitute a list of rules for women, proscribing behaviors that do not cooperate with male desire. These laws join the rhetoric of Book One as another means of disciplining women, all the while implicating women as both criminals and judges. The lady's necessary otherness embitters the male clerical voice, generating a form of jealousy among other negative emotions. Toril Moi argues that "however hard he tries to master her by his discourse, he will always suffer in the knowledge that her consciousness is not his.... The beloved becomes enigmatic precisely in so far as the lover perceives her as a secretive space which must at all costs be penetrated."[39] The analogy of penetration is polyvalent here: Andreas's lady must be available to the lover's gaze. Without her reflection, the lover's identity is at risk; unless she reflects his self-vision, he is in danger of extinction. Lovers need eyes so that they can see themselves reflected. In Andreas's dialogue and trial series female cooperation is required to constitute masculine identity and achievement.

The inevitable waning of desire is emblemized in the Arthurian tale that concludes Book Two. As in many romances, the British knight requires female aid to achieve the task assigned. "Briton," a lady tells him, "no effort of yours will ever be able to ascertain the object of your search unless you are supported by my help" (271). With her help, the knight wins a hawk through his deeds and obtains the scroll attached to the hawk's perch, on which are written the thirty-one rules of love. Taking the hawk obligates the knight to know and promulgate those rules;

---

[38] Dronke, "Andreas Capellanus," 56, notes that Andreas's figuration of Marie of Champagne "may be part of an elaborate game: the ascription of judgements on questions of love to Marie and other exalted ladies may be as much an invention as Andreas's ascription of such judgements to the god of love, Amor. The citing of fictitious authorities is particularly widespread and resourceful in the twelfth and early thirteenth centuries." Even in this *jeu d'esprit*, Andreas presses his female arbiters into service against female autonomy.

[39] Moi, "Desire in Language," 26.

The 'Sic et Non' of De Amore

once again, action becomes language, and the two together propel the beloved's submission. The rules of love are cited as the lessons distilled from all the love trials, a result of the knight's experience in male–female interaction. In this tale as in others, a successful quest seems to doom desire for the object of the quest. Andreas says that the lady who is the quest's object "rewarded his labours with her love" (285) and summons all to the ensuing sessions of the Arthurian court of love, which will guarantee the rules' universal promulgation. Yet desire seems to rest in the forest of adventure, with the helpful "girl endowed with wondrous beauty" who calls him "carissime" as she sends him back to "sweet Britain" with thirteen kisses and the promise that she'll always be there should he return alone (281). Is this the partitioning or the postponement of desire? Andreas typically has it both ways.

If in Book One Andreas appears as rhetorician and in Book Two as a possible familiar of the legal scene, in Book Three's "sic et non" he wields the cleric's ultimate weapon: hellfire and damnation. Here Andreas pumps up the homiletic and moral traditions. Thus he tells Walter that it pleases God if one does not exploit a chance to sin — that is, once Walter has aroused a woman he will win greater spiritual merit if he abandons her and does not seize the opportunity he has created for himself (287). The Devil created amatory love and its associated iniquities; it is thus a greater good to preserve chastity and virtue (299). To drive home his point, Andreas posts an exhaustive catalogue of women's vices that, as Albrecht Classen says, "outdoes every other misogynist writer in the history of medieval literature and of the Church Fathers," hence implies irony, if not satire, or ultimately a strategy to deal with the central issues of human language and discourse.[40]

Andreas prefaced the *De Amore* with a warning to Walter, for whom all information about love was compiled as an act of male friendship; at the opening of Book Three, Andreas urges Walter to read the work merely as a source of learned recreation (287). Throughout the final book, Andreas continues to make explicit the superiority of male friendship in the Ciceronian mode to heterosexual passion and to celebrate male bonding as the highest human value. Less than half of the third book contains the explicit antifemininism that so many scholars treat as its whole. The traditional categories of misogynistic woman-loathing that Andreas details precisely in this section are liberally sprinkled through Books One and Two. What changes is Book Three's negative erasure of women. Because women are sin, even marriage is to be rejected in favor of, first, homosociality, and finally, love of God. Andreas's unreserved debasement and rejection of human amatory love does not here signal a changed or corrected opinion: the preceding books also reject love. His lengthy condemnation of women is the blatant "non" to Book

---

[40] Albrecht Classen's review of Monson, *Andreas Capellanus, Scholasticism, & the Courtly Tradition*, in *Mediaevistik*, forthcoming

One's argument that erotic desire leads men to enhanced goodness: "Love makes the hirsute barbarian as handsome as can be: it can even enrich the lowest-born with nobility of manners: usually it even endows with humanity the arrogant" (1). This "sic" was continually accompanied by Andreas's caveats: if Love exalts, it is nevertheless warfare, slavery, and suffering.[41] The nobleman in dialogue with his social equal in Book One voices this apparent contradiction: "A man's will cannot be more free than when he is unable to desire separation from what he longs for with all his mental energies. Any person should be delighted if he cannot say no to what he desires with all his strength, as long as it is worth desiring."

In Book Three, Andreas returns to the stance of his Preface and recapitulates love's deleterious effects on a man, concluding with a rhetorical question that presents his forceful argument to Walter:

> When the sword of love really pierces a man, he gets no relief from the agitation of unremitting thought about his partner. There are no riches, no distinction or status in this world that can make him as happy as the possibility of truly enjoying his love to his heart's desire.... Who, then, reveals himself such a fool and madman as to try to obtain what forces him with oppressive serfdom to subject himself to another's dominion, and to be wholly tied to another's will in all things? (291)

To this he adds sin: love abstractly and women concretely are "the source of all evils." Andreas chastens Walter:

> If love causes you to lose the grace of the King of heaven, robs you of absolutely every true friend, and removes from you all the distinctions of this world; if love causes your every breath of praiseworthy fame to die, and swallows all your wealth by its greed, and is the source of all evils as is stated earlier, why do you stupidly seek to love? What blessing could you gain from it which could repay you for all these disadvantages? (321)

Most ironically, Book Three enacts the rhetorical strategies that Andreas previously recommended for a successful suitor: Andreas turns the strategies of a male lover toward Walter. Just as the nobleman in Book One manipulates the noblewoman with his story of the Pleasance — that horrific tale by which the woman confesses to be terrified — Andreas also attempts to intimidate Walter with a catalogue of horrors that await if he foolishly continues to pursue heterosexual union. Now Andreas makes even more explicit the tension between benign male friendship and miserable romantic love:

---

[41] Also note the way Andreas hints that he will come back to this point "on another occasion" (5), alluding to his condemnation of heterosexual love in Book 3.

The 'Sic et Non' of De Amore   167

> If you wish to practice the art of love in accordance with this instruction, according as the careful reading of my little book will prescribe to you, you will obtain in full measure all bodily pleasures. But you will rightly be deprived of God's grace, the company of good men, and the friendship of those who win praise, and you will cause your reputation to suffer great harm, and find it hard to win distinctions in this life (323).

Book Three, and the entire treatise, ends with an exhortation derived from the parable of the Wise and Foolish Virgins (Matt. 25:1–13) that urges Walter to avoid any form of human love. The final sentences of the treatise have bizarre force:

> Sumas ergo, Gualteri, salubrem tibi a nobis propinatam doctrinam et mundi penitus vanitates omittas, ut, quum venerit sponsus nuptias celebrare maiores, et clamor surrexerit in nocte, sis praeparatus cum lampadibus occurrere sibi ornatis secumque ad nuptias introire divinas, nec te oporteat tempore opportunitatis instantis tuae lampadis serotina ornamenta disquirere et ad sponsi domum ianua clausa venire ac verecundam vocem audire.
>
> Studeas ergo, Gualteri, lampades semper ornatas habere, id est caritatis et bonorum operum ornamenta tenere. Memento etiam vigilare semper, ne in peccatis dormiendo te inveniat sponsi repentinus adventus. Cave igitur, Gualteri, amoris exercere mandata et continua vigilatione labora, ut, quum venerit sponsus, inveniat te vigilantem, nec de corporis iuventute confisum mundana delectatio te faciat in peccati dormitione iacere ac de sponsi tarditate securum, quia, eiusdem sponsi voce testante, nescimus diem neque horam.
>
> [Therefore you must accept, Walter, the salutary instruction I set before you, and utterly renounce the empty things of the world. Then, when the Bridegroom comes to celebrate the greater marriage, and a shout is raised in the night, you may be ready to meet Him with your lamps adorned, and in His company make your way to the divine marriage; then you will not have to look for adornment for your lamp too late at the moment of pressing need, nor reach the Bridegroom's house to find the door closed and to hear shaming words.
>
> Be sure, then, Walter, to keep your lamps always trimmed; in other words, hold fast to the adornments of charity and good works. Remember also to keep watch constantly, so that the sudden arrival of the Bridegroom may not find you asleep in sins. So, Walter, beware of carrying out Love's commands. Struggle with constant watchfulness, that when the Bridegroom comes He may find you awake. Do not let delight in this world cause you to trust in your physical vigour and lie asleep in sin, confidently expecting the

Bridegroom to be late. That Bridegroom witnesses in His own words that we know not the day nor the hour (322–24)].

Walter should prepare for the "greater marriage" of the "divine bridegroom" and "keep ... [his] ... lamps always trimmed." The Bridegroom ["sponsus"] is directly invoked six times in this passage, but where is the wise virgin? That role is allocated by Andreas to Walter. Seven times in Book Three, and three times in the ending alone, Andreas specifically addresses the *male person* Walter, with his well-trimmed lamps, who should await the Bridegroom. The parable of the Wise and Foolish Virgins (an exhortation frequently invoked by Bernard among others) links the Apocalypse with the Song of Songs in imagery that typically figures the male soul as virgin and feminine (*anima*), craving God as male *sponsus*. No female servant — no woman at all — appears in Book Three, and Andreas's figuration of Mathew's parable erases even the allegorical presence of the feminine by having Walter assume the wise virgin's disciplined biblical role. This would seem the final "non" to love itself.

Yet the ideal that remains is the "divine marriage." Yearning for love doesn't end. The discipline of passion doesn't cease. At the end of the *De Amore,* love is returned to the yearning, preparation, and postponement with which the tract began. The dilatory role of the feminine earlier in Andreas's tract is now claimed as a proper function of the submissive masculine. The ungendered occlusion of virgins (male and female) is conventional: all human desire is sated in the troping of the spiritual marriage feast. For such mystics as Bernard, all loves merge in One Love. But Andreas erases this conventional erasure. He keeps his human and spiritual categories separate; in his usual "sic et non," Andreas affirms the systematic pursuit of passion but moves the discipline of love from the verbal pursuit of the Lady to the self-disciplined anticipation of the Bridegroom. This final denial of human love in Andreas's literary love dissection is also an affirmation of passion itself. In this ending, one can imagine another reason for Tempier's condemnation of the *De Amore*: the treatise's hyperkinetic rhetoric un-collapses allegoresis and thus undermines mysticism's powerful, often gorgeous swirling of divine and human love.

CHAPTER 7

LANGUAGE FOR LOVERS: LESSONS FROM TROUBADOURS AND MYSTICS

VALERIE M. WILHITE
University of Illinois Urbana-Champaign

The best lovers know they are only as good as the words they speak. A lover might be transformed by love, by the perfection of the beloved, but to become the perfect lover, one who reaches across all distance to unite with the beloved, language must play a crucial role in the transformation. The writings of great lovers, divine and secular, offer many lessons on how to behave as a humble servant to the beloved. The lyrics of troubadours and the texts of Marguerite Porete, Jacopone da Todi, and Angela da Foligno provide definitions of the perfect lover, declarations of love's power to transform the lover, and instructions on how to join the beloved, but they also offer examples of the language that forms the lover.

In order to highlight the similarities between these two discourses, this paper will place the words of troubadours beside the words of mystics. We will begin with the explicit references both lovers make to the power of love to transform the lover. The troubadours and mystics themselves will offer the defining features of how language functions in love as they see it. This paper cannot explore the many particular ways of using language to weaken the space of difference between lover and beloved, but instead will focus on only two: language that suggests physical impossibilities and strings of words that deny difference entirely.

Love, loving, and the beloved transform mystics and troubadours alike. The beloved transforms the lover into someone better, says the poet-lover in Arnaut Daniel's song entitled "En cest sonet coind' e leri," "Tot jorn meillur et esmeri / car la gensor serv e coli / del mon — so ·us dic," (40, ll. 14–24; Each day I become better and more refined / because I serve and revere / the most gracious lady in the world, this I tell you).[1] Gaucelm Faidit tells his beloved, "car m'etz enans e respiegs, e guirensa, / gaug e delitz, caps et comensamens" (71, ll. 5–6; because you are beneficial, my hope and my well-being, joy and pleasure, end and beginning) and for this reason "en amar be meillur outra poder" (71, ll. 12; through love I grow exceptionally better).[2] And Raimbaut d'Aurenga emphasizes: "Si ben en amar leis m'esmer" (143, ll. 33; in loving her I grow fine).[3] Bernart de Ventadorn goes so far as to proclaim that "Ben a mauvais cor e mendic / qui ama e no·s melhura" (82, ll. 17–18; He who loves and does not improve himself certainly has a bad and false heart).[4] The theme is a common one in the lyrics of the troubadours and courtly romances, but it sits perfectly inside the declarations of mystics. Like the troubadours, Jacopone da Todi, writing in Italy in the thirteenth century — where most of the troubadour songbooks we have today were being compiled — composes a song praising divine love in which he addresses her saying, "Amor che dai forma / ad omnia cha forma / la forma toa reforma lom che deformato" (119; Love, You who give form to all / Take poor deformed man / and reform him).[5] Marguerite Porete proclaims:

> Ce don [of his love] occist ma pensee
> Du delit de son amour,
> lequel delit
> me soubhaulce et mue par union
> en la permanable joye
> d'estre de divine Amour.[6]   (346, ll. 116–21)

[This gift of his love kills my thought by the delight of His love, which delight lifts and transforms me through union into the eternal joy of the being of divine love; 201.]

---

[1] *The Poetry of Arnaut Daniel*, ed. James J. Wilhelm (New York: Garland, 1981), 40, ll. 14–24. Translations of troubadours are mine unless otherwise noted. This song is not included in the later editions of Arnaut Daniel by Maurizio Perugi or Martin de Riquer.

[2] "Ges de chanter non aten ni esper," *Les Poèmes de Gaucelm Faidit, Troubadour du XIIe siècle ; suivi de Guilhem Peire de Cazals, Troubadour du XIIIe siècle; et de le Troubadour Arnaut de Tintinhac*, ed. Jean Mouzat. Les Classiques d'oc, 2 (965; Genève: Slatkine Reprints, 1989).

[3] "Ben sai c'a sels seria fer," *The Life and Works of the Troubadour Raimbaut D'Orange*, ed. and trans. Walter Thomas Pattison (Minneapolis: University of Minnesota Press, 1952).

[4] "Lancan folhon bosc e jarric," Bernard De Ventadour, *Chansons d'amour*, ed. Moshe Lazar (1966; Moustier-Ventadour: Carrefour Ventadour, 2001).

[5] "Laus excelencie diuine amoris," *The Lauds*, ed. and trans. Serge Hughes, and Elizabeth Hughes. Classics of Western Spirituality (New York: Paulist Press, 1982), 238; *Il Laudario Jacoponico: [Greek Delta]-Vii-15 Della Biblioteca Civica Angelo Maj di Bergamo*, ed. Jacopone and Giuseppe Mazza (Bergamo: San Marco, 1960), 119.

[6] Old French is taken from *Margaretae Porete Speculum Simplicium Animarum*, ed. Romana Guarnieri and Paul Verdeyen. Corpus Christianorum. Continuatio Mediaevalis, 69 (Turnholt: Brepols, 1986). English translations are those of Ellen L. Babinsky, *The Mirror of Simple Souls*. Classics of Western Spirituality (New York: Paulist Press, 1993).

Language for Lovers

Love, loving, and beloved — divine or earthly — seem for these lyrical poets to elicit a common type of change in the lover-poets. Just as troubadours often repeat the words "esmeri" or "refining" and other verbs of bettering and transformation, Marguerite Porete speaks often of the soul changing or transforming with her consistent use of the word "mue" in her description of the soul.

Further exploration reveals that in fact both troubadours and mystics describe a process that is less a trans-forming but rather an un-forming of the subject. The lover places at the feet of the beloved the lover's will, pleasure, and body parts; that is, all the various elements of the self. One of the most obvious gifts of self the lover can offer is the heart. Arnaut de Maruelh no longer holds his own heart; it is now in the hands of the lady: "Domna valens ab avinens lauzors, / Ren de mon cor non ai mais la bailia / de vos lo tenh ...." (73, ll. 29–31; Noble lady of gracious praise I have no control over my heart: from you I hold it).[7] The heart consistently represents the self in troubadour lyric. Bernart de Ventadorn situates his identity, his being, in the heart, describing a self that is at its most condensed and solid in the *cor*.[8] In "Can la freid' aura venta" Bernart de Ventadorn offers both his will and his heart to his lady: "per amor de la genta / vas cui eu sui aclis, on ai meza m'ententa / e mo coratg' assis ..." (160, ll. 5–8; For love of the noble one towards whom I gravitate, where I have placed my affection, and set my heart ...); but in "Non es meravelha" he offers up a more complete inventory of self: "Cor e cors e saber e sen / e fors' e poder i ai mes" (60, ll. 5–6; heart and body, wisdom and mind and strength and force and power I have placed in it [love]). The features of individual identity have been handed over to the beloved.

In the text that led Marguerite Porete to the flames, *Mirouer des simples ames,* Marguerite creates a dialogue which gives a voice to the allegorical figures of Reason, Love, and the Soul. Here too the figures speak of a soul who relinquishes the will, for Love says of the Soul, "car son vouloir n'est mie a elle ne en elle, mais ainçoys est en celui qui l'ayme, et ce n'est mie son oeuvre ainçoys est l'oeuvre de toute la Trinité, qui oeuvre en telle Ame a sa voulenté" (96, ll. 25–28; for her will is no longer her own nor in her, but instead is in the One who loves her, and is not her work but the work of the whole Trinity, Who works at its pleasure in such a soul; 109), continuing further, "Or est ung commun vouloir, comem feu et flambe, le vouloir de l'amant et celluy de l'amie, car Amour a muee ceste Ame en luy" (96, ll. 9–11; Now there is one common will, as fire and flame, as the will of the Lover and the one who is loved, for Love has transformed this Soul into Love herself; 109).

---

[7] "L'ensenhamens e·l pretz e la valors" *Les Poésies Lyriques du Troubadour Arnaut de Mareuil,* ed. R. C. Johnston (Paris: E. Droz, 1935).

[8] Eric Jager discusses the semantic inheritance of the language of the heart by medieval authors in *The Book of the Heart* (Chicago: University of Chicago, 2000). See in particular the introduction and first chapter, "Origins."

As the lover gives his parts to the beloved, the distance, or difference, between lover and beloved weakens. Lover and beloved pull closer together. Distance and difference are overcome with this transforming, *muer*, that turns the lover not only into someone different, better, but the Soul also says "tant suis muee" that all individuality and unique, separate identity is lost. She can have no name for she has no difference. Marguerite Porete's Soul speaks of the experience afforded by such selflessness and union: "Hee! Tres doulce pure divine Amour, dit ceste Ame, comment c'est une doulve muance de ce que je suis muee en la chose que j'ayme mieulx que moy! Et tant suis muee, que je en au perdu mon nom pour amer, qui si pou puis amer: c'st en amour car je n'ayme fors que Amour" (96; Ah! Very sweet Pure Divine Love, says this Soul, how it is a sweet transformation by which I am transformed into the thing which I love better than myself! And I am so transformed that I have lost my name in it for the sake of Love, I who am able to love so little; 109). The name as marker of unique identity is completely lost. Such is the power and purpose of love (cf. Galatians 2:20).

In the compilation of texts left by Angela da Foligno, Angela recounts the story of her own transforming and experience of the divine to the Brother Arnaldo who transcribes her words which will become the *Libro della Beata Angela da Foligno*. In her account she provides an outline of what she calls "the degree of transforming love" in which she too emphasizes the loss of the lover's individual identity: "Et alora la vertù de l'amore transforma l'amante ne l'amato e l'amato ne l'amante" (687; Then the power of love transforms the lover into the Beloved and the Beloved into the lover; 301).[9] A transformation takes place, demolishing all boundaries between loving subject and beloved object. The two entities become blurred through this transformation. Self is lost; the beloved alone remains. It is in this sense a deconstruction, an un-forming of self. Mystics and troubadours agree that some sort of transformation takes place in the loving subject. The process is one of deconstruction, and it is this common goal — for it is a goal and not a passive result — that brings these two lovers to speak of love with similar words. Love and loving alone do not effect change of mental state, but alterations in the components of being a loving subject. The common goal of love to the point of a total eclipsing of the self and the role of language in deconstructing the self is the common link between these two types of lovers. Love of words and language games are what allow mystics and troubadours to become perfect lovers.

To strive to become the perfect lover is to lose all selfish preoccupations, to disappear. Just as the construction of the self happens in the world, through language, and as a process, so too does the deconstruction of self. The deconstructive

---

[9] Angela of Foligno, *Complete Works*, trans. with an introduction by Paul Lachance. Preface by Romana Guarnieri. Classics of Western Spirituality (New York: Paulist Press, 1993); *Il Libro Della Beata Angela da Foligno*, ed. Ludger Thier and Abele Calufetti. 2nd ed. Spicilegium Bonaventurianum, 25 (Grottaferrata (Rome): Editiones Collegii S. Bonaventurae ad Clara Aquas, 1985).

Language for Lovers 173

tools of which we find traces in the works of the mystics and the troubadours center on three particular fields of play: the body, the imagination, and language.

Attempts to deconstruct the self by devaluing the body begin with acts — in speech and body — which put the human form center stage. Both extreme asceticism and self-inflicted woundings offer clear examples of subjects whose desire to minimize the importance or role of the body and the bodily in the construction of self-identity leads them to a grand preoccupation with all things bodily. Hagiographies and the texts of mystics and songs of troubadours indicate that lovers do undertake some of the other methods a subject employs to destroy the self. Ariel Glucklich tracks the mystifying question of why one would expect pain to lead to identification with God in his study *Sacred Pain*. Glucklich admits that "Ascetics and mystics know that they possess effective techniques, short of raw pain, for unmaking their own profane selves: First is a rigid diet, then isolation, sleepless nights (vigils), ongoing prayer or chanting, hard physical work, and other psychotropic techniques."[10] He does not make too much of the uses of language, though he does include prayer and chanting in the list; his specification that it is "ongoing" indicates that it has more to do with the strain of the practice rather than the language involved and so fits the other items in his list. Glucklich presents his objective in the following terms:

> *Sacred Pain* argues that religious individuals have hurt themselves because the pain they produced was meaningful and is not only subject to verbal communication but also figures in our ability to empathize and share. In other words, the symbolic and experiential efficacy of pain derives from the way it bridges 'raw' sensation with our highest qualities as human beings in a community of other humans. (44)

By claiming that pain is key in connecting humans with symbol, he has pitted himself against the very well-known declaration by Elaine Scarry in *The Body in Pain* which posits that pain is "language-destroying."[11] Glucklich says "the hurting body does not suffer silently. It offers a potential voice, if one has the tools to make the soul listen" (*Sacred Pain*, 42). He suggests that "religiously-conceived pain" can "potentially be transformed into good pain: educational, healing, bonding with God" (40). However, many are the mystics who claim that language falls away along with all things worldly when union with God is achieved. Bruce Holsinger's chapter "The Musical Body in Pain" in *Music, Body, and Desire in Medieval Culture* attempts to widen his scope to "a number of approaches to the

---

[10] Ariel Glucklich, *Sacred Pain: Hurting the Body for the Sake of the Soul* (Oxford and New York: Oxford University Press, 2001), 43.

[11] Elaine Scarry, *The Body in Pain: The Making and Unmaking of the World* (New York: Oxford University Press, 1985), 11.

musical body in pain" which allows him to mention flagellants whose *laudi* did indeed allow for pain to "produce painful music as public, civic spectacle" while recognizing that the musicality in devotional practice could also serve to alter the experience of the practicant.[12] The subject that undergoes great pain in order to alter his or her state of being is different from those occasions when self-injury is used as spectacle. For the practicing subject the goal is indeed to alter the mind, and so many claim that the experience is accompanied by the loss of the power to speak. As Scarry's work suggests, self and language are in symbiosis and lost simultaneously.

Hurting the body with God in mind is about devaluing all the elements of individual selfhood. Jerome Kroll and Bernard Bachrach have recently proposed another reason for the widespread use of self-inflicted pain in the Western Christian religious tradition in their book *The Mystic Mind*. They posit as their fundamental hypothesis "that one major and heretofore overlooked motivation for medieval heroic ascetic behaviors is the effectiveness of self-injurious behaviors in bringing about an altered state of consciousness."[13] While Glucklich stresses the effects of pain within community and with God, Kroll and Bachrach focus on mental states; self-induced pain serves a very intimate purpose working on the mind of the subject. Kroll and Bachrach build their book upon the idea that mystics of the Western Christian tradition, at least during the Middle Ages, "employed harsh self-injurious practices as a method of inducing altered states of consciousness," and this because "Western Christianity during much of the Middle Ages did not have available . . . as strong a tradition of meditative practices as those found in Eastern religions" (*Mystic Mind*, 2). If pain was used by so many of those seeking to destroy the self, it is because it was a method available to them. Caroline Walker Bynum suggests that the "peculiarly bodily" focus of spirituality in the Middle Ages was because "theology and natural philosophy saw persons as, in some real sense, body as well as soul."[14] Not only, then, is pain a method available to medieval ascetics, but the body itself holds meaning in a particular way for the medieval subject.

While descriptions of extreme asceticism and self-inflicted physical pain — the bodily means of altering the state of the mystic — are more readily found in hagiographies than in the writings of mystics, traces of the significance of the body in the construction of selfhood are represented in mystical texts and

---

[12] Bruce W. Holsinger, *Music, Body, and Desire in Medieval Culture: Hildegard of Bingen to Chaucer* (Stanford: Stanford University Press, 2001), 198–99. See particularly "Musicality and Suffering," 196–216.

[13] Jerome Kroll and Bernard S. Bachrach, *The Mystic Mind: The Psychology of Medieval Mystics and Ascetics* (New York: Routledge, 2005).

[14] Caroline Walker Bynum, *Fragmentation and Redemption: Essays on Gender and the Human Body in Medieval Religion* (New York: Zone Books, 1991), 183.

Language for Lovers

even in troubadour lyric. Angela da Foligno in her book of visions describes an experience prompted by looking at the crucifixion:

> Ma in questo cognoscimento de la croze m'era dacto tanto fuoco che, stando apresso de la croxe, me spolgiai tute le vestimente e tuta me ofresi a lui. Et avegnaché con tremore, ma alori promisi a lui de observare castitade perpetua, e de non ofender a lui con algun di mie menbri, e accusando li peccati de tuti i membri. (137)

> [Nonetheless, this perception of the meaning of the cross set me so afire that, standing near the cross, I stripped myself of all my clothing and offered my whole self to him. Although very fearful, I promised him then to maintain perpetual chastity and not to offend him again with any of my bodily members, accusing each of these one by one. (126)]

Angela da Foligno strips herself of all that had been draped on her; once stripped she offers herself completely to God. Her bodily members she doffs one by one by giving them a name, an identity apart from her own. She explains that she was "iluminata e fòme insingnata la via de la croxe in questo modo, zioè ch'io mi spolgiàse e fosse piui liziera, e nuda a la croxe andàse, . . ." (139; inspired with the thought that if I wanted to go to the cross, I would need to strip myself in order to be lighter and go naked to it . . .; 126). She would need to rid herself even "my very self." The clothes, then the shell of the body, must be lost. Jacopone da Todi admits he had once foolishly thought the rational and the bodily through the senses offered a means of finding God:

> Auerte cognosuto
> Credeua per intellecto
> Gustato per affecto
> Uiso per simiglianza
> Credendo auer tenuto
> Ti cosi perfecto
> Prouato quel dilecto
> Amor de smesuranza
> Or par me che so fallanza
> Non ei quel chio credeua
> Tenendo non auea
> Ueritate senza errore   (64, ll. 5–16)

> [I once thought that reason had led me to You, and that through feeling I sensed your presence, caught a glimpse of You in similitudes, knew You in Your perfection. I know now that I was wrong, that that truth was flawed. (265)]

In this *lauda*, the opening suggests that for one who has truly arrived, joined the beloved, all intellect, sensory perception, sense of self and self-consciousness, "are swept into infinity."[15] The state and space of union is devoid of all a self can produce or access. As he says in opening the *lauda*, "Love beyond all telling, Goodness beyond imagining."

In claiming that this experience of love is "Sopra omne lengua amore / bontate senza figura" (64; Love beyond all telling, Goodness beyond imagining; 265).[16] Jacopone highlights the two other means of self destruction commonly used by good lovers: language and imagination. Angela da Foligno explains that one day she heard God say "Io te voglio mostrare la mia potenzia" (261, 263; I want to show you something of my power; 169–170), and this is her account of what occurred:

> Et incontenenti furono aperti li ochi de l'anima e vedeva una plenitudine de Dio, ne la quale conprendeva tuto lo mondo, zioè oltra mare e di qua da mare e l'abisso, lo mare e tute le cose. Et in tute queste cose no se dizernèa se no la divina potenzia, et inpertanto in modo al tuto inenarabile.   (263)

> [And immediately the eyes of my soul were opened, and in a vision I beheld the fullness of God in which I beheld and comprehended the whole of creation, that is what is on this side and what is beyond the sea, the abyss, the sea itself, and everything else. And in everything that I saw, I could perceive nothing except the presence of the power of God and in a manner totally indescribable. (169–170)]

Angela uses the imaginary as a method of reducing her own worth to the smallest grain for she continues saying, "E conprendea tuto lo mondo quaxi una picola cosa" (263; Wherefore I understood how small is the whole of creation; 169–170). She has lost herself in the immensity and grandeur of the imaginary. Angela loses herself less by crushing her physicality than by creating and focusing on images of the divine. The book we have today is a collection of visions and reflections Angela da Foligno dictated to the Franciscan Brother Arnaldo. Imagining is the method Angela relies on the most, as she puts it,

> E pregava Dio che li dovèse dar di se inperziò chera cusì seca d'ogno bene. E aloro fono aperti i ochi de l'anima e vedeva l'amore che veniva pianamente verso se, . . . Et incontenente che pervenne a lei, parve a lei apertamente che vedèse con i ochi de l'anima più che non se può vedere con i ochi del corpo . . . . (299)

---

[15] Jacopone da Todi, "Self-Annihilation and Charity Lead the Soul to What Lies Beyond Knowledge and Language," *The Lauds*, trans. Hughes, 265.

[16] Line 1. Mazza, *Il Laudario Jacoponico:*, 64.

Language for Lovers

[She prayed to God that he give her something of himself for she felt very dry and deprived of every good. And then the eyes of her soul were opened and she had a vision of love gently advancing toward her ... And suddenly she saw it coming toward her with the eyes of her soul, more clearly than can be seen with the eyes of the body, ... (182)]

As she recounts what she has seen, she, paradoxically, consistently claims the impossibility of speaking her visions by adding preambles or postscripts to the descriptions of her visions:

> Ancora me disse a me, frate scriptore, essa fedele de Cristo, exponiéndome tute queste cose scrite, che tanta pasione vide l'anima sua, che quantonque santa Maria ne vedèse più che nulo santo in molti modi como essa asegnava, inpertanto essa intendeva che per nessuno modo Ella la potesse dire, né santo alcuno.   (293)

> [At this point, Christ's faithful one, in an explanation of the above, told me, brother scribe, that her soul had seen so much of the passion that it understood that even though the Blessed Virgin had seen more of it and mentioned more of its details than any other saint, still she herself could not — neither could any other saint — find words to express it. (180)]

The passion is shown to her in such a way that the power of the image goes beyond the power of the tongue: "Questo dolore acuto, fo sì grande che lingua no zi basta a dire nì cuore a pensare ..." (295, 297; This acute pain, so intense that the tongue cannot express it nor is the heart great enough to imagine it; 181). Language ceases to have any power; "Love beyond telling":

> E vego et intendo che quelle operazione divine e quelo profondissimo abisso, nullo anzolo e nula criatura è sì larga e capaze che la possa comprenderé; e tuta queste cosse cue ora dico si può sì male dire e meno dire, che sono biastemare quelle.   (381)

> [I am convinced that there is no saint, angel, or creature which has anywhere near the capacity to understand these divine workings and that extremely deep abyss. And everything I am saying now is so badly and weakly said that it is a blasphemy against these things. (381)]

Angela da Foligno dictates her visions to Brother Arnaldo, but her ecstasy comes from the moments of her rapture, the moments when she "sees" the glory of God, the suffering of Christ. Angela seems much more interested in the imaginary than in the rhetorical.

This manipulation of the law of language, of the signifier-signified relationship, is the method of self-destruction chosen by at least some troubadours and numerous mystics like Jacopone da Todi, Marguerite Porete, Teresa d'Avila, and even Thérèse de Lisieux. Even Marguerite d'Oingt, whose *Speculum* focuses on the image of an intricately decorated book placed in the heart and covered with letters, mirrors, and colors, believes the act of writing directs the heart and the mind to God: "Je n'ai escrit ces choses manqué por ce que quant mes cuers seroyt espanduz parmi le munde que je pensaso en cetes choses, por ce que puisso retorner mon cuer a mon creatour et retrayre du mundo" (142; I did not write these things but so, when my heart was wandering the world, that I think about these things, so that I could return my heart to my creator and retire from the world).[17] She claims that she who has had visions wrote them all in her heart until it was so full she was unable to eat or sleep and so "elle se pensa que s'ela metoyt en escrit ces choses que sos cuers en seroyt plus alegiez" (142; She thought that if she wrote those things down her heart would be freed of the burden). The need to speak, to write, to make some utterance before the ineffable has less to do with successful and truthful communication than it does with the effect of love. For Marguerite Porete, one of the effects of love is the desire to speak about it:

> Mais j'en vueil parler et n'en sçay que dire. Non pourtant, dame Amour, dist elle, mon amour est de tel arbiter, quie j'aime mieulx a oïr chose mesdire de vous, que que on ne die aucune chose de vous. Et sans faille ce fais je: j'en mesdis, car tout ce que j'en dis n'est fors que mesdire de la bonté de vous. (46, ll. 123–28)

> [But I want to speak about it and I don't know what to say about it. Nevertheless, Lady Love, she says, my love is so certain that I would prefer to hear something slanderous about you than that one should say nothing about you. And without fail I do this: I slander because everything I say is nothing but slander about your goodness. (91)]

When facing the beloved, language fails. Speech, all speech is slander. In *Mystical Languages of Unsaying*, Michael Sells finds there are three options open to the one who faces "the primary dilemma of transcendence."[18] The first response is silence.

Angela admits that "e ziò ch'io dico me pare dire niente, over dire malle. E poi dìsseme: parme de biastemare" (361; Everything I say now about it seems to say nothing or to be badly said. It seems that whatever I say about it is blasphemy; 205), and ultimately decides there is no way to talk about God or union with the divine:

---

[17] Antonin Duraffour, *Les Oeuvres De Marguerite d'Oingt*. Publications de l'Institut de Linguistique Romane de Lyon, 21 (Paris: Les Belles Lettres, 1965). English translations are my own.

[18] Michael Anthony Sells, *Mystical Languages of Unsaying* (Chicago: University of Chicago Press, 1994), 2.

Language for Lovers

> E perciò non si può dire nulla assolutamente, e perché non si può trovare nessuna parola che esprima queste cose divine e nessun pensiero e nessuna intelligenzia può estenderi ad esse, tanto soperchiano ogni cosa, como Dio per chivele non si può comendare, inperzioché Dio al postuto non si può comendare. E dizea la predita fedele de Cristo con grandísima certeza e dava at intendere che Dio non si può per nessuno modo comendare. (385, 387)

> [Therefore, there is absolutely nothing that can be said about this experience, for no words can be found or invented to express or explain it; no expansion of thought or mind can possibly reach to those things, they are so far beyond everything—for there is nothing which can explain God; I repeat there is absolutely nothing which can explain God. Christ's faithful one affirmed with utmost certitude and wanted it understood that there is absolutely nothing which can explain God. (213)][19]

And yet Marguerite writes — pieces into a series of words the understanding she has of the divine that ultimately leads to her death by fire; Angela speaks to her confessor for hours, and Bernart de Ventadorn claims he cannot stop himself from singing or speaking. In "Can lo boschatges es floritz" Bernard de Ventadorn suggests his heart and mouth do all the trouble / love-making. He knows better than to speak his love, but his mouth talks too much:

> Ar sui de leis trop eissernitz
> Lenga, per que potz tan parlar
> Que de menhs me sol acuzar
> Si que.m sui per las dens feritz.   (224, ll. 17–22)

> [I am too bold. Tongue, why can you talk so much? She usually blames me for less so that and so I have hurt myself through my teeth.]

The second response to an encounter with perfection is scientifically, surgically, to filter the entity into parts: elements of common non-transcendence and others of transcendence. The third response to the ideal beloved is that which interests us: "The third response begins with the refusal to solve the dilemma posed by the attempt to refer to the transcendent through a distinction between two kinds of name. The dilemma is accepted as a genuine *aporia*, that is, as unresolvable; but this acceptance, instead of leading to silence, leads to a new mode of discourse."[20] Language can be used to speak God and the ideal lady, just not *of* the ideal, the divine. As Albrecht Classen notes in his introduction to this volume, the response

---

[19] *Complete Works*, ed. Lachance, 213, *Il Libro della Beata Angela Da Foligno*, ed. Thier and Calufetti,385, 87.

[20] Sells, *Mystical Languages of Unsaying*, 2.

of the lover before the beloved constitutes one of the fundamental reasons for an overlap between the discourse of the religious and secular lover, "[…] because the erotic escapes easy definition and remains elusive to the intellectual and rational efforts to approach it with rational terms."[21] It is the nature of the divine and the erotic but also the nature of language that allows for the similarities in mystical and troubadour literatures. Signs can no longer fully capture the power of reference necessary to refer to a signified once we enter the realm of perfection:

> Qui be remira ni ve
> Olhs e gola, fron e faz,
> Aissi son finas beutatz
> Que mais ni menhs no i cove,
> Cors long, dreih e covinen,
> Gen afliban, conhd'e gai.
> Om no·l pot lauzar tan gen
> Com la saup formar Natura.   (118, ll. 41–48)

[For whosoever looks and observes her eyes, her neck, her forehead and face, her beauty is so fine that neither more nor less would be appropriate to add, her slender body, straight and attractive, nobly adorned, charming and joyous. No person can praise her so well as Nature made her.][22]

The sign cannot work as it does for the common, mundane thing; it simply cannot reach the perfection that nature created. Angela da Foligno describes a scene in which the divine himself appropriates the sign as he refutes the efficacy of normal sign with its divorce from its signified, and indeed the whole nature of signifying — the standing in for, and pointing toward, something outside. God responds to Angela's wish for a sign saying, "Questo che tu adimandi è uno segno che te darìa senpre letizia quando lo vedèsi e tocàsi, ma non te trarìa de dubio e in *cotale* segno poresti esser inganata."(205; This sign which you are asking for is one which would always give you joy whenever you see it or touch it, but it would not take away your doubt. Furthermore, in *such* a sign you could be deceived; 149). Instead of "such" a sign, God proposes he place inside her heart a sign of his kind:

> E questo è lo segno lo quale laso entro ne l'anima tua, lo quale è melgio che quelo lo qualle adimandasti: Làsote uno amore di me, per lo quale l'anima tua continuamente serà calda di me.   (207)

---

[21] See the introduction to this volume by Albrecht Classen, "Introduction," 15.
[22] "Conortz era sai eu be," *Bernard De Ventadour, Chansons d'amour*, ed. Lazar.

[Here then is the sign which I deposit in the depths of your soul, one better than the one you asked for: I deposit in you a love of me so great that your soul will be continually burning for me. (50)]

Love is what he places in her heart — the thing itself, the "authentic sign" – his presence itself is more than sign, it is the thing, and yet, he says, a sign of it. The sign that speaks, that signifies, points to something not there — something that might have been there, but is no longer. The sign is fleeting, dependent on those moments when she "sees" or "touches" it, that is, uses the tools of the imagination or the body. In this scene God describes the "meaning event" as defined by Sells: "Meaning event indicates that moment when the meaning has become identical with existence, but such identity is not only asserted, it is performed" (*Mystical Language*, 9). The type of sign God speaks of no longer points to the signified, but is truly the thing itself — as one would expect.

In so many of the most interesting emotionally charged and semantically complex moments of mystical or *fin' amor* literature are examples of language no longer following the laws of grammar, logic, or linguistics. Mystics and troubadours fall into a practice of *apophasis:* "rather than pointing to an object, apophatic language attempts to evoke in the reader an event that is — in its movement beyond structures of self and other, subject and object — structurally analogous to the event of mystical union"[23] and so beyond the laws of language, beyond grammar.

Ultimately, the very way of language is what allows mystics and troubadours alike to appropriate it as a tool in the path to union with the beloved. To become the ideal lover selfishness must be replaced with selflessness. The solid identity of the lover as unique, as distant in quality, space, and potentiality from the beloved must be overcome. Distinction and difference must be overcome; language, the product of difference, is key to success. One means of breaking down the spatial distance and with it the distinctiveness of identity can be found in a declaration which functions like the Russian matryoshka dolls that hold smaller dolls inside. In words, in grammar, each container can turn into the content — something not possible in the finitude of the physical world. Again and again we hear troubadour and mystic evoke a variation on the same image. Arnaut de Maruelh refers frequently to visions of the beloved, and even to her image carried inside his heart: "Amors, que mi a pres, / m'en fai plus enveios, / que· m te vostras faissos / dedinz e mon coratge" (128, ll. 24–27; Love, which has taken hold of me, makes me desire, for it has put the image of your face inside of my heart).[24] Peire Vidal also claims Love has forced him to place the lady in his heart: "Qu'ins en mon cor m'a fait Amors escrire / Sa gran beutat, don res non es a dire, / E son gent cors ben fait e

---

[23] Sells, *Mystical Languages of Unsaying*, 10.
[24] "franq e norrimens,"*Les Poésies Lyriques du Troubadour Arnaut De Mareuil.*

ben assis!" (ll. 16–18; For Love has made to be written inside my heart her great beauty, about which there is nothing to be said, and about her noble body well-formed and well-set).[25] Yet in the song "Una chanso ai faita mortamen" the poet-lover explains that he is the one who does not have his heart in his possession at all: "Qu' anc nueg ni jorn, de ser ni de mati, / Non tinc mon cor ni nulh mon pessamen!" (ll. 3–4 ; For no night nor day, nor by evening nor by morning, do I have my heart nor by any means my thoughts).[26] Bernart de Ventadorn is penetrated to the *cor*(e) by his beloved; the lady reaches the lover through the eyes in "En cossirer et en esmai":

> Negus jois al meu no s' eschai,
> Can ma domna·m garda ni·m ve,
> Que·l seus bels douz semblans me vai
> Al cor, que m' adous' e·m reve!   (218, ll. 41–44)

[No joy can reach mine when my lady looks at me and sees me. Then her sweet beautiful image goes to my heart and softens and revives me.]

He claims in "Lancan folhon bosc e jarric" that this image remains in his heart always, "e port el cor, con que m'estei, / sa beutat e sa fachura"(84, ll. 39–40; and I carry in my heart, wherever I am, her beauty and image). Raimbaut d'Aurenga enjoys carrying his beloved in his heart:

> Dompna, d' als non ai a parlar
> Mas de vos, dompna, que baisar
> Vos cuig, dompna, quand aug nomnar
> Vos, dompna, que ses vestimen
> En mon cor, dompna, vos esgar;
> C' ades mi·us veig inz dompn' estar
> Vostre bel nou cors covinen.   (185, ll. 43–49)

[Lady, of other affairs I have not to speak, but only of you. For I think I am kissing you, lady, when I hear your name mentioned, you, lady, whom I watch without clothing in my heart. For now I see your beautiful, attractive, pure body.]

Angela da Foligno adds further dimension to the image saying, "pensàndome poi che Dio m'aveva fate le predate cose ch'el mio cuor senpre fosse nel cuor de Dio e lo cueor de Dio senpre fosse nel cuor mio" (139; I thought that since God had conceded me this aforesaid favor, my heart would always be within God's heart,

---

[25] "Per mielhs sofrir lo maltrait e l'" afan," Peire Vidal, *Poesie*, ed. Silvio Avalle D'Arco. Documenti di Filologia, 4 (Milan and Naples: R. Ricciardi, 1960).

[26] Peire Vidal, "Per mielhs sofrir," *Poesie*, ed. D'Arco, 19, ll. 3,4.

Language for Lovers 183

and God's heart always within me; 126). The heart holds inside it the thing which holds, inside it, the heart. Teresa d'Avila also takes up both the position of container and contained in her poem "Muero porque no muero" which begins "Vivo sin vivir en mí" (again cf. Galatians 2:20):

> Vivo ya fuera de mí
> Después que muero de amor
> Porque vivo en el Señor
> ...
> Esta divina prisión
> Del amor con que yo vivo
> Ha hecho a Dios mi cautivo
> Y libre mi corazón;
> Y causa en mí tal pasión
> Ver a Dios mi prisionero,
> Que muero porque no muero.
>
> [I already live outside of me
> After I die of love;
> For I live in the Lord,
> ...
> This divine prison
> Of the love with which I live
> Has made of God my prisoner,
> And free my heart;
> And it causes such great pity
> To see God my prisoner,
> That I die because I do not die.[27]]

Teresa d'Avila's poem offer lines that function as a diptych with contradictory halves. How linguistically bold to declare "que muero porque no muero." While what usually follows the word "porque" or "because" is a reason or a summing of the parts that equal the thing that precedes it, here the reason is simply a negation of what came before.

These passages broach what Sells calls the "high end of the scale of performative intensity."[28] These are moments in which "the mystical discourse turns relentlessly upon its own propositions and generates distinctive paradoxes that include within themselves a large number of radical transformations, particularly in the area of temporal and spatial relationships" (3). In a remarkable passage,

---

[27] Ll. 4–6, 11–17, Santa Teresa de Jesus, *Obras Completas, Edicion Manual*, ed. Efren de la Madre de Dios and Otger Steggink (Madrid: Biblioteca de Autores Cristianos, 1997), 654. Translations mine.

[28] Sells, *Mystical Languages of Unsaying*, 3.

Marguerite Porete explains "Comment ceste Ame noe en la mer de joye" (How this Soul swims in the sea of joy). The division between container / contained blurs:

> Telle Ame, dit Amour, nage en la mer de joye, c'est en la mer de delices fluans et decourans de la Divinité, et sin e sent nulle joye, car elle mesmes et joye, et sin age et flue en joy, sans sentir nulle joye, car elle demoure en Joye, et Joye demoure en elle; c'est elle mesmes joye opar la vertuz de Joye, qui l'a muee en luy. (26)

> [swims in the sea of joy, that is in the sea of delights flowing and running out of the Divinity. And so she feels no joy, for she is joy itself. She swims and flows in joy without feeling any joy, for she dwells in Joy and Joy dwells in her. She is Joy itself by the virtue of Joy which transforms her into Joy itself. (85)]

What contains the soul resides inside her. The permeability between the Joy which envelops the soul and the inner essence of the soul means there is no skin to sense the division. The essence without is that which is within. The boundary simply becomes meaningless; it disappears, and difference dissolves.

The troubadour Arnaut de Maruelh also suggests that his will or desire reside inside him and yet are not his:

> Qu' aissi m' ave, dona.l genser que sia,
> Qu' us deziriers, qu' ins en mon cor s' abranda,
> Cosselh' e.m ditz qu' ie·us am e·us serv' e·us blanda,
> E vol que·m lays d' enquerr' autra paria
> Per vos en cuy an tug bon ayp repaire!   (11, ll. 8–12)

> [Like this it happened to me, most gracious lady that exists, that a desire which in my heart sparked, advises and tells me to love you and to serve and woo you, and it wishes that I leave off pursuing other companions for you in whom all good finds its home.][29]

The lover admits that it was desire that inspired his love and *cortezia,* but it is not his, but "us deziriers." It is a fluid and unattached abstract figure. He cannot claim it as his own. It is this unclaimed and unspecified desire that inspires the love that he has for his lady. This desire enters into his heart with a spark or flame and "cosselh e·m ditz" what he should feel, what he should do, and how he should behave. The matryoshka doll in infinity breaks down not only the physical laws of space, but, as shown in these passages, raises questions regarding the property rights of identity and the place of the will in the self.

---

[29] "Aissi cum selh que tem qu'Amors l'aucia," *Poésies Lyriques,* ed. Johnston

Marguerite Porete has the voice of Reason, confused by the paradoxes of mystical discourse, ask Love "Et que peut ce estre, dame Amour, dit Raison, que ceste Ame peut vouloir ce que ce livre dit, qui desja a dit devant qu'elle n'a point de voulenté?" (26, ll. 17–19; And how can it be, Lady Love, says Reason, that this Soul can will what this book says, when before it said that she had no more will?; 85). Reason here expects the world and words to function according to the standards and rules she knows. She would do well to have put to memory the lesson of Hugh of St. Victor discussed in the introduction to this volume: "The divine deeper meaning can never be absurd, never false.... the deeper meaning admits no contradiction, is always harmonious, always true."[30] The context offers the clue as to how to understand the way language is meaning here. While G. Ronald Murphy stresses the "poetic context" in his "The Language of Love," included in this volume, it is a theological context that here determines the way language means. The confusion described by Murphy fits our Reason, and perhaps some readers, equally well: "If the poetic context is not considered, the puzzlement faced by a reader whose overall understanding of a passage is being influenced by an exclusively linguistic analysis of a name is increased."[31] The linguistic and grammatical laws can be respected in mystical discourse even as the laws of logic are abandoned. To do so, however, means to resort to quite a bit of play. And so Love answers in this way:

> Raison, dit Amour, ce n'est mie sa voulenté qui le vieult, mais ainçoys est la voulenté de Dieu, qui le vieult en elle; car ceste Amen e demoure mie en Amour qui ce lui face vouloir par nul desirer. Ainçoys demoure Amour en elle, qui a prinse sa voulenté et pource fait Amour sa voulenté d'elle, et adonc oeuvre Amour en elle sans elle, par quoy il n'est mesaise qui en elle puisse demourer.   (26, ll. 20–26)

> [Reason, says Love, it is no longer her will which wills, but now the will of God wills in her; for this Soul dwells not in love which causes her to will this through desiring something. Instead, Love dwells in her who seized her will, and Love accomplishes Love's will in her. Thus Love works in her without her, which is why no anxiety can remain in her. (85)]

The physical and metaphorical heart as container has been traded for the will. Love attempts to explain to reason how it is the soul at one with God and Love that can at once "will" when it is without a "will" at all. How can a being without the stuff of willing perform the act of willing? A split is introduced between

---

[30] This passage is quoted in the introduction to this volume, Classen, "Introduction," 00
[31] See the chapter by G. Ronald Murphy in this volume.

"to will" the predicate, and the "will" as thing.[32] The linguistic split allows for a union of souls. The soul joined with the Godhead has no will, for as Love reminds Reason, and us, over and over, this soul has nothing, "n'a nyent." Nor can this soul act in any way that distinguishes her from God—there is no distinct self to act. Thus Love clarifies the paradox by using the language of container / contained in regard to will. In so doing, we are able to see the significance of containment in the process of deconstructing the self. Once the physical boundaries have been penetrated, determining where the will begins and ends becomes more difficult.

The containment of the soul, the image of container / contained, leads to a complete breakdown of binaries, for in Marguerite Porete's *Mirouer* Love explains, "Donc par cestuy entendement scet ceste Ame tout et sin e scet neant. Elle veult tout, dit Amour, et si ne veult neant; car ceste Ame, dit Amour, veult si parfaictement la voulenté de Dieu, qu'elle ne scet, ne ne peut, ne ne veult en son vouloir que la voulenté de Dieu, tant l'a Amour mise en forte prison" (64, 66, ll. 7–12; Thus through this intellect this Soul knows all and so knows nothing. She wills all things, says Love, and so wills nothing; for this Soul, says Love, wills so perfectly the will of God that she neither knows, nor is able, nor wills in her own will except the will of God, because Love holds her in strong captivity; 98). Here the play is between the two terms normally placed on opposite ends of a spectrum: all and nothing. In attempting to define the divine, the difference, the binary system on which language is based, proves unworthy of the task. Definitions of perfection cannot be made in a single word or even a single phrase. Reason asks Love to "Hee, Amour, dit Raison, nomez ceste Ame par son droit non, donnez en aux actifz aucune congnoissance (34, ll. 3–4; name this Soul by her right name, give to the Actives some understanding of it; 87). But she is in perfection and so beyond the binary on which definitions are built. Love answers that she "can be named" by twelve names. There is no single name matching the identity of this perfect soul. Instead she lists the twelve names possible within the broad space of her identification:

> La tres merveilleuce.
> La non congnue.
> La plus innocent[e] des filles de Jheruzalem.
> Celle sur qui toute Saincte Esglise est fondee.
> L'enluminee de congnoissance.
> L'aournee d'amour.
> La vive de louenge.
> L'adnientie en toutes choses par humilité.
> La paisible en divin estre par divine voulenté

---

[32] See M. Djuth, "Will," *Augustine Through the Ages: An Encyclopedia*, ed. Allen D. Fitzgerald (Grand Rapids, MI, and Cambridge: W. B. Eerdmans, 1999), 881–85.

Language for Lovers

> Celle qui ne vieult nient, for la divine voulenté
> La remplie et assovye sans nulle defaillance de divine bonté,
> Par l'œuvre de la Trinité
> son dernier non cest obliance.   (34, 36, ll. 7–19)

> [The very marvelous One.
> The Not Understood.
> Most Innocent of the Daughters of Jerusalem.
> She upon whom the Holy Church is founded.
> Illuminated by Understanding.
> Adorned by Love.
> Living by Praise.
> Annihilated in all things through Humility.
> At peace in divine being through divine will.
> She who wills nothing except the divine will.
> Filled and satisfied without any lack by divine goodness
> through the work of the Trinity.
> Her last name is: Oblivion, Forgotten.   (88)

The definition of God provided in Marguerite's *Mirouer* absorbs everything. It is as though all the words in the human vocabulary simply do not suffice for he is "tout par tout, tout puissant, toute sapience, et toute bonté. Il est nostre pere, nostre frere et nostre loyal amy. Il est sans commencement. Il est incomprehensible fors que de luy mesmes. Il est sans fin, trios personnes et ung seul Dieu; et tel est, dit ceste Ame l'amy de noz ames" (22; He is everywhere present, omnipotent, omniscient, and total goodness. He is our Father, our Brother and our Loyal Lover. He is without beginning. He is incomprehensible except by Himself. He is without end, three persons and one God; and as such, says this Soul, He is the Lover of our souls; 84). In this series the definitions show no regard for the possible contradictions that may be found within.

Perhaps one of the most stunning strings of definitions in this style is found in the poetry of another French mystic, this one from the modern world. The poem, "La rosée divine," begins:

> Mon doux Jésus, sur le sein de ta Mère
> Tu m'apparais tout rayonnant d'Amour.
> L'Amour, voilà l'ineffable mystère
> Qui t'exila du céleste Séjour.

[My sweet Jesus, on the breast of your mother you appear to me completely beaming with love. Love, that is the ineffable mystery which exiled you from the heavenly sojourn.][33]

"La Rosée divine" opens with the description of Jesus with his mother where she says "Tu m'apparais tout rayonnant d'Amour." In the following lines her thought moves on the level of the word, rather than the image or concept, for she continues: "L'Amour, voilà l'ineffable mystère / qui t'exila du céleste Séjour." The word "Amour" is the same but the concept is different: while in the first it is the love which Christ radiates, what follows is the love which is the reason for Christ's incarnation and death, no longer the passive actor in the relationship but a force. This is a type of love she discusses in stanza four saying, "l'amour te pousse a souffrir" and in the poem "Vivre d'amour" saying, "la charité me presse."[34] Just as Reason had to learn in Marguerite's *Mirouer*, words work in a unique way in the world of Thérèse. It would seem the word functions on its own, without the difference in signified that the context has introduced. She moves through the images and the various meanings of the word without regard for what the word had meant in the particular instance. She attempts to break down the power of the word to limit reality.

In the second stanza Thérèse launches into a detailed identification of Jesus with the Rose. She repeatedly employs the copula: "C'est du matin la rosée bienfaisant . . . qui . . . fait entrouvrir la fleur" (236, ll.13–16; It is the beneficent morning dew that makes the flower open; 38); then: "C'est toi, Jésus, la fleur à peine éclose, . . . C'est toi, Jésus, la ravissante Rose" (236, ll. 17–19; It is you Jesus, the flower slightly opened, ... It is you, Jesus, the ravishing rose; 38). The close-up of the baby flower pulls back to reveal Mary's place in the picture: "Ton doux soleil, c'est le sein de Marie / Et ta Rosée, c'est le Lait Virginal!" (236, 23–24; Your sweet sun, it is the breast of Mary, and your dew, it's the virginal milk!; 38). These are nothing less than simple equations in which Jesus is equal to the Rose, Mary's breast to the sun. Here Thérèse only plays with the equations possible through language of things usually not brought together, equating the dew with the mother's milk and then says, "Ton sang divin, c'est le Lait Virginal." The dew once defined as the virginal milk is also the divine blood shed on the cross, and in stanza five the dew loses all uniqueness for it is now the "verbe fait Hostie, / Prêtre eternal, Agneau sacerdotal, / Le fils de Dieu, c'est le fils de Marie / Le pain de l'Ange est le Lait Virginal" (236, ll. 37–40; The

---

[33] Thérèse de Lisieux, *The Poetry of Saint Thérèse of Lisieux*, ed. and trans. Donald Kinney (Washington, DC: ICS Publications Institute of Carmelite Studies, 1996), 236; Engl. trans. on 37, 38.
[34] 260, ll. 59

Language for Lovers

Word made Host, the eternal priest, the sacerdotal lamb, the son of God is the son of Mary, and the Angel's bread is the virginal milk; 38).[35]

Thérèse abandons the equalizing unit of "C'est," simply allowing the poem to give way to a series of objects in which things are linked in a flurry that seems to intend a flattening of all difference. She closes this ecstatic maneuvering exclaiming: "Moi faible enfant, je ne vois au ciboire / que la couleur, la figure du Lait / Mais c'est le Lait qui convient a l'enfance / Et de Jésus l'Amour est sans égal / O tendre Amour! Insondable puissance / Ma blanche Hostie, c'est le Lait Virginal!" (6; 3–8). An important transformation in her use of language has occurred between her first lines which spoke of Love and these lines of the fifth stanza. While in the first stanza the word led her to move from one essence of Love to the other, here the word is left spinning as she abandons the possibility of the meaningful signifier and moves instead through a list of the words, the many signifiers, which should not be brought together — bread is not milk — seemingly infinite and therefore meaningless, which refer to the One signified. Thérèse celebrates the simplicity of a unity which overrides rhetorical incompatibility.

The blurring of difference also allows Angela of Foligno to say "tu sii io e io sia tu"(581; I am you and you are me; 126). Through the breaking down of binaries of difference the beloved and the lover have become one.

Just as all words are not enough to signify the divine, so too, for the lover, do all things point back to the beloved. When Arnaut de Maruelh thinks he is contemplating something else, he finds his mind looking once again upon his lady.

> Can cug pensar en autra res,
> De vos ai messatje cortes,
> Mon cor, q'es lai vostr' ostaliers;
> Me ven de vos sai messatgiers,
> Qu·m ditz e·m remembre'e·m retrae
> Vostre gen cors cuende e gay....[36]

[When I think I am contemplating something else, I have a courtly message from you: it's my heart, that is your guest there, that comes to me as a messenger, to tell me, to remind me, to return my mind to your noble body, gracious and joyous.]

---

[35] For a discussion of this metaphor, see Friedrich Ohly, "Dew and Pearl: A Lecture," idem, *Sensus Spiritualis: Studies in Medieval Significs and the Philology of Culture*, ed. and with an epilogue by Samuel P. Jaffe, trans. Kenneth J. Northcott (orig. 1973; Chicago and London: The University of Chicago Press, 2005), 234–50.

[36] *Les Saluts d'amour du troubadour Arnaud de Mareuil*, ed. Pierre Bec. Bibliothèque méridionale, 31 (Toulouse: É. Privat, 1961), no. 1, ll. 79–84.

The lover is enveloped in the realm of the beloved. Nothing else can pull the troubadour's eye away from the lady. He is consumed by her completely.

For troubadour and mystic, the beloved, love, and loving alone are important. The words of the lover do not serve a communicative function so much as they allow for the lover to exercise the limits of the self, and ultimately destroy difference, the most significant of obstacles separating lover and beloved. The common goal of troubadour and mystic is to arrive at a selfless state, and the use of words to reach this state of selflessness explains the common usage of uncommon wordings. The two lovers demonstrate that it is through words that one becomes a lover and that to master the art of love one must master the art of words.

CHAPTER 8

LA DAME ET L'AMOUR: LES MOTS POUR DIRE LA BEAUTÉ ET LA PASSION. D'APRÈS UN CHOIX DES *CHANSONS* DE GUILLAUME D'AQUITAINE ET DES *LAIS* DE MARIE DE FRANCE

(THE LADY AND LOVE: WORDS TO SAY BEAUTY AND PASSION. ACCORDING TO A SELECTION OF *LES CHANSONS* BY GUILLAUME D'AQUITAINE AND OF *LES LAIS* BY MARIE DE FRANCE)

ANNA KUKUŁKA-WOJTASIK
Nicolas Copernicus University, Torun, Poland

Le paradoxe des amants qui aiment sans s'aimer l'un l'autre n'est qu'une vérité partielle et ne résout point l'énigme de la littérature courtoise qui est à la fois manifestation et instrument d'agir du vaste courant social et littéraire qu'est la courtoisie (*cortezia*).[1] Il est vrai qu'elle est hautement stéréotypée et que les mêmes motifs reviennent de façon récurrente répondant à un schéma préconçu. Nous allons examiner un seul motif, celui du portrait de la dame aimée, dans deux genres différents: la chanson (*canso*) et le lai. La rhétorique de l'aveu amoureux de la chanson des troubadours et des trouvères diverge nécessairement de celle du conte versifié où le *je* autodiégétique du poète amant est remplacé par

---

[1] Il existe des définitions multiples de *courtois*, de *courtoisie*, de *fin'amor*, à la fois mode de vie et mode d'écrire. Nous en citons, à titre d'exemple, celles de J. Frappier, de A. J. Denomy, de M. Lazar et de Ch. Baladier. Elles se trouvent *in extenso* dans les Annexes. Nous y signalons aussi les distinctions entre *courtoisie*, *courtois* et *fin'amor*.

les pronoms *il, elle, ils* de l'histoire et le *je*, s'il apparaît, est celui de narrateur, commentateur ou moralisateur. Le troubadour chante sa dame et son amour en son nom et pour son propre compte dans l'espoir d'une récompense, tandis que le romancier conte son histoire qu'il prétend vraie, pour bien apprendre et enseigner (par exemple Chrétien de Troyes, dans le prologue du *Conte d'Erec*), ou, et c'est le cas de Marie de France, pour la faire perdurer ("pur remambrance," *Les Lais, Prologue*, 35)[2] et aussi pour en tirer plaisir comme elle le dit dans l'épilogue de *Milon*: "De lur amur et de lur bien / Firent un lai li auncien, / E jeo, ki l'ai mis en escrit, / Al recunter mult me delit" (*Milun*, 531–34) (changes tous les autres cas en concordance avec cet modèle). Le problème épineux du destinataire du chant et du conte courtois se trouve à l'origine d'un malaise critique.

S'il nous était possible de considérer la *canso* comme une missive amoureuse dont le destinataire direct serait la dame, uniquement, et de voir le destinataire du conte dans un large public aristocratique, l'objectif du troubadour et celui du conteur seraient nécessairement divergents. Cependant, la missive du troubadour est une missive publique et le poète chantant son amour s'adresse aussi bien à sa dame qu'à son public.[3] Son objectif est donc double: gagner l'amour de sa dame et la gloire du poète. Le conte et la *canso* possèdent donc un dénominateur commun qui est de chanter l'amour qui se veut vrai et authentique et cela dans le but d'en tirer de la gloire: dans les deux cas cet amour est présenté comme réellement vécu puisque le garant de son authenticité est d' une part le *je* amoureux du poète et de l'autre la véracité de l'histoire racontée que le conteur-jongleur ne manque jamais de rappeler, prétendant en avoir pris la connaissance dans un livre ou par ouï-dire.

Si dans le cas de la *canso* nous pouvons parler de la rhétorique de l'aveu, dans celui du conte ou du lai, c'est la rhétorique de l'agencement, du rassemblement, de la *bele conjointure*[4] d'un récit déjà connu et vrai qu'il ne s'agit que de bien présenter. Marie elle-même parle du "pris" qu'elle recherche: elle pensait "D'aukune bone estoire faire" (*Prologue*, 29), la traduisant "de latin en romaunz," mais, puisque tant d'autres s'y sont essayés, elle craignit de n'en tirer plus aucune gloire. Elle

---

[2] Toutes les citations de Marie de France viennent de l'édition de Jean Rychner, ed., *Les Lais de Marie de France*. Les Classiques français du moyen âge, 87 (Paris: Honoré Champion, 1966).

[3] Analysant la chanson IX de Guilhem, Jean Charles Payen écrit dans son essai *Le Prince d'Aquitaine: Essai sur Guillaume IX, son œuvre et son érotique* (Paris: H. Champion, 1980), 123: "Elle (la chanson) n'est apparemment écrite pour personne, hormis pour son auteur lui-même et pour une bien-aimée qui n'est jamais présentée comme une dédicatrice. Mais la création n'en est pas moins un acte public. L'éloge a besoin d'un auditoire le plus vaste qui puisse être. La célébration de la dame sera d'autant plus éclatante que son poète sera plus renommé." Cette observation vaut bien pour tous les autres cas.

[4] Le terme de *conjointure*, ambigu et sujet à maintes interprétations, est de Chrétien de Troyes, *Erec et Enide*, publiés par Mario Roque. Les Classiques francais du moyen âge, 80 (Paris: Champion, 1970), vs 13. Voir Douglas Kelley, *The Art of Medieval French Romance* (Madison: The University of Wisconsin Press, 1992), 15–31.

décida donc de sauver de l'oubli les aventures qu'elle avait entendu conter (*Prologue*, 30–40). Elle entreprit "des lais assembler, / par rime faire e reconter" (*Prologue*, 47–8). Elle souligne, comme Chrétien, son contemporain, son temps et son labeur pour les mettre en vers: "Rime en ai e fait ditié / soventes feiz en ai veillié" (*Prologue*, 41–42). Le problème de l'originalité ne se pose pas, au contraire, pour que l'aventure soit vraie, même si, de fait, elle était originale, il fallait lui inventer une source, plus ou moins imaginaire. Le travail propre de l'auteur consistait justement dans le fait d'"assembler" les aventures qu'il prétendait connaître d'autres sources. Dans la *canso*, où pourtant le *je* chante sa souffrance et sa joie d'aimer, nous ne trouvons, non plus, aucune recherche d'originalité; au contraire, nous avons l'impression que le poète se cache derrière les stéréotypes et utilise sciemment les structures connues, les motifs conventionnels pour, paradoxalement, donner du prix à sa poésie.[5]

L'expression littéraire de la *fin'amor*,[6] la *bon'amor* de Guillaume, traduite dans le français moderne comme l'amour pur, parfait ou noble, est soumise à plusieurs règles et contraintes, voire paradoxes. Individuelle et secrète, elle devient une missive publique, et en tant que telle doit obéir à un règlement et à un certain nombre de prescriptions, aussi bien littéraires que sociales. Ce message d'amour du poète amant qui veut par son chant conquérir à la fois et l'amour de la dame (ce qui est un objectif intime) et la gloire (objectif mondain, social), ce qui peut paraître incompatible, est l'œuvre d'un art d'écrire très spécial possédant sa propre rhétorique et une casuistique amoureuse appropriée. La chanson, œuvre de cour, devait être conforme à un nombre de conventions sociales déterminant la position du poète par rapport à sa dame et à son public.

Si nous comparons les requêtes amoureuses de Guillaume d'Aquitaine et celles de Bernard de Ventadour, par exemple, nous verrons, d'un côté, l'audace et l'orgueil d'un grand seigneur qui rêve de mettre les mains sous le manteau de sa dame et, de l'autre, la timidité soumise d'un troubadour qui crie son désir et n'ose rien demander à sa dame: elle pourrait le faire ressusciter des morts mais: "Dirai com? No sui tan arditz" (Dirai-je comment? Je ne suis pas si audacieux; Ventadour, *Chanson* 42: IV, 32).[7] Le souci de bien écrire, de trouver les mots et les rimes les plus réussis, en somme de former (peut-on dire créer?) une belle chanson est commun à toute la génération des troubadours et des trouvères. Le premier des

---

[5] Cf. Jean Frappier, *Amour courtois et Table ronde*. Publications romanes et françaises, 126 (Genève: Librairie Droz, 1973), 6: "Qu'on ne se laisse pas égarer par l'impression de monotonie que n'est pas sans causer le lyrisme courtois! Cette poésie, inséparable de la musique, ne l'oublions pas, cherche son originalité non dans le renouvellement de l'inspiration, mais dans un agencement subtil de clichés, une architecture de mots, d'expressions, d'images traditionnels, de formes sonores."

[6] Voir Annexes: *fin'amor*.

[7] Bernart de Ventadorn, *Chansons d'amour*, éd. critique avec traduction, introduction, notes et glossaire par Moshe Lazar. Bibliothèque française et romane. Sér. B: Éditions critiques de textes, 4 (Paris: Klincksieck, 1966).

troubadours, Guillaume, s'en vante dans la *Chanson* VII: "Del vers vos dig que mais en vau / Qui ben l'enten ni plus l'esgau, / (tourjours espace a les deux cotes) Que-l mot son fag tug per egau / Cominalmens, / E-l sonetz, qu'ieu mezeis me-n lau, / Bos e valens" ((Je vous dis, au sujet de ce "vers," que celui-là en vaut davantage qui l'entend et y prend plaisir; car tous les couplets sont exactement réglés sur la même mesure, et la mélodie, j'ai le droit de m'en vanter, en est bonne et belle; Guillaume, *Chanson VII*: VII, 37–43).[8] Bernard de Ventadour en parle aussi, et presque dans les mêmes termes, dans la *Chanson* 29, par exemple: "Faihz es lo vers tot a randa, / si que motz no'i deschapdolha" (Chanson est parfaitement achevée, sans qu'un seul mot y soit défectueux; Ventadour, 29: VI, 36–37). Ce motif revient aussi dans d'autres chansons, par exemple *Chanson* XVI, 26. Comme nous voyons, les préoccupations des conteurs et des troubadours dans le domaine de l'art d'écrire sont semblables: il s'agissait de bien présenter le texte, choisir le mot le plus juste, le plus sonore, y ajouter de la musique agréable à écouter et facile à commémorer, quant au sujet lui-même, Amour, et les motifs accompagnants sous-jacents, ils étaient imposés et incontournables.

L'objet de notre examen sont les portraits des dames aimées, telles que les peint le troubadour amoureux dans le chant et dans le conte, le protagoniste amant qui voit pour la première fois sa dame et en tombe amoureux. Il s'avère pourtant que l'ami ne voit pas sa dame ou la voit mal et c'est le narrateur et / ou d'autres personnages qui la décrivent. Le portrait amoureux est un motif récurrent, fortement stéréotypé, présent dans tout œuvre courtoise, dont l'analyse nous permettra, espérons-nous, d'appréhender la part d'intime, de lyrique et d'imaginaire, mais aussi, et peut-être surtout, de symbolique, dans cette rhétorique amoureuse qu'on perçoit, d'habitude, si conventionnelle et si pétrifiée. Pour le champ de notre analyse nous avons choisi *Les Chansons* de Guillaume IX d'Aquitaine et *Les Lais* de Marie de France pour deux raisons: *primo*: ils sont tous les deux représentants de la première génération, respectivement, des troubadours et des conteurs (le lai peut être considéré comme un petit conte d'une aventure d'amour); *secundo*: ils ont en commun quelques traits caractéristiques: une diversité de registres, ils parlent d'amours différents, bons et mauvais; se distinguent par un raffinement intellectuel et artistique: leur œuvre est imbue d'une certaine authenticité et d'une fraîcheur qui leur sont particulières; et, enfin, leurs portraits ne sont pas statiques, ils jouent un rôle dans l'aventure amoureuse du couple. Le choix de ces deux auteurs présente encore un autre avantage: leur œuvre est restreinte. Dans le cas de Guillaume nous pouvons parler de quatre *Chansons*, de la VII à la X, qui constituent le cycle dit de Maubergeonne, celui

---

[8] Guillaume IX, Duc d'Aquitaine (1076–1127), *Chansons*, éd. Alfred Jeanroy. Deuxième édition revue. Les Classiques français du moyen âge, 9 (Paris: Librairie ancienne Edouard Champion, 1927). Toutes les citations de Guillaume se réfèrent à cette édition.

La Dame et L'amour

de la *bon'amor*, chanté par un poète amoureux et soumis.[9] La rupture de ton, de thèmes, de rhétorique par rapport aux six chansons précédentes nous autorise à considérer ces quatre chansons comme un cycle à part et à y chercher le portrait de la dame, le premier en date de la littérature courtoise. L'œuvre de Marie se limite aux douze lais,[10] dont nous avons choisi trois: *Guigemar*, *Equitan* et *Eliduc* présentant trois sortes d'amour différentes.

Guilhem de Peitieus, Guillaume IX, duc d'Aquitaine fut le premier troubadour, premier poète qui parla de la *bon'amor*, amour dévotion, amour adoration, amour fidélité, exaltation et désir. Nous savons beaucoup sur ce grand prince, personnage historique mais nous connaissons peu le poète: son œuvre conservée ne comprend que les onze chansons dont le ton disparate rend vaine toute recherche d'une évolution: il est vain de chercher les raisons de la conversion de cet hédoniste éhonté en amant courtois, de même qu'il est impossible de suivre les étapes de cette transformation.[11] Nous ne pouvons que constater que dans

---

[9] Cf. Frede Jensen, *Provençal Philology and the Poetry of Guillaume de Poitier*. Études romanes de l'Université d'Odense, 13 (Odense: Odense University Press, 1983), 10: "Of Guillaume's literary production, a total of eleven poems have survived. They are divided by Diez and Jeanroy into three different categories: the first group (I–VI) comprises humorous and at times crude or obscene compositions in which is to be found *mais foudat no'i a de sen* 'more folly than reason'. The second group (VII–X), couched in a more idealistic vein and reflecting the feudal concept of courtly love, shows this powerful lord as submitted to his lady and capable of a more elevated sensivity, while the last group, consisting of only one poem (XI), strikes different and more serious chord, that of a sincere repentance."

[10] Marie de France était-elle réellement l'auteur, et l'auteur unique, des douze lais qui lui sont généralement attribués? Il existe un nombre de lais anonymes qui présentent des ressemblances réelles avec ceux de Marie. Voir à ce sujet, par exemple, Donald Maddox, "Rewriting Marie de France: The Anonymous '*Lai du conseil*,'" *Speculum* 80, 2 (2005): 399–437; spécialement 399–403.

[11] Il existe plusieurs hypothèses concernant les sources et l'origine de la *fin'amor*. Il faudrait surtout y mentionner la "théorie arabe," (celle de la poésie arabo-andalouse [*zadjal*]) et celle de la poésie médio-latine utilisée dans le cadre de la tradition liturgique, mais il est possible, aussi, de chercher ces sources dans le conditionnement familial et la vie même du premier troubadour. Voir à ce sujet, par exemple, Pierre Bec, *Le comte de Poitiers, premier troubadour. A l'aube d'un verbe et d'une érotique* (Montpellier: Université de Montpellier III, Centre d'études occitanes, 2004), 32–45: "(. . .) il (Reto Bezzola) insiste surtout sur les amours mystiques de Fortunat, évêque de Poitiers et poète latin (530–600), et de Radegonde, femme de Clotaire Ier, retirée dans un couvent fondée par elle à Poitiers. C'est cette passion sublimée qui aurait pu servir de point de départ à la conception de la *fin'amor* et de la dame objet de culte: la poésie de Fortunat fait en effet 'à la femme une place capitale et mène droit déjà à la conception de l'urbanité médiévale et moderne que nous appelons la courtoisie' (. . .). A cela s'ajouterait l'influence exemplaire de l'abbaye de Fontevrault fondée en 1103 par Robert d'Arbrissel (et confirmée par le pape en 1105), donc au temps de Guillaume IX, abbaye qui groupait une communauté d'hommes et une communauté de femmes placées sous l'autorité d'une abbesse: celle-ci commandait donc aux hommes, auprès desquels elle faisait figure de *domina*. La première femme du comte de Poitiers, Ermengarde, s'y retira et sa seconde, Philippa, y mourut. Cette prééminence de la dame aurait-elle eu une influence sur la constitution de la vénération troubadouresque de la *domna*? D'après Bezzola, ce seraient ces circonstances qui auraient donné à Guillaume le désir d'opposer au mysticisme ascétique de l'époque 'un mysticisme mondain, une élévation spirituelle de l'amour du chevalier rivalisant avec l'attraction qu'exerçaient sur les âmes l'amour mystique et la soumission à la dame que propageait Fontevrault." Voir aussi Paul Zumthor, "An Overview: Why the Troubadours?," *A Handbook of the Troubadours*, eds. F. R. P. Akehurst and Judith M. Davis (Berkeley, Los Angeles, and London: University of California Press, 1995), 11–18.

la *Chanson* VII le ton change radicalement: le chanteur ne s'adresse plus à ses *companhos* pour les faire rire, l'objectif devient différent. C'est dans cette chanson que pour la première fois apparaît la reverdie, une référence au printemps qui deviendra un lieu commun dans la poésie courtoise. Le ton devient grave, *Amor* dont l'importance est rehaussée par A majuscule devient une valeur primordiale et l'image de la femme change radicalement.

Les portraits des dames possèdent leur propre symbolique et portent l'empreinte de leur peintre: ils montrent non seulement la grandeur de l'amour inspirée mais aussi la personnalité de l'amant. Celui de la *dompna*, peint par Guilhem, possède une importance toute particulière puisqu'il est le premier de la longue galerie des portraits amoureux de la littérature courtoise. Le peintre de ce portrait est le troubadour doté d'une personnalité fulgurante et haute en couleurs qui dote sa *dompna* d'une beauté et d'une puissance particulières de sorte que l'image de la dame reflète l'image propre de l'amant: son *je* est toujours présent.

Dans les chansons choisies, comme dans toute *canso*, le destinataire est la dame et le public, et c'est autant pour faire l'éloge de sa dame et pour célébrer son amour pour elle, que pour rechercher sa propre gloire et pour parfaire sa poésie que le poète chante devant un auditoire aussi vaste que possible. Il est notoire que ses chansons, les premières connues, comportent déjà tout le code de l'amour parfait, la future *fin'amor* qui apparaît dans la *Chanson* VIII sous le terme de *bon'amor*. Les règles d'amour codifiées au XIIe siècle par André le Chapelain, contemporain de Chrétien de Troyes, se font déjà jour dans les chansons de Guillaume qui devient serviteur de sa dame dans le sens ambivalent du terme: en tant qu'ami et en tant que poète. Ces deux services se veulent parfaits: il lui incombe, de par l'amour qui devient sa raison d'être et d'agir, le désir ardent de la perfection. Il désire exceller et dans le service vassalique passionnel et dans la poésie qu'il crée. Cette tendance à la perfection semble un élément distinctif de l'activité poétique et chevaleresque des troubadours et trouvères dont le prince est le premier, et déjà arrivé à sa maîtrise, représentant.[12] Le portrait de la dame commence à se faire dessiner à mesure que se forge l'amour du poète dont l'exaltation remplace le récit, parfois grossier, des exploits amoureux des chansons précédentes.

La *dompna* de Guilhem, bien que son nom et son histoire dussent être bien connus de l'auditoire, n'apparaît pas sous son nom dans la poésie, nous la retrouvons dans la chanson VII sous le *senhal* "Mon Esteve" (Guillaume, VII: IX, 47) et dans la X sous celui de "mon Bon Vezi" (Guillaume, X: V, 26). Ces deux *senhals*, mystérieux, car ils masculinisent la *dompna*, la présentant en tant que seigneur

---

[12] Etait-il effectivement le premier des troubadours? Il est sûrement le premier dont les chansons se sont conservées. Le fait de la maîtrise parfaite de la forme de sa poésie pourrait témoigner de l'existence d'une école poétique dont Guillaume serait un disciple. Certes, c'est plausible mais nous ne disposons d'aucun texte pour prouver cette hypothèse. Voir à ce sujet Bec, *Le comte de Poitiers*, 24–28, qui parle d'Eble II de Ventadour et de son école poétique.

féodal, pourraient représenter la même personne, la Maubergeonne,[13] bien que cette identification, en ce qui concerne Mon Estève, soit contestée. Dans la première des chansons d'amour, la chanson VII, la présence de la dame n'est que signalée par l'énigmatique *senhal* Mon Esteve: le poème célèbre l'Amour et la poésie. S'il est possible de reprocher à cette chanson un manque de cohérence, la casuistique courtoise, voire mondaine, s'y trouve déjà dans toute son étendue. Après la reverdie de la première strophe d'ouverture le poète parle de son échec amoureux. Il se plaint amèrement d'avoir échoué mais, dans ses regrets, pointe de l'ironie. Lui, qui a si peu de joie, presque rien, ne sait-il, dans son cœur, que "tout est vain"? Ne connaît-il pas le proverbe qui dit, et qui dit vrai, "A bon coratge bon poder" (Guillaume, VII: IV, 23)? Puis il parle de la soumission et de l'obéissance quasi religieuse qu'il voue à *Amor*, pour passer, sans transition, à faire éloge de sa chanson, de ses vers et de sa musique bonne et belle, "bos et valens" (Guillaume, VII: VII, 42). Les règles du service amoureux poétique sont là: d'une part c'est la soumission à *Amor* et l'obéissance à son règlement, de l'autre, la recherche esthétique. C'est aussi bien le refus de la vilenie qu'une certaine éthique de malheur,[14] où le poète se présente en malheureux, celui qui souffre ayant subi un échec, et cette esthétique du malheur deviendra vite un lieu commun de la poésie amoureuse. Le poème est loin d'être clair, plusieurs vers demeurent obscurs. Qui est Mon Esteve, qui, comme il est suggéré dans la strophe précédente, semble vivre à Narbonne? Le poète lui dédie sa chanson, précisant, par deux fois, que lui-même ne s'y rend pas, et exprime son voeu que ce soit elle, sa poésie, garante de son éloge. Eloge de l'amour, de la dame, ou celui de la poésie?

Le premier portrait, très particulier, car il est plus portrait du poète que de la dame, apparaît dans la chanson VIII.[15] Le poète y fait figure de serviteur de sa dame dans le sens féodal: il est un vassal fidèle mais ardent et impatient qui revendique ouvertement ses droits d'amant. Dans cette chanson nouvelle, la *chansoneta*

---

[13] La Maubergeonne, dite la *Dangeirosa*, est un personnage historique: elle fut femme d'Aimeric Ier, vicomte de Châtellerault. Guillaume maria son fils Guillaume à la fille de la Maubergeonne, Ainor: ils seront parents de la célèbre Aliénor d'Aquitaine.

[14] Cf. Payen, *Le Prince d'Aquitaine*, 109–10: "L'amant est par nécessité courtois, c'est-à-dire apte à des actes qui soient à la fois élégants et méritoires. Il répugne au langage des vilains, qui trahit la rustrerie et l'indélicatesse. Toute une éthique du *melhurar* prend racine dans ces quelques vers, dont le ton n'a plus à voir avec celui des premières chansons."

[15] L'attribution de cette chanson à Guillaume est parfois contestée (p. ex. *The Poetry of William VII, Count of Poitiers, IX Duke of Aquitaine*, ed. and trans. Gerald A. Bond. Garland Library of Medieval Literature, 4 [New York, London: Garland, 1982] place cette *chansoneta* en dehors du corps propre des *Chansons*) mais la maîtrise du code courtois et artistique, la désinvolture et l'ironie qui y percent ne laissent, nous semble-t-il, de doute qu'il est son auteur. Cf. Payen, *Le Prince d'Aquitaine*, 113: "Est-ce à cause de sa singularité par rapport à l'ensemble que ce texte n'a été conservé que par le manuscrit C? Son attribution ne fait pourtant pas de doute: sa ferveur et son ironie trahissent puissamment la main du comte de Poitiers." Voir à ce sujet aussi: Bec, *Le comte de Poitiers*, 217–20, sous-chapitre "Chansoneta." Bec conclut, 220: "Pour revenir au débat sur l'attribution ou non de cette pièce à Guillaume, je dirai que le problème me semble pratiquement insoluble."

nueva, qu'il se dépêche de finir avant que le temps l'en empêche, sa dame le met à l'épreuve, l'épreuve du désir. Il n'est pas ivre, pourtant il semble l'être, il ne peut pas vivre sans elle. Car cet amour—désir est si fort que, s'il reste inassouvi, le poète — ami en mourra. Cependant, assure-t-il, jamais, quoiqu'elle lui reproche, il ne voudra s'affranchir de son joug. Il le dit avec son clin d'œil habituel car il le jure sur la tête de Saint Grégoire et ce juron irrespectueux nous rappelle la personnalité de ce prince moqueur qui ne se départit jamais de son ironie.[16] Son amour, dit-il, est d'une grandeur et d'une puissance qui le font frissonner et trembler (Guillaume,VIII:VI, 31), sa passion le fait souffrir mortellement (Guillaume,VIII: VI, 23). Le *moi* du poète occupe toute la scène du poème, il se plaint, il souffre, il se soumet à l'épreuve qui le fait mourir mais, même s'il ne cherche pas à s'affranchir de son joug, il essaie bien de remédier à son malheur. Une sorte de menace semble planer sur la dame si elle repousse son amour: le fait-elle pour entrer dans les ordres? "Qual pro y auretz, dompna conja, / Si votr'amors mi deslonja? / Par queus vulhatz metre monja" (Guillaume,VIII: IV,19–21). Dans la strophe suivante il la menace d'entrer lui-même dans le cloître: "Qual pro y auretz, s'ieu m'enclostre / E no-m retenetz per vostre" (Guillaume, VIII: V, 26–27). S'il n'envisage pas de renoncer à son amour, il semble n'en pas donner, non plus, le droit à sa dame: si elle refuse de lui accorder son amour, il ne lui reste qu'à se faire nonne. La promesse du bonheur illumine la fin de ce poème: tout le *joy* du monde sera le leur si son amour est partagé: "Totz le joys del mon es nostre, Dompna, s'amduy nos amam" (Guillaume,VIII: V, 27–28), promet-il à sa dame. La dame qui inspire cet amour profond et fidèle apparaît dans le texte sous les termes de *dona, bona dompna, bona dompna, dompna conja, dompna*. Elle y paraît, comme nous le voyons, cinq fois, dans toutes les strophes (*coblas*), sauf dans la dernière, celle de l'envoi où à la *bona dompna*, dame parfaite des strophes précédentes, correspond la *bon'amor,* l'amour parfait. C'est pour la première fois que dans la *canso* des troubadours apparaît le terme même de la *bon'amor,* qui deviendra, dans les poèmes de ses successeurs, troubadours et trouvères, la *fin'amor,* cet amour fidélité et dévotion. A la *bona dompna* la *bon'amor,* à la dame parfaite le service parfait, à la plus noble des dames, le plus noble des amours: elle surpasse toutes les autres, donc elle est digne d'un culte qui l'honore, d'un sentiment plein de respect, de soumission (feinte ou réelle), d'une passion inspirée par le haut idéal de vertu et de beauté qu'elle incarne.[17] Dans cette chanson la dame reste anonyme: nous ne savons rien ou presque rien sur elle, le poète ne confie à son auditoire que peu d'informations. Nous apprenons que sa dame "plus ez blanca qu'evori, / Per qu'ieu autra non azori" (Guillaume,VIII: III, 13–14). L'argument peut, aujourd'hui, paraître léger, mais à l'époque la blancheur de peau était la première des qualités qui, à côté de

---

[16] Cf. Payen, *Le Prince d'Aquitaine,* 113–14.
[17] Cette définition nous renvoie à la notion même de la *cortezia,* celle formulée par Moshe Lazar où le prix et la valeur de la dame sont les éléments primordiaux. Voir Annexes, 215.

la gentillesse, faisait le prix de la dame. Par contre, la forme de cette chanson est réellement légère. De fait, ce n'est pas une *canso*, une chanson, c'est une chansonnette, *una chansoneta*, comme l'appelle le poète lui-même dans son premier vers d'introduction. Ses vers sont courts, heptasyllabiques, les rimes féminines, elle ne compte que six strophes et son rythme est gai, presque dansant, emprunté, paraît-il, à une chanson populaire. Elle est cependant *nueva*, nouvelle dans le ton et dans l'expression, elle ne vante ni le plaisir, ni les exploits amoureux; la rhétorique populaire du *gab* y est totalement absente, le poète y introduit la casuistique amoureuse caractéristique de la littérature courtoise, celle de l'amour pur qui révèle ici son caractère double: il est fait d'épreuves et de souffrances mais aussi du *joy*. Ce *joy*, du seul fait qu'il est espéré longtemps et exige des sacrifices, se divinise, devient grandiose, sublime. Pourtant ce *joy* reste charnel, l'amour du duc est un désir violent, puissant dans ses pulsions, témoin ce souhait ardent du baiser de la dame "en cambr' o sotz ram" (Guillaume, VIII: III, 18). La dame dont la silhouette se faufile dans les vers, plus blanche qu'ivoire, la seule que le poète désire, semblant refuser son amour au poète, est cause de sa souffrance, mais, s'ils s'aiment réciproquement, tout le *joy* du monde sera le leur.

    La chanson suivante, la IXème, montre le poète soumis, adorant sa dame. Il en peint dans des termes hyperboliques un portrait qui la déifie et qui reste néanmoins d'une sincérité touchante. La dame y apparaît dans toute sa grâce et dans toute sa beauté. Elle est dotée de puissances divines de charme, de bonté, et de magnificence capables de changer le jour en nuit et le bonheur en malheur. Elle devient ainsi une déesse rayonnante et puissante qui régit l'existence du poète, mais son règne s'étend sur tous ceux qu'elle accueille, tous doivent lui être soumis. C'est le plus beau des portraits, et aussi le plus puissant. Laissons parler le poète: "Totz joys li deu humiliar, / Et tota ricor obezir / Mi dons, per son belh plazent aculhir / E per son belh plazent esguar; / Et deu hom mais cent ans durar / Qui-l joy de s'amor pot sazir. / Per son joy pot malautz sanar, / E per sa ira sas morir / E savis hom enfolezir / E belhs hom sa beutat mudar / E-l plus cortes vilanejar / E totz vilas encortezir." (Guillaume, IX: IV–V, 18–30). (Toute joie doit s'humilier devant elle / Et toute noblesse doit s'incliner / Devant ma dame, a cause de son doux accueil / Et de son regard bel et plaisant; / Il aura plus de cent ans à vivre, / Celui qui peut savourer la joie de son amour. / Par sa joie, le malade peut guérir / Et par sa colère mourir l'homme sain / Et devenir fou le sage / Et le bellâtre perdre sa beauté / Et le plus courtois devenir vilain / Et tout vilain se faire courtois).

    Il est difficile de rester insensible à cette image de la dame construite savamment d'antonymes familiers: malade-sain, fou-sage, beau-laid, vilain-courtois. La louange que le poète offre à sa dame, qui reste ici abstraite, devient une célébration universelle de la Dame dont il faut implorer la grâce, qu'il faut craindre et exalter. Ce panégyrique semble dénié par la strophe suivante où le poète revendique ses droits de l'amant qui désire posséder pour lui seul celle que lui-même et tous doivent célébrer: puisqu'elle est la plus belle au monde il veut l'avoir auprès de lui pour rafraîchir son cœur et garder son corps de vieillir: "A mos ops la vueilh retenir, / per lo cor dedins refescar / E per la carn renovellar, / Que no puesca envellezir" (Guillaume, IX: VI, 33–36). Il promet à sa dame, si elle daigne lui donner son amour, de n'agir que selon son plaisir, de rehausser son prix et de chanter son éloge: "Si-m vol mi dons s'amor donar, / Pres suy del penr' et del grazir / E del celar e del blandir / E de sos plazrs dir et far / E de sos pretz tener en car / E de son laus enavantir" (Guillaume, IX: VII, 37–42). Dans la dernière strophe il investit sa dame du pouvoir seigneurial en se présentant devant elle humble et craintif, pour revenir dans les derniers vers à l'image de la dame consolatrice dont il espère la guérison de son mal: "Mas elha-m deum mo mielhs triar, / Pus sap qu'ab lieys ai a guerir" (Guillaume, IX: VIII, 47–48). Un clin d'œil ironique qui ouvre la seconde strophe où il s'adresse directement à son auditoire, ses *companhos*, protestant qu'il n'aimait ni *gaber* ni se vanter: "Ieu, so sabetz, no-m dey gabar / Ni de grans laus no-m say formir" (Guillaume,IX: II, vs 7–8) nous renseigne sur la nature de ce *ieu* qui garde toujours ses distances. Les clins d'œil, épars dans la chanson, vers les *companhos* nous révèlent la nature incorrigible de ce prince qui ne se départit pas totalement de ses habitudes et de ses plaisirs d'autrefois. Il sait que ses *gabs* ne sont pas oubliés, et que ses strophes licencieuses sont bien connues de ceux à qui il chante maintenant sa dévotion amoureuse[18] et il s'y réfère en plaisantant: il n'a jamais aimé ni se moquer (*gabar*) des autres ni se vanter de ses exploits.

Toutes les chansons de Guillaume possèdent ce caractère double où le sublime de la vénération se mêle à la crudité du désir et où, jamais, une distance ironique par rapport à ses aveux ne fait défaut.[19] La dernière des chansons du cycle de la Maubergeonne, la Chanson X n'échappe pas à la règle: aux images délicates du printemps naissant de la strophe première et à la métaphore d'une branche d'aubépine tremblante (strophe III) symbolisant la fragilité de l'amour succède ce souhait désinvolte, témoignage de l'arrogance de ce prince troubadour qui n'hésite pas de prier Dieu de lui laisser réaliser son désir: "Enquer me lais Dieus viure tan / C'aja mas manz soz so mantel," de mettre les mains sous le manteau de la dame (Guillaume, X: IV, 23–24).[20] La chanson ferait partie de l'histoire du couple

---

[18] Cf. Payen, *Le Prince d'Aquitaine*, 120: "Le comte de Poitiers, à la cantonade, prétend être incapable de *gab*. Mais l'incise *so sabetz* s'adresse sans doute d'abord à son auditoire immédiat, celui des *companhos* qui connaissent les chansons antérieures; et de toute façon, Guillaume IX sait très bien que la postérité n'oubliera pas la verve de ses *nugae*. Il se moque de ses auditeurs en les prenant à parti: touche provocatrice qu'il ne faudrait pourtant pas surestimer."

[19] Voir à ce sujet Sarah Kay, *Courtly Contradictions: The Emergence of the Literary Object in the Twelfth Century*. Figurae (Stanford: Stanford University Press, 2001), 44: "Throughout the subsequent tradition, and however great the increasing weight of convention upon it, troubadours will retain a sense that they are crazy to sing of love as they do and that therefore they are inevitably at odds with the commonsense attitudes of others."

[20] Les motifs de la rhétorique amoureuse y sont bien présents: les motifs printaniers, ainsi que la soumission et la timidité du poète attendant dans l'angoisse la décision de sa dame qui deviendront

qui devait être agitée puisque le poète y parle de la "guerra." Cependant, c'est le poème de *nos*, de *nostr'amor* vécu ensemble, du poète et de sa dame devenue son amante. Elle y est présente sous le *senhal* "Bon *Vezi*," et, par ailleurs, elle n'apparaît dans le texte que dans l'adjectif possessif *sa* (*drudari*) et *son* (*anel*). Le poème, comme les précédents d'ailleurs, reste énigmatique. Il est, tout semble l'indiquer, un poème de réconciliation avec la dame que, après des jours et des nuits d'angoisse, le poète retrouve dans un geste de tendresse (*drudari*) et de soumission (*anel*) qu'elle lui accorde: "Enquer me membra d'un mati / Que nos fezem de guerra fi, / E que –m donet un don tant gran, / Sa drudari e son anel" (Guillaume, X: IV, 19–22). La dame y est donc une amante, sûrement ombrageuse, mais qui vit sa liaison amoureuse avec son poète, au su et au vu de tous.

Le poète s'y présente en amant angoissé qui attend le messager sans pouvoir dormir ni rire, mais la dame lui est déjà acquise: sûr de sa possession il n'espère qu'une bonne fin à leur querelle: "De lai don plus m'es bon et bel / Non vei messager ni sagel, / Per que mos cors non dorn ni ri, / Ni no m'aus traire adenan, / Tro qe sacha ben de la fi / S'el' es aissi com eu deman (Guillaume, X: II, 7–12). Guillaume y fait rapprochement entre l'amour et la poésie, il parle du *lati* (latin) des oiseaux qui chantent leurs amours, chacun dans son langage, selon les règles *del novel chant*, comme les poètes, dont le langage est étrange (*estraing lati*) et le poète s'en méfie. La chanson semble l'illustration de ce circuit fermé que forment l'amour et la poésie où la perfection de l'un correspond à celle de l'autre: Guillaume est le poète et ami comblé pour qui la poésie et l'amour font corps. Les autres se vantent d'amour et de poésie, lui, il les possède: "Nos n'avem la pessa e-l coutel" (X: V, 30).

Le texte est obscur et se prête à plusieurs interprétations,[21] ce qui nous intéresse ici est la réapparition dans le dernier vers du pronom *nos*. L'identification de ce *nous* pose problème: il peut signifier, entre autres, soit *pluralis majestaticus*, soit le poète et l'amant, soit le poète et son amie, soit l'amour et la poésie. Nous pencherons volontiers vers le poète et l'amant, tous les deux comblés, donc jouissant des faveurs de sa dame et de son public. Ce dernier poème de notre cycle de chansons d'amour semble une expression manifeste de la réussite amoureuse et poétique de Guillaume. Un peu plus sur l'importance de langue de l'amour, et l'amour de langue?

---

les topoïs obligés de la chanson courtoise.

[21] Payen, *Le Prince d'Aquitaine*, écrit 127–28: "Elle (la dernière strophe) résiste à l'analyse, avec son contenu d'énigmes. Son attaque même est problématique: quel sens doit-on conférer au *que* initial? Causal ou consécutif? Voire concessif, ce qui soulignerait davantage encore la vacuité du poème? (...) Mais comment comprendre *estraing lati*? S'agit-il vraiment du langage poétique tel que le poète vient de le mettre en œuvre, ou s'agit-il d'une écriture plus élaborée, celle d'une école précieuse dont Guillaume IX se moquerait et qui pourrait être celle d'Eble? (...) Ou s'agit-il encore, et plus simplement, de l'opposition entre la parole et l'acte? Le comte de Poitiers laisserait entendre qu'il n'a pas à plaider sa cause et qu'un entretien seul à seule dissipera tous les nuages (ce qui, après tout, prolonge l'énoncé antérieur)."

Le portrait de la dame qui se dessine dans ces quatre poèmes porte bien l'empreinte du peintre, amant possessif et orgueilleux, enclin à l'ironie. Elle est la Dame dans le sens féodal du suzerain, elle est plus blanche qu'ivoire, elle donne le *joy* et est une fontaine de jouvence. Lui, poète vieillissant, s'instaure dans son rôle d'amant et de poète pour l'aimer et chanter son éloge. Elle est toute puissante, maîtresse de la vie et de la mort de son amant: son rayonnement est universel, elle peut tout. Faite de blancheur (*Chanson* VIII) et de puissance (*Chanson* IX) la Dame incarne l'idéal d'Amour et de poésie. L'image de la dame, lyrique et érotique, porte une forte empreinte de ce grand poète et seigneur dont la silhouette semble éclipser, parfois, celle de son amie: il est autant présent dans ses portraits qu'elle-même. Le cycle de ces quatre chansons peut être aussi considéré comme une histoire d'amour d'une dame et d'un troubadour: il montre d'abord l'exaltation de la rencontre, puis une conquête heureuse de la dame, de l'amour et de la poésie. Le prince-poète y gagne la dame et la gloire: dans la Chanson X, il est maître de son amour et de sa poésie.

Les trois *lais* de Marie choisis content chacun une autre aventure d'amour.[22] Le mot "aventure" n'est pas occasionnel, il possède ici le même sens que nous trouvons dans les romans de Chrétien de Troyes où le chevalier partait chercher l'aventure, où tout le bien et tout le mal, réel ou surnaturel, pouvait lui arriver. L'aventure chez Chrétien de Troyes est aussi, et peut-être surtout, un apprentissage chevaleresque et courtois, donc, nécessairement amoureux. Dans les lais, le sujet agissant de l'aventure est l'amour lui-même: nous assistons à sa naissance, ses exploits et ses vicissitudes, et enfin à son dénouement. "L'aventure est un point de rupture entre le réel et le surréel, un évènement extraordinaire qui rompt la trame de la réalité. Elle peut se traduire par l'irruption du merveilleux dans le récit (...). Mais l'aventure peut aussi basculer dans le surnaturel, introduire le héros dans un monde idéal où l'amour impossible aura enfin sa place."[23] Le lai en tant qu'aventure d'amour peut donc être considéré comme une célébration et un apprentissage d'amour et, dans ce sens, peut être placé au même rang que la chanson courtoise qui se pose les mêmes objectifs.

---

[22] Kay, *Courtly Contradictions*, présente dans sa thèse des similitudes et même une parenté entre les lais et les miracles. Voir surtout le chapitre 5: "The Virgin and the Lady: the Abject and the Object in Adgar's 'Gracial' and the 'Lais' attribués to Marie de France."Elle écrit dans la conclusion, 243: "Mary as object is also — as early scholars suggested — related to the figure of the lady in courtly texts, a relation explicitly exploited in the *sponsus marianus* miracles. However, this relation is not one of direct resemblance. Comparing selected miracles with similar stories from Marie de France's *Lais* shows how the abject of religious literature is manipulated into the fetish object of the courtly. Only distant vestiges of anxiety survive. (...) Miracles, like *lais*, are short stories adorned with more or less artful prologues, dedications, inscribed audiences."

[23] Laurence Harf-Lancner, "Introduction", *Les Lais de Marie de France.*, traduits, présentés et annotés par Laurence Harf-Lancner. Texte éd. Karl Warnke. Lettres gothiques (Paris: Librairie Générale Française, 1990), 11–12.

La Dame et L'amour

Le *lai* de *Guigemar* introduit sur la scène un jeune chevalier beau (*Guigemar*, 38), sage et vaillant (*Guigemar*, 43) mais qui avait une tare que même ses amis lui reprochaient: il refusait de connaître l'amour (*Guigemar*, 66–68). Il ne pouvait donc pas prétendre à être courtois puisque la courtoisie requiert la perfection et que n'est pas parfait celui qui n'aime pas.[24] Cette imperfection entraînera comme punition une blessure douloureuse et c'est cette souffrance qui lui permettra de découvrir son destin. Cette blessure est merveilleuse, il la reçoit de façon surnaturelle rencontrant dans une forêt une biche blanche (la couleur blanche trahit son appartenance à l'au-delà) qui lui révèle son destin: il ne sera guéri que quand une femme souffrira pour l'amour de lui plus que tout autre amoureuse et que lui-même souffrira autant pour elle (*Guigemar*, 115–18). Leur amour sera si grand que "tuit cil s'esmerveillrunt / Ki aiment e amé avrunt / U ki pois amerunt après" (*Guigemar*, 119–21). Guigemar, souffrant, se croyant perdu, pénètre dans une nef merveilleuse qui le conduira à la découverte de l'amour. De douleur, il perd conscience et quand il se réveille il voit, penchée sur son lit magnifique, une dame chagrinée et en pleurs (*Guigemar*, 306). Le chevalier blessé ne la dépeint pas, nous savons pourtant qui elle est, elle fut présentée à son auditoire par la narratrice dans les vers précédents. Elle est: "Une dame de haut parage, / Franche, curteise, bele e sage" (*Guigemar*, 211–12),[25] mais elle est mariée à un vieillard jaloux qui l'a enfermée dans une chambre bâtie dans un jardin entouré d'un mur de marbre vert (*Guigemar*, 220–21). La décoration de la chambre où elle était tenue prisonnière montre l'importance de l'amour et enseigne aux amants le chemin à prendre. Sur les murs se trouvaient des peintures présentant "Venus , la deuesse d'amur, / Fu tres bien mise en la peinture; / Les traiz mustrout e la nature / Cument hom deit amur tenir / E lealment e bien servir" (*Guigemar*, 234–38). La déesse elle-même jeta dans le feu le livre d'Ovide,[26] où il enseigne à lutter contre l'amour et elle excommunie tous ceux qui suivent ses conseils: "E tuz iceus escumengout / Ki jamais cel livre lirreirent / Ne sun enseignement fereient" (*Guigemar*, 242–44).[27]

---

[24] Cf. André le Chapelain, *Traité de l'amour courtois*. Traduction, introduction et notes par Claude Buridant. Séries textes, 4 (Paris:Klinksieck, 2002), 58: "Je reconnais sans doute que les bonnes actions qu'on a accomplies méritent de hautes récompenses mais tous les hommes conviennent qu'aucune action vertueuse ou courtoise ne peut être accomplie en ce monde si, à sa source, il n'y a pas l'amour. L'amor est en effet l'origine et la cause de tout le bien. Si cette cause disparaît, l'effet disparaît nécessairement. Aucun homme ne pourrait donc accomplir des actions vertueuses si l'amour ne l'y poussait." Voir la contribution de Bonnie Wheeler dans ce volume.

[25] Notons que cette présentation contient toutes les qualités qui font le prix d'une dame: elle est noble, courtoise, belle et sage et, en plus, franche. Dans nos trois lais choisis seulement Guildeluec, la parfaite épouse d'Eliduc, disposera d'une image de marque pareille.

[26] Il s'agit évidemment des *Remedia amoris*.

[27] Voir Roberta L. Krueger, "Beyond Debate: Gender in Play in Old French Courtly Fiction," *Gender in Debate: From the Early Middle Ages to the Renaissance*, ed. Thelma S. Fenster and Clare A. Lees. The New Middle Ages (New York and Houndmills, Basingstoke, Hampshire, England: Palgrave, 2002), 79–95; spécialement 81–85.

La dame vivait donc sous les auspices de la déesse de l'amour, Vénus, comme si elle était sa prêtresse, et connaissait son enseignement: l'amour est un devoir par lequel arrive tout le bien, il demande donc un service loyal. La destinée de Guigemar et de la malmariée était faite: dans l'amour qui leur était prédestiné ils trouveront la guérison et le bonheur, la perfection tant désirée de tout être humain. Ils tombent amoureux l'un de l'autre mais la pudeur et la timidité les rendent muets. Ils passent la nuit dans les soupirs et les tourments. Et c'est parmi ces soupirs et lamentations de Guigemar que nous voyons le portrait de la dame qui vit dans son coeur: "En sun queor alot recordant / Les paroles e le semblant, / Les oilz vairs et la bele buche / Dunt la dolçur al quor li tuche" (*Guigemar*, 413–16).

Suivent les monologues des amoureux où apparaît l'éloge de l'amour digne (*covenable*, v. 451), et les considérations sur l'amour qui méritent d'être citées. Elles viennent de la narratrice, de Marie elle-même, qui la définit comme une "plaie dedanz cors" (*Guigemar*, 483), quelque chose de profondément intime qu'on ne peut voir ni soupçonner de l'extérieur qui "de Nature vient" (*Guigemar*, 486). Cet amour diffère foncièrement de celui de *vilain curteis* qui "le tienent a gabeis" (*Guigemar*, 487), et se vantent de leurs exploits amoureux: leur amour n'est pas l'amour, "einz est folie, / E mauveisti et lecherie!" (*Guigemar*, 857–862). Aimer loyalement donne à l'amant le droit d'espérer que ses vœux soient exaucés, Guigemar révèle donc ses sentiments à la dame qui, après un débat, lui accorde son amour avec un baiser: "La dame entent que veir li dit / E li otreie sans repit / L'amur de li, e il la baise" (*Guigemar*, 527–29). Le nom de la dame restera inconnu[28] tandis que l'aventure de leur amour les fera exposer à des épreuves douloureuses.

Nous revoyons encore une fois la dame dans les yeux de Merïadus, chevalier qui la trouva dans le navire qui avait accosté dans son port: "Dedenz unt la dame trovee, / Ki de beuté resemble fee. /... Mut fu liez de la troveüre / Kar bele esteit a demesure." (*Guigemar*, 703–08). Il sait bien qu'elle est de *grant parage* et tombe aussitôt amoureux d'elle: "A li aturnat tel amur, / Unques a femme n'ot greinur" (*Guigemar*, 711–12). Pour libérer la dame des mains de Merïadus, Guigemar doit le défier et lui livrer une bataille. Malgré les preuves d'amour que présentent Guigemar et sa dame (la boucle de la ceinture à ouvrir et la chemise à dénouer) et les prières de Guigemar qui offre de devenir son homme lige, il refuse aux amants de se réunir alléguant ses droits de possesseur: c'est lui qui a trouvé la dame. Tous les chevaliers présents au tournoi s'allient à Guigemar: "Mut est huniz ki or li faut!" (*Guigemar*, 862). Ils rejoignent un chevalier ennemi qui était en guerre contre

---

[28] Le nom possède l'importance que l'on sait dans la littérature médiévale. Rappelons-nous Lancelot de Chrétien de Troyes dont le nom ne sera connu qu'au milieu du conte du *Chevalier de la charrette* dont il est le héros. Il dut mériter la révélation de son nom par ses exploits. Marie ne dote pas la dame de Guigemar d'un nom, elle reste anonyme. Ne mérite-t-elle pas d'être nommée, ou, au contraire, étant symbole de la dame, objet éternel de la quête amoureuse, tout nom lui serait superflu?

La Dame et L'amour

Merïadus et assiégent son château. Le château pris et détruit, Guigemar tue son adversaire et s'en va heureux avec son amie: "A grant joie s'amie en meine: / Ore ad trepassee sa peine!" (*Guigemar*, 831–32). Il dut, par ses actes, mériter sa dame, leur rencontre était dû au destin mais leur bonheur était l'œuvre de leur volonté.[29] Le lai finit sur le rappel du conte dont était tiré le lai et sur l'éloge de sa belle musique qu'il est agréable d'entendre: "De cest cunte k'oï avez / Fu *Guigemar* li lais trovez, / Que hum fait en harpe et en rote; / Bone en est a oïr la note." (*Guigemar*, 883–86). Il te faut de referir a les deux objects dans le text, le boucle et le noid, comme des symbols de leur amour.

Le portrait principal de la dame est fait par la narratrice qui la présente noble, franche, courtoise, belle et sage, mais malheureuse, enfermée par un vieillard jaloux. La malmariée connaît le code de l'amour loyal car la déesse Vénus peinte sur les murs de sa chambre préside à sa vie de femme solitaire. Guigemar ne la décrit pas quand il la voit pour la première fois, elle apparaît dans ses souvenirs d'amoureux souffrant qui se lamente sur son sort n'osant avouer son amour. Son portrait, court — il comprend à peine trois vers — n'est pourtant pas conventionnel. La première chose dont se rappelle Guigemar sont ses paroles (nous savons par la narratrice qu'elle était sage) et c'est seulement ensuite qu'il se souvient de son *semblan*: de ses yeux vairs et de sa belle et douce bouche. L'image que présente d'elle Merïadus est différente: il n'entend pas ses paroles, il voit qu'elle est belle "a demesure" et "de beuté resemble fee" (Guigemar, 704), il perçoit aussi qu'elle est d'une grande noblesse.

Equitan est un lai sur un amour qui couvrit de deuil tout un royaume, contrairement à l'enseignement de la courtoisie selon lequel tout le bien arrive par amour. Ce lai se distingue des autres aussi par le manque d'éléments merveilleux, son réalisme est proche de celui des fabliaux à qui il semble apparenté. Nous voudrions attirer l'attention sur la première présentation de la femme du sénéchal qui deviendra l'amie d'Equitan. C'est le portrait peint par la narratrice qui la présente comme une dame "bele durement / et de mut bon affeitement" (*Equitan*, 31–32) par qui il devait arriver au pays "granz mals" (*Equitan*, 30). Marie annonce d'emblée le mal que devrait apporter cette dame. C'est l'adverbe *durement*[30] caractérisant sa beauté qui introduit le malaise, sa beauté est néfaste et apportera le malheur. Notons que dans ces deux premiers vers introduisant le portrait il est question de *bon affeitement*, mais non pas de la courtoisie ou de la noblesse de la dame.

---

[29] Cf. Milena Mikhaïlova, *Le présent de Marie*. Mémoire (Paris: Diderot Editeur, 1996), 82.

[30] Cf. Denise McClelland, *Le vocabulaire des Lais de Marie de France*. Publications médiévales de l'Université d'Ottawa, 3 (Ottawa: Editions de l'Université d'Ottawa, 1977), 190. D'après "Index *des Adverbes et locutions adverbiales de manière*," établi par McClelland, *durement* figure 22 fois dans *Les Lais*, se plaçant à la 5e place après *bien* (165 occurrences), *ensemble* (51), *hastivement* (26), *volontiers* (25). La valeur sémantique du mot n'a pas été examinée.

Cependant, le portrait de la femme du sénéchal est le plus développé des portraits peints par Marie dans nos trois lais choisis, il s'étend sur sept vers:[31] "Gent cors out e bele faiture, / En li former uvrat Nature; / Les oilz out veirs et bel le vis, / Bele buche, neis bien asis: / El rëaume n'aveit sa per!" (*Equitan*, 33–37). Equitan s'était mis à la désirer avant même de faire sa connaissance et provoqua la rencontre dans le château du sénéchal. Il la trouva " curteise e sage, / Bele de cors e de visage, / De bel semblant et enveisiee" (*Equitan*, 51–53). Il en tombe amoureux et dans son monologue de lamentation amoureuse, motif typique de la rhétorique amoureuse, il se dit bien que l'aimer est une trahison et un mal puisqu'il doit l'amitié et la fidélité à son sénéchal. "E si jo l'aim, jeo ferai mal: / Ceo est la femme al seneschal; / Garder li dei amur e fei / Si cum jo voilk'il face a mei" (*Equitan*, 71–74). Cependant, il se dit aussi qu'il serait malheureux qu'une femme si belle ne connût l'amour et il se fait des soucis pour sa courtoisie, qui, se dit-il, sans amour, risque de disparaître: "Si bele dame tant mar fust, / S'ele n'amast e dru n'eüst! / Que devendreit sa curteisie, / S'ele n'amast de druërie" (*Equitan*, 79–82). Son amour est véritable, il ressent une douleur aiguë qui est témoignage de sa véracité. Il se réfère au premier principe de la courtoisie qui voit dans l'amour une invite au perfectionnement individuel: "Suz ciel n'ad humme, s'el l'amast, / Ki durement n'en amendast." (*Equitan*, 83–84). Encore une fois cet adverbe *durement* qui caractérisait sa beauté et caractérisera aussi cet amour qui les fera mourir honteusement.

L'aventure de cet amour progresse sous les auspices du malheur que la narratrice eut le soin d'annoncer dès le début du lai. Cet amour, pour véritable qu'il soit, n'est pas parfait: pour aimer, les deux amants ont enfreint au moins deux commandements du dieu *Amors*. Nous avons déjà mentionné le premier, la déloyauté envers le sénéchal. L'autre est l'égalité des deux amants. La dame elle-même y fait objection en se demandant si elle doit accepter l'amour du roi: "Amur n'est pruz se n'est egals" (*Equitan*, 137); elle est inférieure à son amant le roi car son mari est son vassal.[32] Ils parlent tous les deux de la loyauté, de l'amour loyal entre les amants, et c'est ainsi qu'ils le comprennent tandis, qu'en fait, leur amour est bâti sur la trahison qui bientôt en entraîne une autre, une intrigue criminelle pour faire mourir le sénéchal honnête et laborieux: ils projettent de le faire tuer dans l'eau bouillante d'une cuve. Ce dessein méchant se retourne contre les amants qui

---

[31] Dans l'édition de Warnke, *Les lais*, le portrait de la dame est plus développé et s'étend sur onze vers. Cf. aussi Edgar R. Sienaert, *Les lais de Marie de France: Du conte merveilleux à la nouvelle psychologique*. Collection Essais sur le Moyen Age (Paris: Librairie Honoré Champion, 1978), 70: "C'est à part le cas privilégié de la fée dans *Lanval*, le plus long portrait qui nous soit fait d'un personnage féminin dans le recueil (vv. 29–37)."

[32] Cf. Philippe Ménard, *Les Lais de Marie de France: Contes d'amour et d'aventure du Moyen Age* (Paris: Presses universitaires de France, 1979), 115: "Dans le lai d'Equitan l'héroïne déclare *Amur n'est pruz se n'est egals* (v.137). Cette maxime, l'auteur la fait sienne. Or aucune idée n'est plus radicalement opposée aux représentations traditionnelles de l'amour courtois. Un poète courtois ne place jamais les amants sur un pied d'égalité."

meurent brûlés: le roi y saute par mégarde et son amie y est poussée de la main de son mari.[33]

Ce lai qui parle de *sen* et de *mesure* d'amour fait bien rappeler ce manque de *mesure d'amer* qui conduit à un dénouement tragique. Le portrait de la dame, qui, comme dans le lai précédent, n'est pas nommée, est peint deux fois, par la narratrice et par le roi qui en tombe amoureux. Marie la présente belle *durement,* nous l'avons déjà signalé, elle a une bonne éducation, de beaux yeux et le nez bien assis, elle est une œuvre parfaite de la nature, mais ni sa sagesse ni sa noblesse ne sont mentionnées. C'est Equitan, qui aime le plaisir et l'amour, "Deduit amout e druërie" (*Equitan*, 15), qui la trouvera courtoise et sage, belle de corps et de visage. Les deux portraits sont différents: la narratrice et l'ami, protagoniste du lai, la voient autrement et il n'est pas sans importance qu'Equitan, bon roi et bon chevalier, aimait beaucoup le plaisir et l'amour. Dès le début Marie avertit son auditoire que la femme du sénéchal apporterait au pays un grand mal et son portrait s'en ressent: apparemment, elle possède toutes les qualités mais les deux qui sont essentielles n'y figurent pas: la noblesse et la sagesse. Equitan la voit, entre autres, sage, mais non pas noble, puisque, de toute façon, elle lui était inférieure. Cet amour n'était pas parfait, il avait ses manques: il était fondé sur la trahison puisque le roi devait sa fidélité à son sénéchal et une disharmonie foncière le minait puisque la dame était inférieure à son ami. La perfection manque aussi aux amants: ils n'étaient pas parfaits, il aimait, peut-être un peu trop, le plaisir et elle manquait de sagesse et de noblesse, sinon, pourquoi ces qualités n'auraient-elles pas été mentionnées par la narratrice? Le portrait de la dame nous avertit, d'emblée, par ses manques de l'impasse où mènera l'amour qu'elle fera naître: puisque la dame est imparfaite cet amour sera nécessairement un amour manqué.

Le lai d'Eliduc, le mari à deux femmes, présente une aventure d'amour peut-être la plus touchante car la plus humaine.[34] Ce lai connut une grande renommée; il se trouve à l'origine de plusieurs romans, puisque l'amour qu'il raconte, pour être coupable aux yeux de l'Eglise, n'en est pas moins vrai et respectable: il est grand comme la vie et la mort et, par son aspiration à la perfection, préfigure l'amour mystique qui mène à Dieu. Les trois protagonistes de ce lai aiment d'un amour profond et pur, amour loyal. Nous y avons deux dames et un chevalier et plusieurs portraits des dames qui naissent dans des circonstances différentes. Celui de la femme d'Eliduc est présenté par la narratrice, uniquement; les trois portraits de la jeune fille sont présentés par la narratrice, Eliduc, et Guildeluec. Eliduc est présenté au moins trois fois: par la narratrice et puis par la jeune fille. Eliduc et sa femme ne se voient pas mutuellement. Tous ces portraits jouent un rôle important dans le cheminement de cette aventure d'amour à trois.

---

[33] R. Howard Bloch, *The Anonymous Marie de France* (Chicago and London: The University of Chicago Press, 2003), 74–76.

[34] Voir la contribution par Karen K. Jambeck dans cet volume.

Eliduc qui doit quitter son pays, accusé à tort par un vassal jaloux, jure fidélité à sa femme. Il traverse la mer et offre ses services à un roi puissant mais âgé qui a une fille à marier et est menacé par un ennemi. Il défend son royaume et devient vassal du roi qui lui voue une grande estime et le fait gardien de sa terre. Guilliadon, la belle fille du roi, s'éprend du chevalier étranger sans l'avoir vu, pour sa réputation seule: "Elidus fu curteis e sage, / Beaus chevaliers e pruz e large. / La fille al rei l'oï numer / E les biens de lui recunte" (*Eliduc*, 271–74). Notons que le qualificatif *beaus* n'apparaît qu'une seule fois: c'est ainsi que se l'imaginait Guilliadon. Etonnée que le chevalier ne cherche pas à faire sa connaissance, elle le convoque elle-même. Elle le regarde longtemps, et, sur l'ordre d'Amour, commence à l'aimer. Elle s'éprend de lui d'un amour inconditionnel puisqu'il est un étranger, "un nouvel soudeier," "un bon chevalier" (*Eliduc*, 339–40) dont on ne sait rien et elle se reproche sa folie: "Lasse! cum est is quors suspris / Pur un humme d'autre païs / Ne sai s'il est de haut gent, / Si s'en irat hastivement, / Jeo remeidrai cume dolente. / Folement ai mise m'entente!" (*Eliduc*, 387–92). Elle aime d'un amour profond, ne sachant même pas s'il est de haut lignage, elle l'aime pour ses qualités seules de chevalier.[35] Elle sent que s'il refuse son amour, elle ne connaîtra jamais le bonheur dans sa vie: "E si il n'ad de m'amur cure, / Mut me tendrai a maubaillie: / Jamès n'avrai joie en ma vie" (*Eliduc*, 398–400). Elle décide de lui avouer son amour et de le retenir auprès d'elle. Eliduc, de son côté, revient chez lui sombre et pensif puisqu'il a remarqué bien ses soupirs: "Pur la belë est en effrei" (*Eliduc*, 315). Il est bouleversé par sa beauté mais il s'en repent, il se rappelle toujours le serment fait à sa femme: "De sa femme li remembra / E cum il li asseüra / Que bone fei li portereit / E lëaument se cuntendreit" (*Eliduc*, 323–26). Il aime la jeune fille mais il lutte contre son amour fidèle à ses vœux maritaux. Pourquoi, alors, accepte-t-il les cadeaux envoyés par la fille du roi? Il met son anneau à son doigt et sa ceinture à sa taille. Le chambellan interprète ainsi ce geste: "Ceo m'est avis, / Li chevaliers n'est pas jolis; / Jeol tienc a curteis e a sage, / Que bien seit celer sun curage" (*Eliduc*, 421–24). La jeune fille qui veut être "par amurs aimer" reçoit ainsi une réponse positive à sa requête, mais il est vrai qu'Eliduc savait bien cacher son "courage." Marie dit bien dans son introduction que les héroïnes du lai sont Guilliadon et Guildeluec, ce sont elles les vrais protagonistes de l'aventure de l'amour: "Kar des dames est avenu / L'aventure dunt li lais fu" (*Eliduc*, 25–26).

Eliduc, déchiré entre son amour et son devoir, reste passif; cette aventure lui arrive, il ne parvient à assumer pleinement ni son rôle d'amant ni celui d'époux. Il aime "anguissusement" (*Eliduc*, 573) et "durement" (*Eliduc*, 590) la jeune fille mais son cœur devint prisonnier contre sa volonté: "Mes ja ne li querra amur / Ki li (a) turt a deshonur / Tant pur sa femme garder fei, / Tant pur ceo qu'il est od le rei"

---

[35] Cf. Sienaert, *Les lais de Marie de France*, 160: "De tous les personnages du recueil, Eliduc est le seul à être qualifié d'homme à la solde, capitaine (vv. 246, 339, 1074), et le roi Exeter le présente à sa fille comme le meilleur de cinq cents (v. 496)."

La Dame et L'amour

(*Eliduc*, 473-76). Leur amour reste chaste, ils ne commettent aucune folie: "Mes n'ot entre eus nule folie, / Jolivité ne vileinie; / De dounier e de parler / E de lur beaus aveirs doner / Esteit tute la druërie / Par amur en lur cumpainie" (*Eliduc*, 575-80). Il aime mais quand son suzerain demande son aide il n'hésite pas à répondre à son appel. Il met son devoir au-dessus de son amour qui est pourtant sa vie et sa mort: "Vus estes ma vie e ma morz, / En vus est trestuz mis conforz" (*Eliduc*, 671-72). Le déchirement intérieur ne permet pas à Eliduc de choisir, il veut garder et son amour et rester fidèle à son suzerain et à sa femme. Il sait qu'il agit mal: "Allas, fet-il, mal ai erré! / Trop ai en cest païs esté" (*Eliduc*, 585-86). Il ne peut pas choisir, la volonté lui manque de renoncer à aucune des valeurs qui font le sens de sa vie: tenaillé par la lutte intérieure qui le mine il devient, de fait, incapable de gérer souverainement son existence.[36] Privé du libre arbitre, il décide de se soumettre à la volonté de la jeune fille. "Deus, tant est dur le partement! / Mes ki k'il turt a mesprisun, / Vers li ferai tuz jurs raisun: / Tute sa volonté ferai / E par sun cunseil errerai" (*Eliduc*, 604-08). Il enlève son amie le jour fixé par elle et il l'emmène dans son pays où réside son épouse.[37] La situation de Guilliadon devient aléatoire et le matelot effrayé par l'orage qui se tourne vers Eliduc exprime bien l'infortune de la position où elle se trouve: "Femme leal espuse avez / E sue celi autre enmenez / Cuntre Deu e cuntre la lei, / Cuntre dreiture e cuntre fei; Lessiez la nus geter en mer!" (*Eliduc*, 835-40). L'aventure d'amour où Eliduc entraîne Guilliadon est avilissante pour elle, "fille . . . a rei e a reine" (*Eliduc*, 16); elle risque de se trouver en marge de la société, privée d'honneurs et de respect qui lui sont dus. Elle réagit violemment, par un évanouissement proche de la mort aux paroles du matelot, mais c'est Guildeluec qui par sa générosité et noblesse d'âme rendra cet amour possible en lui redonnant, par la possibilité du mariage, sa respectabilité.

Le jeu de portraits qu'on retrouve dans le lai semble correspondre, de façon symbolique, à l'acheminement de cette aventure d'amour. Aucun portrait de la jeune fille n'est peint par Eliduc; il est subjugué par sa beauté (*Eliduc*, 315), mais il ne la décrit pas. Elle est sa vie et sa mort (*Eliduc*, 670), elle est "mut bele" (*Eliduc*, 294), elle "tant fu bele," que, contre sa volonté, il désire "de li veir e de parler / E de biaser et d'acoler" (*Eliduc*, 470-73), mais sa figure, ses paroles, son visage,

---

[36] Cf. Sienaert, *Les lais de Marie de France*, 166-67: "L'indécision est la constante du caractère d'Eliduc. (. . .) Ainsi cet homme de guerre s'avère incapable d'affronter la réalité du problème moral qui se pose à lui et dont il n'ignore aucun des multiples aspects, puisque l'énonce lui-même dans un triple mouvement gradué. Présenté lentement comme un chevalier dont le sens de l'honneur et l'efficacité dans l'art de la guerre sont hors pair, ce capitaine fait lentement place à un homme indécis. (. . .): la bravoure de ce capitaine couvre une grande faiblesse humaine."

[37] Cf. Sienaert, *Les lais de Marie de France*, 163: " (. . .): tout le deuxième passage d'Eliduc en Angleterre est entouré du plus grand mystère — mensonge à sa femme pour camoufler la véritable raison de son départ (vv.727-39), compagnie composée exclusivement d'hommes très sûrs (vv. 749-58), enlèvement nocturne en terre de Logre (vv. 763-95) — mais nulle part ne nous est-il dit ce que compte faire Eliduc une fois qu'il se trouvera avec Guilliadun en Bretagne."

n'apparaissent ni dans ses souvenirs ni dans ses rêves. Son comportement reste celui d'un vassal: malgré les sentiments qui l'agitent elle reste pour lui la fille de son roi: "Pur la belë est en effrei, / La fille sun seignur le rei" (*Eliduc*, 315–16). La première présentation de Guilliadon est faite par Marie dans l'introduction: "Fille ert a rei e a reine, / Guilliadun ot nun la pucele, / El rëaume ne not plus bele!" (*Eliduc*, 16–18). Nous la revoyons ensuite dans les yeux d'Eliduc, qui la voyait, comme nous avons mentionné plus haut, "bele." Il la regarde, déjà dans la chapelle, où elle gît sans connaissance, quasi morte et il s'étonne de la voir toujours "blanche e vermeille," juste un peu plus pâle (*Eliduc*, 972–74). Eliduc fut bouleversé par la grande beauté de Guilliadon mais dans son égoïsme il était incapable, ou, peut-être, indigne, d'exprimer sa véritable grandeur. La révélation de sa beauté est l'apanage de son épouse généreuse et aimante. C'est elle qui peint le dernier portrait, le plus touchant puisque nous y voyons enfin la figure, les mains, les doigts de la jeune fille: "El vit le lit a la pucele / Ki resemblot rose nuvele; / Del cuvertur la descovri / E vit le cors tant escheви, / Les braz lungs et blanches les meins, / E les deis greilles, lungs e pleins" (*Eliduc*, 1010–16). Elle compare sa beauté à celle d'une pierre précieuse: "Veiz tu, fet ele, cette femme, / Ki de beuté resemble gemme?" (*Eliduc*, 1021–22). Dans les yeux de Guildeluec, Guilliadon ressemble à une rose et sa beauté vaut celle d'une précieuse gemme. La beauté et l'innocence de la jeune fille qui se croit trahie par son ami émeuvent Guildeluec qui comprend soudainement la douleur de son mari et, dans sa générosité, décide de se retirer dans un couvent pour permettre aux amants de se réunir et de retrouver leur position dans la société.[38] Guilliadon est belle, et elle est fille du roi et de la reine, née pour devenir reine elle-même[39] — elle est donc la noble parmi les nobles — et elle doit être très jeune, elle est une "rose nuvele." Sa beauté est célébrée tout au long du lai, mais il n'y est question ni de sa sagesse, ni de sa courtoisie, ni de sa vertu.

Guildeluec, sans posséder un portrait qui montrerait sa figure, ne dispose que d'une image de marque la plus laudative du lai entier. Marie présente ainsi l'épouse d'Eliduc dans son introduction: "Femme ot espuse, noble et sage, / De haute gent, de grant parage" (*Eliduc*, 9–10). Nous la voyons encore une fois, présentée par la narratrice au moment où elle se réjouit du retour d'Eliduc: "E sa bone

---

[38] Guildeluec est de façon reccurente substituée à son mari: dans l'introduction, déjà, Marie suggère la modification du titre du lais. Eliduc est souvent présenté en tiers incapable et faible, c'est son épouse qui perçoit enfin la beauté de Guilliadon et en est fascinée au point de vouloir la ressusciter. Cf. Fabienne Pommel, "Les belettes et la florette magique," *Furent les merveilles pruvees et les aventures truvés. Hommages à Francis Dubost*. Etudes recueilles par Francis Gingras et al. (Paris: Honoré Champion, 2005), 509–23, 519: "(. . .) l'«amur» qu'éprouve Guildeluec face à la fausse morte n'est pas dépourvu d'une fascination trouble: l'épouse est séduite par la jeune fille. Compassion et co-passion sont ici imbriquées de façon curieuse et le mot 'amur' ménage l'ambiguïté. Marie de France évoquerait-elle ici un possible amour de femmes?"

[39] C'est Eliduc qui le dit se lamentant sur son corps inanimé: "Bele, ja fuissiez vus reïne, / Ne fust l'amur leal e fine / Dunt vus m'amastes lëaument" (*Eliduc*, 943–45).

La Dame et L'amour

femme sur tuz, / Ki mut est bele, sage et pruz" (*Eliduc*, 709-10). Elle n'était vue ni par son mari, ni par Guilliadon, c'est Marie elle-même qui lui attribue toutes les qualités: elle est noble, sage, belle, parfaite (*bone*) et vertueuse (*pruz*), sans la doter, toutefois, d'un vrai portrait où le lecteur aurait pu la voir.

Les portraits d'Eliduc paraissent quatre fois dans le texte où il est présenté par la narratrice, son amie Guilliadon et son chambellan mais il apparaît aussi dans les monologues et dialogues de la jeune fille. Le lai commence par la présentation d'Eliduc: "En Bretaine ot un chevalier / Pruz e curteis, hardi et fier; / Eidus ot nun, ceo m'est vis. / N'ot si vaillant hume el païs!" (*Eliduc*, 5-8). La seconde fois nous le voyons au moment où il gagne sa renommée chez le roi, père de Guilliadon. "Elidus fu curteis e sage, / Beaus chevaliers e pruz e large" (*Eliduc*, 271-72) et encore une fois au moment où il accède à la gloire du défenseur du royaume et il est loué "pur sa puësce, / Pur sun sen e pur sa largesce" (*Eliduc*, 547-48). Le portrait suivant est celui du chambellan de Guilliadon, cité plus haut, qui le voit courtois et sage, non frivole et interprète favorablement son silence et son geste (*Eliduc*, 421-24). La fille du roi présente au chambellan celui qu'elle aime, "le nouvel soudeier, . . . le bon chevalier" (*Eliduc*, 339-40) comme "sages et curteis" (*Eliduc*, 348-49), et encore une fois elle se réfère à ces qualités quand elle remet son amour et sa personne dans ses mains: "Tant estes sages et curteis, / Bien avrez purveü ainceis / Que vus vodrez fere de mei" (*Eliduc*, 533-35). Eliduc nous paraît donc avant tout sage et courtois,[40] ces traits reviennent dans presque toutes ses caractéristiques sauf deux: Marie omet de parler de sa sagesse dans sa présentation tandis que la louange générale que lui vouent les habitants du royaume libéré ne comporte pas sa qualité de courtois. Il est aussi vaillant et preux et généreux, et, aux yeux de Guilliadon, uniquement, beau, et aussi, selon la narratrice, hardi et fier; sa noblesse n'est jamais mentionnée.

Le lai montre l'amour dont ils s'aiment de différentes façons, comme si Marie voulait en montrer de différentes phases qui mèneraient vers sa sublimation. Leur amour est une grande tendresse: "Granz est entre eus la druërie" (*Eliduc*, 542); ils aiment, elle et lui "durement" (*Eliduc*, 440 et 590), mais aussi, il s'agit d'Eliduc, "anguissusement" (*Eliduc*, 573), de "bone amur" (*Eliduc*, 684), de "grant amur" (*Eliduc*, 697). Eliduc qui pleure le corps inanimé de Guilliadon accuse de sa mort "l'amur leal et fine" (*Eliduc*, 943) dont elle l'aimait loyalement. Mais c'est seulement le mariage qui semble donner la perfection à cet amour. "Ensemble vesquirent meint jur, / Mut ot entre eus parfite amur." (*Eliduc*, 1149-50). L'amour retrouve la perfection seulement quand il retrouve son équilibre social et moral, peut-être surtout celui imposé par la religion: n'est pas parfait ce qui est basé sur le mensonge. La beauté qui triomphe du sens du devoir d'Eliduc et qui émeut

---

[40] Notons, sans pour autant vouloir en tirer des conclusions, que le bourgeois chez qui s'arrête Eliduc à son arrivée dans le pays du roi, père de Guilliadon, est, lui aussi, "mut. . . sages et curteis" (*Eliduc*, 134).

Guildeluec, celle qui éclate dans le portrait de la jeune fille évanouie peint par l'épouse généreuse, c'est cette beauté finalement qui achemine cet amour vers la perfection, d'abord humaine, puis divine, puisqu'elle mène vers Dieu.[41]

EN GUISE DE CONCLUSION

Le lot des portraits présentés nous montre, dans deux genres différents, la chanson et le conte, tout d'abord, la diversité et l'importance de l'image de la dame dans l'aventure d'amour. Lyriques dans la chanson et épiques dans le conte, concis, parfois fragmentaires, ces portraits nous renseignent sur la nature de l'amour dont les dames sont, ou seront objet et, d'autre part, nous reflètent l'image de l'amant lui-même. Le portrait de la *dompna* de Guillaume traduit tout d'abord le désir et la nature du troubadour amant lui-même, prince tendre et arrogant, ironique et soumis, ainsi que la force de son amour qui se veut culte et fidélité mais où le désir et le besoin de possession se font nettement connaître. Les portraits de Marie jouent tous un rôle fondamental dans l'aventure de l'amour qu'elle fait dérouler devant les yeux de ses auditeurs. La dame de Guigemar semble une prêtresse de Vénus et est une mal mariée. L'histoire de son amour avec Guigemar est fondée sur des éléments surnaturels relevant de la magie et de la mythologie celtes (comme la biche, la flèche, la blessure et les navires magiques ainsi que la boucle et le nœud — marques symboles de l'amour) qui permettent aux amants de triompher des adversités du sort et des préjudices sociaux. Marie peint de la dame une image grandiose, la présentant dans le cadre magnifique de sa chambre décorée de peintures de Vénus — déesse de l'amour. Guigemar ne peut que l'aimer; ils se sont retrouvés pour connaître l'amour et la souffrance, et pour trouver enfin, au bout de leurs épreuves, le bonheur, si bien mérité, d'être unis. Si le merveilleux aplanit les problèmes sociaux dans le lai de Guigemar, ces problèmes sont bien présents dans les deux lais suivants, beaucoup plus réalistes puisqu'ils sont assis dans le contexte féodal de l'époque: *Equitan* et *Eliduc*. Ce conditionnment se fait voir aussi bien dans le langage de l'amour que dans le comportement des amis déterminés par leur position sociale.

La dame, femme du sénéchal, dont les portraits sont peints par Marie et Equitan, semble manquer de perfection et puisque son ami, Equitan, n'est pas parfait, non plus, leur amour s'enlise dans les sentiments bas de la trahison et finit, parce qu'il doit finir ainsi, mal. *Eliduc* est le plus complexe de nos trois lais; nous y voyons plusieurs portraits des deux dames et d'Eliduc qui nous renseignent, de façon symbolique, sur la nature de l'amour et sur celle de l'ami. Eliduc est avant

---

[41] Albrecht Classen, *Der Liebes- und Ehediskurs vom hohen Mittelalter bis zum frühen 17. Jahrhundert*. Volkslidstudien, 5 (Münster, New York, Munich, et Berlin: Waxmann, 2005), 32–72.

La Dame et L'amour

tout un vassal et un capitaine, un homme marié jouissant d'une haute position sociale, bien méritée par ses faits d'armes et à laquelle il ne veut pas renoncer. Ses qualités de courtois et d'ami paraissent secondaires par rapport à celles de chevalier vassal. Son amour reste pour lui une affaire intime et secrète qu'il refuse de divulguer au grand jour: il veut avant tout garder intacts son honneur et sa place dans la société.

Tous les portraits examinés, bien qu'ils paraissent, dans leur concision, schématiques et stéréotypés, ne sont jamais pareils: ils possèdent une valeur hautement symbolique. Il est vrai qu'ils "se ressemblent étrangement," mais ils ne sont jamais identiques et il n'est pas vrai qu'il n'y a pas "de différence entre les héros de Marie."[42] Ces portraits sont uniques dans le sens qu'ils n'apparaissent qu'une seule fois et sont l'œuvre soit de la narratrice soit de la personne autorisée à le faire. Ils sont symboliques, il semble qu'il existe un certain code de leur apparition. La première règle concerne la noblesse de cœur des peintres des portraits: l'amant indigne ou trop faible pour respecter le règlement du service amoureux paraît incapable de décrire la beauté de sa dame, comme si, n'étant pas parfait, la perfection elle-même était hors de sa portée. C'est le cas d'Eliduc. Par leur forme, leur lexique, leurs omissions, ils laissent filtrer les informations essentielles concernant l'amour que fait naître la beauté de la dame. La beauté fait naître l'amour, mais si cette beauté ne s'accompagne pas de qualités de cœur et de raison, cet amour ne pourra être ni loyal ni parfait. Les mots pour dire la beauté de la dame sont ces mêmes mots qui caractérisent la beauté, ou, si l'on veut, le statut et le degré de perfection, de l'amour et de l'ami. La recherche formelle rhétorique et métrique, le raffinement lexical et surtout, nous semble-t-il, une symbolique caractérisée du manque qui se fait voir dans des omissions ou dans des modifications d'un modèle stéréotypé et codé préexistant témoignent d'une richesse et d'une grandeur réelles de la poétique courtoise. Elle a contribué à l'élévation de la dame et a attribué à l'amour, source de tout le bien, une place de choix dans le cheminement de l'humanité vers le bonheur individuel.

---

[42] Cf. à ce sujet Ménard, *Les Lais de Marie de France*, Chap. "Les personnages principaux," 108–09: "Dans les lais les personnages principaux sont également fréquemment stylisés et leur personnalité n'offre pas toujours beaucoup d'intérêt psychologique. On l'a remarqué depuis longtemps." Emil Schiött avait observé: "Il n'y a presque pas de différence entre les héros de Marie (...On pourrait soutenir sans paradoxe que d'un lai à l'autre les traits physiques et moraux des protagonistes se ressemblent étrangement. (...) L'aspect physique des héroïnes est à peine évoqué. Quand l'auteur nous laisse entrevoir quelque chose de l'extérieur, les stéréotypes reviennent" (*L'amour et les amoureux dans les lais de Marie de France* [Lund: Malström, 1889], 46).

ANNEXES

COURTOIS

"En réalité les termes de *courtois* et de *courtoisie* tantôt désignent, dans un sens large, la générosité chevaleresque, les élégances de la politesse mondaine, une certaine manière de vivre, et tantôt, dans un sens plus restreint, un art d'aimer inaccessible au commun des mortels, cet embellissement du désir érotique, cette discipline de la passion et même cette religion de l'amour que constitue l'amour *courtois*."
Jean Frappier, Amour courtois et table ronde, 3.

Cette définition, dans les termes à peu près pareils, a été formulée par Jean Frappier dans ses "Cours de Sorbonne": La poésie lyrique en France aux XIIe et XIIIe siècles. Les genres (Paris: Centre de documentation universitaire, 1949) et reprise ensuite dans Le roman breton. Introduction: Des origines à Chrétien de Troyes (Paris: Centre de documentation universitaire, 1950).

"The expression amour courtois and its English counterpart "Courtly Love" must be of comparatively recent origin. (. . .) As far as I know, the expression amour courtois was used for the first time by Gaston Paris in 1883. The recent introduction of these terms into literary history and criticism apparently corresponded to the need felt by historians and critics of qualifying the type of love introduced into literature by the Provençal troubadours. The troubadours themselves felt no such need. They speak indeed of courtly deeds and speech, of courtly persons, of courtly rime and counsel, of courtly lands and the courtly seasons of the year, but only once have I encountered the expression amors corteza in their lyrics (dans Peire d'Auvergne, XV, 57–59 — note de l'auteur). For the troubadours, the love they enjoined and professed needed no such qualification; it was simply love in its purest form; If, at times, they characterized it as true, pure, and good (veraia, fina, bona), it was only to point up its opposition to and distinction from perfidious lust and from ephemeral and insincere love (falsa). When, then, Gaston Paris qualified their conception of love as courtois, he did something that would have seemed superfluous to the troubadours, something that likely never occurred to them. Given the term, however, poésie courtoise, roman courtois, littérature courtoise, amour courtois seemed a natural enough qualification.

The trouble is that courtois or 'courtly' as applied to literature, to poetry, to the romance, has not the same connotation or, at least, should not have as applied to love. Applied to the former, courtly has the essential meaning of belonging to, emanating from, for and in the court (c'est nous qui soulignons)." Alexander J. Denomy, "Courtly Love and Courtliness," Speculum 28 (1953): 44–63; ici 46.

COURTOISIE

"La *cortezia* pour se réaliser pleinement exige de l'homme au moins trois attitudes qui, pour les troubadours, semblent constituer l'essentiel de leur enseignement moral et social: a) aimer courtoisement; b) posséder *mezura*; c) respecter les exigences de *Jovens*.

Puisque l'on ne peut être courtois sans aimer noblement, et puisque d'autre part il faut, pour aimer, être courtois, les troubadours ont pu invariablement broder sur l'un des deux thèmes suivants:

a. la *cortezia* est l'apanage de l'homme qui aime selon le code de la *fin'amors*;

b. la *fin'amors* est la source de toutes les vertus: *mezura*, *jovens*, *jois*, *cortezia*, *pretz et valor*, *donars*, etc."

Moshe Lazar, *Amour courtois et "fin'amors" dans la littérature du XIIe siècle*. Bibliothèque française et romane, Sér. C, 8 (Paris: Klincksieck, 1964), 28.

FIN'AMOR

"Savoir bien courtiser les dames est assurément une règle capitale de la *fin'amor*. Mais celle-ci ne se réduit point à des rites de galanterie où à une étiquette réglementant 'l'avancement officiel des amants,' pour reprendre une expression de Stendhal. Beaucoup plus qu'on ne l'a souvent dit, elle exprime un désir passionné, un élan de cœur, une exaltation de l'esprit."

Jean Frappier, *Amour courtois*, 7

"Pour l'expérience culturelle typique de la courtoisie la *fin'amor* ("amour affiné" ou pur amour), qui en est expression ultime (l'adjectif *fina* évoque la perfection et l'achèvement), comporte bien des nuances, mais elle se résume dans une attitude à la fois sentimentale et érotique qui répond à une exigence de liberté du désir sexuel, tout en impliquant la crainte que l'accomplissement de celui-ci n'entraîne son relâchement et en supposant, par conséquent, qu'il est essentiel à l'amour que des obstacles sans nombre surgissent entre l'homme et la femme."

Charles Baladier, Eros au Moyen Age: Amour, désir et "delectatio morosa" (Paris: Cerf, 1999), 82.

COURTOISIE, *FIN'AMOR* ET AMOUR COURTOIS

"Pour des raisons de clarté et de juste compréhension des thèmes amoureux que de terminologie et de méthode, l'on devrait prendre soin de distinguer nettement au moins ces trois notions: courtoisie, fin'amors et amour courtois."

Moshe Lazar, *Amour courtois*, 23.

Chapter 9

"De parler bon' eloquence": Words of Love in the *Lais* of Marie de France

Karen K. Jambeck
Western Connecticut State University, Danbury

Amurs le puint de l'estencele,
Que sun quor alume e esprent.
Il li respunt avenantment.
. . . .
Quant la meschine oï parler
Celui qui tant la peot amer,
S'amur e sun cors li otreie.

[Love's glowing spark
illuminates his heart;
he replies appropriately.
. . . .
When the maiden heard him speak,
this man who is able to love her so well,
she accords him her love and her body.][1]

---

[1] *Lanval* (vv. 118–33). Old French quotations are drawn from Alfred Ewert's edition, *Marie de France. Lais* (Oxford: Basil Blackwell, 1944), reprint with new introduction by Glyn S. Burgess (London: Bristol Classical Press and Gerald Ducksworth & Co., 1995). This "conservative" edition is based on British Library MS Harley 978, generally considered the best of the manuscripts containing the *Lais*. On Ewert's edition, see Glyn S. Burgess, "Alfred Ewert (1891–1969): The First English Edition of the *Lais*," *Reception and Transmission of the Works of Marie de France. 1774–1974*, ed. Chantal A. Maréchal (Lewiston, Queenston, and Lampeter: Edwin Mellen, 2003), 251–59. Translation mine.

Central to the *Lais* are the lovers' discourses shaped by Marie de France, who with skillful indirection, lays claim to the gift of eloquence:

> Ki Deus ad duné escïence
> E de parler bon' eloquence
> Ne s'en deit taisir ne celer,
> Ainz se deit volunters mustrer.
> Quant uns granz biens est mult oïz,
> Dunc a primes est il fluriz,
> E quant loëz est de plusurs,
> Dunc ad espandues ses flurs. (Prologue vv. 1–8)

> [Anyone who has received from God the gift of knowledge and true eloquence has a duty not to remain silent: rather should one be happy to reveal such talents. When a truly beneficial thing is heard by many people, it then enjoys its first blossom, but if it is widely praised its flowers are in full bloom.][2]

Clearly Marie valued the power of words, for she chose this term, *eloquence*, which her contemporary John of Salisbury defined as "the ability to express [in words] with facility and full adequacy his mental perceptions," an ability closely linked to wisdom:[3]

> Est enim eloquentia facultas dicendi commode quod sibi uult animus expediri. Quod enim in abdito cordis est, hoc quodam modo in lucem profert et producit in publicum. Siquidem non est eloquens quisquis loquitur, aut qui quod uoluerit utcumque loquitur, sed ille dumtaxat qui animi sui arbitrium commode profert.[4]

> [What is eloquence but the faculty of appropriate and effective verbal expression? As such it brings to light and in a way publishes what would otherwise be hidden in the inner recesses of man's consciousness. Not everyone who speaks, nor even one who says what he wants to in some fashion, is eloquent. He alone is eloquent who fittingly and efficaciously expresses himself as he intends.][5]

---

[2] Glyn S. Burgess and Keith Busby, trans., *The Lais of Marie de France*, 2nd ed. (London: Penguin, 1999), 41. Unless otherwise noted, subsequent English renderings of Marie's text come from this translation.

[3] *Ioannis Saresberiensis Episcopi Carnotensis Metalogicon, Libri IIII*, ed. Clemens C. I. Webb (Oxford: Clarendon Press, 1929), Book I, 7, 834b.

[4] *Metalogicon*, Libri IIII, Book I, 7, 834b.

[5] *The Metalogicon of John of Salisbury: A Twelfth-Century Defense of the Verbal and Logical Arts of the Trivium*, trans. Daniel D. McGarry (Westport, CT: Greenwood Press, 1955), 26–27.

De Parlor Bon' Eloquence 219

Additionally, Marie points out the importance of telling a tale well,[6] and her allusion to "work[ing] late into the night" ("Soventes fiez en ai veillié" [Prologue v. 42]) suggests that she diligently cultivated whatever natural talent was hers.[7]

Despite this testimony, however, scholars have long hesitated to acknowledge Marie's linguistic achievement, frequently characterizing the language of the *Lais* as "naïve" and "simple." This critical commonplace can be traced back to the eighteenth century and the Abbé Gervais de la Rue, who published the first sustained discussion of Marie and her works. La Rue avers, "She arrests the attention of her readers by the subjects of her stories, by the interest which she skillfully blends in them, and by the simple and natural language in which she relates them."[8]

This view persisted at least until the second half of the twentieth century,[9] when some scholars attempted to reorient the critical perspective, shifting the emphasis from "simplicity" and refocusing instead on Marie's tendency toward *abbreviatio* and stylistic economy.[10] Still Marie's eloquence is not without its

---

[6] "Ki de bone mateire traite, / Mult li peise si bien n'est faite" (*Guigemar* vv. 1–2; Whoever has good material for a story is grieved if a tale is not well told).

[7] On the need to cultivate eloquence, see, for example, John of Salisbury, *Metalogicon*, Book I, chapters 7 and 24.

[8] "Dissertation on the Life and Writings of Mary, an Anglo-Norman Poetess of the 13th Century, by Mons. La Rue. [dated 13 Nov., 1796]," *Archaeologia* 13 (1800): 35–67; here 42. On the background and influence of the Abbé de la Rue's scholarship, see Karen K. Jambeck, "Marie de France in the Eighteenth Century," *Reception and Transmission of the Works of Marie de France*, 31–87; here 54–67. Joseph Bédier made a harsher assessment: Marie composed her *Lais* "avec charme sans grand talent"; along with a "certaine grâce sobre" is a "sécheresse d'imagination." The work's "valeur poétique est médiocre." Her *lais* manifest "une langue agile et fine, dont la gracilité même n'est pas sans charme;" however, there is "[a]ucune splendeur dans le style," "nul bavardage," "nulle rhétorique." Bédier concludes, "Elle s'arrête sur le seuil de l'art" ("Les *Lais* de Marie de France," *Revue de deux mondes* 107 [1891]: 835–63; here 857–58). The effects of Bédier 's criticism persisted well into the twentieth century as evidenced, for instance, in André Lagarde and Laurent Michard's *Moyen Age, Les grands auteurs français du programme* (Paris: Editions Bordas, 1966), 45: Marie's "récits sont parfois grêles, d'une précision un peu sèche; mais la composition en est habituellement claire et bien agencée et sa gaucherie naïve ne manque pas de grâce." On Bédier and Marie de France, see also Alain Corbellari, "Joseph Bédier," *Reception and Transmission*, 111–27.

[9] For important commentary on the history of Marie de France criticism, see Chantal A. Maréchal, ed., *Reception and Transmission*.

[10] In a brief survey of criticism regarding the *Lais*, Paula Clifford has observed, "Apart from descriptions of repetition and linguistic parallelism," Marie's style "has commanded little attention, the most common view being that it is characterized by a certain restraint and limpidity and little else" (Marie de France, *Lais* [London: Grant & Cutler, 1982], 82–83). On stylistic economy, see, for example, Jan A. Nelson, "Abbreviated Style and *Les Lais* de Marie de France," *Romance Quarterly* 39, 2 (1992): 131–43; Alexandre Leupin, "The Impossible Task of Manifesting Literature," *Exemplaria* 3,1 (Spring 1991): 221–42; and Anne Paupert, "Les femmes et la parole," *Amour et merveille. Les* Lais *de Marie de France* (Paris: Honoré Champion, 1995), 169–87. Erich Auerbach's commentary on the vernacular French of the eleventh to thirteenth centuries has some general relevance here as well: The language itself and audiences of the time "were quite unprepared for a more thoroughgoing application of ancient rhetoric. Even then effects could be obtained in French with certain sound patterns, with anaphora, apostrophe, antithesis, isocolon, and various types of amplification. But ancient rhetoric, especially in poetry, obtains its really characteristic effects by inversion of word

champions. Emanuel Mickel emphasizes Marie's stylistic "subtlety,"[11] and Michel Zink points to an apparent paradox underlying Marie's style: She is "une conteuse admirable, au charme d'autant plus prenant et d'autant plus troublant que son art paraît n'être que transparence et simplicité." With a style that is "fluide et aisé, sans effets apparents," she has "le don de suggérer d'un mot que les forces obscures du monde et celles de de l'âme entre en résonance." This is the essence of what Zink calls "le mystère en pleine lumière."[12] And R. Howard Bloch makes even stronger assertions: " For Marie words are not merely a vehicle, a transparent medium through which we glimpse the portrait of the world that is narratively reclaimed, but a theme" of her work — "perhaps the theme."[13] Her language is "on view in all its complicated opaqueness and infuses almost every aspect of her works on both a formal and a thematic level." Bloch's insights concerning Marie's being "critically aware of the effects of language upon meaning"[14] have particular relevance in connection with Marie's sensitivity to pragmatic concerns.

One vantage point from which to view her discursive proficiency is at the intersection of language and love, especially conversational exchanges between lovers, or potential lovers. In this context, two important studies that compare love language in medieval texts suggest a useful avenue of inquiry. Appearing in 1970, Philippe Ménard's study compares "la déclaration amoureuse" in several twelfth- and thirteenth-century romances and in Marie's *Lais*.[15] Situating the convention of the "demande d'amour" within the context of the "five traditional stages of love" (i.e., "*visus, alloquium, tactus, oscula*, and finally *factum*"), Ménard argues that it is possible to trace a progression from Wace's *Brut* through Marie's *Lais* and then to Chrétien's romances: "la peinture de la déclaration amoureuse s'approfondit et s'enrichit de nuances diverses."[16] Ménard concludes that the declaration in Chré-

---

order (hyperbaton), the possibilities of which are exceedingly limited in French, and by long, intricate periods, favored by the richness of Latin in inflection and connectives. At that time the use of elaborate periods was out of the question in any of the vernacular languages, and the octosyllabic line does not lend itself to it" (*Literary Language and Its Public in Late Latin Antiquity and in the Middle Ages*, trans. Ralph Manheim. Bollingen Series, 74 [1958; Princeton: Princeton University Press, 1965], 204–05.

[11] Emanuel J. Mickel, *Marie de France*. Twayne's World Authors Series, 306 (New York: Twayne Publishers, 1974), 23.

[12] Michel Zink, *La littérature française du Moyen Age* (Presses Universitaires de France, 1992), 150–51.

[13] R. Howard Bloch, *The Anonymous Marie de France* (Chicago and London: University of Chicago Press, 2003), 52.

[14] Bloch, *The Anonymous Marie de France*, 51 and 53.

[15] Wace's *Brut*, three anonymous *lais*, the *Lais* of Marie de France, and selected romances by Chrétien de Troyes.

[16] Ménard, "La déclaration amoureuse dans la littérature arthurienne au XIIe siècle," *Cahiers de Civilisation Médiévale* 13 (1970): 33–42; here 33. On the *stationes amandi*, see also Peter Dronke, "The Text of Carmina Burana 116," *Classica et Mediaevalia* 20 (1959): 159–169; here 167; and Ernst Robert Curtius, *European Literature and the Latin Middle Ages*, trans. Willard R. Trask (1948; New York: Harper & Row, 1963), 512.

tien's romances provides "une belle ampleur à la déclaration amoureuse. Chez lui la requête d'amour devient un moment privilégié pour la peinture du sentiment de l'amour."[17] As for the *Lais*, Ménard observes, Marie "se contente d'une rapide évocation"; one would wish that "la poétesse fût moins laconique."[18]

Thirty years after the appearance of Ménard's study, Thomas Honegger published an article[19] that also compares love speeches, this time in four medieval and early modern texts, including Marie's *lai* of *Lanval*.[20] Applying concepts drawn from pragmatics, Honegger examines the ways writers "exploit the potential inherent in opening moves [in love] relationships for the purpose of plot motivation and protagonist characterization."[21]

These two comparative studies are especially valuable because Ménard and Honegger identify central characteristics of the love declaration in several medieval romances and in Marie's *lais*. For instance, in the Latin-based and Latin-influenced works by male, most frequently clerical, authors, these attenuated vows of love often assume a declamatory, oratorical, or deliberative style brimming with rhetorical figures, which may or may not be appropriate to the male characters who speak them.[22] Both studies also conclude that avowals of love in Marie's *lais* do not fit this mold.[23] Thus in identifying several basic features of the typical declaration, Ménard's and Honegger's studies show how avowals of love in Marie's *lais* diverge from this tradition. In other words, by learning what Marie's "declarations" are not, we begin to see what they are: they are briefer, less rhetorical, more diverse, spoken by women as well as men,[24] more focused on the interaction, and

---

17 Ménard, "La déclaration," 42.
18 Ménard "La déclaration," 35–38.
19 Thomas Honegger, "'But-þat þou louye me, Sertes y dye fore loue of þe': Towards a Typology of Opening Moves in Courtly Amorous Interaction," *Journal of Historical Pragmatics* 1, 1 (2000): 117–50.
20 *Lanval*, *Cligès*, *Gawain and the Green Knight*, and *Romeo and Juliet*.
21 Honegger describes "opening moves in lovers' interactions" as "interactional proposals by interactant A to interactant B that can be interpreted as an invitation to initiate a love relationship" ("'But-þat þou louye me, Sertes y dye fore loue of þe'," 145, note 1).
22 See also Karen Pratt's and Bonnie Wheeler's contribution to this volume. For an analysis of the "burlesque of deliberative oratory as either mere rationalization or as a substitute for action" in *Yvain*, see Tony Hunt, *Chrétien de Troyes. Yvain*. Critical Guides to French Texts, 55 (London: Grant & Cutler, 1986), 59–60.
23 Ménard, for instance, observes that in the ten declarations in the *lais* there is no "stereotypical schema" ("La déclaration," 35). Elsewhere he cautions, "on suivrait une mauvaise voie, si l'on voulait ranger à toute force dans ce cadre les peintures amoureuses que nous offrent les lais" (*Les* Lais *de Marie de France*. 2nd ed. [Paris: Presses Universitaires de France, 1995], 121).
24 The declaration, according to Ménard ("La déclaration amoureuse") and Honegger ("'But-þat þou louye me, Sertes y dye fore loue of þe'"), is a male prerogative. Paupert has noted that in the *Lais*, "Les déclarations d'amour au féminin sont très directes et suivies d'un effet presque immédiate" (179). For an analysis of the "wooing woman" motif, see Judith Weiss, "The Wooing Woman in Anglo-Norman Romance," *Romance in Medieval England*, ed. Maldwyn Mills, Jennifer Fellows, and Carol Meale (Cambridge: D. S. Brewer, 1991), 149–61.

less focused on the psychological state of the male declarer (e.g., on his timidity, uncertainty, anxiety, suffering).

Inasmuch as these conventions belong to the Latin literary tradition, it is significant to recall that in the Prologue of the *Lais*, Marie states that although she had considered translating a "good Latin story" ("De aukune bone estoire faire / E de latin en romaunz traire" [vv. 2–29]), she rejected the idea, opting instead for *lais* she had heard and does not want to be forgotten:

> Des lais pensai, k'oï aveie;
> Ne dutai pas, bien le saveie,
> Ke pur remambrance les firent
> Des aventures k'il oïrent
> Cil ki primes les comencierent
> E ki avant les enveierent.
> Plusurs en ai e oï conter,
> Ne[s] voil laisser në oblïer. (vv. 33–40).

[So I thought of lays which I had heard and did not doubt, for I know full well that they were composed by those who first began them and put them into circulation, to perpetuate the memory of adventures they had heard. I myself have heard a number of them and do not wish to overlook or neglect them.]

In bypassing Latin sources, Marie avoids the typical romance model of declaration, or "opening move," and focuses instead on the exchanges between lovers. The following analysis centers on lovers' initial interactions — miniature discourses — in which hearts are opened and deep emotions revealed, and thoughts are expressed "fittingly and efficaciously."[25]

Commentators like John of Salisbury, and Cicero before him, recognized that eloquence was a "natural talent" that was enhanced by cultivation. In this connection, it is significant that Marie would have had access to several resources for enriching her verbal facility. In triglossic twelfth-century England[26] and in the Angevin empire, a sophisticated vernacular literature appeared alongside the Latin productions.[27] Those associated with twelfth-century aristocratic

---

[25] In accordance with John of Salisbury's definition of *eloquence*. See, for example, the translator's glossing of "commode," (e.g., "fittingly, appropriately, and effectively"). See also *commoditas*: "fitness, appropriate effectiveness, easy adequacy" (*The Metalogicon of John of Salisbury*, trans. McGarry, 26–27).

[26] In addition to French, English, and Latin, Celtic languages were also present in some areas. See also the contribution to this volume by Harry Peters, who focuses on the trilingual situation in Gower's poetry.

[27] For influence of Latin works on medieval vernaculars, see, for example, Auerbach, *Literary Language and Its Public in Late Latin Antiquity and in the Middle Ages*, 270–94; A. G. Rigg, *A History of Anglo-Latin Literature 1066–1422* (Cambridge and New York: Cambridge University Press, 1992);

networks, as Marie seems to have been, would have been familiar with various literary and language models: literary romances and *chansons de geste*;[28] saints' lives; religious texts, for instance, psalters and books of hours connected with religious rites; sermons;[29] and letters and the *artes dictaminis*, which flourished from the eleventh to the thirteenth centuries.[30] Such works would have provided Marie with a means of enriching her verbal repertoire and cultivating and fostering her natural talent.

That Marie knew and drew upon such resources is apparent, for allusions and references in her *lais* indicate that, in addition to Breton materials, she had knowledge of various other sources.[31] In the Prologue, for instance, Marie cites Priscian (v. 10), who was well known for his grammatical treatises. Four of his works enjoyed popularity during the twelfth century: the *Institutiones grammaticae*, which survives in more than a thousand manuscripts; the *De metris fabularum Terentii*; the *De praeexercitamentis rhetoricis*; and the *Partitiones duodecim versuum Aeneidos principalium*, a grammatical explication of analysis of the first twelve lines of Virgil's *Aeneid*.[32] As James J. Murphy has observed, during the Middle Ages grammatical instruction "included a considerable treatment of the

---

and M. T. Clanchy, *From Memory to Written Record: England 1066-1307*, 2nd ed. (Oxford: Blackwell, 1993), 12–16.

[28] On the survival of classical materials, see, for example, the early and still valuable studies by Edmond Faral, *Recherches sur les sources latines des contes et romans courtois du moyen âge* (1913; Paris, Honoré Champion, 1967), 381–85; and Charles Homer Haskins, *The Renaissance of the Twelfth Century* (1927; Harvard University Press, 2001).

[29] On the "contributions" of predication to linguistic and literary development, see, for example, G. R. Owst, *Literature and Pulpit in Medieval England: a Neglected Chapter in the History of English Letters & of the English People*. 2nd ed. (Oxford: Basil Blackwell, 1961), 2–4.

[30] See the pioneering study of Albrecht Classen, "Female Epistolary Literature from Antiquity to the Present," *Studia Neophilologica* 60 (1988), 3–13; and Joan M. Ferrante's insightful "Chapter 1: Women in Correspondence," eadem, *To the Glory of Her Sex: Women's Roles in the Composition of Medieval Texts*. Women of Letters (Bloomington and Indianapolis: Indiana University Press, 1997), 10–35. On correspondence between aristocratic women and prelates like Baudri de Borgueil and Hildebert of Lavardin, see, for example, Reto R. Bezzola, *Les origines et la formation de la littérature courtoise en Occident (500–1200)*, 3 parts in 5 vols. Bibliothèque de l'École des hautes études.... Sciences historiques et philologiques 286, 313, 319–20 (Paris: É. Champion, 1944–1963). Vol. 2, part 2 (1960); and Gerald Bond, *The Loving Subject: Desire, Eloquence, and Power in Romanesque France*. Middle Ages Series (Philadelphia: University of Pennsylvania Press), 1995. On the rise of the letters and the *artes dictamines* in this period, see Giles Constable, *Letters and Letter Collections*. Typologie des sources du Moyen Age occidental, 17 (Turnhout: Brepols, 1976).

[31] This list would be expanded if we were to take into account the other works attributed to Marie de France: the *Fables*, the *Espurgatoire seint Patriz*, and perhaps, as has been recently suggested, the *Vie de seint Audree*. See, for example, Mickel, *Marie de France*, 144, note 4; and most recently June Hall McCash, "*La vie seinte Audree*: A Fourth Text by Marie de France?" *Speculum* 77.3 (2000): 744–77.

[32] James J. Murphy, *Rhetoric in the Middle Ages. A History of Rhetorical Theory from St. Augustine to the Renaissance* (Berkeley and Los Angeles: University of California Press, 1974), 71–72. See also R. W. Hunt, "Studies in Priscian in the Eleventh and Twelfth Centuries," *Medieval and Renaissance Studies* 1 (1941): 194–231; 2 (1950): 1–56.

principle of ornamental variation," even at the beginning level, and "elementary education in the tropes and figures was always a fundamental part" of the teaching.[33] Significantly, too, Gunnar Biller's 1916 study of "courtly style" demonstrated that Marie's *lais* include rhetorical tropes, schemes, and figures (e.g. chiasmus, anaphora, polyptoton, parallelism, formulae, metaphors, metonomy, periphrasis, and classical and Biblical allusions).[34] Moreover, as Suzanne Reynolds has shown," classical literary texts constituted "an essential part of grammatical instruction," particularly "in the earlier stages of learning Latin."[35]

Marie's references to and echoes of Latin-based and Latin-influenced works (whether in Latin or in vernacular translation like the *Roman d'Enéas* , Wace's *Brut*, Geoffrey of Monmouth's *Historia regum Britanniae*, Gaimar's *Estoire des Engleis*) have received considerable attention.[36] Moreover, not only does Marie refer to Ovid's book (*Guigemar* v. 239), but her work has also been seen to manifest a complex relationship to Ovid or the Ovidian tradition.[37] So, too, the *lais* also contain mentions of mythical and historico-mythical figures (e.g., Venus, Octavian, and Semiramis),[38] along with Biblical and liturgical resonances: the parable of the talents[39] and "l'ovre Salemun."[40] Additionally, the psalter carried by the old woman in *Yonec* (v. 59) and the correspondence described in *Milun* demonstrate Marie's familiarity with the liturgical literature and the epistolary genre.[41]

An additional catalyst stimulating linguistic formation in the twelfth-century Anglo-French Angevin empire — a factor that sharpened Marie's verbal sensitivity — is the heightened awareness of language endemic to elite speech communities. In his *Origins of Courtliness*, Stephen Jaeger has described increasing

---

[33] Murphy, *Rhetoric in the Middle Ages*, 191.

[34] See, for example, Gunnar Biller, *Etude sur le style des premiers romans français en vers (1150–75)* (1916; Geneva: Slatkine, 1974), 29 et passim.

[35] Suzanne Reynolds, *Medieval Reading: Grammar, Rhetoric and the Classical Text* (Cambridge and New York: Cambridge University Press, 1996), 11.

[36] For a brief survey, see Mickel, *Marie de France*, 22.

[37] See, for example, Robert W. Hanning, "Courtly Contexts for Urban *Cultus*: Responses to Ovid in Chretien's *Cligès* and Marie's *Guigemar*," *Symposium* 35 (1981–1982): 34–56; and Sunhee Kim Gertz, *Echoes and Reflections: Memory and Memorials in Ovid and Marie de France*. Faux Titre, 232 (Amsterdam and New York: Rodopi, 2003).

[38] Karen K. Jambeck, "'Femmes et tere': Marie de France and the Discourses in *Lanval*," *Discourses on Love, Marriage, and Transgression in Medieval and Early Modern Europe*, ed. Albrecht Classen. Medieval and Renaissance Texts and Studies 278 (Tempe: Arizona Center for Medieval and Renaissance Studies, 2004), 109–45; here 119–21.

[39] See Brewster E. Fitz, "The Prologue to the *Lais* of Marie de France and the Parable of the Talents: Gloss and Monetary Metaphor," *Modern Language Notes* 90 (1975): 558–64.

[40] *Guigemar* (v. 172). On the possible connection between "Salemun" and the Song of Songs, see Alfred Ewert, ed., *Marie de France. Lais*, 166.

[41] Chantal A. Maréchal, unpublished paper, "Le lai de Milun: un exemple d'auto-écriture." International Courtly Literature Society, Seventh Congress, University of Massachusetts, Amherst. July 30, 1992.

De Parlor Bon' Eloquence 225

emphasis on conduct and language appropriate to the medieval court,[42] and such ideas and ideals of courtly behavior and courtly language are prevalent in the works of Marie and many of her contemporaries.[43] In fact, in his analysis of the semantic field of the term *corteis* in the twelfth century, Glyn Burgess concludes,

> To be *courtois* is to provide the right answer at the time of need, to hit on the solution to a problem. It requires that one be a quick thinker, acting swiftly with no desire to offend others. One must tell the truth, pick the right moment for action, show the necessary skill if specific abilities are demanded, manifest gratitude where appropriate, offer hospitality, show sensitivity and understanding where the circumstances are of a delicate or exacting nature. *Courtoisie* is a capacity to handle other people and to say the right thing at the right time.
>
> *Courtoisie* is attractive to the opposite sex and will thus come close at times to what we call charm, the ability to offer a pleasant greeting and to speak in an agreeable way. The person who is *courtois* knows how to handle himself or herself in society and can therefore make an important contribution to society by raising standards of behavior.[44]

One locus of Marie's eloquence is the verbal interaction between lovers, which lends itself to pragmatic explication, especially in the context of politeness theory. Here it is possible to see the intricate ways in which she shapes speakers' words, contexts, and strategies to exploit the interplay between explicitness and implicitness in the process of generating meaning.[45]

---

[42] C. Stephen Jaeger, *The Origins of Courtliness. Civilizing Trends and the Formation of Courtly Ideals: 939–1210*. The Middle Ages Series (Philadelphia: University of Pennsylvania Press, 1985), 116. For a later manifestation, see David Burnley, "Courtly Speech in Chaucer," *Poetica* 24 (1986): 16–38.

[43] Here, it is important to distinguish between courtly conduct and language and the more controversial concept of courtly love. See, for example, Sarah Kay, "Courts, Clerks, and Courtly Love," *The Cambridge Companion to Medieval Romance*, ed. Roberta L. Krueger (Cambridge and New York: Cambridge University Press, 2000), 81–96.

[44] "The Term 'courtois' in Twelfth-Century French," *Etudes de lexicologie, lexicographie et stylistique offerts en hommage à Georges Matoré*, textes réunis par Irène Tamba (Paris: Société pour l'Information Grammaticale, Université de Paris-Sorbonne, 1987), 105–22; here 118–19.

[45] See, for example, Jef Verschueren, *Understanding Pragmatics* (London and New York: Arnold, and New York: Oxford University Press, 1999), 156; and Stephen C. Levinson, *Pragmatics* (Cambridge and New York: Cambridge University Press, 1983), 11ff.; see also 126.

PRAGMATICS AND *POLITENESS*

In analyzing the language of interaction, pragmatics and in particular "politeness phenomena" are especially useful. According to the classic study by Penelope Brown and Stephen C. Levinson, "politeness" centers on "public self image and sense of self" and is universally present across cultures.[46] As will become apparent, the distance between classical principles and contemporary research in sociolinguistics and pragmatics is perhaps not so great. In his *De Officiis*, for instance, Cicero, who greatly influenced John of Salisbury, observes, "maximeque curandum est, ut eos, quibuscum sermonem conferemus, et vereri et diligere videamur" (We must also take the greatest care to show courtesy and consideration toward those with whom we converse).[47] Cicero goes on to outline several emulable "qualities" of conversation that anticipate pragmatic principles, especially the politeness strategies described by Brown and Levinson: "observe the topic of conversation"; maintain an appropriate tone; keep to the topic, taking care that it does "not drift off to other channels"; "be respectful"; and "be agreeable." To be avoided are the following: strong emotions; "offensive language"; "dogmatic" statements; "debar[ring]" others from speaking, "for each should have his turn"; and "reproof," which, when it cannot be avoided, should be "mild" and accompanied by an "explanation that it is for the good of the person reproved."[48]

A branch of pragmatics, *Politeness Theory*, examines the choices in language made in the course of situated language use; the focus is on "public self image and sense of self." Central to Brown and Levinson's approach to politeness is the concept of *face*, which is the "respect that an individual has for himself or herself, and the need to maintain that 'self-esteem'" in public or in private situations.[49] Face consists of dual desires or "wants": the first of these, *negative face*, is the desire for "freedom of action and freedom from imposition"; the second, *positive face*, is

---

[46] Penelope Brown and Stephen C. Levinson assert that these principles "[are] of a universal yet 'social sort'"; the "mutual knowledge of other members' public self image and the social necessity to orient oneself to it in interaction are universal," while particular linguistic realizations are "culture-specific, group specific, and even idiosyncratic" (*Politeness: Some Universals in Language Usage*. Studies in Interactional Sociolinguistics, 4 [Cambridge: Cambridge University Press, 1987], 56 and 61–64).

[47] (Book 1, XXXVIII, para. 136). Pointing out the importance of speaking well in conversation and noting that there are no established guidelines as there are for oratory, Cicero makes these observations. For the Latin with English translation, see Cicero, *De officiis*, trans. Walter Miller (Cambridge, MA, and London: Harvard University Press, 1913), 138–39.

[48] *De Officiis*, 136–41.

[49] Brown and Levinson, *Politeness*, 61. See also Erving Goffman, *Interactional Ritual* (New York: Anchor Books, 1967), 10. For overviews and critiques of Politeness Theory, see, for example, Gino Eelen, *A Critique of Politeness Theories* (Manchester, UK, and Northampton, MA: St Jerome Publishing, 2001); and Richard Watts, *Politeness* (Cambridge and New York: Cambridge University Press, 2003).

the desire to "be appreciated and approved of." Inasmuch as face is "emotionally invested" and "must be constantly attended to in interaction," people generally "cooperate in maintaining face," such cooperation "being based on mutual vulnerability of face."[50]

According to Brown's and Levinson's research on politeness, face, with its concerns for public self image and sense of self, is universal and at the same time social. Additionally, although each culture has relatively few conventionalized formulae, in practice there is an "enormously open-ended inventory of means for realizing politeness."[51] Any utterance, or speech act, in an exchange may have face-threatening potential, either offending against self-respect or entailing an obligation on the part of the addressee. Indeed, simply beginning a conversation can be threatening to both speaker and addressee because the latter may not want to participate. Any act that puts face wants at risk is *a face-threatening act*, a verbal act that infringes on the hearer's need to maintain his or her self-esteem, and to be respected. Among the speech acts that can threaten the addressee's *negative face* are orders, requests, and coercion; similarly *positive face wants* are threatened by criticisms, disagreements, challenges, and utterances that communicate out-of-control emotions. In addition, certain acts can threaten the speaker's face (e.g., rejected requests, unwilling promises and offers, and confessions).[52] For a variety of reasons, a speaker may decide to perform a potentially threatening speech act either explicitly (a *bald on-record* face- threatening act) or moderated by mitigating or redressive politeness strategies:[53] *positive politeness*[54] aims at making the addressee feel appreciated and *negative politeness*[55] attempts to minimize any sense of imposition. Moreover, in navigating the complex weighting process of bringing appropriate politeness strategies to bear — ascertaining the degree of the potential threat and negotiating sociological and psychological variables — some individuals are more capable than others.[56]

---

[50] Brown and Levinson, *Politeness*, 61–63.

[51] Brown and Levinson, *Politeness*, 86; see also 13–15 and 25–27.

[52] Brown and Levinson, *Politeness*, 61–68.

[53] According to Brown and Levinson, *Politeness*, 85, the term *strategy* "impl[ies] a rational element while covering both (a) innovative plans of action, which may still be (but need not be) unconscious, and (b) routines — that is, previously constructed plans whose original rational origin is still preserved in their construction, despite their present automatic application as ready-made programmes."

[54] Positive politeness is not limited as is negative politeness, which "is restricted to the imposition." Positive politeness addresses the hearer's "perennial desire that his wants ... should be thought of as desirable," and the sphere of redress is widened to the appreciation of alter's wants in general or to the expression of similarity between ego's and alter's wants" (Brown and Levinson, *Politeness*, 101). For descriptions of fifteen strategies related to positive politeness, see Brown and Levinson, 103–29.

[55] Brown and Levinson describe ten strategies related to negative politeness (*Politeness*, 129–211).

[56] Brown and Levinson, *Politeness*, 68–84.

Thus, within the context of pragmatics and politeness theory, a conversation can be viewed as an *exchange*, that is, a coherent and cohesive unit of discourse with a tripartite structure consisting of an opening turn or move that introduces a topic, a response, and a possible follow-up.[57] The *Lais* contain a wide variety of such conversations in which lovers express deep-seated emotions and nuanced states of mind in a series of conversational turns. An analysis of exchanges drawn from *Lanval*, *Yonec*, and *Equitan* illustrates Marie's skill in sequencing and exploiting language in the delicate and dynamic process of making meaning,[58] an important feature of her eloquence.

LANVAL

In the *lai* of *Lanval*, two closely parallel and contrasting exchanges occur: one between Lanval and a remarkable *dameisele*, and a second between Lanval and Arthur's queen. These brief discourses are particularly instructive because of the clear contrasts between them. In the first instance, the narrator explains, Lanval is alone and dispirited; having ridden out from the court, he has sought out the solitude of the countryside after a disappointing turn of events. Of all Arthur's knights, Lanval is the only one to have been forgotten when the king distributed fiefs and wives during the celebration of a victorious battle. An alien in Britain, without resources or connections, Lanval contemplates his state as he rests in a grassy meadow. His solitary meditation is interrupted when two beautiful and elegantly arrayed maidens approach and invite him to speak with their mistress.[59]

This encounter with the messengers, who gracefully invite Lanval to accompany them, serves as a prelude, or a pre-sequence,[60] to the actual exchange between Lanval and the lady. In terms of pragmatics, this invitation functions in

---

[57] "[M]inimally two part structure," an exchange "can consist of up to five moves, though such long exchanges are comparatively rare" (Malcolm Coulthard, *An Introduction to Discourse Analysis*. 2nd ed. [1977; Burnt Mill, Harlow, Essex: Longman Group, 1985], 136).

[58] On the application of such methods to historical texts, see for example, *Historical Pragmatics: Pragmatic Developments in the History of English*, ed. Andreas H. Jucker. Pragmatics & Beyond, new series 35 (Amsterdam and Philadelphia: John Benjamins, 1995); *Historical Dialogue Analysis*, ed. Andreas H. Jucker, Gerd Fritz, and Franz Lebsanft. Pragmatics and Beyond, new series, 66 (Amsterdam and Philadelphia: John Benjamins, 1999), 13–14; and Tim William Machan, *English in the Middle Ages* (Oxford and New York: Oxford University Press, 2003), esp. 151–60.

[59] "Pre-sequences and 'fishings' . . . allow the off-record negotiation of business with face implications well in advance of the possible on-record transaction. Thus nearly all of the structural predispositions that have been studied under the rubric of preference and many aspects of pre-sequence seem to be motivated by face considerations" (Brown and Levinson, *Politeness*, 40).

[60] This explanation of lines 69–76 is based upon Honegger's perceptive analysis, which was the first to identify the encounter as a pre-sequence ("'But-þat þou louye me, Sertes y dye fore loue of þe'," 126). Cf. also Honegger's commentary on the following lines (138). On the concept of pre-sequence and "pre-invitation," see also Levinson, *Pragmatics*, 345–64.

several significant ways. It prepares Lanval for his interaction with the sender of the invitation, who, the messengers indicate, is most worthy: "tant est pruz e sage e bele" (v. 72). Such an invitation, then, takes on the value of politeness directed at positive face. Second, the fact that the maidens are envoys lessens the potential infringement upon Lanval's negative face by allowing him freedom to act: a rejection of the invitation they bear would not threaten their positive face directly. Finally, by informing Lanval that the "paveilluns" is nearby and that they will take him there safely (vv.75–76), they minimize the potential imposition upon him.

It is in this context that Lanval accompanies the maidens to a glorious pavilion, and upon entering he encounters a young woman, surrounded by opulence and luxury. She is clearly a personage of considerable standing; her beauty surpasses the best in nature and her possessions are costly beyond compare. In a conversational turn represented by six lines of the *lai*, the lady exhibits a firm command of appropriate speech:

> "Lanval," fet ele, "beus amis,
> Pur vus vient jeo fors de ma tere;
> De luinz vus sui venue quere.
> Se vus estes pruz e curteis,
> Emperere ne quens ne reis
> N'ot unkes tant joie ne bien;
> Kar jo vus aim sur tute rien." (vv. 110–16)

> ["Lanval," she said, "fair friend, for you I came from my country. I have come far in search of you, and if you are worthy and courtly no emperor, counts, or king will have felt as much joy nor happiness as you, for I love you above all else."]

Addressing Lanval by name suggests that she knows something about him; she also calls him "fair friend" ("beus amis" [v. 10]), a compliment conjoined with a group identity marker that signals inclusion and solidarity.[61] Additionally, her use of *vus* suggests both respect and an initial goal of mutual formality.[62] From the outset, she is attentive to Lanval's positive face. When she also invites him to sit near her, allowing him an opportunity to accept or decline and waiting for his response, she also takes into account his negative face, and it is only after he is seated that she begins to speak again. Her comments are brief and deftly

---

[61] Positive Politeness 4: "Use in-group identity markers." This and subsequent politeness strategies are identified here by the number assigned to each by Brown and Levinson (*Politeness*, 103–29; here 107–12). Subsequent notations will generally be restricted to the first appearance of each strategy.

[62] On the distinction between deference and mutuality in connection with honorifics, including formal pronouns, see Brown and Levinson, *Politeness*, 23–24.

sequenced. Utilizing the respectful *vus*, she explains that because of him she has come from another land ("ma terre"), traveling far to seek him out.[63] In these few words, she has implemented three realizations of positive politeness, which demonstrate her regard for him. And each of these manifestations of positive politeness is heightened because of the lady's obvious status.

She then goes on to make a sensitive off-record offer: "If you are wise and courtly, no emperor, count, or king will have felt as much joy or happiness as you" (vv. 113–16). Cast in a hypothetical *if* clause, the statement is less a questioning of Lanval's virtues than an indirect way of indicating that he will be rewarded for his virtue, the resulting benefits also being phrased indirectly. The statement has no sense of *quid pro quo*, nor does it function as a negotiating tactic. Requiring nothing of him, the statement recognizes, and allows him an opportunity to express, his merit — merit, which Lanval and Marie's audience know, had gone unappreciated by the king. In a technical sense, the *if* clause functions as a "possibility marker," which serves to affirm the knight's virtues and to function as a hedge,[64] softening the illocutionary force of the lady's statement: if he wishes, the virtuous Lanval will experience more joy than an emperor or king.[65] This mode of offering without obligating, or coercing, the potential recipient attends to both positive (acceptance and affiliation) and negative face (freedom to act).[66]

Only after expressing concern for Lanval's self-respect as well as his need for autonomy does the lady reveal her love: "Kar jo vus aim sur tute rien" (v. 116). This disclosure does not have the force of a request, for, in point of fact, she asks nothing but offers all, apparently out of loving generosity. If Lanval decides to accept this good fortune, it is up to him to determine what, if anything, he might do in return. Inspired by love, he replies with similar generosity of spirit. The extradiegetic narrator foregrounds this reply by observing that Lanval speaks appropriately ("avenantment"):

"Bele," fet il, "si vus pleiseit
E cele joie me aveneit
Que vus me vousissez amer,

---

[63] That she has come from another land, and perhaps from another world, suggests that she has esteem and concern for him. Positive Politeness 15: "Give gifts," combined with Positive Politeness 1: "Notice, attend to [the addressee]." On combining strategies, see Brown and Levinson, *Politeness*, 17.

[64] See, for example, Brown and Levinson, *Politeness*, 153, 173, and 272.

[65] In connection with this "non-coercive offer," see Honegger, who reaches similar conclusions with differences in explanation and in purpose ("'But-þat þou louye me, Sertes y dye fore loue of þe'," 126).

[66] Positive Politeness 10: "Offer, promise," combined with Negative Politeness 1: "Be conventionally indirect," allows the addressee options. On contextual ambiguity for the purpose of indirection, see Brown and Levinson, *Politeness*, 132 and 172. On the *if*-clause's "function[ing] pragmatically as a hedge on the force of the speech act," see Brown and Levinson, *Politeness*, 272.

Ne savrïez rien comander
Que jeo ne face a mien poeir,
Turt a folie u a saveir.
Jeo f[e]rai voz comandemenz,
Pur vus guerpirai tutes genz.
Jamés ne queor de vus partir:
Ceo est la rien que plus desir." (vv, 121–30)

[Fair one, if it were pleasing to you and this joy befell me, that you would wish to love me, you could ask nothing — whether frivolous or wise — that I would not do to the best of my ability. I will fulfill your requests. I will reject all others. Never do I want to part from you. This is what I most desire.] (Translation mine)

Perceiving that she is beautiful, manifesting both exterior and interior beauty — "tant est pruz e sage e bele" — which is also reflected in her words, Lanval is inspired by love. He addresses her as "bele," a compliment that echoes her initial words to him ("beus amis"); such repetition implies agreement and movement toward solidarity,[67] and he also employs the respectful *vus*.[68] Acknowledging the lady's superior status, Lanval responds with negative politeness, maintaining respectful distance. He begins with great indirection, couching the first three ideas in a hypothetical *if* clause that functions as a hedge.[69] The first part of the clause — "if it were to please you" — stresses her freedom to act and to choose. The next element of the *if* clause loosely connects a second idea to the first by means of the conjunction *and*: in this construction — "if this joy were to befall me" — Lanval assumes the position of direct object; he assigns no agency to himself. It is only in the third component of the clause, an adjective clause, that he delicately identifies the source of his potential joy by means of a subjunctive verb "vousissez": "that you would wish to love me." Thus he indicates that he understands, and appreciates, the generosity of her offer.[70]

Cautiously, with great attention to the lady's negative face, the landless knight who has no material resources offers her all that he has — his love, his loyalty, and his willingness to do her bidding. He expresses the indirection with conditional

---

[67] Positive Politeness 5: "Seek agreement." One means of working toward this goal is "repeating part or all of what the preceding speaker has said in a conversation" (Brown and Levinson, *Politeness*, 112).

[68] Negative Politeness 5: "Give deference."

[69] Negative Politeness 2: "Question, hedge." Here the *if*-clause functions as a hedge, minimizing any imposition and recognizing her freedom of choice; he is fully aware that she is under no obligation to him. On hedges, see Brown and Levinson, *Politeness*, 145–72.

[70] Negative Politeness 3: "Be pessimistic," that is, do not "presume / assume" about the addressee's wants"; maintain "ritual distance" from the addressee (Brown and Levinson, 144). See also the effect of hedges (Brown and Levinson, *Politeness*, 273).

and subjunctive verbs,[71] his focus remaining consistently on her wishes: "Ne *savrïez* rien comander / Que jeo ne *face* a mien poeir" (vv. 124–25). Then shifting to the future tense and declarative statements, he offers the following: "I will fulfill your requests. I will reject all others." He concludes by making two assertions using the declarative verbs "queor " and "desir": "Never do I want to part from you. This is what I most desire." Thus, openly declaring his volition without making any assumptions about her or requesting anything of her, he assures her that he would enter into a love relationship with faithfulness and commitment, acting of his own free will. Upon hearing his words, the lady responds wordlessly:

> Quant la meschine oï parler
> Celui que tant la peot amer,
> S'amur e sun cors li otreie. (vv. 131–33)

> [When the maiden heard him speak, this man who is able to love her so well, she accords him her love and her body.] (Translation mine)

Noting approval, the narrator comments, "Ore est Lanval en dreite voie!" (v. 134; Now Lanval was on the right path!).

While scholars have tended to ignore the significance of the lady's language, attributing all to her otherworldly or faerie qualities, in terms of pragmatics her language is more than apt. And, as Albrecht Classen has observed, "in both religion and literary discourses medieval women often held their own," "not only because of their economic, political, religious, and sometimes even military might, but particularly because they know how to control language and utilize communicative tools to their best advantage."[72] Notably, in composing the interaction between the lady and Lanval, Marie succeeds in communicating much about the two characters and the nature of their relationship, which is based upon mutual respect, generosity of spirit, and willing cooperation.

Standing in stark contrast to this exchange between Lanval and the lady is a second, which also centers on love.[73] Here again, the narrator takes care in contextualizing the exchange. This time, however, there is no pre-sequence or transitional invitation; in fact, there is nothing that would prepare Lanval for the encounter. The scene opens with an almost chilling stillness. The extradiegetic narrator focuses on the queen as she silently gazes down from her tower window at the *vergier*, where the household knights — among them Lanval, who with great reluctance had been persuaded by his companions to join them — are gathered.

---

[71] Brown and Levinson, *Politeness*, 173–75.
[72] "Introduction," *Discourses on Love, Marriage, and Transgression*, 1–42; here 20.
[73] Honegger has observed that each of the openings to these exchanges consists of six lines and the two passages roughly parallel each other, though inversely ("'But-þat þou louye me, Sertes y dye fore loue of þe'," 129).

Unobserved by the knights, the queen quickly prepares to strike. Summoning more than thirty of her most beautiful, refined, and richly garbed maidens, she leads them to the garden, where the *dameiseles* and the knights gladly engage in conversation, which, the narrator emphasizes with litotes, is not *vilains* ("uncourtly") (vv. 243–52). Lanval, however, withdraws from the group to think in solitude about his absent beloved. Seeing him alone, the queen pursues him and wordlessly sits down beside him.[74]

Although she has intruded upon his private space, the queen offers no apology or redress, nor does she make any effort to ascertain his emotional state. Suddenly, with no regard for his negative face, she reveals her feelings for him: "tut sun curage li mustra" (v. 262).[75] Addressing him by name, she abruptly launches into her proposition:

> "Lanval, mut vus ai honuré
> E mut cheri e mut amé.
> Tute m'amur poëz aveir.
> Kar me dites vostre voleir!
> Ma drüerie vus otrei.
> Mut devez estre lié de mei." (vv. 263–68)

> ["Lanval, I have honoured, cherished, and loved you much. You may have all my love: just tell me what you desire! I grant you my love and you should be glad to have me."]

While the queen's first words to Lanval — "honor," "cherish," and "love" — might appear to be intended as positive politeness, she undercuts any positive perlocutionary effect with her self-focus. This assertion comprised of three first-person verbs highlights the queen and her desire and has little to do with Lanval, except as passive object, here the syntactic direct object.

Her bald on-record proffering of *amur*,[76] followed by an imperative — "tell me what you want" — is followed, with no pause for an answer, by "I grant you my love." What at first glance appears to be the offering of a gift is in actuality a granting (*otreier*), which, presented as a *fait accompli*, provides no real option for

---

[74] On the queen's lack of courtly conduct, see also Judith R. Rothschild, "Manipulative Gestures and Behaviors in the *Lais* of Marie de France," *The Spirit of the Court: Selected Proceedings of the Fourth Congress of the International Courtly Literature Society (Toronto 1983)*, ed. Glyn S. Burgess and R. A. Taylor (Woodbridge, Suffolk: D. S. Brewer, 1985), 283–88.

[75] Raising emotional topics constitutes a face-threatening act (Brown and Levinson, *Politeness*, 66–67).
   The queen's direct, and abrupt, approach contrasts sharply with the graceful invitation that begins to prepare Lanval for his conversation with the lady in her pavilion.

[76] On the ambiguity of the terms *dru* and *druerie*, see Roger Dubuis, "*Dru* et *drüerie* dans le *Tristan* de Béroul," *Mélanges de langue et littérature françaises du moyen âge offerts à Pierre Jonin*. Senefiance, no. 7 (Aix-en-Provence: Publications du CUERMA; Paris: Champion, 1979), 349–54.

Lanval, and infringes upon his freedom of choice.[77] The queen's lack of regard for Lanval's face has already been conveyed by her failure to interpret his separating himself from the group as indicative of his wanting to be alone. Oblivious to his wishes, however, the queen continues without pausing: "You should be [very] glad to have me." Yet again, the queen's words, this time an imperative, intensified with the adverb *mut*, threaten Lanval's negative face.[78] This grant, the queen's love, presented with no redressive measures, would clearly entail future obligations on Lanval's part; moreover, her instructions — that he is to feel gratitude — further restrict Lanval's freedom and make explicit the fact that her love is not without strings.[79] Significantly, this arrangement of bald on-record face threats closely parallels, though inversely, the carefully sequenced face-affirming statements and sensitively indirect offers communicated to Lanval by the lady at the beginning of the *lai*.

One touchstone for gauging the queen's unremitting aggressiveness is the temptation scene in *Gawain and the Green Knight*, where the infamous Bertilak's wife repeatedly attempts to seduce Gawain. However, whereas Bertilak's wife moderates her repeated attempts at seduction with sufficient indirection and negative politeness to permit "evasive non-compliance" on Gawain's part,[80] the queen's bald on-record face-threatening acts, unleavened with redressive politeness, allow the stunned Lanval few alternatives. Left with no room to evade or decline gracefully, he responds. Although he begins with the honorific "Dame," he resorts to an imperative followed by an assertion: "lessez m'ester! / Jeo n'ai cure de vus amer" (vv. 269–70; leave me be! I have no desire to love you). These words, which represent Lanval's feeble attempt to salvage his own face which has been sorely neglected by the queen, constitute on-record threats to the queen's positive face. Still, however taken aback Lanval may be, he manages to summon up some redressive politeness, giving reasons for his refusal:[81] "I have long served the king and do not want to betray my faith. Neither you nor your love will ever lead me to wrong my lord."

---

[77] Brown and Levinson, *Politeness*, 65–66.

[78] In connection with the queen's utterances, Ménard has observed, "on sent dans ces mots de la hauteur et une certaine condescendence" (*Les Lais*, 125). Pragmatics and Politeness Theory help to explain such impressions.

[79] Speech acts "that predicate some future act of H [the addressee], and in so doing put some pressure on H [the addressee] to do (or refrain from doing) the act" (Brown and Levinson, *Politeness*, 65, 66, and 270).

[80] Machan, *English in the Middle Ages*, 151–60. See also Kim Sydow Campbell, "A Lesson in Polite Non-Compliance: Gawain's Conversational Strategies in Fit 3 of *Gawain and the Green Knight*," *Language Quarterly* 28 (1990): 53–62.

[81] "Giv[ing] overwhelming reasons" addresses negative face; the speaker "can claim that he has compelling reasons for doing the face threatening act (Brown and Levinson, *Politeness*, 189).

Nonetheless, in this encounter the fundamental principle of mutual maintaining of face has been violated,[82] and both the knight and the queen have sustained serious losses. Moreover, the reason Lanval gives for declining — that is, his loyalty to the king (vv. 271–74) — cannot but be interpreted as a further insult by the unfaithful queen. The face threats escalate. Her angry words, inept attempts to salvage her own face, become a series of pointedly face-threatening acts directed at Lanval[83] as she confronts him:

> Vus n'amez gueres cel delit;
> Asez le m'ad hum dit sovent
> Que des femmez n'avez talent.
> Vallez avez bien afeitiez,
> Ensemble od eus vus deduiez.
> Vileins cuarz, mauveis failliz,
> Mut est mi sires maubailliz
> Que pres de lui vus ad suffert;
> Mun escïent que Deus en pert!" (vv. 278–86)

[You do not like this kind of pleasure. I have been told often enough that you have no desire for women. You have well-trained young men and enjoy yourself with them. Base coward, wicked recreant, my lord is extremely unfortunate to have suffered you near him. I think he may have lost his salvation because of it!]

Here, her accusation of homosexuality and her insults — "vileins cuarz" and "mauveis failliz" — echo those of Lavine's mother — "sodomite" and "couart" — in the *Roman d'Eneas*,[84] suggesting a particular cultural potency in Marie's twelfth-century context.

Clearly distressed, Lanval is not slow to reply. In attempting to preserve his positive face, he denies her accusations and gives yet another reason for refus-

---

[82] On "social breakdown" and "affrontery," see Brown and Levinson, *Politeness*, 62. As Brown and Levinson point out, "Normally everyone's face depends upon everyone else's face being maintained, and since people can be expected to defend their faces if threatened, and in defending their own to threaten others' faces, it is in general in every participant's best interest to maintain each others' face" (61).

[83] On face-threatening acts that indicate a "speaker does not care about addressee's face," including insults and terms of address that are threatening or embarrassing, see Brown and Levinson, *Politeness*, 66–67.

[84] See, for example, *Le Roman d'Eneas. Edition critique d'après le manuscrit B. N. fr. 60*, ed. and trans. Aimé Petit (Paris: Librairie Générale de France, 1997), vv. 8621–65. For further discussions of this topic, see Raymond Cormier's contribution to this volume. On the conventional aspect of the terms and accusations, see John H. Yunk, ed. and trans., *Eneas. A Twelfth-Century Romance* (New York and London: Columbia University Press, 1974), 226, note 147; and Faral, 131–32. See also Suzanne Kocher, "Accusations of Gay and Straight Sexual Transgression in the *Roman de la Violette*," *Discourses on Love, Marriage, and Transgression*, 189–210.

ing the queen, this time uttering words that he will doubly regret. Forgetting his promise to his beloved, he declares that he loves "a woman whose lowliest servant is far superior to the queen" (vv. 299–300). Thus, in the course of explaining, Lanval goes too far, making an invidious comparison, yet another threat to the queen's positive face.[85] The final damage is done. After the queen's initial disregard for Lanval's face, politeness has waned on both sides as each has hastened to save his or her own face. Such lack of concern for the other's face results in affrontery and "social breakdown."[86] The queen subsequently makes a false accusation to the king which leads to Lanval's being charged with misdeeds against his lord.[87] There is no hope for redress.

As in the case of Lanval and the lady, in the course of this dynamic exchange each participant exposes features of his or her own character, and defines the nature of the relationship. The conversation between Lanval and the queen has resulted in a sorry impasse: any possibility for repair, if ever there were one, has been destroyed. Bent on revenge, the queen will do her best to destroy Lanval's reputation, and possibly Lanval himself. Lack of care for face and person has led to conflict between Lanval and the queen, a breach between vassal and lord, disharmony among the barons of the kingdom, and a rift between Lanval and his beloved.

YONEC

In *Yonec*, the narrator is attentive to the context for the lovers' exchange, explaining the conditions of an arranged marriage (vv. 81–84): for seven years the wife has endured unhappiness and loneliness; her husband, the aging lord of Caerwent, had married her because she was beautiful and because he wanted an heir. This loveless marriage, the wife laments, had been arranged by her family and others (vv. 81–84). One day as she is bemoaning her unfortunate lot, a hawk flies through the narrow window of the tower where the lady is a virtual prisoner. Alighting in her chamber, the hawk transforms into a "chevler bel et gent" (v. 115; a fair and noble knight). He calmly and patiently waits, silently acknowledging that he has intruded upon her. Meanwhile, the lady's anxiety is apparent in her somatic reactions and gestures: she trembles and covers her head. When the knight, who is very courteous ("Mut fu curteis li chevaliers" [v. 119]), finally speaks, he does so in a calm, reassuring way, expressing concern for her. He addresses her first,

---

[85] See Brown and Levinson, *Politeness*, 66.
[86] Brown and Levinson, *Politeness*, 62 and 66.
[87] Arthur begins with the following accusation: "Vassal, vus me avez mut mesfait! / ... / De me hunir et aviler" (vv. 363–65; Vassal, you have seriously wronged me ... by shaming and dishonoring me).

employing an honorific[88] and the polite *vus*-form of the verb: "'Dame,' fet il, 'n'eiez poür!'" (v. 121; Lady, do not be afraid!).[89] While the verb is an imperative, it is not a "power-backed command"; rather, the message is solicitous, and when a directive is "primarily in the addressee's interest" and when the speaker "conveys that he does care about the addressee's positive face," as the knight does in regard to the lady, no redress is required.[90]

The hawk-knight, Muldumarec, continues, "Gentil oisel ad en ostur; / Si li segrei [vus] sunt oscur" (vv. 122–23; The hawk is a noble bird, even if its secrets remain a mystery to you). Avoiding the first person pronoun, he "impersonalizes," a strategy[91] that avoids imposing upon the lady's negative face. He follows this statement with a second set of unredressed imperatives, which, linked by the coordinating conjunction *si*, are directed toward the lady's interests and her positive face.[92] The first — "Gardez ke seiez a seür" (v. 124; Be assured that you are safe) — expresses concern for her well-being. In the second — "Si fetes de mei vostre ami!"(v. 125; and make me your friend [translation mine]), — the ambiguity of "ami," which can signify "friend" as well as "lover,"[93] is a form of indirectness, an off-record strategy that softens negative face threats and here emphasizes the offer of caring affection, friendship and potentially love, as contributing to her welfare.[94] Additionally, the hawk-knight will also reveal that he has come in response to her wishes. Expressed in terms of both positive and negative politeness, Muldumarec's offering, a gift, should she choose to accept it, from a person of status and power, is not unlike the offer made by Lanval's lady, who asks nothing in return.[95]

Moreover, the pronominal emphasis on the second person *vus*-form and the relative lack of first-person pronouns reinforces this focus on the addressee rather

---

[88] Such an honorific can indicate mutual respect and address positive face when one of superior status confers it (Brown and Levinson, *Politeness*, 178).

[89] The rather heavy use of exclamation marks here reflects the interpretation of the editor (and at times the translators). There is no comparable punctuation, indeed virtually no punctuation, in British Library MS Harley 978, the base text of Ewert's edition.

[90] "Doing the face-threatening act is primarily in the addressee's interest" as in "sympathetic advice or warnings" (Brown and Levinson, *Politeness*, 98).

[91] Negative Politeness 7: "Impersonalize" speaker and addressee.

[92] On imperatives that address positive face and do not require redress, see Brown and Levinson, *Politeness*, 98.

[93] Examining the semantic field of *ami(e)*, which occurs 128 times in Rychner's edition, Denise McClelland identifies three main significations: a polite term that "peut exprimer une sympathie instinctive vers quelqu'un . . . dans son sens d'amitié." It also "tourne toutefois autour du sentiment amoureux et se trouve renforcée d'une abondance d'adjectifs possessifs qui en soulignent la tonalité tendre et intime," but this term "n'a pas forcément une connotation sexuelle" (*Le Vocabulaire des Lais de Marie de France*. Publications médiévales de l'Université d'Ottawa, 3 [Ottawa: Editions de l'Université d'Ottawa, 1977], 62–64).

[94] On purposeful ambiguity, indirectness, and off-record strategies, see Brown and Levinson, *Politeness*, 225, 211, and 229–33.

[95] Positive Politeness 10: "Offer, promise." See also Brown and Levinson, *Politeness*, 233.

than the speaker and relinquishes agency to the lady, acknowledging her freedom to accept or reject him as an "ami." Thus, like Lanval's lady, this extraordinary knight offers more than he asks. Placing himself and his affection, loyalty, and trustworthiness at her disposal, he affirms that the locus of control remains with her. He then goes on to explain,

> Jeo vus ai lungement amé
> E en mun quor mut desiré;
> Unques femme fors vus n'amai
> Ne jamés autre ne amerai.
> Mes ne poeie a vus venir
> Ne fors de mun païs eissir,
> Si vus ne me eüssez requis.
> Or puis bien estre vostre amis. (vv. 127–34)

[This is the reason I came here. I have loved you for a long time and desired you greatly in my heart. I have never loved any woman but you, nor shall I ever love another. Yet I could not come to you nor leave my country, unless you had wished for me; but now I can be your beloved.]

In speaking to the lady, the knight is most respectful of face. By providing a reason for his actions, he employs positive politeness,[96] which precedes his explanation of his longstanding love for her, thus attending to her needs and giving a gift of affection.[97] In addition, he also communicates cooperation and reciprocity, indicating that he has "knowledge of and sensitivity to" the lady's wishes, which he wants to see fulfilled.[98] In this way he suggests that they are "cooperatively involved in the relevant activity" and that they "share goals in some domain."[99] It is at this point that he promises his loyalty, and then offers himself and his love. Here the polyptoton — "amé," "aimai," "amaerai," and even "amis" — underscores the strength of the hawk-knight's devotion. Indicating that he has noticed and is

---

[96] Positive Politeness 13: "Give (or ask for) reasons."

[97] Positive Politeness 9: "Assert or presuppose speaker's knowledge of and concern for addressee's wants" combined with Positive Politeness 15: "Give gifts."

[98] Brown and Levinson, *Politeness*, 125. Positive Politeness 7: "Presuppose / raise / assert common ground," in combination with Positive Politeness 9: "Assert or presuppose speaker's knowledge of and concern for addressee's wants" in combination with Positive Politeness 13: "Give (or ask for) reasons" and Positive Politeness 15: "Give gifts" (e.g., acts that address the addressee's "wants to be liked, admired, cared about, understood, listened to, and so on." On combined strategies, see, for example, Brown and Levinson, *Politeness*, 17.

[99] Positive Politeness 14: "Assume or assert reciprocity." This indicates the speaker's "willingness to fit one's own wants in with the wants" of the other; the speaker thus states or implies that "he believes reciprocity to be prevailing between "them," and that they are "somehow locked into a state of mutual helping" (Brown and Levinson, *Politeness*, 125). This approach can also soften a threat to negative face by eliminating "the debt" (Brown and Levinson, *Politeness*, 129).

responding to her desires and needs, he offers her friendship and affection like that she has heard of in stories and that she has fervently desired.[100] Thus, like the narrow window through which the hawk has entered the lady's chamber, her longing has provided a point of entry and a passageway to mutual desire.

Muldumarec's words have the appropriate perlocutionary effect of reassuring the lady. Now reassured ("raseüra"—here the narrator echoes the knight's first words to her, "seizez a seür"—the lady responds first with gestural, then spoken, affirmation. Her response is recorded in *style indirect libre*, a feature of Marie's narrative in which indirect discourse "blend[s] narrator's and character's voices in a way that retains the character's 'paroles d'origine'":[101] "E dit qu'ele *en ferat* sun dru," (v. 138; and she said she would make him her lover). These words repeat Muldumarec's formulation (" Si *fetes de mei* vostre ami!" [v. 125] — emphasis mine), thereby reinforcing the reciprocity, mutuality, and accord.[102] Additionally, by substituting "dru" for "ami" she disambiguates the nature of the love and underscores reciprocity.[103] She also adds that their mutual love is dependent upon his belief in God ("S'en Deu creïst" [v. 139]), who makes such love possible"; this qualification ensures both a Christianizing component and a spiritual dimension to the love.

So great is the harmony between the two that Muldumarec readily agrees: "'Lady,' he said, 'you are right.'" Reiterating the verb she used earlier (*croire*), he indicates his deep and shared belief in the Christian deity, whom he associates with freedom from sin.[104] He also explicitly confirms what was implicit in her statement,

---

[100] Positive Politeness 1: "Notice or attend to hearer (his interests, wants, goods, needs)." Positive Politeness 10: "Offer, promise." Positive Politeness 15: "Give gifts," that is, those that address the "wants to be liked, admired, cared about, understood, listened to, and so on." On the motif of the dream fulfilled, see Michelle A. Freeman, "The Changing Figure of the Male: The Revenge of the Female Storyteller," In Quest of Marie de France, ed. Chantal A. Maréchal (Lewiston, Queenston, and Lampeter: Edwin Mellen, 1992), 59–106, 243–61.

[101] On this stylistic feature, see, for example, Matilda Tomaryn Bruckner, *Shaping Romance: Interpretation, Truth, and Closure in Twelfth-Century French Fictions*. Middle Ages Series (Philadelphia: University of Pennsylvania Press, 1993), esp. 188–91; Jean Rychner, "La présence et le point de vue du narrateur dans deux récits courts: Le *Lai de Lanval* et *la Châtelaine de Vergi*," *Vox Romanica* 39 (1980): 86–103; Manuel Bruña Cuevas, "Le style indirect libre chez Marie de France," *Revue de linguistique romane* 52 (1988): 421–46; and Jean Rychner, "Le discours subjectif dans les *Lais* de Marie de France: A propos d'une étude récente," *Revue de linguistique romane* 53 (1989): 57–83. McCash describes this stylistic feature as "one of Marie's most distinctive characteristics ("*La vie seinte Audree*," 744–77; here 764).

[102] Positive Politeness 5: "Seek agreement."

[103] Repetition indicates solidarity and reciprocity (Brown and Levinson, *Politeness*, 112–13). On this sense of *dru*, see Dubuis, "Dru et Drüerie," 349–54. Like the lady in *Lanval*, the knight's physical appearance accords with his virtuous nature: "Kar mut esteit de grant beauté: / Unkes nul jur de sun eé / Si beals chevalier ne esgarda / Ne jamés si bel ne verra"(vv. 141–44; He was very handsome and never in her life had she seen such a handsome knight, nor would she ever again).

[104] "Jeo crei mut bien al Creatur, / Que nus geta de la tristur, / U Adam nus mist, nostre pere, / Par le mors de la pumme amere" (vv. 149–52 ; I do believe in the Creator who set us free from the sorrow in which our ancestor Adam put us by biting the bitter apple).

that is, the fundamental importance of complete, absolute trust between them: "Ne vodreie pur nule rien / Que de mei i ait acheisun, / Mescreauncë u suspesçun" (vv. 146–48; I would not on any account want guilt, distrust, or suspicion to attach to me). Thus he successfully indicates that he shares her desires and her values. Then assuming her "semblant," an event that often puzzles readers, Muldumarec demonstrates his complete agreement in an ultimate "point of view operation," which constitutes "a personal centre shift,"[105] in which he speaks as if he were the lady. In doing so, he symbolically enacts his complete accord: he is at one with her.[106] The narrator describes the couple with unmistakable approval: "unke si bel cuple ne vi" (v. 192; I never saw so fair a couple). This mutuality is ever present in the couple's relationship, up to the time that the knight is mortally wounded as a result of the trap contrived by the lord of Caerwent. Just as Muldumarec reassures her when he first appears, so too he comforts ("ducement cunfortee") her as he is dying, giving her gifts that will protect her and foretelling that she will bear his son, who will be wise and worthy, and who in time will learn the story of his father's unjust death and will ultimately restore order.[107]

EQUITAN

Hovering somewhere between love story and *fabliau*,[108] *Equitan* is perhaps the most discomfiting of Marie's *lais*. It begins with the narrator's depiction of Equitan, a justiciar, king, and lord of "Nauns":

> Equitan fu mut de grant pris
> E mut amez en sun païs;
> Deduit amout e druerie:

---

[105] On assuming the other's perspective, see Brown and Levinson, *Politeness*, 118–19.

[106] The speaker and the addressee "belong to some set of persons who share specific wants, including goals and values." The speaker "can claim common perspective" (Brown and Levinson, *Politeness*, 103).

[107] In this connection, see also Sharon Kinoshita's analysis of *Yonec* from a post-colonial perspective: "Colonial Possessions: Wales and the Anglo-Norman Imaginary in the *Lais* of Marie de France," *Discourses on Love, Marriage, and Transgression*, ed. Albrecht Classen, 147–62.

[108] See, for example, Joachim Schulze, "*Equitan*: höfische Existenz zwischen hoher Forderung und menschlicher Gewöhnlichkeit." *Romanische Forschungen* 94 (1982): 60–66; Judith R. Rothschild, "Marie de France's *Equitan* and *Chaitivel*: *fin'amors* or *fabliau*?" *The Words of Medieval Women: Creativity, Influence, Imagination*, ed. Constance H. Berman, Charles W. Cornell, and eadem (Morgantown: West Virginia University Press, 1985), 113–21; and Glyn S. Burgess, "Two Cases of *mesure* in the *Lais* of Marie de France," *Zeitschrift für romanische Philologie*. Special Vol.: *Sprach- und literaturwissenschaftliche Beiträge vom frühen bis zum ausgehenden Mittelalter*, ed. Kurt Baldinger (Tübingen: Niemeyer, 1977): 198–208.

De Parlor Bon' Eloquence

> Pur ceo maintint chevalerie.
> Cil met[ent] lur vie en nu[n]cure
> Que d'amur n'unt sen e mesure;
> Tels est la mesure de amer
> Que nul n'i deit reisun garder. (vv. 13–20)

[The king was a man of great renown and was well loved in his country; he loved pleasure and amorous encounters and for this reason he practiced chivalry. Those who do not know love's meaning and degree are neglectful of their lives; such is the quality of love that no one is obliged to be reasonable in regard to it.] (translation mine)

This passage, in which information about Equitan is combined with a generalized observation on the nature of *amur*, a polyptoton based on *amer* (vv. 13–20), and a concurrent exploitation of the broad semantic field of *aimer*, foreshadows the polyvalence and multidimensionality of love in this *lai*. Immediately following this information are two additional facts: First, Equitan's "brave and loyal" seneschal was the one who governed the king's land and "administer[ed] its justice." Second, except for fulfilling his duty in time of war, the king would never "forsake his hunting, his pleasure, or his river sport, whatever the need might have been" (vv. 1–28).

In establishing the specific context for the subsequent exchange, the narrator points out that the king has become infatuated with the incomparably beautiful wife of his faithful seneschal. In fact, even before Equitan sees the seneschal's wife, we are told, "he conceived a desire for her." He contrives to meet her, and love for her "catches him unawares." He spends a sleepless night weighing his love for the lady — and his uncertainty regarding whether or not she would take him as her lover — against his love for his vassal, the seneschal. To love her would be to act "wrongly," he knows, for he understands his true obligation in regard to the steward: "Garder li dei amur e fei, / Si cume jeo voil k'il face a mei" (vv. 73–74; I ought to keep faith with him and love him, just as I want him to do with me). Here he alludes to the ethical standard of mutual loyalty between lord and vassal, which is explicitly described in Marie's fable of the body politic:

> — e chescun franc humme le deit saveir —
> nul [hum] ne peot aver honur
> ki hunte fet a sun seigneur,
> ne li sire tut ensement,
> pur qu'il voille hunir sa gent;

si l'un a l'autrë est failliz,
ambdur en erent maubailliz. (Fable 27, vv. 20–26)[109]

[Every honest man must know this: no man can have honor if he dishonors his lord; so, too, for the lord who would wish to shame his vassals. If one or the other is disloyal, both are harmed.] (translation mine)

However, the king is torn between ethical considerations and his attraction to the steward's wife. The actual encounter, moreover, is preceded not only by ethical dilemma and self-justifying rationalization, but also by contrivance and duplicity. Claiming illness, Equitan absents himself from a hunt with the seneschal, whereupon the seneschal's wife is summoned on the pretext of tending to the ailing king.

The extended exchange begins with the first expression of the king's desire reported in *style indirect libre*, which, as noted earlier, can be seen as a reliable account of his thoughts and words. Without preparation, Equitan lays bares his innermost feelings, revealing the true nature of his malady:

Saver li fet qu'il meort pur li;
Del tut li peot faire confort
E bien li peot doner [l]a mort. (vv. 114–16)

[He lets her know he is dying because of her; she can give him comfort or, truly, she can bring him death.] (Translation mine)

This bald on-record face-threatening act is exacerbated by coercion:[110] She is the cause of his suffering, and she will be the agent of his solace or his death. The clausal isocolon combined with antithetical rhyme words—"li peot faire confort" / " li peot doner la mort"—highlights both the starkly manipulative tactic and the intense emotion, which serves to escalate the threat to face.[111] Like Lanval, who is accosted by the queen, the seneschal's wife must respond. However, in spite of this threat to negative face, and despite the lack of indirection or redressive measures on the king's part, she is quick-witted enough to reply in terms designed to satisfy the king's negative and positive face. Beginning with the

---

[109] Marie de France, *Les Fables, edition critique*, ed. Charles Brucker (Louvain: Peeters, 1991), 142. On the body politic and the principles of lordship in Marie's *Fables*, see Karen K. Jambeck, "The *Fables* of Marie de France: A Mirror of Princes," *In Quest of Marie de France*, ed. Chantal A. Maréchal, 59–106.

[110] Avoiding coercion is a principle of negative politeness (Brown and Levinson, *Politeness*, 172–73).

[111] Strong emotions can threaten negative face (Brown and Levinson, *Politeness*, 66–67).

De Parlor Bon' Eloquence

honorific "sire," she explains that she must have time to think ("respit") because at this time she does not know what to do (vv. 119–21).[112]

Significantly, she does not terminate the conversation. Moreover, she continues with what appears to be a neutral observation by way of explanation, a politeness strategy designed to mitigate a threat to the king's positive face:[113]

> Vus estes rei de grant noblesce,
> Ne sui mie de teu richesce
> Que [a] mei [vus] deiez arester
> De drüerie ne vus de amer. (vv. 121–24)

> [You are a king of great nobility, I am not wealthy enough to be the object of your love or passion.]

The lady's deferential acknowledgment of his superior position and her inferior financial, and implicitly social, status introduces a new element. And at this point, the nature of the exchange diverges markedly from the exchanges discussed above. The lady's first response is evasive, yet does not foreclose continuing the conversation. Indeed, the exchange takes on the characteristics of bargaining, a fact to which the King later calls attention: "Ainz est bargaine de burgeis" (vv. 152; This is the sort of deal struck between merchants).

Given this cue, it is not surprising that within the framework of negotiation patterns exhibited in bargaining, this exchange between Equitan and the seneschal's wife has its own coherence and logic, and concerns regarding face take on a new dimension. In a pragmatic analysis of the dynamics of bargaining in early texts, Monika Becker has identified the following stages:[114] After the goods are offered or the availability is questioned, the actual bargaining process has recognizable phases: 1) "demand for price," 2) "pre-bargain warm-up," which "deal[s] with prices that are not meant to be serious or by discussing the quality of goods and therefore weakening or strengthening the participants' position"; 3) the "central unit of sales talk — " that is, 'buying and selling'" — consists of "serious bargaining," "agreement upon price and amount," and "negotiating the terms of payments." The "final step is handing over the goods."[115]

Viewing the exchange between the seneschal's wife and Equitan in the context of negotiation and the pragmatics of bargaining provides important insights not only into their exchange, but also into their relationship. Thus, seen in this light, the king's initial comments take on a new character; he can be perceived

---

[112] Negative Politeness 5: "Give deference."
[113] Positive Politeness 13: "Give (or ask for) reasons."
[114] Monika Becker, "'If ye wyll bergayne wullen cloth or othir marchandaise...': Bargaining in Early Modern Language Textbooks," *Journal of Historical Pragmatics* 3, 2 (2002): 273–97.
[115] Becker, "'If ye wyll bergayne wullen'," 282–83.

as trying to determine the "availability" of the lady and her favors. So, too, when she replies that she does not know what to do and needs time to think, she not only signals an interest in what the king is proposing, but she also begins a "pre-bargaining warm-up," exploring what he might be willing to concede and making sure to avoid "stating a firm price."[116]

In a series of hypothetical *if* clauses accompanied with subjunctive and conditional verbs — off-record strategies to avoid face threats — she explores the price indirectly:

> S'avïez fait vostre talent,
> Jeo sai de veir, ne dut nïent,
> Tost me avrïez entrelaissie[e],
> Jeo sereie mut empeiree.
> Së [is]si fust que vus amasse
> E vostre requeste otreiasse,
> Ne sereit pas üel partie
> Entre nus deus la drüerie.
> Pur ceo quë estes rei puissaunz
> Et mi sire est de vus tenaunz,
> Quidereiez, a mun espeir,
> Le danger de l'amur aveir.   (vv. 125–36)

[If you had your way with me, I know well and I am in no doubt that you would soon abandon me and I should be very much worse off. If it should come about that I loved you and granted your request, your love would not be shared equally. Because you are a powerful king and my husband is your vassal, you would expect, as I see it, to be the lord and master in love as well.]

With an impersonalized generalization,[117] a strategy that serves to mitigate threats to positive face, she tests possible terms, suggesting the need for fairness: "Amur n'est pruz se n'est egals" (v. 137; love is not worthy [or worthwhile] if it is not equal [translation mine]). Notably, *egal* also includes the sense of measurability.[118] Thus she works toward cooperation by intimating that she is seeking

---

[116] On hesitations and delays as a means of evasion and a strategy for allowing the speaker to make the request or offer more acceptable, see Brown and Levinson, *Politeness*, 39. In the bargain, Becker observes, a word or two "can indicate the participant's willingness to enter into this game," although both parties refrain from stating specific terms as long as possible ("'If ye wyll bergayne'," 282).

[117] Negative Politeness 8: "State the face-threatening act as a general rule."

[118] According to McClelland, *Le Vocabulair*, 191 and 49, the term is used only once in the *Lais*. For definitions of *igal / egal* as "gleich," "eben," "glatt," see Adolf Tobler, and Erhard Lommatzsch, *Altfranzösisches Wörterbuch* (Berlin: Weidmannsche Buchhandlung; Wiesbaden: Franz Steiner, 1925–).

De Parlor Bon' Eloquence 245

equitable terms, while nonetheless being vigilant so that they will also be to her advantage.

Continuing with indirection, she offers another generalization, thereby avoiding an *I–versus–you* conflict,[119] and she proceeds to press the idea of worth and value:

> Meuz vaut un povre[s] hum lëals,
> Si en sei ad sen e valur.
> [E] greinur joie est de s'amur
> Quë il n'est de prince u de rei,
> Quant il n'ad lëauté en sei. (vv. 138–42)

> [A poor man, if he is loyal, and possesses wisdom and merit, is of greater worth and his love more joyful than that of a prince or king who lacks loyalty.]

In this thinly-veiled reference to her husband and her current status, she implies that if certain terms are not met she may well be better off with what she now has. In this inadvertent or unconscious allusion she also places her potential faithlessness, and his as well, in the foreground participating in this transaction. It is worth recalling here that in the introduction to the *lai*, Equitan's loyalty is notably absent from the list of qualities attributed to this pleasure-seeking king.

Again, indirectly by means of impersonalizing with "aukuns" and "li riches hum" instead of *je* and *vus*,[120] she points out the disadvantages of loving a wealthy man who need not fear losing his lady to another:

> Si aukuns aime plus ha[u]tement
> Que [a] sa richesce nen apent,
> Cil se dut[e] de tute rien.
> Li riches hum requid[e] bien
> Que nuls ne li toille s'amie
> Qu'il volt amer par seignurie.' (vv. 143–48)

> [If anyone places his love higher than is appropriate for his own station in life, he must fear all manner of things.[121] The powerful man is convinced that no one can steal away his beloved over whom he intends to exercise his seigneurial right.]

---

[119] Avoiding *I* and *you* is a negative politeness strategy (Brown and Levinson, *Politeness*, 190).
[120] Negative Politeness 7: "Impersonalize" speaker and addressee.
[121] Negative Politeness 8: "State the face threatening act as a general rule" combined with the *if* clause as a hedge (Brown and Levinson, *Politeness*, 206). See also Brown and Levinson, *Politeness*, 153, 173, and 272.

This generalization, of course, is an exact description of Equitan's goal. The lady cannot but notice that she is in a strong negotiating position, and she takes advantage of it. Pressing for loyalty and control,[122] she establishes her terms with off-record strategies combined with negative politeness to offset the face threat of possible rejection.

The king enters into the off-record negotiations aggressively. Despite the lady's indirectness, she has threatened his face; however, he recovers saying, "Cil ne sunt mie fin curteis" (v. 151; Such men are not truly courtly). He then questions her tactics, drawing an analogy between her approach and the "bargaine de burgeis."[123] By generalizing and by utilizing a hypothetical *if* clause (i.e., if a lady is wise, courtly, of noble disposition and heart), he proceeds to call into question, albeit with discreet indirection, the lady's worthiness and her worth (in Becker's terms, "the quality of the goods"). And despite his apparent emphasis on virtues, material possessions ("cloak" and "castle") and the dual meanings of *chiere* ("precious" and "of high price or cost") are notably present:

> Suz ciel n'ad dame, s'ele est sage,
> Curteise e franche de curage,
> Pur quei d'amer se tienge chiere,
> Que ele ne seit mie novelere,
> Si ele n'eüst fors sul sun mantel,
> Que uns riches princes de chastel
> Ne se deüst pur li pener
> E lëalment e bien amer. (vv. 155–62)

> [Any wise and courtly lady of noble disposition, who sets a high price on her love and is not fickle, deserves to be sought after by a rich prince in his castle, and loved well and loyally, even if her only possession is her mantle.]

Through generalization, he emphasizes indirectly and off-record the qualities that he would insist upon (e.g., *sagesse*, *curteisie*, and *franchise*). Then, continuing with an aphoristic generalization (one that ironically foreshadows the conclusion of this *lai* in which the lady's deceit turns back upon her), he also specifies attributes that are unacceptable: "Those who are fickle [*novelier*] in love and resort to trickery [*trichier*] end up becoming a laughing-stock and are deceived [*sunt gabé e deceü*] in their turn" (vv. 163–65). Having attended to negative face by means of indirection, he concludes, "De plusurs l'avum nus veü" (v.166; We have seen many

---

[122] In tension with "self-interest and control" is another principle: "In spite of conflictive potential underlying sales talk, both parties have to cooperate to come to an agreement, otherwise the negotiation fails" (Becker, "'If ye wyll bergayne'," 286).

[123] Negative Politeness 8: "State the face-threatening act as a general rule."

De Parlor Bon' Eloquence 247

cases of this). The inclusive pronoun "nus" highlights solidarity, implies common ground and cooperation, and addresses positive face.[124]

Then, addressing her with an honorific that also expresses affection and solidarity, he indicates that he is ready to agree: "Ma chiere dame, a vus m'otrei!" (v. 169; My dearest lady, I surrender myself to you!).[125] In terms of Becker's phases of negotiation, it is at this point that the interlocutors can be seen to enter into "the central sales unit" — the "serious bargaining," the "agreement upon price and amount," and the "negotiat[ion] of terms of payment."[126] He concedes: she need not consider him as king; "I will be," he says "vostre hum e vostre ami!" He then reiterates the specifics:

> Seürement vus jur et di
> Que jeo ferai vostre pleisir.
> Ne me laissez pur vus murir!
> Vus seiez dame e jeo servant,
> Vus orguilluse e jeo preiant. (vv. 172–76)
>
> [I swear to you in all honesty that I shall do your bidding (Do not let me die because of you!): you can be the mistress and I the servant; you the haughty one and I the suppliant.][127]

In agreeing to the lady's terms, Equitan presents special privileges; in Becker's formulation, he can be seen to "foreground the mutual advantage of a having a successful bargain." In addition, the king's entreaty, formulated as an imperative, stresses the high value of the addressee's participation or friendship.[128] Significantly, in conceding, he does not forget about his own interests (i.e., "Do not let me die because of you!"). Here Becker's principle concerning the paradoxical nature of bargaining is clearly illustrated: "In spite of conflictive potential underlying sales talk [i.e., each negotiator seeks the advantage], both parties have to cooperate to come to an agreement, otherwise the negotiation fails."[129]

When the king persists, she finally agrees to his offer: "Que de s'amur l'aseüra, / E el sun cors li otria" (vv. 179–80; and with an exchange of rings and pledges "they take possession of each other").[130] On the analogy of the commercial

---

[124] Positive Politeness 12: "Include both speaker and addressee," by using the inclusive *we* (Brown and Levinson, *Politeness*, 127). On emphasizing cooperation in bargaining, see also Becker, "'If ye wyll bergayne'," 286.
[125] Brown and Levinson, *Politeness*, 178.
[126] See Becker, "'If ye wyll bergayne wullen'," 282–83.
[127] Translation from Burgess and Busby with my punctuation.
[128] See, for example, Becker, "'If ye wyll bergayne wullen'," 287; and Brown and Levinson, *Politeness*, 97.
[129] Becker, "'If ye wyll bergayne wullen'," 286.
[130] "Par lur anels s'entresaisirent, / Lur fiaunce s'entreplevirent" (vv. 181–82).

negotiation, "the bargaining ends with payment" and "the goods are handed over."[131] At the end of this exchange the narrator interjects, "Bien les tiendrent, mut s'entramerent," (v. 183; They kept their promises well; they loved each other very much).[132] Thus they adhere to their agreement, each seemingly satisfied with the negotiated terms. To this, however, the narrator adds, "Puis mururent e finerent" (v. 184; Then they died). Here, it is worth noting that the verb *finer* has among its range of meanings "to die," to pass away," "to yield to death," and of relevance in this context, "to pay a fine," and "to pay the penalty."[133] This initial exchange between Equitan and the seneschal's wife not only adheres to the generic structure of negotiation and bargain, a form that appears again in Marie's fables,[134] it also incorporates politeness in a fitting manner. Moreover, their conversation exploits a mercantile register: these negotiations for personal gratification and personal gain are thematized through terms of commercial transaction.[135] Most importantly, juxtaposing the love affair with business affairs highlights the self-interest of Equitan and the seneschal's wife.

In this *lai*, love is commodified; *amur* and *druerie* are subject to barter, and virtue is in short supply. And, as might be expected, the negotiated match does not last. The lady's doubts, so evident in her initial comments, persist. She lacks faith in the mutuality of their love. And although Equitan resists his councilors' urgings to take a wife (implicitly to provide an heir), she fears that he might desert her and marry the daughter of a king (vv. 215–16). In a highly emotional state the seneschal's wife echoes Equitan's earlier plea, which turns out to be prophetic: "E jeo, lasse! que devendrai? / Pur vus m'estuet aveir la mort, / Car jeo ne sai autre cunfort" (vv. 218–20; What would become of me, unhappy wretch? Through you my death is inevitable. For I know of no other consolation). When the king assures her that were she not already married, he would wed her, she quickly devises a plan to murder her husband and engages the king as an accomplice. The murder scheme, which involves two tubs of boiling water, recoils back upon them, and the king and the seneschal's wife suffer the doom intended for her husband.

As indicated in the early lines of *Equitan*, love is powerful and multivariate. Because of the desires of Equitan and the seneschal's wife, the personal love and

---

[131] Becker, "'If ye wyll bergayne wullen'," 282–83.

[132] Translation mine. Judith Rothschild has noted the selfishness and cupidity of the lovers ("Marie de France's *Equitan* and *Chaitivel*," 113–21).

[133] Alan Hindley, Frederick W. Langley, and Brian J. Levy, *Old French-English Dictionary* (Cambridge and New York: Cambridge University Press, 2000), 319. See also A. J. Greimas, *Dictionnaire de l'ancien francais* (Paris: Larousse, 1979), 267: "finir, se terminer," "mourir," "terminer une affaire en payant, payer."

[134] See for example Marie de France, *Les Fables*: "Le Paysan et son cheval" (Fable 47) and "L'Homme, le cheval et le bouc" (Fable 64).

[135] Among these are *bargaine de burgeis*, *bergeyner*, *richesce*, *riche homme* ("an aristocrat" and "a man of means"), *grant fieu*, *valeur*, *chier* ("dear to one's heart" and "expensive," "costly," "expensive," "of high price," *purchacier* ("to seek, search for" and "to procure, purchase"), *finer*, *entresaisir*.

De Parlor Bon' Eloquence

loyalty between lord and vassal, and between husband and wife, are violated. So too because of their *druerie*, the bond between king and subjects — those by whom he was "well loved" — has been severed, not only as a result of his death, but also as a consequence of his failure to marry and provide an heir.

That Equitan and the seneschal's wife would not escape unscathed is also intimated through Marie's careful management of *sententiae* that thematize ethical conduct: danger for both lord and vassal inheres in breaching the feudal bond; one who deceives is in turn deceived; and misfortune rebounds upon the perpetrator of evil. Such varied reiteration, expressed in both dialogue and narrative in what can be seen as a kind of intermittent *commoratio*, coincides with the moral perspective established in the introduction: this was a tale composed for posterity by the ancient Bretons, who through "prüesce," "curteisie," and "noblesce," composed *lais* so the "aventures" would not be forgotten (vv. 1–8). Eloquently attentive to face, Marie skillfully expresses a moral perspective through indirection rather than direct instruction, which is potentially face-threatening.[136]

THE POWER OF ELOQUENCE

Marie's aristocratic audience — not only the king, whom she describes as "nobles," "pruz," and "curteis,"[137] but also "cunte, barun e chivaler," and the ladies[138] — would have recognized, if not analyzed, the effects of such linguistic operations. They would undoubtedly have appreciated the harmonious accords, the affronts, and the negotiations encoded in these exchanges. As noted earlier, the semantic range of the term *courtois* includes a language component: *courtoisie* is the ability to "show sensitivity and understanding where the circumstances are of a delicate or exacting nature"; it is "a capacity to handle other people and to say the right thing at the right time."[139] In broad strokes, these are some of the main principles underlying pragmatic politeness, and, whether her characters abide by or transgress them, they are hallmarks of Marie's eloquence.

In his introduction to this book, Albrecht Classen points out Walther von der Vogelweide's insights into the nature of love: "love is the joy of two hearts"; when it is shared by both, "love is present."[140] The joy, central to the meaning of love for Walther, is created and maintained through shared experience. So, too, as lovers

---

[136] See, for example, Brown and Levinson, *Politeness*, 65–67.

[137] "En l'honur de vus, nobles reis, / Ki tant estes pruz e curteis" (Prologue vv. 43–44; In your honour, noble king, you who are so worthy and courtly).

[138] Denis Piramus, *La Vie Seint Edmund le rei. Poème anglo-normand du XIIe siècle*, ed. Hilding Kjellman (Göteborg: Wettergren & Kerber, 1935; repr. Geneva: Slatkine, 1974), vv. 42–50.

[139] Burgess, "The Term 'courtois' in Twelfth-Century French," 118–19.

[140] Quoted in Classen, "Introduction," 22.

exchange words, their assumptions, inferences, and contexts inform the collaborative process of constructing meaning, one that surpasses any lexical meaning the words might have out of context. Here the parallels with Robert Sternberg's research on love relationships are striking: "Relationships are constructions, and they decay over time if they are not maintained and improved;" thus, loving relationships must constantly be built and rebuilt. Significant to this process is expression, without which "the greatest of loves can die."[141] Constructing a love relationship, like constructing shared meaning, must be recapitulated in a recursive process that, Sternberg argues, must go on for the lifetime of the love itself.

Certainly, one of the truths of the *lais*, one upon which Marie firmly insists, is the truth that they express about love:[142] "Les contes ke jo sai verrais, / Dunt li Bretun unt fait les lais, / Vos conterai assez briefment" (*Guigemar*, vv. 19–21; I shall relate briefly stories that I know to be true and from which the Bretons made their *lais*). Ménard describes the highest love in Marie's work as "absolute," "total," and "reciprocal."[143] In the *Lais*, the most admirable love partakes of the following qualities: strengthened by an uncompromising integrity, it is founded upon loyalty that is maintained and believed in by both partners. It is cooperative and collaborative. This love is also freely given, and it focuses clearly on the other. Finally, the superiority of such love is immediately apparent to one who, guided by *prudentia*, the cornerstone of all virtues, is capable of sharing it.[144]

These words of love are expertly deployed by an author who understood that she possessed the gift of eloquence. Pragmatic analysis, which illustrates the ways in which linguistic realizations of politeness function in regard to face, one's own face and that of the other, also reveals the ways in which Marie deftly exploits language. By correlating words to thoughts, feelings, and assumptions; by expressing the couple's exchanges with subtle variation and finely-pointed linguistic and pragmatic cues; and by offering a glimpse into intimate moments and strong emotions, Marie depicts two participants in the process of constructing pragmatic meaning that defines to some extent the nature of their relationship. Through the interplay of words, couples collaborate harmoniously or fall hopelessly into discord. Thus the queen's first words to Lanval focus on her face at his expense.

---

[141] Robert J. Sternberg, "Triangulating Love," *The Psychology of Love*, ed. idem and Michael L. Barnes (New Haven and London: Yale University Press, 1988), 119–38; here 136 and 138.

[142] The critical commentary on the varieties of love depicted in Marie's *Lais* is extensive. For an excellent analysis of love in Marie's *lais*, see Glyn S. Burgess, *Les* Lais *de Marie de France: Text and Context* (Athens, GA: University of Georgia Press, 1987), 134–78.

[143] Ménard, *Les Lais*, 123.

[144] On *prudentia* and its importance in Marie's *Fables*, see Karen K. Jambeck, "Truth and Deception in the *Fables* of Marie de France," *Literary Aspects of Courtly Literature: Selected Papers from the Seventh Triennial Congress of the International Courtly Literature Society, University of Massachusetts, Amherst, USA, 27 July–1 August 1992*, ed. Donald Maddox and Sara Sturm-Maddox (Cambridge: D. S. Brewer, 1994), 221–30.

So too Equitan is so preoccupied with his positive face that he neglects to concern himself with the face needs of the seneschal's wife; she must negotiate for herself. On the other hand, Lanval and his lady, and Muldamarec and the lady of Caerwent exemplify cooperative attention to face that bespeaks mutual respect. Appropriately, Marie's otherworldly characters model particularly graceful language, providing the best examples of generosity in love and ideal eloquence. Whether or not her characters are adept at politeness, in giving them words and voice, Marie expertly represents nuances of speech to indicate the dynamic evolution of a relationship, capturing some of the reasons for successes and failures. A person skilled in politeness, as Brown and Levinson conclude, one who is proficient at assessing "the varying scales for ranking power, distance," and relative weights of face threats and "the circumstances in which they vary," and who then employs congruous language, is "considered to be graced with 'tact', 'charm', 'poise'."[145] To this list we might add eloquence, which allows one to express thoughts, feelings, and wisdom "fittingly and efficaciously."[146]

In the *Lais* private exchanges lead to actions that have wide implications for the couple and for others as well.[147] Failure to attend to face on the part of Arthur's queen leads not only to a legal accusation against Lanval, but also a rupture in the orderly functioning of the kingdom. So great is the disturbance that balance can be restored only by the generous intervention by Lanval's lady. The joyful love of the hawk-knight and the lady in the tower cannot long exist in a society where marriages arranged by families for dynastic purposes deprive individuals of love and companionship. Similarly, the passion shared by Equitan and the seneschal's wife destroys feudal loyalties, potentially endangers the kingdom, and finally leads to the downfall of the lovers.

That Marie's *Lais* run counter to much of the twelfth- and thirteenth-century literary production is no doubt linked to her decision not to translate a Latin "estoire," a task, she says, that had been undertaken by others ("Itant s'en sunt altre entremis" [Prologue v. 32]). By turning away from the materials of antiquity, Marie was liberated not only from the traditional declaration, but also

---

[145] Brown and Levinson, *Politeness*, 78.
[146] John of Salisbury's definition (*The Metalogicon*, trans. McGarry, 26–27). See also the definition of *eloquence* in the *OED*: "The action, practice, or art of expressing thought with fluency, force and appropriateness so as to appeal to reason or more than feelings," and "speech or verbal expression in general, the quality of being eloquent."
[147] For an extensive study of communication in medieval German literature, with relevance for medieval European literature, such as Andreas Capellanus's *De amore*, see Albrecht Classen, *Verzweiflung und Hoffnung: Die Suche nach der kommunikativen Gemeinschaft in der deutschen Literatur des Mittlelalters*. Beihefte zur Mediaevistik, 1 (Frankfurt a. M., Berlin, et al.: Peter Lang, 2002). See also *Speaking in the Middle Ages*, ed. Jean E. Godsall-Myers. Cultures, Beliefs and Traditions, 16 (Leiden and Boston: Brill, 2003).

from other constraints — certain plots, characters, and stylistic features [148] — and from their overt and covert themes of political and military power and lineage. [149] Given the "biopolitics" of twelfth-century England and France, with its emphasis on cognatic bonds, individual desires pose a threat: adulterous desire can "falsify genealogy," by "obscur[ing] true paternity" and "the desire of those who are as yet unmarried opens almost infinite possibilities of the recombination, of (mis) match." [150]

Marie's veering away from Latin texts allowed her, then, the opportunity to explore questions inherent in the "inner workings of the feudal model of marriage," especially in relation to, or in conflict with, desire." [151] The questions raised by Marie's *lais* and the discussions they must have engendered were most probably set in even higher relief by a new direction in ecclesiastical policy. During the second half of the twelfth century, especially with the papacy of Alexander III, the Church emphasized consent in marriage, with an increasing acceptance of an individual's choice; thus a vow (a speech act) along with consummation were seen as constituting a valid marriage. While this Church policy did not lead to a radical transformation of marriage practices among the aristocracy, it allowed for new horizons of thought about love and about language. In fact, as James A. Brundage has argued, it is probable that Pope Alexander's marriage decretals and the love poetry of the time both reflect "a dawning consciousness of the importance of individual choice, coupled with a new awareness of marriage as a personal relationship." [152]

---

[148] See, for example, Michelle Freeman, "Marie de France's Poetics of Silence: The Implications for a Feminine *Translatio*," *Publications of the Modern Language Association* 99, 5 (Oct. 1984): 860–83.

[149] Christopher Baswell argues that "Feminine erotic agency destabilizes," potentially "undermin[ing] the progress of political history and chivalric values in the romances of Antiquity" ("Marvels of Translation and Crises of Transition in the Romances of Antiquity," *The Cambridge Companion to Medieval Romance*, ed. Robert A. Krueger, 29–44; here 40).

[150] Bloch, *Etymologies*, 131.

[151] See, for example, Bloch, *Etymologies*, 131 and 193.

[152] James A. Brundage, *Sex, Law, and Marriage in the Middle Ages* (Aldershot, Hampshire, Great Britain; Brookfield, VT: Variorum, 1993), 333–36. While a public ceremony, parental consent, or priestly blessing were considered desirable, they were not absolutely essential to a valid marriage. On the importance of the consent of the two individuals to be married along with increasing emphasis on free choice, see, for example, Brundage, *Sex, Law, and Marriage*, 325, and 333–36; Michael M. Sheehan, "Choice of Marriage Partners in the Middle Ages: Development and Mode of Application of a Theory of Marriage," *Studies in Medieval and Renaissance History* n.s. 1 (1978): 3–33; here 7–15; J. Gillingham, "Love, Marriage and Politics in the Twelfth Century," *Forum for Modern Language Studies* 25 (1989): 292–303; here 294–95; and D. L. d'Avray, *Medieval Marriage. Symbolism and Social Reality* (Oxford and New York: Oxford University Press, 2005), 96 and 99. For the relevance of these trends in connection with *Lanval*, see Jambeck, "'Femmes et tere'," 132. For a consideration of discourse on marriage in Marie's *Lais*, see Albrecht Classen, *Der Liebes- und Ehediskurs vom hohen Mittelalter bis zum frühen 17. Jahrhundert*. Volksliedstudien, 5 (Münster, New York, Munich, and Berlin: Waxmann, 2005), 32–72.

De Parlor Bon' Eloquence

Well attuned to the power of words and the pragmatic force of verbal interchange, Marie would no doubt have considered not only the range of emotions associated with love, but also the theoretical and practical ramifications of desire. Moreover, these skillfully-wrought exchanges between women and men bear timeless witness to Marie's command of words and the power of her eloquence.

CHAPTER 10

THE RHETORIC OF LOVE IN THE ROMANCES OF GAUTIER D'ARRAS

KAREN PRATT
King's College London

"Caitive, lasse en fin me clain
Quant il ne set comment je l'aim!
Molt par en ai le cuer amer
Qu'il ne set con jel puis amer;
Il nel puet savoir par nul fuer,
Por ce ai molt amer le cuer."
    (Athanaïs, *Eracle*, 3911–16)[1]

[In sum, I call myself a pitiable wretch since he does not know how much I love him. My heart is very bitter indeed, for he does not know how much I am capable of loving him. There is no way of letting him know, this is why my heart is so bitter.]

"Icil qui aime finement
N'en puet partir legierement;
Ne s'en part mie quant il veut
Cil qui de fine amor se deut."
    (Paridés, *Eracle*, 4929–32)

[Whoever loves truly cannot give love up lightly; he cannot give it up whenever he wishes, the man who suffers from true love.]

---

[1] Quotations from the works of Gautier d'Arras are taken from my forthcoming edition and translation of *Eracle*. King's College London Medieval Studies (London: King's College London Centre for Late Antique and Medieval Studies, 2006), and from Penny Eley's edition and translation of *Ille et Galeron*, King's College London Medieval Studies, 13 (London: King's College London Centre for Late Antique and Medieval Studies, 1996).

The male and female lovers in Gautier d'Arras's twelfth-century romance *Eracle* are well versed in the art of rhetoric. True to the theme of this volume, "words of love and love of words," they revel in the pleasures of chiasmus, whilst also delighting in anaphora, parallelism, *correctio*, *exclamatio*, antithesis, metaphor, and personification, to name but a few stylistic ornaments both easy and difficult.[2] However, in neither of the above examples are the lovers addressing each other, for, as we shall see, words of love in romances occur more frequently in lovers' monologues or in narratorial commentary than in amatory dialogue. This phenomenon may result from the influence on romance narratives of lyric poetry. For in lyric, words of love are normally addressed to an absent beloved and the focus is on the emotions of the (usually) *male* speaking subject. Moreover, his desire for his lady is overshadowed by his desire for competitive discourse, keen as he is to outdo both rival lovers and rival wordsmiths. The joys of reciprocated love are rarely expressed by lyric poets; similarly in Gautier's romances consummated love is attended by silence rather than by a profusion of words:

> Cil n'ont de parler nul loisir,
> Et fine amors les fait taisir
> Ce c'orent empensé a dire.   (*Eracle*, 4593–95)

> [They had no time to talk and true love prevented them from saying what they had planned to say.]

The ecstasy of union, whether with a worldly lover or with God, is clearly ineffable, producing only silence (see Albrecht Classen, Introduction, 15–16), yet in contrast lovers' suffering produces a torrent of words in the form of highly appreciated love literature, as Gautier perceptively remarks in *Ille et Galeron*:

> Bien lor ira s'il suit l'ordure;
> Mes s'autrement n'alast l'amors,
> Li lais ne fust pas si en cours
> Nel prisaissent tot li baron.
> Grant cose est d'Ille a Galeron.   (*Ille*, 927–31)

> [Things would go well for them if love followed the proper sequence; but if their love had not taken another direction, this lay would not be so popular or so highly esteemed by all noblemen. The story of Ille and Galeron is no trifling matter.]

---

[2] See Karen Pratt, *Meister Otte's Eraclius as an Adaptation of Eracle by Gautier d'Arras*. Göppinger Arbeiten zur Germanistik, 392 (Göppingen: Kümmerle, 1987), chap. 11 on rhetoric.

This essay will focus on the complex rhetoric and dialectic which Gautier employed in his two extant works, *Eracle* and *Ille et Galeron*, in order to explore a favorite topic of medieval romance — love. Beginning with verbal exchanges between lovers, the brevity of which betrays an awareness of the dangers of deceitful eloquence, I shall then consider his far more frequent love monologues, which frequently take the form of internal dialogue. The dialectical analysis of the protagonists' feelings not only reveals the verbal pleasures characters share with their author, but also gives us insights into medieval notions of subjectivity and the importance of speech in the quest for emotional self knowledge. Gautier's significant contribution to twelfth-century love casuistry and the moral issues it raises will be further appreciated through an analysis of his narrators' observations on the passions. This narratorial commentary on love, although not couched in direct speech, nevertheless represents a form of dialogue — with Gautier's own literary predecessors and competitors. Here the homosocial aspect dentified in the works of troubadour poets[3] is clearly at work as the author from Arras debates with his colleagues the nature of love and attempts to outdo their literary virtuosity.[4]

In order to assess Gautier's role in the development of amatory rhetoric in the twelfth century we must first consider the issue of the relative chronology of key near-contemporary French texts. References in his prologues and epilogues to various patrons indicate that Gautier was clearly a contemporary of Chrétien de Troyes, sharing with him the patronage of Marie de Champagne. Also, an analysis of the two poets' use of banal repeated rhymes shows that Gautier's versification is closer to Chrétien's than to that of any other twelfth-century writer.[5] Furthermore, the coincidence of more striking rhymes and diction suggests direct influence, although not necessarily by Chrétien on Gautier, as earlier critics have assumed.[6] The only direct evidence for the dating of Gautier's two works comes from allusions to potential patrons he wished to flatter. Thibaut of Blois, Marie de Champagne, and Baudouin of Hainault are mentioned in *Eracle*, and Beatrice of

---

[3] See Simon Gaunt, *Gender and Genre in Medieval French Literature* (Cambridge: Cambridge University Press, 1995), 135–47.

[4] This is exactly the same phenomenon as in Dante's considerably later *Vita Nuova*, trans. with intr. Barbara Reynolds (London: Penguin, 1969). Here the poet encourages many male poet friends to reflect upon the nature of love together with him, using verse and prose in this prosimetrum: see, for instance, his comment to the sonnet in the third chapter, 33: "This sonnet drew replies from many, who all had different opinions as to its meaning. Among those who replied was someone whom I call my closest friend; he wrote a sonnet beginning: *In my opinion you beheld all virtue.*"

[5] See Maurice Delbouille, "A propos de rimes familières à Chrétien de Troyes et à Gautier d'Arras," *Etudes de langue et littérature du moyen âge: mélanges offerts à Félix Lecoy* (Paris: Champion, 1973), 55–65.

[6] See Guy Raynaud de Lage, "De quelques images de Chrétien de Troyes chez Gautier d'Arras," *Studi di filologia romanza offerti a Silvio Pellegrini* (Padua: Liviana, 1971), 489–94; Corinne Pierreville, *Gautier d'Arras, l'autre Chrétien* (Paris: Champion, 2001), chap. 1.

Burgundy, the empress of Rome, and Thibaut are named in *Ille et Galeron*. Assuming that Thibaut, son of Thibaut (*Eracle*, 6524), was Thibaut V (1152-1191) and Baudouin was Baudouin V of Hainault (1171-1195) we have a *terminus post quem* of 1159, when Marie became countess of Champagne, and a *terminus ante quem* of 1191 (Thibaut's death). However, whilst it is generally assumed that *Eracle* was composed first in its entirety, Gautier's reference to multiple dedicatees who seem to have intervened at different stages in the composition process[7] may suggest that he began *Eracle* for Thibaut (perhaps as early as 1152), continued it under the encouragement of Marie, broke off to compose *Ille*, and then returned to finish *Eracle* at the instigation of Baudouin V.[8] Penny Eley argues that the two extant manuscripts of *Ille et Galeron* (P and W) represent respectively an early and a revised version of the work.[9] She dates P with its fulsome praise of Beatrice in the prologue to the early 1170s, and W, with its shortened prologue and an epilogue claiming that the author began the work for Beatrice but finished it for Thibaut (V of Blois) (ed. Lefèvre, 6592w-92x), to around 1180.[10] Corinne Pierreville argues that Thibaut V may have commissioned *Eracle* from Gautier ca. 1165 in the aftermath of the Second Crusade. His aim would have been to celebrate his brother's achievements in the Holy Land, implying that Henri le Libéral had followed in the footsteps of Eracle. Moreover, marriage negotiations linking Thibaut, Marie, and Baudouin from 1171 onward and especially in 1179 and 1181 make this the likely period for the completion of *Eracle*.[11] Noting that Gautier was probably active over some twenty years (1165-1184) at courts which Chrétien de Troyes also frequented, Pierreville embarks on a detailed intertextual examination of the two authors' works and arrives at the following relative chronology: *Erec et Enide* — first part of *Eracle* — *Ille et Galeron* — *Cligés* — completion of *Eracle* — *Chevalier de la Charette* — *Chevalier au lion* — *Conte du Graal*.[12] Thus Chrétien both influenced and was influenced by Gautier's writing. Pierreville does not explain exactly how Chrétien might have become acquainted with Gautier's unfinished

---

[7] See the edition of MS W of *Ille et Galeron* by Yves Lefèvre. Les Classiques français du moyen âge, 109 (Paris: Champion, 1988), 6592-92a; 6592w-92x; *Eracle*, 6523-31.

[8] It is not clear, however, how dependent Gautier was on patronage and how literally one should take these references to supposed interventions by famous nobles.

[9] Eley's edition is based on manuscript P, whereas the Lefèvre edition is based on W.

[10] Eley (ed. xxii) further suggests that Gautier moved to a new patron when Beatrice went to Italy in 1174.

[11] See Pierreville, *Gautier d'Arras*, 13-14.

[12] Of course the dating of Chrétien's romances is not established; whilst the *terminus ante quem* for the *Conte du Graal* is 1191, the death of Philip of Flanders, the only solid *terminus post quem* (relevant to the *Charette* and later works) is 1159, when Marie acquired the title of Countess of Champagne. Although some scholars have preferred earlier dating, Hunt and Luttrell have both argued for Chrétien's main literary activity in the 1180s, which would make Gautier almost certainly his predecessor. See Claude Luttrell, *The Creation of the First Arthurian Romance: A Quest* (London: Arnold, 1974); Tony Hunt, "Redating Chrestien de Troyes," *Bibliographical Bulletin of the International Arthurian Society* 30 (1978): 209-37.

Eracle, but whereas some scholars have objected that it would be illogical for Gautier to mention an unfinished work in his epilogue to *Ille*,[13] her hypothesis stands if one accepts that only manuscript W contains the reference to *Eracle* as a prior composition,[14] and it is probable that by the time Gautier revised this romance *Eracle* was complete. However, there is an allusion in the prologues to both P (180–84) and W (120–24) to the plot of *Eracle* (see Eley ed., xix), which would be incomprehensible unless the audience was already familiar with the earlier work about Heraclius.

Whereas Pierreville's demonstration of the influence of Gautier's romances on Chrétien's is convincing, her evidence for the influence of *Cligés* on *Eracle* is open to debate (see below).[15] Indeed, her analysis would have benefited from more detailed examination of the two rivals' possible precursors, especially Wace, the author of the *Eneas*, and Thomas in his *Tristan*.[16] For the purpose of the following discusssion it will be assumed that Gautier, a cleric trained in the trivial arts, knew the *romans antiques* (especially the *Eneas*), *Piramus et Tisbé*, the clerical version of *Floire et Blancheflor*, Thomas's *Tristan*, and the *Lais* of Marie de France (whose *Eliduc* provided a source for *Ille et Galeron*).[17] His relationship with Chrétien de Troyes, however, may well be that of precursor rather than imitator.

It is my aim to show that in this illustrious company the poet of Arras exhibits considerable originality and rhetorical virtuosity in his portrayal of love and its devotees.

In the central episode of the biographical romance *Eracle*, Gautier portrays a young virgin named Athanaïs married to the emperor Laïs, who against the advice of Eracle locks her in a tower when he goes to war. Outraged by this unjust treatment, Athanaïs rebels, falling for young Paridés, who fears that his lower social status will be an impediment to love. After a rendezvous arranged by an old woman, the adultery is revealed, but this time Laïs follows Eracle's advice and divorces Athanaïs, allowing her to marry Paridés. It seems that Gautier, like

---

[13] See William C. Calin, "On the Chronology of Gautier d'Arras," *Modern Language Quarterly* 20 (1959): 181–96.

[14] Lefèvre ed., 6952–52a. There remains the issue of whether "s'entremettre" in line 6952 implies that *Eracle* was merely begun first or completed first.

[15] The brief mention in the epilogue to *Cligés* that Byzantine emperors were forced to lock up their wives is in my view best understood as a sly allusion to the plot of *Eracle*, although Pierreville (*Gautier d'Arras*, 58) thinks that Gautier was given the idea for the central section of his *Eracle* when he heard/read the final lines of Chrétien's romance. Whether the name of Cligés's uncle Alis gave rise to Laïs or vice versa is unprovable. However, the name Laïs probably came first, since it can be more easily justified by context, rhyming as it does with Athanaïs, a name Gautier found in his source.

[16] Although we have no definite dates for Thomas, it is likely that his *Tristan* predates both Chrétien's *Cligés* and Gautier's *Ille et Galeron*. See Gustav Adolf Beckmann, "Der Tristandichter Thomas und Gautier d'Arras," *Romanistisches Jahrbuch* 15 (1963): 87–104.

[17] See Eley ed., xxx–xxiv. This would give a pre-1180s dating for Marie's *Lais*.

Marie de France in many of her *lais*, believes that a *mal mariée* should be allowed some happiness, provided that her new love is true and courtly.

Ille et Galeron, on the other hand, treats the subject of the man loved by two women. The impossible situation in which the man finds himself is solved, as in Marie's *Eliduc*, by Ille's first wife Galeron becoming a nun. Unlike Eliduc, however, Ille is not an adulterer, and is free to love and marry Ganor only once Galeron has withdrawn into a convent. Prior to this though, the bliss of Ille's first marriage is ruined by his loss of an eye in a tournament,[18] leading to his loss of self-esteem, already precarious because of his lower social status. Fortunately, both of Ille's women agree that nobility of heart is more important than class or bodily perfection, a view shared by the countess of Narbonne in Andreas Capellanus's *De amore*.[19] Thus, in contrast to Andreas, but like Chrétien in all his romances except for the *Charette*, Gautier promotes an *amour courtois conjugal*, seeing no incompatibility between true love, "amors fine" (*Ille*, 4817), and marriage.

When analyzing the amorous words spoken by Gautier's lovers we might expect to find some of the arguments contained in Andreas Capellanus's model dialogues (Book 1, chapter 6). However, in twelfth-century romance, unlike the lyric, eloquence is rarely employed to persuade a reluctant lover or to express undying love to him/her.[20] The consummation of Athanaïs's love for Paridés in *Eracle* is in fact described briefly by the narrator (4583–604), and when she speaks it is only to voice concern for their souls and fear of punishment (4605–27). Her desire is expressed solely through the action of kissing. Paridés is equally brief, though his words (4631–39) do affirm his love and gratitude for the gift of the empress's body as he offers to be her vassal in a gesture of homage:

"Mon cors et m'ame vos en doing
Par ces deus mains que je chi joing." (*Eracle*, 4633–34)

[in joining my two hands together I hereby grant you my body and my soul.]

Their conversation ends with Athanaïs warning him not to become ungrateful as other lovers do, a sentiment with which Paridés concurs. In this respect Paridés differs from Chrétien's Yvain (*Yvain*, 1972–74), who offers himself to Laudine as

---

[18] Though in Ms. W Ille loses his eye during warfare.
[19] Book 2, chapter 7, judgment 15. According to Eley (ed., xxxv), the version in manuscript W of *Ille et Galeron* is likely to be Andreas's source, and in this article I shall assume that Andreas humorously adapted literary texts such as Gautier's romances rather than that he influenced them. See Michael D. Cherniss, "The Literary Comedy of Andreas Capellanus," *Modern Philology* 73 (1975): 223–37; for a recent discussion of the intertextual processes in Andreas's treatise, see Don A. Monson, *Andreas Capellanus, Scholasticism, and the Courtly Tradition* (Washington, DC: The Catholic University of America Press, 2005), 86–121. See also the contribution to this volume by Bonnie Wheeler.
[20] For an exception to this rule, see the case of Ganor in *Ille et Galeron* discussed below.

her vassal, but then lets her down.[21] Indeed, his speech to Laudine professing his love (2015–32) is one of the longest and most rhetorically sophisticated in twelfth-century French romance, yet as we soon realize, Yvain's sincerity as a husband does not match his deceptive eloquence.[22] Medieval writers, whose profession involved spinning words to produce cultural/artificial representations of feelings, were acutely aware of the dangers of language. This may be why they usually gave only brief dialogue to *genuine* lovers, with actions speaking louder than words. Moreover, in *Eracle* professions of love seem more sincere for being made to third parties. Both Paridés and Athanaïs disclose their passion first to the *vieille* (old woman) and then, more movingly, to the emperor and Eracle as they fight for their lives. The chiastic lines (4929–32) quoted at the beginning of this article are taken from that heart-rending scene, reminiscent of the lovers' interview with the emir in *Floire et Blancheflor* and provoking a similar degree of pathos in both the intra- and extra-diegetic audiences.[23]

Just as the protagonists of *Eracle* express their love for each other more readily to third persons, needing a go-between to unite them, so Ille and Galeron are brought together by Galeron's brother, the duke, to whom they have individually divulged their love. On their wedding night Gautier employs the usual ineffability topos to justify both the brief depiction of their joy (1526–29) and the total absence of amatory dialogue.

Yet one of Gautier's characters does give voice to her feelings. Ganor, Ille's second beloved, like Fénice in *Cligés*,[24] shows less reticence than her female predecessor. Having noted Ille's pleasing physique despite his ocular disability, Ganor, the emperor's daughter, expresses her desire unambiguously:

---

[21] References to *Yvain* are from the edition by T.B.W. Reid (Manchester: Manchester University Press, 1942; repr. 1967).

[22] See Joan Tasker Grimbert, *Yvain dans le miroir: une poétique de la réflexion dans le Chevalier au lion de Chrétien de Troyes* (Amsterdam: John Benjamins, 1988), who argues that Yvain's deception is not malicious, but of the self—he acquires true understanding of love and *courtoisie* with maturity.

[23] *Le Conte de Floire et Blancheflor*, edited by Jean-Luc Leclanche. Les Classiques français du moyen âge, 105 (Paris: Champion, 1980), 2777ff.; Lynn Shutters, "Christian Love or Pagan Transgression? Marriage and Conversion in *Floire et Blancheflor*," *Discourses on Love, Marriage, and Transgression in Medieval and Early Modern Literature*, ed. Albrecht Classen. Medieval and Renaissance Texts and Studies, 278 (Tempe, AZ: Arizona Center for Medieval and Renaissance Studies, 2004), 85–108; here 99.

[24] In their presentation of the birth of love there are some striking parallels between Gautier's *Ille et Galeron* and Chrétien's *Cligés*. The duke's role is similar to that of Guinevere, who brings together Alexandre and Soredamors; the love affairs between Ille and his two wives bear some resemblance to the courtship first of Cligés's parents, then of Cligés and Fénice. Other common features are the protagonists' elaborate monologues expressing their doubts and suffering, and the fact that Ganor, like Fénice, proves to be more forward in her love-making than the older woman. Many of these similarities may, however, derive from a common source, Thomas's *Tristan*.

> "Amis, li vostre fais me plaist.
> Drois est que vostre bouce baist
> Fille de roi et de roïne
> Et k'ele soit a vous acline." (*Ille*, 3345–48)

[My friend, your actions please me. Rightfully your lips should kiss the daughter of a king and queen and she should be at your command.]

Ille gets the hint, but, being married, cannot reciprocate, and when he takes leave of Ganor he hopes that his inferior lineage will make his departure easier for her to bear. True to form, the emperor's daughter makes it clear in a forthright, almost humorous speech, that she loves Ille for himself, not for his father (i.e., genetic inheritance):

> Mais voel je vostre pere avoir
> Ou vos amer por vostre pere?
> Plus ameroie, biaux dous frere,
> Por vous les vos, faus et estous,
> Que vos tot seul por aus trestos.
> De vostre pere a moi que taint?
> Sont dont por vostre pere ataint
> Li sospir qui de parfont vienent
> Et qui si prés del cuer me tienent?
> Onques de lui ne me sovint
> Quant ceste volentés me vint
> De vos amer, de vos joïr. (*Ille*, 4726–37)

[Do I mean to marry your father or to love you for your father's sake? Fair gentle brother, I would rather love your whole family, traitors and heroes alike, for your sake, than you alone for the sake of all of them. What has your father got to do with me? These sighs which well up from deep inside and which grip me so close to the heart, are they heaved for your father? He was never in my thoughts when I found myself wanting to love you, to make much of you.]

Showing much in common with the dialogues of Andreas Capellanus in which lovers deny the importance of social status, Ganor's speech just quoted employs all the strategies of persuasive rhetoric she can muster: chiasmus (4726–27, 4729–30), rhetorical questions (4726–27, 4731, 4732–34), hyperbole (4728–30), binomial expressions (4728, 4729), antithesis (4733–34), and anaphora (4737). Yet despite her eloquence, the usual claim that she will die for love, and the fact that she faints in Ille's arms, Ganor is abandoned until her beloved is able to marry her honorably.

The Rhetoric of Love

With the exception of Ganor's profession of love, just analyzed, Gautier's protagonists reserve their powers of eloquence for internal debate rather than for conversation with their beloveds. His male lovers, Paridés and Ille, investigate in lengthy monologues their feelings of social inadequacy and their fear of rejection by a proud lady. Paridés at first concludes that his suffering for love is *folie*, and, like Chrétien's Soredamours, he tries to deny his love.[25] In a second monologue, he debates with himself over the reasons for the empress's patent interest in him– is it his athletic and musical skills or his beautiful eyes?[26] Then he accuses himself of pride:

> "— Si est, espoir, por tes biaus iex.
> — Or esce folie et orgiex
> Quant tu cuides ne ne cuidas
> Que fust por toi! — Je ne cuiç pas;
> Ainc ne cuidai que fust por moi.
> — Esta en toi! — Que dis 'en toi'?
> Las! je ne puis en moi ester;
> Mes cuers ne se velt arester,
> Ains m'a relenqui des hui main . . ."   (*Eracle*, 3745–53)

[— Perhaps it's for your good looks? — This is sheer folly and pride if you think or thought that it was because of you. — I do not think, nor did I ever think that it was because of me. — Calm down! — What do you mean, calm down? Alas, I cannot calm down, my heart will not stay put. It abandoned me this morning. . . .]

Through polyptoton on the verb *cuidier* Paridés expresses his fear of false belief induced by overconfidence in love. More important, though, the internal dialogue and commonplace notion that the lover's heart leaves his body to be with the beloved enables Gautier to explore the fragmentation of the subject's identity, made more apparent in times of emotional turmoil.[27] Here Paridés goes on to acknowledge his love, looks forward to the night when he will be able to lament freely, but also utters a rather misogynistic generalization about the punishments women of high status mete out to inferior men who dare to love them (3754–798b). Thus, like Jean de Meun in his Continuation of the *Roman de la Rose*, Gautier

---

[25] Compare *Eracle*, 3499–515, and *Cligés*, 469–515, ed. Alexandre Micha. Les Classiques français du moyen âge, 84 (Paris: Champion, 1975).

[26] In another case of female scopophilia (compare Lavine as discussed by Raymond Cormier's article in this volume), Athanaïs has fallen in love with the sight of Paridés. The fact that he is a harpist links him with Tristan, and illustrates further the complex music/magic/love explored by Linda Zaerr in this volume.

[27] The phrase "ester en toi" literally means "stay in yourself," yet Paridés's use of *correctio* questions the very notion of subjecthood and its inviolability.

explores through inner dialogue the conflicted feelings of a medieval male in the throes of love, whose attraction to the female is tainted by culturally induced misogyny.[28]

In a third monologue of seventy lines Gautier gives novel expression to several traditional ideas about love. Weakened by the usual Ovidian amatory symptoms, including a lack of sleep and food, not to mention the loss of his heart, Paridés rails against Love's choice of feeble victims. This is why, he says, no one has respect for love any more, for love is like the man who jumps over a hedge at its lowest point (*Eracle*, 3975–77). In another unusual comparison Paridés accuses Amors of being a painter who has dyed his heart yellow:

> "Amors, ainc mais ne fus si male,
> Mais molt est gaune te tainture;
> Amors, tu ses molt de painture,[29]
> Tu en as si mon cuer vestu..."   (*Eracle*, 3980–83)

[Love, never before were you so cruel, your paint is very yellow indeed. Love, you are an expert in painting, for you have so coated my heart in it....]

Like Paridés, Ille expresses his inferiority complex in lengthy monologues (*Ille*, 1309–72). Through him Gautier suggests again that love[30] produces loss of agency and personal identity:

> "Las! s'a çou tenir me pooie,
> N'aroie mal; garie seroie.
> Mais ne sui pas del tot a moi,
> Et cil qui mie n'est a soi
> N'oevre pas tot si com il veut,
> Ains fait sovent dont mout se delt
> E las! caitis, com je me duel!
> Je faç tot el que je ne voel."   (*Ille*, 1343–50)

[Alas! if I could keep to this, I would feel no pain: I would be cured. But I am not altogether my own man, and anyone who is not his own man does not

---

[28] On Jean de Meun, see Tracy Adams's contribution in this volume. Despite Gautier's creation of impressive female characters, he does not escape the misogyny endemic in medieval clerical culture. See Pratt, *Meister Otte's Eraclius*, 288–91; R. Howard Bloch, *Medieval Misogyny and The Invention of Western Romantic Love* (Chicago and London: The University of Chicago Press, 1991).

[29] The *B* reading *pointure* could be a Picard graphy for *painture* or may mean "stitching," thus indicating that the metaphor here relates to the dyeing and sewing of garments rather than painting. A similar metaphor is used in *Ille et Galeron*, 6262–73, in which the tunic stitched by love is described "Fist les coustures et les pointes" (made the seams and the stitches, 6268).

[30] Linda Marie Zaerr, in her contribution to this volume, poignantly calls it "some force from outside," 317

act entirely as he wishes; instead he often does things which make him very unhappy. Alas, poor wretch, how unhappy I am! What I am doing is quite the opposite of what I want.]

Whilst Gautier's rhetoric here on suffering and volition is reminiscent of Thomas's *Tristan*,[31] he also includes his own colorful criticism of love personified. This time Love is accused of behaving like a madman who strikes the wrong man in response to an attack:

"Or si me vent autrui mesfait
Tot ausi com li dervés fait,
Qui ja ne toucera celui
Qui feru l'a, ains fiert autrui." (*Ille*, 1361–64).

[So now she is making me pay for someone else's misdeed, just like the madman who will never touch the person who has struck him, but strikes someone else instead.]

Thus the poet's unusual wit and humor lighten the almost academic, rhetorical complexity of the protagonists' soliloquies.

Gautier's skill in producing elaborate monologues in the form of internal dialogue is not confined to his male lovers. In Athanaïs he has created a worthy successor to the eloquently introspective Lavine, as aspects of the empress (love versus reason, or her desire versus her conscience) debate the possibility of her committing adultery. Her first monologue, extending over 180 lines (3543–720), is a *tour de force* of rhetoric and dialectic, in which Gautier allows her to examine her feelings and ultimately to justify her eventual infidelity. First, she argues that it is her imprisonment that makes her susceptible to love, and that Paridés is a worthy suitor (3601–12), a soul-mate who shares a private language with her (3618–27).[32] Her priority, therefore, is to inform him discreetly of her interest (3575–96).[33] Her imaginary interlocutor begins with purely practical objections, yet it gradually becomes identifiable with her conscience when it raises moral issues such as her ingratitude towards her husband, who lifted her out of poverty. However, Athanaïs's "desire" blames Laïs for her distress (as indeed Eracle will do

---

[31] Turin, 158–59, in Thomas, *Les Fragments du Roman de Tristan: Poème du XII*[e] *siècle*, ed. Bartina Wind. Textes littéraires français (Geneva: Droz; Paris: Minard, 1960), 75.

[32] She compares their situation to that of children, who can communicate without others understanding them. For further remarks on the special language of lovers, see the essay by Christopher R. Clason in this volume.

[33] This passage contains some verbal parallels with the "Godefroiz de Leigni" section of Chrétien's *Charrete* (6835–41), ed. Mario Roques. Les Classiques français du moyen âge, 86 (Paris: Champion, 1981); see Pratt, *Meister Otte's Eraclius*, 39–40.

later [4999])[34] and, in a stichomythic exchange similar to Paridés's words quoted above (3750–51), the empress overrules her conscience, preferring love to honor:

> "— Je pert m'onor, mais n'en puis mais.
> — Si pués. — Comment? — Esta em pais.
> — Je nel puis trover en mon cuer." (*Eracle*, 3673–75)

[—I am going to lose my honor, but I cannot do otherwise.—Yes you can—How?—Calm down.—I can find no calm in my heart]

Reminded of the consequences of sin by her alter ego, Athanaïs nevertheless persists in her plan to take a lover, claiming (rather shockingly) that God will be understanding about the adultery, as true love ennobles, endowing the lover with all courtly virtues:

> "Mais cui Amors tient asés prés,
> Orguel li taut et felounie
> Et fausseté et vilonie,
> Et si l'estruit de grant largece,
> De cortoisie et de prouece;
> Et s'en amor a un mesfait,
> Ces coses font vers Diu bon plait,
> Qu'il aime honor et cortoisie
> Et fine Larguece est s'amie.
> Or amerai, si serai large,
> Car Amors fine le m'encarge
> Que je le soie, et jel serai,
> Et sor içou si aquerrai." (*Eracle*, 3710–22)

[but when Love chooses someone as her companion, she removes from him all pride, treachery, dishonesty, and wickedness and teaches him great generosity, courtesy and nobility; and if under the influence of love one makes a mistake, God easily forgives such things, for He loves honor and courtesy, and pure generosity is his beloved. So I shall love and I shall be generous, for true love obliges me to be so, and so I shall be, and on this basis I shall reap my reward]

---

[34] In a subsequent internal dialogue (3867–919) she justifies her adultery with the young man by comparing herself to a bird, which when released from its trap naturally seeks the companionship of birds it would not otherwise frequent (3882–90).

The Rhetoric of Love 267

Thus through the examination of her feelings by means of dialectical reasoning the once naïve orphan girl arrives at a deeper, more mature understanding of herself and her values.[35]

Although it is possible to read Athanaïs's apology for illicit love ironically, the poet allowing his protagonist through her specious arguments to condemn her own behavior,[36] it is interesting to note that similar courtly defenses of love are used to describe the unimpeachable conjugal love between Ille and Galeron:

> K'amors n'a cose en soi commune,
> Mais que largece et cortoisie,
> Francise et jeu sans vilonie.
> C'est d'amors fine li commans,
> Qu'on truist çou en tos amans   (*Ille*, 3372–76)

[Because there is nothing in love which can be shared around [or nothing base], except generosity and courtliness, nobility and fair play. This is true love's commandment, that this should be found in all lovers.]

Besides, the fact that Athanaïs was chosen by God's elect, Eracle, to be a perfect bride and was, as the eponymous hero maintains, corrupted only by false imprisonment, suggests that in *Eracle* Gautier has a similar attitude toward a *mal mariée* as that of Marie de France in *Guigemar*. It is notable that in twelfth-century French literature only a female author and Gautier d'Arras allow "true love" to triumph with narrative impunity over the conventions of Christian marriage and society.[37]

Although Gautier's enthusiasm for love casuistry is displayed in amatory monologues and internal dialogues, his love of words is most apparent in passages of narratorial commentary, in which his sympathy for lovers and fascination with their psychological turmoil is again displayed. In particular, Ille's painful conflict between love for his wife and pity or *caritas* for Ganor receives extensive treat-

---

[35] Athanaïs's path toward self-knowledge may well be modeled on that of Lavine in the *Eneas* (see Cormier's contribution in this volume). See also Classen, Introduction, 15–21, on the power of words to facilitate greater personal insight and comprehension of the apophatic.

[36] Pierreville, *Gautier d'Arras*, 212–19, detects strong criticism of the adultery in Gautier's choice of a rather sordid subterranean love-nest at the old woman's house for the consummation of the relationship. However, see Friedrich Wolfzettel, "Wahrheit der Geschichte und Wahrheit der Frau: *Honor de feme* und weibliche *aventure* im altfranzösichen Roman," *Zeitschrift für romanische Philologie* 104 (1988): 197–217; here 197–206, for a more positive evaluation of Gautier's female protagonist's emotional journey.

[37] It is also notable that Marie in *Eliduc* and Gautier in *Ille et Galeron* are the only twelfth-century French writers to treat the theme of the man between two women, although the Tristan material furnishes both male and female versions of a person torn between two lovers. See also Parzival among Belakane, Herzeloyde, and Ampflise in Wolfram von Eschenbach's *Parzival* (ca. 1205). Cf. also the contribution to this volume by Anna Kukułka-Wojtasik.

ment (4644–74). Ille is presented as torn between opposing emotions personified, as if literally being pulled in different directions by the two women.[38] On one side of the tug-of-war is Ganor's love for him, represented by "Feme et Amors" (4658), i.e., female charms and love, which accuse him of treating her discourteously; on the other side are "Prestre, raisons, drois et lois" (4656: priests, reason, right, and the law), all supporting Galeron's cause. Although, according to the narrator, extra-marital courtly love usually prevails over Christian marriage, the wife triumphs in this case, but not before Ille is further torn apart by two forms of pity. In a lengthy prayer to God (4790–872), Ille presents himself as victim of "doble pitiés" (4850, 4857), one born of love for Galeron, the other compassion for the woman he thinks will die of unrequited love — a struggle summed up as "Pitié de cha, Pitié de la" (Pity on this side and pity on that [4871]).[39]

Even when Galeron has become a nun, Ille is still torn between his two loves. This time Gautier adopts the unusual metaphor of a tower being defended by its long-term occupant and attacked by a newcomer — Ille's heart is occupied by love for his wife, whilst Ganor's love besieges it. The narrator even reports the debate between the two loves as the first argues its right to the tower, whilst the second claims that a nun has no need of such a building (5611–55):

> Einsi est de ces .ii. amours:
> Li cuers Ille est la haute tours.
> Dedens qui est? L'amors premiere,
> Qui del tenir est coustumiere;
> Ne mais l'amors de la pucele,
> Qui est dehors, sovent l'apele,
> Dist li c'a tort est la dedens
> Et veut mostrer par argumens
> Et prover k'amors de nonain
> N'a droit en cuer de castelain... (*Ille*, 5632–41)

> [This is how it was with these two loves: Ille's heart was the lofty tower. Who was inside? The first love, which held it by force of custom; except that his love for the maiden, which was outside, frequently accused her, saying she had no right to be there inside, and intended to demonstrate logically and prove that love for a nun has no title to the heart of a castellan....]

---

[38] This allegorical representation of inner conflict anticipates the more sophisticated, extended allegory employed by Jean de Meun as he analyzes out the contradictory impulses which Guillaume de Lorris had largely repressed in his lover; see Tracy Adams's contribution to this volume, 380–81.

[39] Not only does the rhetorical elaboration of terms such as "doloir, voloir, desirier" remind one again of Thomas's *Tristan*, but Gautier's version unusually presents the *marital* love as truly courtly: "amors fine" (4817 and cf. 3375).

Thus in an inversion of the usual metaphor in which the woman's body is besieged like a castle, Gautier presents his male protagonist's heart being fought over by two female "knights."

In amatory dialogue, monologues, and narratorial commentary Gautier d'Arras stamps his own mark on the love casuistry of the late twelfth century. Employing rather clichéd Ovidian metaphors found also in the *lais* of Marie de France, in the *romans antiques*[40] and in Chrétien's works, he portrays love as an aggressor, inflicting a wound which only the beloved's medicine can heal (*Ille*, 1211, 1370). Despite the feminine gender of love in Old French, Gautier follows the trend of imagining love's activities as masculine: love is a hunter setting traps (*Ille*, 6530r, ed. Lefèvre) or Cupid, the military leader shooting arrows or setting fire to lovers with his torch (*Eracle*, 4688–98). More original, though in gender terms is his depiction of Love as a rider on a female horse, digging its spurs into Ganor's side (*Ille*, 3410–11) or involved in the female activity of sewing a tunic to clothe Ganor in suffering (*Ille*, 6262–73, cf. *Eracle*, 3983). His treatment of the ennobling effects of love *is* fairly traditional: the chivalry topos, whereby knights are inspired to great feats of arms by ladies (*Ille*, 3917–22), is a popular feature of courtly romance, found also in Marie's *Chaitivel*. Likewise, Ille's criticism of contemporary lovers in the same speech (3915–30) has much in common with the Golden Age topos present in the prologue to *Yvain*.[41] Moreover, Gautier, like other writers,[42] claims that only the *fin'amans* in his audience can appreciate what lovers feel (*Eracle*, 3823–30; 4588–92),[43] a key indicator being their subjective experience of time (*Ille*, 3414–20). However, Gautier also *takes issue* with other poets. For instance, he disagrees with those ("li auquant," *Eracle*, 3520) who claim that the heart can be divided in two, stating instead that love will not make do with less than the whole heart. Yet whilst Chrétien in *Yvain* (2658–59) argues that when the lover loses his heart to his beloved, he fashions a replacement heart from hope, Gautier claims that Love occasionally releases its grip to allow the lover to go about his ordinary business. Describing the love-sick Paridés, he says:

Il a les mains a l'estrument,
Ne mais li cuers n'i est nïent;

---

[40] Another debt to the *Eneas* are the lover's symptoms (see Raymond Cormier's contribution to this volume, 114–15), including that of "yawning" or (as Eley suggests for *Ille*, 3325) open-mouthed sighing.

[41] This may, however, be a borrowing by Chrétien from Gautier.

[42] Notably Gottfried von Strassburg, who invokes his ideal audience's "noble hearts" in the prologue to his *Tristan* (see Albrecht Classen, "Introduction," 6).

[43] The originality of *Eracle*, 3823–30, lies not in the general claim, but in the specific comparison employed: the uninitiated can no more appreciate love than a blind man can distinguish between the colors red and green (*Eracle*, 3826–30). It is unclear whether or not Gautier is playing here with the idea, found also in Andreas Capellanus (*De amore*, I, 5), that a blind man is incapable of love.

> N'i a del cuer ne tant ne quant;
> Et se le dient li auquant
> Qu'on depart bien sen cuer en deus
> Si l'envoie on en divers leus,
> A ce c'on tient et a s'amie;
> Mais qui çou fait, il n'aime mie.
> Amors n'a cure de lanchier[44]
> S'ele n'a tout le cuer entier
> Ne de cuer malvais a parchon,
> C' Amors n'a cure de garçon.
> Je sai c'on pense bien sor jor
> Souvent en el que en amor,
> Une heure plus, une heure mains,
> Qu'Amors alasque bien ses mains;
> Car ele est france et debonaire,
> Et amans a tel cose a faire
> Qu'il ne poroit faire a nul fuer
> S'il n'i avoit un poi del cuer,
> Se ce n'estoit par grant usage.
> Trestout son cuer et son corage
> A cil aillors qu'a l'estrument,
> Si harpe molt bien nequedent. (*Eracle*, 3517–40)[45]

[His hands were on his instrument but his heart was not in it at all; not even a tiny part of his heart was in it. Yet some say that one can easily split one's heart into two and send each part off to different places, to what one is concentrating on at the time and to one's beloved, but whoever does this is not really in love! Love is not interested in shooting her arrow if she doesn't have the whole heart; nor does she take any part of a vile heart, since Love is not interested in those who are inconstant. I know that during the day one often thinks of things other than love, because Love loosens her grip for long or short periods. For she is noble and generous and lovers have things to do that they would not be able to accomplish in any way if they did not have a small part of their heart in it, unless they were functioning out of pure habit. Paridés's whole heart and mind were focused on matters other than his instrument, but he nevertheless played very well.]

---

[44] The rhyme here is problematic: Ms. A has *lanchier*, which may well be the original reading; B has *tencier* and only the inferior Ms. T reads *rentier*, producing a richer rhyme with *entier*. The latter could be a scribal reminiscence of Chrétien's *Cligés*, 3114, copied later in the same manuscript. The adoption by previous editors of the T reading has misleadingly strengthened the argument for the borrowing by Gautier of rhyme pairs from Chrétien's *Cligés*.

[45] As Beckmann, "Der Tristandichter Thomas und Gautier d'Arras," points out, Paridés is a harp player like Tristan.

The Rhetoric of Love 271

The similarity of rhymes here with Fénice's famous condemnation of Yseut in *Cligés* (3112–24, esp. 3113–14 and 3119–22) has led some critics to suggest that Gautier is borrowing from Chrétien. If this is the case — and the direction of influence has not been convincingly established — then Gautier is clearly rewriting his colleague. For in *Cligés* Fénice is talking about the sharing of her *body* between two men:

Amors en li [Yseult] trop vilena,
Que ses cuers fu a un entiers,
Et ses cors fu a deus rentiers   (3112–14)

[Love behaved basely in her case, for her heart was given to one alone, whilst her body was used by two men],

whereas Gautier is denying the possibility of dividing up the *heart*.[46] Behind both of these texts, however, lies the influence of Thomas's *Tristan*,[47] and a recognition of this helps us further to appreciate the contribution of Gautier to twelfth-century writing on love. Particularly in *Ille et Galeron*, Gautier has imitated Thomas's detailed exploration of the suffering induced by his four protagonists' *estrange amor*.[48] Ille, like Tristan and Iseut, experiences being torn between marriage and love. However, Gautier's stroke of genius is to cast Ganor, a woman, also in the role of Tristan, both characters being jealous of their beloved's commitment to the marital bed (*Ille*, 5216). Thomas's description of Tristan's situation:

---

[46] The rhyme *parchon/garçon* in *Eracle*, 3527–28, is echoed in *Cligés*, 3121–22: "Ja mes cors n'iert voir garçoniers/ N'il n'i avra deus parçoniers" [Never will my body be a real slut / and will never be shared by two men] and in *Ille et Galeron*, 1285–88:
  Ne cuidés ja que garçonier
  Soient ja d'amor parçonier,
  Ne ja n'en seront parçonieres
  Celes qui en sont garçonieres.
[Do not imagine that men of easy virtue could ever have a share in love, and love will never be shared by women of easy virtue.]
However, although the context in *Ille* refers to people of easy virtue, as does Fénice, for Gautier the word *parçon* and cognates has the meaning of "partaker in" in these cases. Thus the relationship between these passages from Gautier's romances and *Cligés* is unclear, and there may be a closer parallel between Chrétien's use of *rentier* (3114) and *parçoniers* (3122) and the rhyme *meteier/parçonier* in *Eneas*, 3827–28 (ed. J.-J. Salverda de Grave, 2 vols. Les Classiques français du moyen âge, 44, 62 [Paris: Champion, 1925 and 1929]), where *meteier* has a similar meaning to *rentier*.
[47] See Beckmann, "Der Tristandichter Thomas und Gautier d'Arras" on the banishment scene in Thomas's *Tristan* as a source for the divorce episode in *Eracle* and for the love triangle in *Ille et Galeron*.
[48] Turin, l. 71, ed. Wind, 72.

> Duble paigne, doble dolur
> Ha dan Tristan por s'amor   (Turin, 109–10)

[Double pain and double grief Lord Tristan has on account of his love]

is clearly echoed in Ganor's lament with its *expolitio* on doubling, in which Gautier attempts to outdo Thomas's rhetoric:

> "Et c'autre prent ce que je voel,
> Ice me double mon torment
> Et me tormente doublement.
> L'uns me poroit assés torbler,
> Et quant vint que l'estut doubler,
> Plus me torment et plus me paine
> Que ne feroit double tierçaine"   (*Ille*, 5222–28)

[And the fact that another is taking what I want, this redoubles my torment and torments me doubly. The one would cause me enough distress, and then when it had to be redoubled, it torments and tortures me more than a double tertian fever would.]

Moreover, Ganor, like Tristan, bewails the fact that another person is sleeping with her beloved and that another woman holds his body as a fief (*Ille et Galeron*, 5216, 5252). Her words constitute a novel feminization of the feudal metaphor, which normally presents the *male* lover as a vassal receiving his lady's body as a fief in return for his service![49]

The rhetoric employed by Gautier d'Arras in his protagonists' speech, especially their monologues, is highly sophisticated and often original. Moreover, his dialectical treatment of conflicted emotions within allegorized interior dialogues reveals a witty yet sympathetic approach to the travails of the human heart. In narratorial commentary on the plight of lovers Gautier makes a significant contribution to the elaboration of love casuistry in twelfth-century romance, often introducing striking gender inversions. Although working within a tradition established by Thomas and the *romans antiques*, he nevertheless rewrote it creatively, and indeed, along with Chrétien and others, no doubt furnished Andreas Capellanus with courtly exemplifications of "that thing we call love". If Gautier was familiar with some of the romances of Chrétien de Troyes, he was no slavish imitator. Indeed, most of the resemblances between the two are likely to be the

---

[49] A good example is the châtelaine de Vergi. However, note that Paridés offers his body as a fief to Athanaïs in return for hers (4633–34, quoted above) — a clear indication of the reciprocity of their love and of Gautier's consistent inversion of gender stereotypes.

result of Chrétien's playful imitation of his colleague, as the parody of the prologue to *Ille et Galeron* in the *Charette* prologue seems to suggest.[50]

Whatever their relationship, the amatory rhetoric of the Champenois poet cannot be appreciated fully without taking into account the love of words of his rival from Arras. Moreover, Gautier's presentation in *Ille et Galeron* of marital love as truly courtly, and in *Eracle* of an adulterous love succesfully and eloquently defended by a strong-willed woman, makes him a key participant in debates about love in twelfth-century French literature. Finally, the romances of Gautier d'Arras demonstrate how inextricably linked love and rhetoric were in medieval cultural production and how richly fruitful the chiastic paradigm "words of love / love of words" was in the development of courtly discourse.

---

[50] Chrétien makes fun of Gautier's overblown flattery of Beatrice in his apophatic encomium of Marie de Champagne. This parody may have led Gautier to reduce his praise of Beatrice in the version of *Ille* copied in manuscript W.

CHAPTER 11

THE BITTERNESS OF LOVE ON THE SEA: ISOLDE'S AMOROUS DISCOURSE VIEWED THROUGH GOTTFRIED'S CRYSTALLINE TRANSPARENCY

CHRISTOPHER R. CLASON
Oakland University, Rochester, MI

In *The Game of Love*,[1] Laura Kendrick illustrates a basic tension in thirteenth-century verbal art between models of interpretation, over "what extratextual model of order would be used to explain the meaning of written signs: oral culture's acentric idea of order as a series of temporary standoffs or indeterminacies in an ever-shifting configuration of competing, physically present forces, or literate (chiefly ecclesiastical) culture's idea of order as a stable hierarchy of forces centered on and controlled by one physically absent ruler" (15). The control of interpretation supports and augments power, and although Augustine's prescription for the return to a "still center of pure meaning" (Kendrick, 2) becomes the dominant intellectual tendency of the later Middle Ages and a weapon serving the Church's supremacy, there is a host of impulses affecting medieval thought on this issue, arising from authors of antiquity such as Lucretius, Varro, and Ovid, through Isidore of Seville to Rhabanus Maurus that aim toward "the extreme richness of signification, the variety and the arbitrary nature" of language — here, the Latin lexicon (Kendrick, 5). Kendrick then shows that many troubadour lyrics celebrate this ambiguity, through riddles, acrostics, puns, and other linguistic indeterminacies, evincing subversive intentions that require the elucidation of a good interpreter: "The troubadours realized what we scholars — preceded by

---

[1] Laura Kendrick, *The Game of Love: Troubadour Wordplay* (Berkeley, Los Angeles, and London: University of California Press, 1988).

contemporary artists — have been reemphasizing in the past few decades: that the meaning of a sign is determined by its use in a particular context, and that the most important context is the mind of the interpreter. As the Archpriest of Hita put it, words serve understanding (or interpretation), not the reverse" (21–22).[2]

Perhaps no other work of medieval epic literature better illustrates Kendrick's discursive connections among love, power, and interpretation than Gottfried's *Tristan*.[3] For years critics have debated its many ambiguities and indeterminacies, ensuring its status as one of the most intriguing texts of the German Middle Ages. The role of knowledge and its relationship to language and "truth" has become one important area of discussion: opinions range from those who consider the epic poem outside the rational realm, either as a work of irony,[4] of mysticism,[5] of revolution against the prevailing courtly culture,[6] or even of a new kind of religion,[7] to those who delve deeply into the language and logical patterns Gottfried presents, in an effort to unveil the epistemological secrets that may lie therein.[8] Several have pondered each section, line, and word

---

[2] Kendrick's reference to the Archpriest of Hita stems from Juan Ruiz, *Libro de buen amor: Arcipreste de Hita*, ed. G .B. Gybbon-Monypenny (Madrid: Castalia, 1988).

[3] Gottfried von Straßburg, *Tristan*, ed. Friedrich Ranke, trans. Rüdiger Krohn, 3 vols. (Stuttgart: Reclam 1980, 1993); all English translations from Gottfried von Straßburg, *Tristan*, trans. A. T. Hatto (1960; London, New York, et al.: Penguin, 1967), to which the subsequent page listings in brackets refer.

[4] E. g., D[ennis] H. Green, *Irony in the Medieval Romance* (Cambridge et al.: Cambridge University Press, 1979), 111–18.

[5] See, for example, Hermann Kunisch, "*edelez herze — edeliu sêle*: vom Verhältnis höfischer Dichtung zur Mystik, *Mediaevalia litteraria: Festschrift für Helmut de Boor zum 80. Geburtstag*, ed. Ursula Hennig and Herbert Kolb (Munich: Beck, 1971), 413–50.

[6] See W. T. H. Jackson, "The Court of the Poet and the Court of the King," *The Medieval Court in Europe*, ed. Edward E. Haymes. Houston German Studies, 6 (Munich: Fink, 1986), 26–40.

[7] See especially the discussions of this concept in Walter Haug, "Gottfrieds von Straßburg *Tristan*: Sexueller Sündenfall oder erotische Utopie?" *Akten des VII. Internationalen Germanisten-Kongresses Göttingen 1985*, vol. I (Tübingen: Niemeyer, 1986), 41–52; and Nigel Harris, "God, Religion and Ambiguity in *Tristan*," *A Companion to Gottfried von Strassburg's "Tristan,"* ed. Will Hasty. Studies in German Literature, Linguistics and Culture (Rochester, NY and Woodbridge, UK: Camden House, 2003), 113–36.

[8] E. g., Wolfgang Jupé, *Die List im Tristanroman Gottfrieds von Straßburg: Intellektualität und Liebe oder die Suche nach dem Wesen der individuellen Existenz*. Germanische Bibliothek. Dritte Reihe: Untersuchungen und Einzeldarstellungen (Heidelberg: Carl Winter, 1976); Joan Ferrante, "'Ez ist ein zunge dunket mich': Fiction, Deception and Self-Deception in Gottfried's *Tristan*," *Gottfried von Strassburg and the Medieval Tristan Legend: Papers from an Anglo-North American Symposium*, ed. Adrian Stevens and Roy Wisbey. Arthurian Studies, 33 (Cambridge: D. S. Brewer, and London: University of London Institute of Germanic Studies, 1990), 171–80; Rüdiger Schnell, *Suche nach Wahrheit: Gottfrieds "Tristan und Isold" als erkenntniskritischer Roman*. Hermaea: Germanistische Forschungen, Neue Folge, 67 (Tübingen: Max Niemeyer, 1992); Eckart Conrad Lutz, "*lesen — unmüezec wesen*: Überlegungen zu lese- und erkenntnistheoretischen Implikationen von Gottfrieds Schreiben," *Der "Tristan" Gottfrieds von Straßburg: Symposion Santiago de Compostela, 5. bis 8. April 2000*, ed. Christoph Huber and Victor Millet (Tübingen: Niemeyer, 2002), 295–313.

of the prologue,[9] searching for one key concept that will make sense out of the many contradictory thoughts expressed there, while others have concentrated on certain key scenes in which language, deception, and discovery are primarily important. It seems that the search is inexhaustible, and spawns ever more creative and stimulating perspectives.

One of the most provocative aspects of *Tristan* remains the characters' strategic use of language and communication, of which both Tristan and Isolde prove themselves masters.[10] Tristan's capabilities of beguiling his associates and concealing the truth accompany his brilliant talent for speaking a large variety of languages, a capacity already evident in his earliest years. As an auditory alternative to linguistic communication, Tristan also possesses legendary skill at playing stringed instruments, the most important aspect of which becomes his musical ability to distract, mollify, and mesmerize others.[11] Isolde, as well, proves uncommonly adept at music and, more importantly, at verbally sketching alternative and ambiguous versions of reality and coloring them with illusory but convincing hues.[12] Purposeful ambiguity informs the basic communicative negotiations between the lovers and the court, granting a decisive advantage to the former.

While the lovers customarily work as a team in deceiving the court, they nevertheless ply their arts on each other as well at certain points in the narrative. This troublesome fact seems to contradict one of the text's most emphasized axioms on love: how can one integrate the lovers' rhetorical manipulation of the "truth" with Gottfried's insistence that love be "cristallîn" (16983; of crystal [264]), and completely transparent? In other words, can ambiguity serve clarity? As we will see, this question provides an important perspective on the scene in which the lovers admit their feelings for one another. Since this formulation of the problem is couched in terms of communicative strategies and epistemology, in this essay I would like to address the specific methods and goals of the communication made in this scene, in conjunction with the essential content of the communicated message. Ultimately, this investigation seeks to reconcile perceived and narrated reality, which on the textual surface appear to be in almost constant conflict.

---

[9] The most influential commentary on the prologue is still Albrecht Schöne, "Zu Gottfrieds 'Tristan'-Prolog," *Deutsche Vierteljahrschrift für Literaturwissenschaft und Geistesgeschichte* 29 (1955): 447–74.

[10] See Albrecht Classen, *Verzweiflung und Hoffnung: die Suche nach der kommunikativen Gemeinschaft in der deutschen Literatur des Mittelalters*. Beihefte zur Mediaevistik, 1 (Frankfurt a. M. and New York: Peter Lang, 2002), 279–358.

[11] See W. T. H. Jackson, "Tristan the Artist in Gottfried's Poem," *Tristan and Isolde: A Casebook*, ed. Joan Tasker Grimbert. Arthurian Characters and Themes (1995; New York and London: Routledge, 2002), 125–46.

[12] See Albrecht Classen, "Female Agency and Power in Gottfried von Strassburg's *Tristan*: The Irish Queen Isolde: New Perspectives," *Tristania* 23 (2004): 39–60.

The scene in question is well known to all who have heard or read the tale, and Gottfried includes in it the famous word-play also found in his primary source, the *Tristan* of Thomas of Bretagne:[13] after imbibing the *minne*-potion on board a skiff traversing the Irish Sea, Tristan and Isolde experience the pain of love deeply and intensely, but at first suffer in silence (11707–874). Apart, each feels "zwîvel unde scham" (11733; doubt and shame [195]) while they hide their feelings from one another. The discourse in this section of the text is one of concealment, solitude, division, and inaction, and each lover evinces the elementary struggle between *minne* and *êre* that runs throughout the poem. When, finally, Tristan poses a compassionate question to Isolde, "waz wirret iu?" (11984; what is vexing you? [199]), her thrice-repeated response, the phoneme "*lameir*," (11986–88) expresses three possible alternatives in Old French: "love," "bitterness," and "the sea."[14] The ambiguity of language that is an essential part of word-play does not surprise the reader here; quite the contrary: such play courses through the entire work, as a part of the complex epistemology Gottfried communicates through rhetorical devices, discourse, irony, and other literary techniques. However, the response also reflects a kind of communication in this epic poem that lovers practice, but other courtiers do not.[15] A much earlier instance in which the ambiguity of language conveys a lover's communication occurs at the beginning of the relationship between Tristan's parents, Blancheflor and Rivalin. Clearly, Cupid's arrow has struck both of them powerfully, and Blancheflor's protest during their first exchange of words, that "an einem vriunde mîn, dem besten den ich ie gewan, dâ habet ihr mich beswaeret an," (754–56; you [Rivalin] have annoyed me through

---

[13] See Ulrike Jantzen and Niels Kröner, "Zum neugefundenen *Tristan*-Fragment des Thomas d'Angleterre: Editionskritik und Vergleich mit Gottfrieds Bearbeitung," *Euphorion* 91 (1997): 291–309; Gérard J. Brault, "*L'amer, l'amer, la mer:* la scène des aveux dans le *Tristan* de Thomas à la lumière du fragment de Carlisle," *Miscellanea Mediaevalia: mélanges offerts à Philippe Ménard*, vol. I, ed. J. Claude Faucon, Alain Labbé, and Danielle Quéruel. Nouvelle bibliothèque du Moyen Âge, 46 (Paris: Champion, 1998), 215–26; Nicola Zotz, "Programmatische Vieldeutigkeit und verschlüsselte Eindeutigkeit: Das Liebesbekenntnis bei Thomas und Gottfried von Straßburg (mit einer neuen Übersetzung des Carlisle-Fragments)," *Germanisch-Romanische Monatsschrift* 50 (2000): 1–19; and Christopher Young, "Der Minnetrank als Literarisierungsprozeß bei Gottfried von Straßburg," *Der "Tristan" Gottfrieds von Straßburg: Symposion Santiago de Compostela*, 257–79.

[14] The origins of the word-play, its form "mit lothringischer Schreibung und Aussprache" and its previous use in Thomas and in Chrétien's *Cligès* are shown by Lambertus Okken, *Kommentar zum Tristan-Roman Gottfrieds von Strassburg*, 2nd ed., vol. I. Amsterdamer Publikationen zur Sprache und Literatur, 57 (Amsterdam and Atlanta: Rodopi, 1996), 486.

[15] Schnell, *Suche nach Wahrheit*, 127–49, treats the discursive/epistemological environments of the court and the lovers as a "doppelte Wahrheit ," the correct understanding of which is dependent on the character's knowledge of a speaker's "*intentio*." However, Classen (*Verzweiflung und Hoffnung*, 289) sees especially the scene under consideration as evidence for the following: "der Liebestrank hat . . . Isolde dazu bewegt, die Suche nach dem Kommunikationspartner aufzunehmen, der hier durch das sprachliche Rätsel getestet wird." Through this process the lovers establish a unique communicative community, in which Isolde plays a particularly important role. The scene I investigate here shows her educating Tristan, in order that he can take his place as her partner.

The Bitterness of Love on the Sea

a friend of mine, the best I ever had [51]) sets him off on an immediate search for the true significance behind her complaint. At first, Rivalin believes she may be expressing enmity or anger. He does not immediately realize, as the narrator asserts, that "der vriunt, des sî gewuoc, daz was ir herze, in dem sî truoc von sînen schulden ungemach, daz was der vriunt, von dem sî sprach" (767-70; the friend she referred to was her heart, in which he made her suffer: that was the friend she spoke of [51]). In the course of pondering her words, however, his thoughts engage the puzzle she has presented him in the context of the other signs she has shown, and the narrator relates the thoroughness of his considerations in detail:

> ir gruoz, ir rede betrahte er gâr,
> ir sûft, ir segen, al ir gebâr
> daz marcte er al besunder
> und begunde iedoch hier under
> ir siuften unde ir süezen segen
> ûf den wec der minne wegen:
> er kam binamen an den wân,
> diu zwei diu waeren getân
> durch niht niwan durch minne. (797-805)

[He considered her greeting, her words; he examined her sigh minutely, her farewell, her whole behaviour, and so doing began to construe both her sigh and her sweet benediction as manifestations of love, and indeed arrived at the belief that both had been uttered with love alone in mind. (52)]

This "clear" conclusion comes to Rivalin after he has willingly entered into the ambivalent linguistic space Blancheflor has prepared for him. The possibilities implicit in the ambiguity caress and seduce his thoughts more and more, as Gottfried reports:

> daz enzunte ouch sîne sinne,
> daz sî sâ wider vuoren
> und nâmen Blanschefluoren
> und vuorten sî mit in zehant
> in Riwalînes herzen lant
> und crônden sî dar inne
> im z'einer küniginne" (806-12)

[This fired his spirit too, so that it returned and took Blancheflor and led her straightway into the land of his heart and crowned her there as his queen. (52)]

In the meantime the pain of love in his heart begins to oppress him, placing him into the same emotional state to which her riddle refers. His inner turmoil compels him to focus entirely upon the ambiguity of the visual and verbal signs he encounters, and the more he immerses himself in amorous notions the more he delivers himself over to the seduction:

iezuo wolt er benamen dan
und al zehant sô wolte er dar,
unz er sich alsô gâr verwar
in den stricken sîner trahte,
daz er dannen niene mahte. (836–40)

[At one moment he was off in one direction, then suddenly off in another, till he had so ensnared himself in the toils of his own desire that he was powerless to escape. (52)]

While the power of love shakes, churns, and agitates his heart, he is nonetheless completely and ineluctably of one mind with the idea that she loves him and vice versa. In a most significant sense, she has taught him to "read" signs in a new way, and the pedagogical process succeeds in both teaching and seducing Rivalin.

Here as in a number of other passages, through the narration of events in the tale of Tristan's parents, Gottfried prepares the reader for aspects of the lovers' situations and experiences.[16] Thus, when Tristan hears Isolde utter the phoneme "lameir," he begins to ponder the possibilities of the meaning, as his father had when Blancheflor presented her riddle to him. Love has already arisen in Tristan's breast, but since he is unsure of Isolde's disposition toward him he feels that he must proceed with his analysis.[17] One must keep in mind that, until this point, Tristan has succeeded again and again in his exploits through his mastery of strategic language. In virtually all previous situations where Tristan has felt endangered or where he has needed subterfuge to take an advantage, his eloquence in many tongues, his impressive good breeding, his knowledge of when to speak and when to remain silent, his stratagems have all been in the service of self and performed alone or with the aid of unwitting accomplices. Through language and the manipulation of signs Tristan has established and maintained his personal control

---

[16] See, for example, Alois Wolf, *Gottfried von Strassburg und die Mythe von Tristan und Isolde* (Darmstadt: Wissenschaftliche Buchgesellschaft, 1989), 111–22.

[17] Albrecht Classen refers to this as an epistemological event: "Isoldes Erklärung löst jedoch einen reflexiven Denkprozeß in ihm aus, der höchst bedeutungsvoll das nachfolgende Geschehen bestimmen wird;" see Albrecht Classen, "Sprache und Gesellschaft: kommunikative Strategien in Gottfrieds von Strassburg 'Tristan,'" *Europäische Literaturen im Mittelalter: Mélanges en l'honneur de Wolfgang Spiewok à l'occasion de son 65ème anniversaire*, ed. Danielle Buschinger. WODAN, 30, Serie 3, Tagungsbände und Sammelschriften, vol. 15; Greifswalder Beiträge zum Mittelalter, 15 (Greifswald: Reineke, 1994), 79–98; here 82.

over his experiences and surroundings, and thus he has exerted a great deal of power over others. Now this position of power and isolation is about to change.[18]

Before imbibing the potion Isolde has been more passive in relations with Tristan, having been his pupil in Ireland and having been tricked into her betrothal to Mark and her subsequent voyage to Cornwall. Now she becomes the active agent in their relationship. To his compassionate question she responds with her homonymic puzzle, which she leaves to Tristan to decipher. It is a provocation to him, since the complex meaning in the phoneme that Isolde utters reflects a verbal sophistication beyond even Tristan's immediate ken. Of course, one must be in possession of some linguistic dexterity to compose a simple "pun" between even two homonyms; but Tristan, along with the audience, must be surprised at the exponential increase in cleverness and erudition implied by the added layer of word-play. The reply Isolde gives is not merely certain, singular and easy, nor is it a lie.[19] Instead, it challenges the questioner to probe further into the matter. Like Blancheflor in her riddle, she permits the respondent to inject his own possibilities and choices and, in one sense, his own identity. The puzzle becomes a mutual project of desire, both sides longing for the correct completion and working together to achieve the result: the correct answer — the word of love, "lameir."

Beyond the linguistic complexity, however, is the provocative numeric significance of "three" that encompasses the riddle. In Gottfried's epic poem thus far, polar oppositions have been the order of the day — witness the prologue, in which *oxymora* set a tone of duality for the earlier sections of the work (e.g., "ir süeze sur, ir liebez leit" [60; its bitter sweet, its dear death {42}], or "sus lebet ir tôt" [238; thus lives their death {44}]). However, in the avowal scene Gottfried introduces several triads of various kinds that shift the mood of the text from "twoness" to "threeness." As we have seen, the formula of the riddle bears its significance as a triad:

Der Minnen vederspil Îsôt,
"lameir" sprach sî "daz ist mîn nôt,
lameir daz swæret mir den muot,
lameir ist, daz mir leide tuot." (11985–88).

---

[18] Ernst Dick ("Gottfried's Isolde: *Coincidentia Oppositorum?*" *Tristania* 12 [1987]: 15–24) also notes this change, although from a slightly different perspective: "This (perplexed Tristan) may not sound very much like the quick-witted Tristan of the earlier episodes, but it does underline the principle of multiple meanings, and its inherent connection with the figure of Isolde" (15).

[19] Classen ("Sprache und Gesellschaft," 81–82) asserts that "[Isolde] will aber ihr Geheimnis nicht verraten und bedient sich daher eines sprachlichen Rätsels, das Tristan zunächst nicht recht ergründen kann;" however, because she actually tells him the truth in such an extraordinary manner, and does not lie as she easily might have, it seems likely that her intention is instead communicative and seductive — she wishes to express to Tristan what is occurring within her and, one must speculate, to transport him amorously to the same level.

["*Lameir* is what distresses me," answered Love's falcon, Isolde, "it is *lameir* that so oppresses me, *lameir* it is that pains me so." (199)]

The image in the first line, Isolde as the falcon of *minne*, presents a standard metaphor of love familiar to all at court, that of the free and soaring, beautifully plumed, avian creature at home in the air and on the land, though not normally at sea.[20] Immediately thereafter follows Isolde's name and then her first usage of "lameir," which, as we know, represents "the sea," as well as "bitterness" and "love." In this central position, the name "Îsôt" provides a juncture for air, land and sea, the three realms that Gottfried combines in the metaphor of the falcon over the water. The amalgamation reflects a further quality of discomfort as well: the strangeness of a falcon in the unfamiliar space reflects the "bitterness" Isolde feels in her newly perceived state of psychological distress. The text in this section depends on the triadic qualities of the word-play to develop fully its multifaceted and interlinked metaphorical fields.

Furthermore, through the three repetitions of the anaphora "lameir," Isolde strongly suggests that Tristan remain open to many possibilities of meaning for unlocking the word-play's secrets. Clearly, with the introduction of the three significations a new potential for association comes into existence, not just "between two," but rather "among three," as, for example, in the triad established by the familial and romantic love shared by Marke, Isolde, and Tristan. Isolde's riddle demands that Tristan break out of old polarities of thought and seek out new and different possibilities. It therefore begins a pedagogical process for Tristan, drawing him into a new communicative and epistemological framework, teaching him how he and an "other," formerly separated by a subject-object duality, can become a new binary subject linked by "lameir."

Tristan's subsequent thoughts evince the beginnings of his psychological transformation. The text observes his process of thinking closely as he weighs each possibility before giving his own response to what Isolde has said, in much the same way Gottfried reports Rivalin's thoughts in response to Blancheflor's word-play. Tristan and Isolde's exchange here becomes perhaps the most important conversation of the epic, for it lays the groundwork for the deep intimacy of their relationship and their unique mode of communication. As Isolde reacts

---

[20] The image of the falcon in medieval literature, such as in the poetry of Der Kürenberger, as well as in Gottfried's *Tristan,* has received much critical attention: see, for example, Irmgard Reiser, "Falkenmotive in der deutschen Lyrik und verwandten Gattungen vom 12. bis zum 16. Jahrhundert," Ph.D. diss. Würzburg 1963, and Ingrid Bennewitz-Behr, "Von Falken, Trappen und Blaufüssen. Kein ornithologischer Beitrag zur Tradition des mittelhochdeutschen Falkenliedes beim Mönch von Salzburg und Heinrich von Mügeln," *Spectrum Medii Aevi: Essays in Early German Literature in Honor of George Fenwick Jones,* ed. William C. McDonald. Göppinger Arbeiten zur Germanistik, 362 (Göppingen: Kümmerle, 1983), 1–20.

to his inquiries about her meaning, Tristan runs through the possibilities in his mind: "lameir" might mean "sea," or "bitterness," or "love." He attempts an analysis by examining each connotation in isolation, as Gottfried describes the process: "er bedâhte unde besach / anclîchen unde cleine / des selben wortes meine" (11989–91; he weighed and examined the meaning of the word most narrowly [199]). The translation "narrowly" conflates two important adverbs, which in Gottfried's original provide a more specific sense: "anclîchen" and "cleine" point not only to Tristan's thoroughness but also to his impulse to split, divide, and segregate the meanings. He is surprised that the single sign "seemed to have a host of meanings" ("der meine der dûhte in ein her" [11996]) where Isolde uses only one phonetic sign. Perhaps it is in the nature of communication and epistemology at court, for example, that complex notions are simplified into more easily understood components, and that one concentrate on only one component at a time; but in the case of the lovers' communication too much is lost in the translation via analysis, dissection, and breaking down the components. Isolde must now give Tristan a lesson in the art of interpreting words of love while maintaining the integrity of the whole communication.

After completing his intellectual analysis, Tristan poses a question to Isolde:

"ich waene" sprach er "schoene Îsôt,
mer unde sûr sint iuwer nôt.
iu smecket mer unde wint.
ich waene, iu diu zwei bitter sint?" (12003–06)

[Surely, fair Isolde, the sharp smack of sea is the cause of your distress? The tang of the sea is too strong for you? Is this what you find so bitter? (199)]

Again, Hatto's translation ("smack" or "tang" of the sea) conflates terms, linking them with the preposition "of," whereas Gottfried seems to be consciously holding them apart without linkage, save for the conjunction "unde." The distinction is subtle, but important. Far more than Hatto makes apparent in his translation, Gottfried's phrasing of Tristan's words, "mer unde sur" and "mer unde wint," implies that these distinct and separate phenomena, by chance occurring simultaneously, are the source of Isolde's distress: 1) there is the sea ("mer") and 2) there is bitterness (implicit in "sur" and "wint"). Tristan's formulation of the question thus reduces the metaphor to two separate possibilities of its meanings, and disconnects them entirely from the third meaning, "love." With this discursive maneuver he is attempting to take control of her metaphor, to force her through his question to eliminate the other two possibilities of her word-play and to avow her love, her *minne*, for him. Isolde refuses to relinquish this control, and she corrects him:

> "nein, hêrre, nein! waz saget ir?
> der dewederez wirret mir,
> mirn smecket weder luft noch sê.
> lameir al eine tuot mir wê." (12007–10)

[No, my lord, no! What are you saying? Neither of them is troubling me, neither the sea nor its tang is too strong for me. It is *lameir* alone that pains me. (199)]

Traditionally this statement has been taken to be Isolde's confession of love to Tristan, followed by his avowal to her — in other words, that "lameir" is equal to "minne," and the word-play loses its combinatory character. But a careful reading of the text reveals another possibility that points in an entirely different direction. While Isolde's statement rejects the individual, separate meanings of "sea" and its "bitterness" as the cause of her inner turmoil, she nevertheless returns to the word-play and reiterates the phoneme "lameir" as the source of her anguish. The sign thus still contains three signified entities simultaneously, each conditioning the metaphorical value of the other, and therefore each part is still indispensable to the whole. Following this rendering of the signs and significations, the passage should be read in the following manner: it is not merely the sea by itself, nor is it the bitterness alone ("der dewederez wirret mir, / mirn smecket weder luft noch sê"), but rather all three in one ("lameir al eine tuot mir wê").[21] The manuscript renders "al eine" orthographically as two elements, perhaps suggesting that "all" and "one" inform the medieval German term for "alone" in this context, supporting a synthetic, rather than analytical, reading of this passage. Hence Isolde's response to Tristan's question seems most likely a subtle and clever exhortation to preserve the "all-in-one" signification of "lameir," in order to interpret it correctly. The lovers must simultaneously embrace all aspects of this phenomenon Isolde refers to as "lameir," since the fathomless sea, the bitterness, and their love are inextricable and resist any attempt to separate one from the other. If Tristan emphasizes one meaning at the expense of the other two, then that is not what Isolde means; hence, neither ("dewederez") the one in isolation not the other in

---

[21] Zotz, "Programmatische Vieldeutigkeit," 11, considers Gottfried the antithesis to Thomas on this point: in her opinion, Thomas seeks the truth in the right combination of the three, whereas Gottfried emphasizes Tristan's separation of the components and the rejection of the two incorrect elements. Similarly, Jantzen and Kröner, "Zum neugefundenen *Tristan*-Fragment ," 299, insist that "Isôt zwei mögliche Übersetzungen für *lameir* verwirft und nur noch die Bedeutung 'minne' übrigläßt." These points of view provide a completely different framing of this scene, giving Tristan the edge in forcing a confession of love from Isolde through his clever question. However, in my opinion, these critics do not fully appreciate Isolde's command of the discourse in this scene, her brilliantly ambiguous riddle, and the fact that her response to Tristan's second question — as to whether the bitterness of the wind on the sea is bothering her — is a repetition of the three-in-one "lameir," and specifically *not* the unambiguous word "minne."

isolation, but rather all three together. Only in this way can the word have a meaning for them.

At this juncture Isolde sheds her former role as Tristan's pupil of language and music[22] (her position, for example, during the "Tantris" episodes), and as an innocent but unwitting accomplice to Tristan's brilliant but self-serving stratagems (e.g., the part she plays in helping Tristan establish his claim as the dragon-slayer). Isolde now takes command of language and interpretation, and not only enables the couple to exercise power over their courtly environment,[23] but to a great degree she can now exercise dominance over Tristan for the first time, reversing their teacher / pupil relationship.[24] She provides instruction for him in how one reads metaphorical, ambivalent language in its entirety, without analyzing it by separating it into components and reducing it to more simple elements. She demonstrates how to perceive what she has said as a whole unit, incorporating all meanings simultaneously. She does not back away from her original statement, nor does she simply "confess" her love for Tristan (*he* will later be the first to speak of "minne," 12017). Instead through her response she challenges the reduction of her "words of love" to a merely intellectual process.

Gottfried expends a mere two lines in recording the inner transformation Tristan experiences at this instant: "dô er des wortes z'ende kam, / minne dar inne vernam" (12011–12). Critics have cited these lines as indications that Tristan discovers love exclusively at the "bottom of the word" (199), eliminating the other two significations in Isolde's word-play. If that were the case, then Isolde's elegant artifice would have very little point, and we might conclude that Tristan has learned nothing from the subtle but effective lesson that Isolde prepares for him. However, when one reads these lines in consonance with the lovers' epistemological method as the perception and incorporation of a developing and dynamic complex of multiple meanings, one senses a much different signification of "ende," that of completion rather than finality, and inclusion rather than omission. The "end" of the word is a communicative-epistemological experience, where the entire word, "*lameir*," has been fully articulated and correctly understood with all its meanings, subtleties and nuances. His previous question established the

---

[22] Linda M. Zaerr sketches Tristan's role as Isolde's tutor for music in her article in this volume, "Songs of Love and Love of Songs: Music and Magic in Medieval Romance."

[23] For Tristan and Isolde power becomes the ability to carry out clandestine *rendezvous* at their whim, and to manipulate the court's investigation into their adultery. Their means of wielding power are primarily communicative, narrative, and epistemological; see Christopher R. Clason, "Intoxicating Illusions and Potent Deceptions: Power, Epistemology and Narration in Gottfried's *Tristan*," *Tristania* 23 (2004): 1–15.

[24] The parallels between this situation and aspects of the medieval love affair of Abelard and Heloise are striking; see Albrecht Classen, "Abaelards *Historia Calamitatum*, der Briefwechsel mit Heloise und Gottfrieds von Straßburg *Tristan*: Historisch-biographische und fiktionale Schicksale: Eine Untersuchung zur Intertextualität im zwölften und dreizehnten Jahrhundert," *arcadia* 35 (2000): 225–53.

connotations "bitterness" and "the sea" in "lameir," but he had not yet come to the point of completion; now he finally arrives, through Isolde's prompting, and finds love therein as well.

Having learned his lesson, Tristan expresses what is on his mind in a whisper: he begins by reiterating Isolde's essential communication, "entriuwen, schoene, als ist ouch mir, / lameir und ir, ir sît min nôt" (12014–15; Faith, lovely woman ... so it is with me, *lameir* and you are what distress me [200]). Gottfried composes once more for the audience a finely crafted sequence of concepts and sounds[25] in these two lines. In his avowal, Tristan links himself with Isolde poetically in the rhyming pronouns "mir" and "ir" and their union through Isolde's phoneme, "lameir." As if to assure his new mentor that he has understood the lesson, Tristan adopts as his own her ambiguous term with its threefold meaning. There is no indication here that Isolde has succumbed to Tristan's superior rhetorical skills, as some critics have asserted;[26] quite the contrary, Tristan seems thoroughly seduced by Isolde's discourse, and he is eager to blurt out his passion, while Isolde remains calm, composed, and silent. Her pupil now quickly avows his love, couching his feelings in the commonplace discourse of love-sickness:

> herzefrouwe, liebe Îsôt,
> ir eine und iuwer minne
> ir habet mir mîne sinne
> gâr verkêret unde benomen
> ich bin ûzer wege komen
> sô starke und alsô sere:
> in erhol mich niemer mêre.
> mich müejet und mich swaeret,
> mir swachet unde unmaeret
> allez, daz mîn ouge siht.
> in al der werlde enist mir niht
> in mînem herzen lieb wan ir. (12016–27)

---

[25] Auditory and acoustic aspects of later medieval "words of love," as well as positions of power women often occupy in medieval lyric poetry, are explored in Albrecht Classen's contribution to this volume, "Love of Discourse and Discourse of Love in Middle High German *Minnesang*: The Case of the Post-Walther Generation in the Thirteenth Century." The poetry of Reinmar von Brennenberg is of particular interest with respect to his use of multiple meanings in order to explore complex emotional reflexes through language. For example, in commenting on Reinmar's use of the verb "meinen" in one of his poems, Classen states that "there are numerous possibilities to interpret the semantic field of 'meinen,' and the poet was obviously fully aware of the complexity of this term, which nicely corresponds to the intricate depth of love itself and his own emotional approach to this phenomenon... individual thirteenth-century poets had an excellent grasp of language and knew how to tease multiple meanings out of one word, hence to correlate love with language and to demonstrate the extent to which individual words of love could also, if not even necessarily so by their very essence, assume an hermeneutic function" (373–74).

[26] See Jantzen and Kröner, "Zum neugefundenen *Tristan*-Fragment."

[My dearest lady, sweet Isolde, you and you alone have turned my wit and robbed me of my reason! I have gone astray so utterly that I shall never find my way again! All that I see irks and oppresses me; it all grows trite and meaningless. Nothing in the wide world is dear to my heart but you. (200)]

Isolde has said much the same thing, more powerfully and more effectively, in one word. Thus, her final contribution to this communication with Tristan is brief and affirms what he has discovered: "herre, als sît ir mir" (12028; So you, sir, are to me [200]). The seduction is complete, and from this point onward the lovers' communication involves a complex process of signs and signification on several levels, which they share exclusively.[27]

This reading of the avowal scene accords with the concept of love as Gottfried develops it from the beginning of the text. The critical literature has attested copiously to the bitterness of love that Gottfried celebrates in the prologue of *Tristan* and the metaphorical values of the sea as a natural, mythic, and psychological space where the lovers are drawn together and where their love first takes seed. But can the ideal of clarity between lovers, which Gottfried also reiterates throughout the text, reconcile with a system of epistemology and communication that encourages ambiguity and multiple significations? Can one employ such language as "lameir" to convey the kind of love symbolized by the bed in the *minnegrotte* (love cave), as Gottfried describes it, "cristallîn, / durchsihtic und durchlûter" (16983–84; of crystal — transparent and translucent! [264])

From the previous reading of the avowal scene, Gottfried's epistemology of love seems to create its own means of perception and understanding. "Clarity," in the lovers' sense of the term, comes about through a communicative and epistemological process that compels them to reject purely cogitative practices such as analysis and reduction, and to understand complex, multiple levels of meaning simultaneously. Each lover is prepared for this particular kind of ambiguity when the other speaks. Other communicative relationships — such as those among the members of the court, for example — demand clarity for mutual understanding and the preservation of the extant power structures. However, it is noteworthy that Gottfried, in the eight instances where he employs various forms of the root "crystal," his symbol for durability, brightness, and clarity, makes only one reference to courtly concerns (6588, describing Tristan's helmet when he is preparing to do battle with the Morhold).[28] Furthermore, when Gottfried employs five variations of the root for "transparent," such as "durchliuhtec" (4902), "durchlûter"

---

[27] See Schnell, *Die Suche nach Wahrheit*, 175–79.
[28] For a complete listing of Gottfried's usage of these terms, see Melvin E. Falk, *Word-Index to Gottfried's* Tristan (Madison: University of Wisconsin Press, 1958), 39. See also Clifton D. Hall, *A Complete Concordance to Gottfried von Strassburg's Tristan* (Lewiston, Queenston, and Lampeter: The Edwin Mellen Press, 1992).

(11726, 16740, 16984), or "durchsichtic" (16984),[29] he invariably connects the quality to poetry or to the lovers, and noticeably not to the court.

The audience encounters one *locus* of the term "durchlûter" immediately preceding the avowal episode. It is of particular interest in the context of ambiguity and clarity, not only because it contributes to setting the following scene, but also because its use sheds crucial light on Gottfried's meaning of the term.

> Nu daz diu maget unde der man,
> Îsôt unde Tristan,
> den tranc getrunken beide, sâ
> was ouch der werlde unmuoze dâ,
> Minne, aller herzen lâgaerîn,
> und sleich z'ir beider herzen in.
> ê sî's ie wurden gewar,
> dô stiez s'ire sigevanen dar
> und zôch sie beide in ir gewalt.
> si wurden ein und einvalt,
> die zwei und zwîvalt wâren ê.
> si zwen enwâren dô niemê
> widerwertic under in.
> Îsôte haz der was dô hin.
> diu süenaerinne Minne
> diu haete ir beider sinne
> von haze gereinet,
> mit liebe alsô vereinet,
> daz ietweder dem anderm was
> durchlûter alse ein spiegelglas.
> sie haeten beide ein herze.
> ir swaere was sîn smerze,
> sîn smerze was ir swaere. (11707–29)

[Now when the maid and the man, Isolde and Tristan, had drunk the draught, in an instant that arch-disturber of tranquility was there, Love, waylayer of all hearts, and she had stolen in! Before they were aware of it she had planted her victorious standard in their two hearts and bowed them beneath her yoke. They who were two and divided now became one and united. No longer were they at variance: Isolde's hatred was gone. Love, the reconciler, had purged their hearts of enmity, and so joined them in affection that each was to the other as limpid as a mirror. They shared a single heart. Her anguish was his pain, his pain her anguish. (195)]

---

[29] Falk, *Word-Index*, 16.

Hatto's translation of "durchlûter" as "limpid," that is, as "clear and transparent" or "lucid," seems particularly appropriate in connection with communication and epistemology, yet the term's juxtaposition with "spiegelglas" ("mirror") is striking, since a mirror does not let light pass through but rather reflects back the subject's image. However, if one considers that love creates a single entity out of the two individuals, looking "into" one's lover is metaphorically comparable to looking into a mirror — one sees a reflection of oneself, as one is, immediate and genuine.[30] Communication between lovers, then, is a communion of hearts and minds, so that *intentio* becomes immediately decipherable — that is, crystal clear — through the discourse of love.[31] While this concept may be familiar in the literature of love, Gottfried's treatment of lovers' discourse as "transparent" and "mirroring" produces a memorable trope, the full meaning of which surpasses the significations of the concept's individual components in isolation.

---

[30] The mirror as a metaphor for spiritual reflection and self-recognition in medieval philosophy and art is discussed by Sabine Melchior-Bonnet, *The Mirror: A History,* trans. Katherine H. Jewett, pref. Jean Delumeau (New York and London: Routledge, 2001), 108–15; later (229–33) she also explores the mirror as metaphor for love, "the encounter with the self by way of alterity" (230).

[31] See Schnell, *Die Suche nach Wahrheit,* 13–56, who considers knowledge of a character's *intentio* as the most important factor in evaluating that character's psychology and behavior. Also, see Albrecht Classen, ed., *Discourses on Love, Marriage, and Transgression in Medieval and Early Modern Literature.* Medieval & Renaissance Texts & Studies, 278 (Tempe, AZ: Arizona Center for Medieval and Renaissance Studies, 2004).

CHAPTER 12

SONGS OF LOVE AND LOVE OF SONGS: MUSIC AND MAGIC IN MEDIEVAL ROMANCE

LINDA MARIE ZAERR
Boise State University, Idaho

Since the ideology of love was often transmitted through performance, music performance is vital to a study of premodern formulations of love. Medieval romances often contain metaperformance elements that illuminate attitudes to love and to performers of the songs and tales of love.[1] Performers represented in romances are not always professional musicians, and it is the protagonists themselves, the lovers, who exhibit the most intriguing patterns of music performance. In this context, the dangerous allure of music performance is sometimes entwined with seduction and magic or trickery, but the association is not always negative, especially early in the romance tradition. Later, when music and magic are explicitly linked they often signal destructive power, but either music or magic in isolation may be benign. By the late fourteenth century there is a tendency to isolate romance protagonists from magic and from any instrumental music but that of the harp, an instrument associated with the redemptive figures of David and

---

[1] Useful and detailed discussions of musical references in medieval French literature are provided by Christopher Page, "Music and Chivalric Fiction in France, 1150–1300," *Proceedings of the Royal Musical Association* 111 (1984–1985): 1–27; idem, *Voices and Instruments of the Middle Ages: Instrumental Practice and Songs in France 1100–1300* (1986; London: Dent, 1987; and Sylvia Huot, "Voices and Instruments in Medieval French Secular Music: On the Use of Literary Texts as Evidence for Performance Practice," *Musica Disciplina* 43 (1989): 63–113. Edmund A. Bowles, "Musical Instruments at the Medieval Banquet," *Revue Belge de Musicologie* 12 (1958): 41–51, also draws on literary texts, as does Edmond Faral, *Les jongleurs en France au moyen âge*. Bibliothèque de l'École des hautes études, Sciences historiques et philologiques, 187 (1910; Paris: Champion, 1971). Pierre Bec, *Vièles ou violes?: Variations philologiques et musicales autour des instruments à archet du moyen âge*. Collections Sapience (Paris: Editions Klincksieck, 1992), draws on a wide range of textual and iconographic sources in his discussion of the vielle.

Orpheus. We can thus trace an increasing distrust of the transformative power of music and magic when connected with words of love.

The mid-eleventh-century Latin *Ruodlieb* from Bavaria is often considered the earliest courtly romance, and it contains a hallmark of many later romances: a detailed description of the protagonist playing harp or vielle in a context deeply associated with love. Annoyed at the bad playing of the professional harper, Ruodlieb asks for another harp. His host supplies him with an excellent harp which her husband had played before he died, one, she adds, "Cuius clangore mea mens languescit amore" (11.32; through its music my thoughts languished from love).[2] Even this early in the romance tradition, the harp is here associated with passionate love.[3]

The poet describes Ruodlieb's performance in technical terms, and then states that the music has power to teach the parts of the body to dance. It possesses a quality that silences the professionals:

> Quam iubet afferri sibi, quam citat is moderari
> . . . . .
> Pulsans mox laeua digitis geminis, modo dextra
> Tangendo chordas dulces reddit nimis odas,
> Multum distincte faciens uariamina quaeque,
> Qu]od pede saltandi manibus neumas uel agendi
> Nescius omnino citus haec perdisceret ambo.
> Qui prius audacter chordas pulsant ioculanter,
> Auscultant illi taciti modulare nec ausi.
> (11.35–44)

> [He has that (harp) brought to him and hastens to tune it.
> (two lines missing)
> Plucking now with two fingers of the left, now with the right,
> by intoning chords, he renders very sweet songs,
> producing many variations with great clarity.
> He who was entirely unversed in moving his feet in a dance
> or in beating time with his hands, learned both of these things quickly.
> Who formerly had boldly struck the chords like gleemen,
> they listened silently and did not dare play.]

---

[2] All quotations and translations are from *Ruodlieb: The Earliest Courtly Novel (after 1050)*, ed. and trans. Edwin H. Zeydel. Studies in the Germanic Languages and Literatures, 23 (Chapel Hill: University of North Carolina Press, 1959).

[3] John Richardson, "*Niuwer David, Niuwer Orpheus*: Transformation and Metamorphosis in Gottfried von Strassburg's *Tristan*," *Tristania* 17 (1996): 85–109; here 89, points out that by this time there was a long secular tradition in which "David and Orpheus symbolized the ideal musician, poet, and lover and were also regarded as the embodiment of masculine beauty." Both figures were also consistently associated with the harp in both iconography and texts.

Songs of Love and Love of Songs

The poet goes on to narrate how Ruodlieb plays again, and this time his nephew dances with his host's daughter. Ruodlieb's music impels the dance, especially in the context of the previous passage, and this dance suddenly causes the two young people to burn with passion:

> Quem per sistema siue diastema dando responsa
> Dum mirabiliter operaretur ue decenter,
> Surrexit iuuenis, quo contra surgit herilis.
> Ille uelut falcho se girat et haec ut hirundo;
> Ast ubi conueniunt, citius se praeteriebant;
> I]s se mouisse, set cernitur illa natasse, /
> Neutrum saltasse neumas manibus uariasse
> Nemo corrigere quo posset, si uoluisset.
> Tunc signum dederant, ibi multi quod doluerunt,
> Deponendo manus, finitus sit quia rithmus.
> Insimul et resident et in alterutrum nimis ardent
> Lege maritali cupientes consociari. (11.48–59)

> [While he carries this out with runs and phrases
> in an admirable and decorous way, and performs the response,
> the young man arose and the young lady too.
> He turns in the manner of a falcon and she like a swallow.
> But when they came together, they passed one another again quickly;
> he seemed to move (glide) along, she to float.
> Neither in dancing nor in beating varied time with the hands
> could anyone improve upon them, had he wished to.
> Then they gave a signal by dropping their hands
> (which many there present bemoaned) that the dance was over.
> Together they sit down and are strongly aglow for one another,
> desiring to be united by the law of marriage.]

These elements resonate with many later romances, but the context complicates the episode. Immediately before this passage, at a lunch where the nephew and the girl eat from the same dish and cup (10.65), the companions are entertained by Ruodlieb's little dog, who performs various tricks and identifies a thief. This is followed by amusement with trained birds in cages that are being taught to sing. Music performance, by association with this other entertainment, becomes a kind of trickery to be marveled at. This trivialization of the episode is underscored by an earlier description of two performing bears dancing:

> Mimi quando fides digitis tangunt modulantes,
> Illi saltabant neumas pedibus uariabant;
> Interdum saliunt seseque superiaciebant,
> Alterutrum dorso se portabant residendo,

Amplexando se luctando deiciunt se;
Cum plebs altisonam fecit girando choream,
Accurrunt et se mulieribus applicuere,
Quae gracili uoce cecinerunt deliciose,
Inser]tisque suis harum manibus speciosis
Erecti calcant pedetemptim, murmure trinsant,
Vt mirarentur, bibi circum qui graderentur,
Non irascantur, quodcunque mali paterentur. (5.84–98)

[When mimes touch the strings with their fingers and play,
they (the bears) danced and varied the music with their paws.
Sometimes they leap and turned somersaults
and sit down and carry each other on their backs,
and embrace and wrestle and throw each other on the ground.
As soon as the people have started a round dance with song and gyrations,
they run up and join the women,
who sang with gentle voices and pleasingly,
and they join their paws with the delicate hands of the women.
In an upright position they move step by step and growl and bellow,
so that those who are taking their steps and making their turns are amazed.
Nor are the people angry, no matter what evil they suffer.]

In this early romance, love, magical animals, and entertainment are all light features to be marveled at, and the romance breaks off before Ruodlieb himself is seriously involved in love.

The idea that music or story performance could evoke love is frequently expressed in thirteenth-century French romances.[4] *Le Bel Inconnu*, for example, is

---

[4] Song performance and romance performance are not always clearly distinguished in medieval romance texts. In *Flamenca*, for example, the minstrel performance lumps together "violadura," "canzo," "descort," and "lais," and all are apparently presented musically.

Qui saup novella violadura,
ni canzo ni descort ni lais,
al plus que poc avan si trais.
L'uns viola<.l> lais del Cabrefoil,
e l'autre cel de Tintagoil;
l'us cantet cel dels Fins Amanz,
e l'autre cel que fes Ivans.
L'us menet arpa, l'autre viula;
l'us flaütella, l'autre siula;
l'us mena giga, l'autre rota;
l'us diz los motz e l'autre.ls nota;   (600–610)

[Whoever knew a new piece for the [vielle],
a song, a descort, or lay,
he pressed forward as much as he could.
One played the lay of the Honeysuckle,

structured as a narrative song designed to win the love of a lady.[5] The poem ends with an implication that if the lady will show him a gracious countenance ("un biau sanblant mostrer" [6255]), the narrator can make the story turn out happily. Performance and love thus influence one another.

In the epilogue to *Le Roman du Castelain de Couci et de La Dame de Fayel*, too, the author indicates that he has hidden his name in an "engien" (8252).[6] When his lady solves the puzzle, he hopes to be "bien guerredonné" (8259). The whole romance, as a performance, becomes a kind of game or trick revolving around love. Within the romance, songs are also consistently linked with love. The lady is first moved to love when she hears a song Renaut has written for her. Renaut marks the progress of their love by songs which express grief or joy, and his last act before death is to compose a song.

There is no indication that Renaut ever presents his songs directly to his lady. In the one instance where transmission is specified, a minstrel sings the song to the lady. While performance by a messenger of a song designed to elicit love is not universal, it is a common feature in romances. In the thirteenth-century romance *Sone de Nausey*, Papegais performs a song with harp on behalf of her lady. Before she begins, she states that the lai is made up entirely of truths, and that these truths about love are the cause of their coming:

> another the one of Tintagel;
> one sang of the Noble Lovers,
> and another which Yvain composed.
> One played the harp; another the viol;
> another, the flute; another, a fife;
> one played a rebeck; another, a rote;
> one sang the words; another played notes]

The Romance of Flamenca, ed. and trans. E. D. Blodgett. Garland Library of Medieval Literature, 101 A (New York: Garland, 1995). Later in the passage, some of the narratives are mentioned, including a number of romances with which we are familiar.

[5] The romance begins:
Cele qui m'a en sa baillie,
cui ja d'amors sans trecerie
m'a doné sens de cançon faire —
por li veul un roumant estraire
d'un molt biel conte d'aventure.
(1–5)

[For her who holds me in her dominion, who has given me understanding to make a song about love without falsehood, for her I want to construct a romance from a beautiful tale of adventure.]

All passages from this text are quoted from Renaut de Bâgé, *Le Bel Inconnu (Li Biaus Descouneüs; The Fair Unknown)*, ed. Karen Louise Fresco, trans. Colleen P. Donagher. Garland Library of Medieval Literature, 77 (New York: Garland, 1992).

[6] *Le Roman du Castelain de Couci et de La Dame de Fayel par Jakemes*, ed. John E. Matzke and Maurice Delbouille (Paris: Société des Anciens Textes Français, 1936).

> Et quant ot la harpe saisie,
> Au roi est errant repairie,
> Se li dist: 'Sire, .I. lai orres
> Qui tous est fais de verités.
> Ensi est ma dame avenu,
> Pour quoi nous sommes chi venu.'[7] (15971–76)

[And when she had taken the harp, she returned quickly to the king and said, "Sire, you will hear a lai which is composed entirely of truths. Thus it happened to my lady, and for this reason we have come here."]

The song, which is 153 lines long, is quoted in full. Her listeners pay careful attention and respond with tears and weeping specifically for the reason that "on set bien que c'est vretés" (16148), they know well that it is true. Her song is valued for being true about love, and she wins the prize based on the "verités" of her performance (16198). The song performance eventually brings about the union of the lovers.

This emphasis on truth in song performance is a key element in the romance motif of the courtly protagonist disguised or brought up as a jongleur.[8] Here, ironically, trickery or deception in the form of a disguise is in some way subverted by a musical performance which reveals some truth about the protagonist. In *Daurel et Beton*, the young nobleman Beton is brought up as a jongleur by Daurel, but Beton's demeanor causes others to suspect he must be noble. His music performance for the princess he is later to marry reveals him to be a nobleman, not because of the content or quality of his performance, but because he refuses to accept money, whereas any true jongleur would accept payment.

The passage is important in initially linking Beton with the princess who is the direct audience of the performance, but it also reveals an important difference in motivation between the courtly amateur performer and the professional minstrel. The passage emphasizes how much Beton enjoys himself when he performs music:

> 'De bels verses sai, dona, vueilh que n'aujatz.'
> E dit sos verses e fon ben escoltatz;
> Lo rei l'auzi que l'era amagatz
> Entorn la cambra e.il reïna delatz,
> Et ab lor so .c. cavaliers prezatz.
> Que tuh escolto cossi s'es deportatz.
> Una gran pessa s'es laïns deportatz,

---

[7] *Sone von Nausay*, ed. Moritz Goldschmidt. Bibliothek des Litterarischen Vereins in Stuttgart, 216 (Tübingen: Litterarischer Verein in Stuttgart, 1899).

[8] Page, *Voices and Instruments*, 158, identifies this feature in his typology of musical references in French narrative fiction.

Cana e vihola, es se fort alegratz.⁹
(1498–1505)

["I know some lovely verses, lady, and I would like for you to hear them." He sang his verses, and she listened well. The king, who was hidden in the chamber, heard him, and the lovely queen, and a hundred excellent knights with them. They all heard how much he was enjoying himself. He remained there for a long time disporting himself. He sings and plays vielle and enjoys himself very much.]

The terminology describing Beton's enjoyment of music might equally describe enjoyment of love. There is a quality of authenticity in Beton's performance and his interaction with the princess which is very different from that of a professional earning his living. Daurel recognizes this when he advises Beton to become skilled in instrumental music, not to earn money, but because it will help him to achieve happiness (1414–15). When a courtly amateur performs in a romance, there is a directness, a truth that comes through clearly even when the performer is disguised.

In *Galeran de Bretagne*, this clarity allows Fresne to reveal herself to her lover through the agency of a song he has previously taught her. Though this early thirteenth-century romance is clearly based on Marie de France's "Lai le Fresne," *Galeran* is developed in greater detail, focusing more equally on the two lovers. A key transformation from Marie's version is the development of the two protagonists as musicians and the structural role music plays in their final union.

Before the lovers have parted, Galeran tells Fresne he has composed a new lai which he would like to teach her. He refers to it as a "deduit," a light amusement or pleasant story, a labor, not of love, but of ingenuity:

Fresne, fait il, j'ay esprouvé
Mon engin a un novel lay,
Si desir moult que sans delay
Tout le deduit vous en apreigne.¹⁰
(2278–81)

["Fresne," he said, "I have tried out my ingenuity with a new lai, and I am eager to teach you the whole tale without delay."]

---

⁹ *A Critical Edition of the Old Provençal Epic Daurel et Beton*, ed. Arthur S. Kimmel. University of North Carolina. Studies in the Romance Languages and Literatures, 108 (Chapel Hill: University of North Carolina Press, 1971).

¹⁰ *Jean Renart: Galeran de Bretagne, roman du XIIIe siècle*, ed. Lucien Foulet. Les classiques français du moyen âge, 37 (Paris: Champion, 1925).

Fresne suggests that he begin the lai, and then she will learn it on her harp ("Mais commenciez je herperay / Et en ma harpe l'aprenray" [2295–96]). She learns the piece by listening to his singing, but also by watching his fingers on the harp, including the preliminary tuning which forms a part of lai performance in a number of romances:

> Il commence, celle l'escoute,
> Qu'en la harpe ses doiz i boute.
> Quant les notes a entendues
> Au pletron les a estendues,
> Et atrempee a droit point.
> (2297–301)

> [He begins, and she listens, paying attention to how his fingers strike the harp. When he has listened to the pitches, he tunes them up with a tuning key so that they are tuned perfectly.]

The lai is a song in praise of love, telling how love is full of adversity but culminates in joy. Galeran sings and plays it until Fresne knows both the melody and the words, a distinction specified several times, both parts being integral to "knowing" the lai, and both learned simultaneously:

> Doulx est li chans et doulx li diz,
> Et cil li chante tant et note
> Qu'elle scet le dit et la note;
> A sa harpe l'a accordee
> Qui estoit d'argent encordee.
> Bien scet le lay tout sans mentir,
> (2316–21)

> [Sweet is the melody and sweet are the words, and he sings and plays the lai until she knows both the words and the melody. Then she tunes her harp, strung with silver, to accord with the lai. To tell the truth, she knows the lai very well.]

This episode lays the groundwork for the culmination of the romance. When Galeran is about to marry Fresne's twin sister, Fresne gains admission to the wedding feast disguised as a jongleur, with her harp hanging from her neck and carrying her cushion. When she arrives, she immediately sings a song of her own composition, a song which expresses directly and honestly her own situation, not a song about others (such as the real jongleurs sing), but an authentic song about her own situation with respect to love:

"Je voiz aux noces mon amy :
Plus dolente de moy n'y va!"
Ceste note premiers trova
Fresne, qui de chanter se peine.
(6976–79)

["At the wedding feast I see my lover. No one alive can be more grief-stricken than I!" Fresne, who put all her efforts into singing, composed this piece.]

The other minstrels immediately stop playing. All their musical technique is worth as little compared to her harp playing as the voice of a wolf compared to a vielle.[11] It is her genuineness that shames the professionals.

Fresne amazes and moves all her audience, including Galeran, with her playing and singing, but his final recognition of her comes when she plays the song he has taught her:

Par un doulx lay le desconforte;
Les autres laiz, celuy a pris
Que Galeren li a apris.
El dit ne mesprent n'en la note :
De Galeren le Breton note.
Si l'escoutent toutes et tuit;
Des moz n'entent nulz le deduit
Fors que dui; mais li chans est doulx,
Si les fait entendre a li tous.
(6996–7004)

[Then she saddens him with a sweet lai. She leaves aside the other [lais] and takes up the one which Galeran had taught her. She performs the song and does not mangle it, the piece by Galeran the Breton. Thus they listen to her, each and every one. Of the words, only two understand the delight, but the song is sweet, and is causes everyone to listen to her.]

Fresne is revealed more clearly in her disguise than if she had come as herself, but only to her lover. Like Beton, she sings a song uniquely grounded in her own love, and the story of the song (of adversity in love followed by joy) is very much the story

---

11   Car tous leurs sons et leur maniere
        Vallent vers la harpe aussi peu
        Com vers vïelle voix de leu;
        (6984–86)

[For all their music and their technique was worth as little compared to the harp as the voice of a wolf compared to a vielle.]

of this romance. In medieval romance, a protagonist may most effectively express her own identity and be recognized by her lover in the guise of a jongleur.

This aspect is particularly evident in the *Roman de Horn*, probably composed ca. 1170. Christopher Page acknowledges that "there is nothing new about the figure of the amateur string-player in royal society," but he suggests that what is new in this romance is "the tacit but unmistakable admission ... that refined love is the passion which music most readily stimulates and feeds."[12] He makes this comment in connection with the famous detailed account of a lai performance, but what is particularly interesting in this account is not simply the way in which Horn's love is revealed in his music performance, but the way his performance of music strips away his disguise. Others do not notice the revelation, but Horn is reminded of himself and becomes more himself after his performance. Immediately after this episode, he turns down an offer of marriage to the Irish princess Lenburc and sets off to rescue his beloved Rigmel from an unwanted marriage.

In this section of the romance, Horn is living in disguise in Ireland. One day a small group of courtiers are entertaining themselves, and the princess Lenburc sings several pieces with harp. She comments that she has heard a magnificent lai, but she knows only half and would give a great deal to learn the rest. She explains that Baltof from Brittany composed it for his sister, the beautiful Rigmel. Lenburc goes on to explain that she has heard of Rigmel and of the great love between Horn and Rigmel:

> 'Oïl,' coe dit Lenburc, 'tut m'est bien recunté.
> Baltof, [le] fiz Hunlaf, rei de nobilité,
> Ki en Bretaigne maint, kar çoe est s(a)'herité,
> Le fist de sa sorur, Rimel od grant beauté.
> Mut en avez oï parler en cest regné
> E de l'amur de Horn ke ele ad taunt amé —
> Si ad dreit, kar n'est hom qui taunt eit de bunté,
> Cum cil Horn ad en sei; bien m'a esté nuncié.'[13]
> (2791–98)

["Listen," said Lenburc, "the whole thing was thoroughly recounted to me. Baltof (the son of the noble King Hunlaf) who maintained his inheritance in Brittany, composed it [the lai] about his sister, the very beautiful Rigmel. I have heard quite a bit about her in this country and about the love of Horn, whom she loved so much — as she ought to have, since there was never a man who had so much nobility as this Horn. I heard about it in detail.]

---

[12] Page, *Voices and Instruments*, 5.
[13] *The Romance of Horn by Thomas*, ed. Mildred Pope, 2 vols. Anglo-Norman Text Society, IX–X and XII–XIII (Oxford: Blackwell, 1955 and 1964).

Ironically unaware of Horn's true identity, Lenburc has nonetheless reminded him of that identity and linked him in love with Rigmel through her characterization of the lai. It is significant that she knows only half of the lai. Like Rigmel, she loves Horn, but her limitation in music performance symbolizes her incapacity for the kind of love relationship implied by the lai.

The text of the lai is not addressed anywhere. Rather, the description focuses on the technical virtuosity of Horn's performance, a skill which causes others to love him:

> Lors prent la harpe a sei, qu'il la veut atemprer.
> Deus! ki dunc l'esgardast cum la sout manïer,
> Cum ces cordes tuchout, cum les feseit trembler,
> Asquantes feiz chanter asquantes organer,
> De l'armonie del ciel li poüst remembrer!
> Sur tuz homes k'i sunt fet cist a merveiller.
> Quant ses notes ot fait si la prent a munter
> E tut par autres tuns les cordes fait soner:
> Mut se merveillent tuit qu'il la sout si bailler.
> E quant li out (is)si fait, si cummence a noter
> Le lai dunt or ains dis, de Baltof, haut e cler,
> Si cum sunt cil bretun d'itiel fait costumier.
> Apres en l'estrument fet les cordes suner,
> Tut issi cum en voiz l'aveit did tut premier:
> Tut le lai lur ad fait, n'i vout rien retailler.
> E deus! cum li oianz le porent dunc amer!
> (2830–45)

[Then he took the harp to himself to tune it. Heavens! whoever saw him as he handled it, how he touched those strings and made them sound, sometimes in a tune, sometimes together, might remember the harmony of the spheres. He did things to be marvelled at of all men. When he had set his strings, he took up the harp and made the strings sound in other tones. All wondered much that he knew this so well. And when he had done this, he began to sing loud and clear the *lai* which was once told of Baltof that the Bretons are used to tell. Afterwards, he made the strings of the instrument sound as his voice had sung before. He performed for them the whole *lai* and omitted none of it. Heavens! how those that heard could love him!][14]

As we might expect, Horn's companions are astonished by the performance, and Lenburc immediately requests to have Horn teach her the lai, having fallen

---

[14] This celebrated description of a lai performance is very technical, and translations vary widely. This translation is from *Medieval English Songs*, ed. E. J. Dobson and Frank L. Harrison (London and Boston: Farber and Farber, 1979), 87.

passionately in love with him as a result of the performance. Horn's performance has simultaneously put him back in touch with his own identity and love while it has deepened the consequences of his deception by stimulating a love response to an identity that is not his own. In this passage, music performance by a protagonist serves both to clarify truth about love and to seduce through deception.

Tristan is the quintessential courtly amateur disguised as a minstrel, a role best explored in Gottfried von Strassburg's early thirteenth-century version of the story (ca. 1210), which is the first full version of the early part of the legend and the account that provides the fullest thematic development of music. In this account, Tristan twice disguises himself as a professional minstrel, and in both cases the disguise highlights an affiliation of music with trickery. The first time, seeking healing in Ireland, he describes his performance skills in these terms:

> ich was ein höfscher spilman
> und kunde genuoge
> höfscheit unde vuoge.
> sprechen unde swîgen,
> lîren unde gîgen,
> harpfen unde rotten,
> schimpfen unde spotten,
> daz kunde ich allez alsô wol,
> als sô getân liut von rehte sol.[15] (7560–68)

> [I was a court minstrel and was master of many accomplishments and courtly ways, such as talking and letting others talk, playing the lyre, fiddle, harp, and crowd, and jesting and joking. I was well versed in it all as such folk have to be.][16]

The description includes several instruments, yet in the story we see him playing only harp. Earlier in Cornwall, he has already revealed his musical skill to Mark with his harp playing, though there too he claims skill in other instruments

---

[15] *Gottfried von Strassburg: Tristan*, nach dem Text von Friedrich Ranke neu herausgegeben, ins Neuhochdeutsche übersetzt, mit einem Stellenkommentar und einem Nachwort von Rüdiger Krohn, 3vols. (Stuttgart: Reclam, 1980); for the most recent developments in research on Gottfried's romance, see *Der "Tristan" Gottfrieds von Straßburg: Symposion Santiago de Compostela, 5. bis 8. April 2000*, ed. Christoph Huber and Victor Millet (Tübingen: Niemeyer, 2002). See also Gottfried von Straßburg, *Tristan*. Vol. 1: *Text*, ed. Karl Marold. Unveränderter fünfter Abdruck nach dem dritten, mit einem auf Grund von Friedrich Rankes Kollationen verbesserten kritischen Apparat besorgt und mit einem erweiterten Nachwort versehen von Werner Schröder. Vol. 2: *Übersetzung* von Peter Knecht. Mit einer Einleitung von Tomas Tomasek (Berlin and New York: de Gruyter, 2004).

[16] Translations of this text are from *Gottfried von Strassburg: Tristan*, trans. A. T. Hatto (Harmondsworth, Middlesex: Penguin, 1960).

(3675–82).[17] It is typical of romance protagonists that in the story they are seen playing either harp or vielle, however many other instruments they may know.[18]

The harp, in fact, becomes emblematic of Tristan even when he uses it to disguise his identity. The harp is the instrument most closely associated with both the classical Orpheus and the Biblical David. Hannes Kästner has demonstrated that Gottfried's Tristan represents a new model for the heroic figure based on strong parallels with Orpheus and David, both of whom embody the "Bann- und Zauberkraft der Musik" (spell power and magic power of music).[19] John Richardson suggests that Gottfried reinvents the Orpheus/David figure in the secular terms of a religion of love,[20] and Anna Sziráky goes even further in linking *Minne* and music in Gottfried's poem, discussing a system of musically-directed code in *Tristan*.[21] In all discussions, Tristan's harp playing is linked with transformative power and with love.

As a minstrel in Ireland, Tristan instructs Isolde so well in music and deportment that she gains remarkable ability to charm. At this point, however, there is no mention of love on the part of either Tristan or Isolde. The hero's fine performance on harp and subsequent instruction of the heroine serve as a prelude to love, but the harp playing itself and the instruction in music do not directly bring about love. Interactions in the realm of love are expressed metaphorically through music before they appear in the plot.

Tristan's appearance to Isolde and her family as a minstrel, however, further functions as a metaphorical expression of another characteristic of his association with Isolde: deception. Even as his music reveals him to Isolde throughout the romance, it functions also to deceive others, to trick them. It is in the guise of a minstrel that Tristan wins the right to Isolde in Ireland, pretending that he has other goals. His deception of others as a minstrel foreshadows the ongoing deception surrounding his love with Isolde.

---

[17] A survey of instruments referred to in this romance is provided by Ian F. Finlay, "Musical Instruments in Gotfrid von Strassburg's 'Tristan und Isolde'," *Galpin Society Journal* 5 (1952): 39–43; see also Martin van Schaik, "Musik, Aufführungspraxis und Instrumente im Tristan-Roman Gottfrieds von Straßburg," Lambertus Okken, *Kommentar zum Tristan-Roman Gottfrieds von Strassburg*. Amsterdamer Publikationen zur Sprache und Literatur, 58 (Amsterdam: Editions Rodopi, 1985), 163–224; Peter K. Stein, "Die Musik in Gottfrieds von Strassburg *Tristan* — Ihre Bedeutung im epischen Gefüge," idem, *Tristan-Studien*, ed. Ingrid Bennewitz (1979; Stuttgart: S. Hirzel, 2001), 323–98.

[18] The patterns reflected in the choice of harp or vielle in medieval romance are fascinating, but perhaps best explored in another context.

[19] Hannes Kästner, *Harfe und Schwert: Der höfische Spielmann bei Gottfried von Straßburg*. Untersuchungen zur deutschen Literaturgeschichte, 30 (Tübingen: Max Niemeyer Verlag, 1981), 77.

[20] Richardson, "*Niuwer David, Niuwer Orpheus.*"

[21] Anna Sziráky, *Éros Lógos Musiké: Gottfrieds 'Tristan' oder eine utopische renovatio der Dichtersprache und der Welt aus dem Geiste der Minne und Musik?* Wiener Arbeiten zur germanischen Altertumskunde und Philologie, 38 (Bern, Berlin, et al.: Peter Lang, 2003); her work, however, suffers from an excessively esoteric and fanciful approach to her topic, see the review by Albrecht Classen, *Tristania* XXII (2003): 114–19.

This association of his minstrel role with trickery is underscored in the episode of the harp and the rote, Tristan's second appearance in a minstrel disguise. Jennifer Looper, building on the work of Thérèse Saint-Paul,[22] usefully discusses the two instrument choices in this episode and the difference implied between the two musicians.[23] But the carefully limned similarity between the two figures is equally striking, and the structure of the incident stresses the similarity. Both Gandin and Tristan use musical performance to win Isolde by trickery. Both perform lais ("leich," 13198, 13321, 13326, etc.), stories of love, and Gandin even requests Tristan to play "den leich von Dîdône" (the lai of Dido [13347]). Both play only after knowing their payment.[24] At the end of the episode, Tristan comments explicitly on the parallel between himself and Gandin in a speech filled with terms of trickery and deception:

"nein nein" sprach Tristan "gouch Gandîn!
vriunt, ir stât an des gouches zil.
wan daz ir mit dem rottenspil
dem künege Marke ertruget an,
daz vüere ich mit der harpfen dan.
ir truget, nu sît ouch ir betrogen.
Tristan der hât iu nâch gezogen,
biz daz er iuch beswichen hât."
(13412–19)

["You are wrong," retorted Tristan. "You are the fool, Gandin! You are the one who has been fooled! Since what you tricked from Mark with your rote, I now take away with my harp! Deceiver that you are, you have now been duped in return. Tristan followed after you till now he has outwitted you!"]

Just before Gottfried's poem breaks off, Tristan again uses song to win a woman deceitfully. In Arundel, when Tristan sings of his love for Isolde people naturally assume he means Isolde of the White Hands, the only Isolde they know. Gottfried states that the song is a key element in Tristan's duplicity:

---

[22] Thérèse Saint-Paul, "La 'Harpe et la Rote' dans le Sir Tristrem," *"Musique, littérature et société au Moyen Âge": Actes du Colloque 14–19 mars 1980*, ed. Danielle Buschinger and André Crépin (Paris: H. Champion, 1980), 467–80.

[23] Jennifer Looper, "L'épisode de la Harpe et de la Rote dans la légende de Tristan: Étude sur le symbolisme de deux instruments de musique," *Cahiers de civilisation médiévale* 38.4 (1995): 345–52.

[24] When Mark asks him to play, Gandin replies, "hêrre, ine wil, / ine wizze danne umbe waz" (Sire, I will not, unless first I know my reward [13190–91]). He agrees to the promise of anything he wants with the binding phrase "Diz sî" (13197). When Tristan, disguised as an Irish minstrel, approaches Gandin, he requests passage to Ireland. When Gandin offers him the finest clothes in the pavilion if he will play, Tristan responds similarly: "deist getan" (At your service [13356]).

und al der trügeheite,
die Tristan an si leite,
sô was ie daz diu volleist,
diu ir herze allermeist
an Tristandes liebe twanc,
daz er daz alsô gerne sanc:
"Îsôt ma drûe, Îsôt m'amie,
en vûs ma mort, en vûs ma vie!"
daz lockete ir herze allez dar.
daz was, daz ir die liebe bar.
(19403-12)

[But of all the duplicity to which Tristan subjected her the crowning deed that compelled her to love him was that he liked to sing: *Isot ma drue, Isot mamie, en vus ma mort, en vus ma vie!* This kept luring her heart toward him, this it was that engendered her affection.]

The trickery accomplished by music in this passage is not far removed from magic. In discussing the symbolic rôle of music in Gottfried's *Tristan*, Danielle Buschinger points to an association of music with magic:

Le thème de la musique qui à l'origine était peut-être un thème magique, le résidu d'un mythe faisant allusion à la puissance magique du chant, de la musique qui permet comme dans le mythe d'Orphée d'entrer en communication avec l'Autre monde, est présent dans toute la tradition.[25]

[The theme of music, which at its origin was perhaps a magic theme, the residue of a myth making allusion to the magical power of song, of music which permits one, as in the myth of Orpheus, to enter into communication with the Other World, is present in the entire tradition.]

This association between music and magic is alluded to in Gottfried's text. Before the second excursion to Ireland, Mark's courtiers suggest that Tristan is a "zouberaere," a magician:

si begunden vil swinde
reden ze sînen dingen
und in ze maere bringen,
er waere ein zouberaere.
diu vorderen maere,

---

[25] Danielle Buschinger, "La musique dans le Tristan de Thomas et le Tristan de Gottfried: Quelques jalons," *"Musique, littérature et société au Moyen Âge"*, 171–85; here 182; cf. also Gary Tomlinson, *Music in Renaissance Magic: Toward a Historiography of Others* (Chicago: University of Chicago Press, 1993).

> wie er ir vînt Môrolden sluoc,
> wie sich sîn dinc z'Îrlant getruoc,
> des begunden s'under in dô jehen,
> ez waere ûz zoubere geschehen.
> (8328–36)

[They began to run him down and hint that he was a sorcerer. His past deeds — how he had slain their enemy Morold, how his affair had passed off in Ireland — had been done by recourse to witchcraft, so they began to declare to one another.]

Gottfried's audience is aware that Tristan has accomplished his success in Ireland by means of music, by the compelling and deceptive power of music.[26] Certainly any pejorative implications are minimized in this text, but it is significant that later in the story Isolde destroys the power of Petitcreiu's little magical bell, a bell which unites the power of music and magic and is linked with deception. The bell, itself a musical instrument, has been transported by a minstrel in a musical instrument, and it is explicitly magical in its capacity to remove sorrow, a power Isolde views as deceptive. Isolde turns away from the relief she could gain from this union of music and magic by destroying the magical component of the bell.[27]

The existence of two Isoldes in Ireland is an indication of how carefully Gottfried avoids too close a link between music and magic in his protagonists. We hear of the beauty of the mother and the daughter, and yet their functions are kept very distinct. While the mother is attracted to Tristan's music and employs him, we do not ever see her playing music or singing. Only the daughter plays music and sings in this account. The mother, on the other hand, is the only character in the tale who actually employs magic:

> Îsôt diu wîse künigîn
> in ein glasevezzelîn
> einen tranc von minnen,
> mit alsô cleinen sinnen
> ûf geleit und vor bedâht,

---

[26] W. T. H. Jackson, "Tristan the Artist in Gottfried's Poem," *Tristan and Isolde: A Casebook*, ed. Joan Tasker Grimbert (1995; New York and London: Routledge, 2002), 125–46; here 125, views *Tristan* in a Christian, and more specifically Boethian, context in which Gottfried sees "the arts, and in particular music, as beneficial for Christian men and women and as leading towards that harmony of the spirit with the eternal which was regarded as the highest good." Hugo Bekker, *Gottfried von Strassburg's* Tristan: *Journey through the Realm of Eros*. Studies in German Literature, Linguistics and Culture, 29 (Columbia, SC: Camden House, 1987), 195, similarly describes the poem in Boethian terms, suggesting that musicians take precedence with Isolde in the realm of Eros.

[27] Albrecht Classen, "Gottfried von Straßburg's *Tristan*, the Eternal Bread, and Love," *Tristania* XXIII (2004): 91–105; here 99, points out how this incident exemplifies "Isolde's courage and deep understanding of the true nature of love."

mit solher crefte vollebrâht:
mit sweme sîn ieman getranc,
den muose er âne sînen danc
vor allen dingen meinen
und er dâ wider in einen.
(11433–42)

[Isolde, the prudent Queen, was brewing in a vial a love-drink so subtly devised and prepared, and endowed with such powers, that with whomever any man drank it he had to love her above all things, whether he wished it or no, and she love him alone.]

The love potion compels love in the same way that music does in some of the contemporary romances.

Drawing on parallels with *Tristan* and the *Roman de Horn*, Christopher Page suggests that the origin of the hero-harpist motif may lie in the fifth-century Latin *Historia Apollonii Regis Tyri*.[28] In this story, the daughter of King Archistrates plays the lyre and sings to cheer the shipwrecked Apollonius: "dulcedine vocis chordarum sonos, melos cum voce miscebat" (she mingled the sound of the strings with her very sweet voice, tune with song).[29] Everyone praises her: "Non potest esse melius, non potest dulcius plus isto, quod audivimus!" (Nothing could be better, nothing could be sweeter than this which we have heard). Only Apollonius remains silent. When the king asks why, he replies that her musical abilities are limited, and if they will pass him the lyre he will demonstrate. His performance is described briefly and in terms similar to the previous description: "Miscetur vox cantu modulata chordis" (In the song his voice blended harmoniously with the strings). The response of the courtiers is almost identical to their previous response: "Non potest melius, non potest dulcius!" (Nothing could be better, nothing could be sweeter!) Their response may not distinguish between the two performances, but the daughter of the king falls in love.

Inter haec filia regis, ut vidit iuvenem omnium artium studiorumque esse cumulatum, vulneris saevo carpitur igne. Incidit in amorem infinitum.

[Meanwhile, when the princess saw that the young man was full of every kind of talent and learning, she was wounded by a fiercely burning passion, and fell very deeply in love.]

---

[28] Page, *Voices and Instruments*, 103–05.
[29] Text and translations throughout are from Elizabeth Archibald, *Apollonius of Tyre: Medieval and Renaissance Themes and Variations. Including the text of the Historia Apollonii Regis Tyri with an English Translation* (Cambridge: D.S. Brewer, 1991); passages in this paragraph are on 128–29.

Although not developed in detail, the key elements in the motif are already here. Music is capable of inspiring love without any recourse. The listener is powerless to prevent it.

It is easy to see origins for the harp-playing hero in this story, but the later part of the *Historia Apollonii* may also have given rise to the thirteenth-century female counterpart: the vielle-playing heroine. The musical talent of Tharsia, Apollonius's daughter, is not developed in detail in the fifth-century text, but the seeds are there. When Tharsia is sent to comfort a stranger, before they recognize each other as father and daughter, she sings for him: "His carminibus coepit modulata voce canere"[30] (In a musical voice she began to sing this song). In the song, Tharsia narrates her misfortunes and sets herself as an example of patient hope. No instrument is mentioned, and the hearer's response is sympathetic but with some irritation.

But by the time the story is told in the thirteenth-century Spanish *Libro de Alexandre*, the dispossessed Tarsiana earns her living as a minstrel playing vielle:

Priso una vïola buena e bien tenprada
e sallió al mercado vïolar per soldada. [31]

[She took a fine *vïola* that was well tuned and went to the market to earn money by fiddling.]

She plays vielle, not harp, and, unlike the harper heroes, she earns her livelihood with her music. Furthermore, she does not play in the refined environment of the court, but in the "mercado." Like the male harpers, however, she sings with her instrument in a way that is authentic ("naturale"):

Començó unos viesos e unos sones tales
que traíen grant dulçor e eran naturales.

[She began to perform words and music that were "natural" and very sweet.]

When she performs for Apolonio, he recognizes that she doesn't perform badly ("que no lo fazie mal"). This contrasts with the earlier version, where no mention is made of her ability as a performer. Tarsia's vielle playing brings her some prestige, but, unlike her male counterparts, she plays to earn money, and she is successful at earning money with her music.

---

[30] Archibald, *Historia Apollonii*, 372.

[31] All quotations and translations from this work are from the music reference appendix in Page, *Voices and Instruments*, 170–71.

Like Tarsia, Josian in the thirteenth-century Anglo-Norman *Boeve de Haumtone* earns her living as a musician, but in this romance, magic also appears among her skills. Josian is an Armenian princess who has converted to Christianity. Capable of some enchantment, she makes a magic belt to keep the evil King Yvor from lying with her. After her marriage with Boeve, however, there is no more mention of her magic. Later, disguised as a man with dark skin, she searches for her husband. When her companion falls ill, she begins to sing about her love for Boeve. Noblemen come from many countries and give her enough horses and clothes to purchase what she needs and to care for her companion for over seven years:

> Un jur se comence Jos*ian* purpenser
> e de B*oun* comence a chant*er.*
> *E* venent li barons p*ar* ample contrez,
> chivals *e* robes donent assez pur achat*er.*
> M*u*lt garda bie*n* Sab*aoth* li guerrer
> jeskes a *set* ans e *trois* mois pleners.[32]
> (2784–89)

(One day, Josian was pondering her situation, and she began to sing about Boeve. Then noblemen came from many countries and gave her enough horses and clothes to buy what she needed. Thus she cared well for Sabaoth the warrior for more than seven years and three months.)

As a professional minstrel, she earns money by performing songs of love, but her songs of love reflect her own real situation. Though an instrument is not specified in the unique Anglo-Norman manuscript, the earliest English version states that Josian plays vielle, and that she has learned to play it as part of her education.

A similar motif appears in *Aucassin et Nicolette*, where the heroine, a Saracen brought up as a Christian, is revealed to be the daughter of the King of Carthage. She evades marriage to a pagan prince by buying a vielle, learning to play it, and disguising herself as a dark-skinned male jongleur:

---

[32] *Der Anglonormannische Boeve de Haumtone*, ed. Albert Stimming. Bibliotheca normannica, 7 (Halle: Max Niemeyer, 1899). A new edition will appear in Leslie Z. Morgan, ed., *La Geste Francor: Chansons de geste of MS. Marc. Fr. XIII*. Medieval and Renaissance Texts and Studies, 256 (Tempe, AZ: Arizona Center for Medieval and Renaissance Studies, forthcoming). See also "Bevis of Hampton," *Four Romances of England: King Horn, Havelok the Dane, Bevis of Hampton, Athelston*, ed. Ronald B. Herzman, Graham Drake, and Eve Saisbury (Kalamazoo: Western Michigan University: Medieval Institute Publications, 1999), 187–340. For a recent social-historical study, see Siobhain Bly Calkin, *Saracens and the Making of English Identity: The Auchinleck Manuscript*. Studies in Medieval History and Culture (New York and London: Routledge, 2005), 61–95.

Ele quist une viële, s'aprist a viëler; tant c'on le vaut marier un jor a un roi, rice paiien; et ele s'enbla la nuit, si vint au port de mer, si se herbega ciés une povre fenme sor le rivage. Si prist une herbe, si en oinst son cief et son visage, si qu'ele fu tote noire et tainte. Et ele fist faire cote et mantel et cemisse et braies, si s'atorna a guise de jogleor; si prist se viele, si vint a un marounier, se fist tant vers lui qu'il le mist en se nef. Il drecierent lor voile, si nagierent tant par haute mer qu'il ariverent en le terre de Provence. Et Nicolete issi fors, si prist se viele, si ala vielant par le païs tant qu'ele vint au castel de Biaucaire, la u Aucassins estoit.[33] (38)

[She bought a vielle and learned to play vielle, until the day came when she would have to marry a powerful pagan king. She avoided that fate by sneaking away at night. She went to the seaport and found lodging with a poor woman on the shore. There she took an herb and smeared it on her face so that she was completely black, and she arranged for a coat and mantle and shirt and breeches, and thus she took on the appearance of a jongleur. She took her vielle, went to a mariner, and arranged with him to take her in his boat. He raised sail and navigated the high sea until they arrived in the land of Provence. Nicolette disembarked. She took her vielle and went through the country playing her vielle until she came to the castle of Beaucaire, the place where Aucassin was living.]

Nicolette here not only earns money with her vielle playing in a non-courtly environment, but she uses that livelihood as the means to return to her lover. When she reaches Aucassin, she remains disguised as a jongleur while she sings and plays for him the true story of their love. As a professional minstrel, she performs a song of love, and by means of the song brings about the consummation of her own love. Here there is an explicit link between music performance by a heroine and subsequent reunion with her lover.

To this point, the music played by romance heroes and heroines is linked with love, may evoke love, or may function as a sublimated version of love, but it functions metaphorically rather than magically. Trickery or deception may be linked with music performance, but the heroes are not directly associated with magic. Heroines may be peripherally affiliated with magic, and they may originate in the Other, but they are not defined in terms of magical power. While their music is linked with love, they do not use music performance to constrain the hero to love.

The figure of the Faerie Lady seems the most likely nexus of music, magic, and love, but sympathetic exemplars of the Faerie Lady tradition are surprisingly

---

[33] *Aucassin et Nicolette*, ed. Mario Roques. Les classiques français du moyen âge, 41 (Paris: Champion, 1982), 36.

Songs of Love and Love of Songs 311

dissociated from music. In both Marie de France's *Lanval*[34] and the later Middle English versions,[35] when the hero is greeted in the lady's pavilion, there is no mention of music.[36] In the English versions, she offers a feast in exactly the terms where we would expect a lady to play harp. Yet, not only does she refrain from music, none of her attendants play music either. There are no songs of love.

As mentioned earlier, *Le Bel Inconnu* is framed as a song of love aiming to transform a lady's view of the singer. If she will love him, then the hero of the story will be reunited with the Pucelle of the Golden Isle. Her love has power to modify his song, and his song has power to invoke her love. Both music and love compel response. Yet within this framework, the Pucelle of the Golden Isle plays no instrument and sings no song. In contrast, the evil clerics who hold Blonde Esmerée captive are expressly linked with a thousand minstrels, and their enchantments are cast by means of music.

The dissociation of the *fée* of the *Ile d'Or* from music becomes explicit when her education is discussed. Peter Haidu has pointed out that here necromancy is substituted for music in the quadrivium:[37]

Arismetiche, dyomotrie,
ingremance et astrenomie
(4939–40)

[Arithmetic, geometry, necromancy, and astronomy]

The *fée* does not exert the power of music, and, though defined as a character in terms of magic, when she considers what "engiens et ars" (2284) she might use to keep Guinglain with her, she chooses not to exert her power of enchantment to compel his love. The *fée* of the *Ile d'Or* may be a morally multivalent figure, but she does not use magic to coerce love, and she does not employ the power of music at all.

The English romance tradition, at its height in the fourteenth and fifteenth centuries, derives largely from the earlier French tradition, and in the English romances we may see the extent to which magic had fallen into disapprobation.[38]

---

[34] *Les Lais de Marie de France*, ed. Jean Rychner. Les classiques français du moyen âge, 93 (Paris: Champion, 1983). See the contribution to this volume by Karen K. Jambeck.

[35] *Sir Launfal*, ed. Alan Joseph Bliss. Nelson's Medieval Library (London: Thomas Nelson and Sons, 1960).

[36] During the supper in *Lanval*, there is an "entremés" (185), but it is ambiguous whether or not this constitutes a musical entertainment.

[37] Peter Haidu, "Realism, Convention, Fictionality and the Theory of Genres in *Le Bel Inconnu*," *L'Esprit Créateur* 12 (1972): 37–60; here 48.

[38] Alan Kors and Edward Peters, eds., *Witchcraft Europe?: 400–1700. A Documentary History*, 2nd ed. rev. by Edward Peters (1972; Philadelphia: University of Pennsylvania Press, 2001), 4, point out that "many contemporary observers from the fourteenth century on looked upon manifest diabolical

In *Lybeaus Desconus*, the fifteenth-century English version of *Le Bel Inconnu*, the *fée* of the *Ile d'Or* becomes an evil seductress. She uses music in conjunction with magic to compel the hero to linger with her for a year:

> For the faire lady
> Cowthe more of sorcerye
> Than other suche fyve;
> She made hym suche melodye
> Off all maner mynstralsye
> That any man myght discryue.
> Whan he sawe hir face
> Hym thought that he was
> Jn paradice on lyve;
> With false lies and fayre
> Th[u]s she blered his eye:
> Evill mote she thryve![39]   (1485–96)

[For the fair lady knew more sorcery than five like her. Using all kinds of minstrelsy, she performed such melodies for him that no one could describe them. When he saw her face, it seemed to him that he was alive in Paradise. Thus she bleared his eyes with false and lovely lies. May she fare badly!]

The Faerie Lady has become evil, and the disapproval is expressed in the combination of music with magic. Like the evil clerics, the lady now employs coercive magic and music.

In isolation, music is not aligned with evil. Sir Orfeo's magnificent harping is set against the enervating magic of the King of Faerie in *Sir Orfeo*.[40] Orfeo approaches the king's court as a professional minstrel. His music does not compel the king to release Heurodis. Instead, he elicits the offer of a reward, thus establishing a contract by means of which he can redeem his wife.

Since the English romance tradition is significantly later than its continental origins, it is instructive to trace the development in England of two thirteenth-century tales of minstrel disguise. Josian's fate in the Middle English *Sir Beues* manuscripts may be indicative of a broader trend in the romance tradition. Though surprisingly stable in most respects, the manuscripts exhibit a dramatic transformation of Josian.

In the earliest English version of the story, the Auchinleck manuscript from the early fourteenth century, Josian is given an independence and initiative that

---

sorcery and witchcraft as quantitatively and qualitatively the single greatest threat to Christian European civilization."

[39] *Lybeaus Desconus*, ed. M. Mills. Early English Text Society Publications, original series, 261 (London: Oxford University Press, 1969).

[40] *Sir Orfeo*, ed. Alan Joseph Bliss. 2nd ed. (1954; Oxford: Clarendon Press, 1966).

Songs of Love and Love of Songs

go well beyond known sources. Here Josian's skill with herbs and music is significantly more developed than in the Anglo-Norman version. Having been trained in medicine and surgery by the great masters of Bologna and Toledo, she eats an herb that makes her look like a leper while pretending to relieve herself, thus repelling an unwanted captor. Later a lengthy passage discusses her music performance when her companion is ill. She does not sing about her own love, as she had in the Anglo-Norman version, but she plays vielle throughout the city, exactly as a professional performer would do, and, like a professional performer, for the purpose of earning a living:

> while iosian was in ermonie
> she hadde lerned of minstralcie
> vpon a fithele for to play
> staumpes notes garibles gay
> tho she kouthe no beter red
> boute in to the bourgh ano(n) she yed
> and boughte afithele so saith the tale
> for fourti panes of one me(n)strale
> and alle the while that saber lay
> iosian eueriche aday
> yede aboute the cite with inne
> here sostenaunse for to winne[41] (3905–16)

[When Josian was in Armenia, she had studied music and learned to play estampies, melodies, and cheerful tunes (?) on a vielle. When she had no better solution, she went at once into the city and bought a vielle, as the tale tells, for forty pence from a minstrel. And all the while that Saber lay sick, Josian, every day, went about in the city to win their sustenance.]

Though the exact relationship among the manuscripts has not been determined, it is possible to trace a gradual diminution of Josian's active role through the fifteenth-century manuscripts and the early sixteenth-century print editions. By the early fifteenth century, she loses all ability to play music. Gradually, she even loses all association with enchantment and all herbal lore.

The fate of Tristan and Isolde, not as lovers but as musicians, deserves attention as well. Rather than exploring the complex reticulation of the tradition, consider the late fifteenth-century account by Malory. While many factors may affect Tristram's representation here, it is significant that his harp playing is drastically diminished. On his expedition to Ireland, he does not claim to be a minstrel. The

---

[41] National Library of Scotland Advocates' MS. 19.2.1, fol. 197r (my transcription; line numbers from *The Romance of Sir Beues of Hamtoun*, ed. Eugen Kölbing. Early English Text Society, extra series 46, 48, 65 (London: Kegan Paul, Trench, and Trübner, 1885–1894).

text says only, ". . . at his aryvayle he sate and harped in his bedde a merry lay: suche one herde they never none in Irelonde before that tyme. And whan hit was tolde the kynge and quene of suche a syke knyght that was suche an harper, anone the kynge sente for hym and lette serche hys woundys."[42] In this version, Tristram falls in love with Isode because she heals him, and his harp playing is linked with her attachment to him, but the whole matter is contained in one brief sentence: "And there Tramtryste lerned hir to harpe and she began to have a grete fantasy unto him" (259). Though his harp is mentioned peripherally a few times in the *Morte Darthur*, the only other time we actually see him playing his harp is during his madness, when a former harp student looks after him, bringing him food and drink and a harp:

> And otherwhyle, whan he founde the harpe that the lady sente hym, than wolde he harpe and play thereuppon and wepe togydirs. And somtyme, whan he was in the wood, the lady wyst nat where he was. Than wolde she sette hir downe and play upon the harpe, and anone sir Trystramys wolde com to the harpe and harkyn thereto, and somtyme he wolde harpe hymselff (305).

Here the harp is associated with insanity brought on by love. In Malory's version of the story, there is no episode with Gandin, no Petitcreiu, and, although Tristram teaches Isode harp, we never see her playing music.

It may be that in an era that loathed and was fascinated by magic, music may have been felt to contain a power too close to that of enchantment. There are close etymological links between Old French *canter* and *encanter* and between Middle English *chaunt* and *chantement*, links which linger in such modern terms as "incantation."

Musician protagonists do appear in the fourteenth- and fifteenth-century English romance, but the terms are very different from their earlier continental counterparts. Male protagonists are often skilled in music and hunting, while central female figures are accomplished in music and healing, but it is the women we most often see performing in the narrative.

In many tales, a knight encounters a maiden in a castle, often a mysterious or distant castle, and frequently the heroine heals him. At a meal or just after the meal, she plays music for the hero, sometimes in the hall and sometimes in a chamber. There may be a hint of magic associated with her, but the magic remains elusive. Where an instrument is specified, it is normally harp or psaltery, instruments associated with the biblical King David, not lute and not vielle, instruments which may carry some associations with the East and lack the prestige of harp, at least in the north.

---

[42] *Malory: Works*, ed. Eugène Vinaver. 2nd ed. (1947; Oxford: Oxford University Press, 1971), 238.

A lady harping at a feast is a harbinger of love in the English romances, but it is perhaps surprising that the couple do not consummate their love on the evening of the harp playing. When the couple are married or brought together, the otherworld associations of the castle and the maiden are dropped; as soon as the marriage is arranged, she abruptly abandons all associations with magic and stops playing harp, even at exactly analogous feasts. Professional musicians are likely to play at the marriage feast, but they are described more in terms of their number and the lavish rewards given them than in terms of their music and its power.

In *Sir Degrevant*, for example, though the hero is skilled in music performance,[43] it is Mildor we actually see playing and singing. At a tête-a-tête feast in her chamber, amid a setting of almost other-worldly splendor, she plays and sings while they eat. The poet is sufficiently aware of the technical realities of the situation to specify that she alternates eating and singing:

And euer Mildor sett
And harped notys full suete,
And otherwhile scho ete
Als hir will ware.
Scho sang songes a-boue,
And other mirthis ynewe,
In the chambyrs of loue
Thus thay sla kare.
(1432–1440)

[And always Mildor sat and harped very sweet melodies, though sometimes she ate when she felt like it. She also sang songs and performed plenty of other entertainments. In the chamber of love, thus they killed care.]

---

[43]　　　He was faire and free,
And gretly gaf hym to glee:
To cetoyle and to sawtree
And gytternyng full gaye;
Wele to playe on a rotte,
To syng many newe note,
And of harpyng, wele I wote,
He wane the pryse aye.
(33–40)

[He was fair and noble, and greatly given to music: to citole and psaltery and gay playing on the gittern; to playing the rote well, to singing many new melodies; and in harping, I know well, he always won the prize.]

Quotations from the text are from the Lincoln MS and are quoted from *The Romance of Sir Degrevant* ed. L.F. Casson. Early English Text Society Publications, old series, 221 (London: Oxford University Press, 1949).

Though they feast in "the chambyrs of loue," she refuses to have sex until they are married, at which point there is no mention of her music, or even the power or beauty of the minstrel's performances. We only hear that minstrels are lavishly rewarded at the wedding feast.

> Alle the mynstrals in the haulle
> He gaffe tham robis of palle,
> And other gyftis with-alle —
> Germentes alle halle.
> (1877–80)

[He gave all the minstrels in the hall robes of rich cloth, and also other gifts — whole garments.]

In this romance, music symbolizes Mildor's power to engage Degrevant's love. When that love is consummated, her music disappears.

In the "forbidden land" in *Eger and Grime*, the lady plays for Eger after his combat with Sir Gray Steele and heals him, saying that if he won't stay with her, his own lady will have to "doe to your wouns as I wold haue done" (327).[44] The healing and music cannot lead to sexual union for Eger, but must be transferred to the appropriate lady. When Grime arrives, on the other hand, she plays for him and gives him the information he needs to defeat Sir Gray Steele. When he returns wounded, she heals him, but does not play music for him; instead she arranges their marriage. Sexual love takes the place of music, and the other-world atmosphere disappears with the appearance of a father and real-life wedding arrangements.

Power is sometimes attributed to harping, but not explicitly power to induce love. In *Sir Degaré*, for example, the lady sits with the hero on a bed and plays harp. He falls asleep "For murthe of notes so sschille" (842).[45] The next morning she teases him for sleeping like a beast, and he excuses himself:

> Certes the murie harpe hit made,
> Elles misdo nowt I ne hade;
> (858–59)

[Certainly the merry harp caused it, or I would not have misbehaved.]

---

[44] *Eger and Grime: a Parallel-Text Edition of the Percy and the Huntington-Laing Versions of the Romance*, ed. James Ralston Caldwell. Harvard Studies in Comparative Literature 9 (Cambridge, MA: Harvard University Press, 1933). Quotations are from the Percy Folio.

[45] *The Middle English Breton Lays*, ed. Anne Laskaya and Eve Salisbury. Middle English Texts Series (Kalamazoo: Medieval Institute Publications, 1995). This edition is based on the Auchinleck Manuscript.

Songs of Love and Love of Songs

Some of the later manuscripts, when magical powers were increasingly suspect, suggest that the wine may have been at fault rather than the notes of the harp.[46]

Music, magic, poetic words and love are all relational. All exert potentially dangerous power by provoking impulses within an individual. If irrational forces lie dormant within, who is responsible for releasing them? Many of the medieval romances touch on this question, discussing at length a personified figure of Love, a love who removes the heart and transfers it elsewhere. The individual is not responsible for the transformations effected by love, but rather some force from outside. Both music and magic function as metaphors for such a force, and both in turn are anchored in the power of words. Acknowledging these connections, we may characterize attitudes to love expressed in medieval romance by exploring protagonists' affiliations with music, language, and magic, and trace shifting attitudes to powers capable of drastic transformation.

---

[46] In Ms. Rawl. Poet. 34, for example, Degaré explains (my transcription)
The notys of thy harp yt mad
other ells the good wyn that y hadd
(fol. 16r)

[The melodies of your harp caused it, or else the good wine that I had.]

Chapter 13

The Language and Culture of Joy

Siegfried Christoph
University of Wisconsin-Parkside, Kenosha

If philology, the love of words, characterizes much of medieval epistemology, from Augustine's *Confessions* to Isidore's *Etymologiae*,[1] then the words of love characterize much of the ethos which occupied the literatures of the Middle Ages. In many cases, whether in the lyrics of *Minnesang* (courtly love) or in romances like *Tristan*, love is the central theme, the subject and object of desire. Yet even philologists can be tempted to gloss over the seemingly self-evident, the familiar, the presumably unchanged, on the way to the real nuggets which throw light into the recesses of a presumed otherness. Wolfram's *zwîvel*, for example, or Erec's *verligen*[2] suggest a truly different experiential universe from our modern one.

More often than not, ideas associated with 'love' anchor so much of the medieval conceptual universe that we begin to take their pervasiveness for granted. We are assured by a false sense of seeming familiarity, a more or less unbroken continuity of essential meaning, and hence a vicarious kinship with a world long ago and far away.

There is a danger, however, in making self-evident assumptions based upon tradition, continuity of meaning, and universality of human experience. In the

---

[1] For general discussions, see Roswitha Klinck, *Die lateinische Etymologie des Mittelalters*. Medium Aevum: Philologische Studien, 17 (Munich: W. Fink, 1970), Hennig Brinkmann, *Mittelalterliche Hermeneutik* (Tübingen, M. Niemeyer, 1980), and Marcia Colish, *The Mirror of Language: A Study in the Medieval Theory of Knowledge* (New Haven: Yale University Press, 1968). More recently, see also Georges Matoré, *Le vocabulaire et la société médiévale* (Paris: Presses universitaires de France, 1985), Ottfrid Ehrismann, Albrecht Classen, et al., *Ehre und Mut, Âventiure und Minne: höfische Wortgeschichten aus dem Mittelalter* (Munich: C.H. Beck, 1995), and Vivien Law, *The History of Linguistics in Europe from Plato to 1600* (Cambridge: Cambridge University Press, 2003).

[2] James A. Rushing, "Erec's Uxoriousness," *Discourses on Love, Marriage, and Transgression in Medieval and Early Modern Literature*, ed. Albrecht Classen. Medieval and Renaissance Texts and Studies, 278 (Tempe, AZ: Arizona Center for Medieval and Renaissance Studies, 2004), 163–80.

case of love, for example, Anders Nygren observed: "In the history of doctrine, comprehensive and painstaking work has been devoted to the elucidation of quite peripheral details, while this central question of love has been largely left to one side, as though the meaning and structure of the Christian idea of love were self-evident and unambiguous and were sufficiently defined by the mere mention of the word 'love'."[3]

'Joy,' Middle High German (MHG) *vröude*, is one of the principal terms which readers encounter in the constellation of concepts associated with love, particularly in its characteristic medieval manifestation of 'courtly love.' Even if, as Denis de Rougemont declared, "[. . .] toute idée de l'homme est une idée de l'amour" (every idea of man is an idea of love),[4] that fact alone falls short of explanation and runs the very risk of self-evidence against which Nygren warned. It is against this background that so much of the emotive language of the Middle Ages seems at once familiar and strange, inviting modern readers to look beyond appearances to explore nuances of difference.

When looking at the term 'joy' in this sense, there are a number of questions which transcend etymology, meaning, or context. The idea of 'joy,' which figures so prominently in the affective language of medieval writers, is by dint of usage alone obviously crucial to the way in which idealized medieval people of a certain status and breeding viewed themselves in relation to others.[5] What exactly is 'joy,' however? How does it differ from the many other terms which express euphoria? How, if at all, is it more or less than what it means to us today, assuming of course that we have any clearer sense than our forebears of what 'joy' means to and in our lives?

In the following I would like to approach the concept of 'joy' from a philological perspective, to situate it within the semantic field of words relating to love, and, finally, to apply both approaches to a specific context, the episode of the 'Joie de la Curt' ('Joy of the court') in Hartmann von Aue's *Erec* (ca. 1170). A brief lexical overview will help to lay the foundation for further discussion.[6]

When considering the meaning(s) of MHG terms, there are a number of stations on which the philologist has to call. The first, and by no means always

---

[3] Anders Nygren, *Agape and Eros*, trans. A. G. Hebert (New York: Macmillan, 1932), 27.

[4] Denis de Rougemont, *Les myths de l'amour* (1939; Paris: Gallimard, 1967), 4.

[5] On the importance of *vröude* to chivalric demeanor, for example, see particularly Hans-Werner Eroms, *Vreude bei Hartmann von Aue*. Medium Aevum: Philologische Studien, 20 (Munich: W. Fink, 1970). See also more recently Arno Mentzel-Reuters, *Vröude: Artusbild, Fortuna- und Gralkonzeption in der "Crône" des Heinrich von dem Türlin als Verteidigung des höfischen Lebensideals*. Europäische Hochschulschriften. Reihe I: Deutsche Sprache und Literatur, 1134 (Frankfurt am Main and New York: Peter Lang, 1989).

[6] For parallel studies regarding the terms 'joie' or 'joians,' see Katarzyna Dybel, *Être heureux au moyen âge: D'après le roman arthurien en prose du XIIIe siècle*. Synthema, 2 (Louvain, Paris, and Dudley, MA: Peeters, 2004); see the review by Albrecht Classen in *Mediaevistik* 19 (2006): 431–32.

the most self-evident, is New High German (NHG). If the word survives with its meaning more or less intact, so much the better. In the case of MHG *vröude* and NHG *Freude* there is an apparently clear lineage in form, meaning, and usage. Secondly, one is obliged to consider Old French (OF), particularly since so much of the courtly vocabulary was adapted or translated from French sources. This relationship between German and French is, as we shall see in the particular case of Hartmann von Aue, explicit and fundamental in the case of OF *joie* and MHG *vröude*. Thirdly, one needs often to consider modern English (E) as a linguistic recipient of Germanic and Romance traditions. In this case, it is far easier to discuss OF *joie* in relation to English *joy* than to MHG *vröude*. Last, but not least, due consideration needs to be given to Latin, both in terms of its lexical contributions[7] and in consideration of the influence which the medieval church, and Medieval Latin as its principal language of expression, had on vernacular culture.[8]

Lexically, then, MHG *vröude*, and its NHG heir, *Freude*, can be discussed within the context of E *joy*, via OF *joie*. This does not, of course, tell us whether such a translation always and in every sense renders the meaning of the medieval original under study. But the original, too, stands somewhere along a continuum of meaning and usage,[9] unless it is a clearly incontrovertible neologism.

A first step toward a more differentiated understanding of *vröude* hence involves etymology. Kluge takes as conceptual point of departure the base form of Old High German (OHG) *vrô* in the meaning of *flink*, E 'agile,' 'brisk' or 'nimble,' which led to the abstract formation, *vröude*.[10] Saran went further to point out *vröude*'s etymological relation to the ideas of Old Norse (ON) 'quick' (*frâr*), E 'lively, fresh' (*frow*) and to posit the possibility of an "Anschluß an die Wurzel ie. *preu-* 'springen, hüpfen'" ('a connection to the Indo-European root *preu-* to leap, hop') to make a plausible leap to the secondary, now primary, meaning of "fröhlich gestimmt," 'to be in a joyous mood.'[11]

---

[7] The issue of L. *honos/honestum* and its relationship to OF *enor* and MHG *êre*, both in its etymological and semantic implications, is a much-debated example. For a thorough discussion of the Latin context, see Friedrich Klose, "Die Bedeutung von 'honos' und 'honestum,'" Ph.D. diss. University of Breslau, 1933; Dybel, *Être heureux*, 2004.

[8] On the relationship between religious and secular conceptualization, see, for example, Justus Hashagen, "Mittelhochdeutsche Laienethik als Forschungsproblem," *Zeitschrift für Kirchengeschichte* 60 (1941): 67–74.

[9] For a general discussion, see Wolfgang Stammler, "Ideenwandel in Sprache und Literatur des deutschen Mittelalters," *Deutsche Vierteljahresschrift für Literaturwissenschaft und Geistesgeschichte* 2 (1924): 753–69; and Elmar Seebold, *Etymologie: eine Einführung am Beispiel der deutschen Sprache*. Beck'sche Elementarbücher (Munich: C. H. Beck, 1981).

[10] Friedrich Kluge and Walther Mitzka, *Etymologisches Wörterbuch der deutschen Sprache*. 19th ed. (Berlin: de Gruyter, 1963).

[11] Franz Saran, *Das Übersetzen aus dem Mittelhochdeutschen*. 5th ed. rev. Bert Nagel (Tübingen: Niemeyer, 1975).

OF *joie*, and its modern English heir, *joy*, derives almost certainly from Latin (L) *gaudium*, 'joy, rejoicing' in the sense of a state of happiness, pleasurable emotion.[12] While the L *gaudium* appears to have survived largely in its religious meanings and context, there are perhaps some intriguing remnants. English, for example, still has the term *gaudy* for both a 'rejoicing' and of course for something flashy, showy. Although the *Oxford Etymological Dictionary* derives the 'flashy' *gaudy* from the weld plant, which was used to produce a particularly vivid yellowish green dye, *gaudy green*, it does not seem too far-fetched to draw a conceptual relationship to something which, here figuratively, 'jumps out' at one, hence the connection among *gaudium*, *vröude* and *gaudy*. German, too, retains a certain indebtedness to the original Latin *gaudium*. Most Germans know, for example, that a 'good time' is meant when a Bavarian speaks of a *Gaudi*. According to the *Oxford English Dictionary*, *Gaudy* is "a grand feast or entertainment; *esp.* an annual dinner in commemoration of some event in the history of a college."[13]

The point of the connection among *gaudium*, *joie*, and *vröude* is important, because a plausible case can be made for a very particular vernacular usage of medieval *vröude/joie*, a usage which rests in turn on different meanings for L *gaudium*. First, however, a recapitulation of the preliminary considerations.

Unlike much of the courtly vocabulary which was imported or translated from French to assert or reinforce a sense of genteel pedigree, MHG *vröude* had enjoyed a long history of usage. In the sense of feeling or expressing 'joy,' *vröude* is not much different from OHG *frewida* or *frouwida*, deriving in turn from the attributive *frô*. Things get a little more interesting when *vröude* is seen in its underlying sense of quickness, suddenness. This is critical to a fundamental aspect of MHG *vröude* as it relates to courtly culture and its literatures.

What characterizes the term *vröude* is its expressiveness. This is seen in both its compounded forms, MHG and NHG, as well as in its delimited semantic fields. MHG compounds refer to *vröudenhôchgezît*, a 'joyous feast,' or its modern English analogue, 'gay old time,' *vröudenbraht* or *vröudenschal*, a 'joyous shout.' Modern German refers to *Freudenschrei*, a 'joyous shout' in much the same way. Add to that the compounds *Freudensprung*, 'leap of joy,' *Freudentanz*, 'dance of joy,' and we can see the expressiveness, the physical exuberance which seems to distinguish *vröude/joie* from more statically euphoric terms like *gladness* or

---

[12] While specific discussion of L *gaudium* goes beyond the scope of this paper, it should be noted that there are distinctions among the similar affective terms *delectatio*, *gaudium*, and *laetitia*. These differences are discussed, for example, in Thomas Aquinas, "Treatise on the Passions" *The Summa Theologica*, trans. Laurence Shapcote, 2nd ed. rev. Daniel J. Sullivan. Great Books of the Western World, 17-18 (Chicago: Encyclopædia Britannica, 1990), and Baruch Spinoza's *Ethica*, in vol. 1 of *The Collected Writings of Spinoza*, trans. Edwin Curley (Princeton: Princeton University Press, 1985).

[13] [13] Cited from the CD-ROM version, available online through most library catalogues, sec. ed. 1989. It can also mean: "Dainties, luxurious viands."

happiness.[14] This is the context in which Hartmann uses *vröude*: "von vreuden er ûf spranc" ('He leapt up for joy,' *Erec*, 4545).[15] The very expressiveness of *vröude/joie* is characteristic of its general meaning, as well as its specific meaning in the context of love. Joy is not only an emotional state, but it is also very much something to be exchanged, as in *Freude nehmen an*, 'to take joy in' and *Freude geben*, 'to give joy.' This semantic context offers a transition to the relationship between *vröude/joie* and *minne*.

The question is not whether *vröude/joie* have a place in the vocabulary of love, but rather in what sense. The relationship between *vröude/joie* and love is clear from its compound forms. MHG refers to the beloved as *vröudenstern*, 'star of joy,' *vröudentrôst*, 'joyous solace,' and *vröudenschatz*, 'joyous treasure.'[16]

Context further cements the role of *vröude/joie* in the deliberation of love and lovers: "ir minne condwierte / mir vröude in daz herze mîn" ('Her love conveyed joy into my heart,' *Parzival*, 495); "Minne, diu der werelde ir vröude mêret, / seht, diu brâhte in troumes wîs die vrouwen mîn" ('Love, which increases the world's joy, see how it brought my lady as in a dream,' Heinrich von Morungen);[17] "dû bist mîner vröude bilde, ich schouwe, sueze, dich, / vür alle wîp dû vröuwest mich" ('You are the image of my joy; / I see you, dear; you bring me joy before all others,' Witzlaw von Rügen);[18] "rehtiu minne vröude hât, sô veiliu minne trûric stât" ('True love has joy, / just as false love stays sad,' *Freidanks Bescheidenheit*).[19]

Of course, the fact that *vröude/joie* plays an integral part of the panoply of feelings which are associated with love says little about the nature of the cause or effect occasioned by, or producing, *vröude/joie*. This also involves the distinction between spiritual and secular joy.

In its spiritual context, joy is the emotion and state which characterizes the Christian's reflection upon the rapture, the joy of salvation, the Kingdom of God, the certain prospect of eternal life, and, in general, all of the things relating to the hereafter. It is a joy of contemplated anticipation which makes this mortal coil

---

[14] See G. F. Benecke, Wilhelm Müller, and Friedrich Zarncke, *Mittelhochdeutsches Wörterbuch* (1854–1866; Stuttgart: S. Hirzel, 1990), for related terms, e.g. *sælde, wunne, hohe muot*, or *munst*.

[15] All references to *Erec* are from Hartmann von Aue, *Erec*, 5th rev. ed. Ludwig Wolff. Altdeutsche Textbibliothek, 39 (Tübingen: Niemeyer, 1972).

[16] The fact that these are also common references to the Virgin Mary further underscores the relationship between *minne*-cult and Mariology. The classic study for the West remains Anselm Salzer, *Die Sinnbilder und Beiworte Mariens in der deutschen Literatur und lateinischen Hymnenpoesie des Mittelalters* (1886–1894; Darmstadt: Wissenschaftliche Buchgesellschaft, 1967). More recently, see also *Marienlexikon*, ed. Remigius Bäumer and Leo Scheffczyk (St. Ottilien: Eos, 1988–1994).

[17] Heinrich von Morungen, "Mir ist geschehen als einem kindelîne," *Des Minnesangs Frühling*. Unter Benutzung der Ausgaben von Karl Lachmann und Moriz Haupt, Friedrich Vogt und Carl von Kraus. 38th rev. ed. Hugo Moser und Helmut Tervooren (Stuttgart: Hirzel, 1988), 145, 9–10.

[18] Wetzlaw von Rügen, "Wol ûf, ir stolzen helde," *Minnesinger: Deutsche Liederdichter des 12., 13. und 14. Jahrhunderts I - IV*, ed. Friedrich von der Hagen (Leipzig: J. A. Barth, 1838-1861), 78-85.

[19] *Freidanks Bescheidenheit: Mittelhochdeutsch/Neuhochdeutsch*, ed. Wolfgang Spiewok.. Greifswalder Beiträge zum Mittelalter, 48 (Greifswald: Reineke, 1996), 98, 11.

bearable and bears witness to our faith. As E. Catherine Dunn noted in her study of medieval English drama: "The spirit of medieval religious drama seems to be an affirmative perspective on the faith, a rich intermingling of intelligence and emotion creating confidence and hope in a vale of tears."[20] This affirmative quality of joy remains a fundamental aspect of the Christian experience. As recently as 1975, notion of a Christian joy is explicitly cited both descriptively and prescriptively. It was during that Jubilee Year that Pope Paul VI wrote the apostolic exhortation *Gaudete in Domino*, in which he characterized joy as "the most noble expression of happiness:"

> When he awakens to the world, does not man feel, in addition to the natural desire to understand and take possession of it, the desire to find within it his fulfillment and happiness? As everyone knows, there are several degrees of this "happiness." Its most noble expression is joy, or "happiness" in the strict sense, when man, on the level of his higher faculties, finds his peace and satisfaction in the possession of a known and loved good. Thus, man experiences joy when he finds himself in harmony with nature, and especially in the encounter, sharing and communion with other people. All the more does he know spiritual joy or happiness when his spirit enters into possession of God, known and loved as the supreme and immutable good. Poets, artists, thinkers, but also ordinary men and women, simply disposed to a certain inner light have been able and still are able, in the times before Christ and in our own time and among us, to experience something of the joy of God.[21]

At the other extreme, joy in its most carnal aspect is nothing less than sexual pleasure, as its Latin usage attests: "*Voluptas* [...] and *gaudium* [...] commonly have a sexual implication."[22] In modern times, Catholic teaching has come to acknowledge the relationship between sex and pleasure, as the Vatican II document, *Gaudium et spes*, confirms:

> [True love] is uniquely expressed and perfected through the appropriate enterprise of matrimony. The actions within marriage by which the couple are united intimately and chastely are noble and worthy ones. Expressed in a manner which is truly human, these actions promote that mutual self-giving by which spouses enrich each other with a joyful and a ready will.[23]

---

[20] E. Catherine Dunn, "Popular Devotion in the Vernacular Drama of Medieval England," *Medievalia et Humanistica*, n.s. 4 (1973): 55–68; here 65.

[21] Paul VI, *On Christian Joy: Apostolic Exhortation* (Washington, DC: US Catholic Bishops Conference, 1975), 7.

[22] J(ames) N(oel) Adams, *The Latin Sexual Vocabulary* (Baltimore, MD: Johns Hopkins University Press, 1990), 197–98.

[23] Paul VI, *Constitution on the Church in the Modern World ['Gaudium et Spes']* (Washington, DC: United States Catholic Conference, 1965), I/49. For a broader discussion, see Joseph E. Kerns,

The Language and Culture of Joy

An interesting perspective on this relationship among social change, the church, and carnal love in the Middle Ages is presented in Tom Radcliffe's "fictional" review:

> Neither political nor technological change came to an end in the Dark Ages, and by the end of the early Middle Ages there was a class of people with sufficient leisure time that sex became a serious problem. An ordinary human being with time and wealth enough to enjoy a life of leisure has opportunities for sexual indulgences that would rarely be available to someone scrabbling a subsistence living out of hard soil or a harder peasantry.[24]

The importance of joyfulness as an affective value is reflected also in the Rabbinic tradition, which understood that "virtues are not only dispositions to *act* in a certain way but also permanent dispositions to *feel* a certain way."[25] The study of the Torah, for example, is attended by and expressive of joy, insofar as it establishes an intimate relationship between student and God. In fact, the Rabbinic tradition celebrates the ecstatic nature of extreme joy in its implicit relationship to the erotic: "The rabbinic ethos [. . .] was but a Jewish version of the erotic Llanguage that Socrates and his disciples used to express their love of wisdom, namely, philosophia. In both cases the erotic pursuit of wisdom is an intense joy and delight that accompanies pure theoretical activity."[26]

Somewhere between the sacred and the profane we find the range of meanings which attend *joie* and *vröude*. *Vröude* is associated often and intimately with religious happiness, for example:

> von disem ellende
> vuor er gedultecliche.
> zuo dem gotes rîche
> Wart er mit himelvreuden grôz
> brâht in Abrahâmes schôz: [*Barlaam und Josaphat*, 14328–34][27]

[From this desolation he went patiently to God's kingdom; was brought with great heavenly joy to the bosom of Abraham]

The Theology of Marriage: The Historical Development of Christian Attitudes Toward Sex and Sanctity in Marriage (New York: Sheed and Ward, 1964), and Robert Kaiser, *The Politics of Sex and Religion: A Case History in the Development of Doctrine, 1962–1984* (Kansas City: Leaven Press, 1985).

[24] Tom Radcliffe, "A Fictional Review on the History of Sex," *Monadnock Review*, www.monadnock.net/essays/hogarth.html (last accessed on April 11, 2006).

[25] Hava Tirosh-Samuelson, *Happiness in Premodern Judaism: Virtue, Knowledge, and Well-Being*. Monographs of the Hebrew Union College, 29 (Cincinnati: Hebrew Union College Press, 2003), 125.

[26] Tirosh-Samuelson, *Happiness in Premodern Judaism*, 117.

[27] Rudolf von Ems, *Barlaam und Josaphat*, ed. Franz Pfeiffer. Deutsche Neudrucke: Texte des Mittelalters (1843; Berlin: de Gruyter, 1965).

Heavenly joy surpasses all other joy:

> ez geschach nie solch fröude
> menschlîcher beschöude
> ân die himelfröud dâ oben:
> für alle fröud muoz man die loben: [*Der heilige Georg*, 703–06][28]

[There was never such joy to human eyes without heaven's joy above: Praise be to it above all joys]

Eternal joy awaits us in the hereafter: "Frew dich, sel meine, frewe dich: an dem nehsten suntag so bist du in den ewigen freuden" ('Rejoice, my soul, rejoice: On the next Sunday you will be in eternal joy;' *Engeltaler Schwesternbuch*, 13–14).[29]

At the same time, *vröude* is linked intimately with *minne* (courtly love), in particular the *vröude* which the beloved is able to grant or withhold: "mîn vröide an der vil schoenen lît, / nâch der mîn herze wüete" ('My joy lies with the beautiful one after whom my heart yearn;' Albrecht von Johansdorf, 11, 3–4); "tugende hât si michels mê, danne ich gesagen kunne. / si ist leides ende und liebes trôst und aller vröiden ein wunne" ('She has more virtue than I can say. She is the end of suffering and love's solace and a delight to all joy;' Dietmar von Eist, 9.7–8); "Der ich dâ her gedienet hân, dur die wil ich mit vröiden sîn" ('The one whom I have served, on her account I will have joy;' Hartmann von Aue, 3. 1–2);[30] "ir har, ir stirne, ir tinne ir wange, ir munt, ir kinne, / den vröuderichen ostertac, / der lachend in ir ougen lac, / do kam diu rehte minne, diu ware viuraerinne" ('Her hair, her brow, her forehead, her cheek, her mouth, her chin, the joyful Easter Day which lay laughing in her eyes, there came righteous love, the true inflamer;' Gottfried von Strassburg, *Tristan*, 925–30).

Common to the several usages of 'joy,' again, is the notion of expressiveness, of energy. This can be illustrated by considering the physical, exuberant contexts in which *vröude* is invoked: "man sach dâ vreude unde schal" ('Joy and noise were seen there,' *Parzival*, 222,14); "mîn herze nâch vreuden schrei" ('My heart shouted for joy;' Wolfram von Eschenbach, *Parzival*, 374,10); "dâ was wünne und êre, / vreude und michel rîterschaft / und alles des diu überkraft / des man zem lîbe gerte" ('There was delight and honor, joy and much chivalry, and all in abundance that the body desired;' Hartmann von Aue, *Iwein*, 2442–45); "von vreuden er ûf spranc" ('He jumped up for joy,' *Erec*, 4545); "Michel froude dâ was / in des

---

[28] Reinbot von Durne, *Der heilige Georg*, ed. Carl von Kraus. Germanische Bibliothek. Dritte Abteilung, Kritische Ausgaben altdeutscher Texte, 1 (Heidelberg: C. Winter, 1907).

[29] *Der Nonne von Engelthal Büchlein von der Genaden Überlast*, ed. Karl Gustav Theodor Schröder. Bibliothek des Litterarischen Vereins in Stuttgart: 108 (Tübingen: Litterarischer Verein in Stuttgart, 1871).

[30] Cited, respectively, in *Des Minnesangs Frühling*.

kuniges palas / von sange und von seitspile" ('There was much joy in the king's palace from singing and string playing,' Heinrich von Veldeke, *Eneit*, 12917–21); "bûhurt, tanzen huop sich hîe ... sô was ir vreude sus grôz, zen vrouwen si giengen / die si schône emphiengen" ('Jousting, dancing began ... in this way their joy was so great, they approached the ladies, who received them well;' Hartmann von Aue, *Erec*, 2142–49). Again we find a vividly sensory, even sensual, context for *vröude*.[31]

This brings me to the last reflection on love of words. The extremes to which *vröude* refers carry over into a contrast of English meanings which are woefully familiar to those who deal with the consequences of semantic change like E *lust* and NHG *Lust*. While the German *Lust* refers generically to pleasure, diversion, enjoyment, amusement, and entertainment, the English *lust* has evolved to a much more restrictive, and principally carnal, connotation. This is despite the fact that English and German *lust/Lust* are cognate, deriving from OHG *lust*, 'yearning, pleasure, joy, sensual longing.' Since the early sixteenth century English 'lust' appears in the sense of 'excessive, inordinate desire' and in particular 'sexual desire.' The OED cites William Tindale's translations of the New Testament for both innovations. Here again we are faced with the tension between sensual and generic pleasure. In all respects, however, it is important to see in *vröude*, as in *Lust*, the element of dynamic expressiveness, of conscious diversion from the ordinary, the mundane. We can illustrate this, as in the case of *vröude*, by the German compound forms *Lustspiel* (comedy), *Lustgarten* (pleasure grove), or *Lustfahrt* (pleasure trip).[32]

To summarize at this point the several aspects of *vröude* that have a distinct bearing on the relationship between joy and love: *vröude* in its most general sense refers to a feeling of pleasure, happiness. Its singular characteristic is one of expressiveness, rather than contemplativeness, as for example MHG *wunne* might be. Moreover, *vröude* is not only a feeling, it is also something which can be given or taken away.

Subsumed under the general meaning of *vröude* is a complex of three related meanings that have to do with the physical and emotional arenas in which *vröude* appears, is felt, and is expressed. The first is spiritual joy, a sense of joy that characterizes the attitude of the Christian believer who acts in accordance with the teachings of Christ and, as such, is in a state of anticipation which will culminate, the Christian hopes, in oneness with Christ after death. The second is arguably

---

[31] [31] These examples, if not further identified, are drawn from the *Mittelhochdeutsche Begriffsdatenbank*, University of Salzburg, online at: http://mhdbdb.sbg.ac.at:8000/ (last accessed on April 12, 2006).

[32] For further examples, see Jakob and Wilhelm Grimm, *Deutsches Wörterbuch*, rev. ed. Deutsche Akademie der Wissenschaften zu Berlin and Akademie der Wissenschaften zu Göttingen (Leipzig: Hirzel, 1965–).

a more profane variant of spiritual joy. It is the sense of *vröude* which is associated with love. The lover is in suspense, infused by the anticipation of his beloved. The beloved thus is the source of *vröude*, since love's reward may be withheld or granted. The sense of anticipation also means that *vröude* characterizes the attitude with which everything is undertaken on behalf of the beloved. The third is the sense of *vröude* which attaches to the court and its members. Here, *vröude* is not only the cheerful, pleasant demeanor which marks the noble knights and ladies. It is the expressiveness of *vröude* which characterizes the environment of diversion, amusement, pleasure, and playfulness.[33] In this sense, *vröude* finds more concrete expression, for example in song and dance, than the no less important virtue of *hohe muot*, high-mindedness.[34]

There is, of course, an interesting area in which the sacred and profane in *vröude* overlap, namely in the sense of anticipation and the degree to which the object which is the source of *vröude* obliges one to be a person of *vröude*.[35] This is also the area in which the sensual aspect of *vröude* enters the picture. In love, the concept of *vröude* evolves very interestingly. It is felt consistently in anticipation of the beloved's reward. There is nothing amusing, pleasant, or playful about being ignored, rebuffed, or slighted by one's beloved. All the lover has is the often vain hope for and anticipation of the beloved's reward. Nonetheless, the lover is obliged to maintain a *vröudenbære* (joyful) countenance, lest despair estrange the lover even further from the beloved. This emotional state of yearning is the essence of *amor de lonh*, 'distant love,' one of the most enduring and powerful attributes of 'courtly love,' such as in the works of the troubadours, particularly Jaufré Rudel (1130–70).[36] It is the anticipation of *vröude* which must guide the lover's exertions. This early stage of love can last a very long time indeed, and it can be marked by any number of setbacks. We have the marvelous case of Ulrich von Liechtenstein's *Frauendienst* (ca. 1260–1270) as a prime example of seemingly unrequited love.[37]

The pinnacle of *vröude* comes with love's reward, which need not — but often does — express itself physically, be it an embrace or other sign of union. Then comes the problem, however, and the place at which the sacred and profane part

---

[33] For a general discussion of the language of courtesy, see C. Stephen Jaeger, *The Origins of Courtliness*. The Middle Ages Series (Philadelphia: University of Pennsylvania Press, 1985), 127–75.

[34] For a seminal discussion of the chivalric virtues, which include *hohe muot*, see Gustav Ehrismann, "Die Grundlagen des ritterlichen Tugendsystems," *Zeitschrift für deutsches Altertum und deutsche Literatur* 56 (1919): 137–216.

[35] See also the contribution to this volume by Connie Scarborough.

[36] See *The Songs of Jaufré Rudel*, ed. and trans. Rupert T. Pickens. Pontifical Institute of Mediaeval Studies Publications, 41 (Toronto: Pontifical Institute of Mediaeval Studies, 1978); for further discussions, see the contribution to this volume by Anna Kukułka-Wojtasik.

[37] *Ulrich von Lichtenstein, Frauendienst*, ed. Franz Viktor Spechtler. Göppinger Arbeiten zur Germanistik, 485 (Göppingen: Kümmerle, 1987). See also the Orgeluse episode in Wolfram von Eschenbach, *Parzival*, and particularly *Mauritius von Craûn*, ed. Heimo Reinitzer. Altdeutsche Textbibliothek, 113 (Tübingen: Max Niemeyer, 2000).

company. The *vröude* of eternal life knows no end. In other words, we do not expect to get bored in, or with the idea of, heaven. While we do not 'expect' to get bored with lovers, reality dictates that *vröude*, by its very nature of being emotionally and physically spontaneous, cannot be maintained or recreated indefinitely by the lovers. There is no reason to believe that medieval lovers were different in that respect from the lovers of any other epoch or culture.

Having proposed a broader context for a discussion of 'joy,' I would like now to apply these observations on the language and culture of *vröude* to an episode which bears its name so conspicuously, the episode of 'The Joy of the Court' in Hartmann von Aue's *Erec*, itself an adaptation of Chrétien de Troye's *Erec et Enide*.

It is not the aim of these observations to propose a new interpretation of the episode. Its allegorical meaning, the lessons which Erec and his wife, indeed the audience, are intended to draw from its example, have been discussed widely and thoroughly. I have no fundamental disagreements with most studies which have tried to relate the episode to the larger work and its meaning(s).[38]

What I am more interested in is the notion of 'joy' to which the episode so clearly draws attention. The episode, which comes late in the work, can be summarized briefly and easily. Erec and Enite arrive at a castle. In a nearby park a knight waits to be challenged. He has already killed eighty knights, whose heads are displayed on poles, and whose widows remain. Erec fights the knight within, defeats him, and thereby releases the knight and his wife from a spell which has kept them in the enchanted garden for years. It turns out that they were bound to stay alone together within the confines of the enchanted park until the knight was defeated.

Hartmann draws attention to the adventure by giving it a name. The attention is compounded by giving it its French name, *Joie de la curt*, and then translating it into German, *vröude des hoves*. Both the French and German names for the adventure are repeated later in the episode, though not contiguously, *Joie de la curt* (9601) some sixteen hundred lines after the adventure is first named, and *des hoves vreude* (9759) some hundred and fifty lines later.

From the time Erec and Enite take the road to the castle of Brandigan to the time when the inhabitants rejoice at the signal that the knight has been defeated and released from his enchantment takes up 1863 lines. The word *vröude*, and its

---

[38] For a review of the older literature, see particularly Christoph Cormeau and Wilhelm Störmer, *Hartmann von Aue. Epoche – Werk –Wirkung*, 2nd rev. ed. Arbeitsbücher zur Literaturgeschichte (Munich: C. H. Beck, 1998), and Petra Hörner, ed., *Hartmann von Aue: Mit einer Bibliographie 1976-1997. Information und Interpretation*, 8 (Frankfurt a.M.: Peter Lang, 1998). More recently, see Walter Haug, "'Joie de la curt'," *Blütezeit: Festschrift für L. Peter Johnson zum 70. Geburtstag*, ed. Mark Chinca (Tübingen: Niemeyer, 2000), 271–90; and Christina Noacco, "La dialectique du don dans la quête de la Joie d'Erec et Enide," *Guerres voyages et quêtes au Moyen Age*, ed. Alain Labbé, Daniel W. Lacroix, and Danielle Quéruel. Colloques, congrès et conférences sur le Moyen Age, 2 (Paris: Champion, 2000), 299–311.

variants, appear thirteen times, of which five refer explicitly to the absence of joy, for example the eighty widows who have been robbed of joy, or Enite whose joy is shattered by the consensus opinion that her husband's head will join the gallery in progress. What, then, does the *Joie/vröude* of the court refer to if the term does not figure prominently in the episode? Indeed, what does it refer to if the campus is not even a court, but rather a park near a court?

With the help of the previous discussion, I believe that the importance — and nature — of *vröude* can be understood in several respects. When Erec, Enite, and Guivreiz — on their way to Arthur's court — come to a split in the road, they choose the "better" one instead of the "right" one.[39] This does not bode well, and Guivreiz sounds an appropriately ominous note as they approach a castle. He rues that they have come this way. Hartmann indulges in some narrative protraction and gives a sumptuous description of the magnificent castle. When Erec finally asks about the name of the castle, Guivreiz keeps up the suspense. Yes, he knows the name, adding: "daz ez got verwâze!"('may God damn it;' 7901). Not surprisingly, his advice to turn back is a red cape to Erec's manhood. In the ensuing, paratactic exchange, the audience's patience is tested as much as Erec's, who finally bursts out: "muget ir mirz durch got nû sagen?" ('For God's sake will you tell me what this is about?;' 7939).

Only now, some two hundred lines after they took a wrong turn, do we learn the adventure's name: *Joie de la curt*, complete with translation, *des hoves vreude*, the 'Joy of the Court.' Yet it is not really the court, as Guivreiz points out immediately: "seht ir den boumgarten / der under dem hûse lît?" ('Do you see the park over there below the house?;' 8009–10). Having thus drawn out the adventure's unveiling and drawn explicitly attention to its name — if not its significance — we have little clue about what exactly it means. By contrast, consider the *Lît marveile* in *Parzival* (566,14). Reader and hero are forewarned by the name. When they get to a bed, something is going to happen . . .

What follows immediately is very much a 'joy of the court' and far from dire, as Guivreiz had warned. Riding into the castle, the three find "vreuden vil" ('much joy;' 8062) with "tanz und aller slahte spil / daz jungen liuten wol gezam" ('dancing and all sorts of amusement fit for young people;' 8063–64). When the people see Erec and Enite their joy dissipates, replaced by sorrow and pity. Erec is not easily discouraged, however. Instead, he greets the inhabitants with laughter, "lachendem munde" (8156), and a song on his lips, "ein viel vrœlîchez liet" (8158).

What transpires at the castle itself is, in every sense of the name, the 'joy of the court.' There is food, lively conversation, and a more than solicitous host.

---

[39] For a discussion of the importance attached to selecting the 'right' path at a junction, see Wolfgang Harms, *Homo viator in bivio: Studien zur Bildlichkeit des Weges*. Medium Aevum: Philologische Studien, 21 (Munich: W. Fink, 1970).

Castle Brandigan and its host, Ivreins, offers everything imaginable to delight palate, ear, and eye.

Nothing in Ivreins' explanation of the adventure and its history really explains what is meant by the 'joy of the court.' Mabonagrin, having been defeated by Erec, gives a long explanation of how he came to be a virtual captive with his wife in the park, waiting for challengers. But that explanation, too, says very little about what is meant by the 'joy of the court.' The theme of the *don contraignant*, the 'constraining promise,' helps to explain that Mabonagrin and his wife were largely responsible for the limbo in which they were forced to exist.[40] This adventure also means to say something about Erec and Enite's own plight, but it is not immediately clear what.

I return now to the several senses in which joy can be understood. In particular, we noted the idea that joy is expressive, that it attaches to action itself as well as disposition to act. Joy is hence something which is, or at least has the potential, to be shared. The joy of love is as emotionally intense and expressive in action as it is fleeting. Fleeting in the sense that the intense physical and emotional anticipation of love's joy cannot be maintained indefinitely, nor can it be recreated in its fundamental aspects except in the sense of diversion, pleasure, amusement. Yet we are obliged to maintain an attitude of, a disposition to be moved by, to create and to communicate joy.

We are clearly invited to consider the notion of joy by the very name of the adventure. There are two passages which, I believe, help to understand what is meant by joy here. In the first passage, Mabonagrin explains the importance of Erec's victory and his own defeat: "ir sêt ze grôzer sælikeit / disem hove her komen, / wan mit mir was im benomen / elliu sîn wünne gar, / und was eht schœner vreuden bar" ('You have brought good fortune to this court, since it was robbed of all happiness on my account and bare of all pleasure and truly bereft of joy;' 9591–94). He continues: "sît daz in mîn abe gie / sô enwart eht hie nie / deheiner slahte spil erhaben: / durch daz in lebende was begraben / mîn jugent unde mî geburt, / sô ist eht Joie de la curt / genzlîchen nider gelegen" ('Since they no longer had me, there was no more amusement, because my youth and high estate were buried alive to them. In this way Joie de la curt had vanished. But now we can pursue it again;' 9596–602). It is a remarkable passage for several reasons. First, it refers to four different words denoting happiness of one sort or another: MHG *sælikeit*, *wünne*, *vreuden*, and *spil*. The idea of pursuing happiness, MHG *phlegen*, is the kind of action, rather than mere disposition, associated with *vreude* or *spil*. Secondly, the passage for the first time since its original naming offers a context for 'Joie de la curt,' the joy of the court. Mabonagrin and his wife selfishly deprived the court of happiness, more particularly the joy which they had the power to give

---

[40] See on this point particularly Noacco, "La dialectique du don."

and share. This is, not coincidentally, the problem of *verligen* that Erec himself also had faced and that had driven him on the series of rehabilitative adventures culminating in the *Joie de la curt*-episode, which ultimately leads to the issue of proper communication, so essential for every society.[41]

Shortly after this, Erec is asked to take the horn and blow it three times, announcing that Mabonagrin has been defeated and thus, paradoxically, released from enchantment. All of the inhabitants rush, "nû îlten si alle" (9652), to the park shouting for joy, "mit vrœlichem schalle" (9653). The importance of blowing the horn lies in the idea of sharing the good news of Mabonagrin's defeat with those who were robbed of joy in the first place by him and his wife.

In these two passages lies a credible explanation of what is meant by the 'joy of the court.' It is the idea that joy is something to be shared. It is furthermore the idea that the joy of love, which represents an intensely intimate sharing between two people, cannot be entire unto itself. It cannot isolate those who enjoy the benefits of love's joy from those with whom they have an obligation to share joy. Not, mind you, the joy of love, but rather the joy of diversion, of pleasure, of amusement, of singing, dancing, wining, dining, parties, visitors, stories, entertainment. Neither Hartmann nor the inhabitants of Brandigan, or — by analogy — Erec's court, would begrudge the couple's enjoyment of love. What they would begrudge is the sense of separation which condemns the court to the tedium of everyday life and its routine practical impositions while the master partakes of joy.

The relationship between *vröude* as a word of love and as an expression of shared celebration within a community, which characterizes the episode of the *Joie de la curt*, suggests a point of contrast to Gottfried von Strassburg's *Tristan*. The waning of expressive *vröude* in the vocabulary of the bonds which bind Tristan and Isolde reflects the absence of *vröude* that comes increasingly to mark the community in which they live. Isolde's love for Tristan does not shirk the cost of joy: "sin wolte doch niht vro sin: / diu getriuwe staete senedaerin, / diu haete ir vröude unde ir leben / sene unde Tristande ergeben" ('She did not want to be joyful; the faithful, steadfast, yearning Isolde had dedicated her joy and her life to longing and Tristan;' *Tristan* 16399–402).

The tension between the public and private spheres becomes especially evident in the *Minnegrotte* (love cave) episode. The lovers at first revel in their exclusive solitude: "ir zweier geselleschaft / diu was in zwein ... hêrhaft" ('Their mutual company was enough for them;' *Tristan* 16863–64). Ultimately, however, there can be no *vröude* in the lovers' union if it cannot celebrate, or be celebrated, within the broader context of the community. The prospect of being reintegrated into the community is also a source of joy, even if it comes at the price of secrecy

---

[41] See Albrecht Classen, *Verzweiflung und Hoffnung: Die Suche nach der kommunikativen Gemeinschaft in der deutschen Literatur des Mittelalters*. Beihefte zur Mediaevistik, 1 (Frankfurt a.M. et al.: Peter Lang, 2002), esp. 109–66; see also Rushing, "Erec's Uxoriousness."

The Language and Culture of Joy

and discretion, i.e., the celebrating joy of their love for each other: "Diz dûhte die gelieben guot / und wurden in ir herzen frô. / die fröude hetens aber dô / vil harter unde mêre / durch got und durch ir êre" ('This seemed good to the lovers, and their hearts were joyful; but the joy was more a matter of God and their honor;' *Tristan* 17698–703). While the reintegration of Mabonagrin and his wife becomes a reason for rejoicing, the lovers' reintegration in *Tristan* is marked by a very different sentiment: "sine wurden aber niemer mê / in allen ir jâren / sô heinlîch, sô s'ê wâren, / nochn gewunnen nie zir fröuden sît / sô guote stat sô vor der zît" ('Yet for the rest of their lives they were never again together as intimately as before, nor did they find a chance for joy again as before;' *Tristan* 17706–10).

However contrived it may feel by contrast, Hartmann's resolution of the conflict between the private joy of love and the public joy of celebration acknowledges the importance of both. The joy of the court is nothing less than a necessary disposition toward, creation of, and sharing of joy. It is not, in the context of *Erec*, an either/or proposition, of choosing between love's joy and the court's joy. Promoting and sharing joy means integrating all aspects of what Huizinga called *homo ludens*, 'playful man.'[42] Being lord and master means having a special responsibility to create and maintain the conditions under which all subjects may partake of joy.

As long as lovers are members of a community, the joyful celebration of love is also a celebration of, by, and for the community. *Vröude* is the common emotional bond which relates the lovers to each other and also the community. In that sense, *vröude* is an indispensable precondition for, and manifestation of, the emotional bond between lovers. Genuine *vröude* implies a mutual respect for the dignity of the lover's person which brings it close to the spiritual quality of religious joy. The 'joy' of love cannot be nurtured or savored, however, in the vacuum of compulsion and at the expense of the *Joie de la curt*.

---

[42] Johan Huizinga, *Homo Ludens: A Study of the Play Element in Culture* (1955; New York: Harper, 1970).

CHAPTER 14

NAMES OF LOVE, LOVE OF NAMES: PARZIVAL'S WOMEN[1]

G. RONALD MURPHY, S.J.
Georgetown University, Washington, DC

The love of words, and the poet's urge to create effective words of love, take an interesting turn in the hands of Wolfram von Eschenbach. In his *Parzival* (ca. 1205),[2] love of words generates a dual outpouring of names: on the one hand, exotic names borrowed from adventures near and far, and on the other, the creation of names-of-love to suit the plot and move the story to its conclusion. Many of the personal names in *Parzival* have been borrowed with some alteration from the vast world of French, German, and classical literature, and even from Hebrew (the "Bâruc" of Baghdad). Such names, geographic as well as personal, contribute at turns an exotic, an oriental, an adventurous, and a mysterious atmosphere to the realm of the *Parzival* epic,[3] which truly attempts an encyclopedic inclusion of the whole fascinating medieval world from Albion to Zazamanc.[4] Wolfram's use of geographic names, however, is not quite the same as his use of persons

---

[1] This article is based broadly on Appendix A of G. Ronald Murphy, S.J., *Gemstone of Paradise: The Holy Grail in Wolfram's Parzival* (New York: Oxford University Press, 2006).

[2] *Parzival, Studienausgabe, Mittelhochdeutscher Text nach der sechsten Ausgabe von Karl Lachmann*. Übersetzt von Peter Knecht, Einführung von Bernd Schirok (Berlin and New York: Walter de Gruyter, 1998). English translations are from the version of Helen M. Mustard and Charles E. Passage, *Parzival by Wolfram von Eschenbach* (New York: Vintage Books, 1961), or are the author's as noted.

[3] The argument can also be made, and should be, that the names, especially geographic ones, need not be tied down to too specific a case without injuring the exotic effect with which they are invested. Albrecht Classen makes a similar argument in the case of the poetry of Oswald von Wolkenstein in the introduction to his contribution to this volume.

[4] For a Bakhtinian approach to the multiplicity of names and languages as de-centering, see Arthur Groos, *Romancing the Grail: Genre, Science and Quest in Wolfram's Parzival* (Ithaca and London: Cornell University Press, 1995), 5–45.

and their names.[5] When it comes to the names of the characters in *Parzival* there are two relatively distinct classes: names borrowed and names created. Failure to make this distinction leads to some of the scholarly (mis-)adventures that can be seen below. When the question of the meaning of a name comes up, it is important to determine whether the name is primarily an obscured borrowing or a created fiction. If the name is borrowed, like Parzival and the Baruch, with exotic and mysterious overtones, it is appropriate to search outside *Parzival* for its possible meaning, with attention to the effects of the tone of its altered sound (especially when the name is that of a distant land, like Zazamanc); one can search medieval letters to locate the word's origin in the world of literature. If the name is Wolfram's creation, however, then, to parallel Christopher Clason's synthesis of Gottfried von Strassburg's *Tristan* in this volume, "the meaning of a sign is determined by its use in a *particular* context"[6] [emphasis mine].

A great deal of work has been done identifying the many origins, medieval, Biblical, Arabic, and classical of the many borrowed and altered names which populate Wolfram's *Parzival*.[7] On the other hand, when it comes to commenting on the meaning of the five critical personal names which are of Wolfram's own poetic invention, and are of great importance to a thorough interpretation of the central thrust driving the text and the plotline — Herzeloyde, Sigûne, Condwîrâmûrs, Cundrîe, and Repanse de Schoie — there is unsatisfying linguistic division. I believe this is because of inappropriate methodology used in approaching the created names. Linguists and etymologists often treat all names equally, each one in isolation, as if it were a standard word whose derivation is to be discerned according to the rules of historical linguistics, a word whose internal composition is to be perceived according to known etymological rules. Some of the results will be seen below. Actually the five names are not derived at all in the strict sense but are fictional: poetic compositions, often created in more than one language, and certainly reflecting Wolfram's deep and compassionate love for words. With some

---

[5] The studies that have identified and categorized the totality of Wolfram's names are principally those of Chandler (below, note 17) and Schröder (below, note 7). My approach differs from theirs in two respects: first, my study is restricted to women's names created by Wolfram (in *Parzival*), and, second, it arrives at a name's meaning not by using a derivational model in isolation from context, but suggests that an invented name's specific meaning, and its function in the plot, is indicated by the poet through analogous vocabulary placed in the surrounding context.

[6] Cf. Christopher R. Clason, "The Bitterness of Love on the Sea," 278. Clason explores the triple meaning of *lameire* (sea, bitterness, love) in its context-given ambiguity as actually fostering clear communication between Tristan and Isolde. The particular context in the story constitutes the vehicle for his exploration of the meaning of *lameire*.

[7] See Werner Schröder, *Die Namen im 'Parzival' und im 'Titurel' Wolframs von Eschenbach* (Berlin and New York: Walter de Gruyter, 1982) for an exhaustive listing and categorization of sources. Schröder takes every name, personal and geographic, and traces it to a category that indicates whence it has been derived and thus also its possible meaning. When it comes to categorizing the unique five names treated in this article, however, he acknowledges them as poetic creations, and does not attempt to force them. His work has not been superseded.

Names of Love, Love of Names 337

poetic freedom, words are altered slightly to create an air of suspended familiarity/unfamiliarity so that the reader can have the pleasure of feeling his or her way to realizing what they mean. The way the reader feels his/her way to the meaning is, as Clason expressed above, by examining them in their *particular context*.

The meaning of the five created names can be thus perceived and felt by the reader because of a poetic device used by Wolfram to intimate to the reader's imagination a gradual but relatively secure recognition of the names' meaning in their immediate context. This poetic technique of Wolfram was first described by Jean Fourquet as 'reprise.'[8] I believe, however, that in relying on the poetic device of reprise, a repetition with some variation, to determine meaning, the location of the reprise can and should be expanded methodologically beyond Fourquet's search for a simple subsequent repetition. The reader of *Parzival* can confidently include a close examination of all of the immediate environment of the word in the text, looking especially to appropriate synonyms and rhymes, to identify the hints and clues which Wolfram has given as to his intent in creating the fictional name. Sometimes Wolfram actually defines the name directly, making the task of interpretation easy, and sometimes he defines indirectly by placing significant actions or synonyms in the surrounding text. If a personal name is without such a defining milieu, it loses a great deal of its power to communicate with and move the reader,[9] but when the immediate context of Wolfram's newly created names is examined, their meaning and function can become clear enough to confirm a poetically intuitive reading. If the poetic context is not considered, the puzzlement faced by a reader whose overall understanding of a passage is being influenced by an exclusively linguistic analysis of a name is increased. The translator, who both confronts word/context and must then transfer meaning to another word/context, will then have to remain in an uncomfortable ("sour" Wolfram would say) state of self-doubt.

This uncomfortable situation was expressed well in their translation by the obviously perplexed Helen Mustard and Charles Passage in their comment[10] on the name Herzeloyde: "The text seems to imply an etymology for 'Herzeloyde' as 'Heart's Sorrow' (herz+leide), but linguistic analysis will not support this poetically appropriate interpretation."

---

[8] See Jean Fourquet, *Wolfram d'Eschenbach et le Conte del Graal: Les divergences de la tradition du Conte del Graal de Chrétien et leur importance pour l'explication du texte du Parzival*. Publications de la Faculté des lettres et sciences humaines de Paris-Sorbonne. Série "Études et méthodes," 17 (Paris: Presses Universitaires de France, 1966).

[9] For the importance of the communicative aspect of *Parzival*, see Albrecht Classen, *Verzweiflung und Hoffnung: Die Suche nach der kommunikativen Gemeinschaft in der deutschen Literatur des Mittelalters*. Beihefte zur Mediaevistik, 1 (Frankfurt a. M., Berlin, et al.: Peter Lang, 2002), 234–35.

[10] *Parzival*, trans. Helen M. Mustard and Charles E. Passage (New York: Vintage Books [Random House], 1961), 78, note 9. All translations of *Parzival* will be quoted from here, unless otherwise noted.

In addition to the particular context, the overall context in the plot should also be consulted as another layer of evidence confirming or not confirming the meaning of poetically created names. I believe that Wolfram's narrative acts as a vehicle to escort Parzival to emotional maturity, i.e., to the capacity to feel sufficient compassion to break through social convention. In this, his poem bears a profound relationship to what one might call the hidden background of the story: the parable of the Good Samaritan.[11] In that story, Luke 10: 25–37, both the Jewish priest and the Levite see the injured man by the side of the road, perhaps react a bit, but simply pass by. The Samaritan, however, both sees and stops to help. He breaks social convention and goes to the aid of a non-Samaritan, someone hostile to Samaritans, a Jew. Why does he act differently from the priest and Levite? Why does he act? Because, as Wolfram would have known it from the Vulgate: "motus est misericordia," "he was moved by pity," literally: he was moved by 'compassionate-heartedness.' Wolfram's challenge in *Parzival*, one might say, is not to praise the Samaritan but rather to suggest to the priest and Levite, with the help of Lady Adventure, the way of emotional growth in *miseri-cordia*. That is, to help expand the confined space of the narrow-hearted,[12] to expand the feelings of those who see, and yet, like the young Parzival and the Levite, are not sufficiently moved by what they see to act, much less to act against honored social convention. The path of emotional growth on which this adventure enters is lined with names that possess the enormous power of indicating the way to the loving compassion that spontaneously[13] emerges from the heart, the kind of strong fellow-feeling that leads the protagonist to becoming a new Samaritan, perhaps best formulated through Parzival's ultimate question to his uncle, "'œheim, waz wirret dier?' (795, 29; "Uncle, what are you suffering from?").[14]

Wolfram assigns this challenging, humanizing role in his *Bildungsroman* to the five women. Parzival is led along the path of exemplification given in the form of the five women for whom, I would like to argue, Wolfram specifically created names that express the nature of this path of the human heart as it goes from inadequate response to being moved, progressing from little to no feelings, on to tears and feelings for other human beings. In analogy to the title of this volume,

---

[11] Roger Sherman Loomis noted this affinity as well; cf. his *The Grail, From Celtic Myth to Christian Symbol* (1963; Princeton: Princeton University Press, 1991), 218–19.

[12] *Parzival* 433, 1–3 (Book 9): "ich wil inz herze dîn zuo dir. / Sô gert ir zengem rûme" ("I want to get into your heart. That's a small, narrow space that you want to get into). The story stretches the space of the heart by letting the reader express the humble sentiment that his emotional space is small and cramped; but equally the heart's space is expandable, as evidenced by the reader's continuing curiosity about what happens next to Parzival: "wie vert der gehiure ... wie vert er nuo?" (433, 8–15; "How fares the handsome one? ... what is happening to him now?"). This is the function of the initial dialogue at the beginning of Book 9. (Cf. also Psalm 118:32.)

[13] This may explain the rule in the Grail community that no one is to tell Parzival when he comes that he is to ask about his host's suffering without any prompting.

[14] See Classen, *Verzweiflung und Hoffnung*, 271–78.

Names of Love, Love of Names 339

we might say, Wolfram's love of names enables him to mark the path to love with names of love. The path goes from the loyal heart's response of sorrow (Herzeloyde), through that of kinship fidelity (Sigûne), and continues with love leading the way (Condwîrâmûrs), on to self-knowledge with its accompanying realization of shame (Cundrîe), and finally ends in overflowing happiness (Repanse de Schoye). I will examine the five names in that order.

Herzeloyde. Chrétien gives her no name in his *Perceval*, but calls her "la veve dame de la gaste forest" (74–75; "the widow lady from the waste forest").[15] The name "Herzeloyde" is Wolfram's poetic creation.

> herzeloyde in kuste und *lief im nach.*
> der werlde *riwe* aldâ geschah.
> dô si *ir sun niht langer sach* ...
> dô *viel* diu frouwe valsches laz
> ûf die erde, aldâ si *jâmer sneit*
> sô daz se ein sterben niht vermeit. (128, 16–23)

> [72; Herzeloyde kissed him and ran after him. Then the sorrow of the world befell. her When she no longer saw her son... then the lady without falsity fell upon the ground, where grief stabbed her until she died]

> deiswâr du heizest Parzivâl.
> der nam ist rehte enmitten durch.
> grôz liebe ier solch *herzen* furch
> mit dîner muoter *triuwe*:
> dîn vater liez ir *riuwe*. (140, 16–20)
> [emphases throughout mine]

> [78; In truth, your name is Parzival, which signifies *right through the middle*. Such a furrow did great love plow in your mother's heart with the plow of her faithfulness. Your father bequeathed her sorrow].

In the first passage I have emphasized the contextual words that give rise to the interpretation of the name as a compound of 'heart' and 'sorrow.' She runs after her child after having kissed him. The world's sorrow then befalls her. When she could see him no longer as he rides away, she fell down on the ground where agonized sorrow so stabbed her that she died. The stabbing of a furrow through the heart expresses the nature of her total commitment in love to her son. In a striking phrase Wolfram comments with great respect on a death caused solely by a

---

[15] Chrétien de Troyes, *Le Conte du Gral (Perceval)* in *Les Romans de Chrétien de Troyes, édités d'apres la copie de Guiot (Bibl. Nat. Fr. 794)*, ed. Félix Lecoy (Paris: Librarie Honoré Champion, 1973).

heart's faithful love; he refers to it as "ir vil getriulîcher tôt" (128, 23) (literally, 'her very loyal death').

In the second passage, Parzival's own name is explained to him by Sigûne as 'right through the middle,' "der nam ist rehte enmitten durch" (140, 17). Then Sigûne explains his mother's name as parallel to her fate, a result of her faithfulness in love: great love plowed a furrow through the heart of your mother's faithfulness: your father left her sorrow. From these passages, including just a hint of the old Germanic belief in fate concealed in the name, passages with their metaphors and synonyms for the cutting pain of sorrow, "jâmer, sneit, riuwe," I believe it is clear from the particular context what Wolfram intended Herzeloyde to mean, and thus "loyde" must be "Leid," and the name can be translated Sorrowful Heart.[16]

A useful summary of etymological research is given by Chandler:

> Already Schulz pointed out that, owing to the consistent spelling of the ending *oy* in Parzival ... it is impossible for this name to be derived from *Leid*, as would seem at first sight the most obvious etymology. Schulz suggested a derivation from Welsh *erch*, 'dismal,' and *llued* or *lluydd*, 'warfare.' Bartsch suggested that the ending *oyde* is derived from the German name-ending *hilt*, through *haut*, *l* in conjunction with *hilt* being common in names (cf. Godalhildis beside Godahildis). *Herze-* he would derive from *hardo*, 'hard.' Alternatively Bartsch suggests that the original form of the name might be Harchehildis (*harc-* from OHG *haruc*, *fanum*) for Harchehildis, the former giving OF Herceleude. Gaston Paris disagrees entirely with the suggestions made by Bartsch, and asserts that Herzeloyde is a form of the OF name Herselot, a view which is held also by Golther and Bruce. Martin agrees with Bartsch that the second half of the name seems to contain the German *hilde* (cf. Rischoide and Mahaute), and he therefore doubts the etymology suggested by Gaston Paris. Martin has no explanation for the former half of the name, (*Herzel-*).[17]

By ignoring the poetic nature and context of the name, the linguistic etymologists end up with a strange division of the word into "Herzel-" and "-oyde" which leads nowhere, not even into the waste forest. What goes completely unnoticed in the etymological discussion is the wonderful and telling rhyme of faithful love with sorrow, of "triuwe" with "riuwe," in 140, 19–20, perfectly describing the feelings of Herzeloyde, whose faithful love, "triuwe," of her son cannot bear the pain ("riuwe")

---

[16] The Grimms' *Deutsches Wörterbuch* lists "herzeleid," giving mainly biblical instances for its use in medieval German, and defines the word as "leid, kummer des herzens" (10:1229).

[17] Frank Chandler, *A Catalogue of the Names of Persons in the German Court Epics* (London: Kings College, Centre for Late Antique and Medieval Studies,1992), 124.

of his leaving her, and the presence, unsurprisingly, in the preceding verse, of her love-furrowed "herzen."

Sigûne. Chrétien has no name for the young woman holding her decapitated[18] knight-lover, but he does refer to her as a young girl, "une pucele" (3419), and then has her identify herself to Perceval as "ta germaine cosine," (3586; your cousin).[19] It seems that her function is to show loyalty as did Herzeloyde; she mourns loving wedding ties even when the marriage did not take place. Her reproof of Parzival and his reply:

> ir lebt, und sît an sælden tôt.
> dô sprach er 'liebiu *niftel* mîn, . . .' (255, 20–21)

[you are alive, and yet as far as salvation is concerned you are dead. Then he said, "my dear cousin . . . .] (trans. mine).

> *der rehten ê diz vingerlîn*
> für got sol mîn geleite sîn.
> daz ist ob mîner triwe ein slôz,
> *vonme herzen mîner ougen vlôz.* (440, 13–16) [emphases mine]

[This ring of true marriage will be my escort before God. This ring is a castle defending my loyalty — the tears that flooded my eyes came from my heart] (trans. mine).

Sigûne accuses Parzival of hardheartedness, risking his ultimate happiness, "sælde," and all he can say in response is to ask her not to be so harsh on him, and he begins this by calling her his "niftel" (his cousin)[20] — Wolfram simply translating Chrétien's French, "cosine," into German, "niftel." The second citation shows Sigûne's wanting the ring to be her escort before God, fortress-like proof that she treated the dead knight with fidelity and that the tears in her eyes really flowed from her heart. This is her function, to show Parzival, albeit in fairly extreme iconography, what compassion and loyalty in the family-initiating world of wooing and lovers is: fidelity and kinship. Thus I think it reasonable to treat the name Sigûne as Wolfram's anagram ("gusine") for "cosine," Parzival's cousin. The name

---

[18] ". . . un chevalier qu'elle tenoit / Qui avoit tranchiee la teste" (3420–3421; the cause of her sorrow was / "a knight whom she was holding / who had his head cut off") (trans. mine).
[19] Wolfram follows and has her identify herself in 140, 22 by saying, "dîn muoter ist mîn muome" ("your mother is related to me [my aunt]") (trans. mine).
[20] For the importance of kinship and family in Wolfram's *Willehalm*, hence by analogy also in *Parzival*, see Sylvia Stevens, *Family in Wolfram von Eschenbach's Willehalm: mîner mâge triwe ist mir wol kuont*. Studies on Themes and Motifs in Literature, 18 (New York, Washington, et al.: Peter Lang, 1997), esp. 9–37.

thus derives from the form of address used by the two cousins in establishing their identities as relatives in the context of their conversations with each other.

The traditional linguistic approach is as follows:

> Schulz suggested a derivation of this name from *cygne,* 'swan,' whilst Bartsch sees in it the feminine of the Old French name Seguin, from OHG Siguwin, a view which Singer shares. Martin compares Sigûne with with Signý, the faithful wife of Loki.[21]

While "swan" may have some charm, I cannot imagine Wolfram associating Sigûne with Signý, since that would make the anointed lover who had died for her love into the highly improbable and unpalatable Loki. Imagining Loki, the sly and selfish murderer of Balder, as the dead knight would mean blending his nasty past history with the love pursuit of Sigûne's devoted knight, and render her iconographic allusion to the Pietà absurd. An allusion to Loki is simply not compatible with the context. "Siguwin," however, might mean "friend of victory" but this too seems rather curious for the name of the weeping gem of a woman named Sigûne. In sum, I find none of these three suggestions really fits the poetic context of Sigûne's repeated iconic role in the epic as Parzival's thoughtful relative, and as the chaste and persistent holder of her fallen knight and lover, the embodiment of familial *pietas.*

Condwîrâmûrs.[22] Chrétien gives her a name, "Blancheflor" ("Blancheflor sa dolce amie;" 2415) which Wolfram obviously did not translate nor take over into his epic poem as "White Flower." In the case of the name "Condwîrâmûrs" we have an etymological explanation by Wolfram himself of the meaning of the name in another context, just as he did with "Parzival." In describing the bravery of Parzival's brother, Wolfram writes:

diu minne condwierte
in sîn manlîch herze hôhen muot,
als si noch dem minne gernden tuot. (736, 6–8)

[Love conducts, guides, and escorts high courage into his manly heart, just as it still does for those who seek for love.]

---

[21] Chandler, *A Catalogue of the Names,* 259–60. Other researchers note that the name Sigûne became an extremely popular name in Germany from 1286 onwards. See also the discussion of Irish sources for European courtly love literature by William Sayers in his contribution to this volume.

[22] Wolfram actually has her name written in two separate compounds, "Condwîr âmûrs," but for clarity's sake the name is written here as one word.

Names of Love, Love of Names   343

The interpreter should consider that love is consistently the subject of the action, rarely the object, in Wolfram's creation of the name Condwîrâmûrs. "Condwir+amurs" means "Love Leads" (leads courage into his heart), and not "Leads to Love," and Wolfram himself gives the explanation for the name in the above instance. Love is thus the source of en-courage-ment, showing the way to increasing maturity and high spiritedness for the warrior. Condwîrâmûrs, i.e., love induces feelings that lead to action, whether this be for Feirefiz or Parzival, for pagan or Christian; and this will be heard in the battle cries of the two brothers when they meet at the end.

The linguistic reflections on the name are not very far off:

> Golther explains this name as an invention from Wolfram from an infinitive plus noun, put together in German style.[23] Bartsch, trying to avoid the infinitive plus noun construction, suggested derivation from *coin de voire amors*, i.e. 'ideal of true love,' a suggestion which is ridiculed by Gaston Paris. According to Singer, the name occurred in Kîôt, who had sometimes *Conduire amors*, 'escort of love' [Geleitung der Liebe] and sometimes *Conduire en amors*, 'escort into love' [Geleitung in die Liebe], thus accounting for the form 'Kondwiren âmûrs' in *Parzival* 327, 20.[24]

Though the observations do consider both love and the idea of escorting or conducting, instead of examining the context, for example, of 736, 6–8 above, Bartsch resorts to idealism, and Singer to two projected forms in a text of the story, Kyot's, that we simply do not have and which probably did not exist.[25] We do have Trevrizent's remark however, referring to the woman he once served for love, which gives another useful example: "ir minne condwirte / mir freude in daz herze mîn" (495, 22–3; "her love conducted joy into my heart.")

Cundrîe. Chrétien has no name for the hideous maiden, but simply describes her as "une demeisele qui vint sor une mule fauve" (3209; "a maiden who came on a tawny mule"). "Cundrîe" is therefore not a borrowing from Chrétien but, once again, a name-creation of Wolfram. I believe we can trust the contextual intuition that her name is to be associated with the immense learning and knowledge she displays. Thus Cundrîe is properly associated by the reader with "kund," to be

---

[23] Chandler, *A Catalogue of the Names*, 164, n. 35, mentions that Golther thought that Wolfram had explained the meaning of the name in 495, 22f.
[24] Chandler, *A Catalogue of the Names*, 164, n. 35.
[25] For a recent reexamination of the Kyot-myth, see Albrecht Classen, "Noch einmal zu Wolframs 'spekulativer' Kyôt -Quelle im Licht jüdischer Kultur und Philosophie des zwölften Jahrhunderts," *Studi Medievali* XLVI (2005): 281–308.

aware of, or to know about.[26] In view of her being aware not only of the names of all the planets, in Arabic and Latin, but also of Parzival's shameful failure, and since she "lets him know," this is an appropriate and telling creation based on "kund."

The linguistic approach bypasses the context of her essential poetic function in the story and goes instead to her appearance:

> Schulz derived this name from the Old French *contruit,* 'misshapen,' whilst Bartsch thought that the Old French *conrée,*[27] 'flame [or tan] colored' (die Lohfarbige), was the root, a derivation with which Gaston Paris disagrees, but which is supported by Martin, who translates *conrée* by the more usual 'woman adorned with jewelry' (die Geschmückte).[28]

If we look at the text surrounding her appearance in the story we can come closer to determining Wolfram's intent in creating the name:

> der meide ir *kunst* des verjach,
> *alle sprâch si wol sprach,*
> *latîn, heidnisch, franzoys.*
> si was der *witze kurtoys,*
> *dîaletike* und *jêometrî*:
> ir wâren ouch die *liste* bî
> von *astronomîe.*
> si hiez Cundrîe:
> *surziere* was ir zuoname (312, 19–27)
>
> [169; The maiden was so learned that she spoke all languages well, Latin, French and heathen (i.e. Arabic). She was versed in dialectic and geometry and even in the science of astronomy. Cundrîe was her name, with surname *la sorcière*).]
>
> diu maget *witze rîche* . . . . (313, 1) (emphasis mine)
> [the maiden rich in intelligence . . . .] (trans. mine)

---

[26] Cf. Jacob and Wilhelm Grimms' *Deutsches Wörterbuch*, Vol. 5 (Leipzig: Hirzel, 1873), 2617–19. The Grimms' dictionary gives the Old High German and Middle High German meaning of the word as similar to "kennend" and "wissend" (knowing about, having knowledge of). Groos, *Romancing the Grail*, 170–96, details Cundrîe's role as the personification of astronomical knowledge.

[27] The verb "conreer" in medieval French meant to arrange, to equip, to put in order, furnish what is necessary, to prepare; "conreé" = equipped. It could be used of soldiers or horses being furnished with equipment for battle, of hides being prepared (tanning) for use, or, in the case of women = "couvrer et vestir," to cover, dress and adorn. From Frédéric Godefroy, *Dictionnaire de l'ancienne Langue Française et de tous ses dialectes du IXe au XVe siècle, composé d'après le dépouillement de tous les plus importants documents, manuscrits ou imprimés* (Paris: F. Vieweg, 1884).

[28] Chandler, *A Catalogue of the Names*, 168.

Repetition of her abilities is not only in the 'reprise' that she is the maiden rich in intelligence, "witze rîche," but also in all the synonyms for intelligence and knowledge, "kunst," "witze," "liste," all parallel to "kund," the root, I believe, of her name. The context surrounds her as a sorceress of cultivated mind by detailing an impressive list of her abilities in the arts and sciences: she has command of Latin, Arabic, and French; she knows dialectics and geometry; all contribute to explaining the significance of her name as designating a person of intelligence and knowledge.[29] No contextual gesture is quite as fine, however, at suggesting the meaning of her name as Wolfram's taking her premier knowledge, that of the planets and the stars in their courses, and rhyming her knowledge of astronomy with her own name: "astronomîe: Cundrîe"!

> ir wâren ouch die liste bî
> von astronomîe,
> si hiez Cundrîe. (312, 24–6)

[she knew well the science of astronomy, her name was Cundry] (trans. mine).

Repanse de Schoye. Chrétien does not give a name to the young girl carrying the Grail. He simply refers to her as a young lady, "une demeisele" (3165)." There is agreement on all sides that the name Wolfram gives her is his own poetic creation in French. There is further agreement, as seen below, that Schoye is "joie," joy or happiness. The difficulty arises in determining the intention of Wolfram in using "Repanse." Could Repanse mean "fullness" or "expanse" so that the name might be understood as a "Fullness of Joy?" The linguists offer several suggestions leading into other directions:

> Schulz thought that the form in *Titurel*, 'Urrepanse', was the original, and he derived this from the Old French *ourer* 'to pray', and *pens*, 'thought', i.e. 'sunk in reverence.' Martin is more inclined to Lachmann's explanation that it is derived from the Old French *répenser*, 'to think again', i.e. 'remembrance of joy'.[30]

Though these are possible, I think once again it is more than useful to look at the context. At her first appearance carrying the Grail, Repanse is described in the section that contains some of the most famous lines in the poem:

> nâch den kom diu künegîn.
> ir antlütze gap den schîn,

---

[29] See also Groos, *Romancing the Grail*, 170–96.
[30] Chandler, *A Catalogue of the Names*, 245.

si wânden alle ez wolde tagen.
Man sach die maget an ir tragen
pfellel von Arâbî.
ûf einem grüenen achmardî
truoc si den *wunsch* von pardîs.
Bêde wurzeln *unde rîs.*
Daz was ein dinc, daz hiez der Grâl,
erden *wunsches überwal.*
Repanse de schoy si hiez ... (235, 15–25; emphasize mine)

[29; "After them came the queen. So radiant was her face that everyone thought the dawn was breaking. She was clothed in a dress of Arabian silk. Upon a deep achmardi [green silk cloth with gold thread] she bore the perfect bliss of Paradise, both root and branch. That was a thing called the Grail, the overflow of earthly bliss. Repanse de Schoye was her name.] (my modification)

The images in the text suggest that there is an exuberant expansion of light and happiness that come out of her and the Grail. First, her face is so radiant with light that people think the dawn is breaking. Then the Grail is described in similar terms. It is the blissful happiness of Paradise, not in primal static form alone, but blissful happiness both in its root and in its expansion from its root into its branches. Finally, the Grail itself is described as blissful joy, "wunsch," in "überwal," literally overflow.[31] The image of expansion and overflow is the dominant one, and helps determine the image behind Wolfram's creation of "Repanse de Schoye." The French word at its base must be, then, *respanche*[32] (modern French "épancher," "répandre") a spilling over, an overflow, and the whole name would then mean "Overflow of Happiness."

To confirm this, a careful examination of the text reveals another close reprise, similar to that in the case of "Cundrîe" above. Immediately preceding the words "Repanse de Schoy" in line 25, we find hidden in plain sight in line 24

---

[31] Translators often render this expression as some form of "transcending earthly happiness." Using the abstract "transcendence" instead of the more concrete "overflow" may be philosophically interesting, but unfortunately it costs the reader the enjoyment of one of the fundamental metaphors of *Parzival*: the flow of water. See also the contribution to this volume by Siegfried Christoph.

[32] The word "respanche" (mod. Fr. "épancher") is ultimately based on a form of "(ex-)pandere," the classical Latin verb for opening wide, spreading, or expanding [its Old French synonym "respandre "(*re+pandere*) has the same meaning]. "Respanche" is used for an overflow, a pouring out or spilling of a liquid, e.g., "Ils respancherent tout le vin," in one case, and in another for generous flow of libations for a sacrifice: "et respanche avec du laict.... du vin, du miel." Godefroy has an elegant definition, albeit with household overtones, of "respandre": letting a liquid flow onto a space on which it expands, "laisser couler un liquide sur un espace où il s'étend." This fits quite well with Wolfram's accompanying images of expansion: light radiation, plant growth, and overflow. Cf. Godefroy, *Dictionnaire de l'ancienne Langue Française*, VII, 108, and X, 558.

the two-word explanation of her name: "wunsches überwal": "Repanse de Schoy sie hiez" ("She was called 'Overflow of Happiness'"). She is thus connected to the outflow of divine pleasure pictured in the Augustinian view of the outflowing of the four rivers of Paradise.[33] When he donned her green cloak at the first Grail banquet, Parzival, though unaware of it, was giving an iconic expression of his destiny to be, one day, a human being capable of human feelings, overflowing with happiness and compassion: a good Samaritan, the healing lord of the Grail, a crusader knight capable of sympathy for his Muslim brother.

If we look again at the invocation made by the author to his muse at the beginning of the pivotal Book 9, we find a lucid image for the author's intent in writing his epic poem, as, in an innovative twist, Wolfram has his story address him. Book 9 begins with a significant command from a woman, Lady Adventure, "frou âventiure": "Open up!" "Tuot ûf."

> 'Tuot ûf.' wem? Wer sît ir?
> 'Ich wil inz herze dîn zuo dir.'
> Sô gert ir zengem rûme. (433, 1–3)
> ["Open up!" To whom? Who are you?
> "I want to get into your heart."
> That's a small, narrow space that you want to get into] (trans. mine).

And then, once the story is inside, the author/reader inquires about the hero Parzival. Lady Adventure is then in the right place to be able to continue with her task to cause some "heart's sorrow" by telling more of the slow growth of the hero — the hero who is every bit as much the author and reader as it is Parzival. In other words, it is the intent of the story itself to get into the author's and readers' hearts, narrow squeeze though that may be, and expand them through sympathy with the adventures of Parzival. The names created by Wolfram for his leading women serve the same purpose as that which he gives to the overall tale itself in the person of Lady Adventure. In a deft textual move reflecting that purpose in the reader and author as well as in Parzival, she goes immediately from the polite (or plural) form in the first line, "tuot," to the intimate form, "dîn," in the second — precisely the path that Parzival will undergo in his asking the question of his uncle. Wolfram thus would have us all, reader and hero, himself as well, arrive at having hearts open to what Albrecht Classen, citing Jürgen Habermas, calls "intersubjektive Anerkennung," the mutual, inter-personal recognition that proceeds from openness and toleration and leads to a genuinely communicative society.[34] This is, in more ancient terminology, the *telos* of having the priest and

---

[33] For a discussion of the role of the Augustinian view of the four rivers of Paradise in Wolfram's *Parzival*, see Murphy, *Gemstone of Paradise, The Holy Grail in Wolfram's Parzival*, chap. 2.

[34] See Classen, *Verzweiflung und Hoffnung*, 235.

Levite arrive at the condition of the heartfelt Samaritan, that of spontaneous compassionate love for one's fellow human being, having been shown the way by the women with names of power.

This analysis of the poetic names given by Wolfram to five forms of love clarifies their function and thereby casts some light, I hope, on Wolfram's depiction of the development of feelings and especially of 'compassionate-heartedness' as the overall inner sequence of the story as love leads the way through sorrow to bliss. The sequence can be written: Herzeloyde, Sigûne, Condwîrâmûrs, Cundrîe, and Repanse de Schoye; more abstractly: maternal affection and pain; fidelity to lover and family; the guiding commitment of husband and wife; painful self-knowledge and shame; and finally, arrival in fraternal style at overflowing happiness. In Wolfram's *Parzival*, women have these feelings innately; men acquire them. Together, they enable the hero to transcend the distance caused by social convention to reach the compassionate and humane world once described in a parable and now called the mountain of the Holy Grail.

CHAPTER 15

WHEN YOUR LOVER IS THE VIRGIN MARY

CONNIE L. SCARBOROUGH
University of Cincinnati

In the *Cantigas de Santa Maria,* Alfonso X the Wise not only praises and exalts the Virgin Mary but also courts her favor by presenting her as the ultimate object of man's affections. To this end, he co-opts many of the rhetorical devices of the courtly love tradition while, at the same time, promoting a political agenda in which he is portrayed as a monarch especially favored by the Heavenly Queen. Just as the protagonists of the miracles confess their undying love and commitment to Holy Mary, so too does Alfonso, in his role both as protagonist of some of the narratives and as director of the collection's composition. From the outset of the work, in his Prologue, Alfonso clearly states his proposal to reject all other women in favor of the Virgin Mary and to dedicate his work to her as if he were her troubadour. He further asserts that he composed the *Cantigas* to assure his own salvation: "sei de pran que, se a ben servir / que non poderei en seu ben falir / de o aver" (1:55; "I know full well that if I serve Her faithfully, I shall never be deprived of Her blessing; 2).[1] And also in the prologue, he expresses his desire that his songs will please Her and that "me dé gualardon com' ela dá / aos que ama" (1:56; She give [him] the reward which She gives to those She loves; 2)

The *Cantigas de Santa Maria* contains over four hundred miracle stories and songs of praise of Holy Mary. It was composed in Galician-Portuguese by Alfonso and his collaborators during the years of the king's reign from 1252 to 1284.[2] Many of the miracles are simply reworkings of Marian legends found in other similar

---

[1] There are in fact two "prologues" to the collection. The one I refer to here is commonly referred to as "Proglogue B." "Prologue A" is largely a listing of the kingdoms under Alfonso's control and identifies him as the composer of the work.

[2] The standard edition for the work in Galician-Portuguese is Walter Mettmann's three-volume set which is most readily available in paperback, published by Castalia in Madrid, 1984–1889 (originally published in Coimbra by the University, 1959–1972).

medieval collections, both those written in the vernaculars and in Latin.[3] However, a significant number of the poems /songs are original to Alfonso's work. In fact, several deal with the miraculous intervention of the Virgin in the king's own life and in the lives of his family members. While Alfonso is usually seen more in the role of editor than as composer of all the texts in the *Castigas de Santa Maria*, one can identity throughout the *Cantigas* a unifying authorial voice whether the songs deal directly with the king or not. Joseph Snow has investigated this singular authorial voice in the collection calling it a single troubadour-like narrative presence in the *Cantigas*. In articles published in 1979[4] and in 1990,[5] Snow convincingly argues that the Alfonsine voice often assumes the posture and rhetoric of the courtly lover in his relationship to Holy Mary. Like all troubadours, Alfonso found in the courtly love tradition a model to interlace mystical love with secular love. These characteristics include, as we shall see: (1) the awe inspired by the beloved lady's / Virgin's lofty qualities; (2) her inaccessibility or physical absence;[6] (3) her power for spiritual and corporeal renewal; (4) the sacrifice undergone by the courtly lover;[7] and (5) the paradisiacal experience as the ultimate reward.[8]

Not only does the king's poetic voice often mimic the conventions of the courtly suitor, but at times it reaches impassioned heights where Alfonso, or one of the protagonists of the narrative, vows to commit himself body and soul to Holy Mary. Moreover, he frequently presents the Heavenly Queen in roles one does not usually associate with the Mother of Christ — e.g., as a jealous suitor, as a great beauty in competition with other women, and as a warrior in the battles for men's souls. By presenting the Virgin in very human guises, we may infer that Alfonso felt a need to humanize the saintly object of his devotion in order to justify his unique attraction to Her, both as woman and as Queen of Heaven. His tone is at once both reverential and amorous. I have already commented on this

---

[3] See Harriet Goldberg, *Motif-Index of Medieval Spanish Folk Narratives*. Medieval and Renaissance Texts and Studies, 162 (Tempe, AZ: Arizona Center for Medieval and Renaissance Studies, 1998), 283; and eadem, *Motif-Index of Folk Narratives in the Pan-Hispanip Romancero*. Medieval and Renaissance Texts and Studies, 206 (Tempe, AZ: Arizona Center for Medieval and Renaissance Studies, 2000), 299–301, all under 'Virgin Mary.'

[4] Joseph Snow, "The Central Role of the Troubadour *Persona* of Alfonso X in the *Cantigas de Santa Maria*," *Bulletin of Hispanic Studies* 56 (1979): 305–16.

[5] Joseph Snow, "Alfonso as Troubadour: The Fact and the Fiction," *Emperor of Culture*, ed. Robert Ignatius Burns, S.J. Middle Ages Series (Philadelphia: University of Pennsylvania Press, 1990), 124–40.

[6] In religious verse, such as Alfonso's, the inaccessibility of a celestial being is often mitigated by a vision of the Virgin, her appearance in one's dreams, or an articulated statue of Mary.

[7] In religious verse, it is most often interpreted as long years of service to the Virgin either as a lay person or as a clergyman or monk. Also quite common is isolation from the rest of world serving Holy Mary as a hermit dedicated to prayer and physical deprivation.

[8] These elements are adapted from Elisa Miruna Ghil's analysis of "Religious Language," *A Handbook of the Troubadours*, eds. F. R. P. Akehurst and Judith M. Davis (Berkeley and Los Angeles: University of California Press, 1995), 441–61.

phenomenon,[9] but here I want to emphasize and carefully examine the specific words and terminology that Alfonso uses to speak about and to Mary. While his discourse at times merely reflects a well-established mode of religious address to a deity or to one's courtly lover, the king also tries to make the Virgin accessible, not only as merciful mother figure for her devotees, but also as desirable woman in earthly terms.

Early in the collection we find examples of Alfonso commingling expressions of religious and profane love.[10] *Cantiga* 16 bears the title "Esta é como Santa maria converteu un cavaleiro namorado, que ss 'ouver' a desasperar porque non podia aver sa amiga" (1:99; This is how Holy Mary converted a knight who was in love and on the verge of despair because he could not have his beloved; 24).[11] This song recounts the tale of a handsome, brave, and virtuous knight who is desperately enamored of a young woman who refuses all his entreaties. The knight confesses his obsession with this woman to a priest, and his confessor tells him that if he truly wishes to win the lady he must pray to Holy Mary for help. Every day, for a year, the knight recites two hundred *Ave Marias*. One day as he prays and pleads his case before the Virgin's altar, the Heavenly Queen appears to him and orders him to "Toll' as mãos dante ta faz / e para-mi mentes, ... / de mi e da outra dona, a que te mais prez / filla qual quiseres, segundo teu semellar" (1:101; Take your hands from your face and look straight at me, ... Between me and the other lady, choose the one who pleases you most, according to your preference; 25). Overcome by Mary's beauty, the knight immediately vows to become a servant of the Virgin and to renounce his infatuation with the lady he has been pursuing. Not only has the knight's original plan backfired, but his continuous devotion to the Virgin has caused him to be smitten by a Holy Cupid, so to speak. But the story does not end here. As with any jealous suitor, Mary does not acquiesce straight away to the knight's profession of love, but demands that he devote as much time and effort to winning her as he had for his former beloved. The Virgin makes her requirements clear when She tells him "Se me por amiga queres aver, mais rafez, tanto que est' ano rezes por mi outra vez / quanto pola outra antano fuste rezar" (1:101; If you wish me for your beloved, you must pray for me another year as much

---

[9] Connie Scarborough, *Women in Thirteenth-Century Spain as Portrayed in Alfonso X's Cantigas de Santa Maria*. Hispanic Literature, 19 (Lewiston, Queenston, and Lampeter: The Edwin Mellen Press, 1993).

[10] For further investigations of this topic, the intertwining of the religious and the secular, see *Geistliches in weltlicher und Weltliches in geistlicher Literatur des Mittelalters*, ed. Christoph Huber, Burghart Wachinger, and Hans-Joachim Ziegeler (Tübingen: Niemeyer, 2000); see the review by Albrecht Classen in *The Medieval Review* 00.08.08 (online).

[11] Quotations are from *Cantigas de Santa Maria*, ed. Walter Mettmann (Madrid: Castalia, 1986–1989). All translations are from Kathleen Kulp-Hill, trans., *Cantigas de Santa Maria: Songs of Holy Mary of Alfonso X, The Wise*. Intro. Connie L. Scarborough. Medieval and Renaissance Texts and Studies, 173 (Tempe: Arizona Center for Medieval and Renaissance Studies, 2000).

as you formerly prayed for the other; 25). At the end of another year of reciting two hundred *Ave Marias* daily to the Virgin, Mary rewards the knight by taking him to be with Her in heaven. Although most of us would not see death as the ultimate prize in love, the fact that he is physically united with his chosen Lady is significant in light of his choice to become exclusively Her suitor.

A review of cantigas involving the Virgin as potential suitor must include Alfonso's version of the classic tale of the statue bride, *Cantiga* 42. The earliest written version of this tale in Western Europe is found in William of Malmesbury's *De Gestis Regum Anglorum* (ca. 1100), where the protagonist is the goddess Venus rather than the Virgin Mary.[12] Alfonso sets his version of the tale in Germany. In the Alfonsine poem, a statue of the Virigin has been placed outside, near a village green, while the church where it was normally housed is undergoing repair. On this green young men gather to play ball and one of the players, in order to safeguard a ring given to him by his lover, places the ring on the statue of the Virgin. As he places the ring on Her finger he is overcome by the beauty of the statue and declares, "Oi mais non m'enchal / Daquela que eu amava, ca eu ben o jur' a Deus / que nunca tan bela cousa viron estes ollos meus; / poren daqui adeante serei eu dos servos teus, / e est' anel tan fremosos ti dou porend' en sinal" (1:161; From this day forth that lady whom I loved means nothing to me, for I swear to God that these eyes of mine have never seen anything so beautiful. Hence from now on I shall be one of your servants and I give you this beautiful ring as pledge; 55). After he utters these words before the Virgin's image, the statue closes its fingers around the ring. The young man is understandably alarmed; his friends see it as a sign from God and tell him that he should enter a convent to serve Our Lady. But he ignores their advice, and returns to his previous love and soon the two are married. However, on the couple's wedding night, the Virgin comes to the bridegroom in a dream and harshly scolds him: "Ai, meu falss' e mentira! / De mi por que te partiste e fuste fillar moller? / Mal te nenbrous a sortella que me dést'; ond' á mester / que a leixes e te vaas comigo a cmo quer, / se non, daqui adeante averás coyta mortal" (1:162; "Oh, my faithless liar! Why did you forsake me and take a wife? You forgot the ring you gave me. Therefore, you must leave your wife and go with me wherever I so will. Otherwise, from now on, you will suffer mortal anguish; 56). Even such a direct threat from the Virgin does not immediately persuade the young man to abandon his wife. When he goes back to sleep, the Virgin appears to him again, this time physically lying between him and his bride in the nuptial bed. Now Mary's threats are even harsher: "Mao, falsso, desleal, / Ves? E por que me leixase e sol vergonna non ás? / Mas se tu meu amor queres, daqui te

---

[12] A version with the Virgin as protagonist is found in Vincent de Beauvais's mid-thirteenth-century collection, *Speculum Historiale*. For a complete review of sources, as well as a classic study of *Cantiga* 42, see John E. Keller, "The Motif of the Statue Bride in the *Cantigas* of Alfonso the Learned," *Studies in Philology* 56 (1959): 453–58.

When Your Lover is the Virgin Mary

levantarás, / e vai-te comigo logo, que non esperes a cras; / erge-te daqui correndo e sal desta casa, sal!" (1:162–63; Wicked, false, unfaithful one, do you understand? Why did you leave me and have no shame of it? If you wish my love, you will arise from here and come at once with me before daybreak. Get up in a hurry and leave this house! Go! 56). This second apparition of the Virgin so frightens the young man that he flees his home immediately wandering in the wilderness until he establishes himself in a hermitage where he devotes the remainder of his days to the service of Holy Mary.

This is another, rather extreme, example of the Virgin as jealous suitor. Also, again it is Mary's beauty that enraptures the young man and blinds him, at least in this case momentarily, to the charms of other women. The persistence of the Virgin in *Cantiga* 42 is remarkable; She literally will not permit her suitor to lie with another woman once he had placed the ring of promise on her finger.

Another excellent example of an impassioned lover of the Virgin is found in *Cantiga* 84. In this song, the protagonist is a knight who, the poet tells us, is very happily married to a young and beautiful lady. The specific words of the text here are quite explicit in describing their relationship, saying that the knight loves his wife dearly and that "ela a el amava que xe perdia o sen" (1:266; She also loved him madly; 108). In spite of his sincere love for his wife, he is even more devoted to the Virgin to the extent that he has a door opened from his house leading directly into the church next door so that he may have ready access to the Virgin's altar at any time. He arises every night after he and his wife have gone to bed and goes into the church to pray to Holy Mary. The wife becomes suspicious of his late-night absences from their bed, but when she asks her husband about where he goes at night, he swears to her that he has never been unfaithful to her.

One day, the wife directly confronts her husband asking him if he loves another woman more than he loves her. The husband confesses that he does indeed love a most beautiful woman more than anything else in the world. Upon hearing this, the wife picks up a knife, plunges it into her breast and dies immediately from the wound. The distraught husband places his wife's lifeless body in their bed and then goes directly to the Virgin's altar to plead that she be returned to him. Mary appears to her devotee and tells him that her Son has agreed to resuscitate his wife because of his great devotion to Her. He returns home to find his wife alive and well. The two then take holy orders so that they may better serve Our Lady.

This cantiga presents a situation of extreme devotion to the Virgin while, at the same time, it implies that one's love for Holy Mary should surpass any other romantic ties to one's loved ones. The song at once celebrates the joy of the happy couple who love each other deeply, and even madly, as the cantiga specifies. But even this example of blissful Christian marriage is inferior to the love of the faithful for the Virgin Mary. She surpasses all other women not only in her purity and mercy, but also in physical beauty. The knight in *Cantiga* 84 cannot spend a night without basking in the physical presence of the Virgin as he worships before her statue. Even the joys of the marriage bed cannot distract him from the love of the other, in this case holy, woman.

Mary is also portrayed as a woman capable of forgiving and, indeed, saving even the darkest of sinners. In *Cantiga* 281, for instance, Alfonso relates the story of a rich man who, owing to a string of bad luck, finds himself impoverished. The devil appears to him in the form of a man who promises to restore all his wealth to him if he will be his vassal. The man readily agrees but the devil asks him, as proof of loyalty, to deny God and all his saints. The man reluctantly agrees to this oath, but when the devil insists that he also deny Holy Mary, he refuses to do so, stating, "Este poder nono ás / que me faças que a negue, nen tanto non me darás / que negue tan bõa dona; ante m' iria matar" (3:55; This power to make me deny Her you do not possess, nor will you give me enough wealth to make me deny such a good Lady. I would die first; 340). The devil accepts this refusal, but also makes the man promise that he will never enter a church as long as he is in his service. The protagonist of the narrative respects this vow not to enter a church until one day, on a journey with the king of France, he is sitting outside the church after the king has gone inside. From his seat outside the church, he sees a statue of Holy Mary who appears to be gesturing for him to enter. Other people witness the miracle of the statue beckoning to the man, but, when the king insists that he do as the statue bids, the man initially refuses, replying that Mary "é m'irada con dereito, a la fe" (3:56; is rightfully angry with [him]; 340). He then confesses that he had become a vassal of the devil and had denied God and the saints, and he publicly swears from this day forward to renounce the devil and pleads for forgiveness for his grievous sin. When the king asks if he had ever renounced his belief in the Virgin, the man replies, in truth, that he never had. The king is so pleased with the man's reply and the sincerity of his repentance that he grants him a large endowment so that he will never be poor again.

Several facets of this text are noteworthy. First, the protagonist is willing to renounce God the Father, Christ his savior, and the host of heavenly saints, but will not agree to blaspheme the Holy Virgin. This singular exception is recognized by the Virgin, who performs the miracle of the articulate statue. This, as is the case for many cantigas, does not follow what has been held to be mainstream canonical theology regarding Mary's role in salvation. Whereas the Church maintains that She serves as our supreme advocate before God, always willing to plead a sinner's cause despite the gravity of the sin, She is not held to be an independent instrument of one's salvation. Nonetheless, in *Cantiga* 281, it is the Virgin's initiative alone which prompts the protagonist to confess and to return to grace. Moreover, Mary represents the ultimate manifestation of his Christian faith because She is the only divine figure that this blasphemous sinner refuses to betray. His last thread of loyalty to the church is love for Holy Mary.

The protagonist of *Cantiga* 295 is a king who renders great homage and service to Holy Mary by composing songs in her honor, writing accounts of her miracles, and commissioning many beautiful statues of Her. The king of this song is a very thinly veiled portrait of King Alfonso himself. It is not uncommon for Alfonso to use the cantiga narratives as vehicles for self-promotion or as proof that the Virgin endorses his political goals, as we will see in this cantiga. In *Cantiga* 295 the king commissions a particularly beautiful statue of Mary and donates it to Her church on Easter; he also invites nuns to come pray before this new image on his behalf. While the nuns are praying, Holy Mary appears to them in a vision, telling them to ask the king to come in person to pray at the altar of her new statue. They dream that when the king arrives the statue kneels down to the ground before him and tries to kiss his hands. But the king refuses to allow Her to pay homage to him and, he, in turn, prostrates himself before the statue saying that it should be he who ought to kiss her hands and feet in gratitude for the mercies She has shown him. She replies that She wishes to kiss his hands "por quanta onrra fazedes a mi sempr' e ao meu / Fillo ... e poren no reino seu / vos meterei pis morrerdes, esto sera sen mentir" (3:87; for the great honor you always pay me and my Son, ... Therefore, I shall place you in his kingdom after you die, this I promise in all truth; 358). When the nuns awake from this vision they go at once to tell the king, who immediately orders a written account of this miraculous occurrence. Our praiseworthy king here is, as I have mentioned, the alter ego of Alfonso, prolific author of Marian miracles. These desires seem to be fulfilled by the Virgin's promise in the final lines of *Cantiga* 295. The king, who is the protagonist of the account, writes about this experience as was Alfonso's practice whenever news of a new miracle reached him. He also specifies that, because of his fervent devotion and service to Our Lady, She rewards him in many ways and adds, "a queno ben comedir" (3:87; he richly deserved it; 358). While we might view this latter statement as pompous, it certainly is in keeping with the king's political agenda and self-promotion. Alfonso's vision of a united and officially Christian Spain at the forefront of a grand Catholic European enterprise was evident in his numerous petitions to the pope over a period of decades to have himself named to the post of Holy Roman Emperor.[13] This king, with Holy Mary by his side, had a grand plan for himself and his kingdom, and cantigas such as *Cantiga* 295 which recognizes the grandeur of this devout and generous servant of the Virgin formed part of Alfono's image-making strategy. It should probably be noted also that *Cantiga* 295 is one of the few cantigas which is repeated in the collection.[14]

---

[13] For a treatment of the king's efforts to have himself named as Holy Roman Emperor, see Joseph O'Callaghan, "Image and Reality: The King Creates his Kingdom," *Emperor of Culture*, ed. Burns, 14–32.

[14] Alfonso repeats this miracle verbatim as *Cantiga* 388.

A number of cantigas deal with illnesses which Alfonso X suffered and relate how he was cured by the Virgin's intervention and divine mercy. Forensic evidence conducted on Alfonso's remains revealed that the king suffered from cancer which disfigured his face as tumors broke through his nasal and sinus cavities.[15] There is also some evidence that he suffered other less life-threatening but nonetheless painful infirmities. Therefore it is not surprising that he dedicated songs to the Virgin in thanksgiving for the times when he was healthy and free from pain. Whereas the Virgin's intervention in these cases of illness could be seen as the actions of a comforting mother or divine physician, Alfonso consistently claims that Mary responds to his pleas for help because of his singular devotion to Her as his peerless Lady. In his songs, Alfonso presents the cure as a type of reward that the Divine Lady bestows on Her most faithful servant and devotee.

In *Cantiga* 367, Alfonso suffers from a tremendous swelling in the legs. Unlike in *Cantiga* 295, previously discussed, Alfonso's identity as central character is not a matter of inference because the very first line of the song names the Wise King as the narrative's protagonist.[16] Despite the horrible swelling in his legs, Alfonso insists on traveling to the newly conquered port city, El Puerto de Santa María, in order to attend the ceremonies to dedicate a new church which he had erected there in honor of the Virgin.[17] On Friday, the evening before the day of the week traditionally dedicated to the Virgin, i.e., Saturday, Alfonso reaches the church and keeps vigil before Holy Mary's altar throughout the night. As matins are about to be sung early Saturday morning, Alfonso is suddenly relieved from the swelling in his legs. All his retinue witness the miracle and sing praises to Holy Mary who "que nos gaanna / de Deus saud' e nos dá alegria" (3:246; wins health for us from God and gives us joy; 447). For Alfonso, this cure implies direct intervention on Mary's part which he regards as his reward for having dedicated yet another church in her honor in territories recently recovered from Moorish occupation.

Near the end of his collection as *Cantiga* 401, Alfonso writes a song which has come to be called the *pitiçon*, or petition. In this poem, Alfonso asks Mary to be his guide and protector and makes a long list of requests to Her. These include protection from the devil; victory over the Moors; defense from false traitors; bad

---

[15] See Maricel E. Preilla, "The Image of Death and Political Ideology in the *Cantigas de Santa Maria*," *Studies in the Cantigas de Santa Maria : Art, Music, and Poetry: Proceedings of the International Symposium on the Cantigas de Santa Maria of Alfonso X, el Sabio (1221-1284) in Commemoration of its 700th Anniversary Year–1981*, ed. Israel J. Katz, John Esten Keller, Samuel G. Armistead, and Joseph Thomas Snow (Madison, WI: Hispanic Seminary of Medieval Studies, 1987), 403–57.

[16] "Como Santa maria do Porto guareçeu al rey Don Affonso d_a grand' enfermedade de que lle ynchavan as pernas" (3:244; How Holy Mary of the Port cured King don Alfonso from a great sickness which caused his legs to swell . . . ; 447).

[17] For the cycle of cantigas involving the capture and settlement of El Puerto de Santa María, see Connie Scarborough, "Las *Cantigas de Santa Maria*, poesía de santuarios: el caso de El Puerto de Santa María," *Alcanate* 1 (1998–1999): 85–97.

advisors, and slanderers; the exercise of good judgment; and the wise management of his wealth. His litany of requests ends with a plea that after he dies he may go to Paradise, where he hopes to live forever in the Virgin's presence. He claims that to be able to spend eternity with the Virgin will be " bon galardon dado" (3:306; a fine reward indeed; 483). While one could simply interpret this statement as reiteration of that part of the Christian creed in which the faithful express hope in an afterlife spent in the presence of God and all the saints, it is significant that Alfonso devotes one of the final songs in his collection of over four hundred to specify that his ultimate wish is to spend eternity with Holy Mary. This *Cantiga* serves as a perfect bookend to the Prologue with which the Wise King began his collection. In the prologue the king vows "e ar / querrei-me leixar de trobar des i / por outra dona, e cuid' a cobrar / per esta quant' enas outras perdi" (1:55; from now on . . . to sing for no other lady, and I think thereby to recover all that I have wasted on the others; 2). According to Alfonso, his days in pursuit of mortal women's affections are over, and his efforts will now be concentrated on writing songs which will please and honor his true love, the Virgin Mary. Just as he ends his petition expressing hope of eternal reward in Heaven with Mary, he ends his prologue with a similar desire: "Onde lle rogo, se ela quiser, / que lle praza do que dela disser / en meus cantares e, se ll'aprouguer, / que me dé gualardon com' ela dá / aos que ama . . . " (1:56; Therefore I pray, if it be Her will, that what I shall say of Her in my songs be pleasing to Her, and if it please Her, that She give me the reward which She gives to those She loves; 2).

Alfonso expresses his love through his songs, both in first-person narratives in which he himself is the direct recipient of the Virgin's grace and through other protagonists who find the love of the Virgin to be the most powerful force in their lives, certainly superior to that felt for any other woman. Alfonso is not only the troubadour of the Virgin, as he himself proclaims in his prologue, but also her champion and cheerleader. He sees eternity with Mary as his ultimate destiny while, on earth, She is his constant companion in his trials both as king and as a man in need of a woman's love and compassion.

The Wise King's most powerful tool, by his own assessment, is composition of texts, for both spiritual and political aims. While the later are most evident in his prose works of history, jurisprudence, and astronomy, his religious verse is also imbued with a consciousness of the power inherent in the king's authorial signature. In the *Cantigas de Santa Maria*, he both adopts and adapts the Galician-Portuguese love song, using its metrical and syntactic conventions for a work of religious devotion. His words, while essentially those of the troubadour to his lady, are nonetheless imbued with a highly personal agenda. This agenda includes not only a covert appeal for his own salvation, but also an ability to adjust religious theme and discourse for personal aggrandizement.

Ultimately, Alfonso had a keen sense of the power of words, that is, words of love, for reaching out to the highest Beloved, the Virgin Mary. Both as a poet and as a devotee of the Virgin, he powerfully blended the sacred with the erotic in his religious poetry, demonstrating, once again, how much medieval poets knew how to embrace the power of words for a plethora of purposes, but, most important, for the transcendence of their physical existence and for unification with the divine. In this sense Alfonso shared much with medieval mystics, especially by using words of love for the transformation of his human existence.[18]

---

[18] See especially Albrecht Classen, "Binary Oppositions of Self and God in Mechthild von Magdeburg's Mystical Visions," *Studies in Spirituality* 7 (1997): 79–98. Also idem, "The Literary Treatment of the Ineffable: Mechthild von Magdeburg, Margaret Ebner, Agnes Blannbekin," *Studies in Spirituality* 8 (1998): 162–87; idem, "Worldly Love — Spiritual Love. The Dialectics of Court Love in the Middle Ages," *Studies in Spirituality* 11 (2001): 166–186; Hildegard Elisabeth Keller, *My Secret is Mine: Studies in Religion and Eros in the German Middle Ages*. Studies in Spirituality, 4 (Leuven: Peeters, 2000).

CHAPTER 16

Love of Discourse and Discourse of Love in Middle High German *Minnesang*: The Case of the Post-Walther Generation from the Thirteenth through the Fifteenth Century[1]

Albrecht Classen
University of Arizona, Tucson

Something amazing happened in early fifteenth-century German poetry. The South-Tyrolean poet Oswald von Wolkenstein (1376/77–1445) embarked on an experiment with words, music, and sound that was, in all likelihood, not repeated until the twentieth century and has, at any rate, truly remained a unique poetic enterprise during his period. In his song Kl. 21 "Ir alten weib" (You Old Women) he develops a most lively hymn on the return of spring and with it the renewed joys of love, dancing, new leaves, flowers, birds, insects, and then also of kissing, collecting of mushrooms, hunting, and many other things one can do only once warmer weather has set in again — an existential experience, no doubt, especially in the Alpine world where he lived. Oswald goes so far as to praise these country entertainments as superior to any courtly arts because the fundamental jubilation about the arrival of spring reminds us of the true meaning of human life. But not satisfied with this bricolage of impressionistic elements, Oswald also includes fragmentary memories of his erotic adventures in Catalonia and Castile; he briefly refers to his visits to Paris and London, and then he sings the praise of

---

[1] I would like to express my gratitude to Christopher Clason, of Oakland University, Rochester, MI, and Raymond Cormier, of Longwood University, Farmville, VA, for their critical reading of my article.

a beautiful young woman. In an outburst of ever new images, combining references to countries that he has visited in the past, the poet suddenly reaches the apogee of his exuberance and breaks into almost incomprehensible verses that seem to be borrowed from nursery rhymes and words incorporated solely for their sound effect. Oswald also mentions several female names, projects the scenario of a chicken yard, and concludes with obviously pornographic allusions. Despite several attempts at translating the last fifteen lines of this unusual poem, Oswald scholars have not succeeded in this linguistic task because it is an impossibility and would, in all likelihood, destroy the aesthetic quality of the original. In fact, Oswald did not want his words to be logical, rational, and comprehensible; instead he played with their sound effects, which in turn allowed him to formulate his sexual fantasies quite openly without specifying in detail what he wishes to accomplish. The onomatopoetic experiment proves to be fascinating even today, and the combination of animal-like utterances with concrete commands to the girls, which again are of unmistakable erotic nature, hardly finds a parallel in medieval and early modern literature:

> Da zissli müssli
> fissli füssli
> henne klüssli
> kompt ins hüssli
> werfen ain tüssli,
> sussa süssli,
> niena grüssli
> wel wir sicher han.
> Clërli, Metzli,
> Elli, Ketzli,
> tünt ain setzli,
> richt eur lëtzli,
> vacht das rëtzli!
> tula hëtzli,
> trutza trätzli,
> der uns freud vergan.[2]

---

[2] *Die Lieder Oswalds von Wolkenstein*, ed. Karl Kurt Klein, 3rd rev. and exp. ed. (1962; Tübingen: Niemeyer, 1987), 72–73, vv. 99–114. Until today there is no English translation of Oswald's songs available, apart from a few songs here and there, see George Fenwick Jones, *Oswald von Wolkenstein*. Twayne's World Author Series, 236 (New York: Twayne, 1973); Alan Robertshaw, *Oswald von Wolkenstein: The Myth and the Man*. Göppinger Arbeiten zur Germanistik, 178 (Göppingen: Kümmerle, 1977). For a brief introduction to Oswald's life and works, see Albrecht Classen, "Oswald von Wolkenstein," *Literary Encyclopedia* (2004) (available only online at: www.litencyc.com/php/speople.php?rec=true&UID=5559; last accessed on March 1, 2006).

Love of Discourse and Discourse of Love 361

Every poet plays with sounds and images, and attempts to combine them in such a way as to create an innovative effect, which in turn might carry meaning. But Oswald, above all, can be credited with transgressing most of the norms characteristic of medieval love poetry, although he was certainly not the first to experiment with onomatopoesis and many other quintessential aspects of poetry.[3] Demonstrating little care about his audience and its ability to comprehend this song in concrete terms, among many others in his rich and enormously diverse œuvre,[4] Oswald offers a fascinating and innovative kaleidoscope of poetic elements which Dieter Kühn has called a "language explosion"[5] and W. T. H. Jackson an "alliterative exuberance."[6] Scholarship has uniformly expressed great admiration for Oswald's artistic, musical, and performative accomplishments, although he borrowed also from the Neidhart tradition and culled material from contemporary folk culture.[7] It might be more appropriate to identify this experimental stanza as Oswald's successful effort to probe the power of lyrical language in its musical dimension and to combine the existential experience of rebirth in spring with the erotic relationship between man and woman. At any rate, his poem serves as an intriguing avenue for the investigation of the significance and deeper meaning of human language, undoubtedly reflecting the chiastic concept of 'words of love and love of words.'

As the brief discussion of this song has indicated, German lyric poetry experienced a tremendous innovation with the highly individualistic contributions by Oswald von Wolkenstein. His fascination with poetic discourse and his ability

---

[3] Albrecht Classen, "Onomatopoesie in der Lyrik von Jehan Vaillant, Oswald von Wolkenstein und Niccolò Soldanieri," *Zeitschrift für deutsche Philologie* 108, 3 (1989): 357–77; idem, "French and Italian Sources for Oswald von Wolkenstein's Onomatopoetic Lyric Poetry," *Fifteenth-Century Studies* 15 (1989): 93–105.

[4] For a study of the Italian connection and Oswald's great interest in foreign languages, see Albrecht Classen, *Zur Rezeption norditalienischer Kultur des Trecento im Werk Oswalds von Wolkenstein (1376/77–1445)*. Göppinger Arbeiten zur Germanistik, 471 (Göppingen: Kümmerle, 1987). See also Burghart Wachinger, "Sprachmischung bei Oswald von Wolkenstein," *Zeitschrift für deutsches Altertum und deutsche Literatur* 106 (1977): 277–96.

[5] Dieter Kühn, *Ich Wolkenstein: eine Biographie*. 8th ed. (1977; Frankfurt a.M.: Insel, 1992), 208; see also Bruno Stäblein, "Das Verhältnis von textlich-musikalischer Gestalt zum Inhalt bei Oswald von Wolkenstein," *Formen mittelalterlicher Literatur: Festschrift Siegfried Beyschlag zu seinem 65. Geburtstag*, ed. Werner und B. Naumann. Göppinger Arbeiten zur Germanistik, 25 (Göppingen: Kümmerle, 1970), 179–95; here quoted from *Oswald von Wolkenstein*, ed. Ulrich Müller. Wege der Forschung, 526 (Darmstadt: Wissenschaftliche Buchgesellschaft, 1980), 262–82; here 278.

[6] W. T. H. Jackson, "Alliteration and Sound Repetition in the Lyrics of Oswald von Wolkenstein," *Formal Aspects of Medieval German Poetry: A Symposium*, ed. Stanley N. Werbow (Austin and London: University of Texas Press, 1969), 43–78; here 56.

[7] Johannes Spicker, *Literarische Stilisierung und artistische Kompetenz bei Oswald von Wolkenstein* (Stuttgart and Leipzig: S. Hirzel, 1993), esp. 159–78. He then concludes: "Die semantische Vermittlung tritt hinter die klangliche Wirkung zurück; die 'ekstatisch-rauschhafte' Ausprägung birgt so affektive Stimulans in ihrer atmosphärischen Unmittelbarkeit" (192; The semantic communication steps into the background behind the vocal effect; the 'ecstatic-frenzied' manifestation thus contains affective stimulation in its atmospheric immediacy).

to combine a wide array of sounds and images are clearly expressed in his erotic love songs, such as Kl. 21, where he freely experimented with sound, imagery, allusions, rhyme schemes, and musical structure. Although certainly not yet a Renaissance poet, Oswald represents a major change in the history of medieval literature, signaling the emergence of the modern world. In light of our observations regarding Kl. 21, here I would like to examine the profound paradigm shift in Middle High German love poetry from the time of Walther von der Vogelweide (ca. 1170–ca. 1230) and Neidhart (ca. 1210–ca. 1240) to the time of Oswald von Wolkenstein (1376/77–1445).[8] The focus will rest on a short selection of outstanding examples, which will illustrate the fascinating power of the poetic word and its epistemological function, as they were realized particularly by late medieval composers of courtly lyrical texts and songs.

Whereas scholarship has previously often relegated late medieval German love poetry to the category of 'epigonal' text production not worthy of serious attention,[9] there are many hopeful indications that we are on the verge of a rediscovery of the thirteenth and fourteenth centuries by means of new aesthetic and ethical criteria in the evaluation of song poetry from that time period.[10] Johannes Janota has recently published a new volume in the series "Geschichte der deutschen Literatur von den Anfängen bis zum Beginn der Neuzeit," and offers a

---

[8] For a parallel study concerning the progression from twelfth- through fourteenth-century German poetry, see, for instance, Jutta Goheen, *Mittelalterliche Liebeslyrik von Neidhart von Reuental bis zu Oswald von Wolkenstein: eine Stilkritik*. Philologische Studien und Quellen, 110 (Berlin: Schmidt, 1984); see also Claudia Händl, *Rollen und pragmatische Einbindung: Analysen zur Wandlung des Minnesangs nach Walther von der Vogelweide*. Göppinger Arbeiten zur Germanistik, 467 (Göppingen: Kümmerle, 1987); focusing on the genre of the 'dawn songs,' Gerdt Rohrbach demonstrates the innovative developments since the early thirteenth century: *Studien zur Erforschung des mittelhochdeutschen Tageliedes: Ein sozialgeschichtlicher Beitrag*. Göppinger Arbeiten zur Germanistik, 462 (Göppingen: Kümmerle, 1986); see also Albrecht Classen, on the development of the German dawn song in the fifteenth and sixteenth centuries, "Das deutsche Tagelied in seinen spätmittelalterlichen und frühneuzeitlichen Varianten," *Etudes Germaniques* 54, 2 (1999), 173–96.

[9] Hubert Heinen, "When Pallor Pales: Reflections on Epigonality in Late 13th–Century Minnesongs," *Medieval Perspectives* IV–V (1989–1999): 53–68, takes a rather traditional approach and argues, taking the example of Johannes Brunwart von Auggen, that "In constrained and uncertain times . . . eschewing innovation and experiment and seizing on clichés and unexciting forms was surely an appropriate way for Brunwart to evoke the imperfectly understood spirit of 'true courtliness' that he may have felt characterized his masters." He ignores the fact, like many others, that poets from later centuries had many more opportunities to preserve their songs, both the good and the bad ones, whereas twelfth- and thirteenth-century poets were much more subject to a historical filter until their poems were finally written down in the early fourteenth century.

[10] For a good summary of older scholarship, together with a critical anysis of the Swiss poet Steinmar's works, see Gesine Lübben, *"Ich singe daz wir alle werden vol": Das Steinmar-Œuvre in der Menesseschen* [sic] *Liederhandschrift* (Stuttgart: M & P Verlag für Wissenschaft und Forschung, 1994); see also Ursel Fischer, *Meister Johans Hadloub: Autorbild und Werkkonzeption der Manessischen Liederhandschrift* (Stuttgart: M & P Verlag für Wissenschaft und Forschung, 1996); for the slightly earlier period, see Eva Willms, *Liebesleid und Sangeslust: Untersuchungen zur deutschen Liebeslyrik des späten 12. und frühen 13. Jahrhunderts*. Münchener Texte und Untersuchungen zur deutschen Literatur des Mittelalters, 94 (Munich: Artemis, 1990).

refreshing overview of individual poets and trends in poetic composition during the late Middle Ages. As to the relevant song poets, he focuses, among others, on Frauenlob, Johannes Hadlaub, Heinrich der Teichner, Hugo von Montfort, and the Mönch von Salzburg. Irrespective of multiple innovations on the lexicological, syntactical, and phraseological level, Janota primarily observes the continuation of the classical Middle High German *Minnesang* combined with a new interest in biographical elements.[11]

However, the true fascination with the epistemological power of the lyric as a highly specialized genre, as reflected by some of Oswald von Wolkenstein's forerunners, still awaits its full investigation because the so-called "classical" period determined by the school of Hohenstaufen poets — mostly collected in the famous *Manessische Liederhandschrift* — predominantly occupies modern German medieval studies.[12] The *Minnesangs Wende* (transformation of German courtly love poetry), as Hugo Kuhn coined the name for the phenomenon, occurred at an auspicious moment, at a time when the Late Middle Ages set in with numerous crises and conflicts, epidemics, and lack of leadership.[13] Nevertheless, it seems questionable to maintain, as Kuhn did, the judgment of the steady and then ultimate decline of *minnesang* until ca. 1300.[14] But we know that Oswald von Wolkenstein created some of the most exciting love poetry ever composed in the entire German Middle Ages, and so we need to ask ourselves where he received his inspiration from, whether he culled material from his German predecessors or contemporary European poets, or whether he was an original innovator.[15] Heinrich von Meissen,

---

[11] Johannes Janota, *Orientierung durch volkssprachige Schriftlichkeit (1280/90–1380–90)*. Geschichte der deutschen Literatur von den Anfängen bis zum Beginn der Neuzeit. Vol. III: Vom späten Mittelalter bis zum Beginn der Neuzeit, ed. Joachim Heinzle (Tübingen: Niemeyer, 2004), 168–71.

[12] See, for example, *Mittelalterliche Lyrik: Probleme der Poetik*, ed. Thomas Cramer and Ingrid Kasten. Philologische Studien und Quellen, 154 (Berlin: Schmidt, 1999); for a historically more differentiated approach, see *Lied im deutschen Mittelalter: Überlieferung, Typen, Gebrauch. Chiemsee-Colloquium 1991*, ed. Cyril Edwards, Ernst Hellgardt, and Norbert H. Ott (Tübingen: Niemeyer, 1996).

[13] Hugo Kuhn, *Minnesangs Wende*. 2nd expanded ed. (Tübingen: Niemeyer, 1967), 1–2: "um 1250 wird, nach manchen Vorbereitungen, eine europäische Epoche, vielleicht die stärkste Wende der mittelalterlichen Geschichte sichtbar — der Beginn dessen, was man in allen Lebensgebieten das Spätmittelalter nennen darf" (since 1250, after many preparations, a new epoch emerged, perhaps the strongest shift in medieval history, the beginning of what is called with regard to every aspect of life the Late Middle Ages).

[14] Hugo Kuhn, *Entwürfe zu einer Literatursystematik des Spätmittelalters* (Tübingen: Niemeyer, 1980; orig. 1968), 54: "Dieser Minnesang stirbt denn auch um 1300 mit den letzten Erinnerungen an seine große Zeit ab. . . . In die Schriftlichkeit rettet den ganzen Minnesang aber eben nur die retrospektive Sammeltätigkeit, die aus dieser Spätproduktion hervorgeht!" (This *minnesong* subsequently dies around 1300 with the last reminiscences of its grand epoch. . . . The entire *minnesong* is preserved in written records only because of this retrospective collection activities, which resulted from this late production). For more recent, rather contradictory perspectives, see Jan-Dirk Müller, *Minnesang und Literaturtheorie*, ed. Ute von Bloh and Armin Schulz (Tübingen: Niemeyer, 2001).

[15] Classen, *Zur Rezeption norditalienischer Kultur des Trecento*. From a musicological perspective, see Lorenz Welker, "Mehrstimmige Sätze bei Oswald von Wolkenstein: eine kommentierte

also known as "Frauenlob" (Praise of Women), active from ca. 1290 to ca. 1318, might well have been a stepping stone toward Oswald because the poet offered a wide array of innovative poetic discussions concerning people's behavior, attitudes, and ideas, and also concerning the nature and effects of love.[16] Historical, social, and economic developments can obviously not necessarily be correlated with literary-historical developments, and vice versa.[17]

The so-called "Wilde Alexander," who is known to us through a handful of fairly traditional courtly love poems, also wrote the most exciting song "Hie vor dô wir kinder wâren" (Long ago when we were still children),[18] for which there are, as far as I can tell, no parallels in European literature. Reflecting on his childhood, the poetic voice laments the change of the world over time. Whereas before they had been able to run around on a meadow and pick flowers, this meadow has been transformed into a pasture for cows: "dâ siht man nu rinder bisen" (1, 7; there you now see cows roaming around). Filled with melancholy, the singer reminisces about the time when they were sitting among the flowers and compared each other's beauty, obviously projecting a group of girls, who also desired to attend the dance where they showed up with wreath on their hair. Alas, however, "alsus gêt diu zît von hin" (2, 7; thus passes time). As part of their enjoyments, the girls collected strawberries, undoubtedly an erotically charged symbol, although late medieval artists often also utilized the strawberry to symbolize Christ's drops of blood.[19] But at the very moment of their carefree happiness, a forester calls out to them and admonishes them to go home. At first the poet does not elaborate on this short scene. Instead, he returns to the strawberry symbolism and informs us that all the girls received "mâsen," or wounds, from them, obviously a reference to the

---

Übersicht," *Jahrbuch der Oswald von Wolkenstein Gesellschaft* 6 (1990/1991): 255–66; Rainer Böhm, "Entdeckung einer französischen Melodievorlage zum Lied *O wunniklicher, wolgezierter mai* (Kl. 100) von Oswald von Wolkenstein," *Jahrbuch der Oswald von Wolkenstein Gesellschaft* 13 (2001/2002): 269–78.

[16] For a brief introduction, see Janota, *Orientierung*, 182–90; he emphasizes, 187: "Mit ungeheurem Anspruch bestimmt Frauenlob die Minne neu, indem er sie als ein kosmologisches, in der Trinität verankertes Prinzip definiert" (With an overwhelming approach, Frauenlob defines courtly love anew by identifying it as a cosmological principle which is anchored in the Trinity). For a solid text edition, see Frauenlob (Heinrich von Meissen), *Leichs, Sangsprüche, Lieder*. Part 1: *Einleitung, Texte*, ed. Karl Stackmann and Karl Bertau. Abhandlungen der Akademie der Wissenschaften in Göttingen. Philologisch-historische Klasse, Dritte Folge, 119 (Göttingen: Vandenhoeck & Ruprecht, 1981); see also Ralf-Henning Steinmetz, *Liebe als universales Prinzip bei Frauenlob: Ein volkssprachlicher Weltentwurf in der europäischen Dichtung um 1300*. Münchener Texte und Untersuchungen zur deutschen Literatur des Mittelalters, 106 (Tübingen: Niemeyer, 1994).

[17] For a broad discussion of the epigonality debate, see Manfred Kern, *Agamemnon weint oder arthurische Metamorphose und trojanische Destruktion im "Göttweiger Trojanerkrieg"*. Erlanger Studien, 104 (Erlangen and Jena: Palm & Enke, 1995).

[18] Quoted from *Deutsche Liederdichter des 13. Jahrhunderts*, ed. Carl von Kraus. Vol. 1: *Text*. 2nd ed., prepared by Gisela Kornrumpf (Tübingen: Niemeyer, 1978), 12–13, no. V.

[19] http://www.nal.usda.gov/pgdic/Strawberry/book/boktwo.htm; see also http://www.forever-bloom.com/site/619770/page/285214 (both last accessed on March 1, 2006).

Love of Discourse and Discourse of Love 365

color stains from the juice (4.1). The consequences of these wounds did not affect the children for a while: "daz was uns ein kintlich spil" (4.3; this was a childish game for us). But then their shepherd shouts at them to watch out for the snakes (4.7), which clearly carries a moral-religious meaning, as William C. McDonald has demonstrated through a careful comparison with a Pauline text.[20]

Whereas the erotic and playful are seemingly idealized in the first part of the song, soon enough tragic elements come to the forefront. One child who wanders off discovers the trails of a snake, calls out in fear, and states that one of their friends will be bitten and will never recover from that wound (5.5), leading to everlasting pain and suffering (5.7). Again the watchman calls out and urges them all to leave the forest, lest they experience the same destiny, which would transform their happiness into sorrow (6.5–7). Finally, shedding all pretenses of enjoying the children's play and their collection of strawberries, the poet observes,

> unde enîlet ir niht balde,
> iu geschiht als ich iu sage:
> weret ir niht bî dem tage
> daz ir den walt rûmet,
> ir versûmet
> iuch und wird iur vröude ein klage (6. 2–7)

> [and if you don't hurry soon,
> it will happen to you as I am going to tell you.
> If you don't leave the forest during the day,
> you will forget about yourself and your joy will turn into lament.]

Concluding the song with an unmistakable allusion to the famous motif of the of the five foolish virgins in the New Testament who missed the Lord and arrived too late, leading to their lament and shame, getting their clothes torn off by the executioner (Matt. 25:1–12), the Wild Alexander signals how easily worldly joys can turn into sorrow and suffering. As the narrative development indicates, the erotic dimension radically turns into a religious allegory of man's sinfulness and the danger of losing one's innocence. Once a snake, or sin, has bitten a child, it can never recover from this wound. As Hugo Kuhn commented, the poet allegorically referred to the Biblical account of Genesis and Adam's and Eve's expulsion from Paradise after they had been seduced by the Devil, or the snake, respectively, to eat the apple.[21] This intricate and not so subtle combination of the religious

---

[20] William C. McDonald, "A Pauline Reading of Der Wilde Alexander's 'Kindheitslied'," *Monatshefte* 76, 2 (1984): 156–75.

[21] *Deutsche Liederdichter*, vol. II, Hugo Kuhn, *Kommentar* (Tübingen: Niemeyer, 1978), 11–12.

with the erotic was not unusual for medieval literature,[22] but the Wild Alexander develops most unusual, highly refreshing imagery, though he also drew certain elements from previous poets such as Neidhart and Walther von der Vogelweide.[23] Most important, however, at first he presents an almost idyllic scene of carefree children playing in a meadow. Both the reference to the strawberries that stain their faces and to cows feeding on the pasture, the latter replacing the former as an indication of the world having grown old, are of highly realistic, yet also deeply symbolic, nature. The playful allusion to children and the danger of being bitten by a snake combine the innocent with the sinful. Moreover, the poet elegantly contrasts the open space where the girls are playing, running from tree to tree, jumping over sticks and stones ("von der tannen zuo der buochen / über stoc und über stein / der wîl daz diu sunne schein" (3.2–4) with the darkness of the forest from where the forester calls out, warning them to return home and to seek shelter (3.6–7). This auditory element is repeated in the following stanza where the poet mentions once again that the children are playing without regard for any dangers ("daz was uns ein kintlich spil," 4.3; this was childish play to us), when their shepherd suddenly shouts at them, warning them of the many snakes hidden in the grass (4.7). In the sixth stanza the poet leaves the childhood scene behind and turns to his audience, offering them the interpretation of his allegory, indicating that the forest (6.1), and obviously also the meadow in the middle of the forest, represent the sinful world, whereas the shepherd obviously represents, although we can only infer this from the previous stanzas, Christ the Savior, the Good Shepherd.[24]

The Wilde Alexander did not offer the same kind of literary firework as Oswald would do about a hundred and twenty years later, but he created a masterpiece of erotic-religious song poetry that still deserves our full respect today. The exuberant employment of alliteration and assonance, the skillful weaving of rhyme schemes, and the almost cinematographic development of the poetic account, enriched with individual images of highly aesthetic character, ultimately establish an entire narrative, which again merges the erotic with the didactic, the religious with the realistic, thus transforming this poem to a literary gem of highly unique quality. The enormously idiosyncratic nature of "Hie vor dô wir kinder wâren" indeed foreshadows some of the innovative strategies in Oswald's

---

[22] Walter Haug, "Gotteserfahrung und Du-Begegnung. Korrespondenzen in der Geschichte der Mystik und der Liebeslyrik," *Geistliches in weltlicher und Weltliches in geistlicher Literatur des Mittelalters*, ed. Christoph Huber, Burghart Wachinger, and Hans-Joachim Ziegeler (Tübingen: Niemeyer, 2000), 195–212.

[23] Fritz Peter Knapp, "Das 'Kindheitslied' des Wilden Alexander und die Alterslyrik Walthers von der Vogelweide," *Methodisch reflektiertes Interpretieren: Festschrift für Hartmut Laufhütte*, ed. Hans-Peter Ecker (Passau: Rother, 1997), 61–74.

[24] Marvin S. Schindler, "Structure and Allegory in Der Wilde Alexander's 'Hie vor do wir kinder waren'," *German Quarterly* 46 (1973): 1–11.

œuvre, although Der Wilde Alexander still harbors strongly medieval values and uses amatory and nature elements not for their own sake, but instead for religious and moral purposes.[25]

Another fascinating experiment with traditional and innovative narrative elements can be discovered in Gottfried von Neifen's poem "'Sol ich disen sumer lanc',"[26] also composed around the middle of the thirteenth century.[27] Even though Hugo Kuhn condemned Gottfried for having created an allegedly poor composition that lacks a clear structure and was the result of naive emotional reactions,[28] and even though German scholarship ever since has mostly disregarded his contributions as imitative,[29] we can observe several intriguing elements that indicate the poet's strong efforts to reach a new level in the meaning of language in its playful, but also hermeneutic sense. The female poetic voice laments the fact that she might be hampered by her own young child during the summer when she really would rather go out dancing and enjoy herself. The reference to the linden tree where the dance would take place proves to be another allusion to Neidhart's various summer songs and to Walther von der Vogelweide's famous "Under the linden,"[30] not uncommon for much of thirteenth-century poetry and beyond.[31] But Gottfried is not content with this intertextual play: instead he also experiments with onomatopoetic elements to reflect the experience of a young mother who has to rock her baby's cradle all night although she would much rather enjoy an erotic adventure:

wigen wagen, gigen gagen,
wenne wil ez tagen?
minne minne, trûte minne, swîc, ich wil dich wagen. (1. 7–9)

---

[25] For further allusions to passages in the Bible utilized by the poet, and for an English translation of the text, see *Eroticism and Love in the Middle Ages*, ed. Albrecht Classen. 5th rev. ed. (1994; Stamford, CT: Thomson Learning, 2004), 185–87.

[26] Quoted from *Deutsche Liederdichter des 13. Jahrhunderts*, ed. von Kraus. Vol. 1: *Text*, 127, no. L.

[27] Kuhn, *Kommentar*, 84–85; for a highly negative evaluation of this poem, see Kuhn, 159–61.

[28] Kuhn, *Kommentar*, 159: "es verträgt keine scharfe Durchleuchtung, weil es empfunden aber nicht durchdacht ist" (it does not warrant a cogent analysis because it is a poem based on imitated emotions, not, however, on original thought). He even speculated that Gottfried might have closely copied a similar poem by Neithart (7.27), here 159, note 5.

[29] Joachim Bumke, *Geschichte der deutschen Literatur im hohen Mittelalter* (Munich: Deutscher Taschenbuch Verlag, 1990), 309–10.

[30] For an insightful study of the impact which Walther's poem had on later poets, even when they resorted to Latin, see Hubert Heinen, "Walther's 'Under der linden,' Its Function, Its Subtexts, and Its Maltreated Maiden," *Medieval German Literature: Proceedings from the 23rd International Congress on Medieval Studies, Kalamazoo, Michigan, May 5–8, 1988*, ed. Albrecht Classen. Göppinger Arbeiten zur Germanistik, 507 (Göppingen: Kümmerle, 1989), 51–73.

[31] Siegfried Beyschlag, *Die Lieder Neidharts: Der Textbestand der Pergament-Handschriften und die Melodien*. Text und Übertragung, Einführung und Worterklärungen, Konkordanz. Edition der Melodien von Horst Brunner (Darmstadt: Wissenschaftliche Buchgesellschaft, 1975), 44–68, et passim.

Whereas the first line is almost untranslatable, since the words imitate the movement of the cradle, the second and the third are very specific in their meaning: "When will it dawn? dear love, beloved love, keep quiet, I want to accept your challenge." Then the mother asks the wet-nurse to take the child from her and to prevent it from crying. Only once the latter has taken over the child does the mother feel safe to go on her erotic adventure. She praises the wet-nurse as her only trustworthy assistant in this dangerous situation: "dû maht mich aleine / mîner sorgen machen frî" (2.5–6; you alone free me of my worries), and then she resumes her refrain: "wigen wagen, gigen gagen, / wenne wil ez tagen?" (5.7–8). Undoubtedly, as Elisabeth Lienert has pointed out, Gottfried experimented with various genre elements and created a satirical parody on the dawn song in which the female voice cannot see her lover because her child forces her to stay next to the cradle.[32] Despite all her efforts in rocking the baby asleep, only the wet-nurse knows how to soothe the child and make it fall asleep. The mother obviously fulfils her parental role, but only grudgingly, and as soon as an opportunity arises, she hands the baby over to another person and runs away to her lover.

Her lack of motherly care would have confirmed older scholarship regarding the absence of emotional bonds between parents and children.[33] However, the comic undertone makes it impossible to draw any certain conclusions about the female figure and her motherly feelings, or lack thereof. More important for our discussion proves to be Gottfried's interest in experimenting with hitherto little used literary themes — a mother rocking her baby asleep — and poetic sound effects imitating the rocking of a cradle: "wigen wagen, gigen gagen."[34] It might certainly be true that Gottfried did not develop new and profound ideas and mostly imitated traditional courtly love song elements which Neidhart had invented first and basically perfected single-handedly. But poetic creativity does

---

[32] Elisabeth Lienert, "Gattungsinterferenzen im späten Minnesang: Gottfrieds von Neifen 'Wiegenlied' als Antitagelied-Parodie," *Zeitschrift für deutsches Altertum und deutsche Literatur* 125, 3 (1996): 264–74.

[33] James A. Schultz, *The Knowledge of Childhood in the German Middle Ages, 1100–1350*. The Middle Ages Series (Philadelphia: University of Pennsylvania Press, 1995); he does not seem to be aware of this poem, however. For a broad revision of the old paradigm established by Philippe Ariès in 1960, see *Childhood in the Middle Ages and the Renaissance: The Results of a Paradigm Shift in the History of Mentality*, ed. Albrecht Classen (Berlin and New York: de Gruyter, 2005).

[34] *Frauenlieder des Mittelalters*, trans. and ed. Ingrid Kasten (Stuttgart: Reclam, 1990), 272, confirms the exceptional nature of this song's theme in medieval lyric poetry. She also emphasizes that it would be erroneous to assume that Gottfried intended his song as a true 'cradle song' because the young mother primarily plays a specifically erotic role in this poem. For further studies of medieval women's poetry, see *Medieval Woman's Song: Cross-Cultural Approaches*, ed. Anne L. Klinck and Ann Marie Rasmussen. The Middle Ages Series (Philadelphia: University of Pennsylvania Press, 2002). However, neither Rasmussen nor Ingrid Kasten, one of her contributors, refer to Gottfried von Nifen. See also Albrecht Classen, *Late-Medieval German Women's Poetry: Secular and Religious Songs*, trans. from the German with introduction, notes and interpretive essay. Library of Medieval Women (Woodbridge, Suffolk, and Rochester, NY: Boydell & Brewer, 2004).

Love of Discourse and Discourse of Love 369

not entirely rely on the genius of an original mind. Instead, it can also include the creative interplay with traditional elements and their reconstruction into a new composition.[35]

In another poem, "Uns jungen mannen sanfte mac" (XLI), Gottfried explored possibilities of operating with onomatopoetic elements to imitate the sounds of threshing flax, which in turn has a specific, though for the male wooer, negative, erotic meaning. Relying on an obvious intertextual strategy, the singer evokes the traditional pastourelle, except that the young man fails to win the girl's love and has to withdraw from her quickly before she might beat him with her wooden instrument.[36]

After having introduced his song with a general comment apparently intended for his male audience only, suggesting that not every effort to win a lady's love might achieve the desired goal (1.1–2), the poet then presents a concrete example involving this flax-threshing farmhand. When he approaches the barn, he hears the sound of her threshing: "wan si dahs / wan si dahs, si dahs, si dahs" (1.5–6), which seems to forebode an unfortunate development for the man. Whereas in traditional pastourelles the wooer encounters a defenseless shepherdess and in most cases then proceeds to rape her,[37] here she is well equipped with a dangerous weapon and obviously threatens him with her thresher: "zehant dô neic diu schœne mir; / von dannen muoste ich kêren" (2.3–4; immediately the beauty greeted me, I had to take my leave) — in a comical way the phallic instrument under female control.[38] With her curt comment that the man would not find a dance there, that is, would not succeed in his erotic adventure ("hien ist der rîben niht," 3.1) and that he decidedly took a wrong path ("ir sint unrehte gangen," 3.2), she aggressively draws a clear demarcation line and even threatens him with violent treatment (3.3–4). Subsequently, she silently resumes her work, but the onomatopoetic refrain — "wan si dahs, / wan si dahs, si dahs, si dahs" (3.5–6) — unmistakably represents an audible warning for the man not to underestimate the woman's strength and the awesome effectiveness of her thresher, a

---

[35] Ulrich Müller, "Klassische Lyrik des deutschen Hochmittelalters — Entfaltung von Minnesang und politischer Lyrik zu weltliterarischem Rang," *Geschichte der deutschen Literatur: Mitte des 12. bis Mitte des 13. Jahrhunderts*, ed. Rolf Bräuer. Geschichte der deutschen Literatur von den Anfängen bis zur Gegenwart, 2 (Berlin: Volk und Wissen, 1990), 503–627; here 601–03, goes so far as to characterize Gottfried's love songs as literary products determined by playful eroticism of the highest caliber (601).

[36] Sabine Christiane Brinkmann, *Die deutschsprachige Pastourelle: 13. bis 16. Jahrhundert*. Göppinger Arbeiten zur Germanistik, 307 (Göppingen: Kümmerle, 1985), 130–53; here 148.

[37] Kathryn Gravdal, *Ravishing Maidens: Writing Rape in Medieval French Literature and Law*. New Cultural Series (Philadelphia: University of Pennsylvania Press, 1991), 104–21; see also Corinne Saunders, *Rape and Ravishment in the Literature of Medieval England* (Woodbridge, Suffolk, and Rochester, NY: D. S. Brewer, 2001), 189–95.

[38] Tomas Tomasek, "Die mittelhochdeutschen Lieder vom Flachsschwingen," *Lied im deutschen Mittelalter*, 115–28.

most humorous, thinly veiled image of a world turned topsy-turvy. Whereas he proves to be on the lookout for sexual gratification, she is concerned only with her work and does not even allow him to interrupt her for one beat of her threshing.

Both the onomatopoetic strategy and the employment of this sophisticated refrain,[39] but also the precise and sophisticated language, elaborately filled with many allusions and semantic implications, confirm that Gottfried had created a poetic masterpiece that can also be countered as a forerunner of Oswald von Wolkenstein's post-medieval love songs. The playful open-endedness of this poem, the curt but decisive exchange of statements between man and woman, her resoluteness in rejecting his seduction attempt, the man's facetious self-pity, and the highly expressive onomatopoetic refrain demonstrate that Gottfried achieved his goal of using poetic language for a dramatic enactment of conflicts between the genders. Whereas traditional courtly love poetry tends to glorify the male perspective, here the opposite is the case and the woman is given sufficient space to make her opinion heard. In fact, she gains our respect for her drastic statements, whereas the wooer appears as a weak fool who thinks that it would be better to stay far away from this dangerous lady who does not want to be interrupted in her heavy farm work and is apparently not interested in any erotic affairs. The beauty and expressivity of Gottfried's song rests not only in the economic use of words and in the subtle dialogue, but also in the powerful utilization of the onomatopoetic refrain, hence in the ludic exploration of sound patterns and their semantic messages.[40] Renate Hausner confirms this observation in her discussion of the refrain in late medieval German poetry:

> der Refrain bringt in der Regel ein verdichtetes Konzentrat der Aussage des Gesamttextes, entweder in Form eines den 'Grundton' des Lieds komprimiert wiedergebenden "überrationalen" Schallgebildes oder in Form eines Ausdrucks, dessen Inhalt implizit jeder Strophe zugrundeliegt, oder in der Form einer Aussage, die die durch die einzelnen Liedstrophen ins Spiel gebrachten unterschiedlichen Aspekte des Grundthemas resümierend zusammenfaßt.[41]
>
> (the refrain normally offers a concentrated essence of the statement underlying the entire text, either in the form of a 'super-rational' body of the sound that reflects, in a compact manner, the 'basic tone' of the song, or in the form of an expression the content of which implicitly underlies each stanza, or in

---

[39] Renate Hausner, "Spiel mit dem Identischen. Studien zum Refrain deutschsprachiger lyrischer Dichtung des 12. und 13. Jahrhunderts," *Sprache — Text — Geschichte*, ed. Peter K. Stein. Göppinger Arbeiten zur Germanistik, 304 (Göppingen: Kümmerle, 1980), 281–384; here 301, note 31.

[40] Tomasek, "Die mittelhochdeutschen Lieder," 128, emphasizes the unique and authentic (original) nature of Gottfried's song: "Vieles deutet darauf hin, daß Neifens Lied von der Flachsschwingerin ein gänzlich eigenständiges Werk ist."

[41] Hausner, "Spiel," 303–04.

the form of a statement which collectively summarizes the various aspects that have been addressed by the individual song stanza.)

In other words, the refrain does not only represent a linguistic-musical phenomenon, but specifically serves to deepen the song's ultimate philosophical, ethical, or moral message.[42] Medieval German poets did not follow any specific pattern in the employment of refrains, but when they use it, this poetic feature normally implies an element of surprise and deliberate appeal to the audience to pay close attention to the song's subtle meaning.[43]

Reinmar von Brennenberg (flourished between 1238 and 1275) also offered a noteworthy poetic experiment in his "Ir munt der liuhtet als der liehte rubîn tuot" (Her Lips Glow as Strongly as the Bright Ruby Does), although in most parts it is determined by rather traditional stylistic elements and linguistic features.[44] After having sung an almost excessive song of praise of his beloved, whose red lips impress him the most, and whose virtues do not find any parallels (stanzas 1 and 2), Reinmar ventures into new territory and meditates on a spiritual response to his love. Turning away from his scopophilic gaze on his lady's body toward his own thoughts and feelings, he admits that he cannot think of anything else than of her. In a noteworthy syntactic parallelism, he emphasizes: "sô denke ich her, sô denke ich hin, / sô denke ich iemer an die reinen süezen minneclîchen" (3.5–6; I am thinking of this and am thinking of that, and constantly think of the pure, sweet, lovely lady). In fact, he is afraid of losing his mind because of his profound love for her whom he compares, in striking parallel to the idealized lady in Dante Alighieri's *Vita Nuova* and, for that matter, his Beatrice in the Divina *Commedia*,[45] to an angel who would come to him secretly (3.8). Subsequently Reinmar employs stunningly impressive images of the sun in its course throughout the day: "sî ist mîn tac, mîn âbentrôt, mîn sunnenbrehen" (3.10; she is my daylight, my evening red sky, my sunset), and concludes with jubilations on the possibility of winning his lady's heart: "ei wol mich wart, wol, iemer wol! wol mich ob mir diu schœne

---

[42] Hausner, "Spiel," 305.

[43] Hausner, "Spiel," 317, and 319: "Der Refrain gleichsam als Sprache gewordenes Ausrufezeichen: das ist die pragmatische Funktion, die der Refrain dank seiner unreglementierten, nicht konventionalisierten Anwendung im deutschsprachigen Raum erfüllen kann" (The refrain is basically an exclamation mark translated into language: this is the pragmatic function which the refrain, thanks to its unregulated, non-conventionalized application in German poetry, can fulfill).

[44] Quoted from *Deutsche Liederdichter des 13. Jahrhunderts*, ed. von Kraus. Vol. 1: *Text*, 327, no. IV.

[45] Dante Alighieri, *La vita nuova (Poems of Youth)*, trans. with an intro. Barbara Reynolds (London: Penguin, 1969); there are too many studies on the women figures in Dante's work to list them all; see, for instance, Victoria Kirkham, "A Canon of Women in Dante's *Commedia*," *Annali d'Italianistica* 7 (1989): 16–41; Molly G. Morrison, "A Journey to *Caritas*: Dante's Idea of Love and Will as Seen through Two Women of the *Divina Commedia*," *The Journal of the Association for the Interdisciplinary Study of the Arts* 1, 1 (1995): 49–57.

wirt!" (3.12; oh, happy me, happy, always happy! happy if I might win the beauty). The following stanza begins, once again, with rather standard expressions of his erotic feelings, but it concludes with a remarkable parallelism of four lines:

> sî ist mir liep und liebet mir für elliu wîp,
> sî ist mir iemer lieber dan mîn selbes lîp,
> sî ist lieb âne zahl, daz spriche ich offenbâr,
> sî ist mîn liehtiu rôse rôt und ouch mîn spilnder sunne klâr. (4.9–12)

> [I love her, and love her more than all other women;
> I will always love her more than myself.
> There is no ending in my love for her, I say this openly;
> she is my bright and red rose and also my clearly shining sun.]

Relying both on the interplay with the same base word of "liep" (dear), the poet intensifies his comparisons from verse to verse, heavily relying on the poetic effects of the 'l'-alliteration and the 'i' and 'ie' assonances. Associating her both with a rose and the sun, he makes us aware that his lady represents the apogee of all earthly and cosmic beauty. Throughout the remaining poem, which consists of fifteen stanzas altogether, Reinmar includes many more similar parallelisms and successfully creates a web of comparisons which strongly project unique impressions of the unfathomable power of love, such as:

> schœn unde liep daz ist ein minneclîchez wîp,
> schœn unde liep ist mînes herzen leitvertrîp,
> schœn unde liep daz machet al mîn trûren laz.
> diu schœne gît mir hôhen muot: diu liebe tuot dem herzen baz. (12.9–12)

> [beauty and love make a lovable woman,
> beauty and love is the joy of my heart,
> beauty and love make all my sorrow go away.
> Beauty gives me high spirits: love best soothes my heart.]

Surprisingly, German scholarship has ignored Reinmar von Brennenberg almost entirely, and he is mostly remembered only for his reflective stanza 13 in the same song in which he reminisces about some of the greatest courtly love poets in the past.[46] However, he was an impressive innovator, after all, who had a solid grasp of

---

[46] This stanza is also quoted in *Dichter über Dichter in mittelhochdeutscher Literatur*, ed. Günther Schweikle. Deutsche Texte, 12 (Tübingen: Niemeyer, 1970), 3–4; Müller, "Klassische Lyrik des deutschen Hochmittelalters," does not mention him at all; Olive Sayce, *The Medieval German Lyric 1150–1300: The Development of Its Themes and Forms in Their European Context* (Oxford: At the Clarendon Press, 1982), touches upon him only fleetingly. The paucity of serious examination of Reinmar's work is best illustrated by the short entry on him in the famous *Verfasserlexikon*, Frieder

traditional *minnesang* and considerably expanded and varied his sources, reaching a new level of poetic insightfulness regarding the hidden power of language as a medium to reflect upon his personal emotions and experiences of love.

This is not to put Reinmar on the same level as Walther von der Vogelweide and Neidhart, on the one hand, and Oswald von Wolkenstein, on the other. But he was keenly aware of the many possibilities of playing with language and of probing the multiple shades of meaning in order to illuminate the potentiality of poetic words and their epistemological significance.

In "Si jehent daz diu minne sanfte lône" (no. V; They Say that Love Offers Soothing Reward), for instance, Reinmar employs a pun based on the verb 'meinen,' which means 'to think,' 'to reflect,' 'to turn one's attention to,' 'to have a grudge against someone,' but also 'to love,' 'to intend,' 'to make it pleasant for someone,' and 'to mean.'[47] The poet raises the crucial question as to whether his love might not have thought of him in the same way as he had thought of her. After all, love is all-powerful: "jâ, si kan ez allez" (1, 5), except denying the lover her favor:

> ... wan daz eine
> daz si mit ir meine
> mich niht meinet als ich sî gemeinet hân. (1.5–7)

> [... except for the one thing
> that she does not keep me in her mind
> as I have thought of her.]

There are numerous alternatives to interpret the semantic field of 'meinen,' and the poet was obviously fully aware of the complexity of this term, which nicely corresponds to the intricate depth of love itself and his own emotional approach to this phenomenon. This gains additional weight in the subsequent discussion of his personal experiences, since the absence of love is equated with death ("swen si hazzet, dest der tôt," 2.4; whomever she hates meets his death). But this was the case with him as well: "alse hât si mich gehazzet sêre" (2.5; she hated me much). Nevertheless he expresses hope that love will look upon him favorably after all (2.7–3, 1).

The remainder of the song consists of general comments about his love for his lady and his hope to catch sight of her, which then would return happiness to him and would inspire him to see his friends again (3, 5–7). Nevertheless, the few lines in which Reinmar operates with various grammatical features of the basic verb 'meinen' signal, once again, that individual thirteenth-century poets had an excellent grasp of language and knew how to tease multiple meanings out of one

---

Schanze, "Reinmar von Brennenberg," *Die deutsche Literatur des Mittelalters: Verfasserlexikon*, 2nd completely rev. ed. Kurt Ruh et al. (Berlin and New York: de Gruyter, 1989), 7, 3–4: 1191–95.

[47] Matthias Lexer, *Mittelhochdeutsches Handwörterbuch*. Vol. 2 (Leipzig: Hirzel, 18), 2080–81.

word, hence to correlate love with language and to demonstrate the extent to which individual words of love could also, if not even necessarily so by their very essence, assume an hermeneutic function.[48] Precisely because of the proximity of meaning of each phrase, the verses open "gaps of indeterminacy" — Wolfgang Iser's term — then they "invite," as Patrick J. Gallacher and Helen Damico observe, "interpretation and provide the means by which reader and author may meet, an encounter in which an experience of 'true' comprehension may occur."[49]

On the other hand, Reinmar reveals this poetic potential only a few times, whereas most of his other songs are predicated on rather traditional concepts of courtly love (*minne*). As in the previous cases, however, these few passages provide powerful insight into the subtle and meaningful transformation of late medieval German love poetry. Some of its best representatives increasingly experimented with formal, linguistic, and also musical elements and here and there achieved a new level of lyrical language that foreshadows Oswald von Wolkenstein's literary genius. Increasingly, late medieval German poets embarked on a metapoetic discourse and addressed lady Love herself, hence also reflected upon their own creative work.

Ulrich von Winterstetten (flourishing in the middle of the thirteenth century), for instance,[50] dedicates his song "Ich wil aber disen sanc" (no. 1) to lady Love herself because he can no longer keep quiet and needs the poetic framework to come to terms with his emotions:

ich mac niht geswîgen mê:
mir ist wirs dann ê.
nie sô sêre mir betwanc
lip unde sinne
diu vil liebe sunder wân (1.3–7)

[I can no longer keep quiet:
I feel worse than ever.
Never before has love
openly tortured me so much
in my body and my mind.]

---

[48] Stanley N. Werbow, "Introduction," *Formal Aspects of Medieval German Poetry*, 3–6; here 5, cites Friedrich Maurer's insightful words, published in the *Festschrift für Jost Trier zum 70. Geburtstag* (1964), in his own translation: "We have learned by now that the intrinsic and main accomplishment of the great *minne* poets was the invention of the forms, the strophic structures and the melody. The development of their art is unfolded in the mastery of ever newer and more magnificent forms and in the most intimate combination of thoughts, of linguistic expression and of strophic forms, that is to say, however, also of the melody."

[49] Patrick J. Gallacher and Helen Damico, "Preface," *Hermeneutics and Medieval Culture*, ed. eidem (Albany: State University of New York Press, 1989), xi–xiii; here xi.

[50] For biographical information, see Kuhn, *Kommentar*, 558–60.

He also formally addressed "Frouwe Minne," whose servant he declares himself to be: "ich bin ir eigen diener iemer her gewesen" (no. II, 4.1). In "Sumer ouget sîne wunne" (no. XVI), Ulrich openly displays the material that he uses to compose his works: "prüeve er wol swer tihten kunne / waz mâterje lît / an dem walde und ûf der heide breit" (1.3–5; he who knows how to compose poetry ought to check for himself what material there is in the forest and on the broad meadow). Subsequently he formulates fairly routine phrases of his woeful suffering from love, but he structures his poem with an intriguing refrain: "est ein altgesprochen wort: / swâ dîn herze wont, dâ lît dîn hort" (1, 8–9; it is an old statement: where your heart lives, there is your treasure). He also incorporated a number of phrases that might be read as a break in the esoteric style of classical Middle High German love poetry. But they seem to serve as key elements to tear the veil of abstract courtly love apart and to remind his audience of the true essence of his poetry, to realize his erotic goals via the infinite power of human language.[51]

Similar tendencies can also be observed in the song poetry by the late medieval Swiss poets, such as Ulrich von Singenberg (flourishing ca. 1209–1228), who delighted in the employment of alliterations, assonances, self-references, and onomatopoetic elements, and explicitly interacted with his audience and fellow poets, such as in "Frowe, sælic frowe."[52] We know that many twelfth- and early thirteenth-century poets also operated with such strategic elements, but Ulrich intensified the metapoetic discourse and indicated a strong degree of self-reflectivity: "Ir welt mir verkêren, / swaz ich singe und och gesage: dast âne wer. / Sold doch ich iuch lêren, / ich beswung iuch sô mit mîner ruoten ber" (III.1–4; You want to distort what I sing and also say: there is no use for it. If I were to teach you, I would whip you with my stick).[53]

This also finds a confirmation in Hugo von Trimberg's didactic verse treatise *Der Renner* (ca. 1300), in which he reflects upon the countless options for people to express themselves. Having served as a schoolmaster for most of his life in Bamberg, Hugo obviously was tired of generations of students babbling, chatting, and making funny noises. But he also ridicules people's vain efforts to communicate: "Sieden, diezen, siusen, singen, / Zwitzern, grellen, snurren, klingen: / Die dœne ich gelernet hân, / die mir vor gar unkunt wâren, / Biz ich kam gein fünfzic jâren" (4–8; to steam, to push, to sweeten up, to sing / to twit, to

---

[51] Sieglinde Hartmann, "Ulrich von Winterstetten und die 'Materie' des Dichtens. Eine Interpretationsstudie zu Lied KLD Nr. XVI," *Ist zwîvel herzen nâchgebûr: Günther Schweikle zum 60. Geburtstag*, ed. Rüdiger Krüger, Jürgen Kühnel, and Joachim Kuolt. Helfant Studien, S 5 (Stuttgart: helfant edition, 1989),105–26; here117.

[52] *Die Schweizer Minnesänger*, ed. Max Schiendorfer. Vol. 1: *Texte* (Tübingen: Niemeyer, 1990), no. 24.

[53] Albrecht Classen, "Der Schweizer Minnesänger Ulrich von Singenberg," *Schweizerisch/Alemannische Perspektiven der neunziger Jahre*, ed. Peter Pabisch. Special Issue of *Schatzkammer* (Vermillion, S.D.: Verlag Schatzkammer, 2000), 107–24.

scream, to babble, to ring: these sounds that had been unfamiliar to me I have learned when I turned fifty).[54]

Ultimately, we also ought to incorporate the love poetry composed by various thirteenth- and fourteenth-century German and Dutch mystical writers, such as Mechthild von Magdeburg and Hadewijch, who transgressed human limitations in their visionary experience of the Godhead and subsequently formulated some of the most amazing erotic images in their song poetry.[55] Of course, this would be the topic of another paper,[56] but I would not want to miss the opportunity to quote at least a few verses from Mechthild's work which strikingly demonstrate the enormous epistemological potentials of mystical approaches to love and the power of poetic language:

> The loving soul betrays her true love in sighing for God.
> She is sold in holy grief for his love.
> She is sought with the host of many tears for her dear Lord,
> Whom she likes so well.
> She is captured in the first experience
> When God kisses her in sweet union.
> She is assailed with many a holy thought
> That she not waver when she mortifies her flesh.
> She is bound by the power of the Holy Spirit,
> And her bliss is indeed many-fold.[57]

As Amy Hollywood has confirmed with respect to Marguerite Porete's (d. 1310) *Mirror of Simple and Annihilated Souls and Those Who Remain Only in Will and Desire of Love*, the text's "authorship is pushed away from the human pen and

---

[54] Hugo von Trimberg, *Der Renner*, ed. Gustav Ehrismann. Mit einem Nachwort und Ergänzungen von Günther Schweikle. Deutsche Neudrucke. Reihe: Texte des Mittelalters (1908; Berlin: de Gruyter, 1970); my attempt to translate these onomatopoetic verses can only be experimental, especially since Hugo did not intend to provide concrete and commonly used verbs. For a recent comprehensive investigation of the treatise, see Rudolf Kilian Weigand, *Der 'Renner' des Hugo von Trimberg: Überlieferung, Quellenabhängigkeit und Struktur einer spätmittelalterlichen Lehrdichtung*. Wissensliteratur im Mittelalter, 35 (Wiesbaden: Reichert, 2000), who offers a detailed description of all manuscripts and the one print from 1549; he also discusses three manuscripts lost today. For a concise English introduction to Hugo, see Jutta Goheen, "Hugo von Trimberg," *Medieval Germany: An Encyclopedia*, ed. John M. Jeep (New York and London: Garland, 2001), 376–77.

[55] Albrecht Classen, "The Literary Treatment of the Ineffable: Mechthild von Magdeburg, Margaret Ebner, Agnes Blannbekin," *Studies in Spirituality* 8 (1998): 162–87; idem, "Die flämische Mystikerin Hadewijch als erotische Liebesdichterin," *Studies in Spirituality* 12 (2002): 23–42; see also Sara S. Poor, *Mechthild of Magdeburg and Her Book: Gender and the Making of Textual Authority*. The Middle Ages Series (Philadelphia: University of Pennsylvania Press, 2004), 17–56.

[56] For comparison's sake, however, consult the contribution to this volume by Connie Scarborough.

[57] Mechthild of Magdeburg, *The Flowing Light of the Godhead*, trans. and intro. Frank Tobin. Preface by Margot Schmidt. The Classics of Western Spirituality (New York and Mahwah, NJ: Paulist Press, 1998), 117.

onto God because he gives the internal image to the Soul that is externalized in the form of the book. The power of God insures that the image interior to the Soul truly portrays God, not just her subjective fantasy."[58] Whereas the secular contemporaries struggled hard to reinvent a lyric language through which the poetic self could fathom the secrets of physical and spiritual love, the mystical poets borrowed from both the world of the courts and the world of the church, and in this regard might well be the most powerful innovators in literary hermeneutics during the late Middle Ages.

Certainly, the mass of both secular and religious love poetry composed in the German late Middle Ages often seems repetitive and trite, but individual pieces indicate the creative potentials and the untiring efforts by numerous representatives, whether they were inspired by their courtly lady, by the human fascination with the infinite potentials of language and music, or by visionary experiences that forced them to cope with the apophatic dilemma.[59]

Altogether, these examples might not quite pave the way toward Oswald's literary, musical, and, perhaps, visionary, accomplishments, but we can be certain that the traditionally negative opinions about German late medieval courtly love poetry require considerable revisions and new critical perspectives. Despite much imitation and repetition dominating thirteenth- and fourteenth-century poetry, the few examples I have dealt with here clearly indicate remarkable and strong efforts by individual composers to embark on new approaches to the timeless topic of (courtly) love and to develop innovative images for its public discourse. Oswald's songs, albeit still anchored in the Middle Ages, definitely belong to a new world, but he had a number of predecessors who more or less successfully delved into the universe of erotic words and realized that this provided them with the access to fundamental hermeneutic insights into the epistemological function of amatory discourse.[60]

As we have learned only recently, however, Oswald in turn was not at all the last great medieval German love poet. Instead, the literary exploration of one of the greatest human emotions — love — evoked many more poetic responses throughout the late, surprisingly strongly blooming Middle Ages. In fact, Johan Huizinga's classic formulation of the *Waning of the Middle Ages*, which is the

---

[58] Amy Hollywood, *The Soul as Virgin Wife: Mechthild of Magdeburg, Marguerite Porete, and Meister Eckhart*. Studies in Spirituality and Theology, 1 (Notre Dame and London: University of Notre Dame Press, 1995), 89–90; see also the contribution to this volume by Valerie Wilhite.

[59] Bruce Milem, *The Unspoken Word: Negative Theology in Meister Eckhart's German Sermons* (Washington, DC: The Catholic University of America Press, 2002), 5–15; Suzanne Conklin Akbari, *Seeing through the Veil: Optical Theory and Medieval Allegory* (Toronto, Buffalo, and London: University of Toronto Press, 2004), 5–20, esp. 17: "Through the metaphor of the seed, language is conceived of as a living thing, able to reproduce meaning by being passed from one text to the next just the human form is reproduced by being passed from one generation to the next."

[60] See also Müller, "Klassische Lyrik," 597.

famous English title of his 1924 monograph, might have been a thorough misconception, because he measured the cultural-literary development with an inappropriate yardstick borrowed from the high Middle Ages.[61] To echo the overarching theme of this volume, fourteenth- and fifteenth-century composers of love poetry demonstrated, via their profound, sometimes even quixotic, words of love, their actual love of words, and hence their deep commitment to gain a new level of human epistemology.[62] They were not, however, the first to do so, and a careful examination of the huge collections of thirteenth- and fourteenth-century Middle High German courtly love poetry, and even of older songs, would yield surprising results. Our few examples have demonstrated that the generations of poets after Walther von der Vogelweide and Neidhart often knew how to explore their own function as poets and how to give words to innovative experiences, both secular and religious, both erotic and mystical. Hence future research is called upon to examine much more closely and with considerably more sensitivity the intimate relationship between late medieval courtly love poetry and contemporary mystical discourse in light of common epistemological operatives and interests.

---

[61] J(ohan) Huizinga, *The Waning of the Middle Ages: A Study of the Forms of Life, Thought and Art in France and the Netherlands in the XIVth and XVth Centuries* (1924; New York: Doubleday Anchor Books, 1954), 119–28. Now see the new translation, *The Autumn of the Middle Ages*, trans. Rodney J. Payton and Ulrich Mammitzsch (Chicago: University of Chicago Press, 1996). For new perspectives on late medieval autobiographical poetry, including Oswald von Wolkenstein's, see Albrecht Classen, *Die autobiographische Lyrik des europäischen Spätmittelalters: Studien zu Hugo von Montfort, Oswald von Wolkenstein, Antonio Pucci, Charles d'Orléans, Thomas Hoccleve, Michel Beheim, Hans Rosenplüt und Alfonso Alvarez de Villasandino*. Amsterdamer Publikationen zur Sprache und Literatur, 91 (Amsterdam and Atlanta: Editions Rodopi, 1991).

[62] Horst Brunner, "Das deutsche Liebeslied um 1400," *Gesammelte Vorträge der 600-Jahrfeier Oswalds von Wolkenstein, Seis am Schlern 1977. Dem Edeln unserm sunderlieben getrewen Hern Oswaltten von Wolkchenstain*, ed. Hans-Dieter Mück and Ulrich Müller. Göppinger Arbeiten zur Germanistik, 206 (Göppingen: Kümmerle, 1978), 105–46; Albrecht Classen, "Lieddichtung und Liederbücher im deutschen Spätmittelalter," *Jahrbuch der Oswald von Wolkenstein Gesellschaft* 12 (2000): 217–28; see also idem, *Deutsche Liederbücher des 15. und 16. Jahrhunderts*. Volksliedstudien, 1 (Münster, New York, Munich, and Berlin: Waxmann, 2001); Bernd Prätorius, *"Liebe hat es so befohlen": Die Liebe im Lied der Frühen Neuzeit*. Europäische Kulturstudien, 16 (Cologne, Weimar, and Vienna: Böhlau, 2004); see now Albrecht Classen's review in *Lied und populäre Kultur: Jahrbuch des Deutschen Volksliedarchivs* 49 (2004): 252–53.

Chapter 17

The Lover and His *Faus Semblant*: Technologies of Confession in the *Roman de la Rose*[1]

Tracy Adams
The University of Auckland, New Zealand

Scholars of medieval literature rarely take seriously the claim of the narrator(s) of the *Roman de la Rose* that the work is an art of love. As interpretations treating the *Rose* as an art of poetry and as a philosophical treatise demonstrate, the meaning of so rich a text cannot be confined to the one professed within the text itself.[2] As for interpretations that do heed the narrator's claim that the *Rose* is an art of love, most have tended to read it as an art of deception intended to amuse by satirizing the pretenses of courtly love rather than offer readers serious instruction.[3]

And yet, the assumptions about the problem of desire/love evinced at various points in the *Rose* correlate so closely with key assumptions of medieval theories of the emotions as partly performative that I will argue in this essay that the text's claim to be an art of love merits re-consideration. What modern readings have taken as a humorously self-conscious assessment of love as inherently deceptive — for example, the emphasis of Amour, the God of Love, upon language, physical appearance, and comportment — can be read as a dramatization of the relationship between the physiological reactions associated with the emotion and

---

[1] I would like to thank Albrecht Classen, Robert Levine, and Christopher Clason, and all the colleagues attending the symposium "Words of Love, Love of Words," for their very helpful comments on this essay.

[2] For example, David Hult, *Self-Fulfilling Prophecies: Readership and Authority in the First Roman de la Rose* (Cambridge: Cambridge University Press, 1986) and idem, *Fortune's Faces: The Roman de la Rose and the Poetics of Contingency* (Baltimore: The Johns Hopkins University Press, 2003).

[3] See Peter Allen, *The Art of Love: Amatory Fiction from Ovid to the Romance of the Rose*. The Middle Ages Series (Philadelphia: University of Pennsylvania Press, 1992).

the cultural templates through which one performs it, as laid out by medieval theories of the emotions. Grounded in the concept of the humors, medieval theories of the emotions depict human beings as easily penetrable by desires they have little power to resist. In his manual of rhetoric, the *Ars Versificatoria* (ca. 1175), Matthew of Vendôme depicts how vulnerable human beings are to their feelings. Love, writes Matthew, is an ephemeral emotion that arrives suddenly, causing great commotion, and pushing the victim to action ("Impulsiva est, quando repentina animi commotione in aliquod factum praecipitamur").[4] Still, as twelfth-century treatises on gesture attest, inner disturbances can be modulated effectively from without through performance, a combination of words and gestures.[5]

Considered from this perspective, the two parts of the *Rose* can be seen to begin with similar assumptions about the physiology of emotion as triggered by powerful forces acting upon the body. However, they go on to dramatize desire/love being pressed into service through performance for two distinct subcultures, the marrying secular aristocracy and the celibate clerical aristocracy. Guillaume's *Rose* illustrates the effacement of self-consciousness necessary to the experience of "sincere" love, dramatizing the participation of the Lover, Amant, in a quasi-ritualistic song and dance that activates certain of the impulses potentially associated with sexual desire, while repressing others, for example, the violent, homoerotic, and misogynistic. In contrast, Jean's Amant is forced into a state of self-consciousness by the allegorical figures who explicate his desire to him, bringing to the surface, so to speak, the contradictory impulses that Guillaume's ritual of love had suppressed and forcing Amant to experience them.[6]

---

[4] Matthew of Vendôme, *Ars versificatoria*, in: *Mathei Vindocinensis Opera*, ed. Franco Munari, 3 vols. (Rome: Edizioni di Storia e Letteratura, 1988), 3:109.

[5] On medieval programs of gesture as means of modulating emotion, see Dom Louis Gougaud, *Dévotions pratiques et ascétiques du moyen âge* (Paris: Desclée de Brouwer, 1925); Richard Trexler, *The Christian at Prayer: An Illustrated Prayer Manual*. Medieval and Renaissance Texts and Studies, 44 (Binghamton, NY: Medieval & Renaissance Texts & Studies, 1987); and Jean-Claude Schmitt, *La raison des gestes dans l'occident medieval* (Paris: Gallimard, 1990). In a description of Hugh of St. Victor's *De institutione novitiorum*, Schmitt writes: "[N]on seulement l'extérieur du corps exprime les mouvements de l'âme (*mentis motus*), mais inversement la discipline du corps et des membres 'étouffe les mouvements désordonnés de l'âme et les appétits illicites' et 'conforte l'âme dans la constance'. Le corps discipliné et notamment le geste discipliné ne sont plus simplement les expressions d'une âme vertueuse, mais les instruments de l'éducation morale du jeune novice" (Not only does the exterior of the body express the movement of the soul [*mentis motus*], but inversely the discipline of the body and the members 'dampens the disordered movements of the soul and illicit appetites and comforts the soul in constancy. The disciplined body and especially the disciplined gesture are not simply the expressions of a virtuous soul, but instruments of moral education for the young novice; 176).

[6] It should also be noted how similar modern and medieval theories of the emotions are. At first glance it would seem that modern theory on performance, which denies the notion of essence, locating "reality" in the performance of a particular state, would see a contradiction between the notions of love based upon theories of the humors. But Rosalind C. Morris suggests that "essence" is not necessarily absent from modern theories, explaining that performance theory in fact can be

In this essay, I will consider the allegorical figure of Faus Semblant, False Seeming, as an extreme version of the self-consciousness promoted within the second part of the *Rose*, and I will argue that this self-consciousness was intended to bring readers to question their own motives about love. Faus Semblant obliges Jean's Amant to confront a paradox left dormant in Guillaume's art of love: to be successful in love, Amant must self-consciously manipulate his persona (that is, present himself as lovable through his clever use of words of love), and yet, to the extent that he is aware of himself as a manipulator of words of love, he must question whether he truly loves or simply wishes to satisfy his selfish desires. Already partially dismantled by the time he encounters Faus Semblant, his love unravels completely once he assumes the traits of this unappealing figure, who "exposes" the structures that allow him to experience his diverse urges as a single powerful emotion. To cast the problem in the terms proposed by this volume, the character suggests that self-reflective lovers must wonder if their words of love are motivated by a love of words rather than genuine emotion.

GUILLAUME'S CONCEPTION OF LOVE

Vernacular love literature in medieval France, like its counterparts in all cultures, dramatized the modulation of powerful and possibly dangerous sexual impulses into emotions that were usable within its different subcultures. The process is perhaps most obvious in love lyrics, where the troubadour transforms inchoate desire into an emotion with a name and characteristics through the performance

---

used to overcome the dichotomy between what we might consider "the given" — what culture thinks of as "natural" — and "the constructed," with a more dialectical sense of how what is socially constructed comes to have the force of the given in individual lives: Rosalind C. Morris, "All Made Up: Performance Theory and the New Anthropology of Sex and Gender," *Annual Review of Anthropology* 24 (1995): 567–92; here 571. Theoretician of the emotions William M. Reddy offers the concept of "emotives" — the words cultures use to discuss their emotions — as an example of the emotions as at least partly performative. He sees emotion as resulting from the relationship between the biological substratum possessed by all human beings and the cultural construction of emotion. See William M. Reddy, *The Navigation of Feeling: A Framework for the History of Emotions* (Cambridge: Cambridge University Press, 2001). When an individual experiences an emotion, it is because this substratum, composed of physiological elements and a collection of associated "thought material" (111) has been activated by a particular event. But the activated material's size and complexity always exceeds the individual's ability to assimilate and articulate it. The activated material is therefore "translated" through socially constructed "emotional regimes," as Reddy calls them, to a level of consciousness. Emotions can be modified by changing the language one uses to discuss them (128). On the modern study of past emotions, see Peter N. Stearns with Carol Z. Stearns, "Emotionology: Clarifying the History of Emotions and Emotional Standards," *The American Historical Review* 90 (1986): 813–36. On medieval perspectives of emotion as theatrical and performative see Albrecht Classen, "Moriz, Tristan, and Ulrich as Master Disguise Artists: Deconstruction and Reenactment of Courtliness in *Moriz von Craûn, Tristan als Mönch*, and Ulrich von Liechtenstein's *Frauendienst*," *Journal of English and Germanic Philology* 103 (2004): 475–504.

of his or her poetry, or, to express the procedure in the familiar troubadour doublet, where he or she undertakes *trobar* followed by *cantar*. Through their *cansos* troubadours showed how to bring the unruly human body into harmony with the cosmos. The romances operate in a similar way with their sometimes lengthy love episodes that halt narrative action to describe desire by means of a pool of common images, using rhyme and rhythm to shape the impulse represented within their narratives by Amor.[7] The vernacular *artes amatoriae*, arts of love, based upon Ovid's *Ars amatoria* and popular in France from the end of the twelfth century, also depict love as performance, teaching potential lovers how to construct a persona that members of the opposite sex will find lovable, under the assumption that in the enactment of the emotion hopeful lovers will experience it. True, Ovid tells his readers to put on a good show: "Est tibi agendus amans, imitandaque vulnera verbis" (611, 54; You must play the lover, and counterfeit heartache with words, 55).[8] But this is only after he has already instructed them to station themselves where they are likely to be smitten by the arrows of Cupid; they are already in the throes of desire when they begin to act out the part of the lover.[9] In other words, they are taught not to simulate an emotion they do not feel, but to act out one that has been authentically aroused within them.

Guillaume also treats love as the management of authentic desire. Near the end of the first part of the *Rose*, Amant finally succeeds in kissing the rose he so madly desires. In outraged response, the allegorical personifications unfavorable to Amant's quest surround the rose, and, to protect it from further violation, they enclose it in a stone tower. Despairing at this new development, Amant begins to lament his pain. Far from satisfying him, the stolen kiss has only increased his desire to an intolerable level, causing him serious physical as well as emotional discomfort:

> Se j'ai la savor essaïe,
> Tant est grainde la covoitise
> Qui esprent mon cuer et atise.
> Or revendront plor et sopir,
> Longues pansees sanz dormir,
> Friçons et pointes et complaintes;

---

[7] Roland Greene, *Post-Petrarchism: Origins and Innovations of the Western Lyric Sequence* (Princeton: Princeton University Press, 1991). Describing the generalizing tendencies of the lyric, Greene writes: "the nature of lyric's ritual dimension, simply stated, is to superpose the subjectivity of the scripted speaker on the reader ... " (5). This tendency he opposes to a fictive element, an "implicit plot that unfolds within a hypothetical world" (11).

[8] Quotes from the *Ars amatoria* and the *Remedia amoris* along with their translations are from *Ovid in Six Volumes, II: The Art of Love, and Other Poems*, trans. J. H. Mozley, rev. G. P. Goold. Loeb Classical Library (1929; Cambridge: Harvard University Press, 1985). Cited by line and page.

[9] See *Ars amatoria*, 19–25.

De tex dolors avré je maintes,
Car je sui en enfer cheoiz.[10]

[Because I have experienced the savor, the desire that overcomes and fans the flame in my heart is all the greater. Now sighs and tears and sleeplessness will come back, shivers and prickings and complaints. I will have many of these pains, because I have fallen into Hell.]

The tears of Guillaume's Amant are not an act, for the text presents them as spontaneous. Modern readers will be suspicious of a "love" that expresses itself in a series of signs that today tend to be associated with sexual frenzy. However, the model informs not only Ovid's love works, but religious depictions of love during the twelfth and thirteenth centuries as well, and the fact that love was believed to manifest itself in its physical symptoms in this different register suggests that desire in its initial movement was perceived as something that could be managed in very different ways.[11] Richard of St. Victor's physical symptoms of his love for God in *Tractatus de quatuor gradibus violentae caritatis* are indistinguishable from those described by Ovid in works like the *Ars amatoria*, the *Remedia amoris*, the *Amores*, and the *Heroides*, and are the same as those experienced by Guillaume's Amant. About the religious lover's physical discomfort, Richard writes that he "desiderio ardet, fervet affectu, aestuat, anhelat, profunde ingemiscens et longa suspiria trahens" (burns with desire, burns with affection, smolders, pants, moans profoundly, and draws long sighs).[12] Like Richard's outward symptoms, those of Amant are not separate from his great love, but prove its intensity.[13]

Amant's body thus contains a "covert" sentiment that his physical form renders "apert" or visible; his symptoms are outward manifestations of the love he is prevented by a series of truculent allegorical characters from expressing. How does an art of love based upon this conception of love function? Just as Amant's body veils a "covert" sentiment, the *Roman de la Rose* itself contains a hidden meaning,

---

[10] *Roman de la Rose*, ed. Félix Lecoy, 3 vols. (Paris: Champion, 1983), 3:3768–75. My translations.

[11] For example, William of St.-Thierry visualizes lust as the downward movement of a force that should be directed upwards. He chastises Ovid for diverting the love placed by in the heart by the Creator to serve an evil end. Ovid's sin was that he taught men to press into madness a power that should be trained towards goodness [*in quandam perurgebat insaniam*]. Guillaume de St-Thierry, *Deux Traités de l'Amour de Dieu: de la Contemplation de Dieu; de la Nature et de la Dignité de l'Amour*, trans. M.-M. Davy (Paris: Vrin, 1953), 72. In this context we might also consider medieval medical literature on love as a physical illness. See Tracy Adams, *Violent Passions: Managing Love in the Old French Verse Romance*. Studies in Arthurian and Courtly Culture (New York: Palgrave Macmillan, 2005), 29–32 and 43–45.

[12] *Patrologiae cursus completus, series Latina*, ed. Jacques-Paul Migne, 221 vols. (Paris: Garnier, 1844–1864), 196:1209C.

[13] C. Stephen Jaeger makes this point in *Ennobling Love: In Search of a Lost Sensibility*. The Middle Ages Series (Philadelphia: University of Pennsylvania Press, 1999), 13–17.

or so its narrator professes: "La verité, qui est coverte / vos sera lores toute overte," he promises, "quant espondre m'oroiz le songe..." (The hidden truth will be made clear to you when you will have heard my explanation of the dream) (lines 2071–73). This verity can be none other than the truth about love, the "art d'amours," for Amour, the God of Love, has commanded the narrator to produce this work, as the narrator announces in the very first lines of the poem, a work within which the "art d'amours est toute enclose." But what does this art of love teach? It teaches potential lovers to efface any consciousness of a possible distinction between the outward physical symptoms of love (which we might think of as lust) and glorious, inwardly authentic love. After an initial movement, construed as an attack by an arrow fired by Amour, Amant is instructed to perform Amour's commandments in his daily life if he wishes to be a successful lover. Through his performance of the commandments with their ritualistic emphasis on personal appearance and behavior, Amant will shape the frenzy of love into a positive emotion:

> Vilenie premierement
> Ce dist Amors, voel et conment
> Que tu gerpisses sanz reprendre,
> Se tu ne velz vers moi mesprendre...
> Or te garde bien de retreire
> Chose de gent qui face a teire.
> N'est pas proece de mesdire...
> Soies cortois et acointables,
> De paroles douz et resnable
> Et au granz genz etaus menus...
> Aprés gardes que tu ne dies
> Ces orz moz ne ces ribaudies...
> Toutes fames ser et honore,
> En aus servir poine et labeure...
> Emprés tot ce d'orgueil te garde...
> Mes qui d'amors se velt pene,
> Il se doit cointement mener.
> Hons qui porchace druerie
> Ne vaut neant sanz cointerie...
> Moine toi bel, selonc ta rente,
> Et de robe et de chaucemente... (lines 2075–130)

[First of all, says Love, I order you to renounce villainy if you don't want to get into trouble with me.... Then keep yourself from saying things about people that it would be better not to say... It is not worthy to talk about people.... Be polite and friendly, using gentle and reasonable words to both noble and lowly people.... After that, watch out that you never say anything obscene .... Honor and serve women.... After that, make sure that you are not proud

.... But he who works hard for love must behave charmingly. Shame on him who seeks a love relationship without being charming.... Conduct yourself well, according to your means in matters of dress and shoes....]

Like Ovid's lovers, Amant has deliberately sought the emotion he suffers from by placing himself in a spot where he is likely to receive one of Cupid's arrows, and, like Ovid's version of the emotion, love within Guillaume's garden is the same thing as sexual desire, a universal, spontaneous, and powerful physical reaction. And, like Ovid's text, Guillaume's demonstrates how the emotion can be trained through performance. Part of the attractive and cheerful crowd gathered in the garden, Amant participates in a ritualized group performance. Ritual reinforces group identity, and as the individuals take part, they lose themselves in the performance, conforming any potentially conflicting desires to the demands of the commandments.

Within a social context that encourages his type of love, Amant experiences his emotion as completely "natural." Or at least he experiences the emotion as natural as long as he does not stop to scrutinize himself in the act of performing as a lover. Susan Crane describes the lingering duality typical among participants in rituals: "A preliminary, underlying conflict exists between a participant's absorption in and resistance to the event itself: typically, people experience both grateful acquiescence to a ritual ... and at the same time an uncomfortable sense of detachment and doubt."[14] This doubt must be suppressed. Reflecting upon oneself as a desiring individual engaged in a ritualistic performance will inevitably increase the sense of detachment and doubt Crane describes. Specifically in the case of the *Rose*, a real danger exists that reflection upon love will reveal sexual desire to be a self-seeking impulse detachable from the inner truth it ostensibly reflects. The unity of inner and outer being so carefully cultivated by Guillaume's art of love will begin to degenerate under scrutiny. As Jean's continuation demonstrates, lovers self-aware enough to discourse at length upon their desire inevitably come up against the impossibility of maintaining that sexual desire is an innocent and spontaneous reflection of love. Reflecting lovers are calculating, a characteristic fervently condemned by Guillaume's Amour.

Of course, the seed of self-interest is present in Amour's list of commandments. After all, he parts from Amant saying,"Or t'ai dit coment n'en quel guise / amanz doit fere mon servise. / Or le fai donques, se tu viaus / de la belle avoir tes aviaus" (2563–66; Now I've told you how a lover should serve me; now do it, if you want to have what you desire from the lovely one). And certainly the God of Love implies that the Lover will be rewarded when he tells him, "Biaus amis, par l'ame mon pere, / nus n'a bien s'il ne le compere; / s'en aime l'en mieuz le chaté / quant

---

[14] Susan Crane, *The Performance of Self: Ritual, Clothing, and Identity During the Hundred Years War* (Philadelphia: University of Pennsylvania Press, 2002), 58–59.

l'en l'a plus chier acheté ...." (2583–86; Dear friend, by my father's soul, no man has good unless he buy it. The goods we love the most are the ones we pay most highly for). But the notion of love as exchange poses nothing more than a quiet threat of an intrusive individual desire smoothed over by ritual; it is left dormant in Guillaume's section.

Guillaume's love paradigm seems to be intended to discourage violence. Amant desires consummation intensely, but the ritual or commandments of love instruct him to behave genteelly — to restrain himself. Indeed, nearly the entirety of Guillaume's narrative is devoted to describing the various obstacles to Amant's attempts to pluck the rose.[15]

JEAN'S CONCEPTION OF LOVE

Jean's section of the *Rose* serves as the *Remedia amoris* to Guillaume's *Ars amatoria*. Guillaume uses words of love to unify interior and exterior manifestations of love (in performing the ritual of love, Amant loves). In his section of the *Rose*, both the art of love hidden within the dream recounted in the text and the love written upon the Lover's body are configured as outward manifestations of interior secrets. In such a poetic universe, Amant remains innocent, his appearance and interior being cleaving together. But with Jean's continuation, Amant encounters a series of characters who convince him that his love is not a reflection of a beautiful emotion; rather, it is nothing more than a set of discrete, selfish, and often unsavory urges, and Amour's commandments are simple instructions in dissimulation. An artificial construction, according to Jean, Guillaume's sort of love can be managed easily when it is fractured into an endless series of glosses — when it is, in effect, analyzed out of existence. As Renate Blumenfeld-Kosinski has observed, Guillaume's text "promises us *the* final key to the text; Jean's, on the other hand,

---

[15] This ongoing directive to restrain oneself and not rape women may seem exaggerated to the modern reader! However, given the habitual violence directed towards women, it is likely that such "restrictions" were earnestly intended. Examples of literature on the violence towards medieval women include Louise O. Vasvári, "'Buon cavallo e mal cavallo vuole spone, e buona femina e mala femina vuol bastone': Medieval Cultural Fictions of Wife-Battering," *Discourses on Love, Marriage, and Transgression in Medieval and Early Modern Literature*, ed. Albrecht Classen. Medieval and Renaissance Texts and Studies, 278 (Tempe, AZ: Arizona Center for Medieval and Renaissance Studies, 2004), 313–36; Kathryn Gravdal, "Poetics of Rape Law in Medieval France," *Rape and Representation*, ed. Lynn A. Higgins and Brenda R. Silver (New York: Columbia University Press, 1991), 207–26 and eadem, *Ravishing Maidens: Writing Rape in Medieval French Literature and Law*. New Cultural Series (Philadelphia: University of Pennsylvania Press, 1991); Henriette Benveniste, "Les enlèvements: stratégies matrimoniales, discours juridique et discours politique en France à la fin du Moyen Age," *Revue Historique* 283 (1990): 13–35; James Brundage's "Rape and Seduction in the Medieval Canon Law," *Sexual Practices and the Medieval Church*, ed. Vern L. Bullough and idem (Buffalo, New York: Prometheus Books, 1982), 41–48.

is a masterpiece of amplification and obfuscation: there is no one meaning in the multiple discourses of his characters."[16]

As Jean reveals that love must be defined as a vast array of different impulses rather than one glorious emotion, he prepares the way for Amant to reconfigure his love as lust, an impulse that can be wrestled with and overcome through literary praxis, as his Amant demonstrates in the romance's final scene.[17] From a medieval pedagogical perspective, literary activity — love of words — was a means of regulating the body's unruly desires.[18] Apprentice clerics began to manage theirs when they took up the study of Latin in the classroom. A force that could be summoned by reading about it, desire was introduced to young students as a theme by their masters in the form of texts like the *Ars amatoria*, the *Remedia amoris*, the *Pamphilus*, and *Piramus and Tisbé*. Although the autobiography of Guibert of Nogent (1053–124) denies any value to Ovidian love writings, it reveals very clearly the immediacy of the relationship between such writings and desire as it was understood by medieval readers.[19] Describing himself as a young man in the monastery he writes:

> After steeping my mind unduly in the study of versemaking, with the result that I put aside for such ridiculous vanities the matters of universal importance in the divine pages, I was so far guided by my folly as to give first place to Ovid and the pastoral poets and to aim at a lover's urbanity in distributions of all types and in a series of letters. Forgetting my proper severity and abandoning the modesty of a monk's calling, my mind was led away by these enticements of a poisonous license, and I considered only if I could render the conversation of the courts in the words of some poet, with no

---

[16] Renate Blumenfeld-Kosinski, "Overt and Covert: Amorous and Interpretive Strategies in the *Roman de la Rose*," *Romania* 11 (1990): 432–53.

[17] Of course, much of medieval literature is filled with contradiction. As Constance Bouchard's study demonstrates, contradiction is indeed embedded in the very structure of medieval literature. See *"Every Valley Shall Be Exalted": The Discourse of Opposites in Twelfth-Century Thought* (Ithaca: Cornell University Press, 2003). In *Courtly Contradictions: The Emergence of the Literary Object in the Twelfth Century* (Stanford: Stanford University Press, 2001), Sarah Kay argues for contradiction as a problem worthy of study in its own right, as a defining structure of the medieval "literary object." On multiple and sometimes contradictory meanings, see also Catherine Brown, *Contrary Things: Exegesis, Dialectic, and the Poetics of Didacticism* (Stanford, CA: Stanford University Press, 1998).

[18] This clerical attitude towards words of love and love of words can be contrasted with Christopher Clason's analysis in his contribution to this volume of the positive use to which Gottfried's Tristan and Isolde put their own love of words. Jan Ziolkowski's *Alan of Lille's Grammar of Sex: The Meaning of Grammar to a Twelfth-Century Intellectual* (Cambridge, MA: Harvard University Press, 1985) discusses the medieval analogy between grammar and sex, esp. 89–107.

[19] In the prologue to his *Tristan*, Gottfried von Straßburg describes love as a kind of metaphorical bread that transforms the lovers and allows them to come to terms with their emotions. Reading about love functions like ingesting bread, or life, and the poet serves as the mediator to breathe new life into the heart of lovers. See Albrecht Classen, "Gottfried von Straßburg's *Tristan*, the Eternal Bread, and Love," *Tristania* XXIII (2004): 91–105.

thought of how much the toil which I loved might hurt the aims of our holy profession. By love of it I was doubly taken captive, being snared both by the wantonness of the sweet words I took from the poets and by those which I poured forth myself, and I was caught by the unrestrained stirring of my flesh through thinking on these things and the like.[20]

The tale of Francesca da Rimini and Paolo Malatesta, the lovers transported by reading about Lancelot and Guenevere, whom Dante discovers in the second ring of Hell, offers one of the best-known versions of all times of the capacity of literature to produce lust.[21] Jean Gerson (1363–1429), too, notes that reading about love creates an immediate physical reaction in the reader. In his critique of the *Rose*, he notes that "fantasie" moves the body, and the more explicit the "fantasie" the more immediate its effect: "Et tout vient de la fantasie: quelle merveille se ung feu couvert de cendres ne brule pas si tost come le sentier a nus? Ainssy est de choses charnelz nueement dictes ou resgardees" (And everything comes from "fantasie": is it any surprise if a fire covered with ashes does not burn as quickly as an open path? So it goes with carnal things nakedly said or viewed).[22]

Why then did teachers introduce Ovid's love writings to their young students, writings that could only have aroused their desires? The pedagogic assumption seems to have been that students could be taught to master their bodies most effectively through the analogous process of mastering Latin literature: being taught to read and write could serve to a large extent to teach them to control the urges Ovidian-style readings aroused. Robert Glendinning writes that love material with its "ironies and moral ambiguities provided what must have seemed a natural medium from the antithetical and manipulative devices of rhetoric, and one which, in the bargain, enabled the practitioner to explore his own interest in and ambivalent attitude toward eros."[23]

Garrett E. P. Epp emphasizes that the medieval students conceived of literary analysis in sexual terms, as male domination: students "are expected to learn

---

[20] John F. Benton, *Self and Society in Medieval France: The Memoirs of Abbott Guibert of Nogent* (Toronto: University of Toronto Press, 1984), 87.

[21] See *The Divine Comedy of Dante Alighieri*, ed. and trans. Robert M. Durling, intro. and notes Ronald L. Martinez and Robert M. Durling, illus. Robert Turner. 2 vols. (New York: Oxford University Press, 1996), 1:90–93; for this phenomenon, see *The Book and the Magic of Reading in the Middle Ages*, ed. Albrecht Classen. Garland Medieval Bibliographies, 24 (New York and London: Garland, 1999).

[22] *Le Débat sur le "Roman de la Rose,"* ed. Eric Hicks (Paris: Champion, 1977), 84.

[23] Robert Glendinning, "Pyramus and Thisbe in the Medieval Classroom," *Speculum* 61 (1986): 51–78, here 54. See also Robert Levine, "How to Rread Walter Map," *Mittellateinisches Jahrbuch* 23 (1988): 91–105. Levine argues that the *De nugis curialium* was a school book, whose elaborate Latin was intended to train students in rhetoric. Its subject matter is bitterly misogynistic, filled with drastic results for heterosexual relationships, but tolerant of homosexuality. Compared to heterosexuality, writes Levine, "homosexuality demands and receives in Walter's stories, no such violent punishment. His comparative tolerance for homosexuality, which, as he suggests in the story, is often to be found among the learned, is, of course, not unique in the Middle Ages" (103).

The Lover and his Faus Semblant

masculine control over their material, avoiding the parallel feminizations of rhetorical and moral vice, learning the proper use of their pens."[24]

In their lengthy reflections upon love, the characters in Jean's continuation explore a number of interests and attitudes toward eros, expounding upon these as a teacher might and helping Amant to re-orient his own emotion. Raison, the first character to appear in part two of the *Rose*, insists that the pleasure associated with sexual relations is nothing more mystical than a trick of Nature for getting people to couple and insists upon a complete separation between desire and friendship.[25] Then, fresh from his encounter with Reason, Amant encounters Ami, who latches on to such innocuous commandments as "refuse to involve yourself in ribaldry and dirty speech" and "those in Love's service should conduct themselves in a refined manner," which in the mouth of Guillaume's Amour represent positive gestures for the amorous, and spins them out to their most extreme conclusions, transforming them into instructions to lovers to create pleasant appearances in order to hide their true motives. Whatever you do, Ami warns Amant, don't let it be known what you really have in mind!

> Mais ne saient pas coustumier
> De dire aus portiers au prumier
> Qu'il se veillent d'aus acoster
> Por la fleur du rosier oster,
> Mais par amor leal et fine,
> De nete pensee enterine.   (Lines 7561–66)

[But do not tell the jailers at first that your design is to deflower the Rose; pretend that the love you feel is fine and pure.]

Under the tutelage of such a teacher, Amant's emotion begins to come apart. Is he one who truly loves, that is, one whose appearance accurately reflects his interior passionate state, itself a reflection of divine love, or is he a master of deception, aiming to seduce through words of love? Early in the discourse of Ami, attention is drawn to the difference between Amant and his friend. Amant, still under the

---

[24] On clerical education and the analogy between control of the language and control of the body, see Garrett E. P. Epp, "Learning to Write with Venus's Pen: Sexual Regulation in Matthew of Vendôme's *Ars versificatoria*" *Desire and Discipline: Sex and Sexuality in the Premodern West*, ed. Jacqueline Murray and Konrad Eisenbichler (Toronto: University of Toronto Press, 1996), 265–79; here 267. Epp discusses Matthew of Vendôme's frequent use of sexually explicit imagery to illustrate the figures of rhetoric in the *Ars versificatoria* (ca. 1175), writing, "Both sexual activity and writing are to be carefully regulated, as they pose parallel dangers to the emerging masculinity of Matthew's young charges" (266).

[25] In the context I am exploring here, Amant's's famously stupid response to Raison's observations that some poetry should be glossed represents a halting but heartfelt attempt to articulate the structure of his life in the garden. There love simply signified; it was not glossed.

sway of Guillaume's Amour, experiences the authentic physical symptoms of a love he expresses rather than feigns. Ami's advice to learn to cry on cue, "vos eulz moilliez / De chaudes lermes . . .," is superfluous at this point, for Amant *has* been crying, but real tears, the result of his deeply-felt longing. This will soon change!

Faus Semblant, a figure who encourages radical scepticism about the relationship between appearance and reality, represents the culminating point of Amant's journey into self-consciousness. About halfway through the work taken as an entirety, Amour, who has gathered his barons, a group representing at least arguably positive qualities like Oiseuse (Idleness), Noblece de Queur (Nobility of Heart), Richece (Wealth), Franchise (Frankness), Pitiez (Pity), Largece (Generosity), Hardement (Bravery), Honor (Honor), Cortoisie (Courtesy), Deliz (Delight), and Simplece (Simplicity), for an assault on the castle, is stunned to find among the number Faus Semblant, deceptively dressed as a Franciscan monk. Faus Semblant incarnates the most extreme possible version of Amour's premise that lovers should enact a role, while the requirement to suffer the pains of love patiently is carried to its most unattractive conclusion in the pale figure of his partner, Atenance Contrainte (Constrained Abstinence). After his initial shock, Amour accedes to the urgings of Atenance Contreinte, an impostor herself in the garb of a Beguine, and the rest of his barons, who want him to accept Faus Semblant as his man. Although Amour remains dubious, he lets himself be convinced that a request for love inevitably involves deception. What one *really* seeks is sexual conquest, but this must be disguised. Without Faus Semblant, the castle enclosing the object of Amant's desire would be quite simply impenetrable.

The figure of Faus Semblant refers to the mid-thirteenth-century conflict between the "seculars" at the University of Paris under the leadership of William of St. Amour and the mendicants. William's attack of 1256, "De periculis novissimorum temporum," a work that ridiculed the friars and viewed mendicancy as the work of the Antichrist, is explicitly mentioned by Faus Semblant. The character also refers to the "Introductio in evangelium aeternum," commonly supposed to have been written by John of Parma, General of the Franciscans. Bringing a whole series of historical references with him, Faus Semblant has long been seen to fit uneasily into this narrative of love and desire.[26] Critics who have read the character in terms of the quest for sexual fulfillment recorded in the *Rose* have seen him as an unambiguously negative aspect of Amant.[27] I would, however, suggest

---

[26] Although a recent article by G. Geltner convincingly makes the case that the character should be seen as a figure of hypocrisy rather than as an antifraternal assault. "Faux Semblants: Antifraternalism Reconsidered in Jean de Meun and Chaucer," *Studies in Philology* 101 (2004): 357–80.

[27] Some of these include Kevin Brownlee's article which while dealing primarily with the *Rose* as "one of the most important literary meditations on the status of language produced during the French Middle Ages," notes that notes that "Love's discourses, both amatory and poetic, appear as inescapably duplicitous when viewed in tandem with Faux Semblant's linguistic practice." "The Problem of Faux Semblant: Language, History, and Truth in the *Roman de la Rose*," *The New Medievalism*,

that, as shady a figure as he undoubtedly is, his primary function in terms of the art of love contained within Jean's *Rose* is to figure the self-reflective individual becoming aware of the welter of conflicting and powerful impulses active inside of himself and of the need to manage them effectively.

Faus Semblant is quickly drawn into a confession by Amour. With the Fourth Lateran Council's injunction for yearly confession along with the new emphasis it placed upon better educating the lay population about Christianity, thorough examinations of the self came to be seen as crucial to Christian moral health.

As Foucault has written, a major tenet of Christianity is the periodic requirement to clean up "the illusions, temptations, and seductions that can occur in the mind" to better understand the "reality of what is going on within ourselves" — and regulate that reality.[28] When the self is understood, the individual can renounce it and hand him or herself over to God. But the imperative to clean up one's "illusions, temptations, and seductions" inevitably results in the confession of a mass of details that assume the meaning into which they are woven by the confessor. The technology of confession, as Karma Lochrie points out, is based upon complicity, and therefore the knowledge it produces is not the work of a single confessing individual. "The 'web of tactics' here is woven around the joint effort at discernment of the confessant's secrets," she writes, "but it involves a complicated mesh of seductions and manipulations on the part of both actors. This constitutes its play and its fascination . . . ."[29] Specifically, the discourse of confession is created by the questions asked of a confessant who is by definition guilty in the eyes of the confessor.[30] All Christians, according to Western

---

ed. Marina Brownlee, Kevin Brownlee, and Stephen G. Nichols, Baltimore: The Johns Hopkins University Press, 1991), 255–71; here 269; and Richard Emmerson and Ronald Herzman's "The Apocalyptic Ages of Hypocrisy: Faus Semblant and Amant in the *Roman de la Rose*," *Speculum* 62, 3 (1987): 612–34. They emphasize that "[t]hose who have argued for the moral inversion inherent in Amant's quest for the Rose have done so by claiming that what is described in the movement of the poem is not merely an excusable fault, at worst the least of the seven deadly sins, but rather an embodiment of the tendency toward sin itself. . . . To make our conclusion even more explicit in this regard, we suggest that yet another level of hypocrisy in the *Roman* is to be discerned in the assumption . . . that the private world of the Lover has no public implications. If even here, in Amant's private world, there are widespread public consequences, then we must attend to the seriousness of the Lover's actions. By setting the quest during the apocalyptic age of hypocrisy, Jean suggested that what is passed off as trivial can be a deadly serious disorder involving the larger community all the more serious to the degree that it masks itself as the good" (632).

[28] Michel Foucault, *Essential Works of Foucault*, trans. Robert Hurley et al., ed. Paul Rabinow, 3 vols. (1994; London: Penguin Books, 1997), 1:178.

[29] Karma Lochrie, *Covert Operations: The Medieval Uses of Secrecy*. The Middle Ages Series (Philadelphia: University of Pennsylvania Press, 1999), 37.

[30] Robert Levine offers the example of Rather of Verona whose "confessions" make him sympathetic to modern readers. Levine does not suggest that Rather's behavior is self-conscious, but hints that he was instinctively aware that confessing one's own guilt makes one more attractive than denying one's own sinfulness. See Robert Levine, "Liudprand of Cremona: History and Debasement in the Tenth Century," *Mittellateinisches Jahrbuch* 26 (1991): 70–84; here 70.

theological teachings, have been guilty of sexual desire since the Fall, when the uncontrollable impulse to couple became the primary sign of humans' disobedience to God. Therefore, during confession they necessarily confess illicit sexual desires. Confessants cannot confess that they are innocent; anyone so audacious would only be considered all the guiltier.

Although it seems paradoxical at first glance that Faus Semblant, whose very existence depends upon keeping his stratagems secret, confesses himself to Amour, the character does not reveal any secrets whatsoever, although he speaks at length. Faus Semblant merely confesses his hypocrisy as per Amour's expectations, reiterating the sins expected of him. The character represents not simple hypocrisy, then, I suggest, but the hypocrisy that arises inevitably from confession. Under questioning, a confessant will unearth a series of plausible ulterior motives, but these may or may not be his own. Trapped in the "complicated mesh of seductions and manipulations on the part of both actors," to repeat Lochrie's formulation, the confessant must confess to lust, which is by definition negative in this context, when asked.

This confessional narrative performs a crucial function in Jean's representation of the psychology of lovers. Because the very procedure of confession must lead to the discovery that the confessant has sinned, a lover cannot possess a pure intention; or at least, self-examination and confession cannot reveal one. Everyone who confesses is *a priori* guilty, and therefore the narrative throws together into one camp 1) those who are undoubtedly truly greedy and hypocritical, and 2) those who are essentially good, but not perfect — who may simply be struggling to suppress ordinary human longings for comfort. The guilty are indistinguishable from their well-intentioned counterparts, even to themselves. Hypocrites might be anywhere, and even worse, wherever they are, they are indiscernible. To Amour's question of where he lives, Faus Semblant replies:

> Parjurs sui; Mais ce que j'afin
> Set l'en enviz devant la fin,
> Car pluseur par moi mort reçurent
> Qui onc mon barat n'aperçurent
> Et reçoivent et recevront
> Qui ja mes ne l'apercevront. (lines 11,141–11,146)

[I am a perjurer. But what I bring about one hardly knows before I finish. Many have died because of me who didn't even recognize my trickery, and many more die and will die who will never even notice.]

Transposed back into the terms of love, Faus Semblant illustrates how effectively the Western clerical model of love renders the emotion impossible. The moment lovers begin to examine themselves within an interrogatory mode that sees them as guilty, they can no longer believe that their love is a glorious experience reflecting divine union. Love in this context can only be a vile consummation of a selfish and animalistic or physical urge.[31] True, love is instigated by sexual desire in Guillaume's garden, but in the garden it is a positive social value. In contrast, in the confessional it is guilty, because once the confessant admits to sexual desire, as he must, he must see himself as motivated by wanton lust rather than a pure and glorious emotion.

---

[31] The problem is parallel to the one Hult observes in the language of courtly lyric in *Self-Fulfilling Prophecies*, 258: "The adequacy of language to express personal unique feelings is severely placed into question when that language is a common, shared instrument. Any artifice can be copied, any voice can be mimed."

CHAPTER 18

WHAT KIND OF WORDS ARE THESE? COURTLY AND MARITAL WORDS OF LOVE IN THE *FRANKLIN'S TALE* AND *SIR GAWAIN AND THE GREEN KNIGHT*

JEAN E. JOST
Bradley University, Peoria, Illinois

> "Much speche way wer expoun / Of druryes greme and grace"
> [And long of love they speke / Its pleasures and its pains.]
> *Sir Gawain and the Green Knight* (1506–07)

When Arveragus woos his reluctant love, the Lady Dorigen in Chaucer's *Franklin's Tale*, he speaks words not fitting a potential spouse, but rather the more devoted, adoring words of a twelfth-century courtly lover. The knight offers her not a traditional medieval marriage, a bondage not to be sought, but a distinctly more advantageous union, a transgressive inversion of normative custom. In a rather different type of digression, Lady Bercilak, the more powerful of the two wooers in *Sir Gawain and the Green Knight*, utilizes similar courtly love rhetoric to entice her prey into a digressive, unsanctioned assignation. She plays off the tradition to produce three creative, sometimes dangerous, sometimes humorous interludes. A thread of deception, in that their charming words of love are less than fully honest, is woven into both love-tapestries, unbeknownst to the potential beloved. In both cases, then, evasive or double-edged courtly love language reverses the expected chivalric intent associated with polite, chivalric refinement.

But perhaps we should not be so surprised at this realistic picture of purportedly chivalric romances belying their courtly ideal, given that the historical reality of their creation was ambiguous if not contradictory in its ideals. C. Stephen Jaeger insightfully remarks that "Courtly literature is not a mimetic mirror but, rather, a mask hiding the reality that produced it."[1] In some subtle fashion, Chaucer and the anonymous *Pearl*-Poet have telescoped through that mask and its chivalric façade to reveal a truer ethos of the times with their unreliable courtly language, indeed a creative literary reversal.

Nevertheless, the refined and over-determined language of the court used in these works, deceptive or not, remains wholly courteous, self-conscious, eloquent, even charming: qualities of civility which accord with the newly emerging ethos of civilization.[2] One drawback to this new way of life is a struggle to restrain impulses and passions and a desire to curry favor with the monarch amidst other courtiers attempting to do the same. Inevitably deceit, intrigue, and manipulation become the *modus operandi* of success. As Jaeger points out,

> The conditions of the inner circle of the ruler's court engender caution, discretion, and calculating foresight. The courtier becomes the master of his every word and act, of his diction and gestures, of the motion of his eyes and the tilt of his head, all of which, when uncontrolled, provide rivals with ammunition against himself. . . . Hence the mask and the disguise become major psychic vestments of the courtier. This produces a refinement and sensitivity unimaginable to men who live in more natural circumstances. One element of this growing refinement, one among many, is the evolution of ethical values and educational ideals.[3]

Is it any wonder that in addition to the ethical values and educational ideals Jaeger notes, the habitual caution, calculation, and self-protection necessary for survival in this hotbed of distrust and dissimulation would produce a precautionary mind-set, a self-conscious awareness of behavior and language, and a tendency to disguise and deceive? And would an author writing within that milieu be immune to such a tendency, or refuse to place such duplicitous language in the mouths of his courtly characters? We would be naive to think otherwise. As Albrecht Classen points out, "The knight in disguise proves to be one of the most

---

[1] C. Stephen Jaeger, *The Origins of Courtliness: Civilizing Trends and the Formation of Courtly Ideals: 939–1210*. The Middle Ages Series (Philadelphia: University of Pennsylvania Press, 1985), x.

[2] Jaeger attributes this transformation to the civilizing forces of education at the court of Otto the Great, instituted by his brother Brun who established five cathedral schools: "By 950 Magdeburg was known as an illustrious school. By 952 the school at Würzburg was in full blossom; by 953 Cologne; by 954 Hildesheim; by 956 Trier. There is a direct connection between the royal court and the rise of these cathedral schools . . . [whose educational goal] was no longer the training of clerics in pastoral duties but rather the training of talented young men, noblemen close to the king above all. Here a humanistic education became an essential part of preparation for service to the empire; the curriculum was adapted to the requirements, both human and practical, of an office" (*Origins of Courtliness*, 4– 5). From such schools emerges the courtly impulse.

[3] Jaeger, *Origins of Courtliness* (7), confirming the opinions of Norbert Elias, *Über den Process der Zivilisation: Soziogenetische und psychogenetische Untersuchungen*. 2nd ed., 2 vols. Suhrkamp Taschenbuch Wissenschaft, 158–59 (1939; Frankfurt: Suhrkamp, 1979).

significant metaphors of late-medieval literature because the creators of these literary figures reflect upon the basic conditions of their society and provide curiously refracted mirror images of the standard representatives of the Arthurian court.... Tristan in Gottfried von Strassburg's *Tristan* demonstrates the enormous potentials of disguise for the realization of the lovers' goals, but the wholesale deception of the entire courtly society becomes noticeable only in thirteenth-century, or postclassical, courtly literature."[4]

Arveragus culls from the troubadour lore of Southern France which calls love an art, bound by definite rules; its precepts are drawn from the originary doctrine of Muslim Spain written down about 1022 by the Andalusian Ibn Hazm in *The Dove's Neck-Ring*,[5] itself derived from the Ovidian *Ars Amatoria* or *The Art of Loving*. This system of rigidly conceived principles ultimately evolved into a ritualistic code of love, contending:

1. A lover is abjectly submissive to his beloved, and "speaks of himself as her slave" (11);

2. Love must be secret, furtive, and transgressive to provide passion and excitement;

3. Thus, "the best partner in a love affair is another man's wife" as she is theoretically unavailable (5);

4. Since the husband must remain deluded for the tryst to continue, no one may be privy to their actions lest gossip betray them;

5. This secret love ennobles the lovers, for "true love and nobility go hand in hand" (10);

6. "Love cannot exist apart from jealousy" (6).

In Andreas Capellanus' famous instantiation, *De Arte Honeste Amandi* or *The Art of Courtly Love* (ca. 1186), the seventh dialogue confirms these tenets in the man's words:

---

[4] Albrecht Classen, "Moriz, Tristan, and Ulrich as Master Disguise Artists: Deconstruction and Reenactment of Courtliness in *Moriz von Craûn, Tristan als Mönch*, and Ulrich von Liechtenstein's *Frauendienst*." *Journal of English and German Philology* 103,4 (2004): 475–504; here 480–81.

[5] A. R. Nykl, ed., *A Book Containing the Risala Known as the Dove's Neck-Ring about Love and Lovers composed by Abu Muhammed 'Ali ibn Hazm al-Andalusi* (Paris: Geuthner, 1931), cited in Andreas Capellanus, *The Art of Courtly Love*, trans. John Jay Parry (1941; Columbia University Press, 1969). But Parry warns, "In his view of love Ibn Hazm is by no means unique among the Arabs. We find similar attitudes in the works of the philosophers who preceded him" (11).

> I am greatly surprised that you wish to misapply the term 'love' to that marital affection which husband and wife are expected to feel for each other after marriage, since everybody knows that love can have no place between husband and wife. . . . For what is love but an inordinate desire to receive passionately a hidden and furtive embrace? . . . [N]obody can make furtive use of what belongs to him.[6]

The response from the arbiter, the Countess of Champagne, concludes and confirms his statement about who can love, saying:

> We declare and we hold as firmly established that love cannot exert its powers between two people who are married to each other. For lovers give each other everything freely, under no compulsion of necessity, but married people are in duty bound to give in to each other's desires and deny themselves to each other in nothing . . . . [A] precept of love tells us that no woman, even if she is married, can be crowned with the reward of the King of Love unless she is seen to be enlisted in the service of Love himself outside the bonds of wedlock. But another rule of Love teaches that no one can be in love with two men. Rightly, therefore, Love cannot acknowledge any rights of his between husband and wife.[7]

Cleverly manipulated fallacies and slanted definitions throughout the treatise themselves reveal a love of deceptive words. But the concept "courtly love" also promises the beloved abject homage, respectful submission, unbounded affection and service, his experiencing of pain and sorrow in her absence, and total deference to her will, albeit without responsibility. Harry Peters' essay "John Gower–Love of Words and Words of Love" in this volume discusses the ambiguity of this elusive phrase "courtly love," which Peters says "can mean almost anything . . . with the linguistic habits of Humpty Dumpty, where the definition of a word shifts according to whatever he wants it to mean."[8] Chaucer, however, accepts and counters the traditional usage, in which the lover, unmarried to his beloved, professes love, adoration, service, submission, and affection. Arveragus offers both courtly love and husbandly responsibility.

As Albrecht Classen points out, "Entscheidend bleibt immer wieder ganz allein die Polarität der Meinungen, wie sie von der Wife of Bath, dem Franklin, dem Clerk, dem Merchant u.a. vertreten werden: Es handelt sich um die Performanz des Ehediskurses, nicht um eine theologisch beeinflusste Strategie, um

---

[6] Andreas Capellanus, *The Art of Courtly Love*, trans. Parry, 100.
[7] Andreas Capellanus, *The Art of Courtly Love*, trans. Parry, 106–07.
[8] Harry Peters, "John Gower: Love of Words and Words of Love," 446. See also the contribution by Anna Kukułka-Wojtasik in this volume.

ideale Ehelehren zu entwickeln."[9] Mary Edith Thomas summarizes the standard accepted interpretation of the marital relationship in the *Franklin's Tale* in these words:

> Whether the final work in the [marriage] group, the *Franklin's Tale*, was presented simply in contrast to the others or intended as a solution of the problem in a happy compromise between husband and wife, the harmonious relationship of Arveragus and Dorigen stands as a condemnation of the domestic infidelity resulting from the attempt to establish either the man's or the woman's authority in marriage.[10]

But this long-held theory more than half a century old fails to catch the nuances so cleverly woven into the story. Rather, the manipulation and slanted definitions of the *Art of Courtly Love* parallel what Bonnie Wheeler calls "textual fissures" or deceptive gaps in the *Franklin's Tale* which constantly threaten to disclose otherwise silent presumptions, including those that privilege dominant class and gender systems:

> Chaucer's notoriously unstable language is particularly slippery in the metonymic constructions of the *Franklin's Tale*. . . . [His] digressive strategies simultaneously unmask chivalric romance as a linguistic encoding of sexual exploitation, just as they map the stress of economic and class competition in this tale. In this respect the *Franklin's Tale* is a shadow play of courtliness — an exaggerated pantomime that the Franklin . . . claims yet fails to comprehend fully.[11]

Perhaps that deferential, submissive tone of homage embodying the courtly love paradigm is a mask for less honorific behavior. Playing the humble, subservient courtly lover himself, the Franklin claims linguistic unworthiness, lacking "Colours of rethoryk,"[12] capable only of "rude speche" (v. 718) and no witty wordlore:

---

[9] Albrecht Classen, *Der Liebes- und Ehediskurs vom hohen Mittelalter bis zum frühen 17. Jahrhundert*. Volksliedstudien 5 (Münster, New York, Munich, and Berlin: Waxman, 2005), 106 (The essential aspect always remains the polarity of opinions, as they are represented by the Wife of Bath, the Franklin, the Clerk, the Merchant, etc. It is the performance of the marriage discourse, not a theologically determined, strategy that advocates an ideal teaching of marriage).

[10] Mary Edith Thomas, *Medieval Skepticism and Chaucer* (New York: Cooper Square Publishers, 1950), 93.

[11] Bonnie Wheeler, "*Trouthe* without Consequences: Rhetoric and Gender in the *Franklin's Tale*," *Feminea Mediaevalia: Representations of the Feminine in Medieval Literature* 1 (1993): 91–116; here 93–94.

[12] *The Riverside Chaucer*, ed. Larry D. Benson (Boston: Houghton Mifflin, 1987), v. 724. Subsequent quotations will be taken from this edition.

> I lerned nevere rethorik, certeyn;
> Thyng that I speke, it moot be bare and pleyn.
> I sleep nevere on the Mount of Pernaso,
> Ne lerned Marcus Tullius Scithero.
> Colours ne knowe I none, withouten drede,
> But swiche colours as growen in the mede. (v. 719–24)

Despite protestations of verbal inadequacy, his words are a ruse. The seemingly humble Franklin crafts highly emotional, powerfully effective words of love which he cleverly infuses into his tale of marriage by presenting a knight who "dide his payne [worked diligently] / To serve a lady in his beste wise" (v.730–31). Of course, courtly love tenets preclude marriage, so Arveragus's daring proposal fusing the two mutually exclusive elements of love and marriage in seeking a "courtly love marriage" is, by both definitions, transgressive, an inversion of both. Perhaps for this reason, and his seemingly whole-hearted sincerity, Dorigen accepts him as both "hir housebonde and hir lord" (v. 741), continuing the courtly love metaphor of Lord and Lady as well as that of husband and wife. The Franklin offers the terms of the contract as follows:

> Of swich lordshipe as men han over hir wyves
> And for to lede to moore in blisse hir lyves,
> Of his free wyl he swoor hire as a knyght
> That nevere in al his lyf he, day ne nyght,
> Ne sholde upon hym take no maistrie
> Agayn hir wyl, ne kithe hire jalousie,
> But hire obeye, and folew hir wyl in al
> As any lovere to his lady shal,
> Save that the name of soveraynetee,
> That wolde he have for shame of his degree. (v.743–52)

Arveragus's words of love are in fact words of power and autonomy for Dorigen, promising Arveragus's subservience and acquiescence to Dorigen's will. Never will he control or force her, but obey and follow her will "As any [courtly] lovere to his lady shal," not merely as any husband to his wife shall. To a Lady not particularly interested in the wifely strictures of marriage, this offer presents a new alternative — a marriage which is not a marriage, but one beyond its usual confines.

The clearly moved Dorigen responds in her own voice with the appellation "Sire," returning his "maistrye," or power, to him, and accepting the role of servant-lover — transgressive for a woman — as he had done; in understanding and appreciation, she returns his promise with her own, likewise blessing it with the marriage pledge:

> Ne wolde nevere God bitwixe us tweyne
> As in my gilt [through my fault], were outher warre or stryf.
> Sire, I wol be youre humble trewe wyf—
> Have heer my trouthe—til that myn herte breste.   (v. 756–59)

Thus both their love speeches are transgressive, albeit differently so; each offers the other excess, more than the norm. Despite this pre-Christian setting, their pre-nuptial vows, hearkening the sometime-fashionable betrothal vows,[13] lead this Franklin and servant of love-words reverently to parody St. Paul's scriptural personification of love with its similar tone, pacing, and intent:

> Love wol nat been constreyned by maistrye.
> Whan maistrie cometh, the God of Love anon
> Beteth hys wynges, and farewel, he is gon!
> Love is a thyng as any spirit free.
> Wommen, of kynde, desiren libertee,
> And nat to be constreyned as a thral [slave];
> And so doon men, if I sooth seyen shal.
> Looke who that is moost pacient in love.
> He is at his avantage al above.
> Pacience is an heigh vertu, certeyn,
> For it venquysseth, as thise clerkes seyn,
> Thynges that rigour sholde nevere atteyne.
> For every word men may nat chide or pleyne.
> Lerneth to suffre, or elles, so moot I goon,
> Ye shul it lerne, wher so ye wole or noon.   (v. 764–78)

This striking rhetoric is reminiscent of Paul's famous passage in 1 Corinthians 13:

> Love is patient, love is kind. It is not jealous, it is not pompous, it is not inflated,
>
> it is not rude, it does not seek its own interests, it is not quick-tempered, it does not brood over injury,
>
> it does not rejoice over wrongdoing but rejoices with the truth.
>
> It bears all things, believes all things, hopes all things, endures all things.

---

[13] The history of betrothal vows is fascinating. Some very brief examples include the Romans' ceremonious bestowal of an exchange of objects (on the man) to begin the process. In 860, Pope Nicholas endorsed the ring and kiss as part of the betrothal ceremony. In 1160, Christina of Markyate, pressured into betrothal vows, refused consummation.

Love never fails. If there are prophecies, they will be brought to nothing, if tongues, they will cease, if knowledge, it will be brought to nothing.[14]

Like Paul's epistle, the Franklin's gently teaches the witnessing audience ways to love successfully; his kindly tone, linguistic structure, personifying imagery, and instructional intent parallel Paul's injunction. But will his subsequent behavior embody his noble ideals? In eloquently espousing the needs of love — courtly, marital, and even Biblical — in a fusion of traditions, the Franklin's idealized words of love implement and instantiate the lovers' double vows.

Arveragus promises Dorigen not merely husbandly devotion and commitment, but the terms of this courtly code, a contract distinctly more idealized and rarified: if she will accept and be his wife, he will swear not only marital love, fidelity, and subservience, but also an equal partnership in marriage, not bound under him in wedlock, but free to do as she pleases as married women could not claim, with no restrictions on her will. Dorigen thus is presented with the best of both worlds: the status of wife, the honor of his battles, the deference of his humility before her, and the economic security of Arveragus's knighthood; but she is also offered a freedom not afforded medieval wives: the primacy of her own will, the service of courtly romance, the praise of a devoted worshiper, the secret passion of a desiring, forbidden lover, and the glorious expression of his obedience and love. These transgressive, excessive, potent words of love and *danger* indeed convince the reluctant Lady to accept her Lord as husband *and* courtly lover.

Not long after, however, Arveragus abdicates his responsibility in becoming no longer the responsible husband he promised to be or even the courtly lover. Yes, he distantly fights for her honor, but fails in the concrete matter of love. As Wheeler notes, "Arveragus promises Dorigen to 'folwe hir wyl in al, / As any lovere to his lady schal' (749–50). Yet he leaves her for two years and Dorigen is filled with grief at his absence."[15] As either husband *or* courtly lover, is he not breaking *trouthe* with her, breaking his promise, when he abandons her — against her will? Despite his courtly words of love, his actions belie his dedication and lead to their dilemma.

Just as Arveragus "Shoop hym to goon and dwelle a yeere or tweyne / In Engelond" (809–10) — shaped his plan of abandonment, so did her friends, seeing her in dangerous and melancholic haunts by the sea, "shopen for to pleyen somwher elles" (897) — shaped theirs of rescue. What it means is that; just as Arveragus shaped his plan to abandon Dorigen, so her friends shaped their plan to rescue her from depression, encourage her to play somewhere else, enjoy life, and stop being depressed at his abandonment. And so they ushered her into the conventional

---

[14] *New American Bible*, 1 Corinthians 13:4–8; here cited from: www.usccb.org/nab/bible/1corinthians/1corinthians13.htm (last accessed on March 1, 2006).

[15] Wheeler, "*Trouthe* without Consequences," 93.

courtly love setting of a May garden with all good intent, where "she ne saugh hym on the daunce go / That was hir housebonde and hir love also" (921–22). Rather, a surrogate courtly lover has claimed the role, the golden Aurelius[16] who expectedly sings complaints, lays, and other courtly songs in such a *derne* secretive way as to elude even Dorigen. His somewhat parodic behavior nevertheless fulfills courtly love expectations, for he "langwissheth as a furye dooth in helle; / And dye he moste, he seyde" (950–51). At the next stage of seduction, he reveals his bursting heart and asks for pity for his "peynes smerte / For with a word ye may me sleen or save.... Have mercy, sweete, or ye wol do me deye!" (974–75, 978).

The shocked Dorigen swears by the God who made her she will "nevere been untrewe wyf" (984); she will not enter into a courtly-love union with him. Nevertheless, perhaps to ease the tension and lessen the burden of rejection, she playfully enters the teasing, leading-on, joking, courtly-love linguistic game, "Syn I yow se so pitously complayne" (991). Clearly she has no intent to fulfill the words of this teasing game, nor does he expect her to, as his reply indicates: "Is ther noon oother grace in yow? ... Madame ... this were an impossibile!" (999).

But her simple game brings Dorigen to her peril. Upon this rejection, Aurelius, in inflated, courtly-love rhetoric, falls upon his knees in excruciating emotion, and prays to Apollo with unrestrained passion and emotional language to "Do this miracle or do myn herte breste" (1056), a kind of suicide wish. His pose, his attitude, and his highly rhetorical tone foreshadow and parallel Dorigen's later unrestrained courtly-love rhetoric.[17] Like Dorigen, this courtly lover "Two yeer and moore lay wrecche" (1102) until his brother rescues him aptly with the greatest courtly-love secrecy, keeping the matter "secree" (1109), and speaking to Aurelius "pryvely" (1137). Furthermore, Aurelius plays the role of courtly love well, for he

1. politely called her "Madame" (which he failed to do at their later assignation until he released her from her promise);

---

[16] Joanne Rice points to the connection between "Aurelianus" and "Orleans" (where Aurelius's brother finds the magician), but not the more obvious linguistic connection to "gold" in her Explanatory Notes to the *Franklin's Tale, The Riverside Chaucer*, l. 938, p. 898. The etymology of "Dorigen" is also of note: related to *Dora*, short for *Theodora* or *Dorothea*, "gift of God," but even more interesting, related to *dorado*, Sp. *gilded*, ME dorre < MFr doree *gilt* < LL deaurare *to gild* < L de- (intensifier) + aurare *to gild*–leading back to *Aurelius*. Arveragus is neither so tractable nor certain. Possibly *ad* or *ar* before *r*, meaning *to* or *toward*; *ver* true, or *verax, veracis* truly speaking; or virago, manlike female, powerful, werewolf [vir wolf] or monster, but highly speculative. From *Webster's New World Dictionary of American English*, 3rd College Edition, ed. Victoria Neufeldt (Cleveland and New York: Simon and Schuster, 1988).

[17] Although many critics admonish Dorigen for her speech of excess emotion and high-blown rhetoric, within the courtly-love context of exaggeration, and in the circumstances, it appears valid and appropriate.

2. acted deferentially, "Heere at youre feet God wolde that I were grave!" (1325);

3. dignified her with the title "my sovereign lady" (1325);

4. acknowledged her favors would only be by her grace, not merited; and

5. "Doun to his maistres feet he fil anon" (1302).

When Aurelius arrives near Orleans in his attempt to win his Lady, Apollo appears to have enacted the miracle, for a prescient clerk tells him "a wonder thyng: / 'I knowe,' quod he, 'the cause of youre comyng'" (1175–76) and promises to remove the rocks. Likewise, the field of deer and plain of jousting knights who disappear when the magician wishes is miraculous. But the rock-removal is not — merely an appearance.

The desperate Aurelius offers an even clearer suicide threat, demanding "To bryngen hym out of his peynes smerte, / Or with a swerd that he wolde slitte his herte" (1259–60), again a foreshadowing of Dorigen's later anguish. When the rocks appear gone, and following two death threats, Aurelius demands satisfaction with an inverted, hypocritical, uncourtly, even disingenuous rationale: "Madame, I speak it for the honour of yow / Moore than to save my hertes lyf right now" (1331–32). His rhetoric is far from that of the idealizing courtly lover at her service, but its content is as deceptive as that rhetoric. Imitating the courtly hyperbole of Aurelius, the equally distraught Dorigen prays to Dame Fortune, as he did to Apollo, seeking escape from her alternatives: "Save oonly deeth or elles dishonour" (1358). His alternatives are pain or death; hers are dishonor or death. Her monologue begins in a high-pitched tone apropos of her courtly-love role and her quandary, and then considers what others have done in her position. She looks outward for direction and courage. During her hundred and one lines, as she focuses on others' stories, she becomes more centered, calmer, and more in control, replacing her own emotional pleas and embellished rhetoric with her narratives of others' plights. Aurelius, on the other hand, remains self-oriented through his prayer, as he emotionally pleads for help from Apollo and his sister Lucina the Bright.

Enter Arveragus, who coolly, dispassionately listens to his wife's dilemma, and bursts into tears. Although he metes out no punishment to her, he contravenes his role as courtly lover and perhaps as husband when he breaks his promise not to exert power or authority over her by issuing three orders:

1. "Ye shul youre trouthe holden, by my fey!" (1474);

2. "I yow forbid, up peyne of deeth,
   That nevere, whil thee lasteth lyf or breeth,
   To no wight tell thou of this aventure" (1481–83);

   3. "Ne make no contenance of hevynesse,
   That folk of yow may demen harm or gesse" (1485–86).

Critics often acknowledge the knight's acceptance of the predicament without rancor or vindictiveness, but seem not to note the overbearing tone with which the Franklin has Arveragus resolve the difficulty. Anne Laskaya, for example, comments that

> The *Franklin's Tale* is comedy, and as such advocates life and mercy, offering an alternative to the moral rigidity of the Man of Law's representation of Custance, the Clerk's Griselde, and the Physician's Virginia. The Franklin-narrator assumes, apparently, that women consist of more than merely maidenheads or wombs, that their value — like men's — lies in living. As the Franklin sees it, "Trouthe [or, more accurately, the appearance of trouthe] is the hyeste thynge that man [or woman] may kepe" (1479), though not at the expense of life itself.[18]

Although his demands may be reasonable enough, he has agreed not to control her actions or levy *maisterie* over her; however, he has just laid out the response to the situation which he demands of her. She has no voice. She has no power. She is his servant, a reversal of the courtly-lover status between male and female. Thus, if the first subversion of the courtly convention is that he has married his lover, the second is that he has controlled her. Thirdly, the expectation of a courtly lover is to remain somewhat aloof from his beloved, and this he has not done. But he is not allowed jealousy, making the third subversion. The Franklin hypothesizes yet a different evaluation, suggesting some of his audience might find Arveragus guilty of putting his wife in jeopardy, forgetting that Arveragus promised not to put his wife anywhere — make her decisions or determine her fate at all.

The spying Aurelius is little better at courtly service. He joins her in walking to his courtly garden and asks her destination:

And she answered, half as she were mad,
"Unto the gardyn, as myn housbonde bad,
My trouthe for to holde — allas, allas!" (1511–13)

This dialogue proves the wife is not in accord with her husband's decision, but acts obediently as a wife, not as a courtly lover allowed the privilege of freedom

---

[18] Anne Laskaya, *Chaucer's Approach to Gender in the Canterbury Tales*. Chaucer Studies, XXIII (Cambridge: D. S. Brewer, 1995), 161.

which he once promised her. Rather, he has dominated her. Next, the squire Aurelius does the right thing for the wrong reason: if he were the true courtly lover, he would woo, but not give his lover an ultimatum or pressure her to succumb to his advances by using her honor as a pawn.[19] He would give her free choice, allow her to determine her own actions. This he does not do. Rather, he considers that the husband has foregone the wife's honor for the sake of truth, and respects that action. He regards the husband's decision more than his courtly lover's well-being, reflecting a kind of deference given to the male, but denied the female. Is he justified? Indeed, viewed from one perspective, the husband's is a noble act. But from another, he has usurped her autonomy by deciding for her, which tarnishes his nobility. Aurelius responds this way:

1. He feels "greet compassioun" (1515) for the unwilling wife and "hire lamentacioun" (1516). He does not feel he owes her autonomy, that justice would preclude him from taking what is not freely given, or that a courtly lover should allow his beloved free choice.

2. He feels compassion for the husband and respect for his having so much integrity that "so looth hym was his wyf sholde breke hir trouthe" (1519). Despite his attraction for the wife, he may ultimately feel a greater respect for or bond with her husband.

3. He has self-respect, believing that to "doon so heigh a cherlyssh wrecchednesse / Agayns franchise and alle gentillesse" (1523–24) would be unworthy of him. It would be a shame to lose your honor for me, he tells Dorigen. He feels he is owed the wife against her will, but does not take her love to save his own reputation and integrity. His conclusion well reveals the emphasis he finds on his own dignity: "Thus kan a squier doon a gentil dede / As wel as kan a knyght, withouten drede" (1543–44).

4. He wants Arveragus's respect. Aurelius instructs Dorigen to tell her husband of Aurelius's generosity in foregoing her love because he sees Arveragus's *gentillesse* to Dorigen, and

Arveragus's acceptance of shame so she won't be foresworn; Aurelius thus would not come between them. Had Aurelius not learned that the husband knew of their assignation, he would not likely have surrendered his prize. This is a

---

[19] This is exactly the same situation in the thirteenth-century Middle High German verse novella "Mauritius von Craûn," where the male lover misunderstands the principles of love and tries to replace it with a business contract, forcing the lady to keep her part of the promise, which ultimately, however, destroys the values of courtly love altogether. See Albrecht Classen, "Twelfth- and Thirteenth-Century Pessimism About Historical Progress: *Mauritius von Craun*, Otto von Freising's *The Two Cities*, and the Metaphor of the Ship," *German Quarterly*, 79,1 (2006): 28–49.

bargain between men, and Dorigen merely the prize. Aurelius clearly summarizes the deal: "And right as frely as he sente hire me, / As frely sente I hir to hym ageyn" (1604–05). She is a pawn handed off between two men, both of whom determine her fate. Despite all courtly-love indicators, she is not the courtly beloved of either, enjoying no freedom of choice or action, and no adoring servitude.

Nor does Dorigen react like a Courtly Lady at her reprieve, as "She thonketh hym [Aurelius] upon hir knees al bare" (1545), a subservient position of humility, not its converse. When she returns to Arveragus, having previously ordered her to do as he willed, now that the danger has passed, "He cherisseth hire as though she were a queene" (1554). He never realizes his broken pledge, his spoken promise to give her autonomy and sovereignty, which he ignored. Aurelius likewise initially treated Dorigen with dignity before their final meeting, but ultimately supplants her with concern for Arveragus, as male bonding controls his final actions.

In a broader perspective, Laskaya compares the *Franklin's Tale's* position on Dorigen's free will with those elsewhere in the *Canterbury Tales:*

> The comedy of the *FT* also reinforces objections to male domination which surface throughout the *CT*s, suggesting that men are more virtuous, or at least more civilized, when they forgive others than when they willfully asset themselves over others as Virginius or Walter do.... Despite these 'answers' to the Man of Law, the Clerk, and the Physician, the *FT* persists in presenting us with a major female character who conforms to men's desires, except, here, conformity is made to appear ridiculous.[20]

Her evaluation is indeed correct, as Dorigen vanishes from the screen in the final moments of the tale, no more than a has-been beloved, abandoned or relegated to insignificance by her two courtly lovers.

Finally, the principles noted above, demarcating the conditions in which a courtly love relationship can most handily be effected, must be reconsidered. First, the lover must be deferential, subservient, and swooning for the beloved. Indeed, this was once the case, but as noted, with his impending success, Aurelius's responses seem to have cooled. Second, the liaison must be secret, but the current assignation is not so, given that Arveragus has sent Dorigen. Third, the best beloved is another man's wife; now this is indeed the case, but when he gives his wife to the suitor, the element of competition melts away. Fourth, the husband must remain deluded; far from being or remaining deluded, the husband is complicit, albeit unwillingly. Fifth, the secret love ennobles the lovers; but far from ennobling Dorigen, the decision to comply and the intent to execute the decision have torn her to pieces. Sixth, love entails jealousy; but after all these years, Aurelius appears more interested in effecting his task and extracting his winnings

---

[20] Laskaya, *Chaucer's Approach to Gender*, 161.

than enraging Arveragus, whom he respects. The conditions of this potential courtly rendezvous are distinctly counter to the Platonic, idealized notions with which Aurelius began his wooing. The reality he envisioned has been countermanded by circumstances beyond his control. The situation, originally romantic, then manipulative and unpleasantly coercive for Dorigen, has evolved into a practical, albeit self-serving, instance of male bonding. Dorigen's three-pronged experience thus counters the traditional lay understanding of idealized courtly love. Robert R. Edwards and Stephen Spector posit an historic explanation for its original instantiation, summarizing C. S. Lewis's argument that

> in medieval life . . . passion was often denounced as wicked, and in feudal society marriage had nothing to do with love. From this cleavage between the Church and court, and between love and marriage . . . emerged the tradition of courtly love, characterized by humility, courtesy, the religion of love, and adultery. Courtly love seemed to exist with equal force as a social practice and as a literary motif.[21]

The Franklin has used this literary motif by inverting it for his own purposes, creating characters who subvert its usual idealized understanding and reveal its more realistic outcome. Thus the tale of courtly lovers who become espoused, of courtly language which has lost its *courtoisie*, of promises unfulfilled or broken has suffered the fate of double transgression: first in its attempt to mix the marital and courtly; and second, in its failure to effect the promised nobility its ideals promulgated. Indeed, a happy resolution is effected, but not through the mode of courtly love the tale first introduced, but rather through the marital love which proves much more sturdy and substantial, more able to weather the storms of life. Not marital discourse, but marital affection resolves the tale insofar as it can be said to reach resolution.

The Lady Bercilak holds distinctly contrary intentions toward Gawain in *Sir Gawain and the Green Knight,* to those Arveragus holds toward his wife Dorigen. The Lady likewise plays the courtly lover—with no husband, but a stranger—through several different inversions. First, her personal motivations and role—as pawn for Morgan le Fay—remain masked and hidden rather than obvious (to her beloved), both a parody and reversal of the traditional *derne* or "secret" meeting and actions of courtly *amores* (hidden from their spouses). Her apparent secret rendezvous beyond the curtains are not so, but fully known to and orchestrated by the supposedly deceived husband. Second, this bold feminine intruder penetrating his sleeping quarters plays an opposite-gendered courtly role. She, rather than her masculine knight, aggressively manipulates

---

[21] *The Olde Daunce: Love, Friendship, Sex, and Marriage in the Medieval World*, ed. Robert R. Edwards and Stephen Spector (Albany: State University of New York Press, 1991), 5.

the relationship, firmly establishes herself in the controlling power position, and devotedly plays the role of servant, adorer, wooer, and potential seducer. Simultaneously, like a courtly lover, she humbly agrees to serve and be used according to her prey's desires, and effectively, if deceptively, utilizes potent "luv-talkyng" to ensnare him.[22]

Capellanus writes his courtly love guide for one "Walter," seeing and creating the love-context from a distinctly male perspective, even when seeming to speak about or in the voice of a woman. Thus, in a third reversal, countering Capellanus's presumptions, Gawain reciprocally adopts the passive, feminine pose to the Lady's masculine one; he becomes shy, reclusive, withdrawing, resisting, and withholding, as the Lady micro-manages each encounter, leading him precisely where she chooses. She sings his praises like a troubadour as he blushes like a maid; she seems to suffer at rejection, and remains persistent in her seduction. Her exaggerated praise of him and his past exploits parallel the troubadour love lyrics, reveling in the lady's lips, or brow, or creamy skin. As J. A. Burrow indicates,

> Seduction scenes of this sort occur also in French romances, where a woman — a damsel, daughter, or wife — makes sexual advances to a knightly guest, often with an ulterior motive.... Gawain's "clean" responses to the lady are threatened, of course, by her physical beauty and sexy dressing (especially on the third morning, ll. 1736–41 and 1760–69); and courtesy compounds his difficulties, for it requires him to employ, in declining her advances, such flattering and conciliatory language that she has every excuse for pressing on.[23]

And indeed she does. Her "lov-talkyng" reveals that she holds, or pretends to hold, Gawain in the ennobled, unrealistically elevated esteem of *Amour*. And yet, in his passivity to her words of love lies a vulnerability to her power, more beloved than lover. R. A. Shoaf describes this phenomenon as:

> ... the rhetoric of feudalism. Gawain becomes the *seruaunt* of Bertilak's Lady: she becomes his sovereign; he pays her homage (*yowre kny3t I becom*). And he makes this gesture, an unmistakable act of fealty, because he is proud of the price that she has put on him. Gawain has sold himself already to the Lady, although he does not yet know it: he has alienated [sic] her the right to determine his identity, and she *will* exercise that right.... He has already paid the Lady. The first installment is his pride. If he is proud of the price that she put on him, Gawain is investing his pride in, or paying it to,

---

[22] Should the lover remain obdurate, Ovid would suggest making the beloved jealous, a tactic to which Lady Bercilak is not forced to resort. See Parry, "Introduction," especially 5, to Andreas Capellanus's *The Art of Courtly Love* for a full discussion of Ovid's influence on the concept.

[23] J. A. Burrow, *The Gawain-Poet* (Horndon, Tavistock, Devon: Northcote House Publishers Ltd., 2001), 48.

her estimate of him. And having bought Gawain's pride, Bertilak's Lady has achieved a major success in the *gomen*, which she and her husband are playing for Gawain's benefit.[24]

Like a courtly lover, the Lady seeks no permanent liaison, but, in another mirrored inversion, is herself married, not seducing a married lover as expected. She feigns a doubtful emotional involvement, an eager assumption of a temporary liaison in which true courtly lovers would accede. Her pretty, idealizing words suggest she also realizes and plays upon Gawain's pride, past reputation, fine words, and previous roles as courtly lover, which first she and then he cleverly utilize:

> "In god fayth," quoþ Gawayn, "gayn hit me þynkkez,
> Þaȝ I be not now he þat ȝe of speken;
> To reche to such reuerence as ȝe reherce here
> I am wyȝe vnworþy, I wot wel myseluen.
> Bi God, I were glad, and yow god þoȝt,
> At saȝe oþer at seruyce þat I sette myȝt
> To þe plesaunce of your prys — hit were a pure ioye." (1241–47)

> [Said Gawain, "In good faith, you've given me praise!
> But I'm hardly that high knight of whom you have spoken.
> To live up to the lauds that you've lavished on me
> I'm incapable quite! You're too kind in your praise!
> But by God, I'd be glad should you grant me the right,
> By some speech or some service to serve one so good.
> I'd be proud; and to please you would please me as well."][25]

Fourth, the feminine courtly seducer whom Gawain and the audience meet is also a word-weaver, as fond of them as Gawain himself, but no lover. As all later discover, the lady is a pretender to the castle of courtly love, and both her gentle words of love and insistently aggressive wooing are tainted with deception. She seeks no liaison for its own sake, but merely entrapment. She acts not out of passion or desire, but out of loyalty to others as she colludes in stimulating his insecurity and instigating his fearful surrender to her wiles and magic.

When Gawain arrives at Bercilak's court, the servants ask his origins: "Þat he beknew cortaysly of þe court þat he were / Þat aþel Arthure þe hende haldez hym one" (903–04; Of the court that he'd come from he courteously told: / He had hailed from the high, famous house of King Arthur). The wily Lord feigns surprise,

---

[24] R. A Shoaf, *The Poem as Green Girdle: Commercium in Sir Gawain and the Green Knight*. University of Florida Monographs: Humanities, 55 (Gainesville: University Presses of Florida, 1984), 40.

[25] *Sir Gawain and the Green Knight*. ed. J. R. R. Tolkien and E. V. Gordon (Oxford: Clarendon Press, 1967). All translations are taken from the *Complete Works of the Pearl-Poet*, ed. and trans. Casey Finch (Berkeley, Los Angeles, and Oxford: University of California Press, 1993).

Courtly and Marital Words of Love 411

already knowing Gawain's identity and background, the first of Bercilak's many deceptions. Gawain's rhetorical reputation precedes him, for his hosts note his "teccheles termes of talkyng noble, / Wich spede is in speche vnspurd may we lerne" (917-18; ... phrases and figures of faultless discourse / We will hear one handy in the high art of speech). But Lady Bercilak knows even more about him than his reputation. She begins her seduction immediately after dinner, at the evensong service, by obviously staring at Gawain to get his attention: "Þenne lyst þe lady to loke on þe knyȝt" (941), a very successful ploy.

For the first time the audience gets a description of the Lady's charms, obviously influenced by Gawain's appraisal, as "Ho ches þurȝ þe chaunsel to cheryche þat hende" (946; To greet that great lady[26] Gawain walked forth). Her description is elaborate "wyth mony cler perlez, / Hir brest and hir bryȝt þrote bare displayed, / Schon schyrer þen snawe þat schedez on hillez" (954-56; ... with fine pearls, / and her beauteous breast and bare neck were exposed, / Where they shone like the snow as it shimmers on hills). Gawain wastes no time picking up her signals, as he "glyȝt on þat gay, þat graciously loked" (970; gazed on that gracious young lady), embraces, courteously kisses and compliments her. Since she remains demure, Gawain becomes the comfortable, if restrained aggressor, the courtly lover. In fact, "he hit quyk askez / To be her seruaunt sothly, if hemself lyked" (975-76; his wishes he stated / To follow them, faithful, their fond servant ever). Indeed, he promises to be the servant of both husband and wife, but his bold statement is perhaps a not-so-veiled invitation to the wife.

By dinner the next day, sitting next to each other,[27] Gawain and the Lady engage in "her dere dalyaunce of her derne wordez ... [And] hor play watz passande vche prynce gomen, / in vayres" (1012, 1014-15; ... dainty dalliance, dear to each other ... Their skill in the sport of speaking all must / Commend). Here in this public space, the discourse is "clene cortays carp closed fro fylþe" (1013; perfectly proper, pure and chaste); the narrator even comments on their fine language. But three mornings later, while others are at the hunt, Lady Bercilak's clever manipulation begins in earnest as she invades his boudoir. The surprised Gawain, peeking at the interloper, decides to feign sleep as he considers the nature of this visit, actively stepping into the game of deceptive words and actions. As this beauty sits on his bed, he rationalizes that he should speak to her, discern her intent: "More semely hit were / To aspye wyth my spelle in space quat ho wolde" (1198-99; I

---

[26] The translation uses "great" for alliterative purposes, but the original *hende* contains the sense of "attractive," "lovely."

[27] Casey Finch, *Works*, 390, l. 1003n, quotes Brian Stone's note on this line: "the formal pairing at table of Gawain and his hostess would appear significant to listeners familiar with folk-tales and romances in which kings offered their wives to guests, usually to test them or gain power over them. Behind the tradition lies the primitive hospitality of wife-sharing with a guest" (*Sir Gawain and the Green Knight*, trans. Brian D. Stone [Harmondsworth: Penguin, 1959]). My reading suggests that this pairing was purposely done by Bercilak, as one more subtle invitation to Gawain.

should surely inquire, / Through discourse discover her desire in good time). And so he pretends to awaken to her charms which the narrator conveniently repeats. Her immediate response is to warn him of danger in sleeping so soundly, a danger she herself inspires and suggests, and laughingly proposes a truce, as if she were an enemy: "Bot true vus may schape, / I schal bynde yow in your bedde, þat be ȝe trayst" (1210–11; A truce you should make, / Or I'll bind you in bed here, yes, be sure of that!). Her "luv-talkyng" is suggestive enough, but also playful enough to be ambiguous. Gawain, not yet sufficiently defensive, well plays the courtly lover:

> Me schal worþe at your wille, and þat me wel lykez
> For I ȝelde me ȝederly, and ȝeȝe after grace,
> And þat is þe best, be my dome, for me byhouez nede: (1214–16)
>
> [I will work what you will; I am well content
> To surrender myself and to sue for your mercy,
> What behooves me I'll heed; I'm beholden to you]

When Gawain asks permission for "her prisoner" to rise and dress, she denies it him, jovially claiming to imprison him in his bed — to talk!

> I schal happe yow here þat oþer half als,
> And syþen karp wyth my knyȝt þat I kaȝt haue;
> For I wene wel, iwysse, Sir Wowen ȝe are,
> Þat alle þe worlde worchipez quere-so ȝe ride;
> Your honour, your hendelayk is hendely praysed...
> I schal ware my whyle wel, quyl hit lastez,
> with tale.
>
> ȝe ar welcum to my cors,
> Yowre awen won to wale,
> Me behouez of fyne force
> Your seruaunt be, and schale.   (1224–28, 1235–40)
>
> [I'll imprison you, pin you down pitilessly here,
> And talk with the true knight I've taken here captive.
> For I know you're the knight whose name is Gawain,
> Who is famous for fortitude far and near,
> For bright courtesy, courage, and kind honor known...
> I will take my time now to talk, to enjoy repartee.
> My body's yours to use.
> I give it gleefully!
> Do with me what you choose:
> Your servant I shall be.]

Courtly and Marital Words of Love

The blatant assertiveness of the Courtly Love Lady takes Gawain by surprise, pushing him into retreat from her partially veiled proposition, albeit politely. As the demure Beloved, he denies her extravagant praise in an attempt to deflect her advances, but she continues to seduce, maintaining "Bot hit ar ladyes inno3e þat leuer wer nowþe / Haf þe, hende, in hor holde, as I þe habbe here" (1251–52; There's no lack of fine ladies who'd love nothing more / Than to have you to hold — as I have — in their arms). But in her most provocative statement, she boldly iterates: "schulde no freke vpon folde bifore yow be chosen" (1275; by heaven I'd have you as husband of choice). The emotionally retreating Gawain, the Beloved in this scene, reminds her that she has a perfectly good, bolder, far better husband already — indeed a double reversal of the courtly love injunction: that the Beloved (Gawain), not the Lover (Lady Bercilak), be married, and that the Lover, not the husband, be praised as the husband is here. The author also plays off of the tradition of "male as pursuer," since this big, strong, powerful knight is clearly intimidated and diminished by the wily, petite female — through her manipulative, softly seductive words of love: power from sweetness rather than force. On the other hand, Gawain willingly switches roles, reverting to conventional expectation in committing to his Lady: "And, soberly your seruuant, my souerayn I holde yow, / And yowre kny3t I becom, and Kryst yow for3elde" (1278–79; As your servant, I say, you're my sovereign, in truth, / Starting now I'm your knight, in the name of Christ). This clarifies part of the game in which they are engaged — the part of which Gawain is aware. The Lady's parting words suggest disappointment, so that Gawain "Ferde lest he hade fayled in fourme of his castes" (1295; Most afraid he had failed in the forms of his speech). But not words of love does the forward lady want, but a more concrete confirmation of her beloved's admiration: Gawain concedes: "I schal kysse at your comaundement" (1303; we will courteously kiss), a gesture that ends their first encounter.

> Once again, the sleeping Gawain is awakened by his beloved, who laughingly flirts with small talk, coyly concluding "'Sir, 3if 3e be Wawen, wonder me þynkkez,' / ... 3et I kende yow of kyssyng,' quoþ þe clere þenne." (1481, 1489; I'm aghast if you're Gawain, the good knight, indeed! / ... (You've failed / In the court-art of kissing). In this second encounter, when the Lady declares none would refuse him a kiss, and anyway, he could constrain any maid, Gawain claims "þrete is vnþryuande in þede þer I lende" (1499; Forcefulness finds little favor in my land). With a bit more "luv-talkyng," Lady Bercilak the seducer connives a kiss from the beloved: Gawain says "I am at your comaundement, to kysse quen yow lykez, / 3e may lach quen yow lyst, and leue quen yow þynkkez" (1501–02; command and I'll kiss you, as courtesy asks. / I'll allow your love if you like). His initial reluctance is overcome by the lady's persistent invitation in a classic seduction of beloved by courtly lover. Interestingly, the Lady describes the courtly love situation in detail:

And of alle cheualry to chose, þe chef þyng alosed
Is þe lel layk of luf, þe lettrure of armes;
For to telle of þis teuelyng of þis trwe kny3te,
Hit is þe tytelet token and tyxt of her werkkez,
How ledes for her lele luf hor lyuez han auntered,
Endured for her drury dulful stoundez,
And after wenged with her walour and voyded her care,
And bro3t blysse into boure with bountees hor awen — (1512–19)

[... in the court of courts' chivalry
The most precious and praised of all practice is love;
When they tell of the trials of true knights, indeed,
Every tale — both the title and text of the work —
Will relate who for love of their lady those knights
Always lay down their lives, always live in distress,
And with valor take vengeance on vicious, mean foes —
All to please and impress the true prize of their hearts!]

Her self-consciousness of the game she is playing and its applicability to Gawain is apparent; she continues her ploy by teasing and egging on Gawain to fall into her seduction: "3et herde I neuer of your hed helde no wordez / Þat euer longed to luf, lasse ne more; ... And teche sum tokenez of trweluf craftes" (1523–24, 1527; would know, my knight, why never one word / In the language of love has yet leapt from your mouth.... Of courtesy's code and the craft of true love). After this mild scolding, the lady's ploy is to posit a self-deprecating statement for her beloved to contradict, and a more direct sexual invitation:

Oþer elles 3e demen me to dille your dalyaunce to herken?
For schame!
I com hider sengel, and sitte
To lerne at yow sum game;
Dos, techez me of your wytte,
Whil my lorde is fro hame. (1529–34)

[Do you deem me too dull lovers' dalliance to learn
For Shame!
Kind sir, to cultivate
Love's courtly ways I came.
My lord's away; I wait
To learn the lovers' game.]

Gawain's response is to say how foolish it would be to teach someone such as she of true love's way, one whose learning and lore in the craft is so deep, one who knows twice as much about love as he. This male beloved, responding to his female lover in an inverted courtly love encounter, now turns the tables and plays the subservient lover:

> I wolde yowre wymyng worche at my myȝt,
> As I am hyȝly bihalden, and euermore wylle
> Be seruaunt to yourseluen, so saue me Dryȝtyn! (1546–48)

> [What you please I'll perform, though, provided I can;
> I am highly beholden; your behest I'll obey
> As a servant a sovereign's so save me my God.]

These deferential words pledging his servitude joyfully end their second encounter despite her enticing words tempting him to sin.

In her third attempt at seduction, the Lady awakes early and dresses for the occasion:

> In a mery mantyle, mete to þe erþe,
> Þat watz furred ful fyne with fellez wel pured,
> No hwez goud on hir hede bot þe haȝer stones
> Trased aboute hir tressour be twenty in clusteres;
> Hir þryuen face and hir þrote þrowen al naked,
> Hir brest bare bifore, and bihinde eke. (1736–41)

> [In a dear full-length dress, which was dainty and gay,
> And a fine, flowing fur; she was fashioned quite well!
> She'd no coif as cover; just clusters of pearls,
> Which hung in her hair in a highly wrought fret.
> Her face was fair, her fine throat exposed;
> Her breast and her back were both bared very low.]

But more than her tempting clothing endangers the knight, since after she takes his face in her hands and kisses him, her deceptive words of love threaten his moral safety:

> For þat prynces of pris depresed hym so þikke,
> Nurned hym so neȝe þe þred, þat nede hym bihoued
> Oþer lach þer hir luf, oþer lodly refuse....
> With luv-laȝyng a lyt he layd hym bysyde
> Alle þe spechez of specialté þat sprange of her mouthe. (1770–72; 1777–78)

> [For that peerless princess pressed him so hard
> And so eagerly urged him that either he must
> Take her favors or refuse her offensively then....

So with love-talk he laughed and eluded each one
Of the fond words of favor that fell from her lips.]

Within the courtly love tradition, such love-talking and its concomitant love-making are acceptable, even a required part of the convention. But in this situation, love-making would violate the hospitality of Gawain's host, the Lord of the Castle: more significantly, they would lead the knight dangerously close to accepting and keeping her magic girdle, not surrendering this prize to Bercilak as promised. The Lady's insistent wooing should have been suspicious to Gawain, had he not been so arrogantly disposed to accept her extravagant praise. Even if he resists her obvious sexual temptation, the more devious one, hoarding her protective green girdle to save his life, proves too compelling to resist. Lady Bercilak's alluring words of love and praise, and even her assertive, desperate coercion prepare the way for his eventual surrender:

> Quoþ þat burde to þe burne, "Blame ȝe disserue
>
> ȝif ȝe luf not þat lyf þat ȝe lye nexte,
> Bifore alle þe wyȝeȝ in þe worlde wounded in hert,
> Bot if ȝe haf a lemman, a leuer, þat yow lykez better,
> And folden fayth to þat fre, festned so harde,
> Þat yow lausen ne lyst — and þat I leue nouþe!   (1779–84)

> [But she sharply said, "You deserve to be blamed
> If you love not the lady who lies here by you,
> In the world the most wounded of women from love!
> For unless you've a lover you're linked to with vows,
> Whom you've sworn to serve with unswerving devotion,
> And would loathe to leave, you are less than polite!"]

Gawain admits he has no other lover, but cannot accept her, or her gold ring, having no compensatory love offering. Indeed, a courtly lover's role is to proffer his beloved such an offering as the lady has proposed, one generally accepted. But after her softening language, she catches him with her next offering, a seeming afterthought — the life-saving girdle from her own waist. He first earnestly refuses while promising not to be her beloved, but her lover, yet another role reversal:

> I am derely to yow biholde
> Bicause of your sembelaunt,
> And euer in hot and colde
> To be your trwe seruaunt.   (1842–45)

> [Yet, madam, I'll remain
> Your servant through and through.

I'll ride through rough and rain,
In truth, your champion true.]

Her fervent entreaty, culminating in the promise that one who wears her belt "myʒt not be slayn for slyʒt vpon erþe" (1854; cannot be killed, not by cunning on earth), finally conquers his reserve. Her insistent and repeated words, seemingly of love, of concern, of assistance, and of salvation, finally wear down his resistance: she has won.

Burrow offers these astute comments about the poet's and the Lady's seduction language:

> In these three scenes ... the poet mainly devotes his lines not to analysing moral issues but to reporting conversations—the kind of conversations between men and women which in his day were known as 'dalyaunce' or 'luf-talkyng' (ll. 1012, 1529), 927). The joy of such talk is that it can mean anything or nothing, so far as serious sexual intentions are concerned. It is this uncertainty that both Gawain and the lady exploit, for their different ends. To give one example, where the lady is sailing exceptionally close to the wind: ... [ll. 1237–4] [You're welcome to *my cors* to do as you like; I must of necessity be your servant, and I shall be.] ... "the lady can claim to be saying, as his hostess, little more than that: 'You are very welcome, and I am entirely at your service.' But in the private bedroom scenes such deference itself strikes a somewhat equivocal note; and the lady's use of 'cors' could be taken as amounting to an actual invitation...."[28]

This clever language-usage carefully ambiguates the intercourse between the Lady and her beloved; it parallels the ambiguously changing role of lover and beloved alternating between Gawain and Lady Bercilak throughout the text.

That Gawain moves from tempted aggressor to wary passive resistor, failing to accept Lady Bercilak's words of love, and her body as his courtly lover, is not because he fails in *cortoisie*, as she teasingly accuses him, but because he more seriously fears the loss of his life, where his attention is currently absorbed. He refuses her transgressive love, but not her transgressive love charm. Not virtue, but distraction and self-protection place him in his less-than-perfect moral locus.

Interestingly, Gawain may also be seen to be in a kind of sanctified courtly love affair with Our Lady, counter to one with the wily and sexual Lady of the Castle. He wears the Virgin's sign, a kind of pennant, not secretly or unobtrusively around his waist for safety, but openly and publicly on his shield for protection.[29] In this way, with the Virgin visible, he plays the more traditional, active, pursuer

---

[28] Burrow, *The Gawain Poet*, 48.
[29] See also the contribution to this volume by Connie Scarborough for parallel examples of the erotic worship of the Virgin Mary within the medieval Spanish context.

male role of supplicator, lover, wooer–the humble and prostrate lover seeking his beloved's favors. Yet Jane Gilbert rightly describes this relationship also as transgressive in its very ontology:

> The Virgin, being of an altogether different order from Gawain, plays the part of his courtly lady. It is her image that he bears on the inside of his shield, where the sight of her revives his courage, should it flag (648–50); a role conventionally given to a knight's secular lady.... Gawain is the Virgin's own knight (1769). She is invoked to protect him from the Lady's blandishments: the potential sexual relationship with the lady and the more abstract one with the Virgin are thus put forward as alternatives. In every way, the Virgin replaces the flesh and blood lady who is the typical romance Knight's inspiration; the relationship with her is carefully constructed as a parallel to the usual sexual love. The virgin belongs, however, to a different ontological order, and Gawain's "sexual" relationship with her therefore echoes the transgressively exogamous desire.[30]

His prayerful words of love are here sincere, if desperate; they are passionate, if not sexual; secretive to both internal and external audience, if not deceptive; devotional, if not courtly. The object of his petition is no wife or paramour, but a virginal maid; his plea not for her body but for his own. This spiritual shadow-relationship with the supernatural Lady, echoing and contrasting with the secular one with the earthly Lady, adds to the richness and sophistication of the poem.

Throughout this work the Gawain-poet plays with the courtly love tenets, cleverly utilizing and reversing them for his own sophisticated purposes. In this courtly-love triangle, the usual, normative masculine role, Gawain's expected locus, is subsumed by the more aggressive and traitorous role of the deceptive Lady of the Castle and the passive and protective role of the truthful but powerful Virgin. As Elisabeth Brewer suggests, "It can scarcely be wondered at that the outburst against women in which Gawain indulges after Bercilak's revelations at the Green chapel is a familiar topos in medieval literature, often taking the form of a reflection on the power of love over the wisest and greatest of men."[31] Why does Gawain indulge in such a misogynist tirade? He has been bested by a woman. He has lost the battle of the poem. While Gawain has survived the physical beheading he so feared, he has lost the intellectual battle with the Lady, and hence the Lord, of the Castle: he misunderstood the game, the role of the green girdle, the trickery behind her sexual flirtation, her true intent in their interactions, her

---

[30] Jane Gilbert, "Gender and Sexual Transgression," *A Companion to the Gawain-Poet*, ed. Derek Brewer and Jonathan Gibson. Arthurian Studies 38 (1997; Woodbridge, Suffolk: D. S. Brewer, 2002), 53–69; here 63–64.

[31] Elisabeth Brewer, "The Sources of *Sir Gawain and the Green Knight*," *A Companion to the Gawain-Poet*, 243–55; here 254.

Courtly and Marital Words of Love

alignment with her husband and Morgana le Fey, and their joint attempt to discredit Arthur's court. No wonder he is ashamed.

And all of his misperceptions can be attributed to his lack of acuity and hence vulnerability to the Lady's sexual innuendo, invitations, and courtly love charms. Her amatory discourse and gestures had little to do with love, and everything to do with deceit, which his naive and arrogant disposition could not comprehend. In his *Vox Clamantis*, John Gower also speculates on the power of love:

> When carnal love holds the mind ensnared, an intelligent man's reason becomes irrational. When the brightness of human intelligence is clouded over by the shadow of the flesh, and the spirit of reason withdraws into the flesh, man's reason stands utterly scorned; it is a slave to the flesh, and scarcely retains the post of handmaiden.[32]

And yet ironically, resentment of that amatory power most often turns those wisest and greatest men to misogyny, a view which self-reflection might reveal as an unreclaimed masculine flaw. That two male authors take their male characters to task for their perceived misogyny and failure to uphold their contracts, both directly and through the courtly love paradigm laced with hypocrisy and deceit, reveals their commitment to honesty, integrity, and fair dealing.

In both *The Franklin's Tale* and *Sir Gawain and the Green Knight,* the mighty power of loving words beats in the heart of the narratives, shaping structure, climax, and *denouement*. However, both creative authors, Chaucer and the *Pearl*-Poet, cleverly invert expectations through courtly-love role-reversals, playing off its courtly expectations, working against the convention; they provide intrigue and suspense through the cognitive dissonance of their inversions. In both texts, verbal description, narration, introspection, and interactive dialogue culminate in an amatory feast of words — a meta-textual focus on loving words, especially words of love. This use and modification of the Courtly Love paradigm evidences these authors' interest in the convention, its ambiguous morality, and its utility within relationships. Both Chaucer and the *Pearl*-Poet conclude that the operation of the Courtly Love tradition, particularly its purposely ambiguous, deceptive, or disloyal love language, does little to nurture amatory relationships between lover and beloved because, despite rhetorically skillful and beautifully crafted loving words and words of love, "Trouthe is the hyeste thyng."

---

[32] *The Major Latin Works of John Gower, Vox Clamantis*, Volume 4, ed. and trans. Eric W. Stockton (Seattle: University of Washington Press, 1962), 201. Again, see Harry Peters's article on John Gower in the present volume.

CHAPTER 19

FROM WORDS OF LOVE TO WORDS OF HATE IN TWO MEDIEVAL FRENCH PROSE ROMANCES

STACEY L. HAHN
Oakland University, Rochester, MI

An evolution regarding the power of words occurs as one passes from the very first French prose romance, the *Prose Lancelot*, written in the early thirteenth century (1225), to Jean d'Arras's late fourteenth-century *Roman de Mélusine* (1393). In the century and a half separating these two works, not only has the ethic of love changed from *fin'amors* to a more pragmatic sort of love based on the material advantages of marriage, but the language of love disappears and is replaced by damaging words of reproach and recrimination that possess within them the power to destroy. Albrecht Classen in his examination of the role of love in late medieval German literature has remarked a narrative shift of focus "away from the dialectics of courtly love" with more attention centered on the factual, biographical aspects of the protagonists.[1] He has observed how in Thüring von Ringoltingen's *Melusine* (1456) the sentimental and erotic characteristics of early romance give way to "a novel fascination with elements such as travel, money, encounters with the foreign, rise in political and economic power, the history of the family and the fate of the generations, fortune, astrology, science and political aspects" (49). The changing historical, political, and cultural climate of the late Middle Ages privileges practical, dramatic questions of power and conquest over *fin'amors* which is personal, private, and intimate.

---

[1] See Albrecht Classen, "Whatever Happened to Courtly Love? The Role of Love in Late Medieval German Literature, with Emphasis on the *Volksbuch*," *Fifteenth-Century Studies* 20 (1993): 35–64; here, 40. See also idem, "Love and Fear of the Foreign: Thüring von Ringoltingen's *Melusine* (1456). A Xenological Analysis," *Foreign Encounters: Case Studies in German Literature*, ed. Mara Wade and Glenn Ehrstine, *Daphnis* 33, 1–2 (2004): 97–122.

As Helen Solterer has observed with respect to Nicole Oresme's coining of the expression *mos actisans* [activating words], there exists "a kind of speech that possesses the force of deeds. These are words that not only make things happen, but that constitute happenings as well."[2] Whereas earlier, a tender phrase such as that pronounced to Lancelot by Guinevere, "biax dous ami " (my dear friend), had the power to inspire Lancelot's earliest chivalric feats of valor, words uttered in the pessimistic and war-ravaged era of Jean d'Arras's *Roman de Mélusine* rarely contain such tender sentiments and slowly give way to words of hatred that end in violence. As the courtly ethic of love service dies away, words take on a life of their own, as if detached from the voice of those who pronounce them. Words that formerly had the power to heal, and to inspire hope, courage, and heroic deeds, now engender death and destruction.[3] The powerful, positive words of love that characterize medieval courtly verse — Chrétien de Troyes's romances, Marie de France's *Lanval, Guigemar, Eliduc, Yonec*, to name just a few — and early prose romance are no longer viable as the ethic of love service gives way to an ethic of marriage and conquest, where passionate love plays a secondary, almost negligible role. In this paper I will explore how the breakdown of the idealistic concept of *fin'amors* brings with it a breakdown in communication that confers upon language a destructive force that parallels a chaotic, troubled world.[4]

Although language plays a more destructive role in *Le Roman de Mélusine* than in the *Prose Lancelot*, both works exhibit what some critics of the *Lancelot-Grail* Cycle describe as the *double esprit*, a term used to characterize the juxtaposition of two contradictory attitudes toward love, the first laudatory and the second condemnatory — which finds poignant expression in Christine de Pizan's *Le livre du duc des vrais amans* (1403–1405).[5] That is, the early portion of the *Lancelot-Grail*,

---

[2] Helen Solterer, "Flaming Words: Verbal Violence in Premodern Paris," *Romanic Review* 86,2 (1995): 356–78; here 357; for a discussion of the political climate of the late fourteenth and fifteenth centuries, see Kate Langdon Forhan, *The Political Theory of Christine de Pizan* (Burlington, VT: Ashgate, 2002), 8.

[3] See Burt Kimmelman, *The Poetics of Authorship in the Later Middle Ages: The Emergence of the Modern Literary Persona*. Studies in the Humanities: Literature — Politics — Society, 21 (New York, Washington, D.C., et al.: Peter Lang, 1996); idem, "Ockham, Chaucer, and the Emergence of Modern Poetics," *The Rhetorical Poetics of the Middle Ages: Reconstructive Polyphony. Essays in Honor of Robert O. Payne*, ed. John M. Hill and Deborah M. Sinnreich-Levi (Madison, NJ: Fairleigh Dickinson University Press, and London: Associated University Press, 2000), 177–205.

[4] Albrecht Classen, *Verzweiflung und Hoffnung: Die Suche nach der kommunikativen Gemeinschaft in der deutschen Literatur des Mittelalters*. Beihefte zur Mediaevistik, 1 (Frankfurt a. M. et al.: Peter Lang, 2002), chap. 8, 401–35.

[5] Christine de Pizan, *Le livre du duc des vrais amans: A Critical Edition*, ed. Thelma Fenster. Medieval and Renaissance Texts and Studies, 124 (Binghamton, NY: Medieval & Renaissance Texts & Studies, 1995). See Myrrha Lot-Borodine, "Le double esprit et l'unité du *Lancelot* en prose," *Etudes sur le Lancelot en prose*, ed. Ferdinand Lot (Paris: Champion, 1954), 443–56; Fanni Bogdanow, "The *double esprit* of the prose *Lancelot*," *Courtly Romance: A Collection of Essays*, ed. Guy Mermier. Medieval and Renaissance Monograph Series, 6 (Detroit: Fifteenth-Century Symposium, 1984), 1–22;

the *Prose Lancelot*, promotes worldly, mundane values such as chivalry, *fin'amors*, and fairy magic, only to deconstruct these values by demonstrating their insufficiency and destructiveness in light of a higher standard, that of the church, in the later, cyclic portion of the work, namely the *Agravain, Queste del Saint Graal*, and *Mort Artu*.[6] This juxtaposition of values is a constant thread throughout medieval literature and in many works that inspired medieval literature, such as Ovid's *Remedia amoris* which acts as a corrective to his Ars amatoria;, in Andreas Capellanus's *Art of Love*, where love is first extolled only to be undermined, in Beroul's *Tristan*, which contrasts with Thomas's more pessimistic vision of love; and in the *Roman de la Rose*. There, as Tracy Adams has indicated in her essay on the lover and *Faus Semblant*, the two parts of the romance seem to be written for two distinct subcultures, the marrying secular aristocracy in the earlier portion written by Guillaume de Lorris and the clerical aristocracy in the latter portion authored by Jean de Meun. Indeed, the medieval cleric, caught between these two distinct subcultures and audiences, was perhaps forced to compromise by titillating his secular readers with juicy tales of love, which he would then diffuse by showing the dangers of such love in order to please the ecclesiastical authorities.[7] In this way the medieval cleric could appeal to both audiences without damaging his reputation and offending his patrons.

The early portions of both prose romances emphasize the positive influence of love, link this love to fairy magic, and open with a tragedy that is rectified thanks to the generosity of a fairy mistress. In the *Prose Lancelot* King Arthur fails to come to the aid of his vassal, Ban of Benoyc, whom the usurper Claudas assails. As a result Ban is forced into exile and dies of grief leaving his wife and son Lancelot defenseless. The Lady of the Lake rescues the young Lancelot, providing him with the material means and education to become a knight, thus procuring for him resources that his newly widowed mother could not provide and thereby allowing him to live up to the potential promised by his privileged lineage. Similarly, in the *Roman de Mélusine*, Raymondin experiences social exile for having accidentally slain his maternal uncle in a boar hunt.[8] He is rescued by Mélusine, who has herself been banished for committing homicide, and together they forge

---

Fritz-Peter Knapp, "De l'aventure profane à l'aventure spirituelle: le double esprit du *Lancelot* en prose," *Cahiers de Civilisation Médiévale (Xe–XIIe siècles)* 32, 3 (1989): 263–66.

[6] Elspeth Kennedy distinguishes between the early *Prose Lancelot* that focuses on the love theme, ends with the death of Galehaut and does not anticipate the adventures of the Grail and a later cyclic version that leads to the adventures of the Grail and *Mort Artu*. See Elspeth Kennedy, *Lancelot and the Grail: A Study of the Prose Lancelot* (Oxford: Clarendon Press, 1986) and the introduction to her non-cyclic edition of the *Prose Lancelot, Lancelot do Lac: The Non-cyclic Old French Prose Romance* (Oxford: Clarendon Press, 1980), 2:41–44.

[7] See the contribution to this volume by Tracy Adams, "The Lover and *Faus Semblant*: Technologies of Confession in the *Roman de la Rose*."

[8] Early in the romance the narrator designates Mélusine's husband as *Raymondin* (which has various spellings) and then later as *Remond*. I shall refer to him as *Raymondin*.

a family of ten sons while Mélusine, like Virgil's crafty Dido, uses the subterfuge of an animal hide to gain land upon which her family will base its dynasty.

Despite these initial similarities, the Lady of the Lake and Mélusine differ in that the Lady of the Lake, although a facilitator of the love affair between Lancelot and Guinevere, remains herself a rather pure and chaste tutelary spirit, despite attempts later on in the romance to pair her up with a male companion. The unmarried Lady of the Lake, Lancelot's guiding protector up until the commencement of the adventures of the Holy Grail, represents the power of *fin'amors* within the context of adultery. She encourages the love between Lancelot and Guinevere because she knows that love is the source of all worldly prowess and that such love will improve the reputation of her adopted son. She even sends the lovers the magical Split Shield, an emblem denoting the perfect physical and spiritual harmony that exists between true lovers, which becomes whole when the couple physically consummates their love. Such love cannot exist within the confines of marriage because the entanglements of marriage and landed property stand in the way of chivalry. In the *Agravain* Bohort makes the following observation when Lancelot offers him the fiefdom of Gaunes, which they conquered in battle:

> Qu'est ce, sire, que vos volez fere? Certes se je volsisse recevoir l'anor del reaume, nel deussiez vos mie soufrir, car si tost come je avrai reaume, il me couvendra laissier toute chevalerie, ou je voille ou non, et ce seroit plus granz honor, se j'estoie povres hom et bons chevaliers, que se je estoie riches rois recreanz. (6:170)[9]

> [What is this, my lord, that you wish to do? Truly, if I wanted to receive the honor of kingship, you should not permit it, for as soon as I have a kingdom, I'll be obliged to give up all knighthood, whether I wish to or not, and I'd have more honor as a landless man but a good knight than as a rich king who had given up knighthood (3:319).[10]]

Earlier in the romance Claudas, an adulterer and king, had forsaken *fin'amors* because he believed it decreased one's life expectancy (1:55). He is unwilling to take the extraordinary risks required of the knight who will undergo dangerous missions in order to prove his love for his lady. The text distinguishes between common adultery, that between Claudas and his vassal Pharien's wife, and the disinterested, faithful bond we discern in *fin'amors* that transcends social conventions, yet works for the good of society via the chivalry such love inspires.

---

[9] All references to the *Prose Lancelot* are based on *Lancelot: roman en prose du XIIIe siècle*, ed. Alexandre Micha. 9 vols. (Paris and Geneva: Droz, 1978–1983).

[10] All translations of the *Prose Lancelot* are based on: *Lancelot-Grail: The Old French Arthurian Vulgate and Post-Vulgate in Translation*, ed. Norris J. Lacy. 5 vols. (New York and London: Garland, 1993–1996).

In addition, adulterous relationships do not often produce offspring since they are not constituted for the purpose of material necessity, but rather on mutual merit. When children are produced outside the confines of marriage in the *Lancelot-Grail*, it is often through some sort of subterfuge, and with the exception of Galaad, Helain le Blanc, and Hector, most of these children come to a bad end.[11] Mélusine, on the other hand, is a married woman whose sexual desires are strictly confined to matrimony and whose marriage bed has been blessed by a bishop. As a result, she and her husband along with four of her sons are graced with male offspring, many of whom are conceived during the wedding nights of their respective marriages. Plentiful progeny is certainly a mark of divine favor and the primary reason for which marriage was created.

The chivalry embodied in the *Prose Lancelot* rests on the premise that *fin'amors* alone represents the path to valor for it is based on free choice and personal merit rather than material gain. It is only later in the cyclic continuation, starting with the adventures of the *Agravain* and culminating with the Quest for the Holy Grail, that this ethic of earthly chivalry is corrected and replaced with the ethic of divine chivalry, which denounces adulterous love in favor of a chaste existence dedicated to serving God. The excesses of Lancelot's adultery, which are eventually exposed, lead to a breakdown in the social order that culminates in the ultimate destruction of the Arthurian realm. Arthur's own lust, which caused him to engender Mordred, adds to the social turmoil when Mordred challenges his father and covets his wife Guinevere so that both father and son kill each other on the battlefield.

In the *Roman de Mélusine*, adultery is entirely absent and *fin'amors*, that is, chivalry based on love service, plays a very minor role, as if it were a mere literary cliché that perfunctorily attaches itself to an impending love affair that will necessarily end in marriage. Marriage and all material goods, whether in the form of progeny or landed property, have intrinsic value. In fact, the primary means of improving one's social status, wealth, and respectability is through marriage, which allows one's lineage and landholdings to expand to territories abroad. Not only is Mélusine herself married, but four of her eldest sons find wives through their adventures and through these wives acquire dynasties and produce children of their own. Her three living sons who do not marry, Geoffrey Big Tooth, Thierry, and Remonnet, exhibit no interest in love at all. One could, then, consider the *Roman de Mélusine* a romance lacking the emotional drama of budding love with its joys, suspense, and disillusions. It is not sexual desire in the form of

---

[11] Merlin assists Utherpendragon in the adulterous seduction of Arthur's mother, Igerne; Lancelot is tricked into engendering Galaad and Bohort into fathering Helain le Blanc by means of magic potions; Ban of Benoyc engenders Hector outside of wedlock as does King Leodigan the False Guinevere, and King Arthur engenders Mordred in an unwitting act of incest.

adultery that leads to social violence and disruption, but rather suppressed rage and family resentments.[12]

Returning to the question of language, we might expect the language of love with its lyrical, emotive qualities to be more pervasive, powerful, and positive in the *Prose Lancelot*, as, indeed, it is. We have a quintessential representation of this in the early stages of Lancelot's love affair with Guinevere, at that second step of the *gradus amoris*, called the *alloquium* (conversation).[13] This event occurs when Lancelot first comes to court as a fair unknown, just after attempting the perilous adventure of removing blades from a wounded knight, a feat no other knight dared to undertake.[14] Guinevere, impressed by Lancelot's courage, asks to see the young knight. In the course of their conversation Guinevere refers to Lancelot as *biax doux ami* (my dear friend).

> *Biax dous amis*, fait ele, vous estes si jovenes hons que l'en vous doit bien pardoner .I. tel mesfait et jel vous pardoins moult volentiers.
>
> "Dame, fait il, vostre merci," et puis il dist: "Dame, fait il, se vous plaisoit, je me tendroie, en quel que lieu que jou alaisse, a vostre chevalier." – Chertes, fait ele, che voel je moult bien.
>
> Dame, fait il, des ore m'en irai a vostre congié.
>
> "Adieu, fait ele, *biax dous amis*." Et il respont entre ses dens: "Grans merchis, dame, quant il vous plaist que je le soie" (7:285–86) (italics mine).
>
> ["*My dear friend*," she said, "you are so young that you can only be forgiven for such a misdeed: of course I forgive you!"
>
> "Thank you, my lady," he said. Then he added, "My lady, if it were agreeable to you, I would, wherever I might be, look upon myself," he said," as your knight."
>
> "Yes," she said, "go right ahead."

---

[12] For a discussion of the theme of violence in the *Roman de Mélusine*, see my Stacey L. Hahn, "Constructive and Destructive Violence in Jean d'Arras' *Roman de Mélusine*, *Violence in Medieval Courtly Literature: A Casebook*, ed. Albrecht Classen (New York and London: Routledge, 2004), 187–205.

[13] This occurs after the *visus* (visual eye contact) but before stage three, *contactus* (touching) and four, *osculum* (feudal kiss), and finally, the fifth and final stage, the *factum* (coitus). For a discussion of the five steps of the medieval love process and its origins, see Lionel J. Friedman, "Gradus amoris," *Romance Philology* 19, 2 (1965): 167–77.

[14] For a treatment of the theme of Lancelot as the fair unknown, see Kennedy, *Lancelot and The Grail*, 10–48.

"My lady," he said, "now, with your leave, I will go."

"Goodbye," she said, "goodbye, *my dear friend*."
And he whispered to himself, "All my thanks, my lady, for letting me be that."] (2:68).

These three simple words, "my dear friend," are enough to sustain Lancelot through all of the adventures that lead up to the fourth step of the *gradus amoris*, the *osculum* (or feudal kiss). It is just before the first kiss that the reader becomes fully aware of the power of Guinevere's words, as we can see from the following conversation.

> ... "Dites moi, fait ele, dont cele amor vient que je vous demant." Et il s'esforce moult de parler au plus qu'il puet et dist: "Dame, des lors que je vous ai dit. — Comment fu ce dont? fait ele. — Dame, fait il, vous le feistes faire, qui de moi feistes vostre ami, se vostre bouce ne me menti. — Mon ami? fait ele. Et comment? — Dame, fait il, je m'en ving devant vous, quant je prins congié de mon seignor le roi tous armés fors de mon chief et de mes mains, si vous commandai a Dieu et dis que j'estoie vostre chevaliers en quelconques lieu que je fuisse; et vous me desistes que vostres chevaliers et vos amis voliés vous que je fuisse; et puis dis "a Dieu, dame" et vous desistes "a Dieu, biax dols amis," ne onques puis del cuer ne me pot issir; et ce fu li mos qui me fera preudome, se jel sui ja; ne onques puis ne fui en si grant meschief que de cest mot ne me membrast. Chis mos me conforte en tous mes anuis, chis mos m'a de tous maus garanti et m'a getei de tous les periex, chis mos m'a saoulé en tous mes fains, chis mos m'a fait riche en toutes mes grans povertés.
>
> Par foi, dist la roine, chi ot mot dit de moult boine eure, et Diex en soit aourés, quant il dire le me fist. Mais je nel pris pas si a chertes comme vous feistes, et a maint chevalier l'ai ge dit ou je ne pensai onques fors le dit. Et vostre pensers ne fu mie villains, anchois fu dols et deboinaires, si vous en est bien avenue que preudomme vous a fait." (8:111–12)

[... "Tell me, where does this love come from that I am asking you about?"

He did his best to reply, and said, "My lady, from the moment I've just told you about."

"How then was that?"

"My lady, you yourself made it happen, by making me your friend, if your words did not lie to me."

"My friend?" she asked. "How was that?"

"My lady," he said, "I came before you, when I took my leave of my lord the king, fully armed but for my head and my hands, and I commended you to God and said that I was your knight in whatever place I might be. And you said that you wanted me to be your knight and your friend. Then I said, 'Farewell, my lady,' and you said, 'Farewell, dear friend.' Since then those words could never leave my heart; those were the words that made me a worthy knight, if I am one; never have I been so badly off that I did not remember those words. They comfort me in all my troubles; they have kept me from all evil and saved me from all dangers; those words satisfied me in all my hunger, and made me rich in my great poverty."
"My word," said the queen, "those were fortunate words, and God be praised for making me say them. But I didn't take them as seriously as you did, and I've said that to many a knight without a thought that went beyond the words."] (2:145)

According to Guinevere's last comment, Lancelot has read more into her words than she intended, indicating that the power of words depends on one's interpretation and on who pronounces the words. Yvain previously addressed these very words to Lancelot right before Lancelot's first interview with Guinevere and they produced no extraordinary effect (7:271). Guinevere's *mos actisans* bring Lancelot's hidden love into the open, thus creating a space for it to blossom and thereby transforming a potentiality into reality, just as the lover in Marie de France's *Yonec* materializes as soon as the unhappily married heroine pronounces her wish for an ideal lover. Words give life to sentiment and feeling, making them real rather than opaque. In other instances certain truths can only be told when the moment is ripe: Guinevere informs Lancelot of the death of Galehaut when they are in bed together which softens the blow (2:75–76).

In both romances the bliss of love, whether outside or within marriage, can last but a brief period owing to the pressures of outside social forces, so that the first part of each romance extols love, while in the second part love disintegrates. This follows a pattern mentioned by Albrecht Classen in the introduction to this volume regarding Andreas Capellanus's *Art of Love* in which lessons on love are forged through the interplay of opposites in the manner of scholastic debate.[15] Henri Fromage, who has done extensive research on the mythological origins of Mélusine, sees strong ties between Guinevere and Mélusine.[16] For Fromage, the attribution of a serpent's body to the figure of Mélusine is a rather late development, one that he ascribes to monastic writers of the twelfth and thirteenth

---

[15] Albrecht Classen, "Introduction: The Quest for Knowledge Within Medieval Literary Discourse The Metaphysical and Philosophical Meaning of Love," 8–9. See also the contribution to this volume by Bonnie Wheeler.
[16] Henri Fromage, "Recherches sur Mélusine," *Mythologie française: bulletin de la société de mythologie française* 177 (1995): 1–26.

From Words of Love to Words of Hate 429

centuries ("Recherches," 13). He perceives traces of Mélusine's serpent body in a description of Guinevere in the long version of the *Prose Lancelot* where the cleric Hélie de Toulouse interprets Galehaut's troublesome dream. Using his skills as an interpreter and knowledge of Merlin's predictions, Hélie forecasts that Guinevere will bring about both Galehaut's and eventually Lancelot's downfall. Here Hélie, using animal imagery, depicts Galehaut as a dragon and Guinevere as a serpent:

> En ceste maniere, fet Merlins, vendra li grands dragons et je sai de voir que c'estes vos, et li serpens qui le vos toldra, ce sera ma dame la roine qui aime le chevalier ou amera tant come dame porra plus amer chevalier (1:57).
>
> [I know for a truth that you are the dragon, and the serpent who will take the knight away from you is my lady the queen, who loves or will love him as much as a lady can love a knight.] (2:254)

Fromage then focuses attention on Lancelot's confession to a hermit during the Grail Quest where Lancelot identifies Guinevere as the source of all his earthly goods:

> "Sire, fet Lancelot, il est einsi que je sui morz de pechié d'une moie dame que je ai amee toute ma vie, et ce est la reine Guenievre, la fame le roi Artus. Ce est cele qui a plenté m'a doné l'or et l'argent et les riches dons que je ai aucune foiz donez as povres chevaliers. Ce est cele qui m'a mis ou grant boban et en la grant hautece ou je sui. Ce est cele por qui amor j'ai faites les granz proeces dont toz li mondes parole. Ce est cele qui m'a fet venir de povreté en richece et de mesaise a toutes les terriannes beneurtez"[17] (66).
>
> ["Sir, it is this way. I have sinned unto death with my lady, she whom I have loved all my life, Queen Guinevere, the wife of King Arthur. It is she who gave me abundance of gold and silver and such rich gifts as I have distributed from time to time among poor knights. It is she who exalted me and set me in the luxury I now enjoy. For her love alone I accomplished the exploits with which the whole world rings. She it is who raised me from poverty to riches and from hardship to the sum of earthly bliss"[18]].

According to Fromage, this passage indicates that Guinevere serves a function very similar to Mélusine's in that she strives to increase her lover's reputation and well-being by endowing him with material goods. Guinevere does this by virtue of her title as queen and consort of King Arthur, whereas Mélusine accomplishes

---

[17] All references to the Quest are based on: *La Queste del Saint Graal: roman du XIIIe siècle*, ed. Albert Pauphilet. Les Classiques français du moyen âge, 33 (Paris: Champion, 1978); here 66.

[18] All translations of the Quest are based on: *The Quest of the Holy Grail*, trans. with an intro. Pauline Maud Matarasso. The Penguin Classics (London: Penguin, 1969); here 89.

the same for her husband by virtue of her supernatural powers. Fromage sees in both Guinevere and Mélusine the remnants of an ancient earth goddess whose fairy powers confer abundance and fertility. With the passage of time these qualities are rationalized, marginalized, and finally condemned by the influence of clerical culture.

If we follow the analogies between the two women further, we observe that they are both denounced, or rather a secret about them is betrayed, by their respective lovers. Lancelot's repudiation of Guinevere occurs during the Quest when he confesses his sins to a hermit. Lancelot's failure to recognize the holy nature of the Grail, which resulted in his shame and the loss of both his horse and his sword, is the result of his adulterous liaison with Guinevere. The hermit extracts for the very first time from Lancelot an avowal that he has sinned with the queen.

> "Sire fet il, vos ne me diriez chose que je ne face, se Diex me done vie."

> "Dont vos requier je, fet li preudons, que vos me creantez que ja mes ne mefferoiz a vostre creator en fesant pechié mortel de la reine ne d'autre dame ne d'autre chose dont vos le doiez corrocier." Et il li creante come loiaux chevaliers. (67)

> ['Sir,' replied Lancelot, 'there is nothing you can say that I will not do, if God gives me life.'

> 'Then I demand of you,' said the good man, 'that you promise me never again to trespass against your Maker by committing mortal sin with the queen, nor with another woman, nor in any other way that might offend Him.' Lancelot plighted his troth as a true knight.] (90)

This renunciation of Guinevere is affirmed a second time at the close of the interview and Lancelot is said to "deplore his sinful love for the queen" (94).

According to the logic of the hermit, the higher law of religion and the social taboo against adultery dictate the repudiation and thus it would cancel out any prior vows of loyalty Lancelot might have made to the queen as a lover, because such a vow would be illegitimate in the first place since Guinevere's marriage vow to Arthur would take precedence.[19] Lancelot's repudiation of Guinevere would therefore not be considered perjury, which in its origins means the breaking of an oath, since an oath of love between them would be invalid. In the case of Raymondin, however, the repudiation is made out of anger and against both his personal promise to Mélusine not to infringe her interdiction that he not see her on Satur-

---

[19] Lancelot was already forced to break his bodily fidelity to Guinevere when he was tricked into engendering Galahad by means of Brisane's magic potion.

days and his wedding vow, an oath taken before society and the church, which mandates that a husband love his wife unconditionally. The main difference between the two repudiations is that Lancelot is forced to do so by the hermit who extracts it as a promise, and he does so in a state of calm reflection and contrition. Raymondin's outburst, however, was motivated by his moral disgust at Geoffrey Big Tooth's slaying of his brother Fromont, a crime which Raymondin associates with his wife's serpent body.

> "Hee, tres faulse serpente, par Dieu, ne toy ne tes fais ne sont que fantosme en ja hoir que tu ayes porté ne vendra a bon chief en la fin. Comment raront les vies ceulx qui sont ars en grief misere ne ton filz qui s'estoit renduz au crucefix? Il n'avoit yssi de toy plus de bien que Fromont. Or est destruit par l'art demoniacle, car tous ceulx qui sont forcennéz de yre sont au commandement des princes d'enfer et par ce fist Gieffroy le grant et horrible et hideux forfeit d'ardoir son frere et les moines, qui mort ne avoient point desservi." (692–94)[20]

> ["Ha, false serpent, by God, you and your deeds are but phantoms and none of the children you have borne will ever amount to anything in the end. How can the lives of those who were so miserably burned and your son who surrendered to the crucifix be brought back to life? The only good thing to come from you was Fromont. Now he is destroyed through the art of the devil, for all those who become crazed by anger are at the commandment of the princes of hell and that is how Geoffrey committed the great, horrible, and hideous deed of burning his brother and the monks who did not deserve to die."][21]

Raymondin conflates his son's moral depravity with his wife's physical deformity. The text explicitly states that Raymondin's rash judgment against his wife is criminal:

> "Las, ma tresdoulce amie, je sui le faulx crueux aspis et vous estes licorne precieuse, je vous ay par mon faulx venin trahie. He! Las, vous m'aviéz mediciné de mon premier crueulx venin! Or le vous ay je crueusement mery quant je vous ay trayee et menty ma foy envers vous. Par Dieu, se je vous pers pour ceste cause, je m'en yray en essil en tel lieu ou on n'ourra jamais nouvelles de moy." (664)

---

[20] All references to Jean d'Arras's *Roman de Mélusine* are from: *Mélusine ou la noble histoire de Lusignan: roman du XIVe siècle*, ed. Jean-Jacques Vincensini. Le Livre de poche, 4566 (Paris: Librairie Générale Française, 2003).

[21] Translations of the *Roman de Mélusine* are mine.

["Alas, my dear, sweet friend, I am the false, cruel asp and you are the precious unicorn; I betrayed you with my false venom. Ah, alas, you cured me of my original cruel venom! And I cruelly paid you back when I betrayed you and broke my promise to you. By God, if I lose you because of this, I will exile myself in such a place where I will never be heard of again."]

If we examine the lesson contained in Marie de France's *Bisclavret*, which treats this theme from a slightly different perspective, we see that a werewolf body is not sufficient grounds for a wife to turn away from her husband if in every other respect he is a virtuous spouse. The same is true for Mélusine who has in no way betrayed her husband despite her serpent body, which becomes the focus of his rage. According to Sylvia Huot, "Mélusine encapsulates within herself the fusion of self and other, a raw potency that is both necessary and impossible to renounce. As such she becomes for Remondin the dangerous embodiment, not only of her own particular conflict between fairyhood and humanity, but also more generally of the crisis of the self."[22] For Huot, Mélusine mirrors Raymondin's own identity crisis born of his guilt for not having come to terms with the involuntary slaying of his maternal uncle and the knowledge that personal identity is a social construct dependent upon "the eye (and speech) of the beholder" ("Dangerous Embodiment," 413).[23]

Although both Lancelot and Raymondin attempt to distance themselves from their beloved through the use of language in communicative strategies, Raymondin's marital status, along with the negative emotional outburst that accompanies his words, make his speech act illegitimate. Raymondin's lack of self-control that borders on hatred has dire consequences, for it banishes Mélusine, the mother of his children, to the realm of the supernatural and thus endangers her eternal salvation, which hangs in the balance until Judgment Day. By denouncing his wife, Raymondin dissolves his marriage contract and destroys his commitment to the words of love that binds these two people together. Raymondin has also acknowledged previously that his spiritual salvation somehow depends upon his wife: "Et toute telle qu'elle est, elle me plaist et sachiéz que c'est ly sourgons de tous mes biens terriens et aussi croy je que c'est la voye premiere du sauvement de lame de moy" ("And I love her just as she is and know that she is the source of all my earthly goods and I also believe that she is the main path of my soul's salvation" [210]). This shared destiny, which transcends marriage, echoes back to the primordial crime that brought them together, the slaying of a father

---

[22] Sylvia Huot, "Dangerous Embodiments: Froissart's *Harton* and Jean d'Arras's *Mélusine*," *Speculum* 78.2 (2003): 400–20; here 411.

[23] According to Huot, "Dangerous Embodiments," 414, Mélusine leads Raymondin to self-knowledge. See also Albrecht Classen, "Die guten Monster im Orient und in Europa. Konfrontation mit dem 'Fremden' als anthropologische Erfahrung im Mittelalter," *Mediaevistik* 9 (1996): 11–37.

figure. Even though Mélusine intentionally slew her father, thinking him guilty of a crime (the betrayal of her mother), whereas Raymondin's act of homicide was accidental, both are culpable in the eyes of the law in so far as the act occurred. As Laurence de Looze has observed, it is the New Testament law of forgiveness that will save both Mélusine and her husband,[24] yet Raymondin's fixation on the body, the scene of the crime, precludes him from transcending the Old Testament law that focuses on the act, rather than "the impalpable world beyond the temporal order" ("Mélusine," 134), which Mélusine signifies.

Because Lancelot's repudiation of Guinevere is sanctioned by a representative of the church, while Raymondin's is not because he is tightly bound to his wife through the sacrament of marriage, Raymondin must make amends for breaking his oath by appealing to the institution that sanctifies marriage, the church. He does this by traveling to Rome where he duly confesses his error to Pope Benedict. The text characterizes Raymondin's wayward speech act as perjury:

Et Remond se confessa a lui au mieux qu'il pot, et quant de ce qu'il s'estoit parjuréz envers sa femme, le pape lui charga tel penitence qu'il lui plot. (728)

[And Raymond confessed to him as best he could and as for his having been perjured toward his wife, the pope charged him with a penance he deemed fitting.]

Raymondin expiates his sin by becoming a hermit and spending the rest of his days praying for the salvation of his wife. It is fitting that a crime committed through speech should be expiated through two additional forms of discourse, confession and prayer, the first of which is speech directed at healing one's inner self, and the second designed to heal the soul of the calumniated person. If Mélusine represents, as Huot implies, a mirror image of Raymondin's own identity, he has sloughed off the material, carnal side of himself through his repudiation of her and he must now, through suffering and loneliness, focus on his inner self through the mediation of prayer which directs words inward. If Mélusine had not ceased to exist in her earthly form, Raymondin might never have embarked on this inward journey. It is, however, a high price that he has to pay, losing both his beloved wife and his family as a social unit, not to speak of Mélusine's victimization.

The above are just a few examples of the way social constructs can have an impact on the power of words. When in the *Lancelot-Grail* Cycle the Grail is removed and the Arthurian world is left to its own devices, the havoc wrought by adultery brings about the eventual decay of Arthur's realm. Lancelot and Guinevere fail to exercise caution in arranging their trysts, thus attracting the attention

---

[24] See Laurence de Looze, "'La fourme du pié toute escripte': Mélusine and the Entrance into History," *Mélusine of Lusignan: Founding Fiction in Late Medieval France*, ed. Donald Maddox and Sara Sturm-Maddox (Athens, GA, and London: University of Georgia Press, 1996), 125–36; here 133.

of Arthur's nephews who, besides wanting to avenge the dishonor done to their uncle because of the adultery, have by now become envious of Lancelot's privileged position at court and therefore plot to catch the couple in *flagrante delicto*.

Since in this world marriage has no privileged position, words of love flourish, inspiring Lancelot and other true lovers to great feats of prowess until the adventures of the Grail bring them to a gradual close. Without marriage and family, words of love are not fixed by social convention and therefore can be denied without the risk of perjury.[25] Lancelot and Guinevere choose in the end to go their separate ways and lead a life of asceticism, thus implying their eventual redemption. But these words of love ring true, and are not predicated on a social contract, hence are the result of a free and voluntary exchange, as we also know from Héloïse in her epistolary exchange with Abelard,[26] and to some extent from Andreas Capellanus's treatise *De amore* with its highly dialectical approach to love, hence also to the words of love.[27]

Such is not the case in the *Roman de Mélusine*. Given the irrevocable nature of the marriage vow with its blood ties, only the violence of death or a symbolic death can separate one spouse from the other.[28] Both romances, however, center on a secret—adultery, incest, pregnancy by trickery in the *Lancelot-Grail*, and Mélusine's hybrid body, which triggers Raymondin's suppressed anger. Language that veils the truth makes all speech suspect until what is hidden is revealed. The secret simmers among Lancelot's rivals (Arthur's jealous nephews) and Raymondin's suspicious brother (the Count of Forez) until it is brought out in the open, only to result in the death of those who speak the truth. In both romances the truth that is revealed leads to the eventual breakdown of the social fabric. When this occurs, however, the seemingly irreparable outcome can be rectified through the healing counter-speech of confession and prayer.

What distinguishes the two romances despite their similarities in structure is the idealism embodied in the language of *fin'amors* evident in the early *Prose Lancelot* and the lack of such sentiments in the *Roman de Mélusine*. Chrétien de

---

[25] For the classical example in Gottfried von Straßburg's *Tristan*, see Christopher R. Clason's contribution to this volume.

[26] See Carmel Posa's essay in this volume.

[27] See Bonnie Wheeler's contribution to this volume, and also Don A. Monson, *Andreas Capellanus, Scholasticism, and the Courtly Tradition* (Washington, DC: The Catholic University of America Press, 2005), 169–97.

[28] Raymondin's desire to break away from Mélusine is not unlike Perceval's desire in Chrétien's *Conte du Graal* to break away from his mother at the expense of her life, a deed for which he later makes amends in Wolfram von Eschenbach's version of the tale (*Parzival*). Regarding this motif of breaking away from an overbearing female figure in Thüring von Ringoltingen's adaptation of Mélusine, see Albrecht Classen, "Women in Fifteenth-Century Literature: Protagonists (Mélusine), Poets (Elizabeth von Nassau-Saarbrücken), and Patrons (Mechthild von Österreich)," *Der Buchstab tödt—der Geist macht lebendig: Festschrift zum 60. Geburtstag von Hans-Gert Roloff*. 2 vols., ed. James Hardin and Jörg Jungmayr (Bern: Peter Lang, 1992), 1:431–58.

From Words of Love to Words of Hate

Troyes's romance *Erec et Enide* established a precedent that allowed the language of *fin'amors* to be integrated within the context of marriage, yet Jean d'Arras tends to minimize this aspect of language, perhaps because it was already hackneyed by the late fourteenth century, as can be observed in works like Alain Chartier's *La Belle Dame sans mercy* (1424), where the flowery language of love is called into question and undermined.[29] In speaking of early fifteenth-century Paris, Helen Solterer indicates that a climate of harangue brought on by the social disarray occasioned by the split in the French court, the schism of the church, and the Hundred Years War left a mark on the writings of major Parisian poets such as Eustache Deschamps, Alain Chartier, Jean Gerson, and Christine de Pizan ("Flaming Words," 359–61). For Solterer "social conflict was expressed and experienced in large measure linguistically" (360). An increase in contentious, vituperative language follows naturally from an environment of division, and it is this atmosphere that seems to be reflected in the harsh words Raymondin uses to denounce his wife and the irreparable damage his words cause her. The harmful, irrevocable nature of Raymondin's speech echoes the acts of violence or retribution that occur against family members within the romance (among them Mélusine, her two sisters, and Presine as objects and causes of retribution, Raymondin, his brother, uncle and foster father, Fromont, Mélusine's father, and Horrible). The division among Mélusine's family members despite the wealth, wisdom, and fecundity she brings them closely parallels the social conflicts of Jean d'Arras's world and the world of his patron, Jean de Berry.[30] Acts of violence

---

[29] A rather different situation emerged, it seems, in fourteenth- and fifteenth-century German lyric poetry, where a new fascination with and willingness to experiment epistemologically with language emerged on numerous occasions; see Albrecht Classen's contribution to this volume. But lyrical poetry is much more individualistic and does not necessarily reflect on social-historical changes. A comparison with the Constance writer Heinrich Wittenwiler's *Ring* (ca. 1400), on the other hand, where a cacophony of voices emerge and drone out each other, ultimately leading to a breakdown of communication and then to an all-engulfing violence, would probably yield the same insights; see Albrecht Classen, *Verzweiflung und Hoffnung*, 401–35; Corinna Laude, *"Daz in swindelt in den sinnen...": Die Poetik der Perspektive bei Heinrich Wittenwiler und Giovanni Boccaccio*. Philologische Studien und Quellen, 173 (Berlin: Schmidt, 2002), 94–102 et passim.

[30] Nadia Margolis, in her comparison of Mélusine to Joan of Arc, implies that Mélusine's split from Raymondin echoes on a smaller scale that between the Duke of Berry and his neighboring adversaries: "Myths in Progress: A Literary-Typological Comparison of Mélusine and Joan of Arc," *Mélusine of Lusignan*, 241–66. She indicates how these women, as "popular figures of enchantment," were "appropriated and refashioned by the hired historians of each realm, Lusignan and Armagnac France, for the common purpose of strengthening national pride and to help combat the English menace during the Hundred Years War..." (243). Margolis demonstrates how "a hierarchical layering of eventually fatal confrontations" trickles down from the political strife that inspired the romance into the personal relationships of the main characters. In the lives of both Joan of Arc and the fictional Mélusine (separated only by a span of some twenty years or more) there is a breaking of covenants (Joan's covenant made to her voices and that between Joan and Charles VII) and denunciation (by Charles VII in the case of Joan and Raymondin in Mélusine's case) that ends in betrayal ("Myths in Progress," 248–49). These conflicts of loyalty reflect the increasing divergence between the ruling families of France and England that were formerly closely linked. According to Langdon Forhan, *The*

that occur within the *Lancelot-Grail* Cycle are directed less at family members (with the exception of King Arthur and Mordred) and concentrate instead on the rift between Arthur's household and Lancelot's; that is, the problem does not concern conflicts within the lineage itself, but rather conflicts between lineages that represent separate ideals, that of King Arthur whose realm embodies the Celtic ideal of love and courtesy, and that of Lancelot, whose lineage triumphs over Arthur's and represents the Christian ideal of the pursuit of the Grail.[31] Here, words are far less provocative in setting off the final cataclysmic chain of events.

The Christian ideal which predominates in the thirteenth century seems to have decayed in the late fourteenth, which can be witnessed in the gradual extinction of the Lusignan family and a return to diabolical origins despite Mélusine's attempts to redeem her world. Raymondin did not keep his promise, and his grandson from the Armenian branch of the family, who attempts the final adventure at the Castle of the Sparrowhawk, has no intention of adhering to the terms of the adventure. Although the young Armenian king is predestined by his bloodline to complete the adventure, and does manage to pass the test by spending three consecutive days and nights watching a sparrowhawk without sleep, his desire to have what is expressly forbidden, Mélior, the lady of the castle, causes him to be brutally beaten by disembodied hands and thus turned away from the castle in shame. The incest implied in the young man's desire for his great-aunt represents a regression to a more barbaric time, a time that predates Christian marriage and *fin'amors*. He even attempts to take his aunt by force when she resists him. The decline and disintegration of the Lusignans may be linked to their inability to keep their word, the linchpin of the social contract, which begins with marriage. This lack of adherence to oaths in a society where language should ideally reflect the divine *logos* parallels the crumbling of the social fabric and the rampant lack of civility so prevalent in the troubled fourteenth and fifteenth centuries.[32]

It is most ironic that Raymondin's grandson had the moral fortitude to forego food and drink in order to keep his three-day vigil, yet could not resist the temptation to possess his aunt. This is rendered even stranger if we consider the inscrip-

---

Political Theory of Christine de Pizan, 8, "Changing views of inheritance, property, sovereignty and the feudal relationship, and family rivalries not far removed from the tradition of the blood-feud added to burgeoning economic competition and complicated the relations of the two emergent nation-states." These internecine confrontations with their twists and turns are reflected in the clash of loyalties among the various members of Mélusine's family.

[31] See Stacy L. Hahn, "Genealogy and Adventure in the Cyclic Prose *Lancelot*," *Conjunctures: Medieval Studies in Honor of Douglas Kelly*, ed. Keith Busby and Norris J. Lacy. Faux Titre, 83 (Amsterdam and Atlanta: Rodopi, 1994), 139–51.

[32] For a discussion of the damaging impact of words on women, particularly with respect to Christine de Pizan who made defamation and verbal injury the subject of many of her polemic and political writings, see Helen Solterer, *The Master and Minerva: Disputing Women in French Medieval Culture* (Berkeley and Los Angeles, University of California Press, 1995).

tion over the portraits of the numerous knights who attempted the adventure and failed:

> Et tel an veilla ceans cest chevalier nostre espervier mais il dormy, et pour tant lui fault tenir compaignie a la dame de cest chastel tant comme il pourra vivre, mais il ne lui fault rien qu'il n'ait a son plaisir, fors seulement le partir de ceans. (802)

> [Here, on this date, this knight kept watch over our sparrowhawk, but he fell asleep, and therefore he must keep the lady of this castle company as long as he shall live. He shall lack for nothing that he might desire except the right to leave the premises.]

Ironically, the young man fails to obtain Mélior's company by succeeding at the adventure, yet to remain enclosed forever with this Mélusinian double would resemble too much the fate of his grandfather. The young man claims he has all the material goods he could wish for and therefore refuses the terms of the adventure, that is, any favor the lady can grant him except for her person. As a result of his transgression, the rest of his lineage up to the ninth generation will gradually become destitute and finally lose their hold on the land. His hope for that which is expressly forbidden — incest with an older mother figure — brings us back to the Oedipus complex, the source of another social taboo. The romance begins with parricide and ends with incest, moves from poverty to wealth and back to poverty again in what seems to be an endless repetitive cycle, taking us beyond language to the murky realm of desire that language cannot contain.

This return to desire results from the failure on the part of language to bridge the gap between self and other, a failure that has long-lasting implications for individuals, families, and society alike. The *Roman de Mélusine* echoes on a smaller scale a general and widespread fourteenth-century frustration with language and its inability to create social harmony through the power of words. In a world where defamation, anger, frustrated passion, and lack of cohesion rule, words either are impotent or they have destructive and negative ramifications.

Chapter 20

John Gower — Love of Words and Words of Love

Harry Peters
University of Sydney

John Gower (ca. 1327–1408) shares with Marie de France the conviction that "anyone who has received from God the gift of knowledge and true eloquence has a duty not to remain silent: rather should one be happy to reveal such talents."[1] However, his eloquence is driven by experiences different from those of Marie, which are described in Karen Jambeck, "'de parler bon eloquence'" in this volume. Living two centuries later, he sees the destructive effects of the first half of the Hundred Years War, survives three major outbreaks of the Black Death (1346–1349, 1360–1362, and 1369), and witnesses the upheaval of the Peasants' Revolt (1381). Drawing on personal assets, he retires to private quarters attached to the Priory of St. Marie Overie, on the south bank of the Thames at Southwark. From here he observes and writes about the affairs of English society.

Gower concludes that he is living in the end age prophesied in the Book of Daniel (2:31–45), where Nebuchadnezzar dreamt of a golden-headed statue which collapses due to its feet of iron and clay.[2] He directs his eloquence into an urgent call for reformation that is evidenced in an illustration attached to two manuscripts of *Vox Clamantis* that are believed to have been written and corrected under his direction (Glasgow Hunterian T.2, 17 and London, Cotton Tiberius A.iv).[3] In

---

[1] *The Lais of Marie de France*, trans. Glyn S. Burgess and Keith Busby (Harmondsworth: Penguin Books, 1986), 41.

[2] G. C. Macaulay, *The Complete Works of John Gower; The English Works* (Oxford: Oxford University Press, 1900), 1:21–34. See also John Gower, *Confessio Amantis*, ed. Russel A. Peck, with Latin trans. Andrew Gallowlay. 3 Vols. (Kalamazoo, MI: Medieval Institute Publications, 2003–2006) (vol. 1 sec. ed.).

[3] G. C. Macaulay, *The Complete Works of John Gower; The Latin Works* (Oxford: Oxford University Press, 1901), frontspiece, lxii–lxiii.

these he is depicted as an archer shooting at the world, armed with a great longbow that contrasts with his elegant dress of a full-length blue coat with brown lining, and a stylish hat. The world is shown as a globe divided into three parts, signifying nobles, clergy, and commoners, and the accompanying text announces that his arrows are the words that he flings against the evil-doers of all classes of the world at this critical point in time:

> Ad mundum mitto mea iacula dumque sagitto
> At ubi iustus erit nulla sagitta ferit
> Sed male viuentes hos vulnero transgredientes
> Conscius ergo sibi se speculetur ibi

> [I hurl my darts at the world, and I shoot my arrows;
> Yet where there is a just man, no arrow strikes.
> But I wound those transgressors who live evilly;
> Therefore, let the one who is conscious of guilt examine himself.]

1. LOVE OF WORDS

Gower can be said to mark the point in the fourteenth century where modern English literature begins. He exemplifies love of words by completing a major work in each language of the contemporary English culture: Latin, French, and English. These are, respectively, *Vox Clamantis*, a social complaint of the times; *Mirour de l'Omme*, a religious commentary on the state of mankind; and *Confessio Amantis*, a confession in English between Amans, a frustrated lover, and Genius, a priest of Venus. In addition to these, he composes two sets of French ballades, namely *Traitié*, eighteen poems that are usually attached to *Confessio Amantis* and which deal with married love, and *Cinkante Balades*, fifty-two poems which reconcile courtly love with divine love.

These works give us a unique window into how an educated Englishman could switch among Latin, French, and English and expect his audience to follow his meaning without having to resort to translations of the French and Latin. It is common knowledge that Chaucer and the other poets of the time were trilingual, but only in the case of Gower do we have the proof on a large scale, amounting to about 12,000 lines of Latin, 32,000 lines of French, and 34,000 lines of English. Such a body of work allows us to follow verbal contexts, allusions, and puns across linguistic boundary lines in a way that is not possible for the other poets.[4]

---

[4] Robert F. Yeager, "Learning to Read in Tongues: Writing Poetry for a Tri-Lingual Culture," *Chaucer and Gower: Difference, Mutuality, Exchange*, ed. idem (Victoria, BC: University of Victoria, 1991), 115–29; here 115–18. For a parallel case in Continental European literature, see Oswald von

John Gower

The choice of language depends on the subject matter and purpose of each work, and is not a linear process where Latin gives way to French, and then French gives way to English. This is seen by the sequence in which the works are composed, as given below.[5]

Pre-1374	*Cinkante Balades (CB)*
ca. 1374–1385	*Mirour de l'Omme (MO)*
	Vox Clamantis (VC)
Post-ca. 1385	*Confessio Amantis (CA)*
	Traitié pour essampler les amants marietz (Traitié)
ca. 1400	*Cronica Tripertita (CT)*
	In Praise of Peace (PP)

Gower's purpose in writing is evidenced by the colophon, entitled *Quia Vnusquisque*, attached to many manuscripts of *VC* and *CA*.[6] In this he explains that he has written three major works for the comfort and instruction of others, driven by the obligation to share with others whatever he has received. He describes *MO* as teaching the way by which a sinner may return to God, *VC* as describing the misfortunes of England during the reign of King Richard II, and *CA* as an instruction on the lines of that of Aristotle to King Alexander, but most of all, concerning the disease of love and infatuation of Amans (*super amorem et infatuatas Amantum passiones fundamentum habet*), a pseudonym that may be read as Everyman.

The greatest example of Gower's love of words is his major English work, *Confessio Amantis*, which is constructed in three levels. The outer, or framing, level is formed by Latin verses that by inference claim moral authority for Gower, a layman, to comment on priestly matters. The Latin apparatus classifies the English text under the seven deadly sins of pride, envy, anger, sloth, avarice, gluttony, and lust, and imitates religious works by setting a headnote for each section, and pointing out the moral of the tales with marginal glosses. The next level is a confessional interaction (in English) between Amans, a frustrated lover, and Genius, a priest of Venus. This immediately places tensions between the Latin frame and the confessional, because moral objectivity is not a quality that we would expect from a servant of Venus. The third level is the tales told by Genius to illustrate sins against love. The tales amount to about one hundred and twenty-two in all, and are used by Genius as prompts whereby Amans may examine his conduct in order to confess his sins.

Wolkenstein (1376/77-1445), whose polyglot and onomatopoetic poems are at the center of Albrecht Classen's contribution to this volume.

[5] John H. Fisher, *John Gower: Moral Philosopher and Friend of Chaucer* (London: Methuen, 1965), x, 71–74, 99–115.

[6] Macaulay, *The Latin Works*, 360.

The love of words, and language, is seen in the conscious use of a vernacular dialect that is descended from Old English and enriched with French loan-words, and by the way in which complex issues are presented to the reader. As to the matter of dialect, there were at the time no books of English grammar, or accepted spelling, and Gower was free to write whatever to his ear and taste sounded authentically English. The opening lines of the Prologue to *CA* are a typical example of Gower's English:

> Of hem that written ous tofore
> The bokes duelle, and we therefore
> Ben tawht of that was write tho.

Every word is from an Old English or Norse root, arranged into flowing octosyllabic couplets. Nevertheless, he includes French loan-words whenever it suits his purpose, or completes the rhyme, as in the tale of "The King and His Steward's Wife," drawn from a French original in the *Roman des Sept Sages*:

> To **trete** upon the **cas** of love,
> So as we tolden hiere above,
> I finde write a wonder thing.
> Of Puile whilom was a king,
> A man of hih **complexioun**
> And yong, bot his **affecioun**
> After the **nature** of his **age**
> Was yit noght falle in his **corage**
> The lust of wommen forto knowe. (V. 2643–51)

The words in bold are from Old French roots and illustrate the point made above of the interlacing of French with English. They are assimilated with ease into the expressional frame of the evolving English language.

The arrangement of English to present complex issues in *CA* is far more nuanced than a surface reading of the text would suggest. By contrast with *MO*, Gower's earlier major work in French in which he spells out every issue explicitly, the three levels of *CA* contain many puzzling inconsistencies foreshadowed by his statement that he intends to avoid dullness, occasioned by "who that al of wisdom writ / It dulleth ofte a mannes wit," and in its place he will offer a book which can be read for pleasure, learning, or both: "I wolde go the middle weie / And write a bok between the tweie, / Somwhat of lust, somwhat of lore" (Prologue, 13–14 and 17–19).

The central challenge of *CA* is to recognize, and resolve, the way in which the three levels, of the Latin frame, the confessional interaction of Amans and Genius, and the tales themselves, do not always mesh. This was once taken as evidence that Gower has lost control of this huge work, which Robert Levine has labeled a "loose and baggy monster," containing "three misleading voices in the text" and which is "the long, bad dream of a sick old man."[7] Against this, other recent scholars propose that the tensions and disjunctions in the work are deliberate.[8]

I would argue that the disjunctions in *CA* function to question the process of identifying sin, and may be seen to predate the modern writings of Michel Foucault, who classifies confession as a process where "the Christian pastoral prescribed as a fundamental duty the task of passing everything having to do with sex through the endless mill of speech."[9] Of course there is more to confession than matters of sex, and he acknowledges it to be "one of the main rituals we rely on for the production of truth . . . . Western man has become a confessing animal."[10] In this wider aspect he is concerned with confession as an act of truth-telling, or *parrhesia*, which he traces from its roots in the ancient and late antique Greek and Roman worlds. The crux of *parrhesia* is a dialogue of trust between two parties, where *both* are truthful, in order that the confessing subject is led to greater self-knowledge.[11]

There is a clear parallel between Foucault's *parrhesia* and *CA*, where the latter functions as a truth-telling exercise at three levels. First, the confession of Amans is facilitated by Venus, through her priest, in order to bring the aged Amans to recognize the absurdity of his infatuation with a young lady. Second, the text, by containing instructions on rulership as well as examining sins against love, becomes a "lesson for princes," and demonstrates the Aristotelian principle that self-governance is a prerequisite to the governing of a people. Finally, the disjunctions which emerge among the Latin apparatus, the dialogue of Amans and Genius, and the tales themselves (often changed from forms that the reader would expect) demand that the reader participate imaginatively in, and make a judgment on, the situations presented in the text. In this way a dialogue is built between the text and the reader, where the text becomes Genius, the confessor, and the reader becomes Amans, or Everyman, in order to prompt greater self-knowledge.

---

[7] Robert Levine, "Gower as Gerontion: Oneiric Autobiography in the *Confessio Amantis*," *Medieaevistik* 5 (1992): 81–96; here 81, 82, 96.

[8] See, for example, Winthrop Wetherbee, "John Gower," *The Cambridge History of Medieval English Literature* (Cambridge: Cambridge University Press, 1999), 589–609; here 603; Siân Echard, "Glossing Gower," *Re-visioning Gower*, ed. R. F. Yeager (Asheville: Pegasus Press, 1998), 237–56; here 238, 249, 251; William Calin, *The French Tradition and the Literature of Medieval England* (Toronto: University of Toronto Press, 1994), 388–93.

[9] Michel Foucault, *The Will to Knowledge: The History of Sexuality*. Vol. I, trans. R. Hurley (Harmondsworth: Penguin, 1998), 21.

[10] Foucault, *The Will to Knowledge*, 58–59.

[11] Thomas Flynn, "Foucault as Parrhesiast: His Last Course at the Collège de France," *The Final Foucault*, ed. James Bernauer and David Rasmussen (Cambridge, MA: MIT Press, 1988), 102–16; here 103.

2. WORDS OF LOVE

The work of Gower which best qualifies as "words of love" is the *Cinkante Balades*, found in a single manuscript known as "Trentham Hall," with an estimated date of composition of 1400. The MS is seen as Gower's last literary act, composed in honor of Henry of Lancaster, the eldest surviving son of John of Gaunt and Blanche of Lancaster, on the occasion of his coronation as Henry IV after he had deposed Richard II in 1399. The MS itself is trilingual, and the contents can be said to echo what J.A.W. Bennett termed, speaking of *CA*, Gower's concern for "'honeste love' in wedlock, *caritas* in the commonwealth."[12] The most extraordinary feature of these poems is that they have to date received no attention in their own right, in marked contrast to the mountain of critical work on *CA*; yet, as I shall demonstrate later, they are capable of yielding significant insights that are not to be found in *CA*.[13]

The importance of these ballades becomes apparent when we review the structure of the MS, as follows:

In Praise of Peace	(Fifty-five stanzas in rhyme royal)	6 folios
Rex celi deus	(Latin verse of 56 lines)	
Cinkante Balades	(Fifty-four ballades in French)	23 folios
Ecce patet tensus	(Latin verse, some lines missing)	
Traitié	(Eighteen ballades in French)	6 folios
Henrice quarti primus	(Latin verse of 12 lines)	

The first surprising aspect of the MS is that, at a time of political crisis in England, Gower saw fit to make the courtly French ballades of *CB* the centerpiece of the work. He was about seventy years old at the time, in poor health and going blind, and Fisher believes that they are his earliest works, composed before 1374 and *Miroir de l'Omme*.[14] A study of the ballades in *CB* demonstrates many variations

---

[12] J. A. W. Bennett, "Gower's 'Honeste Love'," *Patterns of Love and Courtesy; Essays in Memory of C. S. Lewis*, ed. John Lawlor (London: Edward Arnold, 1966), 107–21; here 121.

[13] For general discussion of *CB*, see Robert F. Yeager, *John Gower's Poetic: The Search for a New Arion* (Cambridge: D. S. Brewer, 1990), 66–67 discussing the originality of these ballades; Calin, *The French Tradition*, 380–85, summarizes *CB* as reconciling *fin'amor* and marriage, and 398: "no-one, not even Chaucer himself, is more representative of the Franco-English court culture of the fourteenth century"; Ardis Butterfield, "French Culture and the Ricardian Court," *Essays on Ricardian Literature: In Honour of J. A. Burrow*, ed. A. J. Minnis, Charlotte C. Morse and Thorlac Turville-Petre (Oxford: Clarendon Press, 1997), 82–120; here 107: "the poetry of John Gower is supremely poised between linguistic cultures," and 114: "he handles the stock metaphors (of courtly love) with the ease and subtlety of a native (French) speaker"; and Robert F. Yeager, "John Gower's French," *A Companion to Gower*, ed. Siân Echard (Cambridge: D. S. Brewer, 2004), 137–52, here 146: "nothing similar (*CB*) exists by the hand of an English poet," and 148: "we should see the lovers progressing steadily from empty fictional voices of a thoroughly traditional kind to beings capable of moral choices and a credible affection." Yet despite these praises, there is no published work devoted to *CB*.

[14] Fisher, *John Gower*, 304.

in stanza length and format, by comparison with the absolute regularity of the ballades in *Traitié*, and this, together with an obvious error in the MS in which the fourth and fifth ballades are both given the same number, namely (iv), suggests to me that they were a rushed selection, drawn from a store of poems written across a period of time, with possibly just the last three ballades composed for the occasion to draw the collection together.[15]

The second surprising aspect of the MS is the existence of such ballades. Earlier, in *MO*, Gower renounces his youthful composition of romantic material:

> Jadis trestout m'abandonoie
> au foldelit et veine joye,
> dont ma vesture desguisay
> et les fols ditz d'amours fesoie,
> dont en chantant je carolloie. (27337–41)[16]

> [In olden days I gave myself freely to wantonness and vain joy. I decked myself out in fancy clothes and composed foolish love ditties, which I danced about singing.][17]

The sentiment is repeated later in *CA*, when the persona of Amans admits to a weakness for composing love songs:

> And also I have ofte assaied
> Rondeal, balade and virelai
> For hire on whom myn herte lai ...
> And thus I sang hem forth fulofte
> In hall and ek in chambre aboute. (*CA*, 1.2726–28, 2732–33)

The images of the sober and aging author, most famously named by Chaucer as 'moral Gower' (*Troilus and Criseyde*, V.1856), having once composed love songs to be danced and sung before ladies, are quite delightful, and it is even more delightful to find that he did not destroy his disowned love songs, but presents a selection in this, his last major manuscript. It is tempting to connect the choice of material with his late marriage to Agnes Groundolf in 1397–1398, given the last two lines of the Latin verse that follows *Traitié* in the Trentham MS:

---

[15] I have confirmed this error by checking the Ms. (British Library microfilm, Add. 59495).

[16] G. C. Macaulay, *The Complete Works of John Gower: The French Works* (Oxford: Clarendon Press, 1899), 303; for a critical examination of the topos of recantation, or palinode, see Anita Obermeier, *The History and Anatomy of Auctorial Self-Criticism in the European Middle Ages*. Internationale Forschungen zur Allgemeinen und Vergleichenden Literaturwissenschaft, 32 (Amsterdam and Atlanta: Editions Rodopi, 1999). She refers to Gower once (191), but she does not examine Gower's use of the palinode.

[17] *John Gower, Mirour de l'Omme,* trans. William Burton Wilson, rev. Nancy Wilson Van Baak (East Lansing, MI: Colleagues Press, 1992), 358.

Hinc vetus annorum Gower sub spe meritorum
    Ordine sponsorum tutus adhibo thorum.

[Thus I, Gower, aged in years, in hope of merit,
    go safe to the marriage-bed in the ordinance of the wedded.] [18]

The marriage could be interpreted as a carer/patient relationship, or, in the absence of evidence either way, it could be a case of love. Gower himself suggests the possibility in *CA*, when, before he is dismissed by Venus on account of his age, he is the subject of a dispute by the famous lovers of all ages who follow in her procession:

Bot that the wylde loves rage
In mannes lif forberth non Age;
Whil ther is oyle forto fyre,
The lampe is lyhtly set afire. (CA. 8.2773–76)

The point that these famous lovers are making is that, despite Venus's disowning of aged lovers, aged lovers are not able to disown Venus — there may yet be oil in Gower's lamp (or fond memories on behalf of younger courtiers) when he selects love poetry as the centerpiece of the Trentham MS.

The ballades in *CB* belong to the genre that is loosely termed "courtly love," which can mean almost anything. However, Theresa Tinkle's comparison of this "semiotic abyss" with the linguistic habits of Humpty Dumpty, where the definition of a word shifts according to whatever he wants it to mean, suggests a useful way in which *CB* may be evaluated.[19] I propose to accept her lead and would say that, for Gower, courtly love means the discourse that he presents in *CB*, and nothing more nor less. The discourse that he presents is not the same as, for example, the passionate *Lais* of Marie de France, or the sophistication of Jean de Meun's continuation of the *Romance of the Rose*. Taking another lead, this time from Michel Foucault, we can seek out the competing discourses of love proper to the fourteenth century, accepting that there may be multiple discourses on the topic which compete and overlap in a way that he terms "tactical polyvalence," rather than operating as simple binary oppositions.[20] Then we can position the discourse of Gower's ballades against or within the other discourses of love.

The critical study by Georges Duby identifies two competing discourses of love, which he terms the ecclesiastical model and the lay model of marriage. The ecclesiastical model became the dominant discourse promoted by the Church as

---

[18] Fisher, *John Gower*, 85–86.

[19] Theresa Tinkle, *Medieval Venuses and Cupids: Sexuality, Hermeneutics and English Poetry* (Stanford: Stanford University Press, 1996), 10–11.

[20] Foucault, *The Will to Knowledge*, 100–01.

it sought to extend its control over the civil regime of marriage from the ninth to the twelfth centuries, whereas the lay model developed on the basis of Roman law in ruralized society in support of landed inheritance, and is centered around the concept of "house" where the house comprises a family grouping that has the primary aim of retaining or improving their reputation and possessions.[21] Duby writes specifically about the conditions in northern France; however, his classification of the lay model remains relevant at the time of Gower, and is, in a sense, timeless in all classes of society where power and possessions are counted paramount.[22]

THE LAY MODEL OF THE MARRIAGE DISCOURSE

The lay discourse may be summarized under six points, as follows:

(A) *SUPREMACY OF THE HOUSE*

The needs of the house are paramount, and possessions, rank, and honor must be at least maintained, or better still, enhanced. The house is headed by a senior member who speaks on behalf of all the males who have some claim of inheritance. The concept of "house" can be found at any level of society where power and possessions are involved: for example, in the households of royalty, nobles, merchants, or landed gentry.

(B) *MARRIAGES MUST SERVE THE HOUSE*

Following from (a), sons are married in such a way as to improve the inheritance and to continue the line with legitimate children, while daughters are married in such a way as to maximize the influence of the house.

(C) *GUARD THE HOUSE WITH COMPLEX LEGAL SETTLEMENTS*

To negotiate, make promises, and enter into legal agreements that minimize the risk of impoverishment of the house, secure the rights of daughters married off into other houses, and gain mutual support across houses.

---

[21] Georges Duby, *Love and Marriage in the Middle Ages*, trans. Jane Dunnett (Cambridge: Polity Press, 1994), 6–10.

[22] The lay model of marriage is based on taking, rather than giving. The latter is another discourse of love, also aristocratic, described by C. Stephen Jaeger, in *Ennobling Love: In Search of a Lost Sensibility* (Philadelphia: University of Pennsylvania Press, 1999), ix: "a kind of (public) love that conferred honor on those who practiced it," and 4: "charismatic love is a genuine mode of loving."

(D) TENDENCY TO ENDOGAMY

Marriage amongst cousins is favored, in order to conserve the inheritance.

(E) *DIVORCE ALLOWED*

The society allows only one wife at a time, but permits the husband, or his family group, the power to break off the marriage at will. The material interests of the repudiated wife and her lineage are dependent on the foresight of the legal contract entered into at the time of the marriage (see (c) above).

(F) *DOUBLE STANDARD IN SEXUAL EXPRESSION*

The husband could have other women, before, during, or after marriage, and male virility is extolled. By contrast, the wife should be a virgin at the time of marriage, and should remain faithful to the husband thereafter.

Duby states that this model was challenged by the development of church teaching on matrimony from the ninth to the twelfth centuries, and that it was only gradually Christianized. The lay model is refuted implicitly by Gower in *MO*, in the sections on Adultery and Marriage, where he denounces loveless marriages, marriages for gain, and unfaithfulness in marriage.[23] It is denounced explicitly in *CA*, where Genius warns Amans against marriage for 'covoitise,' motivated by the possession of beauty, manor, fields, or profit.[24] However, there was a large gap between the church's teachings endorsed by Gower, and what men actually did, as can be seen in the following examples taken from the highest levels of the English court.

The matter of adultery and double standards is seen in the affair of King Edward III, who took Alice Perrers as a mistress and fathered children by her, until the attack by Parliament on her position in 1376. Closer to Gower, and Chaucer, is the affair of Edward's fourth son, John of Gaunt, who, after the death of his first wife Blanche of Lancaster, took Katherine Swynford (neé de Ruet, or Roelt, and sister-in-law of Chaucer) as a mistress while her husband was still alive, and subsequently fathered four children by her. At the same time he was marrying Constance of Castile with the expectation of inheriting the throne of her father. After the birth of a daughter, who was later married off into the royal house of Portugal, Constance lived as a virtual exile while Katherine took her place at

---

[23] Macaulay, *The French Works*, 102–106, 199–206.
[24] G. C. Macaulay, *The Complete Works*, 2:15–16.

court.[25] These public affairs throw more light on Gower's presentation of himself as an archer in *Vox Clamantis*, mentioned above, where he is careful to attack the faults rather than to name the persons causing the greatest scandal.

THE ECCLESIASTICAL MODEL OF THE MARRIAGE DISCOURSE

The alternative model of marriage is characterized by Duby as being based primarily upon four features, namely: that marriage is a disturbance of the soul, based on the views of St. Jerome; it is acceptable only as a lesser evil to control sexuality; it is to be directed to procreation rather than pleasure; and, finally, it must be subject to the rituals of the church.[26] This summary is correct as a broad sketch of changes in the marriage discourse from the ninth to the twelfth centuries, but it falls short of being a full description of the teaching of the church as it applied in the fourteenth century. D'Avray argues that the evidence of the surviving sermon literature demonstrates that medieval scholasticism had moved away from Augustine's view that sexual pleasure arose from the original sin of Adam and Eve, and that the emphasis has moved to the blessing of human nature through the incarnation of Christ.[27] In accordance with Foucault's injunction to study the archive of the period, I have expanded Duby's summary into seven points, drawing upon critical works that document the clerical teachings of marriage in fourteenth-century Europe.

(A) *THE MATTER OF MARRIAGE*

The theology of marriage by this time was less ascetic than the twelfth-century model sketched above. Marriage is viewed now as instituted in Paradise between Adam and Eve, where their union is declared by God to be a new body.[28] Further, the church declares marriage to be one of the seven sacraments and likens it to the relationship of Christ with the Church, as His bride. Marriage is also seen as a model of the affective relationship between the individual soul and God.[29] In

---

[25] Sydney Armitage-Smith, *John of Gaunt* (1904; London: Constable, 1964), 129, 390–93; Norman F. Cantor, *The Last Knight* (New York: Free Press, 2004), 60, 79–81, 86, 194–95.

[26] Duby, *Love and Marriage in the Middle Ages*, 10–11.

[27] David L. d'Avray, *Medieval Marriage: Symbolism and Society* (Oxford: Oxford University Press, 2005), 13–14, 168–75; for the aspect of discourse within the broad discussion of marriage throughout the Middle Ages and beyond, see Albrecht Classen, *Der Liebes- und Ehediskurs vom Mittelalter bis zum frühen 17. Jahrhundert*. Volksliedstudien 5 (Münster, New York, Munich, and Berlin: Waxmann, 2005); also *The Medieval Marriage Scene*, ed. Sherry Roush and Cristelle Louise Baskins. Medieval and Renaissance Texts and Studies, 299 (Tempe, AZ: Arizona Center for Medieval and Renaissance Studies, 2005).

[28] Jaroslav Pelikan, *The Growth of Medieval Theology, 600–1300* (Chicago: University of Chicago Press, 1978), 211; and see Genesis 1:27, 2:18 and 2:22–24.

[29] d'Avray, *Medieval Marriage*, 58–61.

addition, marriage reflects the ideal relationship between a king and his subjects, a subject of great concern to both Chaucer and Gower during the instability of the later years of the reign of Richard II.[30]

(B) THE MANNER OF CONTRACTING MARRIAGE

Possibly the most surprising feature of medieval canon law is the insistence that the *consent of both parties* constitutes a valid marriage, prior to any physical consummation.[31] The church sees marriage as a sacrament that is *bestowed mutually by the marriage partners*, rather than the priest or bishop. At the same time, the church requires public celebration of a marriage, to be officiated by a priest at the church door, after reading of the banns to bring to light any impediments.[32] The juxtaposition of these two principles opens the door to the clandestine marriages that bedevilled the church courts, with instances of bigamy or seduction on the strength of a private vow to marry, such that "by far the most common matrimonial cause in the medieval Church courts was the suit brought to enforce a marriage contract."[33]

(C) THE PURPOSE OF MARRIAGE

Marriage is instituted primarily for the procreation of the human race.[34] However, there are exceptions. The prime example is the betrothal and marriage of Mary to Joseph, where the church had come to define Mary as being ever-virgin before and after the birth of Jesus.[35] In normal life, a marriage could be valid even when procreation is not possible, such as the marriage of older people, or even the marriage of an impotent old man to a young woman. The latter cases are classed

---

[30] David Wallace, *Chaucerian Polity* (Stanford: Stanford University Press, 1997), 297.

[31] Neil Cartlidge, *Medieval Marriage: Literary Approaches, 1100–1300* (Cambridge: Brewer, 1997), 16–19; see also R. N. Swanson, *Religion and Devotion in Europe, c.1215–c.1515* (Cambridge: Cambridge University Press, 1995), 33, 239; and James A. Brundage, *Law, Sex and Christian Society in Medieval Europe* (Chicago: University of Chicago Press, 1987), 265, 268–70.

[32] Michael M. Sheehan, *Marriage, Family and Law in Medieval Europe* (Toronto: University of Toronto Press, 1996), 108; and see also d'Avray, *Medieval Marriage*, 118, for the point that the church service (as distinct from the banns) was not mandatory in all countries. For the role of Joseph, see now Mary Dzon, "Joseph and the Amazing Christ-Child of Late-Medieval Legend," *Childhood in the Middle Ages and the Renaissance: The Results of a Paradigm Shift in the History of Mentality*, ed. Albrecht Classen (Berlin and New York: de Gruyter, 2005), 135-57.

[33] R. H. Helmholz, *Marriage Litigation in Medieval England* (London: Cambridge University Press, 1974), 25.

[34] Cartlidge, *Medieval Marriage*, 16–17; also see Genesis 1:28.

[35] Marina Warner, *Alone of All Her Sex: The Myth and Cult of the Virgin Mary* (1976; London: Random House, 2000), 43–45, and Penny S. Gold, "The Marriage of Mary and Joseph in the Twelfth-Century Ideology of Marriage," *Sexual Practices and the Medieval Church*, ed. Vern L. Bullough and James Brundage (Buffalo: Prometheus Books, 1982), 102–17; here 111–15.

as "solace," and in both cases the key point is the consent of the couple (see point (b) above).[36]

(D) THE ALLOWABLE PARTIES

Marriage was forbidden where the parties were related by consanguinity or affinity. The former rule forbade marriage between kindred, which were defined as cousins to the third degree.[37] The latter rule, of affinity, was a relationship created by intercourse, or by a spiritual relationship, e.g., a man would be forbidden to marry the sister of a woman with whom he has had intercourse, or to marry a girl to whom he had stood godfather.[38] The rule of consanguinity could be relaxed by an appeal to the pope for dispensation, as happened in John of Gaunt's first marriage when he took his cousin, Blanche of Lancaster, as his wife.[39]

(E) *THE NORMS OF SEXUAL EXPRESSION*

Marriage is the relationship within which sexuality is legitimized. There are shades of opinion in the medieval church on the status of the sexual act, with some arguing that it simply transforms a deadly sin into a lesser sin, although others stress that marriage is part of God's plan from the beginning of mankind and is not sinful if directed to procreation.[40]

(F) *AUTHORITY VESTED IN THE HUSBAND*

Following from the image of Christ as the groom, and the Church as the bride, and by authority of the Pauline epistles, the husband was authorized to govern the wife.[41] Husbands were exhorted to love their wives as Christ loved the church, and wives were exhorted to honor and obey their husbands, and to behave modestly.

---

[36] Henry Ansgar Kelly, *Love and Marriage in the Age of Chaucer* (Ithaca: Cornell University Press, 1975), 247 and James A. Brundage, "The Problem of Impotence," Bullough and Brundage, *Sexual Practices*, 135–40; here 137. Now see also Classen, *Der Liebes- und Ehediskurs*.

[37] Kelly, *Love and Marriage*, 140–43.

[38] Helmholz, *Marriage Litigation*, 78.

[39] Armitage-Smith, *John of Gaunt*, 14–15; and note d'Avray, *Medieval Marriage*, 94–96, who makes the point that great men could play off the rule of degree against the rule of indissolubility, as it suited them.

[40] Kelly, Love and Marriage:, see chap. 10, "he Too Ardent Lover," esp. 254–56.

[41] See Ephesians 5:21–33 and also Genesis 3:16.

(G) *THE DURATION OF MARRIAGE*

Marriage is a lifelong relationship that can be terminated by death alone. This is seen in the Gospels, where Jesus condemns divorce, but places a limit on marriage as an earthly state that does not apply in heaven.[42]

The ecclesiastical model clashes with the lay model in promoting the consent of the couple above the demands of the house, and in prohibiting marriages amongst kindred, divorce, and extramarital sexual relations. Both models agree on the authority of the husband over the wife and are directed to the production of children; however, the ecclesiastical model views children as the future inheritors of heaven rather than the inheritors of earthly estates. This model is confirmed in the section in *MO* that deals with marriage, but, unfortunately, the positive view of marriage is diluted by the misogynistic claims of the period that, since death came into the world by the sin of Eve, women are weak-minded and less perfect than men. The place of marriage is downgraded further in the section on chastity, which follows immediately after the treatment of marriage in *MO*, and ranks the religious life above the married state.[43]

I propose to compare the discourse found in *CB* against the two discourses of love and marriage that are set out above, in order to establish how far Gower's concept of courtly love contradicts, overlaps, or extends the discourses of marriage. The discourse of *CB* will be extracted in two stages, where the first step is to identify the primary theme of each ballade, and the second step is to consolidate the primary themes into points that are comparable to the lay and ecclesiastical models. Reading the ballades consecutively yields the following primary themes:

(i) The lover surrenders to, and serves the lady — 1, 2, 4a, 4b, 21, 23, 47
(ii) The lover awaits her favor — 3, 16, 22, 24, 26, 27, 31, 32, 33, 34, 36, 38, 39
(iii) The lover rejoices in the surrender of the lady — 5, 45
(iv) The separated lover yearns for the lady's presence — 6, 7, 8, 9, 10, 15
(v) The lover appeals to the lady to be less aloof — 11, 12, 14, 35
(vi) The lover considers himself unworthy of the lady — 13, 14
(vii) The lover complains of the lady's hardness of heart — 17, 18, 19, 20, 28, 30, 37
(viii) The lovers are threatened by slanderers or gossip — 25
(ix) The lover suffers from the lady's anger — 29
(x) The lover finds the lady unfaithful — 40
(xi) The lady rebukes her cheating lover — 41, 42, 43
(xii) The lady surrenders to her idealised lover — 44
(xiii) The lady rejoices secretly when she hears of her lover's exploits — 46

---

[42] See Matthew 5:31–32, 19:3–12, 22:24–30 etc.
[43] Macaulay, *The French Works*, 203–08.

John Gower 453

(xiv) Love is a thankless path, and a form of madness — 48
(xv) Love and marriage rank next to love of God and neighbour — 49
(xvi) True love agrees with nature and reason — 50
(xvii) By courtesy, to serve all ladies, with Our Lady above all — Conclusion

Consolidating these themes yields the following six-point schema, as a summary of Gower's concept of courtly love:

(a) Sovereignty granted to the lady
Themes (i), (ii), (iv), (v), (vi), (vii) — thirty-nine ballades.

The most notable feature of the courtly discourse is the unconditional service of the lady by the lover, in contradiction to the authority of the husband over the "less perfect" wife in the ecclesiastical and lay discourses. This point promotes love as a refining power in opposition to the inequality found in the other discourses. The theme of female sovereignty is found also in *CA* in the "Tale of Florent," where the ugly old dame is transformed into a beautiful young woman when the knight surrenders to her rule.[44]

(b) Idealization of the partner
Themes (iii), (xii), (xiii) — four ballades.

Another commonplace of courtly literature, where the lady is beautiful and gracious, and the man is courteous and valiant.

(c) Emotional madness
Themes (ix), (xiv) — two ballades.

The danger of courtly love is summarized in ballade 48, with the common medieval metaphors of love, where the sweet is bitter, the thorn is soft, the soft rose is a nettle, etc.[45] The risks of self-deception and the abandonment of reason are singled out in the refrain, *en toutz errours amour se justifie*, and the remedy is given in the following ballade as an appeal to balance love with reason, by living within the love of God and neighbor.

(d) Jealousy
Theme (viii) — one ballade.

No collection of courtly poems would be complete without reference to *fals jangle* and *tresfals*, but the point is treated in one ballade only. This is the nearest that we hear of a secret love affair, and there is no reference in any of the ballades in *CB* to adulterous love. The decision to omit adultery from these ballades is

---

[44] Macaulay, *The English Works*, 1:74–86.
[45] See, for example, the litany of over forty inversions in *Carmen de variis in amore*, following ballade XVIII of *Traitié* (missing in the Trentham MS), in Macaulay, *The French Works*, 392, 473.

particularly significant given the forthright condemnation in *VC* where courtly love is named *gallica peccata* (French sins) and the men and women who indulge in it are termed *meretrices* (whores). Stockton's translation is as follows:

> The French sins now clamor to take possession of our households, which have recently fallen prey to them. Now it is permissible for every man to dance attendance upon another's wife, and this is called the noble rank's "love." This is not a vice for laymen, but a great mark of esteem; for a man becomes esteemed through adultery, while his adulterous wife courts dishonour for the sake of gifts. The husband who plays the same game is thereby absolved. Thus men and women now sell themselves as if they were whores, while Venus' generous hand is propitious. [46]

Two points stand out in *VC*, namely, that the concept of courtly love has arrived recently from France and that it is copied from the customs of the nobility. The vulnerability of the nobility could be answered in part by the prevalence of marriages under the lay model, where free consent and love are missing, and the cult of courtly love has been adopted as a substitute for a lack of emotional love in arranged marriages.

(e) Disillusionment
Themes (x), (xi) — four ballades.

Complaints of betrayal are heard, one in the voice of a man whose lady has taken a new lover, and three in the voice of a woman who complains bitterly of a cheating lover. The ratio of these voices recalls the final point of the lay model, where men are more likely to indulge in promiscuous behaviour than women.

(f) Sublimation of courtly love to marriage and Mary
Themes (xv), (xvi), (xvii) — three ballades.

The omission of adultery as a theme in *CB* can be explained by the fact that it is implicitly condemned in ballade 49 (to be discussed below), where Christian love is stated to rest in three points, namely, the love of God, the love of neighbor, and honest love in marriage. Ballade 50 praises the ennobling powers of love, provided that it is guided by reason, and the final (unnumbered) ballade repeats this point, and calls for the exercise of courtesy toward all women, within the

---

[46] Macaulay, *The Latin Works*, *Vox Clamantis*, VII, 157ff, trans. Eric W. Stockton, *The Major Latin Works of John Gower* (Seattle: University of Washington Press, 1962), 22, 258. See also John Gower, *The Minor Latin Works*, ed. and trans. Robert F. Yeager, with *In Praise of Peace*, ed. Michael Livingston (Kalamazoo, MI: Medieval Institute Publications, 2005).

spiritual framework of surrender to Mary, *la plus cherie virgine et miere, en qui gist ma creance.*[47]

The discussion of Gower's discourse of courtly love in greater detail will be undertaken by consideration of three ballades, namely ballade 24 (Sovereignty), ballade 43 (Disillusionment), and ballade 49 (Sublimation). The text of each ballade, followed by my translation, is attached at the end of this paper.

Ballade 24 reveals the lover who is so carried away, presumably by sight and hearing alone, that the lady has become the object of his religious devotion. The refrain and the reference to a statue of stone, *l'image de piere*, suggest that the lover is being ignored by the lady. This could be a pointer to Ovid's version of the tale, where Pygmalion, disgusted by the flint-like behavior of wicked women, carves his statue lovingly from *ivory* and yearns for a beautiful and innocent bride. The statue is transformed to living flesh by Venus in response to his devout prayers, but we are left with the suspicion that the *stone* statue in this ballade presages an unhappy ending. Similarly, if the audience recalls the tale of Pygmalion in *The Romance of the Rose,* they will receive the tale as a warning of the foolishness of loving where love cannot be returned. The religious image re-enters in line 26, *soul apres dieu* ('alone after God'), so that the lover cannot be accused of idolatry, or are we being warned that the loss of reason in the first stanza can be cured only by a return to Christian faith? Just as in *CA*, an apparently simple text dissolves into multiple interpretations that depend on the reader.

Ballade 43 is the complaint of a lady who has been seduced and deceived. The bitterness of her accusation is framed in terms of classical mythology, commencing with the example of Jason who promised marriage in order to seduce Medea and to gain the Golden Fleece with her magical assistance.[48] Medea typifies the woman who is married under the lay model, where she surrenders everything, abandons her family, bears children in a strange land, and restores the youth of Jason's aged father (head of the house). She is worse off, in fact, than under the lay model, because as a foreigner she has no legal protection or enforceable agreement and is powerless to prevent Jason from abandoning her in favor of a new love. The tone of the poem changes in the second stanza when the mask of classical allusion is dropped to bare (literally) the promiscuous behavior of the lover, and closes with a rebuke to Fortune, the personification of change and deception. The third stanza invokes examples of faithful lovers in order to set up the opposition of the lady's faithfulness and the lover's predatory behavior. The closing *envoie* summarizes the misery that can follow for a woman in courtly love when her lover betrays the ideal.

---

[47] See, for example, the discussion of the syncretism of courtly and religious devotion in Warner, *Alone of All Her Sex*, 134–48.

[48] Macaulay, *The English Works*, 2:35–62.

Ballade 49 is the first of the three ballades that summarize and close the collection. Love (*amour*) is introduced in the first stanza as a two-edged sword that must be guided by reason before it can be reckoned to be honorable. In the second stanza the definition of love moves to *bon amour,* identified with the Great Commandment spelt out by Jesus in response to the teacher of the Law, "Thou shalt love the Lord thy God with thy whole heart, and with thy whole soul, and with thy whole mind. This is the greatest and the first commandment. And the second is like to this: thou shalt love thy neighbor as thyself."[49] The point of surprise comes in line 10 where we are told that we should have not just these two, but three, great loves.

The third love is held over to next stanza, where it is revealed to be the living of an honest marriage. In my judgment, this definition of *trois amours* is the most forthright statement on human love in Gower's French and Latin writings. There is a less developed form of this idea in the three concluding ballades of *Traitié*, where in ballade XVI we are told that "en marriage est la perfeccioun; Guardent lour foi cils q'ont celle ordre pris" (in marriage lies perfection; let those who have taken this order hold to this faith). In ballade XVII we are told, against those who allow a third party into the relationship, "a un est une assetz en marriage" (in marriage, one is enough for one), and in ballade XVIII, against those who seek out lovers outside their marriage partner, "n'est pas amant qui son amour mesguie" (he isn't a lover who misdirects his love).

In the *Traitié* ballades there is a sense of anxiety about marriage, where Gower recalls the major negative examples of *CA*, and burdens the point by stressing what should *not* be done. By contrast, in this ballade in *CB*, anxiety has given way to a supreme confidence that the argument speaks for itself, with no explanation required. Here are implied the three finest points that underlie medieval marriage symbolism: that human nature has been redeemed by the incarnation of Christ; a faithful marriage is like the relationship of Christ with the church; and the ideal human marriage is like the indissoluble bond between the individual soul and God.[50]

We hear no more of the inferiority of woman or the superiority of religious vows, and the almost scholastic invocation in line 23 (*je vous ai dit la forme et la matiere*) is clearly a claim of moral authority by Gower, a layman, who has the audacity to place married love on a par with the command to love God and neighbour.

The model of courtly love presented in *CB* accepts emotional love as a transforming power, provided that it does not exceed the rule of reason. The conflict with the matter of male authority is solved neatly by the call to exercise

---

[49] Matthew 22:37–40, and retold with slight differences in Mark 12:28–34 and Luke 10:25–28.
[50] D'Avray, *Medieval Marriage*, 59–65.

droite courtasie toward all women, modelled on devotion to Mary, the Queen of Heaven. The fame of Mary, in medieval religious devotion, lies in her *fiat* (Luke 1:38) to the will of God who, within the limitation of language, is denoted as Father. This, in turn, takes devotion to Mary very close to a justification of the lay model, provided that the head of the house acts primarily for the welfare and happiness of his children. The presence of adultery within courtly love, whether associated with the lay model of marriage or as a reaction against it, is never raised as a possibility in *CB* and is condemned implicitly by the call for *vie honeste* under the rule of marriage.

In conclusion, Gower's love of words is evidenced by his mastery of French and Latin forms, and, most of all, by his "civilizing" of vernacular English as a medium capable of complex expression and, together with Chaucer, setting it into the direction that emerges several centuries later as Standard English. In the matter of words of love he redirects the conventions of *fin'amor* to a view of love that is honest and faithful, that rises above the materialism of the lay model of marriage and does not degenerate into clerical arguments concerning sexuality, consanguinity or gender rulership. Above all, he presents a vision where the love between a man and a woman is committed, emotionally fulfilling, and prefiguring of the indissoluble love of the Court of Heaven.

John Gower — Words of Love (a)

> Balade XXIIII Jeo quide qe ma dame de sa mein
> M'ad deinz le coer escript son propre noun;
> Car quant jeo puiss oïr le chapellein
> Sa letanie dire et sa leçoun,
> Jeo ne sai nomer autre, si le noun;
> Car j'ai le coer de fin amour si plein,
> Q'en lui gist toute ma devocioun:
> Dieus doignt qe jeo ne prie pas en vein!
>
> Pour penser les amours de temps longtein
> Com le priere de Pigmalion   10
> Faisoit miracle, et l'image au darrein
> De piere en char mua de s'oreisoun,
> J'ai graunt espoir de la comparisoun
> Qe par sovent prier serrai certein
> De grace ; et pour si noble reguerdoun
> Dieus doignt qe je ne prie pas en vein!
>
> Com cil qui songe et est en nouncertein,
> Ainz semble a lui qu'il vait tout environ
> Et fait et dit, ensi quant sui soulein,

A moi parlant jeo fais maint question, 20
Despute et puis responde a ma resoun,
Ne sai si jeo sui faie ou chose humein:
Tiel est d'amour ma contemplacion;
Dieus doignt qe je ne prie pas en vein!

A vous, qe m'avetz en subjeccion,
Soul apres dieu si m'estes soverein,
Envoie cette supplicacion:
Dieus doignt qe je ne prie pas en vein!

[I believe that my lady by her power has inscribed her own name in my heart; For when I am able to hear the chaplain reciting his litany and his lesson, I don't know any other name, save hers; Because my heart is so filled with pure love, in it lies all my devotion: God grant that I am not praying in vain!

Reflecting on the loves of times long gone, like the prayer of Pygmalion that caused a miracle, and the image at last changed from stone to flesh through his prayer, I have great hope from the comparison that through frequent prayer I shall be certain of grace; and for so noble a reward God grant that I am not praying in vain!

Like one who dreams and is uncertain, it seems to him that he roams all around speaking and telling, likewise when alone I put many a question to myself; "Can't" and "Can" reply to my thought, I don't know if I am bewitched or human: Such is my preoccupation with love; God grant that I am not praying in vain!

To you, for you hold me in subjection, You are my ruler save God alone, I send you this supplication: God grant that I am not praying in vain!]

John Gower — Words of Love (b)

Balade XLIII Plus tricherous qe Jason a Medée,
A Deianire ou q'Ercules estoit,
Plus q'Eneas, q'avoit Dido lessée,
Plus qe Theseüs, q'Ariagne amoit,
Ou Demophon, quant Phillis oubliot,
Je trieus, helas, q'amer jadis soloie:
Dont chanterai desore en mon endroit,
C'est ma dolour, qe fist ainçois ma joie.

Unqes Ector, q'ama Pantasilée,
En tiele haste a Troie ne s'armoit, 10
Qe tu tout nud n'es deinz le lit couché,

> Amis as toutes, quelqe venir doit,
> Ne poet chaloir, mais q'une femne y soit;
> Si es comun plus qe la halte voie.
> Helas, qe la fortune me deçoit,
> C'est ma dolour, qe fist ainçois ma joie.
>
> De Lancelot si fuissetz remembré,
> Et de Tristrans, com il se contenoit,
> Generides, Florent, Partonopé,
> Chascun de ceaux sa loialté guardoit. 20
> Mais tu, helas, q'est ceo qe te forsvoit
> De moi, q'a toi jammais null jour falsoie?
> Tu est a large et jeo sui en destroit,
> C'est ma dolour, qe fuist ainçois ma joie.
>
> Des toutz les mals tu q'es le plus maloit,
> Ceste compleignte a ton oraille envoie;
> Santé me laist et languor me reçoit,
> C'est ma dolour, qe fuist ainçois ma joie.

[More treacherous than Jason to Medea, or Hercules to Deianeira, more than Aeneas when he deserted Dido, more than Theseus whom Ariadne loved, or Demophon, when he forgot Phillis, I choose, alas, to love what once was: For my part, I shall sing from now on, "This is my sorrow, where once was my joy."

Never did Hector, loved by Penthesilea, arm himself with such haste at Troy, as when you, stark naked, leap into bed, lover to all, whoever may come, not caring, as long as it is a woman; You are more common than a tavern, alas, that Fortune deceived me, this is my sorrow, where once was my joy.

Of Lancelot, it was so remembered, and of Tristram, as it was told, Generides, Florent, Partonope, each of these guarded his integrity. But you, alas, why do you forsake *me*, I have never a day been false to *you*? You prowl at will, and so I am destroyed; this is my sorrow, where once was my joy.

Of all evils, you are by far the worst, I commit this complaint to your hearing; good health deserts me, sickness is my lot; this is my sorrow, where once was my joy.]

John Gower — Words of Love (c)

> Balade XLIX As bons est bon et a les mals malvois
> Amour, qui des natures est regent;
> Mais l'omme qui de reson ad le pois,
> Cil par reson doit amer bonement:

Car qui deinz soi sanz mal penser comprent
De bon amour la verité pleinere,
Lors est amour d'onour la droite miere.
Bon amour doit son dieu amer ainçois,
Qui son dieu aime il aime verraiment,
Si ad de trois amours le primer chois;   10
Et apres dieu il doit secondement
Amer son proesme a soi semblablement;
Car cil q'ensi voet guarder la maniere,
Lors est amour d'onour la droite miere.

Le tierce point dont amour ad la vois,
Amour en son endroit ceo nous aprent
Soubtz matrimoine de les seintes lois,
Par vie honeste et nonpas autrement.
En ces trois pointz gist tout l'experiment
De bon amour, et si j'ensi le quiere,   20
Lors est amour d'onour le droite miere.

De bon amour, pour prendre avisement,
Je vous ai dit la forme et la matiere;
Car quique voet amer honestement,
Lors est amour d'onour la droite miere.

[Love, the ruler of natures, is goodness to the good and evil to the wicked; but the man who has the weight of reason, through reason ought to love diligently: When a man within himself, without evil thought, understands good love as the fullness of truth, then love is the just mother of honor.

Good love ought first to love his God; who loves his God, loves truly, and has chosen the first of three loves; and secondly after God he ought to love his neighbour as himself; for one who so wishes to guard his way, then love is the just mother of honor.

The third point concerning love, love reveals to us in its own manner under the holy laws of marriage, in honest life and not otherwise. In these three points rest all the experience of good love, and so I thus seek it, then love is the just mother of honor.

Of good love, to take advice, I have told you the form and the matter; for whoever wishes to love honestly, then love is the just mother of honor.]

CHAPTER 21

HOW LOVE TOOK REASON TO COURT: DIEGO DE SAN PEDRO'S *PRISON OF LOVE*

SANDA MUNJIC
University of Toronto

Diego de San Pedro's *Cárcel de amor* (*Prison of Love*), written ca. 1482 and published in Seville in 1492,[1] acquired readership throughout western Europe in a number of translations.[2] It is considered the most accomplished example of sentimental fiction, a subgenre of Spanish literature with a distinctly medieval flavor that was cultivated approximately between 1440 and 1550.[3]

---

[1] Carmen Parrilla summarizes the textual history of *Cárcel de amor* in the introduction of her edition of the work (Barcelona: Crítica, 1995), LXXIV–LXXIX. For information on Diego de San Pedro, one can consult Keith Whinnom's introduction to his edition of San Pedro's *Obras completas* (Madrid: Clásicos Castalia, 1985), 1:9–34, and idem, *Diego de San Pedro* (New York: Twayne, 1974).

[2] *Cárcel de amor* was translated into Catalan (*Lo carcer de Amor* in1493, by Bernardí Vallmanyà); Italian (*Carcer d'amore* in 1515 by Lelio Manfredi of Ferrara); French (*Prison d'amour* in 1525, based on the Italian translation, by François d'Assy / d'Arcy); English (*The Castell of Love* ca. 1533, by John Bourchier, Lord Berners); see Joyce Boro, ed., The Castell of Love: A Critical Edition of Lord Berner's Translation (Tempe, AZ: Arizona Center for Medieval and Renaissance Studies, forthcoming); and German (*Gefängnüs der Lieb* in 1625 by Hans Ludwig von Kufstein). According to Whinnom, *Prison of Love* had some seventy editions in Spanish and in translations in the course of the sixteenth and seventeenth centuries (*Prison of Love*, Edinburgh University Press, 1979)l vii–xxxix; here vii–ix. Albrecht Classen identified three additional German editions of *Cárcel de amor* in the *VD 17* (German Books in Print from the Seventeenth Century; available online at www.vd17.de (last accessed on Jan. 10, 2006): according to his sources, Kufstein's translation quoted by Whinnom also exists in a fifth edition dated 1635. The other two German editions of *Cárcel de amor* that Classen identified are Diego Fernández de San Pedro, *Carcell De Amor. Oder / Gefängnüs der Lieb: Darinnen eingebracht wird die traurige und doch sehr schöne Historia / von einem Ritter / Genant Constante, Und der Königlichen Tochter Rigorosa* (Hamburg: Nauman, 1660 and 1675).

[3] I will provide Spanish quotes of the text from Carmen Parilla's edition of *Cárcel de amor*, and English versions from Keith Whinnom's translation, *Prison of Love*. Unless otherwise stated, all other translations are mine.

As the designation of the subgenre suggests, words of love through which the protagonists formulate their amorous feelings proliferate on the pages of sentimental fiction. Leriano, the protagonist of this romance, articulates his love for Laureola, the daughter of King Gaulo and the heiress to the throne of the fictional kingdom of Macedonia. The thematic and compositional parameters according to which Leriano professes his love highlight the fact that *Cárcel de amor* is steeped in the literary tradition of courtly love and in medical theories on erotomania. In addition, a series of debates practiced in the medieval universe — humanist and scholastic debates,[4] the practice of medieval university judicial disputes, and the subgenre of literary debates[5] — all merge in the complex rhetorical style of the *Prison of Love*.[6] Courtly love convention bequeathed to the Spanish sentimental fiction a treatment of love that Sarah Kay describes as "an art of literary composition as much as of emotion."[7] That is to say, a predominantly male-authored sentimental literature that explored through words of love the emotional capacity of the lover was a pretext for his demonstration of literary mastery, a love of words. A different kind of love of words, the one that scholastics manifested in their insistence on linguistic precision and systematic reliance on logical argumentation, was practiced as an essential method in all university training, and particularly so in jurisprudence.[8] The plot of *Cárcel de amor* advances through conflicting situations that need resolution through arguments often expressed

---

[4] Maureen Ihrie, "Discourses of Power in the *Cárcel de amor*," *Hispanofila* 125 (1999): 1–10, studies the plot of the romance as an example of the conflict between scholastics and humanists. She argues that characters in *Cárcel de amor* exemplify stereotypical representations of the advocates of the two pedagogical movements as described in Erika Rummel, *The Humanist-Scholastic Debate in the Renaissance and Reformation* (Cambridge, MA: Harvard University Press, 1995).

[5] Mercedes Roffé, *Cuestión del género en* Grisel y Mirabella *de Juan de Flores* (Newark, DE: Juan de la Cuesta, 1995) analyzes the influence of the university and literary traditions of debate in Flores's sentimental romance.

[6] The work consists of forty-nine segments: a prologue/dedication; eight letters; two cartels (letters of challenge and reply); a harangue; two mother's laments (*plancti*); two political discourses (one by the cardinal and another by the king); a series of monologues; and a debate on the vices and virtues of women that ends the romance.

[7] Sarah Kay speaks about Ovidian inheritance in medieval troubadour poetry, but her comment fits the writerly and psychological self-awareness of the authors of Spanish medieval sentimental fiction as well: "Courts, Clerks, and Courtly Love," *The Cambridge Companion to Medieval Romance*, ed. Roberta L. Krueger (Cambridge: Cambridge University Press, 2000), 81–96; here 87–88.

[8] In "Two Medieval Textbooks in Debate," James Murphy gives an example of a *controversia*, a popular debate format in medieval legal training: "The law required that children support their parents or be imprisoned. Two brothers disagreed. One had a son. His uncle fell on evil days, and in spite of his father's veto the boy supported him. For this reason he was disinherited, but did not protest. He was then adopted by the uncle, who inherited a fortune. The father then fell on evil days, and in spite of the uncle's veto the young man supported him. He was disinherited." The dilemmas to be resolved in *Cárcel de amor* correspond to the paradoxes set up in the cited debate piece. (James Murphy, *Latin Rhetoric and Education in the Middle Ages and Renaissance* [Burlington, VT: Ashgate Publishing Ltd., 2005], No. IV: 1–6; here 2).

in terms that proceed from medieval legal codes.[9] This demonstrates that the scholastic methods of debate and legal vocabulary left their mark on what could be termed the romance's ultimate "philo-logical" enterprise of playing with the meaning, and the persuasive power of words.[10] Hence Mercedes Roffé's observation regarding the representation of characters' speech and thought processes in Juan de Flores's sentimental romance *Grisel y Mirabella* is relevant to *Cárcel de amor* as well: "the characters [...] do not talk, they reason; they do not resolve nor decide, but determine; they do not confront doubts or problems, but *quaestiones* ("[l]os personajes [...] no hablan, *razonan*; no resuelven ni deciden, *determinan*; no enfrentan dudas ni preguntas — sino *questiones*" [*Cuestión del género*, 13]).[11]

In short, *Cárcel de amor* describes the destructive force of passions: to wit, Leriano's suffering in the allegorical prison of love, the uncontrollable alterations in Laureola's behavior, her eventual imprisonment and possible death sentence as the king attempts to follow the strict word of the law, the war that breaks out in the kingdom as Leriano rebels against the king in order to save Laureola's life, and Leriano's final death scene. All of these events unfold as Leriano, with the help of an intermediary called *El Auctor*, attempts to win from Laureola a *galardón*, a reward for his service of love. The storyline of Leriano's unrequited love for Laureola thus provides a sentimental narrative framework for what is the central element of the romance: the rhetorical function of language explored through a

---

[9] In this paper I am interested in how reason and passions play into the formulation of different rhetorical strategies, rather than in the use of specialized legal vocabulary in *Cárcel de amor*. A look at the legal vocabulary and codes informs Pilar Diez de Revenga Torres, "Literary Language and Legal Language: *La cárcel de amor*," *Revista de Investigación Lingüística* 3, 2 (2000): 185–87; and in part Laura Vivanco, "'Parece cuento de historias viejas': *Cárcel de amor* and the *Crónica del Rey don Pedro*," *Bulletin of Spanish Studies* LXXXI (2004): 157–73.

[10] Eugene Vinaver observes in the Arthurian romance the same influences and literary methods we recognize in the Spanish sentimental fiction: "Along with Abelard's device of *sic et non*, romance writers transferred into the secular sphere the scholastic *manifestatio* which helped to make the problem less soluble and the controversies more acute. [...] Courtly love in the twelfth century is primarily a matter of controversy, a rich source of dilemma which it is the poet's task to explore, to elucidate and to discuss often from two opposite points of view without necessarily committing himself to either": "Landmarks in Arthurian Romance," *The Expansion and Transformation of Courtly Literature*, ed. Nathaniel B. Smith and Joseph T. Snow (Athens: University of Georgia Press, 1980), 17–31; here 18.

[11] A number of scholars have contributed to the awareness of the importance of debates and juridical terminology in medieval literature. In addition to Mercedes Roffé, *Questión del género*, other works on the subject in Spanish literature are: José Luis Bermejo Cabrero, *Derecho y pensamiento politico en la literatura española* (Madrid: G. Feijoo, 1980); Ivy A. Corfis, "Judges and Laws of Justice in *Celestina*" (*Studies in Medieval Spanish Literature in Honor of Charles F. Fraker*, ed. Mercedes Vaquero and Alan Deyermond (Madison, WI: The Hispanic Seminary of Medieval Studies, 1995), 75–89; Lilian von der Walde Moheno, *Amor e ilegalidad: Grisel y Mirabella, de Juan de Flores*. Publicaciones Medievalia, 12: Serie Estudios de Lingüística y Literatura, 34 (México: UNAM, El Colegio de México, 1996); Diez de Revenga Torres, "Literary Language and Legal Language," and Vivanco, "'Parece cuento de historias viejas'."

series of debates, arguments, and deliberations.[12] The female protagonist of the romance, Laureola, is the organizing principle for discussions that examine the epistemological function of passions and of reason in medieval sentimental, medical, and judicial context. Leriano's wooing of Laureola, and *El Auctor*'s attempts to interpret Laureola's words and behavior on the basis of medical science, each examine the power of amorous and rational discourses in the sentimental field, while King Gaulo's "wooing" of justice in his attempt to uphold law and order contrasts the persuasive powers of rational and passionate discourses in the field of legal decision-making. Diego de San Pedro has the protagonists of each of these discursive formations see their greatest efforts defeated. Consequently, he suggests that neither the power of passion nor that of reason as respective conceptual pillars of two broadly formulated categories, passionate-sentimental and rational-scientific, can lead to knowledge or certainty.[13] He demonstrates additionally that, in effect, one cannot draw a line that separates passionate from rational motivations, or that distinguishes between emotional and rational decision-making. In that sense, *Cárcel de amor* exemplifies the ways in which love took reason to court — both by introducing rational consideration into a courtly love convention, and by judging the role of reason and of passions in causing social order and disorder.

The sentimental component of *Cárcel de amor* is based on dominant medieval amorous discourses.[14] These are the courtly love concept of a lover's unrequited love for an unresponsive and cruel lady, and medical discourse on love as sickness.[15] Leriano perishes in the allegorical prison of love, afflicted by the torments

---

[12] There are several studies on the uses of rhetoric in *Cárcel de amor*: Keith Whinnom, "Diego de San Pedro's Stylistic Reform," *Bulletin of Hispanic Studies* XXXVII (1960): 1–15; idem, ed., Diego de San Pedro, *Obras completas*, 2:44–66; Joseph Chorpenning, "Rhetoric and Feminism in the *Cárcel de amor*," *Bulletin of Hispanic Studies* 54 (1977): 1–8; Esther Tórrego, "Convención retórica y ficción narrativa en la *Cárcel de amor*," *Nueva revista de filología hispánica* XXXII (1983): 330–39; Ivy A. Corfis, "The *Dispositio* of Diego de San Pedro's *Cárcel de amor*," *Iberorromania* XXI (1985): 32–47; and Sol Miguel-Prendes, "Las cartas de la *Cárcel de amor*," *Hispanófila* 102 (1991): 1–22.

[13] Eukene Lacarra Lanz has addressed the question of scientific and amorous discourses in "Los discursos científico y amoroso en la *Sátira de felice e infelice vida* del Condestable D. Pedro de Portugal," *"Never-ending Adventure": Studies in Medieval and Early Modern Spanish Literature in Honor of Peter N. Dunn*, ed. Edward H. Friedman and Harlan Sturm. Homenajes, 19 (Newark, DE: Juan de la Cuesta, 2002), 109–28. Lacarra studies the tension produced in the *Sátira* by two coexisting discourses: the glosses as a historical or objective discourse, and the sentimental or subjective discourse of the love allegory. Similarly to what I argue in this paper, Lacarra suggests that "ambos discursos fallan porque no pueden superar la irracionalidad del amor" (109) ("both discourses fail because they cannot overcome the irrationality of love").

[14] Studies collected in *Discourses on Love, Marriage and Transgression*, ed. Albrecht Classen. Medieval and Renaissance Texts and Studies, 278 (Tempe, AZ: Arizona Center for Medieval and Renaissance Studies, 2004), deal, from numerous perspectives, with medieval notions of affectivity based on hermeneutic discourse.

[15] Mary F. Wack's study of Constantine the African's *Viaticum* in *Lovesickness in the Middle Ages: The Viaticum and its Commentaries* (Philadelphia: The University of Pennsylvania Press, 1990)

of lovesickness that was caused by the sight of Laureola's beauty. The allegorical prison is constituted of a number of what could be deemed early modern psychological functions that administer to Leriano his pains: the personified affliction, desire, memory, will, and so on.[16] He summons the character named *El Auctor* to help him be released from his torments by soliciting a letter from Laureola as a *galardón*, a reward for his service of love. In an effort to ascertain whether Laureola would be willing at all to requite Leriano's passions, *El Auctor* takes on the task of discovering the true nature of Laureola's sentiments. As a number of scholars have observed, even if Laureola has any feelings for Leriano, she is constrained by the strict social codes of honor from revealing them. *El Auctor* speaks repeatedly to Laureola of Leriano's passion for her, despite her prohibition to do so. Aware of the social constraints that may be the cause for Laureola's rejection of Leriano's pleas, *El Auctor* refuses to believe her words. An expert in love casuistry and an advocate of Leriano's cause, he wishfully surmises that Laureola loves Leriano, but plays the conventional role of a cruel and inaccessible lady. *El Auctor* therefore relies on his ability to read what he interprets as signs of love in Laureola's behavior:

> ... mirava en ella algunas cosas en que se conosce el coraçón enamorado: quando estava sola veía pensativa; quando estava aconpañada, no muy alegre; érale la conpañía aborrecible y la soledad agradable. Más vezes se quexava que estava mal por huir los plazeres; quando era vista, fengía algund dolor; quando la dexavan, dava grandes sospiros; si Leriano se nombrava en su presencia, desatinava lo que dezía, bolvíase súpito colorada y después amarilla, tornávase ronca su boz, secávasele la boca. (17)

> [I fancied that I observed in her certain signs by which the enamoured heart betrays itself: when she was alone, I found her pensive; when among company, none too merry; she abhorred society and found solitude agreeable; often she would complain that she was sick in order to flee the merry-making; when she was in the public eye she would feign that she suffered from some ache; when she was left to herself she would have great sighs; if Leriano was mentioned in her hearing, she would become distracted and talk beside the point, would turn suddenly red, and then pale, her voice would grow husky and her mouth became dry.] (16–17)

---

reviews the tradition of medical conceptualizations of extreme passion as illness. M. R. McVaugh's introductory study to his edition of *Arnaldi de Villanova Opera medica omnia* (Barcelona: Universitat de Barcelona, 1985) reviews the tradition of erotomania with a focus on the writings of Catalan physician Arnalt de Villanova.

[16] Cf. the contribution to this volume by Tracy Adam, and her observations regarding the function of allegorical personifications in the *Roman de la rose*.

In *El Auctor's* judgment, these alterations in Laureola's behavior belie her harsh words of rejection. At the root of *El Auctor's* preference for accepting physical manifestations in the heroine's behavior that strengthen his wishes as more telling than her words that discourage his wishes, is Ovidian teaching that recommends persistence to an ideal lover.[17] This playful principle has a potential of becoming violent as it gives license to a hopeful lover to impose relentlessly on a woman his expression of passion. The precept is exploited in courtly love tradition in different contexts, either as evidence of a lover's quality as a true lover, or as an indication of his inability to perform decorously in the art of courtly love play. The latter is the case with men who try to persuade women to reciprocate their love in Andreas Capellanus's *The Art of Courtly Love*, a work that, along with *Cárcel de amor*, mocks the persuasive power of a medieval lover's discourse.[18] Both works exemplify how the convention that urges a lover's persistence can turn into a practice that refuses to admit a lady's "no" for an answer. Such a crossing of the line from a skillful to a clueless performer in the art of love leads in *Cárcel de*

---

[17] In Book One of *The Art of Love*, Ovid recommends persistence to a lover:

Tempore difficiles ueniunt ad aratra iuuenci,
tempore lenta pati frena docentur equi.
Ferreus assiduo consumitur anulus usu,
interit assidua uomer aduncus humo.
Quid magis est saxo durum, quid mollius unda?
Dura tamen molli saxa cauantur aqua.
Penelopen ipsam, persta modo, tempore uinces:
capta uides sero Pergama, capta tamen.
(*Artis Amatoriae Libri*, ed. Antonio Ramírez de Verger [Madrid: CSIC, 1995], ll. 471–78.

[Time brings obdurate ox to submit to the yoke and the ploughshare,
Time brings the fieriest steed under the bridle and rein.
Even an iron ring is worn by continual usage,
Even the hardest ground crumbles at last from the plough.
What is harder than rock, or what more gentle than water?
Yet the water in time hollows the rigidest stone.
Only persist: you can have more luck than Penelope's suitors.
Though it took a long time, Troy came tumbling down.]

(*The Art of Love*, trans. Rolfe Humphries [Bloomington: Indiana University Press, 1957], 119)

[18] On Andreas Capellanus's *De amore*, see the contribution to this volume by Bonnie Wheeler, as well as Peter Allen's analysis of Capellanus's uses of rhetoric and persuasion in *The Art of Love: Amatory Fiction from Ovid to the Romance of the Rose*. Middle Ages Series (Philadelphia: The University of Pennsylvania Press, 1992), 59–78. See also Catherine Brown, *Contrary Things: Exegesis, Dialectic, and the Poetics of Didacticism* (Stanford: Stanford University Press, 1998); Kathleen Andersen-Wyman, *Andreas Capellanus on Love? Desire, Seduction and Subversion in a Twelfth-Century Latin Text*. Studies in Arthurian and Courtly Cultures (New York and Houndmills, Basingstoke: Palgrave Mcmillan. *The New Middle Ages*, 2007). See also Albrecht Classen's introduction to the present volume, 11–12; and his extensive study of the communicative approach in Andreas's treatise in idem, *Verzweiflung und Hoffnung: Die Suche nach der kommunikativen Gemeinschaft in der deutschen Literatur des Mittelalters*. Beihefte zur Mediaevistik, 1 (Franfurt a. M., Berlin, et al.: Peter Lang, 2002), 53–107.

amor to a series of elaborate negotiations among Leriano, *El Auctor*, and Laureola, until Laureola is convinced to send a letter to Leriano in order to alleviate his love pains. As Laureola hands over her first letter for Leriano, *El Auctor* again comments on her behavior:

> Quienquiera que la oyera pudiera conocer que aquel estudio avié usado poco; ya de enpachada estava encendida; ya de turbada se tornava amarilla; tenía tal alteración y tan sin aliento la habla como si esperara sentencia de muerte; en tal manera le tenblava la voz, que no podía forçar con la discreción al miedo. (27)

> [Anyone who heard her would have recognized that she was quite unstudied in such matters. At one moment her embarrassment made her flush; at the next her perturbation made her pale. She was as distressed and breathless in her speech as though she had been awaiting sentence of death. Her voice trembled so violently that her natural good sense could not overcome her fear.]

In both descriptions of Laureola's distress *El Auctor* points out the change of color between red and pale in her face, change in breathing, and difficulty in speech, all delineated as physical symptoms of lovesickness in medieval medical and fictional texts.[19] *El Auctor* puts his faith in medical science as a tool to help him "read" Laureola. In the first analysis he claims that physical changes he observes in her behavior are "cosas en que se conosce el coraçón enamorado" (17), "signs by which the enamoured heart betrays itself" (16), while in the second instance he explains that Laureola cannot dissimulate her physically manifested passion because she is a novice in the art of love. However, at the end of each description, *El Auctor* grants that those symptoms in her behavior that he wishfully interprets as signifying love could actually connote different passions. Thus he ends the first description by conceding to a possibility that Laureola's behavior was a manifestation of compassion, "por mucho que encobría sus mudanças, forçavala

---

[19] We can compare what *El Auctor* identifies as symptoms of love in Laureola's behavior with Bernardo de Gordonio's description of erotomanic symptoms in male lovers: "Son: que pierde el sueño e el comer e el beuer e se enmagresce todo su cuerpo, saluo los ojos; e tienen pensamientos escondidos e fondos, con suspiros llorosos; e sy oyen cantares de apartamiento de amores, luego comiençan a llorar e se entristeçer; e sy oyen de ayuntamiento de amores, luego comiençan a reyr e a cantar; e el pulso dellos es diuerso e non ordenado, pero es veloz e frequentido e alto sy la muger que ama viniere a el o la nombraren o passare delante del": *Lilio de medicina*, ed. Brian Dutton y Mª. Nieves Sánchez (Madrid: Arco Libros, 1993), 522–23: "These [symptoms] are loss of sleep, appetite and thirst, and the body becomes emaciated, save the eyes. They have deep and dark thoughts with tearful sighs. If they hear songs of lovers' separation, they then begin to cry and become saddened, and if they hear songs of lovers uniting they then begin to laugh and to sing. Their pulse is irregular and disorderly, but it becomes rapid, frequent and high if the woman he loves were to approach him, or if her name were to be mentioned, or if she were to appear in his presence."

la passion piadosa a la disimulación discreta" (17), "though she endeavoured to conceal these signs of emotion, her feelings of compassion overcame her discreet dissimulation" (17). In the second instance, *El Auctor* recognizes that her alterations might be caused by fear, because she reacts "como si esperara sentencia de muerte" (27), "as though she had been awaiting sentence of death" (27). This remark will acquire an ironic note in retrospect, for Laureola will indeed be faced with death as a consequence of events that unfold after she has written a letter to Leriano.

The failure of medical discourse in diagnosis or management of passions is accompanied by a failure of the lover's discourse to win a lady's favor. Through the person of *El Auctor*, Leriano sends letters to Laureola in which he tries to persuade her to requite his love with *galardón*. In the second of four letters that Leriano sends to Laureola, he advises her that, since he has not received any encouragement from her, he is about to die due to his unrequited passion:

> No pudiera pensar que a tal cosa dieras lugar si tus obras no me lo certificaran. Sienpre creí que forçara tu condición piadosa a tu voluntad porfiada, comoquiera que en esto mi vida recibe el daño, mi dicha tiene la culpa. Espantado estó cómo de ti misma no te dueles; dite la libertad, ofrecíte el coraçón, no quise ser nada mío por sello del todo tuyo, pues ¿cómo te querrá servir ni tener amor quien sopiere que tus propias cosas destruyes? Por cierto tú eres tu enemiga; si no me queries remediar porque me salvara yo, deviéraslo hazer porque no te condenaras tú; porque en mi perdición oviese algund bien, deseo que te pese della; mas si el pesar te avié de dar pena, no lo quiero, que pues nunca biviendo te hize servicio, no sería justo que moriendo te causase enojo. Los que ponen los ojos en el sol, quanto más lo miran más se ciegan; y assí quanto yo más contemplo tu hermosura más ciego tengo el sentido; esto digo porque de los desconciertos escritos no te maravilles; verdad es que a tal tienpo, escusado era tal descargo, porque segund quedo, más estó en disposición de acabar la vida que de desculpar las razones. Pero quisiera que lo que tú avías e ver fuera ordenado, porque no ocuparas tu saber en cosa tan fuera de su condición [...]. (25–26)

> [I could never have believed that you would have allowed this to come to pass, had your actions not convinced me. I always believed that your compassionate nature would overcome your obstinate will, even though in this, if it is my life which must be forfeit, it is my luck which must take the blame.

> I am amazed that you have so little pity for yourself: I gave you my freedom, I offered you my heart, I wanted to be in nothing mine so that I might be wholly yours; and now, how can anyone wish to serve you or love you who knows that you destroy what belongs to you? Assuredly, it is you who are your own enemy. If you had no wish to grant me relief, so that I might be

saved, you should have done it for your own sake, so that you should not stand condemned. So that some good may come from my destruction, I wish that it might cause you to repent, and yet, if repentance should cause you pain, I would not have it so, for since in life I never did you any service, it would be wrong if in death I should cause you displeasure. He that gazes upon the sun shall at last be blind, and so it is that the longer I have contemplated your beauty, the blinder has my understanding become. I say this so that you shall not wonder at any foolishness I may have written. It is true that at a time such as this, it is superfluous to offer such an excuse, for I am now left in such a state that I am more disposed to make an end of my life than to offer excuses for what I say. Nevertheless, I wish that what you are to read were more coherent, so that you should not exert your wits on a task so foreign to their nature.] (25)

This rather long quote exemplifies the kind of reasoning that pervades Leriano's amorous discourse presented to Laureola. Of course, it is not out of place to wonder what place should reasoning have in what are Leriano's "words of love," nor whether these words indeed come across as loving. Leriano's communication proceeds through subtle stages of accusing Laureola for his suffering and presenting himself as a victim of her dispassion: he calls her "porfiada," "obstinate," but then blames his own luck for his misfortune, a strategy through which he rhetorically redirects the blame from Laureola's lack of compassion to his own destiny. The rhetorical softening of the initial accusation may serve as an excuse for the speaker, but does not lift the weight of responsibility already impressed upon the accused. Leriano then presents himself as disempowered and generous by claiming that he gave his freedom, his heart, and his entire self to Laureola. His words veil the fact that he might have rewarded Laureola with gifts she never wanted. Leriano attempts to convince Laureola that it is to her own benefit that she reciprocate his love — a proposal resting on an unusual premise that love can be negotiated as a matter of interest. More specifically, Leriano suggests that by reciprocating his love, Laureola would avoid condemnation, and not avert others from loving her — a strange clause if his love for Laureola is supposed to be a secret affair, and if a lover is unlikely to advertise his own competition. Leriano furthermore desires that Laureola would repent so that his own destruction may bear some good. He immediately takes these words back by claiming that he does not wish her repentance if it consists of pain, for once he is dead he does not want to cause her displeasure if, while alive, he never did her service. This rationale progresses through the stages of self-interest (the lover wishes his death to be purposeful) and self-victimization (he doesn't wish his death to be purposeful if that would cause pain to Laureola), to a concealed desire to punish the unresponsive lady (he actually does want her to be in pain, or else he wouldn't be writing her a letter replete with accusations). At the end, Leriano puts in question the validity of his entire discourse. He claims that his understanding is debilitated by the sight of Laureola's beauty, and excuses himself for the senselessness of what he wrote, in order to then invalidate the apology as hardly necessary in what he describes as his "near-death" condition.

Leriano praises Laureola's beauty; he condemns her disposition; he blames her for his suffering, and attempts to persuade her to carry out actions that, in his judgment, would signify an improvement in her disposition, and alleviate the suffering caused to him by her beauty. The finer points of this thought process are plagued with inconsistencies that undermine its external logic. Leriano's letter demonstrates that reasoning is ineffective in the sentimental field, not only because his "blinded understanding" under the force of passion might not allow him to produce sound arguments. More to the point, it is ineffective because he suffuses the art of emotional persuasion with that of logical argumentation and debate. As a matter of fact, Leriano's persuasive strategy amounts to little other than a rhetorical exercise of power. It is therefore not surprising that his letter does not win him Laureola's reciprocate love, but only an outward gesture, her letter, aimed at appeasing his insistence rather than at requiting his passions.[20] This partial success of Leriano's rhetorical strategy in the sentimental field of action will have disastrous effects in the political realm: it will result in Laureola's defamation, her eventual imprisonment and death sentence according to the laws of the kingdom, as well as in Leriano's armed rebellion against the king.

Having undermined the ability of reason to yield appropriate results outside of its jurisdiction, that is, in the realm of passions, San Pedro proceeds to destabilize faith in the ability of reason to function effectively in its proper field, that of legal reasoning. When Persio, Leriano's jealous rival, falsely accuses Laureola to her father the king for ruining his honor, the king, the text reports, "turbado [el rey] de cosa tal, estovo dubdoso y pensativo sin luego determinarse a responder,

---

[20] There are as many similarities as there are differences between Diego de San Pedro's *Cárcel de amor* and Geoffrey Chaucer's *Troilus and Criseyde*. Leriano's sympathetic mediator *El Auctor* is reminiscent of Pandarus's role of a go-between for Troilus and Criseyde. Laureola's letter to Leriano serves the same purpose as Criseyde's letters to Troilus. Rather than express reciprocity of passions, these letters are designed to placate the insistence of the lovers. However, the two authors take very different approaches to courtly love convention. While Chaucer engrosses the reader in the emotional upheaval of the characters, San Pedro problematizes the convention by exposing the manipulations of power that underlie courtly love amorous rhetoric. For Chaucer's *Troilus and Criseyde*, see *The Riverside Chaucer*, ed. Larry D. Benson. 3rd ed. (1987; Oxford: Oxford University Press, 1988). There are certain similarities between Diego de San Pedro's *Cárcel de amor* and Geoffrey Chaucer's *Troilus and Criseyde*. Leriano's sympathetic mediator *El Auctor* in Diego de San Pedro's romance is reminiscent of Pandarus's role of a go-between for Troilus and Criseyde. Laureola's letter to Leriano serves the same purpose as Criseyde's letters to Troilus. Rather than express reciprocity of passions, these letters are designed to placate the insistence of the lovers. However, the two authors take very different approaches to courtly love convention. While Chaucer engrosses the reader in the emotional upheaval of the characters, San Pedro problematizes the convention by exposing the manipulations of power that underlie courtly love amorous rhetoric.

y después que mucho durmió sobre ello, tóvolo por verdad, creyendo segund la virtud y auctoridad de Persio que no le diría otra cosa" (31), "greatly perturbed at such news, was perplexed and pensive, and could not bring himself to make reply. But after he had slept long on the matter, he accepted it as the truth, believing, in view of Persio's nobility and authority, that he would not tell him other than the truth" (31). At this point, the sentimental romance becomes the territory for judicial debate exploring the role of reason, passions, divine law, human testimony, and counsel in the process of delivering justice. This takes place as King Gaulo negotiates the ground between passions and logical argumentation as two possible foundations for determining political and legal resolutions.

As seen in the previous quote, the narrator takes care to demonstrate that the king exercises caution in bringing judgment in the accusation of his daughter. After a judicial ordeal by duel in which Leriano cuts off Persio's right hand, thus providing divine evidence of Persio's guilt and proof of Laureola's and his own innocence, at the intervention of Persio's relatives the king interrupts the duel and spares his life. The king was about to release his daughter from the prison on the basis of the evidence of judicial duel, "a Laureola dava por libre segund lo que vido" (37), "on the evidence of his own eyes, he held Laureola free of blame" (36). However, the king's intentions are cut short when Persio bribes three men to testify before him that Laureola had been meeting with Leriano at night. The king "hizo a cada uno por sí preguntas muy agudas y sotiles para ver si los hallaría mudables o desatinados en lo que respondiesen; [. . .] [pero] quanto más hablavan mejor sabián concertar su mentira, de manera que el rey les dio entera fe" (37–38), "interrogated each one separately, asking acute and subtle questions to see if he could catch them changing their evidence or becoming confused in their answers. But since they must have spent their lives in the study of lying, the more they talked the closer they contrived to make their lies agree, so that the king was completely convinced" (37). Under the force of this overwhelming testimony against Laureola, the king reverses his decision, and again sentences his daughter to death.

In order to save Laureola's life, *El Auctor* proposes a persuasive strategy to Leriano instead of an open rebellion against the king. He introduces the advice by an explicit consideration of the choice of action based either on reason or on emotions: "como viste tu juizio enbargado de passion, conociste que sería lo que obrases no segund lo que sabes, mas segund lo que sientes; y con este discreto conocimiento quesiste antes errar por mi consejo sinple y libre que acertar por el tuyo natural y enpedido" (38), "when you perceived that your wits were paralysed by passion, you realized that your actions would be governed not by what you know but by what you feel. Sensibly acknowledging this fact, you chose to err by acting upon my simple but unprejudiced advice rather than to do [. . .] right by relying on your own judgment, spontaneous but hampered by emotion" (38).[21] While *El Auctor* commends Leriano for not taking action influenced by feelings, he concludes with a surprising conceit: it is better to make mistakes under the guidance of reason than to act correctly steered by emotions. While this paradoxical pronouncement confirms the primacy of rational over emotional decision-making in principle, it undermines the privileged status of reason as a decision-making instrument that leads to appropriate actions.

El Auctor then summons one by one the Cardinal, Laureola's mother the queen, and finally Laureola herself to try to persuade the king to spare his daughter's life. Just as *El Auctor* advocates the reliance on reason to Leriano, the Cardinal stresses to the king that he should seek advice from his counselors to avoid acting passionately, because "mejor aciertan los honbres en las cosas agenas que en las suyas propias, porque el coraçón de cuyo es el caso no puede estar sin ira o cobdiçia o afición o deseo . . ." (44), ". . . men are better judges of other men's affairs then of their own, for the man who is involved in the affair cannot have a heart free from anger or covetousness or affection or desire . . ." (44). The king replies to the Cardinal that his remarks are superfluous, for

> [. . .] quando el coraçón está enbargado de pasión [. . .] están cerrados los oídos al consejo, y en tal tiempo las frutuosas palabras en lugar de amansar acrecientan la saña, porque reverdecen en la memoria la causa della; pero digo que estuviese libre de tal enpedimento, yo creería que dispongo y ordeno sabiamente la muerte de Laureola, lo qual quiero mostraros por causas justas, determinadas segund onrra y justicia. (46)

> [(. . .) when the heart is possessed by passion, then are the ears stopped against counsel, and at such a time fruitful advice, instead of assuaging, increases rage, for it revives in the memory the cause of that anger. But even if I were free of that impediment, I should still believe that I am acting and deciding wisely in the matter of Laureola's death. And this I shall show by logical argument, determined by considerations of honour and justice.] (46)

The king proceeds by explaining that if he were to fail to punish his daughter for causing him dishonor, he would become responsible for dishonoring himself and his entire lineage, and would risk being despised and disobeyed by his subjects and held in contempt by all. Within the honor-based value system of his society, the king's arguments appear logically sound in considering the possible

---

21 I modify Whinnom's translation by removing "what you thought." In my view, this insertion softens the paradox presented in the Spanish original, and is not warranted by San Pedro's text. The following is Whinnom's unmodified translation: "Sensibly acknowledging this fact, you chose to err by acting upon my simple but unprejudiced advice rather than to do *what you thought* right by relying on your own judgment, spontaneous but hampered by emotion" (38, emphasis added).

consequences of disregarding the laws. However, the king's confession of the fact that he is under the influence of passions — "quando el coraçón está embargado de pasión [...] están cerrados los oídos al consejo," "when the heart is possessed by passion, then are the ears stopped against counsel" — problematizes the nature of his motivations. Although his arguments suggest that his decision is based on objective considerations of the law, the king's confession of his anger directed at Laureola and Leriano casts a shadow over his claims to impartiality. Consequently, while *El Auctor* puts in doubt the superiority of rational over emotional deliberation, the king questions the very possibility of distinguishing or separating the two processes.

Ironically, while suggesting that the king should be dispassionate and rely on reason in making his decision, the Cardinal, the queen, and Laureola herself appeal primarily to the king's passions in order to sway his decision. They ask him to consider that Laureola is his daughter, and that his subjects will neither respect nor honor him for being just, but will loathe him for being cruel if he carries out her death sentence. The queen tries to persuade her husband by speaking to him "palabras assí sabias para culpalle como piadosas para amansallo" (48), "wise words to show that he was at fault, and loving words to move him to pity" (48), a rhetorical strategy that fails to substitute for the king's demand for legal evidence. Equally unsuccessful, Laureola pleads to her father in the same manner in which Leriano implored her, suggesting self-interest: "tan convenible te es la piedad de padre como el rigor de justo" (51), "it is as meet that you should show a father's compassion as a law-giver's rigour" (52). Since all the persuasive strategies eventually fail, *El Auctor* encourages Leriano to carry out his original military plan. Through armed rebellion, Leriano eventually saves Laureola from the prison. His men capture one of the false witnesses who, under the threat of torture, confesses to perjury. With this evidence of Laureola's innocence, the king forgives his daughter and accepts her at the court with tears and apologies.

In *Cárcel de amor*, characters' desires, intentions, and personal and public interests are staked against one another in a complex web of clashing social relations, obligations, and implicit and explicit laws. The romance is woven rhetorically into a net of deliberations and arguments that ceaselessly consider the conflicting reasons and often bring the narrative thread to a standstill.[22] Illustrative of the rhetorical style of *Prison of Love* is *El Auctor*'s deliberating at the beginning of the work. When he encounters Leriano led in chains by a wild man, a medieval

---

[22] Peter Dunn effectively describes this quality of *Cárcel de amor*: "... the thematic structure is kept constant as a complex interplay of tensions. [...] These oppositions are sustained on the verbal level by a predominantly antithetical style, and in the temporal sequence they generate a succession of dilemmas. The plot — that is to say, the form in which the action is perceived — is a process of one stark either/or situation leading inexorably to the next": "Narrator as Character in the *Cárcel de amor*," *Modern Language Notes* 94 (1979): 187–99; here 191.

symbol of desire, he considers whether he should follow him: "dexar el camino que levava parecíame desvarío; no hazer el ruego de aquel que assí padecía figurávaseme inhumanidad; en siguille havía peligro y en dexalle flaqueza; con la turbación no sabía escoger lo mejor" (5), ". . . to leave the path I was following seemed to be folly, not to respond to the plea of one who suffered so appeared to be inhuman cruelty; to follow him was perilous, and to abandon him was cowardly; and in my confusion I could not decide which was the better course to choose" (5).

The characters' continuous efforts to assess situations and actions, as well as the underlying causes and reasons for the situations presented or actions considered, turn *Cárcel de amor* into a virtual linguistic maze of ambiguous statements, contradictory reasons, and paradoxical outcomes. Cruelty vs. compassion, concern for the other's misfortune vs. matters of self-interest, are the motifs that are repeated in variations throughout the text. The king has to consider being impartially just by sentencing his daughter to death but risk the label of cruelty, or he can be compassionate but break the letter of the law and thus risk dishonoring himself and undermining his authority. Diego de San Pedro takes care to demonstrate that compassion does not provide an ideal alternative to strict adherence to the letter of the law. When King Gaulo acts compassionately and spares Persio's life in the judicial duel, he provides the ground for Persio's further slander against his innocent daughter. Similarly, when Laureola shows compassion toward Leriano she risks dishonoring herself and her family, as well as jeopardizing her own life. Paradoxically, Laureola's withdrawal of compassion leads to Leriano's to death, but saves her own reputation and life.[23] While *El Auctor* advises other characters on how to act in accordance with reason, he forgoes his own advice. Blinded by sentimental preference that Laureola might be in love with Leriano, he engages in mediation between Leriano and Laureola that unfolds in a series of disastrous events. *El Auctor*'s efforts to resolve the conflicting situations through logical persuasion fail: Laureola is ultimately liberated through the use of force, and Leriano eventually dies of lovesickness. Hence, whether the characters attempt to be rational or (com)passionate, their decisions result in actions that, ironically, defy their ostensible intentions.

The sentimental context and the rhetorical method thus brought together in the fictional space of *Prison of Love* serve to evaluate and to contrast the functioning and the effectiveness of passions and of reason in amorous, medical, and judicial settings. By demonstrating passion's resistance to medical rationalization, and the futility of logic as a tool in verbal formulation of the workings of

---

[23] What I study as a question of rhetorical dilemmas and paradoxes, Dorothy Sherman Severin has addressed as an issue of the romance's structure and theme: "Structural and Thematic Repetitions in Diego de San Pedro's *Cárcel de Amor* and *Arnalte y Lucenda*," *Hispanic Review* 45 (1977): 165–69.

passion, San Pedro problematizes the ability of science and of reason to manage passions. In *Cárcel de amor*, fear and compassion, much like love, are emotions that share similar physical manifestations, which become interchangeable and hence equivocal symptoms of effective medical diagnostics of passions. Used as elements in the lover's persuasive strategy, these emotions fail to win a reward for Leriano's service of love. By having the enamored protagonist die due to the symptoms of unrequited love, San Pedro shows the futility of the persuasive power of amorous discourse to win a reward for a persistent courtly lover. Finally, the king's inability to enforce law and order through rational consideration, as well as his more fundamental difficulty in separating passionate from rational motivation, demonstrates the permeability of the two systems, that of passion and that of reason. The difficult interdependency of reason and passions that underlies sentimental, scientific, and legal discourses woven together into a precarious texture of the medieval social universe roughly amounts, in my analysis, to what Marina Scordilis Brownlee described, in referring to the language of *Cárcel de amor*, as a "system of bankruptcy of discursive generic traditions of the Middle Ages" (172).[24]

I would, however, broaden Scordilis Brownlee's use of the term "generic" to include non-fictional along with the fictional discourses, and consequently to refer beyond the literary to a wider ideological context of Spanish medieval society. That society cultivated with comparable devotion a variety of discourses that coexisted within a tensed reality of contradictions. These were: expressions of love in secular and religious contexts; practice of persuasion in amorous-literary and in rational-scholastic writings; simultaneous idealization and vituperation of women; literary fantasies of secret, adulterous relationships in a society overtly guided by strict codes of honor and by religious teaching that confined sexuality to a reproductive function within the legal space of marriage. These very real paradoxes of the medieval world are the ideological background for the conflicting discourses that constitute the characters' persuasive efforts in *Cárcel de amor*.

Different persuasive strategies, even though failing to influence the characters within the framework of the text, have often solicited an active involvement

---

[24] The very title of Marina Scordilis Brownlees's study of sentimental fiction, *The Severed Word* (Princeton: Princeton University Press, 1990), bears witness to the centrality, as well as to the ambiguity, of language in the plot of the sentimental romance. Departing from the principles of John Searle's speech act theory that "focuses on language as performance [...] by identifying the so-called 'cooperative principle' of a given speech situation" (162), Scordilis Brownlee interprets *Cárcel de amor* as a series of speech act situations that violate such "cooperative principles." Due to the breach of cooperative principle in each speech situation, Scordilis Brownlee maintains that the characters are unable to establish communication. As a result, the critic argues, "[n]ot Leriano, nor Laureola, nor San Pedro the inscribed narrator — only San Pedro the author figure — is left totally fulfilled in his exemplary metalinguistic act. Starting from the perspective of a negative generic *summa*, San Pedro paradoxically makes poetic capital from the very system of bankruptcy of discursive generic traditions of the Middle Ages" (172).

of its readers. A case in point is that of Nicolás Núñez who wrote a continuation to *Cárcel de amor*, published in Burgos in 1496. In his version of the story, Núñez clarified one of the romance's ambiguities — the playfully concealed true nature of Laureola's feelings for Leriano. Núñez resolved the desiring that propels the action of *Cárcel de amor* into a kind of happy ending by establishing that Laureola indeed loved Leriano. His postscript exemplifies how Diego de San Pedro has successfully engaged his readers in the debates that take place in the romance.

The text involves the avid reader in the assessment of the characters' emotions, motivations, and reasons. Thus the readers themselves take on the usually perceived roles of *El Auctor* — the interpreter, author, and mediator — of the king — the cruel judge — of Leriano — the suffering lover — and of Laureola, the unwilling object of desire. As is evident in scholarly interpretations, the common (although not unanimous) reaction of San Pedro's readers was to re-evaluate Laureola's emotions, to reject the persuasiveness of the king's judicial discourse based on reason, and to succumb to the power of pathos contained in Leriano's amorous plaints. The censure of Laureola for her unresponsiveness to Leriano, the exaltation of Leriano as an ideal lover, and the condemnation of the king for his cruelty demonstrate that the persuasive strategy of Leriano's amorous discourse has been far more effective than any of the persuasive strategies used by the king in an attempt to respect justice, or by Laureola in order to protect her honor, let alone her right to feel what she may. As an experiment in persuasive strategies, *Cárcel de amor* has demonstrated, then and now, the enduring powers of the words of love to take reason to court.

INDEX

Abelard, Peter, 5, 8, 31, 130, 134–48, 434
Aelred, 122
Agravain, 423
Alan of Lille, 24
Albrecht von Johansdorf, 326
Alexander III, Pope, 252
Alexander the Great, 441
Alexander, Der Wilde, 44, 364–67
Alfonso X, King, 6, 29, 43–44, 349–58
Andreas Capellanus, 7–8, 14–15, 32–33, 36, 49, 122, 149–68, 196, 262, 272, 397–98, 428, 466
Angela da Foligno, 33, 169, 172, 175–76, 178–80, 182–83, 189
Anselm of Canterbury, St., 4–5, 122
Apollonius of Tyre, 39, 307–8
Apollonius, 59–60
Aquinas, Thomas, 5
Aristotle, 441, 443
Arnaldo da Foligno, 172, 176–77
Arnaut de Maruelh, 171, 181–82, 184, 189
Arunculeia, Vibia, 59
Asclepius, 27
Aucassin et Nicolette, 39, 309–10
Auchinleck manuscript, 312
Augustine, St., 4, 91–93, 122, 319, 449
Ausonius, 81
Barlaam and Josaphat, 325
Baudouin of Hainault, 257–58
Beatrice of Burgundy, 257–58
Bel Inconnu, Le, 38, 294–95, 311

Benedict of Nursia, 133
Bernard of Clairvaux, 42–43, 129–30, 133, 144, 151, 168
Bernardus Silvestris, 27, 115
Bernart de Ventadorn, 33, 170–71, 182, 193–94
Béroul, 423
Bertram of Bordeau, 89
Blanche of Lancaster, 448
Boccaccio, 25, 27
Boethius, 26–27
Boeve de Haumtone, 309
Cattleraid of Froech, Táin bó Fraích, 99
Catullus, 57–59, 61
Charibert, 90
Charles the Bald, 85
Chartier, Alain, 435
Chaucer, Geoffrey, 3, 9, 27, 30, 34, 46–47, 50, 395, 399–408, 419, 445, 448, 457
Childebert, 85
Chilperic, 82, 89–90
Chrétien de Troyes, 23, 36, 42, 104, 106–7, 120, 192, 196, 258, 260–61, 269, 271–73, 329, 422, 434–35
Christine de Pizan, 422, 435
Chrysostom, John, 57
Cicero, 222, 226
Constance of Castile, 448
Cormac Uí, 105
Cormac's Glossary, 105
Daniel, Book of, 439
Daniel, Arnaut, 169–70

Dante Alighieri, 2–3, 9, 11–12, 24, 26, 33, 43, 371, 388
Daurel et Beton, 296
David, King, 291, 303
Deschamps, Eustache, 435
Diego de San Pedro, 49–50, 462–76
Dietmar von Eist, 326
Eckhart, Meister, 15–16
Edward III, King, 448
Eger and Grime, 316
Eleanore of Aquitaine, 112
Engeltaler Schwesternbuch, 326
epithalamium, 54–75
Eriugena, Scotus, 27
Exile of the Sons of Uisnech, 101
Fortunatus, Venantius, 28–29, 69, 75–93
Frauenlob, 363–64
Fredegund, 82
Freidank, 323
Freud, Sigmund, 159
Fulgentius, 115
Gaimar, 224
Galeran de Bretagne, 38–39, 297–300
Galswinth, 82
Gaucelm Faidit, 33, 170
Gautier d'Arras, 36–37, 255–73
Geoffrey of Monmouth, 224
Gerson, Jean, 388, 435
Goscelin, 122
Gottfried von Strassburg, 6, 31, 37–40, 275–89, 302–7, 319, 332–33, 336, 397
Gottfried von Neifen, 44, 367–71
Gower, John, 49, 114, 398, 419, 439–60
Gratian, 152
Gregory the Great, 133
Gregory of Tours, Bishop, 81–82, 89
Groundolf, Agnes, 445
Guibert of Nogent, 387
Guillaume de Lorris, 45–46, 379–86
Guillaume IX d'Aquitaine, 34, 123, 193–202, 212

Hadewijch, 44
Hadlaub, Johannes, 363
Hartmann von Aue, 23, 40–41, 319–20, 326, 329–32
Heilige Georg, Der, 326
Heinrich der Teichner, 363
Heinrich von Veldeke, 114, 118, 326–27
Heliand, 2
Heloise, 31, 37, 129–48, 434
Henry of Lancaster, 444
Henry the Liberal, 258
Hildegard of Bingen, 20, 23, 139
Horace, 77
Hrabanus Maurus (also Rhabanus), 1–2, 275
Hugh of St. Victor, 10, 26, 131
Hugo von Montfort, 363
Hugo von Trimberg, 44, 375–76
Humbert of Rome, 15
Ibn Hazm, 397
Ile d'Or, 311
Instructions of Cormac, 105–06
Isidore of Seville, 275, 319
Ivo of Chartres, 152
Jacopone da Todi, 33, 169–70, 176, 178
Jean d'Arras, 47–49, 422, 435
Jean de Berry, 435
Jean de Meun, 11–14, 27, 45, 50, 263, 380, 386–93, 423, 446
Jerome, St., 449
John, St., 11
John of Gaunt, 448
John of Parma, 390
John of Salisbury, 222
Juan de Flores, 463
Kempe, Margery, 19–20
Lancelot, 11
Libro de Alexandre, 308
Lucan, 83
Lybeaus Desconus, 39, 312
Mai und Beaflor, 36
Malory, 39, 313–14
Manessische Liederhandschrift, 363

Marguerite d'Oingt, 21, 178
Marie de France, 12, 25, 35, 107, 192, 194, 202–13, 217–53, 257, 269, 297, 311, 422, 432, 439, 446
Matthew of Vendôme, 380
Mechthild of Hackeborn, 17–18
Mechthild of Magdeburg, 18–20, 23, 43–44, 376
Menander Rhetor, 55, 68
Mönch von Salzburg, 363
Mort Artu / Morte Darthur, 39, 48, 314, 423
Neidhart, 362, 366–67
Nibelungenlied, 2
Nicholas of Lyra, 5
Núñez, Nicolás, 476
Orpheus, 292, 303
Oswald von Wolkenstein, 44, 359–63, 366–67
Ovid, 61–62, 112, 114, 122, 153, 224, 259, 264, 269, 382–83, 385, 387–88, 397, 423, 466
Pamphilus, 387
Paul VI, Pope, 324
Paul, Saint, 401–02
Paulinus of Nola, 28, 53–74, 81
Pearl, 419
Perrers, Alice, 448
Peter the Venerable, 136
Porete, Margaret, 16–17, 23, 33–34, 169, 171–72, 178–79, 184–89, 376–77
Priscian, 223
Prose Lancelot, 47–48, 421–36
Prudentius, 122
Pseudo-Dionysius, 55, 68
Pursuit of Diarmaid and Gráinne, 102–04
quadrivium, 7
Queste del Saint Graal, 423
Raimbaut d'Aurenga, 33, 170
Reinmar von Brennenberg, 44, 371–74
Richard II, King, 441, 444

Richard of St. Victor, 119, 383
Roelt, *see* Swynford
Roman d'Eneas, 9, 30–31, 111–27, 224, 235
Roman de Horn, 300–2, 307
Roman des Sept Sages, 442
Roman du Castelain de Couci et de La Dame de Fayel, 295
Ruet, *see* Swynford
Ruiz, Juan, 7, 9, 50, 276
Ruodlieb, 38, 292
San Pedro, 50
Sappho, 57–58
Second Battle of Mag Tuired, 96–97, 106
Severus, Sulpicius, 87
Sidonius, 81
Sir Beues, 312
Sir Degrevant, 315
Sir Degaré, 316
Sir Gawain and the Green Knight, 40, 46–47, 395, 408–19
Sir Orfeo, 312
Sone de Nausey, 295
Sophocles, 58
Statius, 28, 54–74
Swynford, Katherine, 448
Tempier, Etienne, 32, 150–51, 168
Theocritus, 57
Theresa d'Avila, 183
Thérèse de Lisieux, 187–89
Thibaut of Blois, 257–58
Thomas de Bretagne, 259, 265, 271–72
Thüring von Ringoltingen, 421–37
Torquatus, Manlius, 59
Tristan, 29, 95
trivium, 7, 152
Ulrich von Liechtenstein, 328
Ulrich von Etzenbach, 36
Ulrich von Singenberg, 44, 375
Ulrich von Winterstetten, 44, 374–75
Virgil, 113, 115, 223, 424
Völuspá, 106
Wace, 220, 224

Wasting Sickness of Cú Chulainn, 99–100
Walther von der Vogelweide, 21–24, 249–50, 362, 366–67, 373
William of Conches, 27
Wolfram von Eschenbach, 15, 36, 41–42, 106, 323, 326, 319, 335–48
William of Malmesbury, 352
William of St. Amour, 390
Wooing of Emer, Tochmarc Emire, 98–99
Wooing of Étaín, 97–98